Computer Accounting with Peachtree by Sage Complete Accounting 2012

Sixteenth Edition

Carol Yacht, M.A.

McGraw-Hill Irwin

The McGraw-Hill Companies

McGraw-Hill
Irwin

COMPUTER ACCOUNTING WITH PEACHTREE BY SAGE COMPLETE ACCOUNTING 2012, 16th EDITION
Carol Yacht

Published by McGraw-Hill/Irwin, a business unit of The McGraw-Hill Companies, Inc., 1221 Avenue of the Americas, New York, NY 10020.
Copyright © 2013, 2012, 2011, 2010 by The McGraw-Hill Companies, Inc. All rights reserved. Printed in the United States of America.

1 2 3 4 5 6 7 8 9 0 RMN/RMN 1 0 9 8 7 6 5 4 3 2

ISBN-13:   978-0-07-802535-8
ISBN-10:   0-07-802535-4

Publisher: *Tim Vertovec*
Executive editor: *Steve Schuetz*
Editorial coordinator: *Danielle Andries*
Senior project manager: *Diane L. Nowaczyk*
Senior buyer: *Michael R. McCormick*
Senior design coordinator: *Joanne Mennemeier*
Marketing manager: *Dean Karampelas*
Media project manager: *Alpana Jolly, Hurix Systems Pvt. Ltd.*

www.mhhe.com

Software Installation

Install the software that tens of thousands of customers choose every year and is accountant recommended. Peachtree software is used by more than 3.1 million small and medium-sized business customers in North America; 6.2 million worldwide.

The Sage family of software products, which includes Peachtree Complete Accounting, is the leading global supplier of business management solutions and services. Sage is a global company with more than 13,600 employees and more than 25 years experience.

1. Sage Academic Site License, information below and on pages v and vi.
2. Peachtree Complete Accounting 2012: Student Version and Educational Version, page iv.

> To register the Student Version software included with the textbook, go online to www.peachtree.com/student/regi.

3. System Requirements, pages iv-vi.
4. Software Installation, page vi.
5. Sage Academic Site License, page vi.
6. Peachtree and Firewalls, page vi.
7. Peachtree Complete Accounting 2012 Installation, pages vi-xv.
8. Expiration date, Student Version, PCA 2012, pages xv-xvi.
9. Setting Global Options. Once global options are set, they are in effect for all Peachtree companies, pages xvi-xviii.
10. Computer Lab Installation, page xviii.
11. File Management, pages xviii-xx.
12. Student Version Software, page xx.
13. Educational Version Software, page xxi.
14. Deleting Peachtree, page xxi-xxii.

SAGE ACADEMIC SITE LICENSE

To obtain a site license for installation on multiple classroom computers, complete the Sage academic site license application at www.mhhe.com/yacht2012; Academic Site License link. The full educational version software is free to schools.

The McGraw-Hill Companies, Inc., *Computer Accounting with Peachtree by Sage Complete Accounting 2012, 16e*

Peachtree Complete Accounting 2012: Student Version and Educational Version

The software included with the textbook is the **Student Version** which can be installed on one computer. To receive a free multi-user **Educational Version**, complete the Sage Academic Site License. The Educational Version can be installed on multiple classroom computers.

The two versions, Student Version for individual installation, and Educational Version for multi-user classroom installation, include the same features. The difference is the Student Version expires after 14 months.

Peachtree Complete Accounting 2012 was used to write the textbook. All Peachtree screen captures are done using Windows 7. Install the software included with the textbook on individual computers. For multi-user installation, complete the Academic Site License from Sage at www.mhhe.com/yacht2012. If you have an earlier version of Peachtree installed (Peachtree Complete Accounting 2011 or lower), see Deleting Peachtree pages xxi-xii.)

SYSTEM REQUIREMENTS: Recommended System Configuration
http://www.peachtree.com/productsservices/complete/system

Recommended System Configuration

- 1 GHz Intel Pentium III (or equivalent) for single user and 1.8 GHz Intel Pentium 4 (or equivalent) for multiple concurrent users.
- 512 MB of RAM for single user and 1GB for multiple users.

Minimum System Requirements

- 1 GHz Intel Pentium III (or equivalent) for single and multiple users.
- 512 MB of RAM for single user or multiple users.
- Windows 7 Home Professional or higher, Vista SP1, XP SP3. (Peachtree does not have a Macintosh version. For Macintosh computers, search for PC compatibility at www.apple.com.)
- 1 GB of disk space for installation.
- Internet Explorer 7.0 required; Internet 8.0 and 9.0 supported.
- Microsoft .NET Framework CLR 3.5. Requires an additional 280 MB to 610 MB.
- At least high color (16-bit) SVGA video; supports 1024x768 resolution with small fonts required.

Higher screen resolution may be used. Higher resolution will not affect how the software functions, but the user interface may look different. For example, if you do not have an <OK> button, press <Enter> to start Bellwether Garden Supply or Stone Arbor Landscaping.

- DVD-ROM.
- USB drive: For backing up data, one USB flash drive is recommended with 2GB of storage space.
- All online features/services require Internet access with at least a 56 Kbps modem.

Integration/Compatibility Requirements

- Excel®, Outlook®, and Word integration requires Microsoft Excel, Outlook, and Word 2003, 2007, or 2010
- Sage Peachtree is certified to meet the Payment Card Industry Data Security Standards (PCI-DSS) for customers who process credit card payments in Sage Peachtree through integration with Sage Exchange. Internet connection required.
- Outlook Sync supported in Exchange 2000 SP2, 2003, 2007 and 2010
- Printers supported by Microsoft Windows XP/Vista/7
- In-product demos require Macromedia® Flash™ Player
- Adobe® Reader® 9.0 required
- Crystal Report® 2008
- SP1 requires installation of Sage Peachtree Premium Accounting or Sage Peachtree Quantum Accounting 2009 or higher. Additional 300 MB of available disk space is required.

Multi-User

- Multi-user environments are supported in Sage Peachtree Complete Accounting and higher
- Multi-user mode is optimized for Windows Server 2003 or Windows Server 2008 client-server networks, and Windows XP/Vista/7 peer-to-peer networks
- A maximum of five licensed named users are allowed. A named user account is granted a license when selected in the user maintenance screen
- 1 GB of disk space for installation of components on server.

IMPORTANT: Read Me—ACADEMIC SITE LICENSE
For classroom installation on multiple computers, complete the Sage academic site license application online at www.mhhe.com/yacht2012; link to Academic Site License.

Terminal Services

- Windows 2003 or 2008 Server along with Remote Desktop Connection or Remote Desktop Web Connection client is required to run in a Windows Terminal Services environment. No more than 5 named users.
- Terminal Server requires additional memory when more than one user is running under Windows Terminal Services. An additional 21 MB RAM is recommended for each additional user.

SOFTWARE INSTALLATION

This section gives you instructions for installing Peachtree Complete Accounting 2012 (PCA) software. *Check with your instructor to see if Peachtree has already been installed in the classroom or computer lab*.

Sage Academic Site License

To install Peachtree Complete Accounting 2012 on multiple classroom computers, complete the site license application at www.mhhe.com/yacht2012; Academic Site License link.

The Student Version software included with the textbook should be installed on one computer.

Peachtree and Firewalls

Peachtree and its database, Pervasive, can be mistakenly identified as an intrusion threat by many firewall and anti-virus programs. If not addressed properly, this may cause installation to fail or Peachtree may not start or run properly.

Go to this website to review information about firewalls and antivirus software, www.peachtree.com/supportTraining/commonIssues/firewall/. The textbook's website at www.mhhe.com/yacht2012 includes more information at the Frequently Asked Questions link to How do I check my Firewall and Antivirus software.

Peachtree Complete Accounting 2012 Installation

Follow these steps to install PCA 2012 on an individual computer (non-networked). The installation steps that follow are consistent with the Windows 7 operating system. If you are using Windows Vista or XP, your steps, and some of the screen illustrations, will differ slightly. For more information, refer to File Management, pages xviii-xx.

Student Version software installation requires that you complete Sage Peachtree's registration process online at www.peachtree.com/student/regi. *Before* **you insert the Peachtree Complete Accounting 2012 DVD included with the textbook, complete Step 1.**

Step 1:   To obtain a serial number for software installation, go online to www.peachtree.com/student/regi. To complete Step 11, page ix, you must use the serial number provided and complete any additional online registration and activation steps.

Step 2:   Insert the Peachtree Complete Accounting 2012 DVD in the DVD drive. If an AutoPlay window appears, click Run autorun.exe. (*Or*, select Browse the DVD. Select autorun.exe.)

Step 3:   At the Welcome to Peachtree Accounting window, select Install Peachtree Accounting. If a User Account Control window appears, click <Yes> with Windows 7; <Continue> with Vista.

NOTE: If a window prompts that your computer is currently using a default network protocol, IPV6, that may cause Peachtree to run slowly, read the information. Then, click <Yes>.

Step 4:   A Preparing to Install window appears. When the scale is complete, the Welcome to Peachtree Accounting window appears. The Welcome to Peachtree Accounting window is shown below.

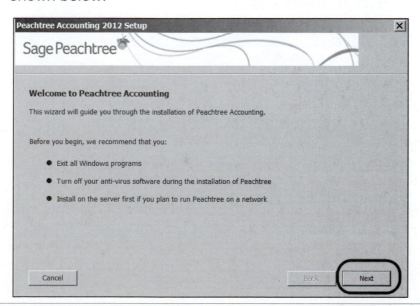

Step 5:   Click .

Step 6:   When the License Agreement window appears, click on the box next to I agree to the terms of the license agreement to place a checkmark.

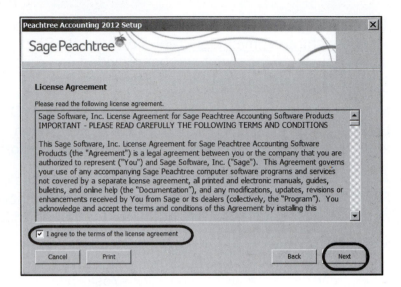

Step 7:   Click .

Step 8:   The Windows Firewall window appears. Accept the default for Yes (Recommended).

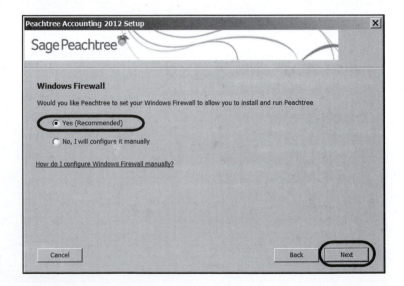

Step 9:   Click [Next]. The Firewall Settings window appears; read the information. You may need to disable your antivirus software. (Refer to page vi, Peachtree and Firewalls.)

Step 10   Click [Next]. The Searching for Previous Installations window appears. This may take several minutes.

Step 11:   The Serial Number window appears. Type the serial number given when you completed Step 1, page vii. If you have *not* obtained the serial number, go online to www.peachtree.com/student/regi.

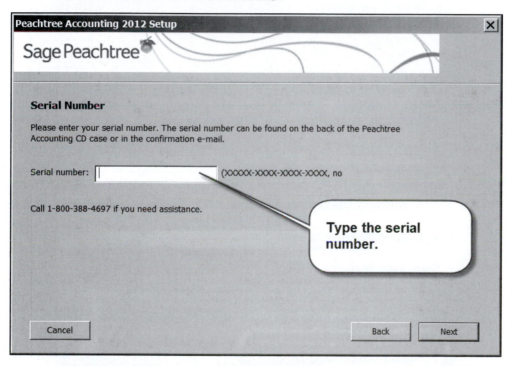

NOTE TO INSTRUCTORS/SCHOOLS: If you are installing the software received with the Sage Academic Site License, type the serial number found on the label within the DVD case.

Step 11:   Click [Next].

Step 12:   The Single Computer or Network window appears. Make the appropriate selection. Yes is the default for individual computers.

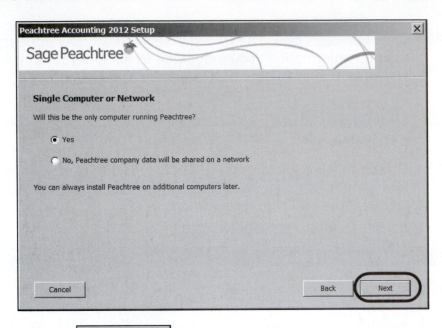

Step 13:   Click Next .

Step 14:   The Choose Peachtree Program Files Location window appears. The author suggests accepting the default installation directory at C:\Program Files (x86)\Sage\Peachtree. (On Windows Vista and XP computers, this location will differ.)

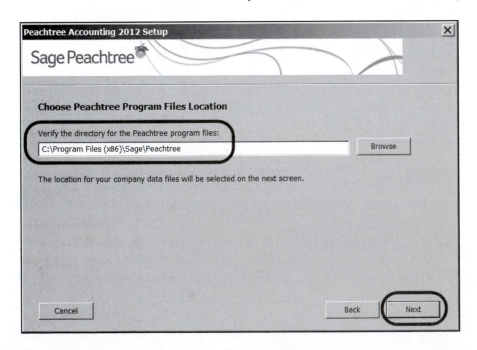

Step 15:   Click [Next].

Step 16:   The Company Data Files Location window appears. Accept the
           default, C:\Sage\Peachtree\Company or click Browse to set
           another location. (*Hint:* Your Company Data Files Location may
           differ. Refer to page xix, step 2.) The Company Data Files
           Location window is shown below.

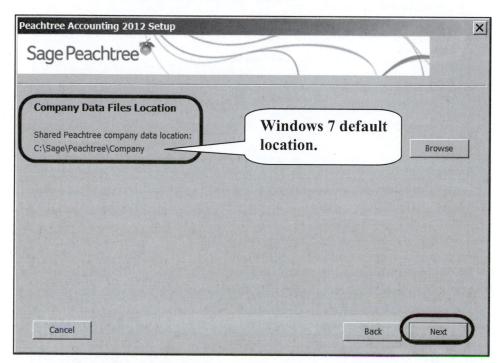

Step 17:   Click [Next]. The Summary window appears. Read the
           information on the Summary window. (*Hint:* Your program files
           and company data files may be in different locations. Refer to
           File Management, pages xviii-xx.) The Summary window is
           shown on the next page.

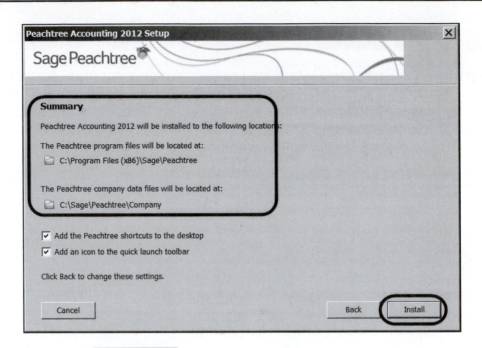

Step 18: Click [Install]. Peachtree starts to install. Be patient. Installation takes several minutes.

Step 19: Read the Installation Completed window. Observe that Start Peachtree Accounting is selected.

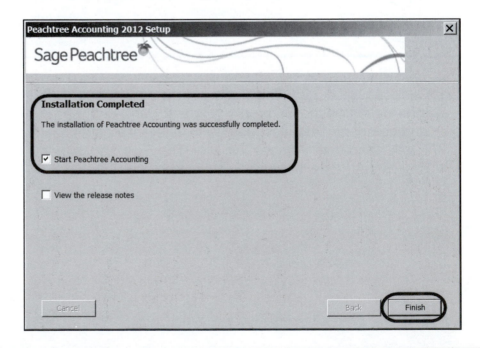

Step 20: Click [Finish]. The Sage Peachtree Student Version *or* Sage Peachtree Educational Version startup window appears. Both versions include the same features.

Student Version software included with textbook:

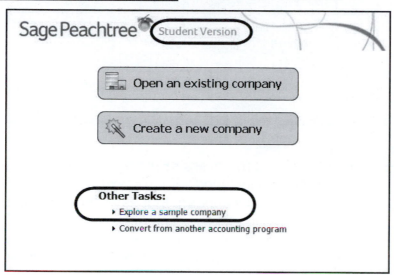

Educational Version software (classroom version received with Academic Site License):

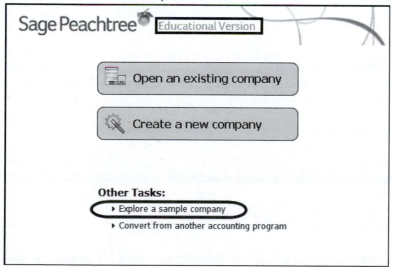

Step 21: If Bellwether Garden Supply is highlighted, go to step 22. *Or,* Select Explore a sample company. Bellwether Garden Supply is the default.

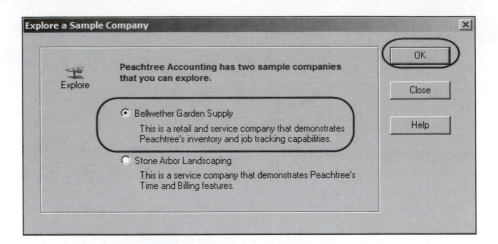

Step 22:   Click (or, press <Enter>). If you installed the Student Version included with the textbook, a Peachtree Accounting window appears that says "You can use this company in the student version of Peachtree for the next 14 months and then it will expire. The company's expiration date can be found in the Company Information section of the System Navigation Center." For more information about the expiration date, refer to page xv-xvi.

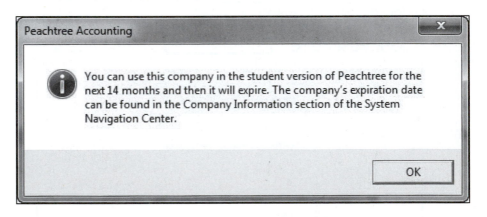

Step 23:   Click [OK] .

Step 24:   If the What's new in Peachtree window appears. Read the information. To read more, select <Next>. Click on the box next to Do not display this screen again. If you selected <Next> your window will differ.

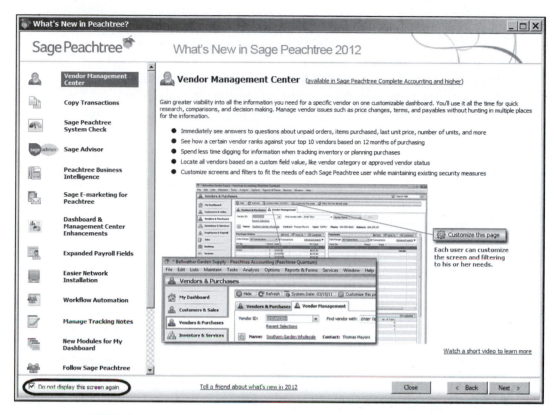

Step 25:   To close the What's New in Sage Peachtree 2012 window, click <Close>. When the window prompts Click OK to exit What's New in Peachtree, click on the box next to Do not display this window again.

Step 26:   Click [OK]. The Bellwether Garden Supply - Peachtree Accounting window appears.

Expiration Date, Student Version, PCA 2012

To see when the Student Version of Peachtree 2012 expires, follow the steps shown on the next page.

1. From the Navigation Bar, select 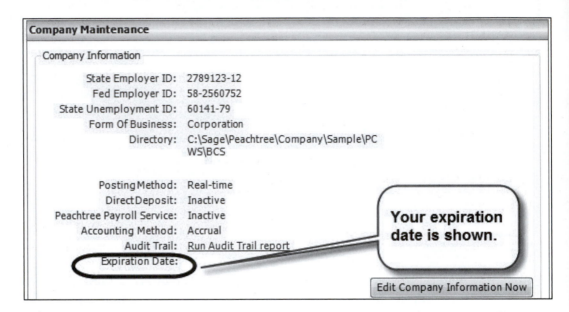 .

2. The Company Maintenance area includes an Expiration Date field. The expiration date is 14 months after the day you installed the software; for example if you installed the software on August 12, 2012, the expiration date is October 12, 2013.

Company Maintenance

Company Information

State Employer ID:	2789123-12
Fed Employer ID:	58-2560752
State Unemployment ID:	60141-79
Form Of Business:	Corporation
Directory:	C:\Sage\Peachtree\Company\Sample\PC WS\BCS
Posting Method:	Real-time
Direct Deposit:	Inactive
Peachtree Payroll Service:	Inactive
Accounting Method:	Accrual
Audit Trail:	Run Audit Trail report
Expiration Date:	

Your expiration date is shown.

Edit Company Information Now

Setting Global Options

Follow these steps to set Peachtree's Global Options. These options will be in effect for all Peachtree companies.

1. From Peachtree's menu bar, select Options; Global. The Accounting tab is selected.

   - In the **Decimal Entry** area, Manual and 2 decimal places should be selected in each field.

   - In the **Hide General Ledger Accounts** area, the boxes *must* be unchecked.

   - In the **Other Options** area, Warn if a record was changed but not saved and Recalculate cash balance automatically in Receipts, Payments, and Payroll Entry should be checked.

Compare your Maintain Global Options/<u>A</u>ccounting window to the one shown below.

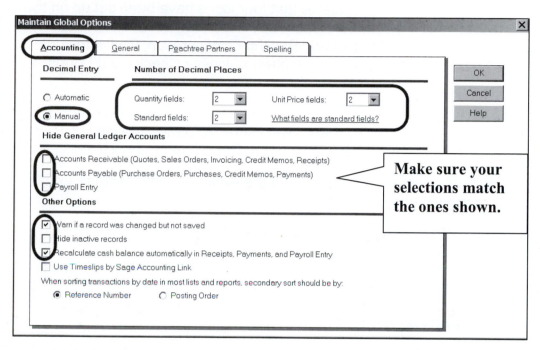

2. Click the <u>G</u>eneral tab. Make sure your screen matches the one shown below.

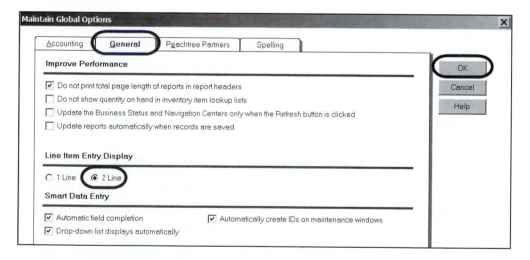

3. Click [OK]. The selections made in global options are now set for all companies.

4.   From Peachtree's menu bar, click File, Exit.

5.   Remove the DVD. Observe that four icons have been set up on the desktop for Peachtree: Peachtree Accounting 2012, Peachtree Accounting 2012 Automatic Backup Configuration, Peachtree Knowledge Center, and Peachtree Business Checks and Forms.

COMPUTER LAB INSTALLATION

Before computer lab installation, make sure all former versions of Peachtree are deleted. Refer to Deleting Peachtree, page xxi-xxii.

For multi-user installations, complete the Academic Site License from Sage at www.mhhe.com/yacht2012.

1.   Peachtree Complete Accounting 2012 should be installed locally. Do *not* put on server.
2.   Install software on local workstation then ghost (replicate) install. You can put the software on a standard lab image.

FILE MANAGEMENT

When Peachtree was installed two directories were set up (refer to steps 14-16, pages x-xi).

1.   **Program Files Location**: The Windows 7 default directory where Peachtree is installed is C:\Program Files (x86)\Sage\Peachtree (step 14, page x). To see the Properties window, right-click on the Peachtree Accounting 2012 desktop icon; left-click Properties, select the Shortcut tab.

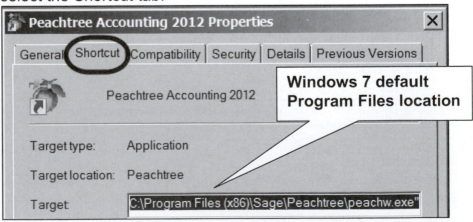

2. **Company Data Files Location**: On Windows 7, the default location
    for company data files is C:\Sage\Peachtree\Company (step 16,
    page xi).

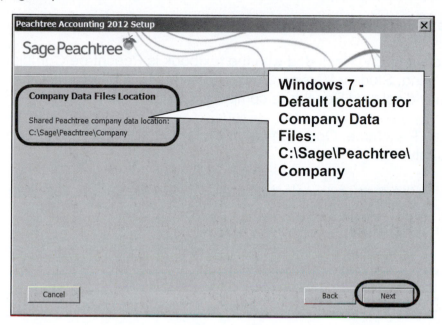

On Windows Vista and XP, the default location for company data is
C:\Program Files\Sage\Peachtree\Company. The directory field on
the Maintain Company Information window shows where company
data is stored (refer to Chapter 1, Comment box on page 23).

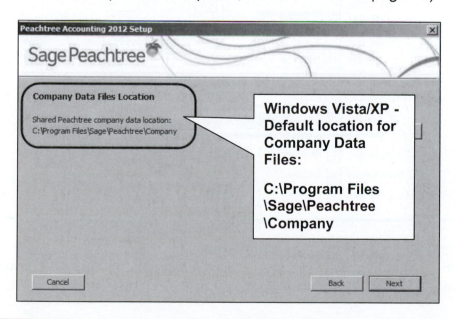

Peachtree files can be backed up (saved) to various locations: the company data files default location, a USB drive, external media, or other location. Detailed steps for backing up are on pages 22-25.

Student Version Software

The software DVD included with the textbook is Peachtree Complete Accounting, Student Version. To see the default location where the currently displayed Peachtree company resides, follow these steps.

1. Start Peachtree. Open the sample company, Bellwether Garden Supply.

2. From the menu bar, select Maintain; Company Information. The Directory field shows where the currently displayed Peachtree company resides.

    Student version directory:

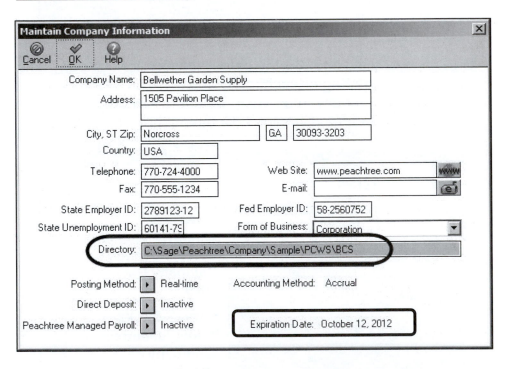

You can use company data in the Student Version of Peachtree for 14 months. After 14 months, the Student Version software expires. Your expiration date will differ from the one shown.

Educational Version Software

If you are working in the computer lab, the default directory for Educational Version differs slightly when compared to the Student Version.

The Maintain Company Information window's Directory field differs slightly. Observe that the default folder for the Educational Version is \PCW**E** not \PCW**S**.

Educational Version Directory:

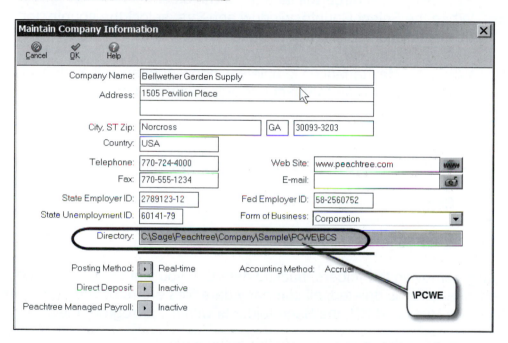

The features of the Student Version and Educational Version are the same, except for the Student Version's 14-month period of use.

DELETING PEACHTREE

Follow these steps to delete Peachtree Complete Accounting 2012. (Use similar steps to delete Peachtree 2011.)

1.   Insert the Peachtree DVD. Select Run autorun.exe.

2. When the Welcome to Peachtree Accounting window appears, select Remove or Modify Peachtree Accounting. When the User Account Control window appears, select <Yes>.

3. Select Peachtree Complete Accounting 2012. A Preparing to Install window appears. Be patient, this will take a few minutes. When a screen prompts that setup has detected an installation of Peachtree Release 2012 on this computer, click <OK>.

4. Select Remove, then click <Next>. A window prompts, This will remove Peachtree Accounting 2012 (all versions), click <OK>. Removing Peachtree will take a few minutes.

5. When the Select Country window appears, select the country for this installation; for example, United States. Click <Next>.

6. When the Maintenance Complete window appears, click <Finish>. Close the Welcome to Peachtree Accounting window.

7. Remove the DVD.

After removal, you may want to delete these two folders:

1. C:\Sage

2. C:\Program Files (x86)\Sage

Before removing the folders, backup data that you want to keep. Once the Sage folder is deleted, all company data files are removed. (*Hint:* In Windows Vista and XP, the Sage folder is within C:\Program Files.)

After removing the folders, empty the recycle bin.

Preface

*Computer Accounting with Peachtree by Sage Complete Accounting 2012, 16*th*Edition,* teaches you how to use Peachtree Complete Accounting 2012 software. For more than 36 years[1], Peachtree by Sage has produced award-winning accounting software. Over 6.2 million customers use Sage software products. More than 13,600 employees work for Sage (http://sage.com/ourbusiness/aboutus). The Sage family of software products, which includes Peachtree Complete Accounting, is the leading global supplier of business management solutions and services. For more information about Sage's worldwide community, refer to page xxxv.

In the United States and Canada, Peachtree is used by more than 3.1 million businesses. Each year, tens of thousands of customers choose accountant-recommended Peachtree by Sage for their business needs. Why? Because Peachtree helps you do more to support the success of your business. Industries that use Peachtree include retail stores, healthcare, human resources/payroll, construction/real estate, transportation/distribution, payment processing, nonprofit, manufacturing, public utilities, legal, medical, and accounting firms.

In *Computer Accounting with Peachtree by Sage Complete Accounting 2012, 16*th*Edition,* you learn about the relationship between Peachtree software and fundamental accounting principles, procedures, and business processes.

Read Me: Multi-User Academic Site License from Sage

To install Peachtree Complete Accounting 2012 on multiple classroom computers, complete the Sage academic site license application at www.mhhe.com/yacht2012; Academic Site License link (refer to pages iii, v-vi). The full Educational Version software is free to schools.

The software included with the textbook is the Student Version which can be installed on one computer.

---

[1]Peachtree Software was available in 1976.

System Requirements: For system requirements, go online to http://www.peachtree.com/productsServices/complete/system/. Refer to pages iv-vi.

PEACHTREE COMPLETE ACCOUNTING 2012

Each textbook includes a copy of the software, Peachtree Complete Accounting 2012 Student Version.

NEW   The software, **Peachtree Complete Accounting 2012 Student Version**, is included with every textbook. For software installation instructions, see pages vi-xv. **Register the Student Version software at www.peachtree.com/student/regi**.

NEW   You can use the student version for **14 months** and then it expires. The company's expiration date can be found in the Company Information section of the System Navigation Center and on the Maintain, Company Information window

NEW   For installation on multiple classroom computers, schools complete the Sage Academic Site License at www.mhhe.com/yacht2012.

NEW   Online Learning Center at www.mhhe.com/yacht2012.

NEW   Bellwether Garden Supply project includes questions and answers for analyzing the sample company data, identifying software features and functions, and reviewing correct and incorrect sample company transactions. The Online Learning Center includes the Bellwether Garden Supply project, www.mhhe.com/yacht2012.

NEW   Peachtree's emphasis on double-entry accounting and business processes is explained throughout the textbook. Accounting skills are applied to all facets of running a business. Students create 12 companies, complete the accounting cycle, and practice computer accounting skills. Assessment is emphasized in every chapter.

NEW   Narrated PowerPoint slides for Chapters 1-18 on the textbook's Online Learning Center at www.mhhe.com/yacht2012. The narrated PowerPoints include chapter review, Peachtree tips, glossary of terms, Assessment Rubrics, Analysis Questions, links to the Going to the Net exercise, and Online Learning Center.

NEW Chapter 8, Stone Arbor Landscaping: Time and Billing. Use Peachtree's time and billing feature to record a time ticket, enter a sales invoice, and record payroll for jobs completed.

NEW Chapters 1-18 include saving Peachtree reports as Adobe Acrobat PDF files, and exporting reports to Excel.

NEW Payroll tax tables for 50 states. Example payroll withholdings are included in Chapter 4, Employees; Chapter 15, Employees, Payroll, and Account Reconciliation; Exercise 15-1, Student Name Sales and Service; Project 2, Sports Emporium; and Project 4, BR Manufacturing, Inc.

NEW End-of-Chapter exercises include Check Your Figures, Analysis Questions and Assessment Rubrics.

NEW File Management includes where Peachtree stores program and company data, including differences between Windows 7 and Vista/XP.

NEW Use Peachtree's import/export feature to copy lists into another company.

NEW Peachtree's modular system design is explained and compared to other accounting information systems.

NEW Workflow diagrams illustrate Peachtree's system design.

NEW An accounting software diagram illustrates where Peachtree fits into the range of accounting software applications.

NEW Peachtree is compared to QuickBooks and Microsoft Dynamics GP.

Computer Accounting with Peachtree by Sage Complete Accounting 2012, 16th Edition, shows you how to set up service, merchandising, nonprofit, and manufacturing businesses. When the textbook is completed, you have a working familiarity with Peachtree Complete Accounting 2012 software. The Part 1, 2, 3, and 4 introductions include a chart showing the chapter number, backup and Excel and Adobe file names, size in kilobytes of each file backed up or saved, and page numbers where each backup, Excel, and Adobe PDF file is completed.

Some of the **new** and continued features included in *Computer Accounting with Peachtree by Sage Complete Accounting 2012, 16e*, are shown on the next two pages.

❋ **NEW!** The software, **Peachtree Complete Accounting 2012, Student Version**, is included with every textbook. Students can use company data for 14 months. Register the Student Version software included with textbook at www.peachtree.com/student/regi.

❋ **NEW! Sage Academic Site License** at www.mhhe.com/yacht2012 for installation on multiple classroom computers.

❋ **NEW!** Backup and restore data from USB flash drive.

❋ **NEW!** Payroll withholding tables for 50 states. Students complete exercises and projects using tax tables for different states.

❋ **NEW!** Source document practice set at www.mhhe.com/yacht2012.

❋ **NEW!** Bellwether Garden Supply project at www.mhhe.com/yacht2012.

❋ **NEW! PDF files**. Steps for saving files in Adobe PDF format, Excel (xlsx), and Peachtree (ptb).

❋ **NEW! Narrated PowerPoint slides for Chapters 1-18** online at www.mhhe.com/2012.

❋ **NEW! Assessment Rubrics** for Chapters 1-18 online at www.mhhe.com/yacht2012.

❋ **Check Your Figures**. In Chapters 1-18 and Projects 1-4, you can verify your work.

❋ **NEW!** Import lists to another company.

❋ **NEW!** Online Feature Quizzes, Flash [demonstration] Videos, and Peachtree videos.

❋ **NEW!** Vendor Management *and* Customer Management.

❋ **NEW!** Inventory & Services *and* Inventory/Service Management.

❋ Peachtree's modular system design is explained—includes how the user interface is organized into general ledger, accounts receivable, accounts payable, inventory, payroll, and job costing.

❋ Appendix B, Accounting Information Systems (AIS)—defines accounting information systems and compares Peachtree to other accounting software applications.

❋ Chapters include learning objectives, exercises, analysis questions, and assessment rubrics.

❋ **NEW!** Watch **flash videos** to review key software features at

www.mhhe.com/yacht2012. The icon indicates there is a flash video.

❋ Chapters include reminders to check the appropriate place in the data. This

icon— —reminds you to check your work.

❋ **NEW! Feature quizzes** at www.mhhe.com/yacht2012 review Peachtree's user interface.

❋ **NEW!** Interactive true/false and multiple choice quizzes.

❋ **NEW!** In Chapters 1-18, export reports to Excel and save files in PDF format.

❋ **Part 2**, Peachtree 2012 for Service Businesses, includes **3 chapters and two projects**—Chapter 9, New Company Setup and Beginning Balances; Chapter 10, Maintaining Accounting Records for Service Businesses; Chapter 11, Completing Quarterly Activities and Closing the Fiscal Year, and Projects 1 and 1A.

❋ **Part 4**, Advanced Peachtree 2012 Applications, includes **3 chapters and three projects**—Chapter 16, Customizing Forms; Chapter 17, Import/Export; and Chapter 18, Microsoft Word and Templates, Projects 3, 4, and 4A.

❋ Software installation is at the beginning of textbook, pages vi-xv.

❋ **NEW! QA templates** online at www.mhhe.com/yacht2012 include end-of-chapter questions and analysis questions.

❋ All instructions, screen captures, and detailed steps are consistent with Windows 7. Peachtree 2012 is compatible with Windows 7/Vista/XP.

❋ Navigation Bar includes Business Status; Customers & Sales, Vendors & Purchases, Inventory & Services, Employees & Payroll, Banking, Company.

❋ Navigation Centers for accessing information, recording transactions, drill down to reports, setup windows, and graphs.

❋ Enhanced Excel Integration.

❋ Expanded purchase orders, receiving reports, sales orders, and shipping notices.

❋ Improved customer and inventory management.

❋ Open multiple companies.

❋ Enhanced prior year reports. Information available for general ledger and financial statements for all closed years.

❋ Real-time error alerts. Alerts if you try to save a transaction with non-standard accounts payable or accounts receivable accounts.

❋ Free online backups for one year.

❋ Cash flow manager.

❋ Improved time and expense tracking.

❋ Payroll wizard.

❋ **NEW!** Enhanced password security, role-based features, audit trail and internal controls.

❋ Daily customer balances on sales and customers windows.

❋ Custom date-range filtering and enhanced report options.

❋ Restore Wizard lets you restore An Existing Company or A New Company.

❋ Smart sort for account identification.

❋ **NEW!** E-mail reports, financial statements, and add attachments.

❋ Design tools for report customization.

❋ Set up **12 new** service, merchandising, nonprofit, and manufacturing businesses, including source document practice set at www.mhhe.com/yacht2012.

What's New in Peachtree 2012?

The Help menu includes the new Peachtree 2012 software features. To see that window, follow these steps:

1. Start Peachtree.
2. Open the sample company, Bellwether Garden Supply. (Detailed steps for installing the software and starting Bellwether are on pages vi-xv.)
3. From Bellwether Garden Supply's menu bar, select Help, What's New in Peachtree.

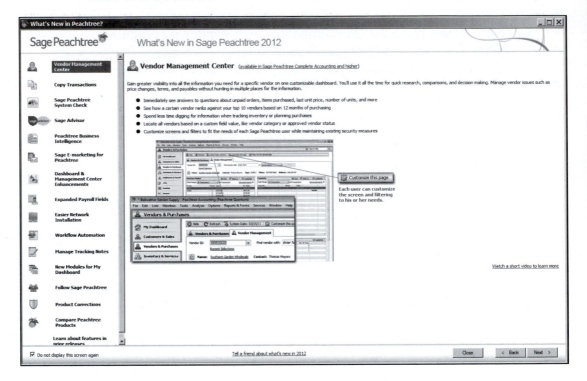

4. On the What's New in Peachtree? window, click Next > to see more. Read the information on these windows to review the new software features. Click < Back to review information. When through, click Close.

PART 1: EXPLORING PEACHTREE COMPLETE ACCOUNTING 2012

There are two sample companies included with the software: Bellwether Garden Supply and Stone Arbor Landscaping. Bellwether Garden Supply is a retail and service company that demonstrates Peachtree's inventory and job tracking capabilities. Stone Arbor Landscaping is a service company that demonstrates time and billing features.

> Each part of the textbook includes an introduction. Refer to pages 1 and 2 for an overview of Part 1. Page 2 includes a chart showing chapter numbers, files backed up and saved, file sizes, and page numbers where work was completed.

Part 1, Chapters 1-8, shows how to export Peachtree reports to Excel and save reports as Adobe PDF files. Peachtree's system design is explained. This includes how Peachtree's user interface is organized into general ledger, accounts receivable, accounts payable, inventory, payroll, and job costing modules.

In Part 1 of the textbook, you complete eight chapters that demonstrate how Peachtree is used. This introduces you to the procedures that will be used with all the chapters of the textbook.

NEW Chapter 1, Introduction to Bellwether Garden Supply, includes Peachtree's Navigation Centers and Restore Wizard for opening new or existing companies. *New menu bar selections are explained. Bellwether Garden Supply is updated to March 2012.*

NEW Chapter 2, Vendors, shows you how to view accounts payable lists and reports from the Vendors & Payables Navigation Center as well as custom date filtering and how to add columns to reports. New sections include Receive Inventory from a Purchase Order and Apply to Purchase Order. Explanation of Peachtree's accounts payable system.

NEW In Chapters 1-18, the summary and review includes Assessment Rubrics.

Chapter 3, Customers, shows you how to view customer lists and reports from the Customers & Sales Navigation Center as well as custom date filtering and how to add columns to reports. Chapter 3 includes Sales Orders and Ship Items from a Sales Order. Explanation of Peachtree's accounts receivable system.

Chapter 4, Employees, shows you how to navigate Peachtree's Employees & Payroll system.

Chapter 5, General Ledger, Inventory, and Internal Control, shows you Peachtree's budget feature, how selected access for security is used, internal controls, and audit trail. Explanation of Peachtree's inventory system is also included.

Chapter 6, Job Cost, shows you how to use Peachtree's job cost system.

Chapter 7, Financial Statements, shows the result of work completed in Chapters 1-6.

NEW In Chapter 8, Stone Arbor Landscaping: Time & Billing, you work with a service company that demonstrates Peachtree's time and billing features. In Exercises 8-1 and 8-2, you record time and billing transactions, including a time ticket that is applied to a sales invoice and payroll entry.

PART 2: PEACHTREE COMPLETE ACCOUNTING 2012 FOR SERVICE BUSINESSES

Chapters 9, 10, 11, Project 1, and Project 1A are included in this section of the textbook. The work completed in Chapter 9 is continued in Chapters 10 and 11. The accounting cycle is completed for the fourth quarter of the year.

For an overview of Part 2, refer to pages 275-278. Pages 277-278 includes a chart showing chapter numbers, files backed up and saved, file sizes, and page numbers where work was completed.

NEW In Chapter 9, New Company Setup and Beginning Balances, you set up two service companies—Mark Foltz Designer and Design by Student Name—with Peachtree's simplified chart of accounts. You use Peachtree's new Company Setup Wizard and enter beginning balances. The companies set up in Chapter 9 continue in Chapters 10 and 11.

In Chapter 10, Maintaining Accounting Records for Service Businesses, you record entries for October in the Write Checks and Receipts windows, use Peachtree's enhanced account reconciliation feature and print reports. You also save reports in Excel and Adobe PDF format.

Chapter 11, Completing Quarterly Activities and Closing the Fiscal Year, you complete transactions for November and December, record adjusting entries, print financial statements, and close the fiscal year.

NEW Exercises 9-1 through 11-2 include three months of transactions, account reconciliation, adjusting entries, financial statements, Peachtree's closing procedure, Check Your Figures, Assessment Rubrics, and Analysis Questions. Peachtree reports are saved as PDF files and exported to Excel.

NEW Project 1, Susan Babbage, Accounting, is a comprehensive project that reviews what you learned in Chapters 9, 10, and 11.

Project 1A, Student-Designed Service Business, shows you how to design a service business from scratch. You set up the business, choose a chart of accounts, create a Balance Sheet, write business transactions, complete the computer accounting cycle, and close the fiscal year.

PART 3: PEACHTREE COMPLETE ACCOUNTING 2012 FOR MERCHANDISING BUSINESSES

Chapters 12, 13, 14, 15, Project 2, and Project 2A are included in this section of the textbook. Students set up two merchandising businesses in Chapter 12—Cynthia's Service Merchandise *and* Student Name Sales and Service. The work started in Chapter 12 is continued in Chapters 13, 14 and 15.

For an overview of Part 3, refer to pages 425-428. Pages 426-428 includes a chart showing chapter numbers, files backed up and saved, file sizes, and page numbers where work was completed.

In Chapter 12, Vendors & Purchases, use Peachtree's accounts payable system, record inventory purchases and payments from vendors, set up vendor defaults to automatically track purchase discounts, and use vendor credit memos for purchase returns.

In Chapter 13, Customers & Sales, use Peachtree's accounts receivable system, record cash and credit sales and receipts from customers, set up customer defaults, use credit memos for sales returns.

Chapter 14, Inventory & Services, shows you how to use Peachtree's inventory system.

NEW Chapter 15, Employees, Payroll and Account Reconciliation, shows Peachtree's payroll system using two states (Arizona and Georgia) as an example for payroll withholdings. You set up payroll defaults, add employee information, learn about automatic payroll tax calculations, and complete payroll entry. Account reconciliation shows you how Peachtree's Accounts Payable, Accounts Receivable, Inventory, and General Ledger systems work together. Chapter 15 includes account reconciliation for both the checking and payroll accounts.

NEW Exercises 12-1 through 15-2 include Check Your Figures, Analysis Questions, and Assessment Rubrics.

NEW Project 2, Sports Emporium, is a comprehensive project that incorporates what you have learned in Chapters 12 through 15. Project 2 includes payroll withholdings for Oregon.

Project 2A, Student-Designed Merchandising Business, asks you to create a merchandising business from scratch.

PART 4: ADVANCED PEACHTREE COMPLETE ACCOUNTING 2012 APPLICATIONS

Chapters 16, 17, 18, Project 3, Project 4, and Project 4A are included in this part of the textbook. Chapter 16, Customizing Forms, shows you how to use Peachtree's design tools. Chapter 17, Import/Export, shows you how to export data from Peachtree to a word processing program and how to import lists into a company. In Chapter 18, Microsoft Word and Templates, you copy a Peachtree report to Word and look at vendor, customer, and employee templates included with the software. Chapter 18 also includes searching Peachtree's Knowledge Center.

> For an overview of Part 4, refer to pages 655-656. Page 656 includes a chart showing chapter numbers, files backed up and saved, file sizes, and page numbers where work was completed.

Chapter 16, Customizing Forms, includes design tools for report customization.

NEW In Exercises 16-1 and 16-2, forms and financial statements are customized.

Chapter 17, Import/Export, includes how to import a chart of accounts into another company and export to a word processing program.

NEW In Exercises 17-1 and 17-2 import lists from Bellwether Garden Supply into the company set up in Chapter 17.

Chapter 18, Microsoft Word and Templates, includes copying reports to Word, using templates, the write letters feature, and search Peachtree's Knowledge Center.

NEW Project 3, Chicago Computer Club, is a nonprofit business.

NEW Project 4, BR Manufacturing, Inc., is the culminating project in your study of Peachtree Complete Accounting 2012. Project 4 includes payroll withholdings for Pennsylvania.

Project 4A, Student-Designed Project, instructs you to write another month's transactions for one of the four projects completed.

Appendix B, Accounting Information Systems (AIS). This appendix defines an accounting information system, and compares Peachtree's user interface and modular system design to other accounting software applications. An accounting software diagram illustrates where Peachtree fits into the range of accounting software applications.

CONVENTIONS USED IN TEXTBOOK

As you work through *Computer Accounting with Peachtree by Sage Complete Accounting 2012, 16e*, you should read and follow the step-by-step instructions. Numerous screen illustrations help you to check your work.

The following conventions are used in this textbook:

1. Information that you type appears in boldface; for example, Type **Supplies** in the Account ID field.
2. Keys on the keyboard that should be pressed appear in angle brackets; for example, <Enter>.
3. When you see this icon , there is a flash video on the textbook website at www.mhhe.com/yacht2012; Student Edition link. Select the appropriate chapter, link to Flash Videos, and then select the video.

4. This icon—🖫—reminds you to check the Peachtree work completed.

5. Unnamed buttons and picture icons are shown as they actually appear on the screen.

   Examples: [Next >] (Next button); [Display] (Display icon)

PEACHTREE'S KNOWLEDGE CENTER

The Knowledge Center offers help for the most frequently asked Peachtree questions. You can search by product, category, keywords, Answer ID or phrases. Feedback can also be emailed to Peachtree.

1. From the desktop, click [Peachtree Knowledge Center].

2. After selecting the Peachtree Knowledge Center, the Sage Peachtree Find Answers page appears. (The web site address is www.peachtree.com/supporttraining/findanswers?WT.mc_id=RD_pe achtree.com/inproduct_KnowledgeCenter.) Link to Search the Knowledgebase.

3. Select Sage Peachtree - [Sage Peachtree].

4. For purposes of this example, type **Import/Export** in the Search field

   | Import/Export | [Search] Hide Options |

5. Click [Search]. A list of documents appears. Link to one or more documents for feedback about Import/Export.

6. Experiment. Change the search field to look at Peachtree's knowledgebase.

The textbook ends with four appendixes: Appendix A, Troubleshooting; Appendix B, Accounting Information Systems; Appendix C, Review of Accounting Principles; and Appendix D, Glossary. Appendixes A and D are included on the textbook's Online Learning Center at www.mhhe.com/yacht2012.

Each chapter in the textbook ends with an index. The index at the end of the textbook is an alphabetic listing of the chapter indexes.

Sage's Worldwide Community
http://sage.com/ourbusiness/aboutus/ourproductsservices

Sage products are classified into the following groups:

- Accounting
- Payroll
- Customer Relationship Management (CRM)
- Financial forecasting
- Payment processing
- Job costing
- Human Resources
- Business intelligence
- Taxation and other products for accountants
- Business stationery
- Development platforms
- E-business
- Enterprise Resource Planning (ERP)

Key facts about Sage include the following:

- More than 13,600 employees
- More than 6 million customers
- Offices in 24 countries around the world
- Advise 1.9 million customers through support contracts
- Manage 33,000 customer calls a day
- Global network of 26,000 business partners and 40,000 accountants

For more information go online to
http://sage.com/ourbusiness/newsroom/companyinformation.

About the Author: <u>carol@carolyacht.com</u>

Carol Yacht is a textbook author and accounting educator. Carol is the author of Peachtree, QuickBooks, Microsoft Dynamics-GP, and Excel textbooks, and the accounting textbook supplement, Carol Yacht's General Ledger and Peachtree DVDs (<u>www.mhhe.com/yacht</u>). Carol taught on the faculties of California State University-Los Angeles, West Los Angeles College, Yavapai College, and Beverly Hills High School. To help students master accounting principles, procedures, and business processes, Carol includes accounting software in her classes.

An early user of accounting software, Carol Yacht started teaching computerized accounting in 1980. Yacht's teaching career includes first and second year accounting courses, accounting information systems, and computer accounting. Since 1989, Yacht's textbooks have been published by McGraw-Hill.

Carol contributes regularly to professional journals and is the Accounting Section Editor for *Business Education Forum*, a publication of the National Business Education Association. She is also the Editor of the American Accounting Association's Teaching, Learning, and Curriculum section's *The Accounting Educator*.

Carol Yacht was an officer of AAA's Two-Year College section and recipient of its Lifetime Achievement Award. She is a member of the Microsoft Dynamics Academic Alliance Advisory Council, worked for IBM Corporation as an education instruction specialist, served on the AAA Commons Editorial Board, and NBEA's Computer Education Task Force. She is a frequent speaker at state, regional, and national conventions.

Carol earned her MA degree from California State University-Los Angeles, BS degree from the University of New Mexico, and AS degree from Temple University.

Acknowledgments

I would like to thank the following colleagues for their help in the preparation of this book: Steve Schuetz; Danielle Andries; Beth Woods, CPA; and Matt Lowenkron. A special thank you to the following professors.

Kathy Blondell, St. Johns River Comm. Coll.
Linda Bolduc, Mt. Wachusett College
Michael Bryan, Tidewater Community Coll.
Jim Burcicki, Penn Foster Career School
Richard Campbell, Rio Grande College
Vickie Campbell, Cape Fear CC
Brenda Catchings, Augusta Technical Coll.
Leonard Cronin, Rochester Comm. College
Susan Crosson, Santa Fe College
Robert Dansby, Columbus Tech. Institute
Alan Davis, Comm. Coll. of Philadelphia
Dave Davis, Vincennes University
Vaun Day, Central Arizona College
Roger Dimick, Lamar Inst. of Technology
George Dorrance, Mission College
Philip Empey, Purdue University-Calumet
Raul Enriquez, Laredo Community College
David R. Fordham, James Madison Univ.
Bill Gaither, Dawson Community College
Harold Gellis, York College of CUNY
Christopher Gilbert, Glendale College
Marina Grau, Houston Community College
Nancy Greene, University of Cincinnati
Joyce Griffin, Kansas City Kansas CC
Bill Guidera, Texas State Technical College
Jim Hale, Vance-Granville Community Coll.
Mary Hauschen, Moraine Park Tech. Coll.
Larry Heldreth, Danville Community College
Mark Henry, Victoria College
Geoffrey Heriot, Greenville Tech. College
Jan Ivansek, Lakeland College
Jeff Jackson, San Jacinto College
Robert Jackson, Ivy Tech State College
Stacy Johnson, Iowa Central Comm. Coll.
Judy Kidder, Mohave Community College
Mary Kline, Black Hawk College
Linda Kropp, Modesto Junior College
Edward Kufuor, ASA Institute
Sara Lagier, American Business College
Jan Lange, MN West Comm. & Tech. Coll.
Connie Lehman, University of Houston
Jim Leonard, Strayer University
Bruce Lindsey, Genesee Community Coll.
Susan Looney, Mohave Community Coll.

Susan Lynn, University of Baltimore
Charles McCord, Portland Comm. College
J. Mike Metzcar, Indiana Wesleyan University
Jack Neymark, Oakton Community College
Cory Ng, Comm. College of Philadelphia
Michelle Nickla, Ivy Tech Community College
Pat Olson, Moraine Park Technical College
Vincent Osaghae, Chicago State University
Michael Papke, Kellogg Community College
Timothy Pearson, West Virginia University
Gerald Peterka, Mt. San Jacinto College
Simon Petravick, Bradley University
Tom Pinckney, Trident Technical College
Susan Pope, University of Akron
Robert Porter, Cape Fear Community College
Shirley Powell, Arkansas State University
Charlotte Pryor, University of Southern Maine
Jeffrey Pullen, Univ. of Maryland Univ. College
Iris Lugo Renta, Interamerican University
Betty J. Reynolds, Arizona Western College
Monique Ring, So. New Hampshire University
Annalee Rothenberg, Tacoma Community Coll.
Helen Roybark, Radford University
Diane Sandefur, Elliott Bookkeeping School
Art Shroeder, Louisiana State University
Joann Segovia, Winona State University
Donald Schwartz, National University
Lee Shook, Chipola College
Mona Stephens, University of Phoenix
Charles Strang, Western New Mexico Univ.
Marilyn St. Clair, Weatherford College
Marie Stewart, Newport Business Institute
Maggie Stone, Pima Community College
Mel Sweet, University of Connecticut
Laurie Swinney, University of Nebraska
Eileen Taylor, North Carolina State University
Greg Thom, Parkland Community College
Tom Turner, Des Moines Area Community Coll.
Jamie Vaught, Southeast Community College
Mazdolyn Winston, Calhoun Community Coll.
W. Brian Voss, Austin Community College
Bruce Whitaker, Diné College
Shandra Ware, Atlanta Technical College
Michele Wiltsie, Hudson Valley Comm. Coll.

Table of Contents

The Timetable for Completion on the next page is a guideline for in-class lecture/discussion/demonstration and hands-on work. Work <u>not</u> completed in class is homework. In most Accounting classes, students can expect to spend approximately two hours outside of class for every hour in class.

Two optional projects are on the textbook's Online Learning Center at www.mhhe.com/yacht2012. Select the Student Edition and then link to Practice Set or Bellwether Garden Supply Project.

The Bellwether Garden Supply project is in question/answer format. The Practice Set includes source documents for setting up and completing the accounting cycle for a merchandising business.

Table of Contents

Part 1

Exploring Peachtree Complete Accounting 2012

Part 1 introduces the basic features of Peachtree Complete Accounting 2012. The purpose of Part 1 is to become familiar with the software rather than test accounting knowledge. Beginning with Chapter 9, computer accounting skills are reviewed in more depth. In Chapters 9-18 and Projects 1-4A, 12 businesses are set up from scratch. Part 1, Chapters 1-8, introduces two sample companies that are included with the software: Bellwether Garden Supply and Stone Arbor Landscaping.

Chapter 1:   Introduction to Bellwether Garden Supply
Chapter 2:   Vendors
Chapter 3:   Customers
Chapter 4:   Employees
Chapter 5:   General Ledger, Inventory, and Internal Control
Chapter 6:   Job Cost
Chapter 7:   Financial Statements
Chapter 8:   Stone Arbor Landscaping—Time & Billing
Online Learning Center–Bellwether Garden Supply Project,
www.mhhe.com/yacht2012, Student Edition

In Chapters 1 through 7, the work completed with Bellwether Garden Supply is cumulative. That means all work within the chapter and end-of-chapter exercises needs to be completed. Throughout Part 1, report illustrations and Check your figure amounts are shown. To insure that your work matches the textbook, complete *both* the work within the chapter and the end-of-chapter exercises. The Online Learning Center at www.mhhe.com/yacht2012, Student Edition link, includes a Bellwether Garden Supply Project.

The instructions in this book were written for Peachtree Complete Accounting 2012 (abbreviated **PCA**). PCA requires Windows 7, Vista Service Pack 1, or XP SP 3. Multi-user mode is optimized for Windows Server 2003 or Windows Server 2008 client-server networks, and Windows XP/Vista/7 peer-to-peer networks.

Windows[1] uses pictures or *icons* to identify tasks. This is known as a *user interface* (*UI*), also known as the *graphical user interface* (*GUI*). For example, PCA uses common icons or symbols to represent tasks: a disk for saving, a question mark for help, a printer for printing, an envelope for email, etc. A *mouse*, *touchpad* or other pointing device is used to perform various tasks. Software design can be described by the acronym *WIMP* -- Windows, Icons, Menus, and Pull-downs.

The chart below shows the size of the backup files, Excel files, and PDF files saved in Part 1–Chapters 1 through 8. (Excel 2007 and 2010 files end in an .xlsx extension; Excel 2003, the extension is .xls.) The textbook shows how to back up to a USB drive. Backups can be made to the desktop, hard drive location, network location or external media.

Chapter	Peachtree Backup (.ptb) Excel (.xlsx) and Adobe (.pdf)	Kilobytes[2]	Page Nos.
1	bgs.ptb[3]	3,306 KB	23-25
	Chapter 1.ptb	3,314 KB	41-42
	Chapter 1_Employee List.xlsx	14 KB	43-45
	Chapter 1_Employee List.pdf	14 KB	45-46
	Exercise 1-2.ptb	3,317 KB	51
	Exercise 1-2_Employee List.xlsx	15 KB	52
	Exercise 1-2_Employee List.pdf	14 KB	52
	Exercise 1-2_Chart of Accounts.xlsx	17 KB	52
	Exercise 1-2_Chart of Accounts.pdf	17 KB	52
2	Chapter 2.ptb	3,435 KB	88
	Chapter 2_Vendor List and Ledgers.xlsx	21 KB	88-90
	Chapter 2_Vendor List.pdf	8 KB	91
	Chapter 2_Vendor Ledgers.pdf	14 KB	91
	Exercise 2-2.ptb	3,460 KB	97
	Exercise 2-2_Vendor List and Ledgers.xlsx	21 KB	97
	Exercise 2-2_Vendor List.pdf		97
	Exercise 2-2_Vendor Ledgers.pdf	47 KB	97
3	Chapter 3.ptb	3,529 KB	135
	Exercise 3-2.ptb	3,531 KB	138
	Exercise 3-2_Customer Ledgers.xlsx	18	138
	Exercise 3-2_Customer Ledgers.pdf	50 KB	138
4	Chapter 4.ptb	3,554	159-160
	Exercise 4-2.ptb	3,577 KB	162
	Exercise 4-2_Payroll Check Register.xlsx	13 KB	162

---

[1] Words that are boldfaced and italicized are defined in Appendix D, Glossary.
[2] Your backup sizes may differ.
[3] This is the first backup and includes starting data for Bellwether Garden Supply.

Chapter	Peachtree Backup (.ptb) Excel (.xlsx) and Adobe (.pdf)	Kilobytes[4]	Page Nos.
4	Exercise 4-2_Payroll Check Register.pdf	58 KB	162
5	Chapter 5.ptb	3,576 KB	198-199
	Exercise 5-2.ptb	3,571 KB	203
	Exercise 5-2_General Ledger Trial Balance.xlsx	15 KB	203
	Exercise 5-2_General Ledger Trial Balance.pdf	56 KB	203
6	Chapter 6.ptb	3,661 KB	218
	Exercise 6-2.ptb[5]	3,680 KB	220
	Exercise 6-2_Job Profitability Report.xlsx	16 KB	221
	Exercise 6-2_Job Profitability Report.pdf	14 KB	221
7	No backups in Chapter 7	--	--
	Chapter 7_Financial Statements.xlsx	37 KB	243
	Chapter 7_Balance Sheet.pdf	12 KB	244
	Chapter 7_Income Statement.pdf	14 KB	244
	Chapter 7_Dept Gross Profit Totals.pdf	8 KB	244
	Chapter 7_Statement of Cash Flow.pdf	11 KB	244
	Chapter 7_Statement of Retained Earnings.pdf	7 KB	244
	Chapter 7_Statement of Changes in Financial Position.pdf	11 KB	244
OLC	Bellwether Garden Supply Project, www.mhhe.com/yacht2012		
8	Chapter 8.ptb	1,674 KB	264
	Chapter 8_Time Ticket Register.xlsx	14 KB	265-267
	Chapter 8_Time Ticket Register.pdf	11 KB	267
	Exercise 8-1.ptb	1,706 KB	271
	Exercise 8-2_Time and Billing Reports.xlsx	33 KB	272
	Exercise 8-2_Job Ledger.pdf	59 KB	272
	Exercise 8-2_Time Ticket Register.pdf	44 KB	272
	Exercise 8-2_Payroll Time Sheet.pdf	43 KB	272

> **Read Me: Problem Backing Up to USB Drive**
> If you encounter difficulties backing up to a   USB drive, backup to the desktop first. Then, copy the backup file from the desktop to the USB drive. Refer to Appendix A, Problem Backing Up to USB Drive or other External Media, pages 756-758.

---

[4]Your backup sizes may differ.
[5]The **Exercise 6-2.ptb** backup file is used in Part 4, Chapters 16, 17, and 18. If necessary, backup to external media. Do *not* delete the Exercise 6-2.ptb file.

Chapter 1

Introduction to Bellwether Garden Supply

LEARNING OBJECTIVES

1. Start Peachtree Complete Accounting 2012 (PCA).[1]
2. Explore the sample company, Bellwether Garden Supply.
3. Make sure global options are set ▶.[2]
4. Back up Bellwether Garden Supply data ▶.
5. Restore data with Peachtree's restore Wizard ▶.
6. Operate Peachtree's menus, drop-down lists, toolbar, and navigation bar.
7. Use Windows Explorer to see file sizes.
8. Export Peachtree reports to Excel, and save reports as Adobe PDF files.
9. Make three backups, save three Excel files, and three PDF files.[3]

Peachtree Complete Accounting 2012 (PCA) is similar to other programs that use Windows. These similarities relate to menus and windows, entering and saving data, and selecting icons. If you are not familiar with Windows, using PCA will help you become familiar with the Windows operating system.

MOUSE AND KEYBOARD BASICS

One of the first decisions is whether to use the mouse or keyboard. The instructions in this book assume that you are using a mouse. When the word click is used in the instructions, it means to use the mouse, but you can also use the keyboard. The instructions below explain how to use the mouse or keyboard.

---

[1] If Peachtree Complete Accounting 2012 is not installed, refer to pages vi-xv. The sample companies must be installed to complete Chapters 1-8.

[2] This icon, ▶ , means there is a Setting Global Options flash video. Go online to www.mhhe.com/yacht2012. Link to Student Edition, select Chapter 1, Flash Videos, Setting Global Options.

[3] Refer to the chart on pages 2-3 for the size of files backed up and saved. Check with your instructor for his or her preference for receiving files–Adobe .pdf, Excel .xlsx, or Peachtree .ptb.

Using the Mouse

➢ To single click: position the mouse cursor over the selection and click the left mouse button once.

➢ To double-click: position the mouse cursor over the selection and click the left mouse button twice, quickly.

➢ Use the right mouse button the same way as the left mouse button.

Using the Keyboard

➢ If there is an underlined letter on the menu bar, hold down the **<Alt>**[4] key and the underlined letter to make the selection. (*Hint:* Press the **<Alt>** key to underline menu bar letters.)

➢ If you have already held down the **<Alt>** key and the underlined letter and more selections appear with underlined letters, just type the underlined letter to select the item.

Using Shortcut Keys

Shortcut keys enable you to perform common operations by using two or more keys together. The shortcut keys are shown below and on the next page.

<Ctrl> + <Letter> Shortcuts	
<Ctrl> + <X>	Cut
<Ctrl> + <C>	Copy
<Ctrl> + <V>	Paste
<Ctrl> + <E>	Delete Record
<Ctrl> + <F>	Find
<Ctrl> + <D>	Find Next
<Ctrl> + <N>	New Company
<Ctrl> + <O>	Open Company
<Ctrl> + <B>	Back Up Company
<Ctrl> + <R>	Restore Company
<Ctrl> + <P>	Print Displayed Report, Invoices, Quotes, etc.

---

[4]The angle brackets are used around words to indicate individual keys on your keyboard; for example, **<Alt>** is for the Alternate key, **<Enter>** for the Enter/Return key, **<Ctrl>** is for the Control key, **<Esc>** is for the Escape key.

Key Shortcuts	
<F1>	Displays the online Help topic for current window
<Shift> + <F1>	Changes mouse pointer to What's This Help selector
<F3>	Find transactions
<F5>	Saves records and posts (or saves) transactions in certain windows
<F7>	Check spelling
<F10>	Toggles between open window and menu bar
<CTRL> + <F4>	Close current document window
<ALT>+<F4>	Closes the application window
<CTRL> + <F6>	Moves to next window
<Shift> + <CTRL>+F6	Moves to the previous window

To learn more about Peachtree's shortcuts, use Peachtree's Help menu. From the menu bar, select Help; Peachtree Accounting Help. Select the Index tab. Type **Keyboard Shortcuts** in the keyword field, then display Peachtree Keyboard Shortcuts. Additional links are listed in the Related topics and What do you want to do next? areas of the help window.

PCA'S STARTUP WINDOW

Peachtree's startup window displays a number of options.

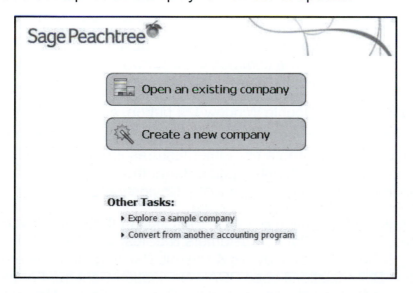

From the startup window, you can Open an existing company, Create a new company, Explore a sample company, and Convert from another accounting program.

The McGraw-Hill Companies, Inc., *Computer Accounting with Peachtree by Sage Complete Accounting 2012, 16e*

Observe that the top-left of the Peachtree Accounting window has four

menu-bar options—.

To exit from the startup window select File; Exit; *or*, click on the ⊠ on the upper right-hand side of the Peachtree Accounting window.

Comment
The illustrations in this textbook were done with Windows 7 and Peachtree Complete Accounting 2012.

THE WINDOWS INTERFACE

One of the benefits of Windows is that it standardizes terms and operations used in software programs. Once you learn how to move around PCA, you also know how to use other Windows applications.

To learn more about the Windows environment, let's look at a PCA window. On the next page, the Peachtree Accounting window shows the **Business Status Navigation Center** (the **dashboard**) and the menu bar for Bellwether Garden Supply.

For now, let's study the parts of Peachtree's Business Status Navigation Center. Some features are common to all software programs that are written for Windows. For example, in the upper right corner there is the Minimize ▬ button, Double Window ⬚ button, and the Exit or Close ▬⊠▬ button. The title bar, window border, and mouse pointer are also common to Windows programs. Other features are specific to PCA: menu bar, toolbar, and the Navigation Bar at the left side of Peachtree's main window which offers access to the Navigation Centers.

PCA includes a Navigation Bar on the left side of the window with seven selections: Business Status, Customers & Sales, Vendors & Purchases, Inventory & Services, Employees & Payroll, Banking, and System. The Navigation Bar selections open PCA's Navigation Centers. For example, the Business Status selection opens the Business Status Navigation Center. The content of the Navigation Centers differ depending on the selection from the Navigation Bar. The Business Status Navigation Center is shown on the next page.

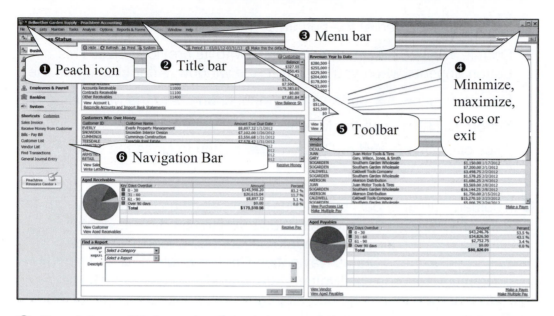

❶ Peach icon: Click on the Peach icon and a menu appears with options such as: Restore, Move, Size, Minimize, Maximize, Close. (Words that are gray are inactive selections.)

❷ **Title Bar**: The bar is at the top of the window. When a company is open in PCA, the name of the company is displayed on the Title Bar. If your window is minimized, you can put your mouse on the Title Bar, click and hold the left mouse button and drag the window around the *desktop*. The title bar shows Bellwether Garden Supply – Peachtree Accounting.

❸ Menu Bar: In PCA 2012, there are 10 (or 11) menu bar selections. If your menu bar selections have underlined letters that means you can make a selection by typing **<Alt>** and the underlined letter. For example, if you press the <Alt> key then press the <F> key, the menu bar shows underlined letters as well as the drop-down menu. You can also click with your left-mouse button on the menu bar headings to see a menu of options.

❹ Minimize ▬, Double Window ⧉, or Maximize ▢, and Close or Exit ✕ buttons: Clicking once on Minimize ▬ reduces the window to a button on the *taskbar*. In Windows 7, the ⊞ Start button and

---

taskbar are located at the bottom of the window. Clicking once on Double Window returns the window to its previous size. This button appears when you maximize the window. After clicking on the Double Window button, the symbol changes to the Maximize button. Click once on the Maximize button to enlarge the window. Click once on the Exit or Close button to close the window, or exit the program.

❺ Toolbar: The gray bar[5] below the Business Status button shows the following selections: Hide, this allows you to hide the Navigation Centers; Refresh, you can update account balances; Print, you can print the Business Status Navigation Center; System Date; Period for accounting records (Bellwether defaults to Period 3 – 03/01/12-03/31/12); Make this the default page; Customize this page. (When Business Status is selected, this toolbar appears.)

⊗ Hide	↻ Refresh	🖨 Print	System Date: 03/15/12	Period 3 - 03/01/12-03/31/12	Make this the default page	Customize this page

❻ Navigation Bar: Peachtree's Navigation Bar includes seven selections. These selections open the Business Status, Customers & Sales, Vendors & Purchases, Inventory & Services, Employees & Payroll, Banking, and System Navigation Centers.

---

[5]Window colors may differ. Check with your instructor if you have a question.

TYPICAL PCA WINDOWS

When you make a Navigation Bar selection, access is provided to the Navigation Center for each area of the program. For example, when Customers & Sales is selected, a workflow diagram is shown for Customers & Sales tasks, and links to related areas. There is also a tab for Customer Management.

The Maintain Customers/Prospects window is shown below, one that is typical of PCA. Information about customers is entered into the Maintain Customers/Prospects window. There are five sections on this window: ❶ the icon bar, ❷ Previous or next record, ❸ drop-down list (down arrow), ❹ tabs, ❺ information about window.

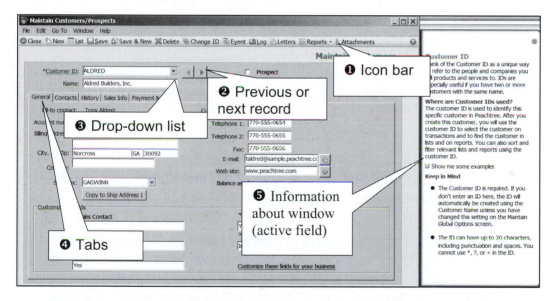

❶ ***Icon bar***[6]: The icon bar shows pictures of commands or additional information that pertains to the window. Some icons are common to all windows while other icons are specific to a particular window.

The icons included in the Maintain Customers/Prospects window are shown on the next page.

---

[6]Notice that familiar business items are used for icons: disk for <u>S</u>ave, an X for Delete, a paperclip for Attachments.

Close: This closes the window without saving any work that has been typed since the last time you saved.

New: New record or customer.

List: List of customers.

Save: This saves information you have entered such as addresses, telephone numbers, contacts for vendors, customers, employees, etc.

Save & New: Save the record and go to a new, blank record.

Delete: If you select this while using a selection from the Maintain menu, the record (customer, vendor, etc.) will be deleted. When you're finished deleting, select Close, in order to delete the records.

Change ID: When a customer record is displayed on the window, you may change the information for that customer.

Event: Select this button in various maintenance windows to create an event. The Create Event window allows you to schedule an event for a customer/prospect, vendor, or employee/sales representative. You can also use the Event log to record notes about telephone calls, meetings, letters, and create a listing of future activity.

Log: This shows you events recorded for an individual over a range of time that you specify. You can *filter* this list to see only certain types of activities and whether they're completed or not. You can mark activities as completed by placing a mark in the far left column. Double-clicking on any of the *line items* will take you to the Create an Event window. Line items appear on many of Peachtree's windows. On color monitors, a magenta line is placed around the row (line item) you select.

Letters Letters: Select this button to process a mail merge for the currently opened record.

Reports ▾ Reports: If you click on the down-arrow on the Reports icon, you can select the following customer reports—Aged Receivables, Customer Transaction History, Customer Ledgers, Items Sold to Customers, Job Ledger, Quote Register, Sales Order Register, and Ticket Listing by Customer. (In this example, Maintain; Customers/ Prospects, Aldred Builders, Inc. is selected as the customer.)

Attachments Attachments: Use this icon to add attachments for this record.

? Help: Selecting this icon gives you information specific to the current window. The fields of the window are often listed at the bottom of the help message. When you have a question about how to use Peachtree, clicking on the Help icon often answers it.

❷ **◄ ►** Previous or Next Record: Click on either the left arrow for the previous record; or the right arrow for the next record.

❸ *Drop-Down List*: The down arrow means that this field contains a list of information from which you can make a selection. Many of PCA's windows have drop-down lists that appear when you click on a down arrow next to a field. You can press **<Enter>** or click on an item to select it from the list.

❹ *Tabs*: The tabs that are shown in the Maintain Customers/Prospects window are General, Contacts, History, Sales Info, Payment & Credit. Once a customer is selected, you can select one of these folders to display information about a customer.

❺ On the right side of maintenance windows, information about the active field is shown. On the Maintain Customers/Prospects window on page 11, information about the CUSTOMER ID field is shown.

THE SAMPLE COMPANY: BELLWETHER GARDEN SUPPLY

Bellwether Garden Supply is one of the sample companies included with PCA. To help you become familiar with the software, the sample company is used.

GETTING STARTED

Follow these steps to start Peachtree Complete Accounting 2012 (PCA):

1. Start PCA. If Peachtree Complete Accounting 2012 is not installed on your computer, refer to pages vi-xv for installing the Peachtree Complete Accounting software that is included with this textbook.

2. When Peachtree Complete Accounting 2012 (PCA) was installed, an icon was created for Peachtree. To start, place the mouse pointer on the Peachtree icon and double-click with the left mouse button. (Or, click Start, All Programs, Peachtree Accounting 2012. Then, click Peachtree Accounting 2012.)

3. The Peachtree Accounting window appears. From the startup window, you can Open an existing company, Create a new company, Explore a sample company, or Convert from another accounting program.

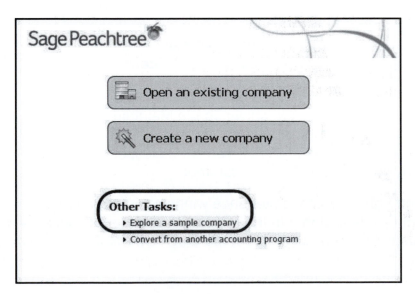

4. Select Explore a sample company.

5. The Explore a Sample Company window appears. PCA 2012 has two sample companies: Bellwether Garden Supply and Stone Arbor Landscaping. In Chapters 1 – 7, you use Bellwether Garden Supply to explore Peachtree. Then, in Chapter 8, you use Stone Arbor Landscaping to see how Peachtree's time and billing feature works. Make sure that Bellwether Garden Supply is selected.

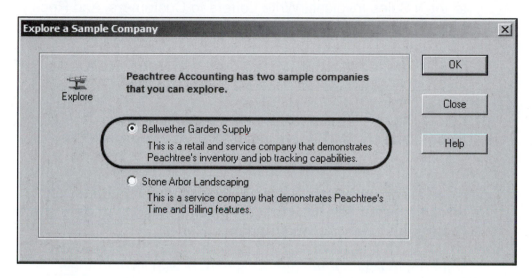

Troubleshooting: Why doesn't my Explore a Sample Company window show the OK, Close, and Help buttons?

Screen resolution affects how Peachtree's windows look. The recommended screen resolution is 1024 X 768 with small fonts (refer to p. iv). You can use a higher resolution but some of the windows will look different. If you do not have an OK button, press <Enter> to start Bellwether Garden Supply.

6. Click [OK]. On the Navigation Bar, select [Business Status]. The Business Status Navigation Center appears. The Business Status Navigation Center, also known as the *Home page* or dashboard, is separated into seven areas. The dashboard lets you see at a glance a variety of general business information. Scroll down the window to see all of it. Each area has underlined links shown in blue font.

a. Account Balances – observe the links from this area are <u>View Account List</u>; <u>Reconcile Accounts and Import Bank Statements</u>; <u>View Balance Sheet</u>. In Peachtree, you can link to reports from the Navigation Centers *or* from the menu bar.

b. Customers Who Owe Money – A customer list is shown with links to <u>View Sales Invoices</u>, <u>Write Letters to Customers</u>, and <u>Receive Money.</u>

c. Aged Receivables – A graph is shown and links to <u>View Customer List</u>; <u>View Aged Receivables Report</u>; and <u>Receive Payment</u>.

d. Find a Report – Observe that fields are included for Category, Report, and Description. (If necessary, scroll down the Home page.)

e. Revenue: Year to Date – A graph shows the first quarter of 2012's revenue and links to <u>View Income Statement</u>; <u>Edit the Budget</u>; and <u>View Account Variance Report</u>.

f. Vendors to Pay – A vendor list is shown with links to <u>View Purchases List</u>, <u>Make Multiple Payments</u>, and <u>Make a Payment</u>s.

g. Aged Payables – A graph is shown and links to <u>View Vendor</u>, <u>View Aged Payables</u>, <u>Makes a Payment</u>, and <u>Make Multiple Payments</u>.

DISPLAY PRODUCT INFORMATION

1. From the menu bar, click Help; About Peachtree Accounting.

   The About Sage Peachtree Accounting window shows the copyright information and the Release, Build, Serial Number, Installed Tax Service, and Registered Tax Service. The Release field shows Sage Peachtree Complete® Accounting 2012; the Build No. is 19.0.00.0906E (E for education) *or* Build No. 19.0.00.0906S (S for student); Serial Number, Educational Version or Student Version; Installed Tax Service 19000101; Registered Tax Service None.

   The About Sage Peachtree Accounting window is shown on the next page for the Educational and Student Versions.

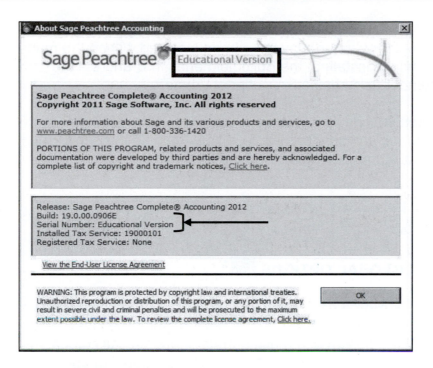

Troubleshooting: On my About Sage Peachtree Accounting window the Build field ends in S (not E), and Serial Number field shows Student Version (not Educational Version). Why?

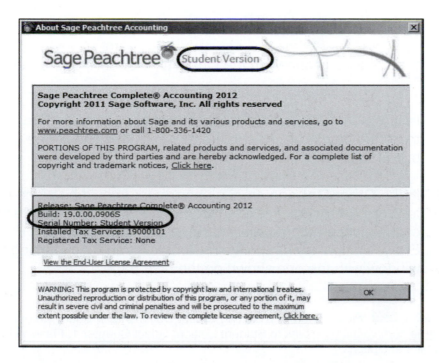

If you are using Peachtree in the classroom or computer lab, the multi-user version may have been installed. When the multi-user version is installed, the Build field ends in E and the the Serial Number field shows Educational Version.

When you install the student version software included with the textbook on your PC, the Build Number field ends in S and the Serial Number field shows Student Version.

2. Click [OK] to close the About Sage Peachtree Accounting window.

SETTING GLOBAL OPTIONS ▶[7]

Peachtree's *global options* are in effect for all Peachtree companies. On pages xvi-xviii, steps are shown for setting global options. They are repeated here so you can make sure they are set. All companies in Chapters 1-18 and Projects 1-4 require these global options.

1. From the menu bar, select Options; Global. The Maintain Global Options window appears. The Accounting tab is selected.

   a. In the **Decimal Entry** area, select Manual.

   b. Make sure 2 is shown in the Quantity, Standard and Unit Price fields.

   c. In the **Hide General Ledger Accounts** area, make sure that there are no checkmarks in the boxes. (To uncheck one of the boxes, click on it.)

   d. In the **Other Options** area, a checkmark should be placed next to Warn if a record was changed but not saved; and Recalculate cash balance automatically in Receipts, Payments, and Payroll Entry. Compare your Maintain Global Options; Accounting tab window with the one shown on the next page.

---

[7]This icon, ▶, means there is a Setting Global Options flash video. Go online to www.mhhe.com/yacht2012. Link to Student Edition, select Chapter 1, Flash Videos, Setting Global Options.

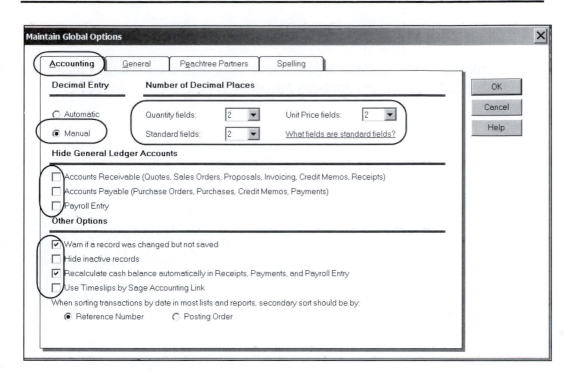

2. Click on the **General** tab. Make sure the Maintain Global Options; General window shows the following selections.

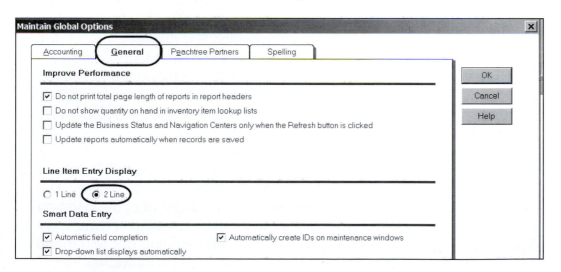

3. Click [OK] to save the global options, which will be in effect for all Peachtree companies.

PEACHTREE'S USER INTERFACE

A User Interface (UI) is the link between a user and a computer program. Peachtree's UI is designed for both Navigation Bar and menu-bar selections.

The user interface is one of the most important parts of any software because it determines how easily you can make the program do what you want. Graphical user interfaces (GUIs) that use windows, icons, and pop-up menus are standard on personal computers.

The **Navigation Bar** appears at the left side of the Peachtree main window and offers access to the **Navigation Centers**. The Navigation Centers provide information about and access to Peachtree. The Navigation Bar includes seven selections: Business Status, Customers & Sales, Vendors & Purchases, Inventory & Services, Employees & Payroll, Banking, and System.

When you click one of the seven selections (for example, Customers & Sales), the panel to the right of the Navigation Bar displays a **workflow diagram** with additional links related to that **module**. Modules organize Peachtree's transaction windows and reports. The menu bar selections, Tasks and Reports & Forms, are also organized by module; for example, the Reports & Forms menu includes Accounts Receivable, Accounts Payable, General Ledger, etc.

Peachtree's modules include Customers & Sales, Vendors & Purchases, Inventory & Services, Employees & Payroll, Banking, and System. The Business Status Navigation Center includes a snapshot of the company. Peachtree's modular design is similar to other accounting software applications. In this textbook, you use PCA's Navigation Bar and menu bar selections to access features of the program. The individual Navigation Bar selections take you to Navigation Centers. For example, if you select Customers & Sales, the Customers & Sales Navigation Center appears.

CHART OF ACCOUNTS

A *chart of accounts* is a list of all the accounts used by a company showing identifying numbers assigned to each account. Peachtree's *general ledger module* is the complete collection of accounts (chart of accounts) of a company, transactions associated with these accounts, and account balances for a specified period. In Chapter 5, General Ledger, Inventory, and Internal Control, you will learn more about Peachtree's general ledger module and the chart of accounts. For now, let's view Bellwether's chart of accounts so that you can familiarize yourself with the accounts that will be used in subsequent chapters.

Follow these steps to display Bellwether's chart of accounts.

1. From the Navigation Bar, select ⌨ **Business Status** . In the Account balances area, link to View Account List. The Account List window appears. The Account List is also called the Chart of Accounts.

Account ID ⟁	Description	Type	Running Balance
10000	Petty Cash	Cash	$327.55
10100	Cash on Hand	Cash	$1,850.45
10200	Regular Checking Account	Cash	$23,389.83
10300	Payroll Checking Account	Cash	$3,711.09
10400	Savings Account	Cash	$7,500.00
11000	Accounts Receivable	Accounts Receivable	$175,383.01
11100	Contracts Receivable	Accounts Receivable	$0.00
11400	Other Receivables	Accounts Receivable	$7,681.84
11500	Allowance for Doubtful Account	Accounts Receivable	($5,000.00)
12000	Inventory	Inventory	$12,854.06
14000	Prepaid Expenses	Other Current Assets	$14,221.30
14100	Employee Advances	Other Current Assets	$3,000.65
14200	Notes Receivable-Current	Other Current Assets	$11,000.00
14700	Other Current Assets	Other Current Assets	$120.00
15000	Furniture and Fixtures	Fixed Assets	$62,769.25
15100	Equipment	Fixed Assets	$38,738.33
15200	Vehicles	Fixed Assets	$86,273.40
15300	Other Depreciable Property	Fixed Assets	$6,200.96
15400	Leasehold Improvements	Fixed Assets	$0.00
15500	Buildings	Fixed Assets	$185,500.00
15600	Building Improvements	Fixed Assets	$26,500.00
16900	Land	Fixed Assets	$0.00
17000	Accum. Depreciation-Furniture	Accumulated Depreciation	($54,680.57)
17100	Accum. Depreciation-Equipment	Accumulated Depreciation	($33,138.11)
17200	Accum. Depreciation-Vehicles	Accumulated Depreciation	($51,585.26)
17300	Accum. Depreciation-Other	Accumulated Depreciation	($3,788.84)
17400	Accum. Depreciation-Leasehold	Accumulated Depreciation	$0.00
17500	Accum. Depreciation-Buildings	Accumulated Depreciation	($34,483.97)
17600	Accum. Depreciation-Bldg Imp	Accumulated Depreciation	($4,926.28)
19000	Deposits	Other Assets	$15,000.00
19100	Organization Costs	Other Assets	$4,995.10
19150	Accum Amortiz - Organiz Costs	Other Assets	($2,000.00)
19200	Notes Receivable- Noncurrent	Other Assets	$5,004.90
19900	Other Noncurrent Assets	Other Assets	$3,333.00
20000	Accounts Payable	Accounts Payable	($80,626.01)
23000	Accrued Expenses	Other Current Liabilities	($3,022.55)
23100	Sales Tax Payable	Other Current Liabilities	($18,017.89)

The Account List's icon bar includes a Send To selection. When you make that selection, you can send the Account List to Excel, E-mail, or PDF (Adobe Acrobat). Exporting Peachtree reports to Microsoft Excel is shown on pages 43-45. Saving PDF files is shown on pages 45-46. The numbers in parentheses are credit balances.

2. Close the Account List by clicking ☒ on its title bar.

BACKING UP BELLWETHER GARDEN SUPPLY ▶[8]

Before making changes to Bellwether Garden Supply, you should back up the sample company data. When using PCA, information is automatically saved to the hard drive of the computer. In a classroom, a number of students may be using the same computer. This means that when you return to the computer lab or classroom, your data will be gone. *Backing up* means saving a copy of the data to a hard drive, network drive, or external media. Backing up insures that you can start where you left off the last time Peachtree was used.

When backing up, you have choices—accept the hard-drive default location or back up to a USB drive (or other external media). In the steps that follow, backups are made to a USB drive also called flash drives, thumb drives, or pen/stick drives. In this book, the term *USB drive* is used to identify USB storage media. USB is an abbreviation of Universal Serial Bus.

---

[8]The arrow indicates there is a flash video. Go online to www.mhhe.com/yacht2012; link to Student Edition, select Chapter 1, Flash Videos, Backup.

Comment: Backing up data to the hard-drive default location

The author suggests backing up the sample company *before* any changes are made. In the textbook, backups are made to **external media** or a USB drive. Backups can also be made to the desktop or other locations.

You may also backup to the default location at C:\Sage\Peachtree\Company\Sample\PCWS\BCS. (*Hint:* To see the default directory where Bellwether is located, from the menu bar select Maintain, Company Information. The Directory field shows the location of the BCS folder. BCS is the folder where Bellwether Garden Supply data is stored.

Education Version directory:

Directory:	C:\Sage\Peachtree\Company\Sample\PCWE\BCS

Student Version directory: | C:\Sage\Peachtree\Company\Sample\PCWS\BCS |

When a back up is made, data is saved to the current point. To distinguish between backups, a different backup name (file name) should be used. Use Peachtree's **restore** feature to retrieve information that was backed up.

In the business world, backups are unique to each business: daily, weekly, monthly. Think of your backups this way and you will see why individual backups at different points in the data are necessary. *You should never leave the computer lab or classroom without backing up your data.*

Follow these steps to back up Bellwether Garden Supply.

The text directions assume that you are backing up to a USB drive. *You can also backup to* the desktop, hard drive, or network location. *One USB flash, thumb or pen drive, CD-R or DVD-R can be used for all backups in the textbook (Chapters 1-18 and the projects).* The chart on pages 2 and 3 (Part 1 introduction) shows the size of each backup made in Chapters 1-8.

1. Insert a USB flash drive into the USB drive.

2. From the Navigation Bar, click [System]. In the Back Up and Restore Data area, click [Back Up Now]. The Back Up Company window appears. If necessary, uncheck the box next to Include company name in the backup file name. Compare your Back Up Company window to the one shown on the next page.

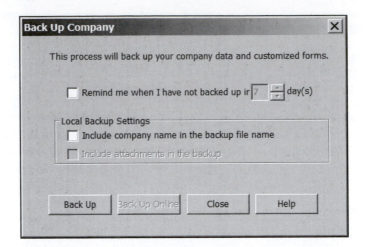

3. Click [Back Up]. The Save Backup for Bellwether Garden Supply as window appears.

4. In the Save in field, select your USB drive. The illustration below shows drive H, which is the location of the author's USB drive. Your USB drive letter may differ. Type **bgs** in the File name field.

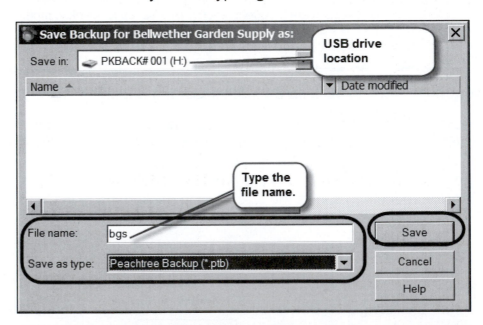

Observe that the Save as type field shows that you are making a Peachtree Backup (*.ptb), which is abbreviated ptb. This is the extension for Peachtree backups.

Comment

If your Save as type field does *not* show Peachtree Backup (*.ptb), follow these steps:

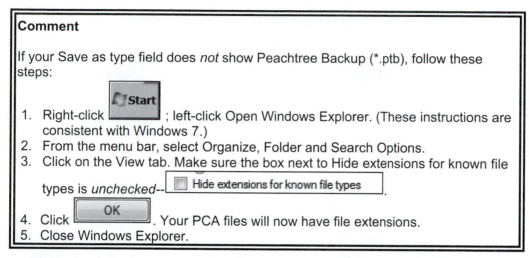

1. Right-click ; left-click Open Windows Explorer. (These instructions are consistent with Windows 7.)
2. From the menu bar, select Organize, Folder and Search Options.
3. Click on the View tab. Make sure the box next to Hide extensions for known file types is *unchecked*-- ☐ Hide extensions for known file types .
4. Click OK . Your PCA files will now have file extensions.
5. Close Windows Explorer.

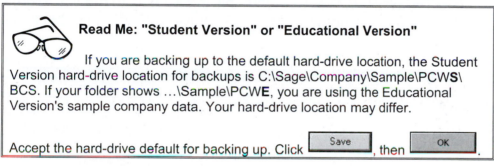

Read Me: "Student Version" or "Educational Version"

If you are backing up to the default hard-drive location, the Student Version hard-drive location for backups is C:\Sage\Company\Sample\PCW**S**\ BCS. If your folder shows ...\Sample\PCW**E**, you are using the Educational Version's sample company data. Your hard-drive location may differ.

Accept the hard-drive default for backing up. Click Save , then OK .

---

5. Click Save .

6. A window appears that says This company backup will require approximately 1 diskette.

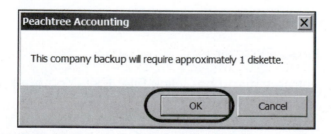

7. Click OK . When the window prompts Please insert the first disk, click OK . When Back Up Company scale is 100% complete, you have successfully backed up the sample company.

Follow these steps to see the size of the backup file.

1. Right-click ![Start]; left-click Open Windows Explorer. The folder icon ![folder icon] also opens Windows Explorer. (*Hint:* This textbook was written with Windows 7. If you are using a different Windows operating system, your start button differs.)

2. Select your USB drive (or the location where you backed up Bellwether Garden Supply).

    The Name of the file is bgs.ptb; the size of the file is 3,306 KB;[9] and File Type is PTB File. Compare this information to the bcs folder on your hard drive, network drive, USB drive, or DVD. Your backup size may differ.

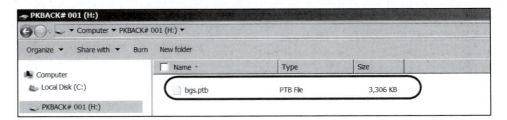

    Refer to the chart on pages 2 and 3 for back up sizes. Peachtree backs up to the current point in the data. The author suggests backing up to a USB flash drive, CD-R, DVD-R, or hard drive location.

Follow these steps to exit Peachtree:

1. Close Windows Explorer.

2. From Peachtree's menu bar, click File; Exit. You are returned to the desktop.

COPYING THE BCS FOLDER TO A CD-RW OR DVD-RW DRIVE

The instructions on pages 22-25 show how to use Peachtree's Back Up feature. Peachtree's Back Up feature works with Restore, which is shown

---

[9]The size of your backup file may differ.

on pages 29-32. *What if your instructor prefers that all the company data files be copied or saved?*

1. Go to your Windows desktop.

2. Put your CD-R or DVD-R into the appropriate drive. In this example, Roxio Easy Media Creator is being used to copy files to a CD-R. An AutoPlay window appears.

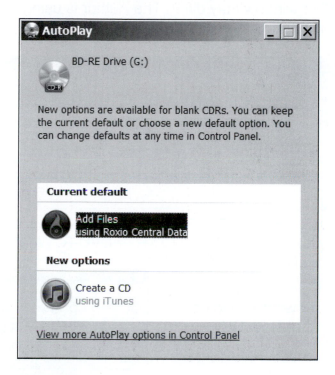

3. Select Add Files.

4. Right-click [Start]; left-click Open Windows Explorer. (*Hint:* In Windows 7, the folder icon [folder icon] also opens Windows Explorer.)

5. Select the location of the BCS folder: C:\Sage\Peachtree\Company\Sample\PCWE (or \PCWS).

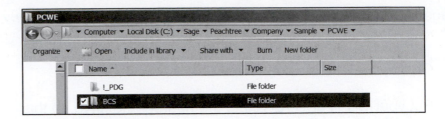

6. Copy/Paste or Drag Drop the BCS folder to the Easy Media Creator window. (Your window may differ. The Author is using Roxio Easy Media Creator software.)

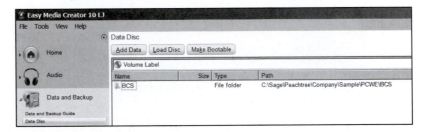

7. Click [ ] to continue. The Project Running window appears while the folder is being copied to the CD-R or DVD-R. When the drive opens, the file is copied. Click

[Done], close the Easy Media Creator window. Do not save the current Data Disc project.

8. Close the Windows Explorer window.

USING WINDOWS EXPLORER

To see the size of the folder you copied, follow these steps.

1. Close your CD or DVD drive. When the AutoPlay window appears, select Open folder to view files using Windows Explorer.

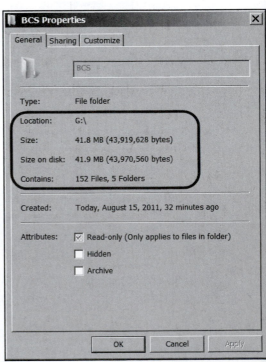

2. On the CD or DVD drive window, there is a Files Currently on the Disc (1) area. Right-click on the BCS folder. Left-click Properties. The BCS Properties window appears. The Location and Size of the BCS folder is shown. (Your file size may differ.)

3. Click [OK] to close the BCS Properties window.

USING PEACHTREE'S RESTORE WIZARD ▶¹⁰

In order to start where you left off the last time you backed up, use Peachtree's Restore Wizard. Your instructor may prefer that you use Windows Explorer to copy/paste instead of Peachtree's Restore feature. You may need to check with your instructor on the preferred method. This textbook shows Peachtree's Restore Wizard.

Follow these steps to use Peachtree's Restore Wizard.

1. Start Peachtree. (*Hint:* If another company opens, from the menu bar select File; Close Company to go to the startup window.) Open the sample company, Bellwether Garden Supply.

 Read Me: What if Bellwether Garden Supply is *not* shown as an existing company *or* when you select Explore a sample company?

Some schools delete company folders from the hard drive. For example, you have a back up file but the company, Bellwether Garden Supply, is *not* listed as a Peachtree company. Follow these steps to restore a company from a backup file.

1. If necessary, click File; Close Company to go to the Startup window. To double-check that Bellwether is *not* listed, select Open an existing company. Make sure Bellwether Garden Supply is *not* listed in the Company Name list. Click [Close].

2. The startup window shows four menu bar options—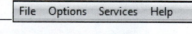. Select File; Restore.
3. Browse to the location of your backup file, select it. Click <Next>.
4. Restore *A New Company*. Compare your Select Company window with the one shown on page 31 step 8. Make sure A New Company is selected and the Company Name field shows Bellwether Garden Supply; click <Next>. Continue with step 10, page 31.

---

¹⁰The arrow indicates a flash video at www.mhhe.com/yacht2012. Select Student Edition; Chapter 1, Flash Videos, Restore.

2. Insert your USB flash drive. The steps that follow assume you are restoring from a USB drive.

3. From the Navigation Bar, click [System]. Click [Restore Now]. The Select Backup File window appears. Click [Browse].

4. The Open Backup File window appears. In the Look in field, select the location of your USB drive. Select the bgs.ptb file.

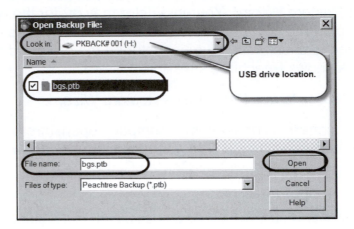

5. Click [Open].

6. The Restore Wizard – Select Backup File window appears showing the location of your backup file, X:\bgs.ptb. (Substitute X for your drive letter.)

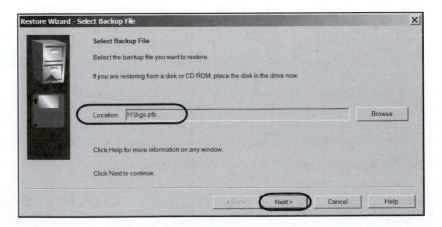

7. Click [Next >].

8. The Select Company window appears. Observe that An Existing Company is the default. The Company Name field shows Bellwether Garden Supply and the Location shows Bellwether's location. Your Location field may differ.

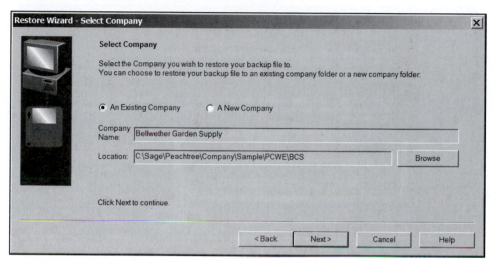

9. Read the information on the Select Company window; click [Next >].

10. The Restore Options window appears. Make sure that the check mark is next to Company Data.

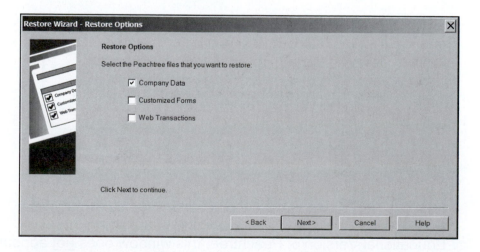

11. On the Restore Options window, click [Next >] .

12. The Confirmation window appears. The From field shows the USB drive location of the backup file. The To field shows the default installation location (your location may differ).

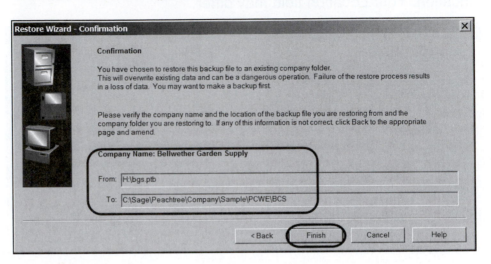

13. Read the information on the Confirmation window, then click [Finish] . Your backup data starts to restore. When the scale is 100% complete, the Bellwether Garden Supply data is restored.

    A window prompts that you can use this company in the student version of Peachtree for the next 14 months and then it will expire.

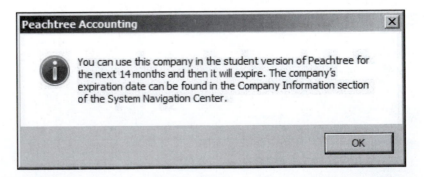

    Click [OK] . The Bellwether Garden Supply - Peachtree Accounting window appears. (*Hint:* If you are using the Educational Version of Peachtree, this window does <u>not</u> appear.)

Once Bellwether's files are restored, you are ready to continue using the sample company. *Remember before you exit PCA, make a backup of your work.*

The following information demonstrates PCA's horizontal menu bar selections. In this book, you are going to use *both* the menu bar selections and the Navigation Bar.

MENU BAR

PCA's menu bar has 10 (or possibly 11) selections: File, Edit, Lists, Maintain, Tasks, Analysis, Options, Reports & Forms, (Services is inactive), Window, and Help. (Once a file is restored, the Services menu appears.) Follow these steps to look at each menu bar selection.

1. From the menu bar, click File to see its menu, *or*, press <Alt> + F to display the File menu. If you use <Alt> + F instead of your mouse, notice that the individual letters on the menu bar are underlined. In this example, the mouse is used. The File menu selections are shown.

   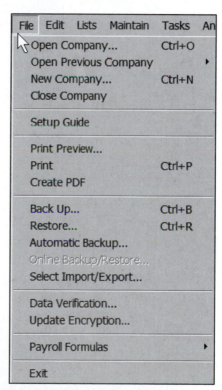

   The File menu allows you to open a company, open previous company, create a new company, close the company, go to the setup guide, print preview, print, create a PDF (Adobe Acrobat) file, Back Up, Restore, Automatic Backup, select import/export, data verification, update encryption, enter payroll formulas, and exit. (The grayed out selection is inactive.)

Menu choices that are followed by an ***ellipsis*** (...) are associated with ***dialog boxes*** or windows that supply information about a window. An arrow (▶) next to a menu item (Open Previous Company and Payroll Formulas) indicates that there is another menu with additional selections. To cancel the drop-down menu, click File or **<Esc>**.

2. The Edit selection shows Find Transactions.

3. Click Lists to see its menu. The Lists selection shows Customers & Sales, Vendors & Purchases, Employees & Payroll, Chart of Accounts, General Journal Entries, Inventory & Services, Jobs, and Time/Expense. The Lists menu is an alternative to using the Navigation Bar.

4. Click Maintain to see its menu.

From the Maintain menu, you can enter, view, or edit required information for your company's customers or prospects, vendors, employees or sales reps, chart of accounts, budgets, inventory items, item prices, job costs, make records inactive, and fixed assets. (Fixed Assets requires that FAS for Peachtree has been purchased.) You can also edit company information; enter memorized transactions; or go to *default* information, sales tax codes, and users (passwords and security). Defaults are commands that PCA automatically selects. Default information automatically displays in windows. You can change the default by choosing another command.

5.   Click Tasks to see its menu.

From the Tasks menu, you can enter quotes and sales orders, sales invoices, invoice time and expenses, receipts, finance charges, select for deposit, issue credit memos, purchase orders, purchases of inventory, select bills to pay, make payments, write checks, transmit electronic payments, issue vendor credit memos, display account registers, record time and expenses, record payroll information, and make general journal entries. You can also make inventory adjustments, assemblies, reconcile bank statements (account reconciliation), void checks, write letters, and enter action items. With the System selection, another menu displays with choices such as post and unpost (available with batch posting), change the accounting period, use the year-end wizard, and purge old or inactive transactions.

File Edit Lists Maintain **Tasks** A
Quotes/Sales Orders ▸
Sales/Invoicing...
Invoice Time and Expenses...
Receipts...
Finance Charge...
Select for Deposit...
Credit Memos...
Select for Purchase Orders...
Purchase Orders...
Purchases/Receive Inventory...
Bills ▸
Select for Payment ▸
Payments...
Write Checks...
Transmit Electronic Payments...
Vendor Credit Memos...
Account Register...
Time/Expense ▸
Select for Payroll Entry...
Payroll Entry...
General Journal Entry...
Inventory Adjustments...
Assemblies...
Account Reconciliation...
Void Checks...
Write Letters ▸
Action Items...
System ▸

6.   Click Analysis to see its menu.

The Analysis menu includes the cash flow manager, collection manager, payment manager, and financial manager.

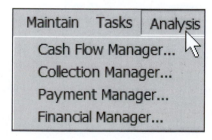

Maintain Tasks **Analysis**
Cash Flow Manager...
Collection Manager...
Payment Manager...
Financial Manager...

7. Click Options to see its menu.

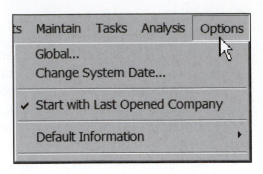

The Options menu includes setting global options, change the system date, start with the Last Opened Company, and enter default information. The checkmark next to Start with Last Opened Company means that each time you start Peachtree, the last company worked with opens.

8. Click Reports & Forms to see its menu.

The Reports & Forms menu allows you to *queue* reports for printing or displaying reports. You can also create and edit the format for forms, reports, and financial statements.

9. Click Window to see its menu. The Window menu allows you to close all windows.

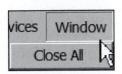

10. Click Help to see its menu.

The Help menu allows you to open a window of context-sensitive help, see what's new in Peachtree, go to the setup guide, open Peachtree's user manuals, go to Show Me How videos, Sage University, Sage Advisor History and Settings, Customer Support and Service, Peachtree on the Web, view or print the License Agreement, and the About Peachtree Accounting window. Select About Peachtree Accounting to display product information. Detailed steps for displaying product information are shown on pages 16-18.

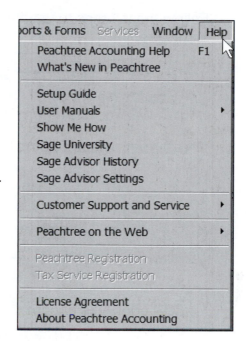

BECOMING AN EMPLOYEE OF BELLWETHER GARDEN SUPPLY

Before adding yourself as an employee of Bellwether Garden Supply, let's use the Navigation Bar to open the Maintain Employees & Sales Reps window. The Navigation Bar selections include: Business Status, Customers & Sales, Vendors & Purchases, Inventory & Services, Employees & Payroll, Banking, and System.

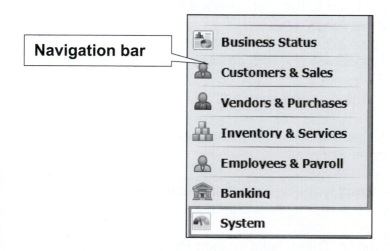

Follow these steps to use the Navigation Bar to add yourself as an employee.

1. On the Navigation Bar, select [Employees & Payroll]. The Employees & Payroll Navigation Center appears. The Employees & Payroll Tasks diagram is shown below.

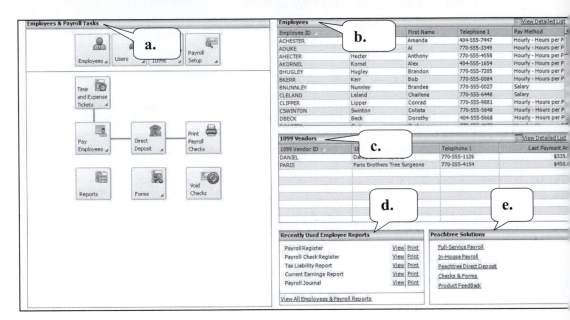

The Employees & Payroll Navigation Center displays information and access points related to the company's employees. It is organized into five sections.

a. Employees & Payroll Tasks: The flowchart shows how Peachtree processes payroll.

b. Employees: The employee list is shown.

c. 1099 Vendors: These are vendors who receive 1099's from Bellwether Garden Supply.

d. Recently Used Employee Reports: This section includes links to payroll reports.

e. Peachtree Solutions: These links include Peachtree's third-party suppliers.

2. Click 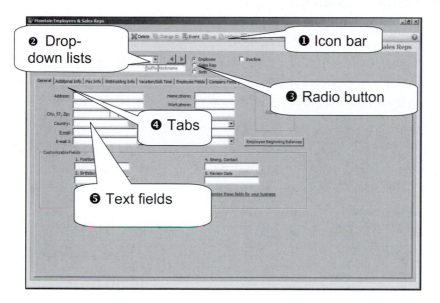 ; New Employee. The Maintain Employees & Sales Reps window appears.

❶ The icon bar at the top of most windows shows graphical representations of commands or functions that are accessible from the window.

❷ Drop-down lists: Click on the down-arrow to see lists. On the Maintain Employees & Sales Reps window, employee IDs are shown.   When you are in the text portion of the field, the cursor changes to an I-bar and a question mark <⌶?>. Type a question mark **<?>** in the field, or click the right mouse button, to display lists.

❸ *Radio Button* or *Option Button:* These buttons allow you to select one by clicking with the mouse. The default is Employee shown by the radio button next to Employee.

❹ Tabs are common to most PCA windows. They provide a subtitle to the various windows that store and organize information. Here, for example, the information you can choose to track is subdivided into categories: General, Additional Info, Pay Info, Withholding Info, Vacation/Sick Time, Employee Fields, and Company Fields.

❺ Text fields are rectangles or fields where information is typed.

Adding Yourself as an Employee

Follow these steps to add yourself as an employee.

1. Type an Employee ID code for yourself in the Employee ID field. For example, in all caps type **CYACHT** (type *the first initial of your first name and your full last name in all capital letters);* and press **<Enter>**.[11]

2. In the Name field, type your first name, press **<Enter>**; type your middle initial, if any, press **<Enter>**, then type your last name. Press **<Enter>** five times.[12]

3. In the Address field, type your street address. There are two lines so you can enter an ATTENTION line or P.O. Box, if necessary. If you are using just one line for your address, press **<Enter>** two times to go to the City, ST, Zip fields.

4. In the City, ST Zip field, type your city, state (two-digits), and zip code, pressing **<Enter>** after each.

5. None of the other information is required. You work with the other fields in Chapter 15, Employees, Payroll, and Account Reconciliation. Click 🖫 Save . To check that your Employee ID has been added, click on the down-arrow in the Employee ID field.

6. Click ⊗ Close to return to the Employees & Payroll Navigation Center.

---

[11]All ID codes are case-sensitive which means that cyacht and CYACHT are considered different codes. Capital letters sort before lowercase letters.

[12]You can use **<Enter>** or **<Tab>** to move between fields. Use **<Shift>+<Enter>** or **<Shift>+<Tab>** to move back a field. You can also hold the **<Alt>** key and press the underlined letter of a text box to move between fields.

BACKING UP CHAPTER 1 DATA

Follow these steps to back up Chapter 1 data:

1. Insert your USB flash drive.

2. From the Navigation Bar, click [System] ;
    [Back Up Now]. Make sure that the box next to Include company
    name in the backup file name is *unchecked*.

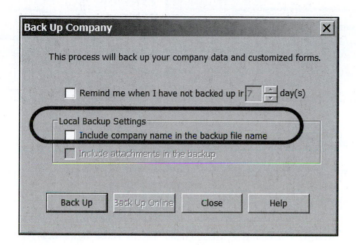

3. Click [Back Up] .

4. In the Save in field, select the appropriate drive letter for your USB
    drive.[13] (*Or,* save to the hard-drive default location or other location.)
    Type **Chapter 1** in the File name field. Compare your Save Backup
    for Bellwether Garden Supply as window with the one shown on the
    next page. (Your Save in field may differ.)

---

[13]If you are having difficulty backing up to USB flash drive, backup to the desktop, then
copy the file to a USB flash drive. Refer to Appendix A, Troubleshooting, pages 756-
758—Problem Backing Up to USB Drive or Other External Media.

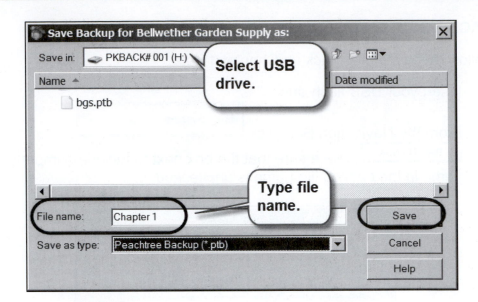

5. Click [Save].

6. When the window prompts This company backup will require approximately 1 diskette, click [OK]. When the window prompts Please insert the first disk, click [OK]. When the Back Up Company scale is 100% complete, you have successfully backed up to the current point in Chapter 1. (Step 6 will differ slightly if you are backing up to the default or other hard-drive location.)

Read Me: Problem Backing Up to USB Drive

If you encounter difficulties backing up to a USB drive, backup to your desktop first. Then copy the backup file from your desktop to a USB drive. Refer to Appendix A, Problem Backing Up to USB Drive or Other External Media, pages 756-758 for detailed steps.

---

7. Continue with the next section, Exporting Peachtree Reports to Microsoft Excel.

EXPORTING PEACHTREE REPORTS TO MICROSOFT EXCEL

On page 40, you added yourself as an employee of Bellwether Garden Supply. To see an Employee List and export the list to Excel, follow these steps. In order to export reports to Excel, you need Excel 2002 or higher.

1. From the Navigation Bar, select Employees & Payroll. In the Recently Used Employee Reports section, link to <u>View All Employees & Payroll Reports</u>. The Select a Report or Form window appears. Select Employee List.

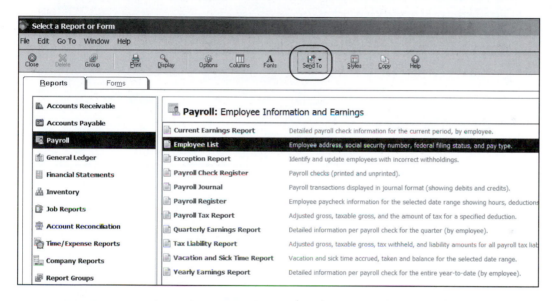

2. On the icon bar, select Send To; then select, Excel.

3. The Modify Report – Employee List window appears. Accept the defaults by clicking [OK].

4. The Copy Report to Excel window appears. Accept the File option, Create a New Microsoft Excel workbook. In the Report header option area, select Show header in Excel worksheet. If necessary, unmark the boxes in the Excel options area. The boxes should be *unchecked*.

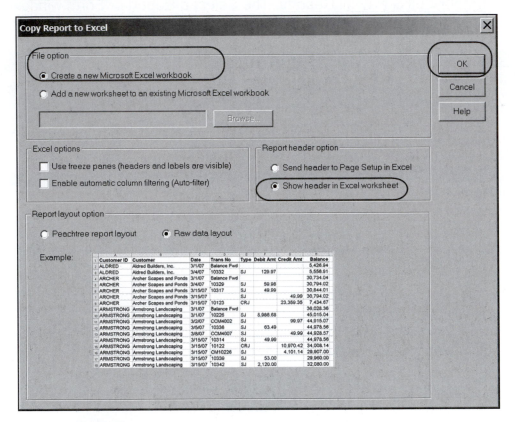

5. Click [OK]. The Copying Employee List to Excel window appears. When the Bellwether Garden Supply Employee List displays, check that your name has been added to the list of employees.

6. Save the Excel worksheet to your USB flash drive. Use **Chapter 1_Employee List.xlsx** as the file name. (If you are using Excel 2003 or earlier, the file extension is .xls.) The Employee List on the next page shows the author's name. Your name should be shown.

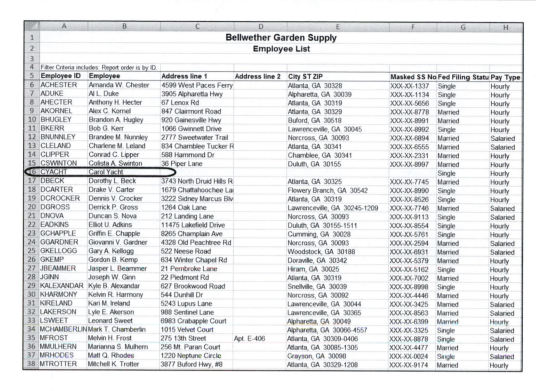

	Employee ID	Employee	Address line 1	Address line 2	City ST ZIP	Masked SS No	Fed Filing Statu	Pay Type
1				Bellwether Garden Supply				
2				Employee List				
3								
4	Filter Criteria includes: Report order is by ID.							
5	Employee ID	Employee	Address line 1	Address line 2	City ST ZIP	Masked SS No	Fed Filing Statu	Pay Type
6	ACHESTER	Amanda W. Chester	4599 West Paces Ferry		Atlanta, GA 30328	XXX-XX-1337	Single	Hourly
7	ADUKE	Al L. Duke	3905 Alpharetta Hwy		Alpharetta, GA 30039	XXX-XX-1134	Single	Hourly
8	AHECTER	Anthony H. Hecter	67 Lenox Rd		Atlanta, GA 30319	XXX-XX-5656	Single	Hourly
9	AKORNEL	Alex C. Kornel	847 Clairmont Road		Atlanta, GA 30329	XXX-XX-8778	Married	Hourly
10	BHUGLEY	Brandon A. Hugley	920 Gainesville Hwy		Buford, GA 30518	XXX-XX-8991	Married	Hourly
11	BKERR	Bob G. Kerr	1066 Gwinnett Drive		Lawrenceville, GA 30045	XXX-XX-8992	Single	Hourly
12	BNUNNLEY	Brandee M. Nunnley	2777 Sweetwater Trail		Norcross, GA 30093	XXX-XX-6894	Married	Salaried
13	CLELAND	Charlene M. Leland	834 Chamblee Tucker R		Atlanta, GA 30341	XXX-XX-6555	Married	Salaried
14	CLIPPER	Conrad C. Lipper	588 Hammond Dr		Chamblee, GA 30341	XXX-XX-2331	Married	Hourly
15	CSWINTON	Colista A. Swinton	36 Piper Lane		Duluth, GA 30155	XXX-XX-8997	Married	Hourly
16	CYACHT	Carol Yacht					Single	Hourly
17	DBECK	Dorothy L. Beck	3743 North Druid Hills R		Atlanta, GA 30325	XXX-XX-7745	Married	Hourly
18	DCARTER	Drake V. Carter	1679 Chattahoochee Lai		Flowery Branch, GA 30542	XXX-XX-8990	Single	Hourly
19	DCROCKER	Dennis V. Crocker	3222 Sidney Marcus Blv		Atlanta, GA 30319	XXX-XX-8526	Single	Hourly
20	DGROSS	Derrick P. Gross	1264 Oak Lane		Lawrenceville, GA 30245-1209	XXX-XX-7746	Married	Salaried
21	DNOVA	Duncan S. Nova	212 Landing Lane		Norcross, GA 30093	XXX-XX-9113	Single	Salaried
22	EADKINS	Elliot U. Adkins	11475 Lakefield Drive		Duluth, GA 30155-1511	XXX-XX-8554	Single	Hourly
23	GCHAPPLE	Griffin E. Chapple	8265 Champlain Ave		Cumming, GA 30028	XXX-XX-5761	Single	Hourly
24	GGARDNER	Giovanni V. Gardner	4328 Old Peachtree Rd		Norcross, GA 30093	XXX-XX-2594	Married	Salaried
25	GKELLOGG	Gary A. Kellogg	522 Neese Road		Woodstock, GA 30188	XXX-XX-6931	Married	Salaried
26	GKEMP	Gordon B. Kemp	634 Winter Chapel Rd		Doraville, GA 30342	XXX-XX-5379	Married	Hourly
27	JBEAMMER	Jasper L. Beammer	21 Pembroke Lane		Hiram, GA 30025	XXX-XX-5162	Single	Hourly
28	JGINN	Joseph W. Ginn	22 Piedmont Rd		Atlanta, GA 30319	XXX-XX-7002	Married	Hourly
29	KALEXANDAR	Kyle B. Alexandar	627 Brookwood Road		Snellville, GA 30039	XXX-XX-8998	Single	Hourly
30	KHARMONY	Kelvin R. Harmony	544 Dunhill Dr		Norcross, GA 30092	XXX-XX-4446	Married	Hourly
31	KIRELAND	Kari M. Ireland	5243 Lupus Lane		Lawrenceville, GA 30044	XXX-XX-3425	Married	Salaried
32	LAKERSON	Lyle E. Akerson	988 Sentinel Lane		Lawrenceville, GA 30365	XXX-XX-8563	Married	Salaried
33	LSWEET	Leonard Sweet	6983 Crabapple Court		Alpharetta, GA 30049	XXX-XX-6399	Married	Hourly
34	MCHAMBERLIN	Mark T. Chamberlin	1015 Velvet Court		Alpharetta, GA 30066-4557	XXX-XX-3325	Single	Salaried
35	MFROST	Melvin H. Frost	275 13th Street	Apt. E-406	Atlanta, GA 30309-0406	XXX-XX-8878	Single	Salaried
36	MMULHERN	Marianna S. Mulhern	256 Mt. Paran Court		Atlanta, GA 30085-1305	XXX-XX-4477	Married	Hourly
37	MRHODES	Matt Q. Rhodes	1220 Neptune Circle		Grayson, GA 30098	XXX-XX-0024	Single	Salaried
38	MTROTTER	Mitchell K. Trotter	3877 Buford Hwy, #8		Atlanta, GA 30329-1208	XXX-XX-9174	Married	Hourly

7. Exit Excel.

SAVING EMPLOYEE LIST AS AN ADOBE PDF FILE

Check with your instructor to see if he or she would like you to save the Employee list as a PDF file. If so, follow these steps.

1. From the Select a Report or Form window, select Send To, PDF. To save reports as PDF files, Adobe Reader must installed. If necessary, go online to www.adobe.com and download the free Adobe Reader. (*Hint:* If you cannot save the Employee List as a PDF file, make sure you have the latest Adobe Reader update.)

The McGraw-Hill Companies, Inc., *Computer Accounting with Peachtree by Sage Complete Accounting 2012, 16e*

2. The Modify Report - Employee List window appears. Click OK .

3. The Save As window appears. If necessary, insert your USB drive. Select the USB drive. Type **Chapter 1_Employee List** in the File name field. Observe that the Save as Type field shows Adobe PDF Files (*.pdf).

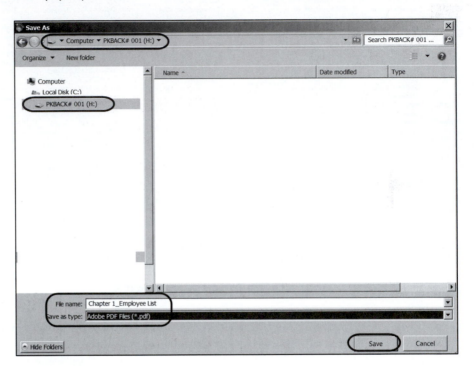

4. Click Save . Close the Select a Report & Form window. Continue or exit Peachtree.

MANUAL VS. COMPUTERIZED ACCOUNTING

Because there are differences between manual and computerized accounting, notice there are several instances where the procedures used in PCA are different than those outlined in the steps of the manual accounting cycle. The steps of the manual accounting cycle shown in most accounting textbooks differ slightly from PCA's computer accounting cycle.

The differences between the Manual and Computer Accounting Cycle are shown on the next two pages. The first step of the Computer Accounting Cycle is setting up a new company, which includes the option for selecting a Chart of Accounts. Starting with Chapter 9 you will set up 11 companies from scratch. In Chapters 1-8 you work with the two sample companies that are included with PCA.

The Manual Accounting Cycle does not include creating a new company. In manual accounting, the chart of accounts is the same as the accounts in the general ledger.

Step five of the manual cycle shows a worksheet. There is no worksheet in the computerized cycle. In PCA you can complete account reconciliation. Account reconciliation automates bank reconciliation. Another important difference is that in the Computer Accounting Cycle, the adjusting entries are journalized and posted before printing the financial statements.

In the computerized cycle, Step 10, change accounting periods, is similar to closing the month manually except that the temporary accounts maintain balances so a post-closing trial balance is not available. PCA tracks income and expense data for an entire year. At the end of the year, all revenue and expense accounts are closed to equity. In all Peachtree companies (including sole proprietorships), a retained earnings account is needed so that posting to the general ledger can be done.

MANUAL ACCOUNTING CYCLE	PCA's COMPUTER ACCOUNTING CYCLE
1. Analyze transactions.	1. Create a new company *or* restore A New Company.
2. Journalize entries.	2. Analyze transactions.
3. Post to the ledger.	3. Journalize entries.
4. Prepare unadjusted trial balance.	4. Post to the ledger.
5. Prepare worksheet.	5. Print general ledger trial balance (unadjusted).
6. Prepare financial statements: income statement, statement of changes in owner's equity, and balance sheet.	6. Account reconciliation: reconciling the bank statement.

7.	Adjust the ledger accounts: journalize and post adjusting entries.	7.	Journalize and post adjusting entries.
8.	Close the temporary accounts: journalize and post the closing entries.	8.	Print the general ledger trial balance (adjusted).
9.	Prepare post-closing trial balance.	9.	Print financial statements: balance sheet, income statement, statement of cash flow, and statement of changes in financial position.
10.	Reverse entries (optional).	10.	Change accounting periods.
	11. Interpret accounting information		

SUMMARY AND REVIEW

Complete the following end-of-chapter activities:

1. Going to the net, pages 48-49.
2. True/make true questions, page 49.
3. Exercises 1-1 and 1-2, pages 50-52.
4. Analysis questions, page 52.
5. Assessment Rubric, page 53.
6. Chapter 1 Index, pages 54-55.

GOING TO THE NET

Comment:

The textbook website at www.mhhe.com/yacht2012 has a link to Textbook Updates. Check this link for updated Going to the Net exercises.

Access the Welcome to Careers in Accounting website at http://www.careers-in-accounting.com/.

Read the article Welcome to Careers in Accounting. (Going to the Net links are on the textbook website at www.mhhe.com/yacht2012; link to Student Edition, select Chapter 1.)

1. List four activities that accountants engage in (not including recording transactions and preparing financial statements).

2. Approximately how many people join public accounting firms each year?

3. What key factors contribute to being hired as an accountant?

True/Make True: The Online Learning Center includes these questions and the analysis question at www.mhhe.com/yacht2012, select Student Edition, Chapter 1, QA Templates.

1. If the menu bar shows an underlined letter, hold down the <Ctrl> key and that letter to make a selection.

2. Peachtree's modular design is similar to other accounting software applications.

3. Peachtree's Restore Wizard allows you to restore existing companies only.

4. The extension used for Adobe files saved in this chapter is .xlsx.

5. In this book, angle brackets are used to indicate individual keys on the keyboard; for example <Tab>.

6. You can close the application you are working with by single clicking with the mouse on the close button (⊠).

7. The Business Status Navigation Center is also called the dashboard.

8. In PCA, some icons are common to all windows while other icons are specific to a particular window.

9. The Navigation Bar is located at the bottom of most Peachtree windows.

10. The extension used for Peachtree backups is .pdf.

Exercise 1-1: Follow the instructions below to complete Exercise 1-1:

1. Start PCA. Open the sample company, Bellwether Garden Supply.

2. Follow these steps to restore your data from the end of Chapter 1:

   a. Insert your USB flash drive. From the System Navigation Center, select | Restore Now |. (The Chapter 1.ptb backup was made on pages 41-42.)

   b. The Select Backup File window appears. Click | Browse |. Go to the Location of your Chapter 1.ptb file and select it. (*Hint:* The File name field shows Chapter 1.ptb.) Click | Open |.

   c. The Select Backup File window shows the location of your backup file. Click | Next > |.

   d. The Select Company window appears. Make sure that the radio button next to An Existing Company is selected. The Company Name field shows Bellwether Garden Supply. The Location field shows the default location on the hard drive for Bellwether Garden Supply. Click | Next > |.

   e. The Restore Options window appears. Make sure that the box next to Company Data is *checked*. Click | Next > |.

   f. The Confirmation window appears. Check the From and To fields to make sure they are correct. Click | Finish |. When the Restore Company scale is 100% complete, your data is restored. (*Hint:* The Student Version of Peachtree prompts that company data can be used for 14 months. After that time the data expires. Click <OK>. Bellwether Garden Supply opens.)

3. Continue using PCA and complete Exercise 1-2.

Exercise 1-2: Follow the instructions below to complete Exercise 1-2:

1. Add Janie Wood as a new employee.

Employee I<u>D</u>:	JWOOD [use all caps]
N<u>a</u>me:	Janie Wood [use upper and lower case]
Address:	1300 West Hudson Drive
City, ST <u>Z</u>ip:	Atlanta, GA 30328

2. Print the Employee List.

    Select .
    In the Employees area, link
    to <u>View Detailed List</u>.

Employees				⊞ View Detailed List
Employee ID ⏶	**Last Name**	**First Name**	**Telephone 1**	**Pay Method**
ACHESTER	Chester	Amanda	404-555-7447	Hourly - Hours
ADUKE	Duke	Al	770-555-3349	Hourly - Hours
AHECTER	Hecter	Anthony	770-555-4558	Hourly - Hours

3. Click 🖶 Print, then make the selections to print. If necessary, click
    on Employee ID to display the list in alphabetical order.)

4. After printing the Employee List, close the Employee List window.

5. Follow these steps to back up Exercise 1-2:

    a. If necessary, insert your USB flash drive.

    b. From the Navigation Bar, click  ;

    c. Click | Back Up |.

    d. In the Save in field, select the USB drive. Type **Exercise 1-2** in
        the File name field.

    e. Click | Save |.

    f. When the window prompts that This company backup will require
        1 diskette, click | OK |. When the window prompts Please
        insert the first disk, click | OK |. When the Back Up
        Company scale is 100% complete, you have successfully backed
        up to the current point. You are returned to the menu bar.

> **Read Me: Problem Backing Up to USB Drive**
> If you encounter difficulties backing up to a USB drive, backup to your desktop first. Then copy the backup file from your desktop to a USB drive. Refer to Appendix A, Problem Backing Up to USB Drive or Other External Media, pages 756-758 for detailed steps.

6. Export the Employee List to Excel. Save. Use **Exercise 1-2_Employee List.xlsx** as the file name. Refer to step 2, page 51, for the Employee List. Click Send To Excel to Create a new Microsoft Excel workbook. (If you are using Excel 2003 or lower, the file extension is .xls.)

7. Save the Employee List as a PDF file. Use **Exercise 1-2_Employee List.pdf** as the file name. Refer to pages 45-46 for saving files as PDFs.

8. Export the Chart of Accounts to Excel. Use **Exercise 1-2_Chart of Accounts.xlsx** as the file name. (Refer to pages 21-22 for displaying the account list or chart of accounts.)

9. Save the Chart of Accounts as a PDF file. Use **Exercise 1-2_Chart of Accounts.pdf** as the file name.

   Check your figures: Account No. 10200, Regular Checking Account: $23,389.83.

> **Comment:** If your instructor would like Peachtree reports attached for grading purposes, see pages 43-46, Exporting Peachtree Report Data to Microsoft Excel or Saving as a PDF File. To export two Peachtree reports to one Excel file, see pages 88-90. For grading purposes, your instructor may prefer receiving an Adobe file (.pdf) or an Excel file (.xlsx). Ask your instructor his or her preference.

10. Exit Excel and Peachtree.

ANALYSIS QUESTIONS:

1. How many menu bar selections does Peachtree Complete Accounting 2012 have? List the menu bar selections that are available.

2. What is the Navigation Bar? Briefly describe its function.

ASSESSMENT RUBRIC

Complete the Assessment Rubric online at www.mhhe.com/yacht2012; Student Edition, select Chapter 1, Assessment Rubric link. To review Peachtree's journals, navigation centers, modules, task windows, and reports complete the blank fields online. The assessment rubrics are also included in the chapter PowerPoint slides.

Chart of Accounts or Account List				
Navigation Bar/Navigation Center	Account ID	Description	Type	Running Balance
		Regular Checking Account		
		Accounts Receivable		
		Prepaid Expenses		
		Buildings		
		Accounts Payable		
		Common Stock		
		Sales - Aviary		
		Product Cost - Aviary		
		Freight		

CHAPTER 1 INDEX

Chapter 2 — Vendors

LEARNING OBJECTIVES

1. Restore data from Exercise 1-2. (This backup was made on page 51.)
2. Enter a purchase order.
3. Apply receipt of inventory to existing purchase order.
4. Enter and post a vendor invoice in the Purchases/Receive Inventory window.
5. Go to the Payments window to pay a vendor.
6. Print a check in payment of the vendor invoice.
7. Add a Terms column to the Vendor Ledgers report.
8. Analyze payments and vendor credit memos.
9. Export the Vendor List and Vendor Ledgers to Excel.
10. Save the Vendor List and Vendor Ledgers as PDF files.
11. Make two backups, save two Excel files, and save three PDF files.[1]

Chapter 2 explains how Peachtree works with vendors. The first thing you do is select **Vendors & Purchases** from the Navigation Bar to go to the Vendors & Purchases Navigation Center.

When Bellwether Garden Supply orders and receives inventory from vendors, Account No. 12000, Inventory, is debited. Accounts Payable and the vendor account are credited.

Vendors offer Bellwether a ***purchase discount*** for purchase invoices paid within a discount period. Purchase discounts are cash discounts from vendors in return for early payment of an invoice; for example, 2% 10, net 30 days. If Bellwether pays an invoice within 10 days, they can deduct two percent from the invoice amount. In Peachtree, the purchase discount is entered when the vendor is paid. If the payment is not made

---

[1]Refer to the chart on page 2 for the size of backups and saved Excel and PDF files.

The McGraw-Hill Companies, Inc., *Computer Accounting with Peachtree by Sage Complete Accounting 2012, 16e*

within 10 days, the full invoice amount is paid within 30 days. In this chapter, you learn how PCA handles accounts payable transactions with vendors.

GETTING STARTED

Follow these steps to start PCA:

1. Start Peachtree.

2. Open the sample company, Bellwether Garden Supply. From PCA's startup window, there are two ways to open Bellwether:

   a. Click [Open an existing company]; select Bellwether Garden Supply, [OK] .

   b. *Or,* in the Other Tasks list, select Explore a sample company; Bellwether Garden Supply, [OK] (*or,* press <Enter>).

   ➢ **Troubleshooting: Bellwether Garden Supply is not listed on Peachtree's Company Name list.**

      Refer to the Read Me box on page 29 to review the steps for restoring *A New Company*. In the section that follows, Restoring Data from Exercise 1-2, steps are shown to restore an existing company (the default) from a USB drive. The steps on page 29 show how to restore a backup file and set up a new company at the same time.

In this textbook, it is assumed Bellwether Garden Supply is included when Peachtree 2012 was installed. Bellwether's hard drive location is C:\Sage\Peachtree\Company\Sample\PCWS\BCS. (*Hint:* Your file location may differ. For more information, refer to File Management, pages xviii-xx.) BCS is the shortened named that Peachtree assigns to Bellwether. If the BCS folder was deleted, you can restore the file from your backup. Refer to the Read Me box on page 29. The next section, Restoring Data from Exercise 1-2, assumes Bellwether can be opened from Peachtree's startup window.

RESTORING DATA FROM EXERCISE 1-2

On page 51, Exercise 1-2 is backed up (saved). In order to begin where you left off, restore the Exercise 1-2.ptb file. Restoring allows you to start where you left off at the end of Chapter 1.

Follow these steps to restore the Exercise 1-2.ptb file. (The Exercise 2.1.ptb backup was made on page 51.)

1. Insert your USB flash drive. From the Navigation Bar, select

   System ; click Restore Now .

2. The Select Backup File window appears. Click Browse . Go to the Location of your Exercise 1-2.ptb file and select it. Click Open .

3. The Select Backup File window shows the location of your backup file, X:\Exercise 1-2.ptb. (Substitute X for your drive letter.) Click Next> .

4. The Select Company window appears. The radio button next to An Existing Company is selected. The Company Name field shows Bellwether Garden Supply. The Location field shows the default location on the hard drive for Bellwether Garden Supply. Click Next> .

5. The Restore Options window appears. Make sure that the box next to Company Data is checked. Click Next> .

6. The Confirmation window appears. Check the From and To fields to make sure they are correct. Click Finish . When the Restore Company scale is 100% complete, your data is restored. (*Hint:* The Student Version of Peachtree prompts that company data can be used for 14 months. After that time the data expires. Click OK . Bellwether Garden Supply opens.)

   To make sure you are starting in the appropriate place in the data (Exercise 1-2 backup), display the Employee list. (*Hint:* From the

Navigation Bar, select [Employees & Payroll]. In the Employees area, link to <u>View Detailed List</u>. Your name and JWOOD should appear. You added yourself as an employee on page 40, and added JWOOD in Exercise 1-2, page 51.)

ACCOUNTS PAYABLE SYSTEM

Peachtree's *Accounts Payable System* provides the summary information needed for the entry that credits Accounts Payable and debits the various asset and expense accounts that the vendor invoices represent. Since Bellwether Garden Supply buys on credit from a number of vendors, the company keeps close track of the amount owed and the due dates of the bills.

Vendor transactions are a five-step process:

1. Maintain Vendors: Set up a new vendor.

2. Purchase Orders: Order items from one of Bellwether's vendors.

3. Purchase Invoices: Receive inventory or services from one of Bellwether's vendors. Apply a purchase order to a purchase invoice.

4. Payments: Pay a vendor or record a cash purchase. (PCA also includes vendor credit memos.)

5. Print Checks: Print a check for payment to a vendor or for expenses.

Before you begin adding accounts payable transactions, examine the Vendors & Purchases Navigation Center. Follow these steps to do that.

1. From the Navigation Bar, select [Vendors & Purchases]. The Vendors & Purchases Navigation Center appears. Vendors & Purchases illustrate Peachtree's *accounts payable module* or accounts payable system. The Vendors & Purchases Navigation Center includes Vendors & Purchases Tasks and its workflow diagram, Vendors, Recently Used Vendor Reports, Aged Payables, and Peachtree Solutions.

Modules organize Peachtree's transaction windows and reports.

When the Navigation Bar's Vendors & Purchases selection is made, Peachtree's accounts payable system is shown. The menu bar selections, Tasks and Reports & Forms, are also organized by module; for example, the Reports & Forms menu includes Accounts Receivable, Accounts Payable, General Ledger, etc. Compare your Vendors & Purchases Navigation Center with the one shown.

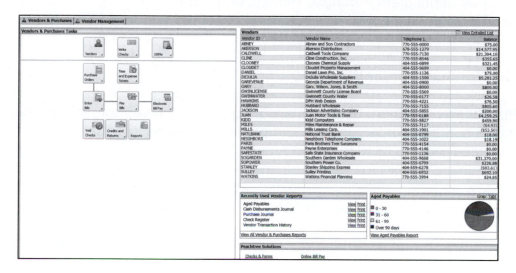

The Vendors & Purchases Navigation Center displays information and access points related to the company's vendors. It includes a summary of vendor information, access to recently used vendor reports, and an overview of the company's aged payables. In addition, the Navigation Center shows the flow of vendor-related tasks. You can also link or drill down to various areas.

The Vendors & Purchases Navigation Center includes two tabs: Vendors & Purchases and Vendor Management. Vendors & Purchases is the default and shows the workflow diagram for Vendors & Purchases Tasks. The Vendor Management tab lists information regarding transactions and history for an individual vendor, including purchase orders, purchases, and payments.

2. If necessary, click on the Vendors & Purchases tab. In the Vendors area (on the right side of the screen), click ABNEY. The Maintain Vendors window appears with information about Abney and Son Contractors.

3. Click [⊗ Close] to return to the Vendors & Purchases Navigation Center.
4. Click on the Vendor Management tab. In the Vendor ID field, select Abney. Vendor Management shows current and historical information about Abney and Son Contractors – Purchase Orders, Payments, Item Purchase History, and Totals.
5. To return to the workflow diagram, select the Vendors & Purchases tab.

The Purchase Order Window

Purchase orders are used to place an order from a vendor. When you post a purchase order, you do not update accounting information. A purchase order is used to request items from a vendor. When the Apply to Purchase Order tab is selected on the Purchases/Receive Inventory window and the transaction is posted, accounting information (inventory, accounts payable subsidiary ledger, general ledger) is updated.

Changing Global Settings for Accounting Behind the Screens

Peachtree is a double-entry accounting system. There is a selection in Options/Global that allows you to hide general ledger accounts. This is called Accounting Behind the Screens. The PCA windows in this book show the general ledger accounts. To check the Accounting Behind the Screens settings, follow the steps shown below.

1. From the menu bar, click Options, then Global. The Accounting tab is selected. The boxes in the Hide General Ledger Accounts section *must* be unchecked. (If necessary, click on the boxes to uncheck them.)

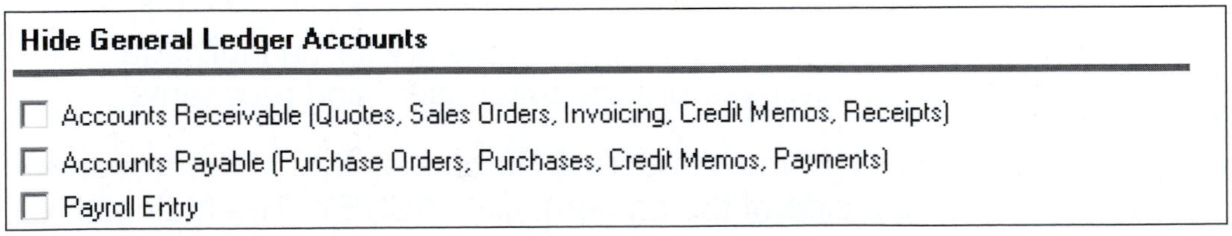

Hide General Ledger Accounts

☐ Accounts Receivable (Quotes, Sales Orders, Invoicing, Credit Memos, Receipts)

☐ Accounts Payable (Purchase Orders, Purchases, Credit Memos, Payments)

☐ Payroll Entry
---

2. Observe that two boxes need to be checked in the Other Options section: Warn if a record was changed but not saved and Recalculate cash balance automatically in Receipts, Payments, and

Payroll Entry. Make sure *both* of these Other Options boxes are checked.

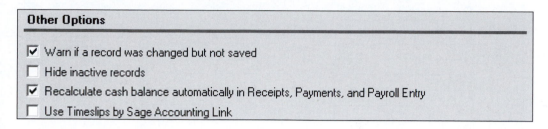

3. Click on the <u>G</u>eneral tab. Make sure your Line Item Entry Display has 2 Line selected; and that the Smart Data Entry area has all three boxes checked.

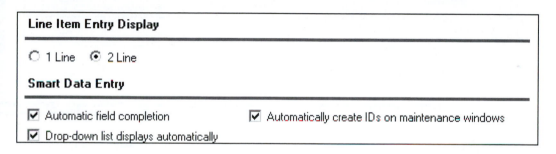

4. Click 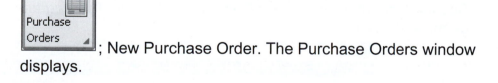 .

5. From the Vendors & Purchases Navigation Center, select
Purchase Orders ; New Purchase Order. The Purchase Orders window displays.

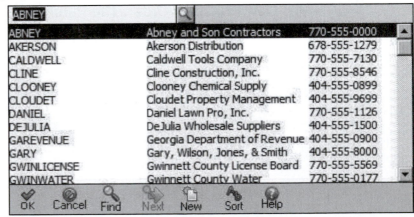

If your Purchase Orders window does *not* show an A/P Account lookup field [A/P Account | 20000] or a GL Account [GL Account] field, the option to hide general ledger accounts is selected. Uncheck the Hide General Ledger Accounts boxes in Options; Global. (*Hint: See the instructions on pages 62-63 steps 1-4, for changing the global settings.*)

6. Your cursor is in the Vendor ID lookup field. Type **A** (use capital A). ABNEY displays in the lookup field.

ABNEY		
ABNEY	Abney and Son Contractors	770-555-0000
AKERSON	Akerson Distribution	678-555-1279
CALDWELL	Caldwell Tools Company	770-555-7130
CLINE	Cline Construction, Inc.	770-555-8546
CLOONEY	Clooney Chemical Supply	404-555-0899
CLOUDET	Cloudet Property Management	404-555-9699
DANIEL	Daniel Lawn Pro, Inc.	770-555-1126
DEJULIA	DeJulia Wholesale Suppliers	404-555-1500
GAREVENUE	Georgia Department of Revenue	404-555-0900
GARY	Gary, Wilson, Jones, & Smith	404-555-8000
GWINLICENSE	Gwinnett County License Board	770-555-5569
GWINWATER	Gwinnett County Water	770-555-0177

OK Cancel Find Next New Sort Help

Comment

If the Vendor ID field is not completed, the Automatic Field Completion option is *not* selected. Click Options, then Global. Click on the <u>G</u>eneral tab. In the Smart Data Entry section, make sure that a check mark is placed next to Automatic field completion. Click OK when you are finished.

7. Click on the <u>D</u>ate field. Highlight the date, then type **28** and press **<Enter>**. Your cursor moves to the <u>G</u>ood thru field. Press **<Enter>** to accept the default. Your cursor moves to the PO No. field.

8. Click on the Quantity field. Type **20** as the Quantity. If necessary, refer to the Comment below.

Comment

If 20.00 does *not* display in the Quantity field, click Options; Global. Make sure that the Decimal Entry shows Manual; and that the Number of decimal places is 2.

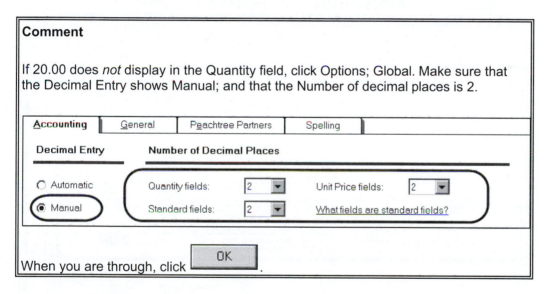

When you are through, click OK.

9. Press **<Enter>**. Your cursor is in the Item field.

10. Click once on the magnifying-glass icon in the Item field. Click AVRY-10150 Bird Bath - Stone Gothic 2pc. The Description field is automatically completed with detailed information.

11. Press the **<Enter>** key and your cursor moves to the GL Account field. Notice that Account No. 12000 is automatically selected. Account No. 12000 is the Inventory account. The word Inventory is also displayed on the line below the Description. (*Hint:* If Inventory is *not* shown, refer to step 1, page 62.)

12. Press the **<Enter>** key to go to the Unit Price field. The Unit Price of 51.95 automatically displays.

13. Press the **<Enter>** key to go to the Amount field. Peachtree calculates the quantity times the unit price and enters the result in the Amount field (20 X $51.95 = $1,039.00).

14. Press the **<Enter>** key to go to the Job field. The Job field is also a lookup field. It contains a list of the jobs and their descriptions. Since Bellwether does not apply this purchase to a job, press the **<Enter>** key to skip this field. Complete the following information:

Quantity: **50**
Item: **AVRY-10100** - Bird House Kit

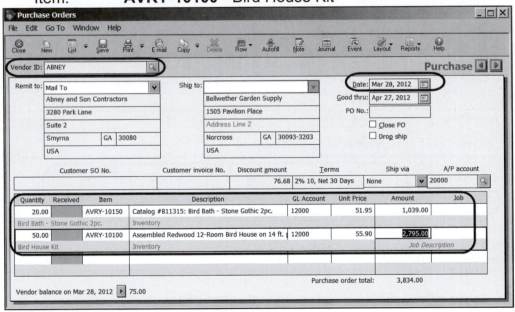

When you selected Abney and Son Contractors, the Vendor Account Balance as of March 28, 2012 also appears on the lower left side of the Purchase Orders window. You can drill down to Abney and Son Contractors vendor ledger by clicking on the right arrow (▶) in the Vendor Balance area. Observe that the icon bar also includes a Reports button. Click on the down-arrow next to the Reports button.

Journal   Event   Layout   Reports

Buyer Report
Inventory Stock Status Report
Items Purchased from Vendors
Job Ledger
Vendor Ledgers

15. Click 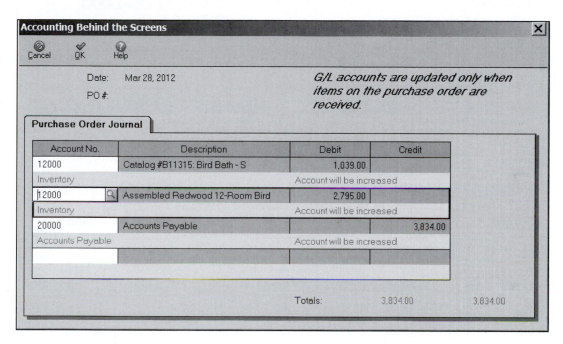 . The Accounting Behind the Screens, Purchase Order Journal window displays. Compare your Accounting Behind the Screens window to the one below. This window shows that Account No. 12000, Inventory, was debited for two items and that Accounts Payable was credited. (The vendor account, Abney and Sons, is also credited.)

Accounting Behind the Screens ⊠

Cancel   OK   Help

Date: Mar 28, 2012

PO #:

G/L accounts are updated only when items on the purchase order are received.

Purchase Order Journal

Account No.	Description	Debit	Credit
12000	Catalog #B11315: Bird Bath - S	1,039.00	
Inventory		Account will be increased	
12000	Assembled Redwood 12-Room Bird	2,795.00	
Inventory		Account will be increased	
20000	Accounts Payable		3,834.00
Accounts Payable		Account will be increased	

Totals: 3,834.00   3,834.00

16. Click OK . You are returned to the Purchase Orders window.

Printing Purchase Orders

When you select Print , PCA prints the purchase order and posts it to the purchase order journal. Follow these steps to print the purchase order:

1. Click Print . (*Or,* click on the down-arrow next to Print and select Print Preview to display the purchase order.)

2. The Print Forms: Purchase Orders window appears. Accept the default for First PO Number 101 by clicking [Print]. (If you selected Print Preview, there is a Print Preview button — [Print Preview].) The purchase order starts to print.

ORDERED BY:			

Bellwether Garden Supply
1505 Pavilion Place
Norcross, GA 30093-3203
USA

Voice: 770-724-4000
Fax: 770-555-1234

PURCHASE ORDER

Purchase Order No.:   101
Date Issued: 3/28/12

To:	Ship To:
Abney and Son Contractors 3280 Park Lane Suite 2 Smyrna, GA 30080 USA	Bellwether Garden Supply 1505 Pavilion Place Norcross, GA 30093-3203 USA

Good Thru	Ship Via	Account No.	Terms
4/27/12	None	BEL005	2% 10, Net 30 Days

Quantity	Item	Description	Unit Cost	Amount
20.00	AVRY-10150	Catalog #B11315: Bird Bath - Stone Gothic 2pc.	51.95	1,039.00
50.00	AVRY-10100	Assembled Redwood 12-Room Bird House on 14 ft. pole. Attracts Purple Martins, Bluebirds and Wrens	55.90	2,795.00
			TOTAL	$3,834.00

Authorized Signature _____

> **Comment**
>
> The purchase order form that printed is called Purchase Order. To print a different form,
> click [Select Form]. Then, select Purchase Order Preprinted as the form to print. When
> you select a different form, the information is the same but the look of the form changes.

3. If you displayed the report, click [Print]. The Purchase Orders
    window is ready for the next entry. (*Hint:* Selecting the Print icon
    saves and posts the purchase order. If you are not connected to a

    printer, click [Save].)

4. Click [Close].

Receive Inventory from a Purchase Order

After you have entered a purchase order, the next step is to receive the
inventory. Peachtree allows you to receive a different quantity for an item
than you originally ordered. In other words, you can receive less than or
more than the originally ordered quantity.

Let's see how Bellwether's purchase orders match up to the inventory
received.

1. From the Vendors & Purchases Navigation Center, select Purchase
    Orders, View and Edit Purchase Orders.

2. Double-click DEJULIA, PO No. 10300. Observe that some of the
    items are received and some are not. For example, six BGS
    Gardening Handbooks (BOOK-11010) have not been received.
    Twelve Clay Flower Pot – 6 in. (POTS-30210) were received.

    PO No. 10300 is shown on the next page.

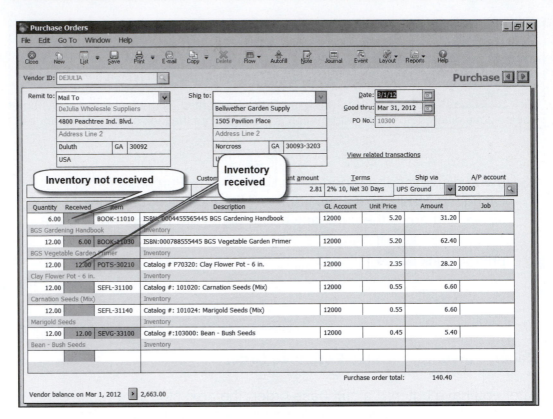

The Received field shows items added to inventory.

3. Select [Reports], Inventory Stock Status Report. The Inventory Stock Status Report shows the inventory items purchased from DeJulia Wholesale Suppliers, item class, stocking units/measures, quantity on hand, minimum stock order, reorder quantity, and the inventory location.

4. Close the Inventory Stock Status Report.

Apply to Purchase Order

To see if inventory items from PO No. 10300 have been applied, follow these steps.

1. On the Purchase Orders window, link to View related transactions.

2. Double-click Purchase 22113. The Purchases/Receive Inventory window appears. This is Peachtree's Purchase Journal. Observe that

some of the items from PO No. 10300 are shown. (The Apply to Purchase Order No. field shows 10300, the PO number.)

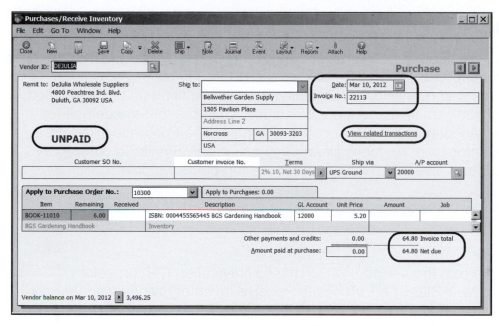

When purchase orders are applied, the transaction appears in Peachtree's Purchase Journal. Click Journal to see how the Purchases Journal was debited and credited. When the Purchases/Receive Inventory window (Purchase Journal) is posted, the vendor, DeJulia Wholesale Suppliers, is updated in the vendor ledger, and the controlling account, Accounts Payable, is updated in the general ledger. Inventory is also updated. Close the Purchase Journal window.

Observe that the Purchases/Receive Inventory window shows Unpaid. Also, the Invoice total and Net due fields show $64.80 (the items received so far). The entire purchase order was for $140.40. As of March 10, Bellwether has not received all the items requested on PO 10300. Payment will be made at a later date.

From the Purchases/Receive Inventory window, link to View related transactions to go to Purchase Order 10300. This is the same Purchase Orders window shown above.

3. Close all windows. (*Hint:* From the menu bar, select Window; Close All.)

The Purchases/Receive Inventory Window

In Peachtree, the Purchases/Receive Inventory window is the Purchase Journal. The Apply to Purchases tab is the default. The lower half of the window shows fields for Quantity, Item (inventory items), Description, GL Account, Unit Price, Amount, and Job. Observe that the default for the A/P Account is 20000, Accounts Payable. The Purchases/Receive Inventory window looks like a purchase order. Similar to other PCA windows, the icon bar appears at the top of the window.

Follow these steps to learn how to process vendor transactions.

1. From the Vendors & Purchases Navigation Center, select ; New Bill. The Purchases/Receive Inventory window appears. Observe that the Apply to Purchases tab is the default. The cursor is in the Vendor ID field.

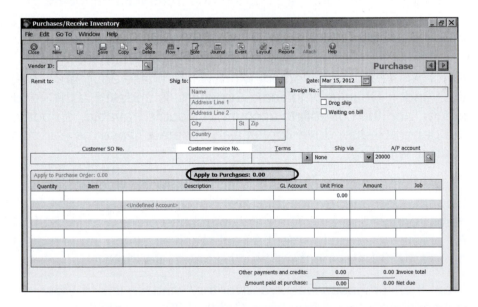

To see more lines in the Quantity/Item/Description table, make the Purchases/Receive Inventory window larger. You can do this by putting your mouse on the bottom border of the window and pulling down. The mouse changes to a double-arrow [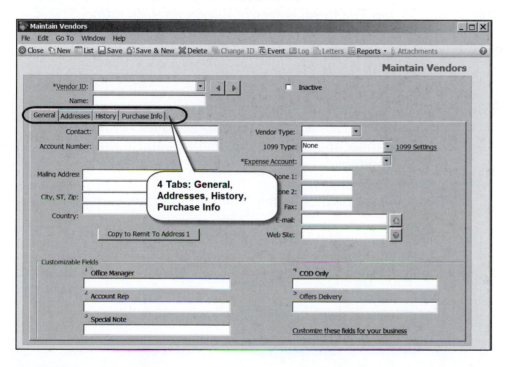]. With the cursor on the bottom border of the window, pull the window down to make it larger. If necessary, repeat this step on the left and right borders.

2. With the cursor in the Vendor ID field, press the plus key **<+>** and the Maintain Vendors window appears.

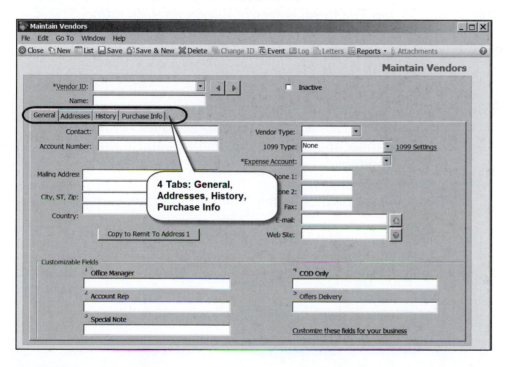

Adding a New Vendor

You are going to enter a new vendor, Armstrong's Landscaping. Since a *coding system* has already been established for Bellwether's vendors, you should continue to use the same one. The coding system used has uppercase letters. To be consistent, Armstrong's Landscaping will use ARMSTRONG. Notice that the name of the company is typed in all capital letters. What if two companies have the same name, such as, Armstrong's Landscaping and Armstrong's Suppliers? They could be coded as ARMSTRONG and ARMSSUPPL.

You should be consistent so that others working with the company can figure out what a customer or vendor code is from the company's name.

This is accomplished when a logical, consistent coding system is followed. Remember codes are *case sensitive* which means that you must type either upper or lowercase letters: ARMSTRONG is not the same as armstrong.

You have choices for coding. Here are some other suggestions for coding Armstrong's Landscaping:

ARM: the first three letters of the company's name.

ARML: the first three letters of a company's name, the first letter of the second word.

ARMSTRONG: An alphabetic code for a company name, using the first word. This is the Vendor ID used for Armstrong's Landscaping and is consistent with Bellwether's other vendors.

Follow these steps to continue in the Maintain Vendors window:

1. Make sure the Maintain Vendors window is displayed. Type **ARMSTRONG** in the Vendor ID field and press **<Enter>**. Your cursor is in the Name field.

2. Type **Armstrong's Landscaping** in the Name field.

3. Press **<Enter>** two times. Your cursor is in the Contact field. The person who handles sales for Armstrong's Landscaping is John Armstrong. Type **John Armstrong** and press **<Enter>**.

4. Your cursor is in the Account Number field. Click on the Vendor type field. (Skip the Account Number and Address fields.) For now, you are going to use only one more field in the Maintain Vendors window: Vendor Type. The Vendor Type field is used for classifying

vendors. You could classify vendors as Service or Supply to indicate what type of goods you purchase from them.

5. Click on the down-arrow in the Vendor Type field. Select SUPPLY.

6. Click on the down-arrow in the Expense Account field. Scroll down the list. Select Account No. 57200, Materials Cost. Press **<Enter>**. When Armstrong's Landscaping is selected as the vendor, Account No. 57200, Materials Cost, will be automatically debited.

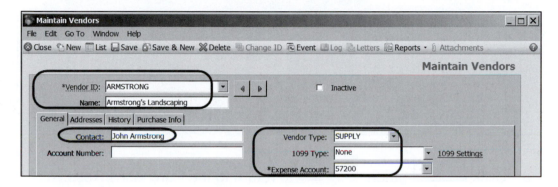

If you need to move between fields to make corrections, use the **<Tab>** key to move forward and the **<Shift> + <Tab>** to move backwards.

7. Click on the Purchase Info tab. Notice that the Vendor ID and Name fields stay the same: ARMSTRONG and Armstrong's Landscaping. Also, observe the Terms and Credit are 2% net 10, 30 days. Purchase discounts are described on page 57.

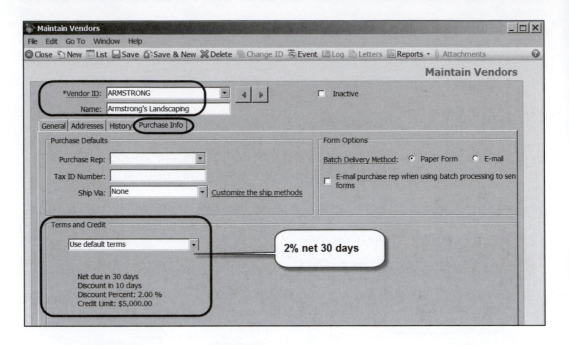

8. Click ![Save] , then ![Close] to return to the Purchases/Receive Inventory window.

Entering a Vendor Invoice

Make sure that the Purchases\Receive Inventory window is displayed and that the cursor is in the Vendor ID field. Follow the steps below to enter the transaction.

Date   *Transaction Description*

03/15/2012   Invoice No. ARM107 was received from
                       Armstrong's Landscaping for the purchase of Plant
                       Food, $45. (*Hint:* Debit Account No. 57200,
                       Materials Cost; Credit Account No. 20000, Accounts
                       Payable/Armstrong's Landscaping.)

1. In the Vendor ID field, click ![icon]. Select ARMSTRONG, Armstrong's Landscaping.

2. Observe that the date is Mar 15, 2012. You are *not* going to change the date. Click on the Invoice No. field. Type **ARM107** and press **<Enter>**.

3. Click on the Quantity field and type **1** and press **<Enter>**.

4. Since you are not purchasing an inventory item, press the **<Enter>** key again.

5. The cursor moves to the Description field. In the Description field, type **Plant Food** and press **<Enter>**.

6. In the GL Account field press **<Enter>** to accept Account No. 57200, the Materials Cost account.

7. In the Unit Price field, type **45** and press **<Enter>**. Compare your Purchases/Receive Inventory window to the one shown below.

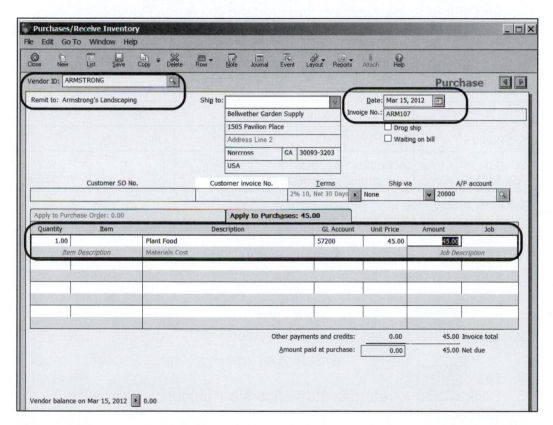

Comment: What if your Purchases/Receive Inventory window does *not* show an A/P Account field or GL Account field?

You should check your settings in the Options/Global selection. Make sure that the boxes in the Hide General Ledger Accounts section are unchecked. These steps were shown on pages 62-63, steps 1-4.

Editing a Journal Entry. Observe that the Purchases/Receive Inventory window includes a [List] icon. Selecting List displays the Purchase List window. From the Purchase List, you can drill down to an entry that you want to edit or change. The Purchases/Receive Inventory window is Peachtree's Purchase Journal. The List icon is included on journal-entry windows.

Posting a Purchase Transaction

When you made this entry in the Purchases/Receive Inventory window, you debited Account No. 57200, Material Costs, which is a General Ledger Cost of Sales account; and credited Accounts Payable/ Armstrong's Landscaping. ARMSTRONG is the vendor account. (To see this account distribution, click [Journal].)

Acct. #	Account Description	Debit	Credit
57200	Materials Cost	45.00	
20000/ ARMSTRONG	Accounts Payable/ Armstrong's Landscaping		45.00

Follow these steps to post this transaction.

1. Make sure the Purchases/Receive Inventory window is displayed as shown on page 77.

2. Click [Save] to post the vendor invoice.

3. Click [Close] to return to the Vendors & Purchases Navigation Center.

PAYMENTS TO VENDORS

When you make a payment to a vendor, use the Payments window. The Payments window is the Cash Disbursements Journal. On pages 73-76, you added a new vendor; then entered and posted an invoice to that vendor on pages 76-78. *Both* the new vendor and invoice *must* be completed *before* a vendor payment can be made.

Date	*Transaction Description*
03/17/2012	Issued Check No. 10215 to Armstrong's Landscaping in payment of Invoice No. ARM107.

Follow these steps to pay the Armstrong's Landscaping invoice:

1. From the Vendors & Purchases Navigation Center, select

   Pay Bills ; Pay Bill. Remember, to enlarge the window use the cursor's double-arrow and pull the window to the left/right or top/bottom.

   There are two parts to the Payments window: the check section at the top; and the invoice section at the bottom.

   The cursor is in the Vendor ID field. Click on the magnifying-glass icon, then select ARMSTRONG, Armstrong's Landscaping. Look at the invoice section. The invoice number ARM107 is shown with the amount that Bellwether owes to Armstrong's Landscaping.

---

2. Click on the <u>D</u>ate field. Type or select **17**.

3. Click on the Pay box for Invoice ARM107. Notice that the check portion of the window is completed. The amount to be paid is 44.10. This is the amount of the invoice less the 2% discount ($45 -.90 = $44.10). Compare your Payments window to the one shown below.

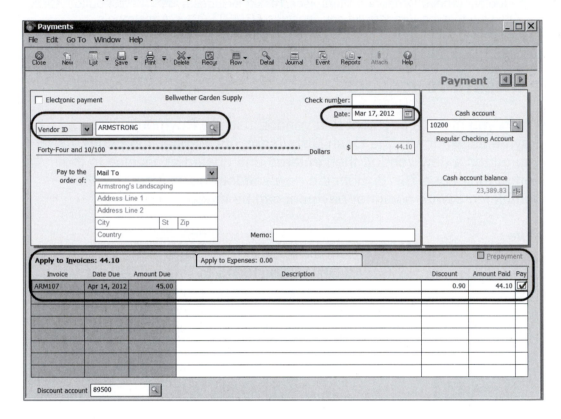

> ➢ **Troubleshooting Tip:** Observe that the Check num<u>b</u>er field is blank. The check number is assigned when you print. Enter a check number if checks are *not* going to be printed. Checks are printed on pages 81-84.

4. To see the Cash Disbursements Journal entry, click ⊞ Journal . Observe the debits and credits (account distribution is shown on the next page below step 6). Click ✓ OK to close Accounting Behind the Screens.

5. Click [Save] to post the Payments window (cash disbursements journal).

6. Click [Close] to return to the Vendors & Purchases Navigation Center.

When you post this payment, the Accounts Payable account is debited for the full invoice amount ($45), which offsets the credit created when you entered the invoice. The cash account is decreased (credited) by the amount of the check ($44.10) and the Discounts Taken account is increased (credited) for the purchase discount ($.90). The purchase discounts account (Account No. 89500 Purchase Disc-Expense Items) was already established for Bellwether Garden Supply.

Acct. #	Account Description	Debit	Credit
20000/ ARMSTRONG	Accounts Payable/Armstrong's Landscaping; Invoice ARM107	45.00	
10200	Regular Checking Account		44.10
89500	Purchase Disc-Expense Items		.90

PRINTING CHECKS

You can print a batch of checks or print one check at a time. Since we have only one check to print, you are going to print an individual check. PCA also has special check forms to use for printing checks. These may be purchased from Sage. Since you do not have check forms, print the check on a blank piece of paper.

Follow these steps to print a check:

1. From the menu bar, select Reports & Forms; Forms, Checks. The Select a Report or Form window appears.

2. Observe that the Forms tab is selected. If necessary, in the Form Types list, select Checks. In the Forms list, OCR AP Laser Preprinted is automatically selected. (If not, select OCR AP Laser Preprinted.)

> **Comment**
>
> Step 2 instructs you to select OCR AP Laser Preprinted as the form to print. If this form does *not* print, select another one. The form you select is tied to the kind of printer you are using. Depending on your printer, you may need to make a different selection.

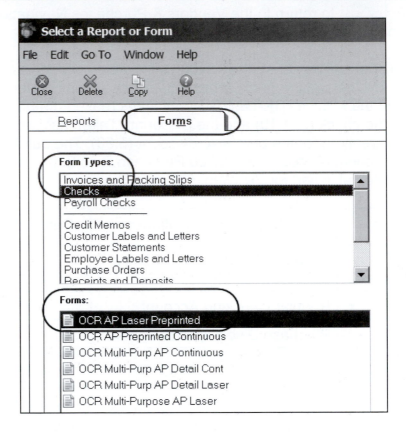

3. Double-click OCR AP Laser Preprinted.

4. The Preview and Print Checks window appears. In the Include checks through field, type or select March 17, 2012.

5. Type **10215** in the Number the first check field.

6. In the Filter vendors by area, select ARMSTRONG to ARMSTRONG in the ID fields.

7. Click ⟨ Refresh List ⟩.

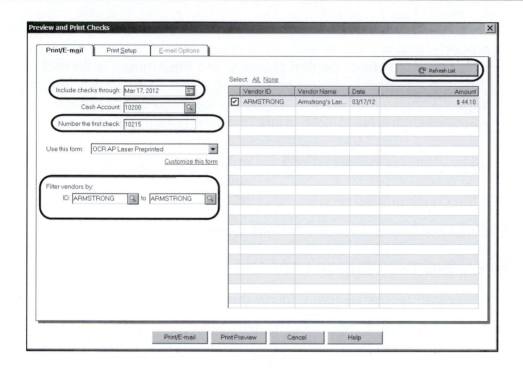

8. Click [Print/E-mail] or [Print Preview]. The check prints or displays. Compare Check No. 10215 to the one shown below. The top half of the check is shown.

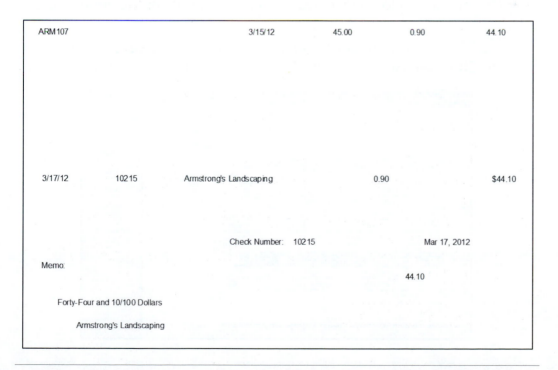

If you print the check, a window displays asking Did the Checks print properly, and is it OK to assign the check numbers to the checks? Make sure the check printed properly and the amount is correct. (See the Payments window on page 80.) The check illustrated on page 83 shows the check stub (top portion) and check portion. When you print Check No. 10215, there is also a bottom portion.

9. If needed, click [Cancel] and make the necessary corrections. If the check printed properly, click [Yes].

10. Close the Select a Report or Form window.

DISPLAYING THE VENDOR LEDGERS

To display the Vendor Ledgers, follow these steps.

1. On the Vendors & Purchases Navigation Center, Recently Used Vendor Reports area, link <u>View All Vendor & Purchases Reports</u>; select Vendor Ledgers, [Display]. (*Or,* link to View next to Vendor Ledgers.)

2. The Vendor Ledgers displays. To see the terms for the vendor, click [Columns]. The Vendor Ledgers/Columns window displays. Scroll down the Show list. Select Terms. (Click on the box to place a checkmark.)

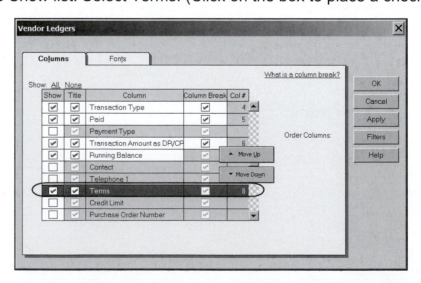

3. Click [OK]. Observe that a Terms column is added to the Vendor Ledgers report. A partial Vendor Ledgers report is shown below.

Bellwether Garden Supply
Vendor Ledgers
For the Period From Mar 1, 2012 to Mar 31, 2012

Filter Criteria includes: Report order is by ID.

Vendor ID / Vendor	Date	Trans No	Type	Paid	Debit Amt	Credit Amt	Balance	Terms
ABNEY	3/1/12	B1000	PJ			75.00	75.00	2% 10, Net 30
Abney and Son Cont	3/9/12	B1015	PJ	*		195.65	270.65	
	3/12/12	VCM30001	PJ	*	195.65		75.00	
	3/15/12		CDJ		50.00	50.00	75.00	
AKERSON	3/1/12	Balance Fw					9,398.75	2% 10, Net 30
Akerson Distribution	3/7/12	VCM30002	PJ	*	27.20		9,371.55	
	3/8/12	4	PJ			5,179.20	14,550.75	
	3/13/12		CDJ		1,000.00	1,000.00	14,550.75	
	3/14/12	B1016	PJ	*			14,577.95	
ARMSTRONG	3/15/12	ARM107	PJ	*		45.00	45.00	2% 10, Net 30
Armstrong's Landsc	3/17/12	10215	CDJ		0.90	0.90	45.00	
	3/17/12	10215	CDJ		45.00		0.00	

The Vendor Ledger is the Accounts Payable subsidiary ledger. When you entered and posted the vendor invoice (pages 76-78) in the Purchases/Receive Inventory window, the Accounts Payable subsidiary ledger for Armstrong's Landscaping was credited for $45. Once the invoice was entered, there is a balance of $45. When you posted the payment (pages 79-81), PCA debited the vendor for the same amount. The balance after posting the payment is zero ($0.00).

VENDOR CREDIT MEMOS

Vendor credit memos are returns to vendors. You can apply vendor credit memos to any existing vendor invoice that has *not* been paid. All entries made on the Vendor Credit Memos window are posted to the general ledger, vendor records, and when applicable, inventory and job records.

You are going to use Peachtree's *drill down* feature to go to the original entry from the vendor ledger. Using the vendor ledger as an example, use drill down to follow the path of an entry to its origin. In Peachtree reports, you can click transactions to drill down to the window that includes the original transaction information.

1. The vendor ledger should be displayed. Using the vendor, Abney and Son Contractors, put your cursor over the 3/9/12 vendor ledger entry. Your cursor changes to a magnifying-glass with a Z (for zoom) in it.

ABNEY	3/1/12	B1000	PJ			75.00	75.00	2% 10, Net 30
Abney and Son Contractors	3/9/12	B1015	ⓩ PJ	*		195.65	270.65	
	3/12/12	VCM30001	PJ	*	195.65		75.00	
	3/15/12		CDJ		50.00	50.00	75.00	

2. To drill down to the 3/9/12 transaction, double-click on it with your left mouse button. The Purchases/Receive Inventory window appears showing the original purchase of inventory items.

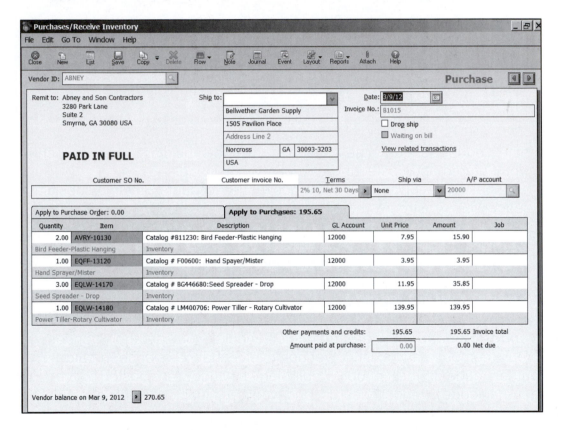

> **Troubleshooting Tip:** On my Purchases/Receive Inventory window, the Quantity, Item, Description, GL Account, Unit Price, and Amount table does *not* show multiple lines. If that is the case, you can use the arrows next to the Job field to scroll through the multiple lines. Try enlarging your screen with the cursor. If that doesn't work, read the next paragraph about screen resolution.

The number of lines on the Quantity, Item, Description, GL Account, Unit Price, and Amount table is determined by your screen resolution. On page iv, the minimum system requirements suggest 1024x768 resolution with small fonts.

3. Click [Close]. You are returned to the Vendor Ledgers. Drill down on the 3/12/12 vendor credit memo (VCM30001). The Vendor Credit Memos window appears. Observe that the Apply to Invoice No. tab shows B1015. This is the same merchandise that was purchased on 3/9/12. (See the Purchases/ Receive inventory window shown on the previous page.) The returned field shows the items returned.

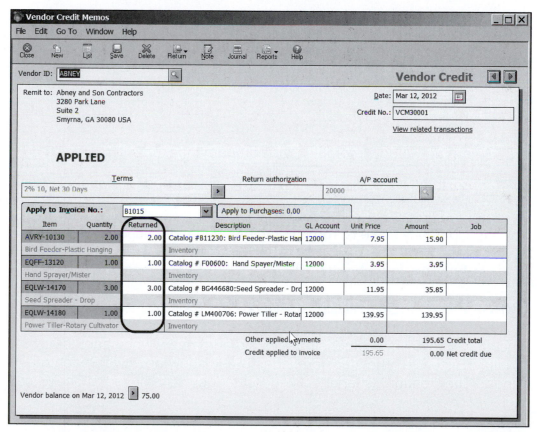

4. Click [Close]. You are returned to the Vendor Ledgers. Click [Close] to return to the Vendors & Purchases Navigation Center.

BACKING UP CHAPTER 2 DATA

Follow these steps to back up Chapter 2 data:

1. Insert your USB flash drive.

2. From the Navigation Bar, click [System] ;
    [Back Up Now]. Make sure that the box next to Include company
    name in the backup file name is *unchecked.*

3. Click [Back Up].

4. In the Save in field, select the appropriate drive letter for your USB
    drive.[2] (*Or,* save to the hard-drive default location or other location.)
    Type **Chapter 2** in the File name field.

5. Click [Save].

6. When the window prompts This company backup will require
    approximately 1 diskette, click [OK]. When the window
    prompts Please insert the first disk, click [OK]. When the Back
    Up Company scale is 100% complete, you have successfully backed
    up to the current point in Chapter 2. (Step 6 will differ slightly if you
    are backing up to the default or other hard-drive location.)

EXPORT TWO PEACHTREE REPORTS TO EXCEL

The steps that follow demonstrate how to add a new worksheet to an
existing Excel file. The steps on pages 89-90 show how two Peachtree
reports, the Vendor List and the Vendor Ledgers, are saved to one Excel
file.

---

[2]If you are having difficulty backing up to USB flash drive, backup to the desktop, then
copy the file to a USB flash drive. Refer to Appendix A, Troubleshooting, pages 756-
758—Problem Backing Up to USB Drive or Other External Media.

1. From the Navigation Bar, click  **Vendors & Purchases** . In the Recently Used Vendor Reports area, link to <u>View All Vendor & Purchases Reports</u>. The Select a Report or Form window appears.

2. Select Vendor List; Se<u>n</u>d To, Excel. When the Modify Report – Vendor List window appears, click OK . (*Hint:* You may want to display the Vendor list, reformat the columns, then from the displayed report click Excel .)

3. The Copy Report to Excel window appears. In the File option area make sure Create a new Microsoft Excel workbook is selected. In the Report header option, Show header in Excel worksheet should also be selected.

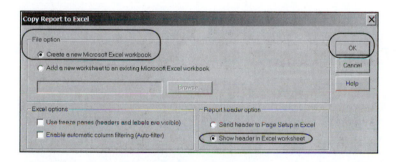

4. Click OK . The report is exported to Microsoft Excel. Bellwether Garden Supply's Vendor List is shown.

5. Save the Vendor List. Use **Chapter 2_Vendor List and Ledgers.xlsx** as the file name. (Excel 2003 ends in the file extension .xls.)

6. Go to Bellwether. (*Hint:* On the Taskbar at the bottom of the screen, click Peachtree, Select a Report or Form.)

7. From the Select a Report or Form window, double-click Vendor Ledgers. The Vendor Ledgers displays.

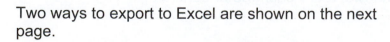

Two ways to export to Excel are shown on the next page.

a. From the Select a Report or Form window, highlight the report and then select Se_n_d To Excel.

b. Display the report and select Excel ⊞ Exce_l_. (This is shown below.)

8. Click ⊞ Exce_l_. On the Copy Report to Excel window, select Add a new worksheet to an existing Microsoft Excel workbook. Select Browse... . Go to the location of the saved file, Chapter 2_Vendor List and Ledgers.xlsx. Select Open .

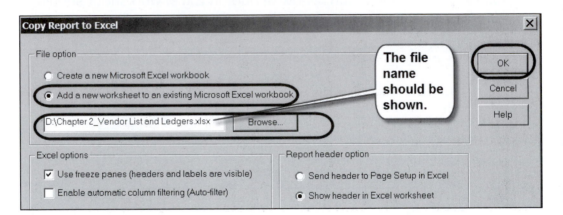

9. Click OK . Bellwether Garden Supply's Vendor Ledgers appear. Observe that the two sheets are shown: Vendor List and Vendor Ledgers (tabs at the bottom of the window.)

10. Save. The Excel file, Chapter 2_Vendor List and Ledgers, includes two sheets: the Vendor List and the Vendor Ledgers. Click ✕ on the title bar to exit Excel and return to Peachtree.

11. Close all windows. Exit Peachtree or continue.

SAVE VENDOR LIST AND VENDOR LEDGERS AS PDF FILES

Follow these steps to save the Vendor List as a PDF file.

1. Go to the Vendor List. From the Reports & Forms menu, select Accounts Payable, double-click Vendor List.

2. The Vendor List appears. On the icon bar, click [PDF]. The Save As window appears. Select the location of your USB drive.

3. Type **Chapter 2_Vendor List** in the File name field.

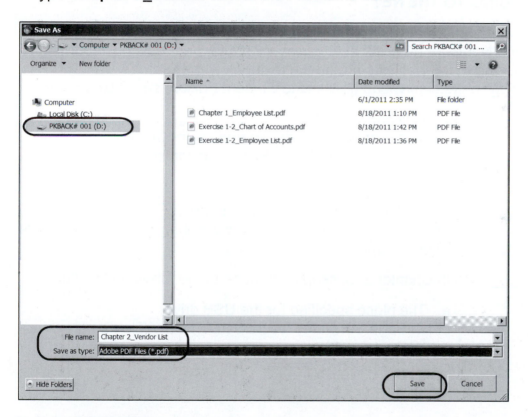

4. Click [Save].

5. Complete similar steps to save the Vendor Ledgers as a PDF file. Use the file name **Chapter 2_Vendor Ledgers.pdf**.

6. Close all windows.

SUMMARY AND REVIEW

Complete the following end-of-chapter activities:

1. Going to the Net, pages 92.
2. Multiple-choice questions, pages 92-94.
3. Exercises 2-1 and 2-2, pages 95-97.
4. Analysis question, page 98.
5. Assessment rubric, page 98.
6. Chapter 2 Index, page 99.

GOING TO THE NET

Access information about the Internet Corporation for Assigned Names and Numbers (ICANN) at http://www.icann.org/en/registries/about.htm. (Going to the Net links are on the textbook website at www.mhhe.com/yacht2012; link to Student Edition, select Chapter 2.)

1. What is a TLD and gTLD?
2. What gTLDs are operated under contract with ICANN?
3. What types of gTLDs are there? Briefly explain sponsored and unsponsored gTLDs.

Multiple Choice Questions: The Online Learning Center includes these questions and the analysis question at www.mhhe.com/yacht2012, select Student Edition, Chapter 2, QA Templates.

_____1. In Chapter 2, backups are made to the following location:

    a. The place specified for the USB drive.
    b. C:\Sage Software\Peachtree\Company\[file name].
    c. X:\Exercise 1A.
    d. D:\Chapter 1_Exercise 1-1.
    e None of the above.

_____2. Cash discounts from vendors in return for early payment of an invoice are called:

    a. Sales discounts.
    b. Returns and allowances.
    c. Purchase discounts.
    d. Markdowns.
    e. None of the above.

_____3. You can enter information within a lookup field by using one or more of the following keys:

    a. Type the **<+>** symbol.
    b. Double-click with the mouse.
    c. a. or b.
    d. Type the invoice number.
    e. None of the above.

_____4. Why is it important that your coding system for vendors be consistent and logical?

    a. All vendors and customers should be identified by 3 digits.
    b. So that others working in your company can determine a vendor code from the company name.
    c. All the vendors and customer numbers are already set up for Bellwether Garden Supply so you don't have to worry about it.
    d. All customers and vendors should be identified by the first eight letters of a company's name.
    e. None of the above.

_____5. Why are purchase orders used?

    a. To post accounting information.
    b. To place an order with a customer.
    c. To update the accounts payable subsidiary system.
    d. To request items from a vendor.
    e. None of the above.

_____6. It is important to use either upper or lowercase letters to identify a vendor because the program:

    a. Is susceptible.
    b. Doesn't recognize numbers.
    c. Doesn't recognize symbols.
    d. Is case sensitive.
    e. None of the above.

_____7. Which window do you use to add a new vendor?

    a. Maintain Vendors.
    b. Purchases/Receive Inventory.
    c. Menu bar.
    d. Select a Report.
    e. None of the above.

_____8. Going from the general ledger to the original entry window is called:

    a. Drill down.
    b. Coding.
    c. Lookup.
    d. None of the above.
    e. All of the above.

_____9. When you make an entry in the Purchases/Receive Inventory window for Armstrong's Landscaping you are debiting and crediting which accounts:

    a. Dr. Accounts Payable/Armstrong's Landscaping
       Cr. Cash in Checking
       Cr. Purchase Discounts
    b. Dr. Cash
       Cr. Accounts Payable
    c. Dr. Cash
       Cr. Sales
    d. Dr. Materials Cost
       Cr. Accounts Payable/Armstrong's Landscaping
    e. None of the above.

_____10. Which of the following Navigation Bar, Vendors & Purchases selections do you use to issue a return of merchandise to a vendor?

    a. Vendors & Purchases Tasks; Purchases/Receive Inventory.
    b. Credits & Returns; New Vendor Credit Memo.
    c. Sales/Invoicing.
    d. Credit Memos.
    e. None of the above.

Exercise 2-1: Follow the instructions below to complete Exercise 2-1.

1. Start PCA. Open Bellwether Garden Supply.

2. Follow these steps to restore your data from the end of Chapter 2:

    a. Insert your USB flash drive. From the System Navigation Center, select $\boxed{\text{Restore Now}}$. (The Chapter 2.ptb backup was made page 88.)

    b. The Select Backup File window appears. Click $\boxed{\text{Browse}}$. Go to the Location of your Chapter 2.ptb file and select it. (*Hint:* The File name field shows Chapter 2.ptb.) Click $\boxed{\text{Open}}$. The Select Backup File window shows the location of your backup file. Click $\boxed{\text{Next >}}$.

    c. The Select Company window appears. Make sure that the radio button next to An Existing Company is selected. The Company Name field shows Bellwether Garden Supply. The Location field shows the default location on the hard drive for Bellwether Garden Supply. Click $\boxed{\text{Next >}}$.[3]

    d. The Restore Options window appears. Make sure that the box next to Company Data is *checked*. Click $\boxed{\text{Next >}}$.

    e. The Confirmation window appears. Check the From and To fields to make sure they are correct. Click $\boxed{\text{Finish}}$. When the Restore Company scale is 100% complete, your data is restored. (*Hint:* The Student Version of Peachtree prompts that company data can be used for 14 months. After that time the data expires. Click $\boxed{\text{OK}}$. Bellwether Garden Supply opens.)

---

[3]If Bellwether Garden Supply is *not* shown in the Company Name field, refer to the Read Me box on page 29.

3. Add the following vendor:

   Vendor ID: POSTOFC
   Name: Post Office Supplies
   Contact: Randall Poston
   Vendor Type: OFFICE
   Expense Account: Account No. 71000, Office Expense

4. Enter the following transaction.

   Date   *Transaction Description*

   03/15/2012   Invoice No. H788 was received from Post Office
                   Supplies for the purchase of five boxes of letter-size
                   file folders, $10.95 each. (*Hint:* Account No. 71000,
                   Office Expense, should be debited.)

5. Post this purchase.

6. Continue with Exercise 2-2.

Exercise 2-2: Follow the instructions below to complete Exercise 2-2.

1. Enter the following transaction.

   Date   *Transaction Description*

   03/18/12   Pay Post Office Supplies for Invoice H788, $53.65.
                 (*Hint:* The payment is less a 2% discount: $54.75 -1.10
                 = $53.65.)

2. Post the Cash Disbursements Journal. (*Hint:* The
   Purchases/Receive Inventory window is the Cash Disbursements
   Journal.)

3. Print Check No. 10216. (*Hint: On the OCR AP Laser Preprinted
   Filter window, select the payment date and vendor.*)

4. Print the Vendor Ledgers. Add a Terms column. Adjust the Vendor
   Ledgers report so that it prints on one page. (*Hint:* Place the mouse
   over the column. The cursor changes to a double-arrow. Adjust the
   column.)

5. Follow these steps to back up Exercise 2-2.

   a. If necessary, insert your USB flash drive.

   b. From the Navigation Bar, click [System];

   Back Up Now .

   c. Click [Back Up].

   d. In the Save in field, select the USB drive. Type **Exercise 2-2** in the File name field.

   e. Click [Save].

   f. When the window prompts that This company backup will require 1 diskette, click [OK]. When the window prompts Please insert the first disk, click [OK]. When the Back Up Company scale is 100% complete, you have successfully backed up to the current point. You are returned to the menu bar.

Read Me: Problem Backing Up to USB Drive

   If you encounter difficulties backing up to a USB drive, backup to your desktop first. Then copy the backup file from your desktop to a USB drive. Refer to Appendix A, Problem Backing Up to USB Drive or Other External Media, pages 756-758 for detailed steps.

---

6. Save two Peachtree reports, the Vendor List and the Vendors Ledgers, to one Excel file. (*Hint:* Refer to pages 89-90, Export Two Peachtree Reports to One Excel File.) Add the terms column to the Vendor Ledgers. Use **Exercise 2-2_Vendor List and Ledgers.xlsx** as the file name.

7. Save the Vendor List and Vendor Ledgers as a PDF file. Use **Exercise 2-2_Vendor List.pdf** and **Exercise 2-2_Vendor Ledgers.pdf** as the file name.

   Check your figures: Vendor Ledgers balance: $80,826.01.

8. Close all windows. Exit Peachtree.

ANALYSIS QUESTION:

With the Vendors & Payables Navigation Center serving as the starting point to perform tasks related to Accounts Payable, list five Vendors & Purchases Tasks.

Briefly describe the Vendor Management Navigation Center.

ASSESSMENT RUBRIC

Complete the Assessment Rubric online at www.mhhe.com/yacht2012; Student Edition, select Chapter 2, Assessment Rubric link. To review Peachtree's journals, navigation centers, modules, and task windows, complete the blank fields online.

Date	Transaction	Navigation Center/Module	Task Window	Journal Dr./Cr.
3/15	Invoice No. H788 was received from Post Office Supplies for the purchase of five boxes of letter-size file folders, $10.95 each.			
3/18	Pay Post Office Supplies for Invoice H788, $53.85			

CHAPTER 2 INDEX

Chapter 3   Customers

LEARNING OBJECTIVES

1. Restore data from Exercise 2-2. (This backup was made on page 97.)
2. Go to the Customers & Sales Navigation Center to enter quotes and sales orders.
3. Enter a sales order.
4. Ship items from a sales order.
5. Enter customer terms.
6. Record a sales invoice on the Sales/Invoicing window.
7. Print a sales invoice.
8. Analyze receipts and customer credit memos.
9. Post a receipt for previously invoiced amounts.
10. Add a Customer Terms column to the Customer Ledgers report.
11. Export Customer Ledgers to Excel.
12. Save the Customer Ledgers as a PDF file.
13. Make two backups, save one Excel file, and one PDF file.[1]

Chapter 3 introduces the basics of how PCA works with customer transactions. First you learn about quotes and *sales orders*. A sales order is a document containing a list of items or services that a customer wants to buy. When a sales order is posted, no accounting information is updated. Once you complete sales orders, you learn how the information entered in customer maintenance is used when posting entries. For example, in the Maintain Customers/Prospects window, you set a range of days within which a customer can receive a discount and set the discount percentage. This information will print on the sales invoices you record. The discount is automatically applied when you enter a receipt within the allotted time. The Collection Manager, included on the Analysis Menu, shows an overview of all outstanding invoices.

---

[1]Refer to the chart on page 2 for the size of backups, and saved Excel and PDF files.

The McGraw-Hill Companies, Inc., *Computer Accounting with Peachtree by Sage Complete Accounting 2012, 16e*

GETTING STARTED

Follow the steps below to start PCA:

1. Start Peachtree. Open the sample company, Bellwether Garden Supply. (If Bellwether Garden Supply is not shown, restore a New Company. Refer to the Read Me box on page 29.)

2. Restore your data from the Exercise 2-2 backup made on page 97.

   a. Insert your USB flash drive. From the Navigation Bar, select

   [System]; click [Restore Now].

   b. The Select Backup File window appears. Click [Browse]. Go to the Location of your Exercise 2-2.ptb file and select it. Click [Open]. The Select Backup File window shows the location of your backup file. Click [Next>].

   c. The Select Company window appears. The radio button next to An Existing Company is selected. The Company name field shows Bellwether Garden Supply. The Location field shows the default location on the hard drive for Bellwether Garden Supply. Click [Next>].

   d. The Restore Options window appears. Make sure that the box next to Company Data is *checked*. Click [Next>].

   e. The Confirmation window appears. Check the From and To fields to make sure they are correct. Click [Finish]. When the Restore Company scale is 100% complete, your data is restored. (*Hint:* The Student Version of Peachtree prompts that company data can be used for 14 months. After that time the data expires. Click [OK]. Bellwether Garden Supply opens.)

💾 To make sure you are starting in the appropriate place in the data (Exercise 2-2 backup) check that these vendors, Armstrong's

Landscaping and Postal Office Supplies, are shown in the Vendors area of the Vendors & Purchases Navigation Center. (*Hint:* You may need to click [🔄 Refresh] to update your Vendors list.) The Vendor Ledgers report should show a zero balance for both Armstrong's Landscaping and Postal Office Supplies.

ACCOUNTS RECEIVABLE SYSTEM

Accounts Receivable represents amounts owed by customers for items or services sold to them when cash is not received at the time of sale. Typically, accounts receivable balances are recorded on sales invoices that include terms of payment. Accounts receivable is used if you are setting up accrued income that customers owe.

The four basic tasks in Accounts Receivable are:

1. Quotes: Allows you to enter a quote for a customer.

2. Sales Orders: Sales orders provide you with a means of tracking backorders for your customers.

3. Sales/Invoicing: When items are ready for shipment, the sales/invoicing window is used.

4. Receipts: Used for recording receipts from customers. (PCA also includes credits and returns.)

Before adding accounts receivable transactions, examine the Customers & Sales Navigation Center. Follow these steps to do that.

1. From the Navigation Bar, select [👤 **Customers & Sales**]. The Customers & Sales Navigation Center displays information and access points related to the company's customers. In Peachtree, this represents the ***accounts receivable module*** or ***accounts receivable system***.

    Modules organize Peachtree's transaction windows and reports. When the Navigation Bar's Customers & Sales selection is made, Peachtree's accounts receivable system is shown. The menu bar selections, Tasks and Reports & Forms, are also organized by module; for example, the Reports & Forms menu includes Accounts

Receivable, Accounts Payable, General Ledger, etc. Peachtree's Customers & Sales Navigation Center has two tabs that display information and access points related to Bellwether's customers.

- The Customers & Sales tab is a summary of customer information, includes access to recently used customer reports and an overview of the company's aged receivables. Scroll down the Customers & Sales window to see the Customers, Recently Used Customer Reports, Aged Receivables, and Peachtree Solutions.

- On the Customer Management tab, you can see lists of information regarding transactions and customer history, including invoices, receipts, and finance charges.

The Customers & Sales Tasks are shown below. Scroll down the window to see the rest of the Customers & Sales Navigation Center.

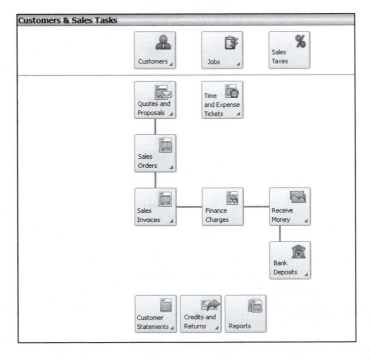

Link to a couple of areas to explore the Customers & Sales Navigation Center. Close any open windows, then continue with the next section. (*Hint:* If multiple windows are open, from the menu bar select Window, Close All.)

2. Click on the 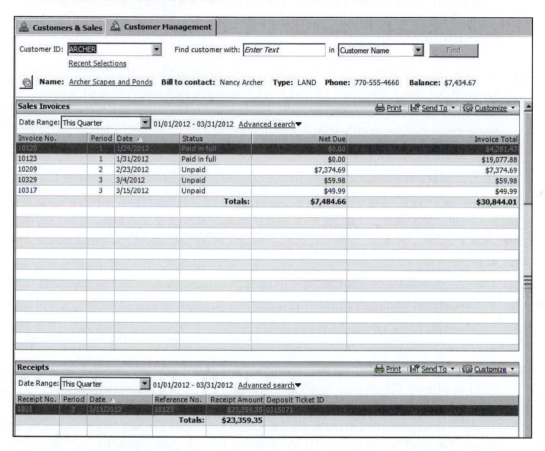 **Customer Management** tab. In the Customer ID field, select ARCHER. Observe that the Sales Invoices area lists this customer's invoices, and the Receipts area shows this customer's payments to Bellwether Garden Supply. Scroll down the screen to see Credit Memos and Totals. A partial Customer Management window is shown below.

Invoice No.	Period	Date	Status	Net Due	Invoice Total
10120	1	1/29/2012	Paid in full	$0.00	$4,281.47
10123	1	1/31/2012	Paid in full	$0.00	$19,077.88
10209	2	2/23/2012	Unpaid	$7,374.69	$7,374.69
10329	3	3/4/2012	Unpaid	$59.98	$59.98
10317	3	3/15/2012	Unpaid	$49.99	$49.99
			Totals:	$7,484.66	$30,844.01

Receipts

Date Range: This Quarter   01/01/2012 - 03/31/2012 Advanced search ▼

Receipt No.	Period	Date	Reference No.	Receipt Amount	Deposit Ticket ID
1038	3	3/15/2012	10123	$23,359.35	0315071
			Totals:	$23,359.35	

Entering a Quote

When you enter a quote for a customer, you are *not* updating any accounting information or inventory amounts. PCA calculates what the total cost of the sale will be for a customer, including sales tax and freight. You can then print the quote for the customer. Follow these steps to enter a sales quote.

1. Select the [≜ **Customers & Sales**] tab. From the Customers & Sales Tasks diagram, click [Quotes and Proposals ◢]; New Quote.

2. The Quotes window displays. Your cursor is in the Customer ID field. Type **D** (use capital D). Dash Business Systems displays. Press the **<Enter>** key.

3. Your cursor is in the Ship to field. Click on the Date field. Accept the default for the Date and Good thru dates by pressing the **<Enter>** key four times. The Quote No. field is blank. This is okay. Peachtree assigns a quote number automatically.

Comment

You can also enter a number that you want to print in the Quote # field. If you assign your own number, PCA sorts numbers one digit at a time. Therefore, it is a good idea to assign numbers with the same number of digits. For example, PCA sorts the following numbers in this order:

   1
   104
   12
   2
   23

---

4. Your cursor should be in the Customer PO field. Observe that this field is blank. Since this customer does not have a purchase order number, you are going to leave this field blank. Click on Quantity field. Type **1** and press **<Enter>**. (If the Quantity field shows .01, refer to the steps 1a. and b. on page 18 for setting two decimal places.)

5. In the Item field, select EQFF-13110 Fertilizer Compression Sprayer. (*Hint: Scroll down the Item list to make this selection, or* you can type the item ID.) The Description, GL Account, Unit Price, Tax, and Amount fields are automatically completed.

> **Comment**
>
> If the GL Account field is not displayed on the Quotes window, you need to check your global settings. Refer to step 1c on page 18 (Chapter 1) to make sure that the boxes in the Hide General Ledger Accounts section are unchecked (see Options/Global).

6. Click on the Quantity field. Type **4** then select EQWT-15120 Garden Hose - 75 ft. for the item. Compare your Quotes window to the one shown below.

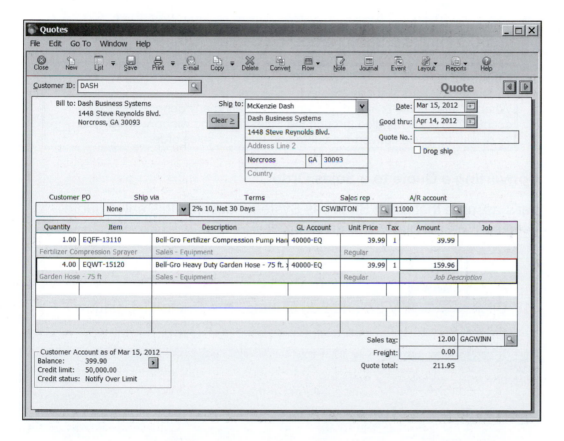

When you selected Dash Business Systems, the Customer Account balance as of March 15, 2012 also appears on the lower left side of the Quotes window, along with the Credit Limit and Credit Status. You can drill down to Dash Business Systems' customer ledger by clicking on the right arrow ( ) in the Customer Account area.

7. To see the journal entry, click 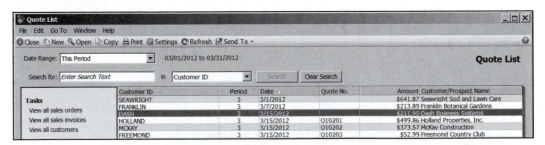Journal. The Quotes Journal lists the sales taxes that are paid for the transaction, the price for each item, and the amount that Bellwether will receive from the customer on this quote. Close the Accounting Behind the Screens window by clicking OK .

8. Click Save to post this sales quote, then click Close to return to the Customers & Sales Navigation Center.

> **Comment**
>
> When a sales quote is saved, you are *not* updating any general ledger accounts. That is handled through the Sales/Invoicing window, which you work with after you convert the quote and print the sales order.

Converting a Quote to a Sales Order

Let's assume that Dash Business Systems accepts this sales quote. Let's convert the quote to a sales order.

1. Click Quotes and Proposals ; View and Edit Quotes. The Quote List window appears.

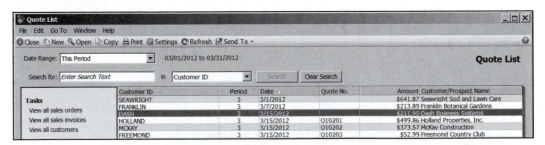

2. Double-click DASH. The Quotes window appears showing the March 15, 2012 quote. Compare this to the Quotes window shown on page 107.

3. Click 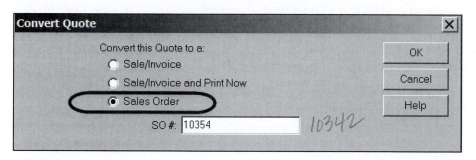. There are three options: Sales/Invoice; Sales/Invoice and Print Now; Sales Order. Click on the radio button next to Sales Order. The SO # field is completed automatically.

Convert Quote	✕
Convert this Quote to a:	OK
○ Sale/Invoice	Cancel
○ Sale/Invoice and Print Now	Help
⊙ Sales Order	
SO #: 10354 *10342*	

4. Click **OK**. A blank Quotes window appears. Click **Close**. You just converted the sales quote to a sales order. Now you can invoice the customer for shipment.

5. Close all windows. (*Hint:* Select Window; Close All.)

Printing (or Displaying) a Sales Order

Printing a sales order gives you the ability to confirm customer orders and fill these orders more efficiently. Follow these steps to print.

1. From the Customers & Sales Navigation Center, select **Sales Orders**; View and Edit Sales Orders. On the Sales Order List window, double-click DASH. The Quote converted to Sales Order No. 10354 displays.

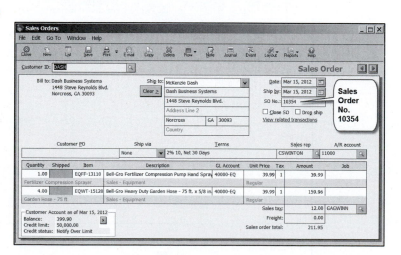

2. Click 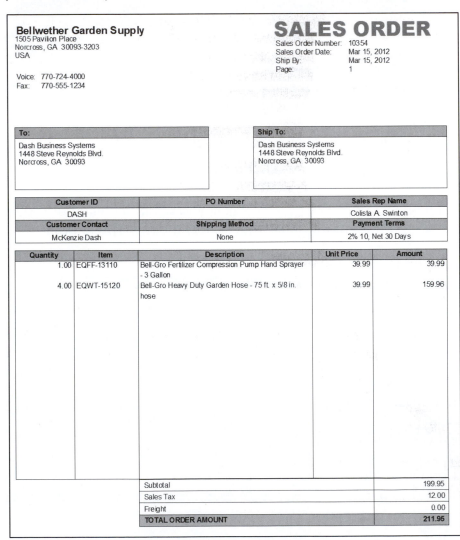. *Or,* click on the down arrow next to Print and select Print Preview. The Print or Preview Forms: Sales Orders window appears. Observe that the Sales Order number is 10354. This agrees with the quote that was converted to a sales order on pages 108-109. Remember, Peachtree automatically assigned the sales order number. (*Hint:* If necessary, click anywhere on the Sales Orders window to activate the Print icon.)

3. Accept the Last used form – Sales Order w/Totals. Click Print (*or* Print Preview). The sales order starts to print or displays.

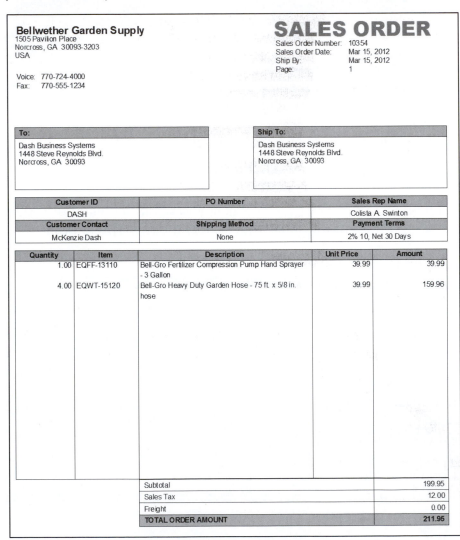

Bellwether Garden Supply
1505 Pavilion Place
Norcross, GA 30093-3203
USA

Voice: 770-724-4000
Fax: 770-555-1234

SALES ORDER

Sales Order Number: 10354
Sales Order Date: Mar 15, 2012
Ship By: Mar 15, 2012
Page: 1

To:	Ship To:
Dash Business Systems 1448 Steve Reynolds Blvd. Norcross, GA 30093	Dash Business Systems 1448 Steve Reynolds Blvd. Norcross, GA 30093

Customer ID	PO Number	Sales Rep Name
DASH		Colista A. Swinton

Customer Contact	Shipping Method	Payment Terms
McKenzie Dash	None	2% 10, Net 30 Days

Quantity	Item	Description	Unit Price	Amount
1.00	EQFF-13110	Bell-Gro Fertilizer Compression Pump Hand Sprayer - 3 Gallon	39.99	39.99
4.00	EQWT-15120	Bell-Gro Heavy Duty Garden Hose - 75 ft. x 5/8 in. hose	39.99	159.96

Subtotal	199.95
Sales Tax	12.00
Freight	0.00
TOTAL ORDER AMOUNT	**211.95**

4. If you previewed the Sales Order, click [Print]. Close all windows.
    (*Hint:* From the menu bar, click Window, Close All.)

Ship Items from a Sales Order

To ship items from a sales order, open the Sales/Invoicing window, select the customer, then choose the open sales order you want to invoice. Once the shipped field is completed, an invoice is created with the appropriate sales tax and the amount of the sale. When the Sales/Invoicing window is saved (posted), accounting information is updated. That includes the accounts receivable controlling account in the general ledger, the customer's subsidiary account in the customer ledger, and inventory amounts.

Follow these steps to ship items from a Sales Order No. 10354.

1. Click [Sales Invoices], New Sales Invoice. The Sales/Invoicing window appears.

2. In the Customer ID field, select DASH, Dash Business Systems.

3. The Apply to Sales Order No. tab is selected. Click on the down-arrow and select number 10354.

4. Type **1** and **4** in the Shipped fields. Once you complete the Shipped fields, the Invoice totals are computed (sales tax and amount paid at sale.)

    Compare your Sales/Invoicing window to the one shown on the next page.

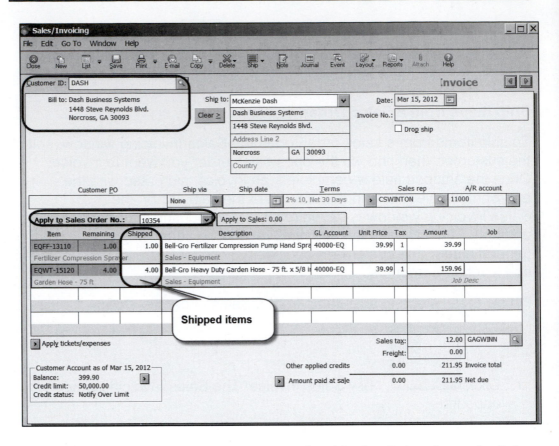

5. To see how this transaction is journalized in the Sales Journal, click
    Journal . After the entry is saved (posted), Cost of Sales is computed.
    Close the Sales Journal window.

6. Click Save to post. Close the Sales/Invoicing window.

THE MAINTAIN CUSTOMERS/PROSPECTS WINDOW

The first step is to select the customer you are going to invoice and to change one item of information: the discount percentage offered for timely payment.

1. From the Customers & Sales Navigation Center, click 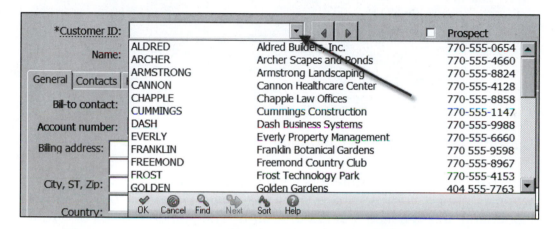;
   New Customer. The Maintain Customers/Prospects window displays.
   The cursor is in the Customer ID field. Notice the down-arrow in this
   field.

2. Click on the down-arrow in the Customer ID field to open the
   customers/prospects list.[2]

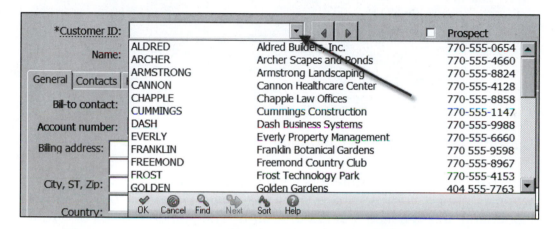

3. The customer file you are going to use is Teesdale Real Estate.
   Scroll down the customer list, then click **TEESDALE** for **Teesdale
   Real Estate** to select it from the list. The Maintain Customers/
   Prospects window shows a completed record for Teesdale Real
   Estate.

   Compare your Maintain Customers/Prospects window to the one
   shown on the next page.

---

[2]There are three ways to open the list in a lookup field. First, make sure that your
cursor is in the Customer ID field: 1) Press the right mouse button; 2) type a question
mark **<?>**; 3) left-click the down-arrow.

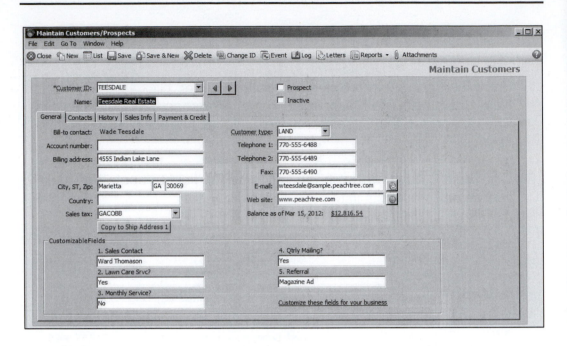

Entering a Discount for a Customer

Because Teesdale Real Estate is such a good customer, Bellwether Garden Supply is going to increase their discount from 2% to 5%. In accounting, this is called a *sales discount*. The standard sales discount for Bellwether is 2% if paid within 10 days. Teesdale's new sales discount is 5% if paid within 15 days. Sales discounts are applied when payment is received from the customer. In Peachtree, sales discounts are applied when payment is received from the customer.

Follow these steps to enter a discount for a customer:

1. The Maintain Customers/Prospects window should be displayed. Click on the Payment & Credit tab.

2. In the Terms and Credit Area (right side of window), click on the down-arrow. Select Customize terms for this customer.

3. If necessary, click on the radio button next to Due in number of days to select it.

4. Click on the Discount in field. Type **15** and press **<Enter>**. The cursor moves to the Discount percent field.

5. Type **5** and press **<Enter>**.[3]

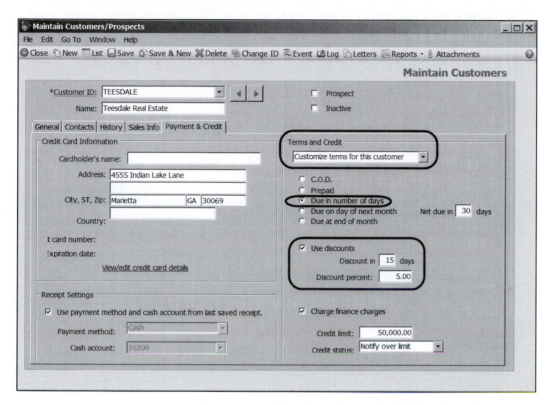

6. Click ⊞ Save .

7. Close the Maintain Customers/Prospects window to return to the Customers & Sales Navigation Center.

Entering a Sale to a Customer

Let's learn how to invoice Teesdale Real Estate. To print or record an invoice in PCA, enter a sales invoice for a customer on the Sales/Invoicing window. Like a Sales Journal, the Sales/Invoicing window is reserved for sales from credit customers. The transaction you are going to enter is shown on the next page.

---

[3]You should have set two decimal places in Chapter 1 (see page 18, 1 a. and b.).

Date   Transaction Description

03/01/12   Bellwether Garden Supply sold 5 hose-end sprayers, $49.95,
            to Teesdale Real Estate, Customer ID, TEESDALE, and
            cleaned the parking lot, $100, for a total of $149.95 plus
            $9.00 sales tax; $158.95.

Follow these steps to learn how to use the Sales/Invoicing window:

1. From the Customers & Sales Navigation Center, click ; New
    Sales Invoice. The Sales/Invoicing window appears.

    Use the Sales/Invoicing window for credit sales from customers. If
    you want to enter a cash sale, use the Receipts window, not the
    Sales/Invoicing window. The Sales/Invoicing window is for credit
    customers only. Here's a way to remember the difference between
    Receipts and Sales/Invoicing: if the transaction involves real money
    (cash or check), enter it in the Receipts window; if the transaction
    involves a credit sale, enter it in the Sales/Invoicing window. The
    Sales/Invoicing window posts to the Sales Journal. The Receipts
    window posts to the Cash Receipts Journal.

    The Sales/Invoicing window should be displayed. The cursor is in the
    <u>C</u>ustomer ID field. Don't worry if you have forgotten Teesdale's
    customer ID number because PCA knows it. The <u>C</u>ustomer ID field
    has a lookup field.

2. With the cursor in the <u>C</u>ustomer ID field, click the right mouse button
    (or type a question mark, **<?>**). You may also click 🔍.

3. Select Teesdale
    Real Estate,
    TEESDALE.

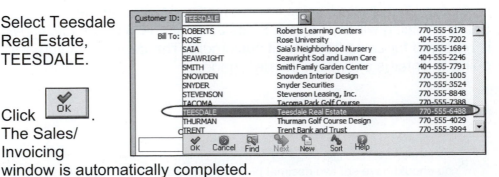

4. Click ✔OK.
    The Sales/
    Invoicing
    window is automatically completed.

Observe that the Bill to and Ship to fields are completed automatically. PCA provides an invoice number when the sales invoice is printed so there is no need to enter an invoice number now.

5. Click on the Date field which defaults to 3/15/12.

   PCA offers flexibility when entering dates. For example, you can enter March 1, 2012 as 030112 and the program will format the date correctly. You can also enter just the day portion of the date and PCA formats the date in the current period. For example, if you're working in March of 2012, you can type 4 in the date field and the program formats the date as March 4, 2012. You can also use the pop-up calendar to click the date.

6. Type **1** (or select 1) for the date and press **<Enter>**. The cursor moves to the Invoice No. field, which you are going to leave blank. Peachtree will assign an invoice number when you print the sales invoice.

7. Click on the Apply to Sales tab.

8. Click on the Quantity field, type **5** and press **<Enter>**. Your cursor goes to the Item lookup field.

9. Click 🔍 to open the list of inventory items.

ADMIN-01000	Bookkeeping/Administrative	<N/A>
AVRY-10050	Prefabricated Birdhouse	
AVRY-10100	Bird House Kit	5.00000
AVRY-10110	Bird House-Pole 14 Ft.	15.00000
AVRY-10120	Bird House-Red 12-Room Unit	4.00000
AVRY-10130	Bird Feeder-Plastic Hanging	12.00000
AVRY-10140	Thistle Bird Seed Mix-6 lb.	29.00000
AVRY-10150	Bird Bath - Stone Gothic 2pc.	2.00000
AVRY-10200	Birdbath-Plastic	

OK   Cancel   Find   Next   New   Sort   Help

There are two ways to enter transaction lines for an invoice:

➤ By Inventory Item: Because the price of each inventory item is stored in the Maintain Inventory Items file, you only have to enter the quantity supplied. The program will compute the credit amount.

➤ By Account Number: If there is no line item set up for a particular commodity you sell, or if you don't use the Inventory module, you can distribute directly against the proper General Ledger account.

10. The Inventory Item list should be open. Let's see what happens if the Sort icon is selected. Click [Sort] which is located at the bottom of the lookup list on the right side.

   By selecting Sort, you change the order of the list. The list was sorted by ID number; now the list is sorted alphabetically by name. This feature is available in all lookup lists.

11. Select Hand Sprayer/Mister as the item for this sale. EQFF-13120 displays in the Item field. (*Hint:* You can also type the item ID.)

12. Your cursor should be in the Description field with the following description highlighted: Bell-Gro Plant All-Purpose Plastic Sprayer/Mister. Since we're not going to add a comment or explanation about this inventory item, press **<Enter>** to move to the GL Account field.

   The default account is Account No. 40000-EQ, Sales – Equipment. The account name, Sales – Equipment, is shown below the transaction line. This account will be credited unless you change the account number in this GL Account field. The debit is automatically made to Accounts Receivable–Teesdale Real Estate.

13. Press **<Enter>** to accept Account No. 40000-EQ. The cursor moves to the Unit Price field and 9.99 is automatically completed. Since the price has been set up in the Maintain Inventory Items file, the unit price is automatically completed for you.

14. Press **<Enter>** to go to the tax field. Type a **<?>** to display the lookup list. Inventory Item tax types are set up in the Maintain Inventory Item file. This lookup list lets you specify certain items as exempt or having special tax situations. There is no need to specify any special tax situation.

15. Press **<Enter>** to go to the Amount field. PCA calculates the total, $49.95, and enters it in the field.

16. Press **<Enter>** to go to the Job field. The job field also has a lookup list. You'll learn about Jobs in more detail in Chapter 6.

17. Press **<Enter>** to go to a new transaction line.

➢ **Troubleshooting Tip:** Observe that the Invoice No. field is blank. The invoice number, similar to the check number, is assigned when you print. Enter an invoice number if you are *not* going to print invoices.

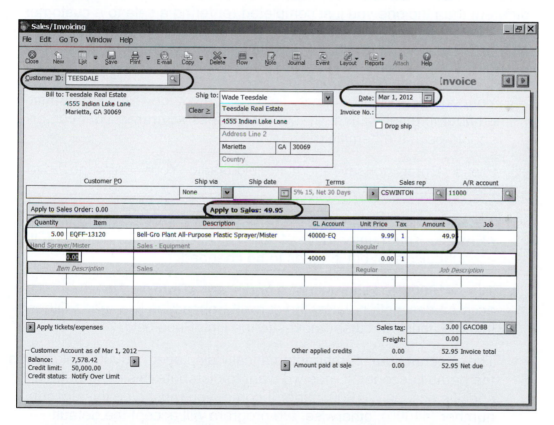

Notice that the Invoice Total and Net Due in the lower right of the window shows $52.95. The Invoice Total displays a running total of the amount that the customer's account in the Accounts Receivable subsidiary ledger is increased (debited). When you add the next transaction line, this figure will increase. In accounting you learn that two things happen when the Accounts Receivable subsidiary ledger is used.

a. The Accounts Receivable controlling account in the General Ledger is increased by the amount of the credit sale.

b. The credit to the applicable revenue account is offset by a debit to the Customer's account in the Accounts Receivable ledger.

Distributing Against a Specific Account

In this part of the transaction, Bellwether Garden Supply contracted with Teesdale Real Estate to clean up their parking lot for $100. Because no Inventory Item is stored in the maintenance records, this transaction is different than the one you just completed (entering a sale to a customer for an inventory item). In this part of the transaction, you need to distribute the amount ($100.00) directly against the Other Income account.

1. Your cursor is in the Quantity field. Since you don't have a quantity number to enter with this transaction, press **<Enter>**. Your cursor should be in the Item field.

2. Press **<Enter>** to leave the Item field blank. Your cursor moves to the Description field.

3. Type **Cleaned parking lot** in the Description field and press **<Enter>**. Your cursor moves to the GL Account field. The default account displays, but it needs to be changed.

4. Type **41000** (for Other Income) and press **<Enter>**. Now the account description below the current transaction line reads Other Income and your cursor moves to the Unit Price field.

   The account number that automatically displayed, 40000, Sales, was the default account. Since we want to distribute this revenue to a specific account, 41000, Other Income, you must type this account number (41000); otherwise, the program will accept the default account number.

5. Press **<Enter>** to skip the Unit Price field because we don't need a unit price. Your cursor moves to the Tax field.

6. Press **<Enter>** to accept the default tax code. Your cursor moves to the Amount field.

7. Type **100** and press **<Enter>** two times. Notice the Sales/Invoicing window shows the two amounts entered for this invoice. The Invoice Total, including sales tax, is $158.95.

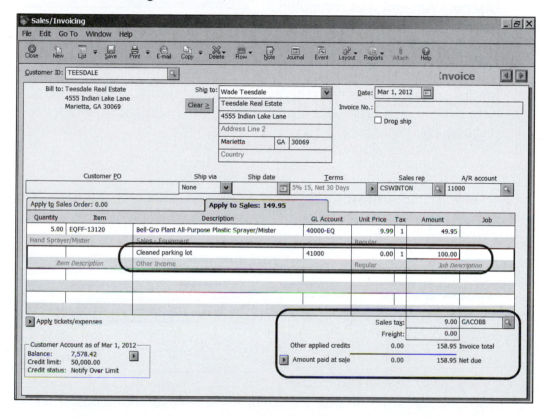

For purposes of this example, the cleaning service is taxed. In some states, services such as cleaning a parking lot would not be subject to sales tax.

Discount Information

At the beginning of this chapter you changed the sales discount for Teesdale Real Estate. Let's check to make sure that the discount information is current for the invoice you just entered.

1. Click on the arrow 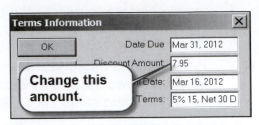 button to the right of <u>T</u>erms. This information is below the Shi<u>p</u> To address. The Terms Information window appears. Since the Discount Amount was computed automatically on the items sold plus sales tax, the Discount Amount of 7.95 needs to be changed. In Peachtree, you can enter a different sales discount amount.

   In this example, the sales discount is calculated on the amount of the items sold which is $149.95. (Refer to the Sales/Invoicing window on page 121.)

   Items sold: $49.95 + $100 = $149.95
   Times sales discount   .05
   Discount Amount   **$7.50**

2. Type **7.50** in the Discount Amount field, then press **<Enter>**.

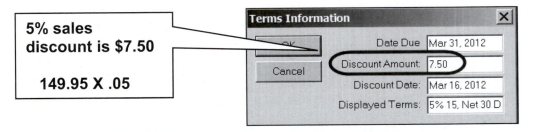

   The Discount Date (March 16, 2012) is the date when the customer must pay to receive the discount. The Displayed Terms are the percentage of discount (5%), the time period in days for receiving the discount (15), and the number of days before the invoice is due (Net 30)—5% 15, Net 30.

3. Click [OK] to close the Terms Information window.

POSTING THE INVOICE

The sample company, Bellwether Garden Supply, uses *real-time posting*. When real-time posting is used, the transactions that you enter are posted when you select the [Save] icon.

There is another type of posting included in PCA. It is called **batch posting**. When using batch posting, the transactions you enter are saved to a temporary holding area where you can review them before posting to the general ledger.

Follow these steps to save and post the invoice:

1. Click 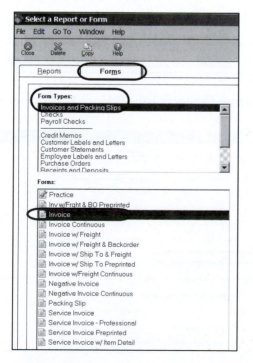. The Sales/Invoicing window is ready for another transaction.

2. Close all windows.

PRINTING (OR DISPLAYING) INVOICES

Follow these steps to print the invoice for Teesdale Real Estate:

1. From the menu bar, select Reports & Forms; Forms, Invoices and Packing Slips.

2. Observe that the Form Types field shows Invoices and Packing Slips highlighted. In the Forms list, select Invoice.

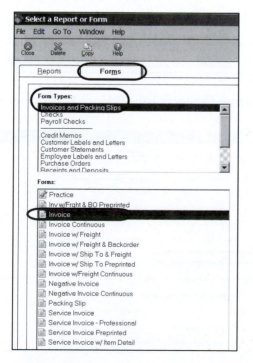

3. Double-click Invoice. The Preview and Print Invoices and Packing Slips window appears.

4. In the Filter customers by field select Teesdale in the ID and to fields.

5. Click 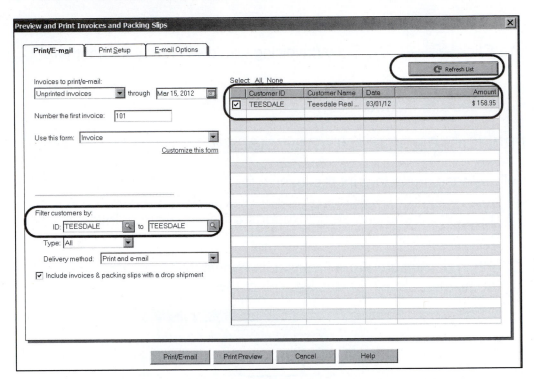 Refresh List .

6. Select the E-mail Options tab. Select Print only a paper copy.

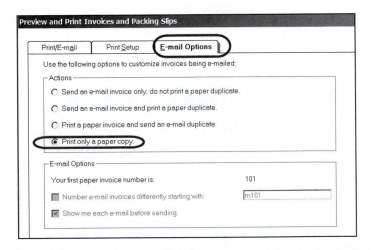

7. Click Print Preview . Compare Invoice 101 to the one shown.

Bellwether Garden Supply
1505 Pavilion Place
Norcross, GA 30093-3203
USA

Voice: 770-724-4000
Fax: 770-555-1234

INVOICE

Invoice Number:	101
Invoice Date:	Mar 1, 2012
Page:	1

Bill To:	Ship to:
Teesdale Real Estate 4555 Indian Lake Lane Marietta, GA 30069	Teesdale Real Estate 4555 Indian Lake Lane Marietta, GA 30069

Customer ID	Customer PO	Payment Terms	
TEESDALE		5% 15, Net 30 Days	
Sales Rep ID	**Shipping Method**	**Ship Date**	**Due Date**
CSWINTON	None		3/31/12

Quantity	Item	Description	Unit Price	Amount
5.00	EQFF-13120	Bell-Gro Plant All-Purpose Plastic Sprayer/Mister	9.99	49.95
		Cleaned parking lot		100.00

Subtotal	149.95
Sales Tax	9.00
Total Invoice Amount	158.95
Payment/Credit Applied	
TOTAL	**158.95**

Check/Credit Memo No:

---

8. Click Print .

> **Read Me:**
>
> When I try to print Invoice 101, a Peachtree Accounting window appears that says There are no forms to preview. What should I do?
>
> 1. Click OK.
> 2. Close the Select a Report and Forms window.
> 3. On the Customers & Sales Navigation Center, select Sales Invoices; View and Edit Sales Invoices.
> 4. Double-click Teesdale, Invoice 101, to go to the Sales/Invoicing window.
> 5. Make the selections to Print from the Sales/Invoicing window. Compare Invoice 101 to the one shown above.
> 6. Close all windows.

Notice the Payment Terms are 5% 15, Net 30 Days. This is the information you entered for Customer Terms on pages 114-115.

9. If you print the invoice, a message displays asking if the invoice printed and emailed properly. When you answer Yes, PCA updates invoice numbers and flags the invoice as printed so that it will not print again. Click Yes .

10. Close all windows.

ENTERING RECEIPTS

Teesdale Real Estate has sent a check in payment of their invoice. Follow these steps to enter the following transaction.

Date   *Transaction Description*

03/15/12   Received Check No. 8818 from Teesdale Real Estate in payment of Invoice No. 101, $151.45. (*Hint:* The sales discount is applied to the items sold in the amount of $149.95. Refer to Discount Information, step 2, page 122.)

The customer payment is calculated like this:

Items sold:	$149.95
5% sales discount:	(7.50)
Sales tax:	9.00
Customer payment:	$151.45

Receive Money

1. From the Customers & Sales Navigation Center, click [Receive Money];
   Receive Money from Customer. The Receipts window appears.

   The Receipts window and Payments window look alike. There is a
   table in the lower half of the window that lists distribution lines for
   the current transaction. There is an icon bar at the top of the
   window. The item descriptions and account descriptions appear
   beneath each transaction line. The title bar identifies the window
   being used. In this case, the title bar says, Receipts.

2. Your cursor is in the Deposit ticket ID field. Type **03/15/12** (the
   receipt date). This Deposit ticket ID field defaults to the current date
   (today's date) and is used to combine receipts for the bank
   reconciliation. Press **<Enter>**.

3. In the Customer ID field, type the Customer ID for Teesdale:
   TEESDALE and press **<Enter>**.

   When you enter a Customer ID, the window shows a list of invoices.
   When the receipt is to pay for invoiced amounts, you can select an
   invoice from the list. The invoice amounts, including discounts,
   complete the Apply to Invoices table.

4. Click on the Reference field. Type **8818** for the customer's check
   number (a Reference number must be entered). Press **<Enter>** key
   two times and the cursor moves to the Date field.

   On your window the Date field displays 3/15/12. This date is
   important because it is used by PCA to determine if a discount
   applies. For example, if the transaction date for the invoice was
   March 1, 2012, and the discount terms were 5% for 10 days, the
   receipt entered with a date of March 12, 2012 would miss qualifying
   for a discount. PCA automatically computes and displays the
   discount amount when one applies.

5. The terms for Teesdale are 5% 15 days, Net 30. Since March 15,
   2012 is within the discount period, accept the March 15, 2012 date.
   Press **<Enter>**. In the Payment method field, select Check. Press
   <Enter>.

6. If the Cash Account field does *not* show Account No. 10200, Regular Checking Account, select it. Press **<Enter>**.

7. If necessary, select the Apply to Invoices tab.

8. Click on the Pay box for Invoice 101.

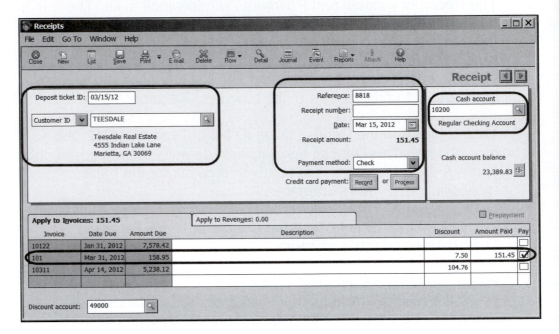

Notice that the Discount field displays the amount of the discount, $7.50. The discount displays because payment was received within the discount period (5%, 15 days). Therefore, the customer gets the 5% discount and the amount is automatically entered in the Discount field. Then, PCA automatically computes the check for the correct amount of the invoice: $151.45 (149.95 – 7.50 + 9.00 = $151.45). The Receipt Amount in the check portion of the Receipts window shows 151.45, Teesdale's invoice minus the 5% discount, plus sales tax.

9. Click [Journal] to see the account distribution in the Cash Receipts Journal.

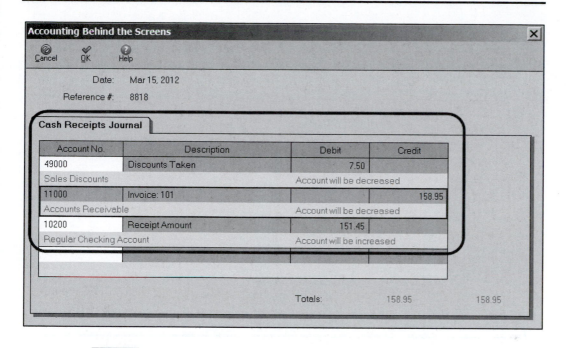

10. Click [OK] to close the Accounting Behind the Screens window.

11. Click [Save] and the receipt is posted.

12. Close the Receipts window to return to Customers & Sales Navigation Center.

ANALYZING CUSTOMER PAYMENTS

How well does Bellwether Garden Supply manage its collections of payments from customers? To look at customers and aging amounts, use the Collection Manager. Follow these steps to learn how to use the Collection Manager:

1. From the menu bar, click Analysis; Collection Manager. The Collection Aging bar graph appears.

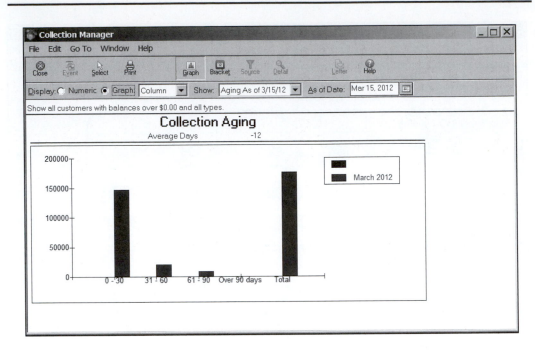

There are four aging brackets along the horizontal or X axis: 0 - 30 days, 31 - 60 days, 61 - 90 days, and over 90 days. The vertical or Y axis shows dollar amounts due.

2. Click [Bracket]. The Total Bracket table is shown below.

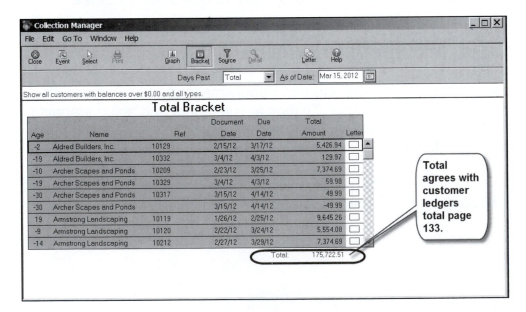

The Total Bracket window shows the age of the invoice in days, the customer name, the reference   (Ref) number, the document date or transaction date, the due date, the total amount due, and whether a letter was sent.

3. Scroll down the window to highlight the invoice for Teesdale Real Estate (Age, -30; Ref, 10311; Amt Due, 5,238.12). Then, click [Source]. The Customer Detail window is shown below.

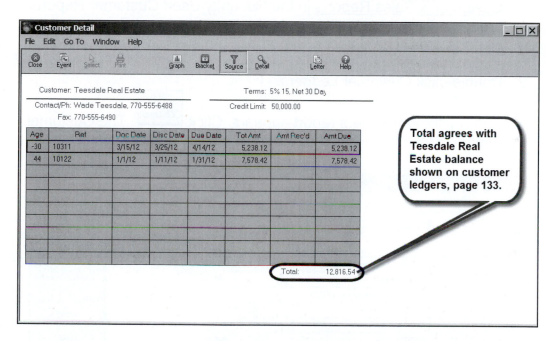

At this level you can see all of Teesdale Real Estate's invoices. If you want to send a collection letter you can do that from this window.   By clicking [Letter] on the icon bar you can send a collection letter. (If you print a letter, Peachtree defaults to a letter addressed to Thurman Golf Course Design.)

4. Click [Close] to exit the Collection Manager.

DISPLAYING THE CUSTOMER LEDGERS

Peachtree's accounts receivable system includes the customer ledgers.
Customer Ledgers lists customers with detail transaction information
including outstanding balances for each customer.

To display the Customer Ledgers, follow these steps.

1. From the Customers & Sales Navigation Center, link to <u>View All</u>
   <u>Customer & Sales Reports</u> in the Recently Used Customer Reports
   area. If necessary, scroll down to the Recently Used Customer
   Reports area. The Select a Report or Forms window appears.

2. Double-click Customer Ledgers.

3. The Customer Ledgers report appears. Click [Columns]. The Customer
   Ledgers/Columns window appears. Select Customer Terms.

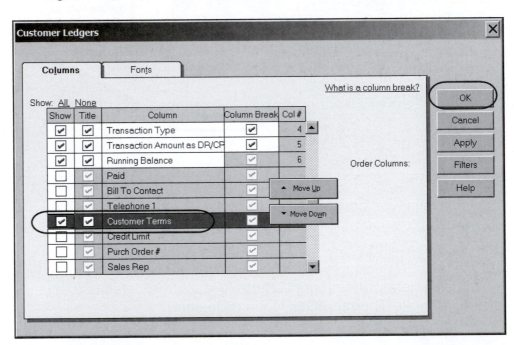

4. Click [OK]. A Terms column is added to the Customer Ledgers
   report. Scroll down the report to TEESDALE. Observe the terms are
   5% 15, Net 30 Days and the account balance is $12,816.54. The
   Customer Detail window on page 131 shows the same balance.

Bellwether Garden Supply
Customer Ledgers
For the Period From Mar 1, 2012 to Mar 31, 2012

Filter Criteria includes: Report order is by Name. Report is printed in Detail Format.

Customer ID Customer	Date	Trans No	Type	Debit Amt	Credit Amt	Balance	Terms
SNOWDEN	3/1/12	Balance Fw				7,161.98	2% 10, Net 30 Days
Snowden Interior Design	3/3/12	10303	SJ	387.63		7,549.61	
	3/4/12	31114	CRJ	1.99	1.99	7,549.61	
	3/4/12	31114	CRJ		387.63	7,161.98	
	3/11/12	10306	SJ	184.29		7,346.27	
SNYDER	3/1/12	Balance Fw				2,981.04	2% 10, Net 30 Days
Snyder Securities	3/4/12	10334	SJ	59.98		3,041.02	
	3/13/12	CC0006	CRJ	99.98	99.98	3,041.02	
STEVENSON	3/8/12	10318	SJ	49.99		49.99	2% 10, Net 30 Days
Stevenson Leasing, Inc.	3/12/12	10118	SJ	7,790.42		7,840.41	
TACOMA	3/1/12	Balance Fw				4,675.57	2% 10, Net 30 Days
Tacoma Park Golf Cours	3/14/12	10322	SJ	49.99		4,725.56	
	3/15/12	10327	SJ	1,049.01		5,774.57	
TEESDALE	3/1/12	Balance Fw				7,578.42	5% 15, Net 30 Days
Teesdale Real Estate	3/1/12	101	SJ	158.95		7,737.37	
	3/15/12	10311	SJ	5,238.12		12,975.49	
	3/15/12	8818	CRJ	7.50	7.50	12,975.49	
→	3/15/12	8818	CRJ		158.95	12,816.54	
THURMAN	3/1/12	Balance Fw				3,610.39	2% 10, Net 30 Days
Thurman Golf Course De	3/15/12	10343	SJ	9,998.00		13,608.39	
TRENT		No Activity				0.00	2% 10, Net 30 Days
Trent Bank and Trust							
WILLIAMS	3/3/12	4452	CRJ	220.31	220.31	0.00	2% 10, Net 30 Days
Williams Industries	3/5/12	10312V	SJ		939.72	-939.72	
	3/15/12	10312	SJ	939.72		0.00	
Report Total				**91,724.16**	**80,942.32**	**175,722.51**	

The Report Total, 175,722.51, agrees with the Total Bracket table's total on page 130.

CREDIT MEMOS

Credit Memos are returns to customers. Use the Credit Memos window to enter credit memos for customer returns and credits. You can apply credit memos to any existing sales invoice. All entries made on this window are posted to the General Ledger, customer records, if appropriate, and to inventory and job records.

The customer ledgers should be displayed on your screen. Scroll up the customer ledger to Saia's Neighborhood Nursery. Observe that Saia's Neighborhood Nursery has a customer credit memo (CCM4003) on 3/14/12.

Follow these steps to see how the credit was applied.

1. The customer ledgers should be displayed. Scroll up the Customer Ledgers window to Saia's Neighborhood Nursery.

2. Double-click on the 3/14/12 CCM4003 transaction to drill down to Credit memos window.

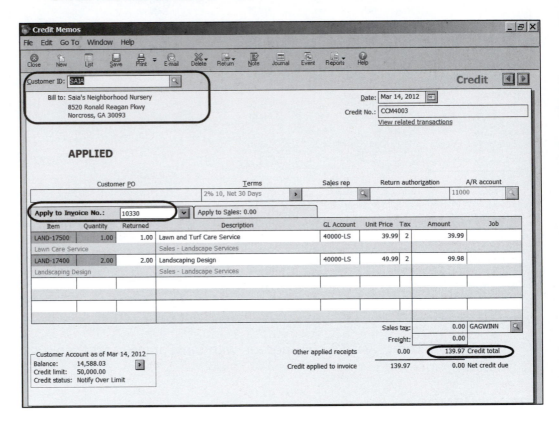

3. Observe that there is a $139.97 Credit total which was applied to Invoice No. 10330. Close the Credit Memos window. You are returned to the Customer Ledgers. The amount of the credit memo is subtracted from the Customer Ledger's balance forward amount: $14,728.00 – 139.97 = $14,588.03.

4. Close all windows.

BACKING UP CHAPTER 3 DATA

Follow these steps to back up Chapter 3 data:

1. Insert your USB flash drive.

2. From the Navigation Bar, click [🔲 **System**] ;
   [Back Up Now]. Make sure that the box next to Include company
   name in the backup file name is *unchecked*.

3. Click [Back Up] .

4. In the Save in field, select the appropriate drive letter for your USB
   drive.[4] (*Or,* save to the hard-drive default location or other location.)
   Type **Chapter 3** in the File name field.

5. Click [Save] .

6. When the window prompts This company backup will require
   approximately 1 diskette, click [OK] . When the window
   prompts Please insert the first disk, click [OK] . When the Back
   Up Company scale is 100% complete, you have successfully backed
   up to the current point in Chapter 3. (Step 6 will differ slightly if you
   are backing up to the default or other hard-drive location.)

SUMMARY AND REVIEW

Complete the following end-of-chapter activities:

1. Going to the net, page 136.
2. Short-answer questions, page 136.
3. Exercises 3-1 and 3-2, pages 137-138.
4. Analysis question, page 138.

---

[4]If you are having difficulty backing up to USB flash drive, backup to the desktop, then
copy the file to a USB flash drive. Refer to Appendix A, Troubleshooting, pages 756-
758—Problem Backing Up to USB Drive or Other External Media.

5. Assessment rubric, pages 138-139.
6. Chapter 3 Index, page 140.

GOING TO THE NET

Access the Financial Accounting Standards Board website at www.fasb.org. Select the About FASB tab; then Our People, link to Members of the FASB. (Going to the Net links are on the textbook website at www.mhhe.com/yacht2012; link to Student Edition, select Chapter 3.)

1. How many board members serve on the Financial Accounting Standards Board? Do they serve part time or full time?
2. What are the qualifications for the board members?

Short-Answer Questions: The Online Learning Center includes these questions and the analysis question at www.mhhe.com/yacht2012, select Student Edition, Chapter 3, QA Templates.

1. What icon(s) can be used to display lookup lists?

2. Describe three ways to open a lookup list.

3. If you want to look at a customer's account, what window do you open? Describe the selections.

4. What is the customer identification for Teesdale Real Estate?

5. What is the sales discount for Teesdale Real Estate?

6. What is the default discount for customers?

7. Describe what happens when you use the Accounts Receivable subsidiary ledger.

8. When you want to print an invoice in PCA, what are the steps?

9. How do you post a sales order to the controlling account in the general ledger and the customer subsidiary ledger?

10. If you receive payment from a customer, what window do you use?

Exercise 3-1: Follow the instructions below to complete Exercise 3-1.

1. Start PCA. Open Bellwether Garden Supply.

2. Restore data from the end of Chapter 3. This backup was made on page 135.

3. Record the following transaction.

Date	Transaction Description
03/03/12	Bellwether Garden Supply sold one Rotary Mower – Riding 4HP to Teesdale Real Estate, Invoice 102, $299.99; plus $18 sales tax; total, $317.99. (*Hint:* Do *not* enter an invoice number. Select the Apply to Sales tab. Type **1** in the Quantity field; select EQLW-14140; Bell-Gro Riding Lawn Mower - 4HP as the Item.)

4. Print or post. (*Hint:* If you print from the Sales/Invoicing window, the sales invoice prints and posts.)

5. Continue with Exercise 3-2.

Exercise 3-2: Follow the instructions below to complete Exercise 3-2.

1. Record the following transaction:

Date	Transaction Description
03/15/12	Received Check No. 9915 in the amount of $302.99 from Teesdale Real Estate in payment of Invoice 102. (*Hint:* Type **3/15/12** in the Deposit ticket ID field. Remember to use the check number in the Reference field. **Calculate the discount on the item sold. On the Receipts window, type the appropriate amount in the Discount field.** *Do* not *include sales tax in the sales discount computation.*)

2. Post the receipt.

3. Print the Customer Ledgers. Add a Customer Terms column to the Customer Ledgers report. Adjust the columns so that the Terms for each customer prints on the same page.

4. Back up Exercise 3-2. Use **Exercise 3-2** as the file name.

5. Export the Customer Ledgers to Excel. Use **Exercise 3-2_Customer Ledgers.xlsx** as the file name. (*Hint:* Refer to pages 43-45, Exporting Peachtree Reports to Microsoft Excel. A Terms column should be included on the Customer Ledgers.)

6. Save the Customer Ledgers as PDF file. Use **Exercise 3-2_Customer Ledgers.pdf** as the file name.

    Check your figures: Customer Ledgers balance, $175,722.51.

7. Exit PCA.

ANALYSIS QUESTION:

With the Customers & Sales Navigation Center serving as the starting point to perform tasks related to Accounts Receivable, list five Customers & Sales tasks.

ASSESSMENT RUBRIC

Complete the Assessment Rubric online at www.mhhe.com/yacht2012; Student Edition, select Chapter 3, Assessment Rubric link. To review Peachtree's journals, navigation centers, modules, and task windows, complete the blank fields online.

Date	Transaction	Navigation Center/Module	Task Window	Journal Dr./Cr.
3/3	Bellwether Garden Supply sold one Rotary Mower - EQLW-14140 to Teesdale Real Estate, Invoice 102, $299.99; plus $18 sales tax.			

Continued

3/15	Received Check No. 9915 in the amount of $302.99 from Teesdale Real Estate.			

CHAPTER 3 INDEX

Chapter
4
Employees

LEARNING OBJECTIVES

1. Restore data from Exercise 3-2. (This backup was made on page 138.)
2. Enter and store information using the Maintain Employees/Sales Rep window.
3. Set up default information for payroll.
4. Store constant information about payroll payment methods.
5. Transfer funds from the regular checking account to the payroll checking account.
6. Enter paychecks in the Payroll Entry window.
7. Print employee paychecks.
8. Make two backups, save one Excel file, and save one PDF file.[1]

In Chapter 4 you learn how PCA processes payroll. Once default and maintain employee information is set up, payroll is a simple process. The first step in setting up payroll is to go to the Employees & Payroll Navigation Center. Peachtree's Employees & Payroll Navigation Center displays information and access points related to the company's employees. It includes a summary of employee information including 1099 vendors and access to recently used employee reports. There is also an area called Peachtree Solutions, with links to additional resources such as checks and forms.

On the left side of the Navigation Center, there is a diagram showing the flow of employee-related tasks. Click the icons to see menus that will take you where you need to go to perform those tasks.

Peachtree's **employees and payroll system** is another example of the software's modular design. Peachtree's modules organize lists,

---

[1]Refer to the chart on pages 2-3 for the size of backup files and saved Excel and PDF files.

The McGraw-Hill Companies, Inc., *Computer Accounting with Peachtree by Sage Complete Accounting 2012, 16e*

transaction windows, and reports related to a specific Navigation Bar selection. In Chapter 2, Vendors, you used Peachtree's accounts payable system. In Chapter 3, Customers, you used Peachtree's accounts receivable system. In this chapter, you see how the payroll system is organized.

Another way to use Peachtree's modules is to select Tasks or Reports & Forms from the menu bar. For example, if you select Tasks from the menu bar, observe that selections for Payroll—Select for Payroll Entry and Payroll Entry—are listed together. If you select Reports & Forms from the menu bar, there is a selection for Payroll. Selections from the Tasks and Reports & Forms menus are also organized by Peachtree's modules.

Some of the information that appears in the Employees & Payroll Navigation Center can be accessed with the drill down feature. Drill down is the act of following a path to its origin for further analysis. In certain Peachtree reports, click on a transaction to drill down to the window that includes the original transaction information. From financial statements, you can drill down to the General Ledger report, and then use drill down again to see original transaction detail. You can also drill down to transaction detail from the Business Status selection, as well as from receipts and payments.

The diagram on the next page describes PCA's payroll process. These steps show how payroll accounting is set up in PCA.

```
                        ╱───────────────╲
                       ╱    Employees     ╲
                        ╲───────────────╱
                                │
                    ┌───────────────────────┐
                    │   Set up Employee      │
                    │     Defaults           │
                    └───────────────────────┘
                                │
                    ┌───────────────────────┐
                    │   Select employees     │
                    └───────────────────────┘
                                │
          ┌──────────────────────────────────────────┐
          │ Enter tax information and define payroll fields │
          └──────────────────────────────────────────┘
                    │
     ╱──────────────╲                         ╱──────────────╲
    ╱   Employee      ╲───────────────────►  ╱   Record        ╲
    ╲   maintenance   ╱                      ╲   transaction   ╱
     ╲──────────────╱                         ╲──────────────╱
            │                                         │
  ┌─────────────────────────┐            ┌─────────────────────────┐
  │ Select employees/sales reps │         │   Select payroll entry   │
  └─────────────────────────┘            └─────────────────────────┘
            │                                         │
  ┌─────────────────────────┐            ┌─────────────────────────────┐
  │ Set up employee rates and special │   │ Enter employee paycheck information │
  │        deductions        │            │   for a specific pay period    │
  └─────────────────────────┘            └─────────────────────────────┘
```

GETTING STARTED

Follow these steps to start PCA:

1. Start Peachtree. Open the sample company, Bellwether Garden
    Supply. (If Bellwether Garden Supply is not shown, restore a New
    Company. Refer to the Read Me box on page 29.)

2. Restore your data from the Exercise 3-2 back up. (The Exercise 3-2.ptb backup was made on page 138.)

   a. Insert your USB flash drive. From the Navigation Bar, select 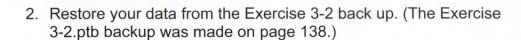; click [Restore Now].

   b. The Select Backup File window appears. Click [Browse]. Go to the Location of your Exercise 3-2.ptb file and select it. Click [Open]. The Select Backup File window shows the location of the backup file. Click [Next >].

   c. The Select Company window appears. The radio button next to An Existing Company is selected. The Company name field shows Bellwether Garden Supply. The Location field shows the default location on the hard drive for Bellwether Garden Supply. Click [Next >].

   d. The Restore Options window appears. Make sure that the box next to Company Data is *checked*. Click [Next >].

   e. The Confirmation window appears. Check the From and To fields to make sure they are correct. Click [Finish]. When the Restore Company scale is 100% complete, your data is restored. (*Hint:* The Student Version of Peachtree prompts that company data can be used for 14 months. After that time the data expires. Click [OK]. Bellwether Garden Supply opens.)

🖫 To make sure you are starting in the appropriate place in the data (Exercise 3-2.ptb backup) check the account balance for Teesdale Real Estate.

1. Go to the Customers & Sales Navigation Center. On the right side of the screen, scroll down to the Customers list; click TEESDALE. The Maintain Customers/Prospects window shows a Balance as of Mar 15, 2012 of $12,816.54.

2. Click <u>$12,816.54</u> to drill down to the Customer Ledgers. Compare your Customers Ledgers report to the one shown below.

Bellwether Garden Supply
Customer Ledgers
For the Period From Mar 1, 2012 to Mar 15, 2012

Filter Criteria includes: 1) IDs: TEESDALE. Report order is by ID. Report is printed in Detail Format.

Customer ID Customer	Date	Trans No	Type	Debit Amt	Credit Amt	Balance
TEESDALE	3/1/12	Balance Fw				7,578.42
Teesdale Real Estate	3/1/12	101	SJ	158.95		7,737.37
	3/3/12	102	SJ	317.99		8,055.36
	3/15/1	10311	SJ	5,238.12		13,293.48
	3/15/1	8818	CRJ	7.50	7.50	13,293.48
	3/15/1	8818	CRJ		158.95	13,134.53
	3/15/1	9915	CRJ	15.00	15.00	13,134.53
	3/15/1	9915	CRJ		317.99	12,816.54
Report Total				**5,737.56**	**499.44**	**12,816.54**

3. Close all windows.

DEFAULT INFORMATION

PCA allows you to set up default information for your business. This information is important for payroll, customer receivables, and vendor payables. Bellwether Garden Supply already has the receivable and payable default information set up. Processing payroll is automatic once defaults are set up correctly.

Follow these steps to set up payroll Default Information:

1. From the Navigation Bar, select 👤 **Employees & Payroll** ; then click

    👤 Employees ▴ , Set Up Employee Defaults. Compare your Employee Defaults window with the one on the next page.

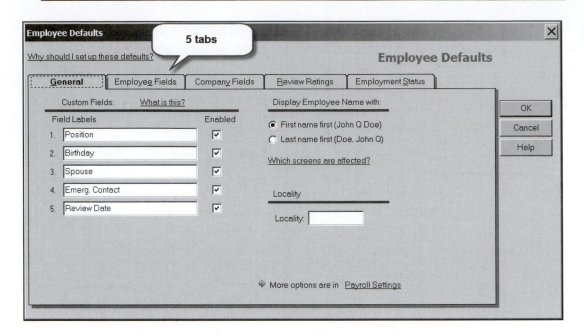

There are five tabs on the Employee Defaults window: General, Employee Fields, Company Fields, Review Ratings, Employment Status. You can set up a lot of information within these tabs. This will make your payroll processing almost automatic.

2. Click on the Employee Fields tab.

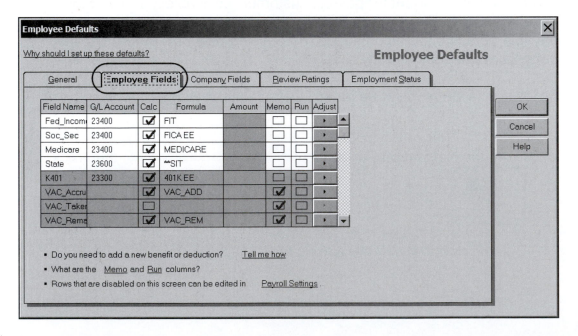

Notice that there are numerous items checked in the Calc column: Fed_Income (FIT), Soc_Sec (FICA EE), Medicare (MEDICARE), State (**SIT), K401 (401K EE), etc. (Scroll down to see the Field Name's complete list.) These fields work together with the payroll tax tables to calculate common employee deductions.

The check marks in the Calc and Memo columns indicate common deductions. Bellwether Garden Supply computes Federal Income Tax, Social Security, Medicare, State Income Taxes, 401K, and vacation deductions. These deductions are calculated according to the appropriate tax tables and formulas entered for payroll deductions, 401K's and vacation calculations.

The accounts affected by paychecks are liability accounts set up specifically to handle these kinds of deductions. Notice that the GL Account field shows the account numbers. All the accounts that are checked off are liability accounts. You can also set up voluntary deductions (called allowances in PCA). Voluntary allowances that are individually entered on the employee paycheck could include gas allowances, union dues, and savings bonds.

There is a Memo column with a place to put check marks for amounts that should not be posted to the company's books. The Memo check box is used when you want the employee record to show amounts not on the company's books. An example would be a restaurant business that needed to show employees' tips.

3. Click on the Company Fields tab. The Company Fields tab is for the employer's portion of Soc_Sec_ER (Social Security), Medicare_ER (Medicare), FUTA_ER (Federal Unemployment Tax Act) SUI_ER (State Unemployment Insurance), and K401_ER (401K contribution). The Employee Defaults/Company Fields window is shown on the next page.

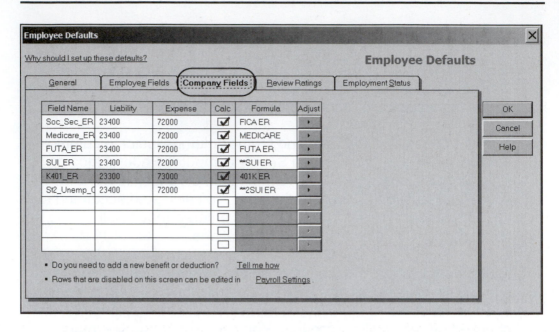

4. Click on the Review Ratings tab. You can add up to 10 performance ratings.

5. Click on the Employment Status tab. This shows different statuses for Bellwether's employees: Current Employee, Terminated, Leave of Absence, etc.

6. Select [OK] to return to the Employees & Payroll Navigation Center.

EMPLOYEE MAINTENANCE

When default information is completed, PCA sets guidelines for processing the company's payroll. On the Maintain Employees/Sales Reps window, information is entered for each employee.

1. From the Employees & Payroll Navigation Center, click [Employees]; View and Edit Employees. The Employee List appears.

2. Double-click BNUNNLEY; Nunnley, Brandee. The Maintain
    Employees & Sales Reps window appears. Let's look at this
    employees' record. (*Hint:* In Chapter 15, you learn about Peachtree's
    payroll features in more detail.)

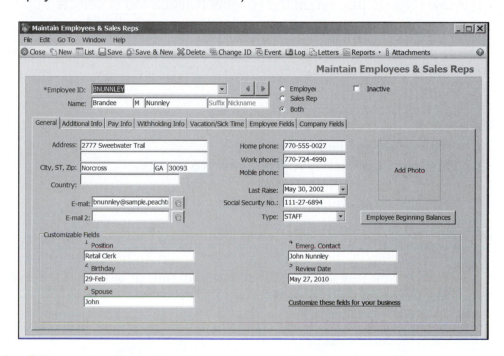

3. Click on the Pay Info tab.

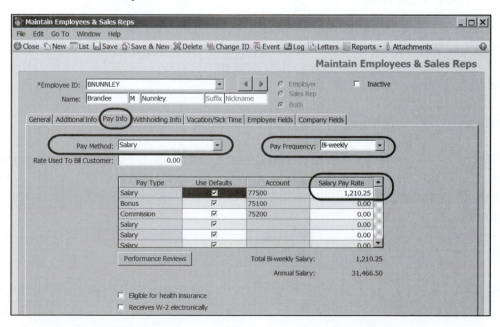

Observe that there is a Performance Reviews button. Select

[Performance Reviews] to see if any information has been added for this employee. On page 148, the Employee Defaults window included a Review Ratings tab. When the Review Ratings tab is selected up to

ten performance ratings can be set up. Click [Close]. You are returned to the Maintain Employees & Sales Reps window; the Pay Info tab is selected.

Notice the following about Ms. Nunnley:

a. She is paid a salary of $1,210.25.
b. She is paid bi-weekly (once every two weeks).

4. Click on the down-arrow in the Employee ID field.

5. Select employee **DCARTER**; **Drake V. Carter**. If necessary, select the Pay Info tab. Notice that Mr. Carter is paid an hourly wage of $9.00; overtime pay of $13.50; and special rate of $18.00. Observe that Mr. Carter is paid bi-weekly.

6. Close all windows.

PAYROLL SYSTEM

Once employee default information is set up, PCA automates the payroll process. Now that you have looked at Bellwether's payroll defaults, you can see how easily PCA computes and prints paychecks for hourly and salaried employees.

Transferring Cash to the Payroll Checking Account

Before making a payroll entry, you need to transfer $8,000 from Account No. 10200, Regular Checking Account; to Account No. 10300, the Payroll Checking Account. The following transaction is recorded in the general journal.

Date	*Transaction Description*
3/29/12	Transfer $8,000 from the regular checking account to the payroll checking account.

Follow these steps to record this transaction in the general journal.

1. From the Navigation Bar, select ; click

    General Journal Entry, New General Journal Entry. The General Journal Entry window appears.

2. Select or type **29** as the date. Click on the Refere<u>n</u>ce field. Type **Transfer** in the Refere<u>n</u>ce field. Press the **<Enter>** key two times.

3. Your cursor is in the GL Account field. Select Account No. 10300, Payroll Checking Account (or you can type **10300**). Press **<Enter>**.

4. Your cursor should be in the Description field. Type **Payroll Checking Account** (or you can type a description) in the Description field. Press **<Enter>**.

5. Type **8000** in the Debit field. Press the **<Enter>** key three times to go to the Account No. field.

6. Your cursor should be in the GL Account field. Select Account No. 10200, Regular Checking Account.

7. Type **Regular Checking Account** in the Description field. Press the **<Enter>** key two times to go to the Credit field.

8. Your cursor is in the Credit field. Type **8000** in the Credit field. Press **<Enter>**. Observe that at the bottom of the General Journal Entry window, the Out of Balance field shows 0.00. This shows that debits equal credits, therefore, out of balance equals zero.

    Compare your General Journal Entry window to the one shown on the next page.

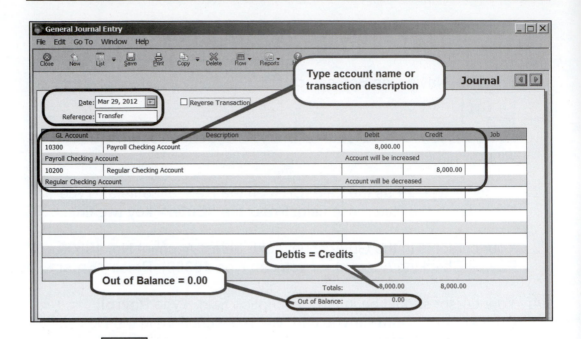

9. Click ![Save] to post the entry to the general ledger.

10. Close the General Journal Entry window.

Payroll Entry for a Salaried Employee

In the next section you enter paychecks for these two employees: Brandee M. Nunnley and Drake V. Carter. When processing payroll checks, the information stored in Default Information and in the Maintain Employees file is important. Processing payroll is simple once you have set the defaults correctly.

Follow these steps to see how a paycheck for a salaried employee is done.

1. From the Navigation Bar, select **Employees & Payroll**;
Pay Employees, Enter Payroll For One Employee. The Payroll Entry window appears.

2. In the Employee ID field, type **BN** for Brandee M. Nunnley and press **<Enter>**.

3. To print a check, leave the Check Number field blank by pressing **<Enter>**. If you type a check number, PCA prints Duplicate on the check.

4. Type **29** in the Date field, then press **<Enter>**. (*Remember you can also click on the Calendar icon* *and select 29. If necessary, enlarge the Payroll Entry window.*) Your cursor goes to the Cash Account field. This check will be charged against the Payroll Checking Account (Account No. 10300) which is displayed in the Cash Account field.

5. Press **<Enter>**. Your cursor is in the Pay Period Ends field. Type **29** then press **<Enter>**. Your cursor goes to the Weeks in Pay Period box. The number 2 is displayed. Ms. Nunnley is on a bi-weekly pay period which means that Ms. Nunnley has two weeks in her pay period.

   Notice that Brandee M. Nunnley has a Salary Amounts table that includes Salary, Bonus, and Commission. If necessary, these amounts can be adjusted. All of the Taxes - Benefits - Liabilities fields that were completed, which include Fed_ Income, Soc_Sec, Medicare and State tax, etc., have been calculated and display as negative amounts. They display as negative amounts because they decrease the check amount. The amounts shown as positive numbers are *not* deducted from the employee's check. Once payroll defaults and employees are set up, payroll processing is easy. Compare your Payroll Entry window for Brandee M. Nunnley to the one shown on the next page. (*Hint:* A partial window is shown. To see all the amounts, scroll down the Amount column.)

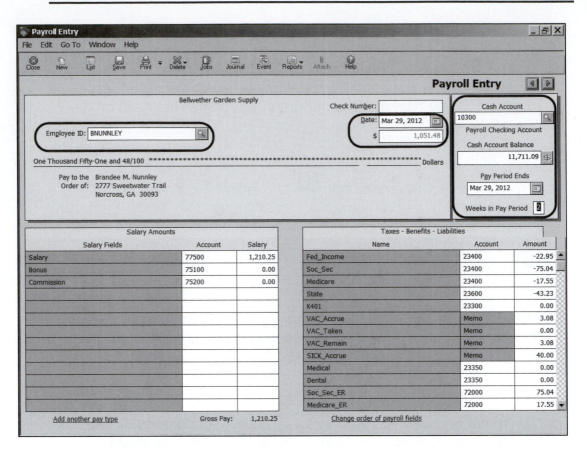

Observe that the Cash Account Balance field on the upper right side of the Payroll Entry window shows 11,711.09. This is because the default is to recalculate the cash balance automatically for receipts, payments, and payroll entries. From the menu bar, select Options, Global, and notice that a check mark <✓> is placed next to the Recalculate cash balance automatically in the Receipts, Payments, and Payroll Entry field. If your balance field does *not* show an amount, then place a check mark in the recalculate cash balance automatically field. Also, notice that Ms. Nunnley's paycheck amount is $1,051.48.

6. Click [Save] to post this payroll entry.

Payroll Entry for an Hourly Employee

1. In the Employee ID field, click [🔍]. Select Drake V. Carter.

2. If necessary, type **29** in the Date field and press **<Enter>** two times.

3. If necessary, type **29** in the Pay Period Ends field.

    Since Drake V. Carter is an hourly employee, the Hours Worked table lists his regular and overtime hours. If necessary, these categories can be adjusted.

4. To see how to adjust the hours that he worked, do the following: in the Hours Worked table, click on Overtime. The Overtime row is highlighted. Make sure your cursor is in the Hours field. Type **3** and press **<Enter>**. Notice that the amounts in the Taxes - Benefits - Liabilities fields are automatically adjusted. The check amount also changed.

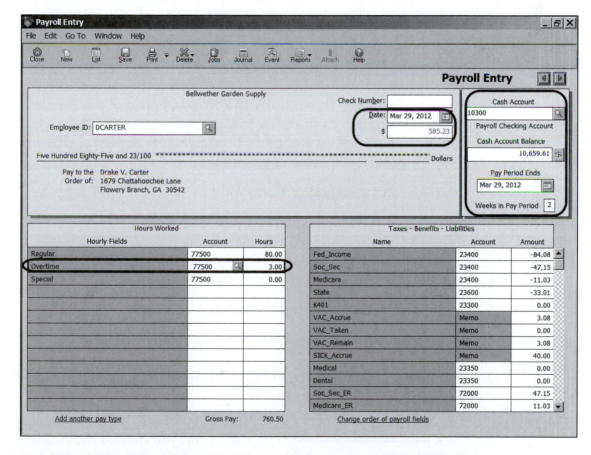

Observe that the Cash Account Balance field on the upper right side of the Payroll Entry window changed to 10,659.61. This is because the default for Peachtree is to recalculate the cash balance automatically for receipts, payments, and payroll entries. (If your Cash Account Balance did *not* automatically recalculate, refer to Chapter 1, page 18 step 1d; Other Options area, Recalculate cash balance automatically in Receipts, Payments, and Payroll Entry should be *checked*.)

5. Select [Save] to post this paycheck. Close the Payroll Entry window.

Printing Payroll Checks

Similar to vendor disbursements, there is a choice: you may print each check as you enter it in the Payroll Entry window or you can print all the checks at once. Batch posting involves printing checks before posting. Real time posting allows you to print checks later. Since real-time posting is used with Bellwether, you print checks later. (You may also use the Preview icon to display checks instead of printing them.) Follow these steps to print the checks previously entered in the Payroll Entry window.

1. From the Recently Used Employee Reports area of the Employees & Payroll Navigation Center, link to <u>View All Employees & Payroll Reports</u>. The Select a Report or Form window appears. Observe that in the <u>R</u>eports list, Payroll is selected.

2. On the Select a Report or Form window, click on the For<u>m</u>s tab.

3. In the Form Types list, select Payroll Checks.

4. In the Forms list, double-click OCR Multi-Purpose PR Laser. The Preview and Print Payroll Checks window appears.

5. In the Include checks through field, select March 29, 2012.

6. Type **1294** in the Number the first check field.

7. In the Filter employees by field, select ID, Brandee M. Nunnley; to Drake V. Carter.

8. Click [Refresh List]. The two employee names, both check marked, appear in the table on the right side of the Preview and Print Payroll Checks window.

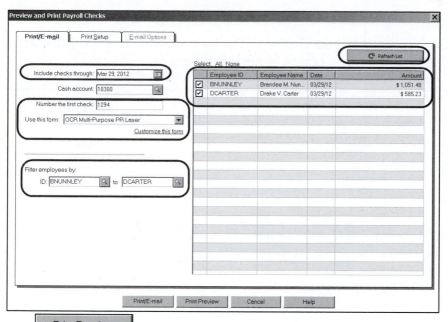

9. Click 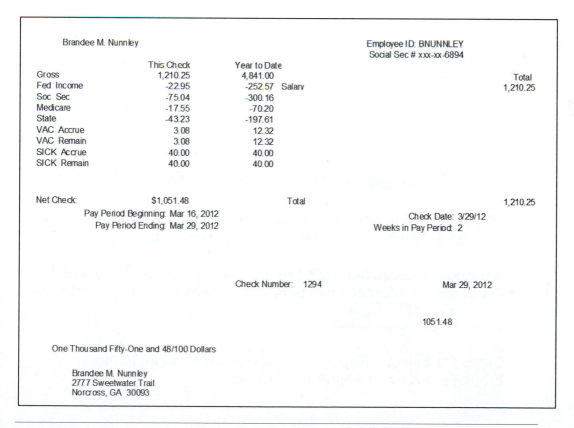 . The Print Preview window appears. The top portion of Brandee M. Nunnley's check is shown below.

Brandee M. Nunnley

Employee ID: BNUNNLEY
Social Sec # xxx-xx-6894

	This Check	Year to Date			
Gross	1,210.25	4,841.00			Total
Fed Income	-22.95	-252.57	Salary		1,210.25
Soc Sec	-75.04	-300.16			
Medicare	-17.55	-70.20			
State	-43.23	-197.61			
VAC Accrue	3.08	12.32			
VAC Remain	3.08	12.32			
SICK Accrue	40.00	40.00			
SICK Remain	40.00	40.00			

Net Check: $1,051.48   Total   1,210.25

Pay Period Beginning: Mar 16, 2012
Pay Period Ending: Mar 29, 2012

Check Date: 3/29/12
Weeks in Pay Period: 2

Check Number: 1294

Mar 29, 2012

1051.48

One Thousand Fifty-One and 48/100 Dollars

Brandee M. Nunnley
2777 Sweetwater Trail
Norcross, GA 30093

10. Click [Next] to see Drake V. Carter's check. The top portion of Drake V. Carter's check is shown below.

Drake V. Carter				Employee ID: DCARTER		
				Social Sec # xxx-xx-8990		
	This Check	Year to Date				
Gross	760.50	2,920.50		Hours	Rate	Total
Fed Income	-84.08	-362.21	Regular	80.00	9.00	720.00
Soc Sec	-47.15	-181.07	Overtime	3.00	13.50	40.50
Medicare	-11.03	-42.35				
State	-33.01	-124.75				
VAC Accrue	3.08	12.32				
VAC Remain	3.08	12.32				
SICK Accrue	40.00	40.00				
SICK Remain	40.00	40.00				
Net Check:	$585.23		Total	83.00		760.50

Pay Period Beginning: Mar 16, 2012
Pay Period Ending: Mar 29, 2012

Check Date: 3/29/12
Weeks in Pay Period: 2

Check Number: 1295

Mar 29, 2012

585.23

Five Hundred Eighty-Five and 23/100 Dollars

Drake V. Carter
1679 Chattahoochee Lane
Flowery Branch, GA 30542

11. Click [Print] to print the Check No. 1294 and 1295.

Observe that the employee statement information (also known as the pay stub) is printed first, then the actual check is printed.

12. A window appears that says Did the Checks print properly and is it is OK to assign the check numbers to the checks? If your checks are correct, click [Yes].

13. Close the Select a Report or Form window to return to the Employees & Payroll Navigation Center.

> **Comment**
>
> In Chapter 15, Employees, Payroll, and Account Reconciliation, you learn how to set the defaults for the payroll accounts. Each employee and employer deduction will be set for individual liability accounts and expense accounts. The sample company is used as an example of automatic payroll processing but does *not* reflect correct payroll accounting procedures.

JOURNAL ENTRY FOR PAYROLL

What happens when you post payroll? In the most common case, the Cash Account that you entered in the Payroll Default window is automatically credited for the net paycheck amount when the payroll check is posted. The employee salary expense account is debited for the gross amount of the check and any deductions used are credited. The following table shows the payroll journal entry for the hourly employee, Drake V. Carter.

Account Description	Debit	Credit
Wages Expense (Regular Hours)	720.00	
Wages Expense (Overtime Hours)	40.50	
Federal Payroll Taxes Payable (Fed_Income)		84.08
Social Security (Soc_Sec for the Employee)		47.15
Medicare (Medicare for the Employee)		11.03
State Payroll Taxes Payable		33.01
Payroll Checking Account		585.23

BACKING UP CHAPTER 4 DATA

Follow these steps to back up Chapter 4 data:

1. Insert your USB flash drive.

2. From the Navigation Bar, click [System]; [Back Up Now]. Make sure that the box next to Include company name in the backup file name is *unchecked*.

3. Click [Back Up].

4. In the Save in field, select the appropriate drive letter for your USB drive.[2] (*Or,* save to the hard-drive default location or other location.) Type **Chapter 4** in the File name field.

5. Click [Save] .

6. When the window prompts This company backup will require approximately 1 diskette, click [OK] . When the window prompts Please insert the first disk, click [OK] . When the Back Up Company scale is 100% complete, you have successfully backed up to the current point in Chapter 4. (Step 6 will differ slightly if you are backing up to the default or other hard-drive location.)

SUMMARY AND REVIEW

Complete the following end-of-chapter activities:

1. Going to the net, pages 160-161
2. Short-answer questions, page 161.
3. Exercises 4-1 and 4-2, pages 161-162.
4. Analysis questions, page 163.
5. Assessment rubric, page 163.
6. Chapter 4 Index, page 164.

GOING TO THE NET

Access the SmartPros website at http://accounting.smartpros.com/ . Move your cursor over Career Center. From the Career Center list, select Career Resources, then link to Effective Salary Negotiation. The URL is http://accounting.smartpros.com/x28536.xml. Read the Effective Salary Negotiation article. Answer the following questions. (Going to the Net links are on the textbook website at www.mhhe.com/yacht2012; link to Student Edition, select Chapter 4.)

---

[2]If you are having difficulty backing up to USB flash drive, backup to the desktop, then copy the file to a USB flash drive. Refer to Appendix A, Troubleshooting, pages 756-758—Problem Backing Up to USB Drive or Other External Media.

1. What skills should you objectively evaluate?

2. List three factors that affect starting salary.

Short-Answer Questions: The Online Learning Center includes these
questions and the analysis question at www.mhhe.com/yacht2012, select
Student Edition, Chapter 4, QA Templates.

1. Draw the diagram that shows how payroll accounting is done in PCA.

2. When setting up payroll defaults, what is the first step?

3. Identify the five tabs on the Employee Defaults window.

4. What is the Maintain Employees/Sales Reps window used for?

5. What do the check marks in the Calc column of the employee
   defaults indicate? Explain.

6. What is the difference in the appearance of the Payroll Entry window
   for an hourly employee and a salaried employee? Explain.

7. Why do the employee deductions display as negative amounts on
   the Payroll Entry window?

8. What are the gross pay amounts for Brandee M. Nunnley and for
   Drake V. Carter? Include Mr. Carter's overtime pay.

9. What is the net pay for Brandee M. Nunnley and for Drake V.
   Carter? Include Mr. Carter's overtime pay.

10. What happens when payroll entries are posted?

Exercise 4-1: Follow the instructions below to complete Exercise 4-1:

1. Start PCA. Open Bellwether Garden Supply.

2. Restore data from the end of Chapter 4. This back up was made on
   pages 159-160.

3. Record the following transaction.

Date	*Transaction Description*
03/29/12	Record paycheck information for Brandon A. Hugley. Mr. Hugley worked 80 regular hours during this pay period.

4. Post the payroll entry.

5. Continue with Exercise 4-2.

Exercise 4-2: Follow the instructions below to complete Exercise 4-2:

1. Record the following transaction:

Date	*Transaction Description*
03/29/12	Record paycheck information for Derrick P. Gross. Mr. Gross is a salaried employee.

2. Post the payroll entry.

3. Print Check Nos. 1296 and 1297. (*Hint: The Include checks through field should show Mar 29, 2012; the Number the first check field should display 1296. If not, type 1296. Click* [C Refresh List]. *Remember to select From Brandon A. Hugley To Derrick P. Gross.*)

4. Print the Payroll Check Register. (*Hint*: In the Recently Used Employee Reports area of the Employees & Payroll Navigation Center, link to <u>Print</u> the Payroll Check Register. Accept the default for This Period.)

5. Close all windows. Back up Exercise 4-2. Use **Exercise 4-2** as the file name.

6. Export the Payroll Check Register to Excel. Use **Exercise 4-2_Payroll Check Register.xlsx** as the file name.

7. Save the Payroll Check Register as a PDF file. Use **Exercise 4-2_Payroll Check Register.pdf** as the file name.

   Check your figures: Payroll Register, 3/1/12 thru 3/31/12, $37,631.02

ANALYSIS QUESTIONS

1. What pay methods does Bellwether Garden Supply use to pay employees? Briefly explain how you determine Bellwether's pay method.

2. Are all employees paid the same way; for example, bi-weekly? Explain how to determine the frequency with which an employee is paid.

ASSESSMENT RUBRIC

Complete the Assessment Rubric online at www.mhhe.com/yacht2012; Student Edition, select Chapter 4, Assessment Rubric link. To review Peachtree's journals, navigation centers, modules, and task windows, complete the blank fields online.

Date	Transaction	Navigation Center/Module	Task Window	Journal Dr./Cr.
3/29	Record paycheck information for Derrick P. Gross.			

CHAPTER 4 INDEX

Chapter 5

General Ledger, Inventory, and Internal Control

LEARNING OBJECTIVES

1. Restore data from Exercise 4-2. (This backup was made on page 162.)
2. Enter a new account in the Chart of Accounts.
3. Look at Peachtree's budget feature.
4. Record and post a General Journal entry to transfer funds.
5. Display the General Ledger Trial Balance.
6. Set up an Inventory Item.
7. Record an inventory adjustment.
8. Look at Peachtree's internal controls, user security and access, and audit trail.
9. Make two backups, save one Excel file, and save one PDF file.

In Chapter 5, the General Ledger Chart of Accounts is used; and you continue to work with the sample company, Bellwether Garden Supply. In Parts 2 and 3 of the textbook (Chapters 9-14 and Projects 1 through 4A), 11 companies are set up. In other words, sample company data is not used. When a new company is set up, the following initial steps are performed: set up a chart of accounts and enter beginning balances or budget amounts.

This chapter also shows how to use PCA's Inventory system. PCA lets you track inventory items both at the purchasing and the sales level. When an inventory item is set up, the General Ledger accounts that are updated by purchases and sales are established. PCA keeps track of cost of goods sold, stock levels, sales prices, and vendors. PCA uses a *perpetual inventory* system. In a perpetual inventory system, an up-to-date record of inventory is maintained, recording each purchase and each sale as they occur.

Another Peachtree feature is user security. On pages 190-198, Security and Internal Control, you look at how Peachtree keeps company data secure.

PEACHTREE HELP: CHART OF ACCOUNTS

In accounting you learn that a chart of accounts is a list of all the accounts used by a company showing the identifying number assigned to each account. PCA includes over 75 sample companies' Charts of Accounts. A Chart of Accounts can be set up from scratch or you can select an industry-specific simplified or extensive Chart of Accounts.

To see the sample Charts of Accounts, follow these steps:

1. Start PCA. Open Bellwether Garden Supply. (If Bellwether Garden Supply is not shown, restore a New Company. Refer to the Read Me box on page 29.)

2. Click Help; Peachtree Accounting Help. The Peachtree Help window appears. Peachtree's help is also called online Help. Peachtree Help topics are displayed in the **HTML** (Hypertext Markup Language) Help Viewer.

3. If necessary, click on the Index tab.

4. In the Type in the keyword to find field, type **sample**. The words, sample charts of accounts, are highlighted.

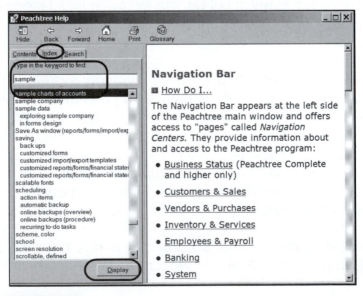

5. Click ▭ Display ▭.

---

6. The right pane shows sample charts of accounts by industry.

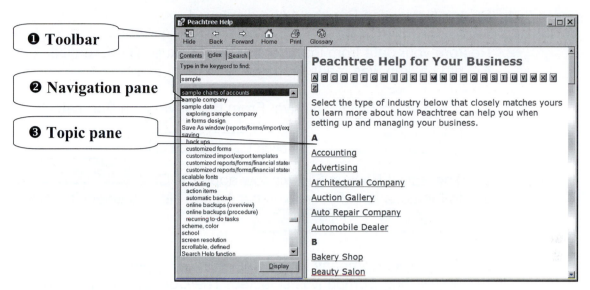

Observe that there are three panes on the Peachtree Help window:

❶ Toolbar is located below the Peachtree Help title bar. The toolbar appears on individual windows and contains buttons that let you perform certain functions within that window.

❷ On the left side of the window is the Navigation pane. It contains three tabs: Contents, Index, and Search. Use the Navigation pane to browse or search for topics.

❸ On the right side of the window is the Topic pane. The topic pane displays each Help topic or Web page selected in the Navigation pane. In this example, the topic pane shows charts of accounts by industry.

7. In the list of sample charts of accounts, click Accounting. The Accounting Agency window appears. Scroll down the window. In the What do you want to do next? area, click Display a sample chart of accounts. A sample chart of accounts for an Accounting Company appears.

8. Click ☒ on the Peachtree Help title bar to close the Help window.

GETTING STARTED

1. PCA 's Navigation Bar should be displayed.

2. Restore your data from the Exercise 4-2 backup. The Exercise 4-2.ptb backup was made on page 162.

   a. Insert your USB flash drive. From the Navigation Bar, select [System]; click [Restore Now].

   b. The Select Backup File window appears. Click [Browse]. Go to the Location of your Exercise 4-2.ptb file and select it. Click [Open], then [Next >].

   c. The Select Company window appears. The radio button next to An Existing Company is selected. The Company name field shows Bellwether Garden Supply. The Location field shows the default location on the hard drive for Bellwether Garden Supply. Click [Next >].

   d. The Restore Options window appears. Make sure that the box next to Company Data is *checked*. Click [Next >].

   e. The Confirmation window appears. Check the From and To fields to make sure they are correct. Click [Finish]. When the Restore Company scale is 100% complete, your data is restored. (*Hint:* The Student Version of Peachtree prompts that company data can be used for 14 months. After that time the data expires. Click [OK]. Bellwether Garden Supply opens.)

   To make sure you are starting in the appropriate place in the data (Exercise 4-2.ptb backup) check the Payroll Check Register. Link to the Payroll Check Register from the Employee's & Payroll Navigation Center. Make sure Check Nos. 1294-1297 are listed. A partial Payroll Check Register is shown on the next page.

		Bellwether Garden Supply		
		Payroll Check Register		
		For the Period From Mar 1, 2012 to Mar 31, 2012		

Filter Criteria includes: Report order is by Check Date. Report is printed in Detail Format.

Reference	Date	Employee	Amount
1287	3/15/12	Susan T. Prichard	559.22
1288	3/15/12	Samuel R. Prather	1,148.62
1289	3/15/12	Thatcher G. Leverne	759.00
1290	3/15/12	Tim O. Maske	1,380.01
1291	3/15/12	Tyler F. Riddell	756.11
1292	3/15/12	Virginia L. Ansell	965.72
1293	3/15/12	Vincent O. Kilborune	759.00
1294	3/29/12	Brandee M. Nunnley	1,051.48
1295	3/29/12	Drake V. Carter	585.23
1296	3/29/12	Brandon A. Hugley	650.25
1297	3/29/12	Derrick P. Gross	1,058.87
		3/1/12 thru 3/31/12	37,631.02
		3/1/12 thru 3/31/12	37,631.02

3. Close all windows.

4. From the Navigation Bar, select 🏛 **Banking** , click

    📚 **Chart of Accounts** , New Account. The Maintain Chart of Accounts window appears.

5. To add a new Money Market account, follow these steps:

    a. In the Account ID field, type **10500** and press **<Enter>**
    b. Your cursor is in the Description field. Type the name of the account **Money Market Fund**, and press **<Enter>**.

c. Your cursor is in the Account Type field. There is a drop-down list indicated by a down arrow. The default Account Type is Cash.

*Account Type: Cash ▼

. In the Account Type field specify the kind of account you are creating; for example, Cash, Cost of Sales, Equity-doesn't close, Equity-gets closed, etc. Select the drop-down list by clicking on the down arrow in the Account Type field to display the list of available account types. Make sure **Cash** is highlighted and press **<Enter>**. *The Account Type is important; it sorts each account on the financial statements.* Compare your Maintain Chart of Accounts window to the one shown below. (The top portion of the Maintain Chart of Accounts window is shown.)

Remember to check the Account Type field. The selection made in the Account Type field classifies accounts on the financial statements.

6. Click [Save] then close the Maintain Chart of Accounts window.

BUDGETS

Bellwether Garden Supply already has a budget set up. To see Bellwether's budget, do the following.

1. From the Navigation Bar, select [Banking] ; [Analysis Tools], View and Edit Budgets.

2. The Maintain Budgets window appears. Observe that the Maintain Budgets window shows an icon bar with an Excel icon—[Excel]. Most Peachtree reports can be exported to Excel.

The author recommends that if you are attaching Peachtree reports in an email to your instructor, Excel attachments be used.

The Maintain Budgets window defaults to Income Statement Accounts. This is shown in the Account Filters/Type field –

The Maintain Budgets window lets you build a forecast of dollar amounts for selected accounts for each fiscal period. You can filter the accounts you budget for by account type (income statement accounts, expenses, etc.). For example, the amount budgeted to Account No. 40000-AV, Sales - Aviary for 3/31/12 was $7,000.00. Let's look at the Income Statement to see how close that amount was to the actual sales for Account No. 40000-AV, Sales - Aviary. (*Hint:* The Total column shows the accumulated total for 1/31/12 through 12/31/12.) A partial Maintain Budgets window is shown below.

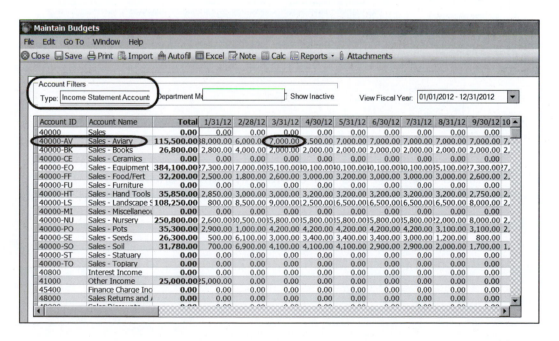

To compare the March 31, 2012 budgeted amount for Account No. 40000, Sales-Aviary to the actual amount, display the <Standard> Income/Budget report. Follow these steps to do that.

1. Minimize the Maintain Budgets window.

2. From the menu bar, select Reports & Forms; Financial Statements. Select <Standard> Income/Budget. The Select a Report or Form window is shown below.

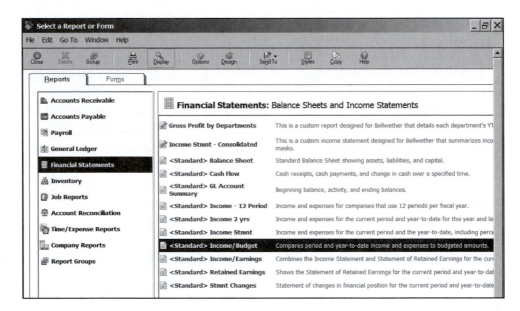

3. Click . The <Standard> Income/Budget window appears. Observe that the title of the report shows Income Statement, Compared with Budget. Observe that Sales - Aviary for the Current Month is 7,127.71. The Current Month Budget shows 7,000.00. A partial The Income Statement, Compared with Budget report's Total Revenues section is shown on the next page.

Current Month Budget and Current Month Variance are also shown for the current month, March 31, 2012, and Year to Date balances.

	Bellwether Garden Supply Income Statement Compared with Budget For the Three Months Ending March 31, 2012					
	Current Month Actual	Current Month Budget	Current Month Variance	Year to Date Actual	Year to Date Budget	Year to Date Variance
Revenues						
Sales	$ 295.00 $	0.00	295.00 $	295.00 $	0.00	295.00
Sales - Aviary	7,127.71	7,000.00	127.71	51,652.86	51,000.00	652.86
Sales - Books	149.75	2,000.00	(1,850.25)	7,293.10	8,800.00	(1,506.90)
Sales - Ceramics	0.00	0.00	0.00	0.00	0.00	0.00
Sales - Equipment	17,848.80	35,100.00	(17,251.20)	60,202.29	79,400.00	(19,197.71)
Sales - Food/Fert	1,006.96	2,600.00	(1,593.04)	5,204.15	6,900.00	(1,695.85)
Sales - Furniture	0.00	0.00	0.00	0.00	0.00	0.00
Sales - Hand Tools	729.67	3,000.00	(2,270.33)	7,058.12	8,850.00	(1,791.88)
Sales - Landscape Services	17,467.43	9,000.00	8,467.43	26,975.53	18,300.00	8,675.53
Sales - Miscellaneous	0.00	0.00	0.00	45.00	0.00	45.00
Sales - Nursery	33,795.03	35,800.00	(2,004.97)	67,637.11	68,900.00	(1,262.89)
Sales - Pots	7,919.31	4,200.00	3,719.31	11,483.74	8,100.00	3,383.74
Sales - Seeds	1,457.43	3,000.00	(1,542.57)	8,661.39	9,600.00	(938.61)
Sales - Soil	724.92	4,100.00	(3,375.08)	9,152.45	11,700.00	(2,547.55)
Sales - Statuary	0.00	0.00	0.00	0.00	0.00	0.00
Sales - Topiary	0.00	0.00	0.00	0.00	0.00	0.00
Interest Income	0.00	0.00	0.00	0.00	0.00	0.00
Other Income	100.00	0.00	100.00	25,600.00	25,000.00	600.00
Finance Charge Income	0.00	0.00	0.00	0.00	0.00	0.00
Sales Returns and Allowances	0.00	0.00	0.00	0.00	0.00	0.00
Sales Discounts	(145.72)	0.00	(145.72)	(155.62)	0.00	(155.62)
Total Revenues	88,476.29	105,800.00	(17,323.71)	281,105.12	296,550.00	(15,444.88)

What does the Income/Budget report show? For the Current Month, March 31, 2012, the budgeted amount of $7,000 was exceeded by the actual sales amount of $7,127.71 for Sales-Aviary. The current month variance is 127.71—sales exceeded the budget by that amount. Amounts shown in parentheses indicate that sales were lower than budgeted amounts.

4. Close all windows.

GENERAL JOURNAL

To open the Money Market Fund, transfer $4,500 from Bellwether's regular checking account to Account No. 10500, Money Market Fund. Also, transfer $1,000 from Bellwether's regular checking account to the payroll checking account (10300, Payroll Checking Account). The transfer of funds is recorded in the General Journal, and then posted to the General Ledger.

Date	Transaction Description
03/15/12	Transfer $4,500 to the Money Market Fund and $1,000 to the Payroll Checking Account from the Regular Checking Account.

Follow these steps to enter the transfer of funds:

1. From the Banking Navigation Center, select , New General Journal Entry. The General Journal Entry window appears.

2. Press **<Enter>** to accept the displayed date (3/15/12) in the Date field.

3. Your cursor is in the Reference field. Type **Transfer** and press **<Enter>** two times.

4. Your cursor is in the GL Account field. Type the account number for the Money Market Fund account, **10500**, and press the **<Enter>** or **<Tab>**. Observe that Money Market Fund appears below the account number.

5. Type **Money Market Fund** in the Description field. In this textbook, the account name is used as the description. You may prefer to type a description instead; for example, Established money market account. When a description is typed, it will repeat automatically on each Description line. Press **<Enter>** or **<Tab>** to go to the Debit field.

6. You are going to increase this account by $4,500. Type a debit amount of **4500** and press **<Enter>** three times. (It doesn't matter whether you type the debit or credit part of the entry first.) Notice that the Totals field displays 4,500.00 below the Debit column. The Out of Balance amount beneath it totals 4,500.00.

7. Your cursor is in the Account No. field. Type **10300** and press **<Enter>**. Payroll Checking Account displays on the line below the account number. Type **Payroll Checking Account** in the Description field. Press **<Enter>** to go to the Debit field.

8. Type **1000** in the Debit field. Press **<Enter>** three times.

9. Your cursor is in the Account No. field. Type **10200**; press **<Enter>**. Type **Regular Checking Account** in the Description field. Press **<Enter>** two times to go to the Credit field.

10. Type **5500** in the Credit field; press **<Enter>**. Notice that the Totals field now displays 5,500.00 beneath the Credit column. The Out of Balance amount equals zero (0.00). This means that the General Journal is in balance and can be posted. Compare your General Journal Entry window to the one shown below.

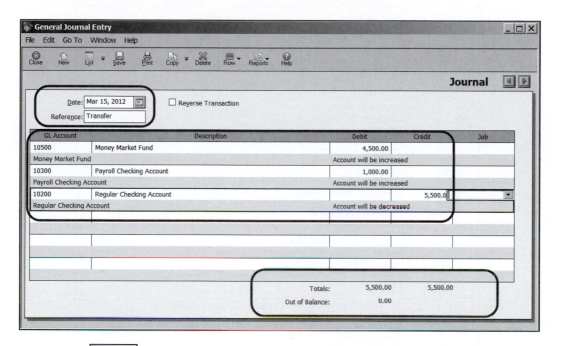

11. Click [Save] to post to the General Ledger. Close the General Journal Entry window.

The General Journal entry that you just completed transferred $4,500 from Bellwether's Regular Checking Account (Account No. 10200) to their Money Market Fund (Account No. 10500) and $1,000 to their Payroll Checking Account (Account No. 10300). To check that the account transfers have been made, follow these steps:

1. From the menu bar, select Reports & Forms, then General Ledger. The Select a Report or Form window displays.

2. In the General Ledger: Account Information List, double-click General Ledger Trial Balance. The General Ledger Trial Balance is shown on the next two pages.

*****EDUCATIONAL VERSION ONLY*****

Bellwether Garden Supply
General Ledger Trial Balance
As of Mar 31, 2012

Filter Criteria includes: Report order is by ID. Report is printed in Detail Format.

Account ID	Account Description	Debit Amt	Credit Amt
10000	Petty Cash	327.55	
10100	Cash on Hand	1,850.45	
10200	Regular Checking Account	10,246.52	
10300	Payroll Checking Account	9,365.26	
10400	Savings Account	7,500.00	
10500	Money Market Fund	4,500.00	
11000	Accounts Receivable	175,594.96	
11400	Other Receivables	7,681.84	
11500	Allowance for Doubtful Accou		5,000.00
12000	Inventory	12,614.61	
14000	Prepaid Expenses	14,221.30	
14100	Employee Advances	3,000.65	
14200	Notes Receivable-Current	11,000.00	
14700	Other Current Assets	120.00	
15000	Furniture and Fixtures	62,769.25	
15100	Equipment	38,738.33	
15200	Vehicles	86,273.40	
15300	Other Depreciable Property	6,200.96	
15500	Buildings	185,500.00	
15600	Building Improvements	26,500.00	
17000	Accum. Depreciation-Furnitur		54,680.57
17100	Accum. Depreciation-Equipm		33,138.11
17200	Accum. Depreciation-Vehicles		51,585.26
17300	Accum. Depreciation-Other		3,788.84
17500	Accum. Depreciation-Building		34,483.97
17600	Accum. Depreciation-Bldg Im		4,926.28
19000	Deposits	15,000.00	
19100	Organization Costs	4,995.10	
19150	Accum Amortiz - Organiz Cos		2,000.00
19200	Notes Receivable- Noncurrent	5,004.90	
19900	Other Noncurrent Assets	3,333.00	
20000	Accounts Payable		80,626.01
23000	Accrued Expenses		3,022.55
23100	Sales Tax Payable		18,056.89
23200	Wages Payable		2,320.30
23300	401 K Deductions Payable		2,490.32
23350	Health Insurance Payable	530.64	
23400	Federal Payroll Taxes Payabl		41,791.17
23500	FUTA Tax Payable		258.20
23600	State Payroll Taxes Payable		6,857.05
23700	SUTA Tax Payable		658.67
23800	Local Payroll Taxes Payable		113.25
23900	Income Taxes Payable		11,045.75
24000	Other Taxes Payable		2,640.15
24100	Current Portion Long-Term D		5,167.00
24300	Contracts Payable- Current		2,000.00
24700	Other Current Liabilities		54.00
27000	Notes Payable-Noncurrent		4,000.00
39003	Common Stock		5,000.00
39004	Paid-in Capital		100,000.00
39005	Retained Earnings		189,037.60
40000	Sales		295.00
40000-AV	Sales - Aviary		51,652.86
40000-BK	Sales - Books		7,293.10
40000-EQ	Sales - Equipment		60,202.29
40000-FF	Sales - Food/Fert		5,204.15
40000-HT	Sales - Hand Tools		7,058.12
40000-LS	Sales - Landscape Services		26,975.53
40000-MI	Sales - Miscellaneous		45.00
40000-NU	Sales - Nursery		67,637.11
40000-PO	Sales - Pots		11,483.74
40000-SE	Sales - Seeds		8,661.39
40000-SO	Sales - Soil		9,152.45

*****EDUCATIONAL VERSION ONLY*****

Bellwether Garden Supply
General Ledger Trial Balance
As of Mar 31, 2012

Filter Criteria includes: Report order is by ID. Report is printed in Detail Format.

Account ID	Account Description	Debit Amt	Credit Amt
41000	Other Income		25,600.00
49000	Sales Discounts	155.62	
50000	Product Cost		68.50
50000-AV	Product Cost - Aviary	20,821.45	
50000-BK	Product Cost - Books	2,361.37	
50000-EQ	Product Cost - Equipment	24,154.95	
50000-FF	Product Cost - Food/Fert	2,060.04	
50000-HT	Product Cost - Hand Tools	2,813.85	
50000-PO	Product Cost - Pots	3,423.60	
50000-SE	Product Cost - Seeds	3,450.65	
50000-SO	Product Cost - Soil	4,075.97	
57000-NU	Direct Labor - Nursery	3,062.50	
57200	Materials Cost	1,397.45	
57200-NU	Materials Cost - Nursery	9,668.50	
57300-LS	Subcontractors - Landscaping	335.50	
57500	Freight	50.00	
60000	Advertising Expense	1,325.00	
61000	Auto Expenses	274.56	
61500	Bad Debt Expense	1,341.09	
62000	Bank Charges	18.00	
64000	Depreciation Expense	8,394.00	
68500	Legal and Professional Expen	510.00	
69000	Licenses Expense	150.00	
70000	Maintenance Expense	75.00	
71000	Office Expense	534.64	
72000	Payroll Tax Exp	15,857.60	
74000	Rent or Lease Expense	1,100.00	
74500	Repairs Expense	3,694.00	
75500	Supplies Expense	2,873.42	
77000	Utilities Expense	303.45	
77500	Wages Expense	138,465.46	
89000	Other Expense	464.90	
89500	Purchase Disc- Expense Item		10.11
	Total:	**946,081.29**	**946,081.29**

On page 176, Account No. 10200, Regular Checking Account, has a debit balance of $10,246.52; Account No. 10300, Payroll Checking Account, has a debit balance of $9,365.26; and Account No. 10500, Money Market Fund, has a debit balance of $4,500.00. This shows that the General Journal entry that you just completed is posted correctly. To see the rest of the General Ledger Trial Balance, scroll down the General Ledger Trial Balance window.

3. Close all windows.

SETTING UP AN INVENTORY ITEM

This part of Chapter 5 explains PCA's Inventory system.

The sample company, Bellwether Garden Supply, has decided to track cleaning supplies as stock inventory items and to bill clients for supplies used. First, you need to enter the cleaning supplies they stock as Inventory Items.

Peachtree's Inventory & Services Navigation Center shows Peachtree's *Inventory* **System**, another module within the software. The Navigation Bar's **Inventory & Services** selection displays information and access points related to the company's inventory items. It includes a summary of item information, access to recently used inventory reports, and a graphic analysis of how the cost of sales is trending. In addition, the Inventory & Services Navigation Center shows the flow of inventory-related tasks and takes you where you need to go to perform those tasks. Observe that drill down links are also available. If necessary, scroll down and across the Inventory & Services Navigation Center window to see all the areas. The Inventory & Services Tasks workflow diagram is shown below.

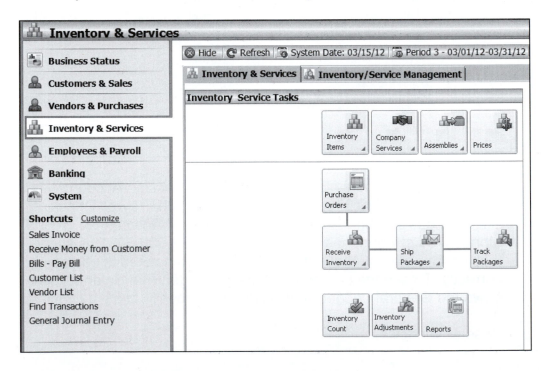

The Inventory & Services Navigation Center also includes an Inventory/Service Management tab. The Inventory and Service Management selection is a dashboard that allows you to quickly find and view information about inventory and service items. This helps you do research, make comparisons, and make decisions regarding the items sold and the services offered by the business.

Follow these steps to set up an Inventory Item:

1. From the Inventory & Services Navigation Center, select ![Inventory Items] ; New Inventory Item. The Maintain Inventory Items window displays.

2. In the Item ID field, type **AVRY-10300** (type a capital A because the ID code is case sensitive--the first four characters should be in uppercase) and press **<Enter>**.

3. In the Description field, type **Oriole Feeder** and press **<Enter>**.

4. Your cursor is in the Item Class field. Select Stock item.

Inventory Types

If you click on the down-arrow next to the Item field, observe that there are several types of Inventory Items:

➢ Stock item: Use this item class for traditional inventory items that are tracked for quantities, average costs, vendors, low stock points, etc. Once an item is assigned to this class, it cannot be changed.

➢ Master Stock Item: Use this item class when you want to set up a group of related stock items that have similar characteristics or attributes. A master stock item is a special item that does not represent inventory you stock but rather contains information (item attributes) shared with a number of substock items generated from it.

➢ Non-stock item: Use this class for items; such as service contracts and office supplies that you buy or sell but do not put into your inventory. Quantities, descriptions, and unit prices are printed on invoices and purchase orders, but quantities on hand are not tracked. You can assign a cost of goods General Ledger account to non-stock items, but it is not affected by a costing method.

➢ Description only: Use this item class when nothing is tracked except the description. For example, "comments" that can be added to sales or purchase transactions are description-only items.

➢ Service: Use this item class for services you perform and sell, such as monthly maintenance work. You can enter a cost for the service, which would include your employee's wage, overhead, materials, and such used in the course of performing the service.

➢ Labor: Use this item class for labor that is part of an assembly item or for outside labor that you use for projects; you can enter a cost for the service. In the case of assembly items, this labor will become part of the cost of goods for the assembled item.

➢ Assembly: Use this class for items that consist of components that can be built or dismantled. For each assembly item, select the Bill of Materials tab, and define the components of the assembly before you click the Save button on the Maintain Inventory Items window. Once a transaction uses an assembly, it cannot be changed.

➢ Activity item: Use this item class for different types of work that are performed for a customer or job. These are very useful for professional businesses, such as law firms, that want to track employee time for a customer and job and then bill the customer. Activity items are used in Time & Billing and are recorded on employee or vendor time tickets.

➢ Charge item: Use this item class to identify items that are expenses recorded by an employee or vendor when various services are performed for a customer or job. Charge items are used in Time & Billing and are recorded on employee or vendor expense tickets. Use charge items when you plan on billing customers for reimbursable expenses, such as parking fees, mileage, and so on.

Follow these steps to continue setting up an Inventory Item:

1. If necessary, press the **<Enter>** key to go to the Description field.

2. Your cursor is in the Description for Sales field. Press the **<Enter>** key to go to the description field. Type **Oriole Feeder** and press **<Enter>**.

3. Your cursor is in the Price Level 1 field. Click on the right arrow button `Price Level 1: 0.00 ▶` in this field. The Multiple Price Levels window appears. In the Price Level 1 row, click on the Price field. Type **15** on the Price Level 1 row, then press **<Enter>**. You can set up ten different sales prices per item.

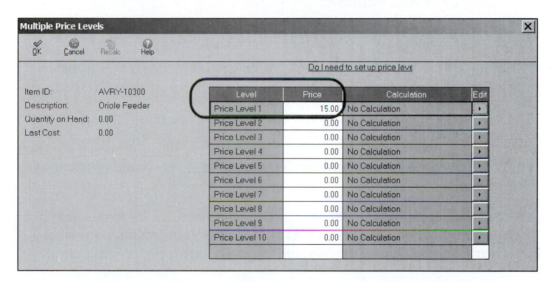

4. Click [OK] to close the Multiple Price Levels window. The Price Level 1 field shows 15.00.

5. Click on the Last Unit Cost field. Type **7** and press **<Enter>**.

6. Observe that the Cost Method is FIFO. Peachtree includes three inventory cost methods: FIFO, LIFO and Average. Press **<Enter>**.

7. Your cursor is in the GL Sales Account field. Click 🔍, then select Account No. 40000-AV, Sales – Aviary, as the sales account. Press **<Enter>**.

8. Accept the default for the GL Inventory Acct, Account No. 12000, Inventory, by pressing **<Enter>**.

9. Your cursor is in the GL Cost of Sales Acct field. Select Account No. 50000-AV, Product Cost – Aviary, as the product cost account. Press **<Enter>**.

10. Click 🔍 in the Item Ta<u>x</u> Type field. Observe that the default, 1, means that this is a regular, taxable item. Press **<Enter>**. The UPC/SKU window appears. Read the information.

11. Click on the Item Type field. The Item Type is a way of classifying similar inventory items for sorting and printing reports. Select SUPPLY. Press **<Enter>**.

12. Your cursor is in the Location field. Select AISLE 1. Press **<Enter>**.

13. Your cursor is in the Stocking U/M field. Select Each and press **<Enter>** two times.

14. Your cursor is in the Minimum Stock field. Type **6** and press **<Enter>**.

15. Your cursor is in the Reorder <u>Q</u>uantity field. Type **6** and press **<Enter>**

16. Select DEJULIA, DeJulia Wholesale Suppliers as the Preferred <u>V</u>endor ID. Leave the Buyer ID field blank. Your Maintain Inventory Items window should agree with the one shown on the next page.

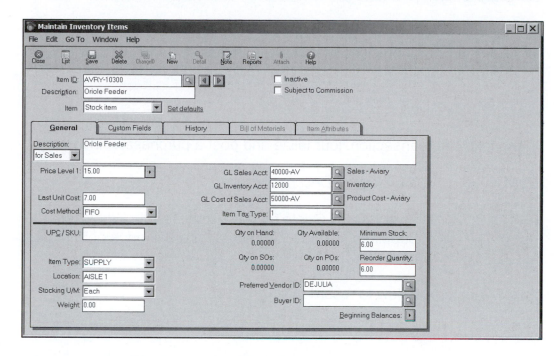

When you purchase inventory stock items from a vendor, this is the Purchases Journal entry: debit the Inventory account and credit Accounts Payable/Vendor account. When you sell Inventory stock items on account, a compound Sales Journal entry is recorded.

➢ Debit Accounts Receivable and Cost of Goods Sales accounts.

➢ Credit Sales, Sales Tax Payable, and Inventory accounts.

The Maintain Inventory Items window should be displayed.

Observe that you set the following account defaults for this stock item:

GL Sales Acct	40000-AV	Sales - Aviary
GL Inventory Acct	12000	Inventory
GL Cost of Sales Acct	50000-AV	Product Cost - Aviary

You also selected a preferred vendor. The Preferred Vendor ID field should display DEJULIA, which is the Vendor ID for DeJulia Wholesale Suppliers. Bellwether purchases oriole feeders from this vendor.

17. Click [Save] then close the Maintian Inventory Items window to return to the Inventory & Services Navigation Center.

INVENTORY AND PURCHASES

In the following transaction, journalize and post a purchase of inventory.

Date   *Transaction Description*

03/17/12   Purchased 6 Oriole feeders from DeJulia Wholesale Suppliers, Invoice No. 55522, at a unit price of $7, for a total of $42.

Follow the steps below to record this transaction.

1. From the Navigation Bar, click [Vendors & Purchases] ; [Enter Bills], New Bill. The Purchases/Receive Inventory window displays. If your GL Account field and A/P Account fields are *not* displayed on the Purchases/Receive Inventory window, see the instructions on page 18, step 1c, Hide General Ledger Accounts area.

2. In the Vendor ID field, type **DEJULIA** and press **<Enter>** (or use the lookup icon to find DeJulia Wholesale Suppliers).

3. Click on the Date field. Type or select **17** as the date.

4. In the Invoice No. field, type **55522** and press **<Enter>**. This is a required field.

5. Click on the Apply to Purchases tab.

6. Click on the Quantity field. Type **6** and press **<Enter>**.

7. Your cursor is in the Item field. Type or select the code you just created, **AVRY-10300** and press **<Enter>** three times. The description and the GL Account automatically default to the information you assigned in the Maintain Inventory Items window.

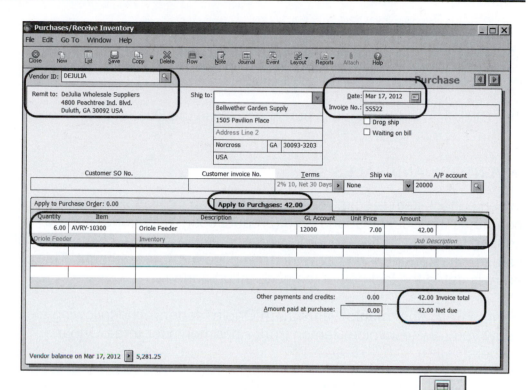

8. To see how this inventory purchase is journalized, click 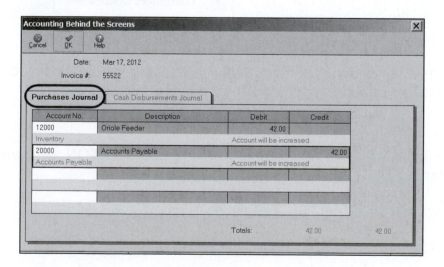 . The Accounting Behind the Screens, Purchases Journal appears: Account No. 12000, Inventory, is debited for 42.00; Account No. 20000, Accounts Payable is credited for 42.00. The vendor, DeJulia Wholesale Suppliers is also credited. The entry to the vendor is shown in the Vendor Ledgers.

9. Click [OK] to return to the Purchases/Receive Inventory window.

10. Click [Save] to post this purchase. Close the Purchases/Receive Inventory window.

INVENTORY AND SALES

When a stock item is sold, PCA updates Accounts Receivable and computes the Cost of Goods Sold (product cost), using one of three costing methods. In the General Ledger, a single entry encompassing all sales in the current period is made to the Product Cost account. This entry is dated the last day of the accounting period.

Henton Park Apartments wants three Oriole feeders. The following steps show you how to invoice Henton Park Apartments for three Oriole feeders.

Date	Transaction Description
03/17/12	Sold three Oriole feeders on account to Henton Park Apartments for $15 each plus sales tax.

1. From the Navigation Bar, click [Customers & Sales] ; [Sales Invoices] , New Sales Invoice. The Sales/Invoicing window displays.

   If the GL Account field and A/R Account field are *not* displayed, refer to the instructions on page 18 step 1c, Hide General Ledger Accounts area.

2. In the Customer ID field, click [🔍] and select **HENTON, Henton Park Apartments**.

3. Type or select **17** as the date. Do not complete the Invoice No. field.

4. Click on the Apply to Sales tab.

5. Click on the Quantity field. Type **3** and press **<Enter>**.

6. The cursor is in the Item field. Type **AVRY-10300** and press **<Enter>** five times.

    PCA computes the amount based on the quantity times the sales price that was established when setting up the inventory item. All the other lines for this invoice are automatically completed based on the inventory item information.

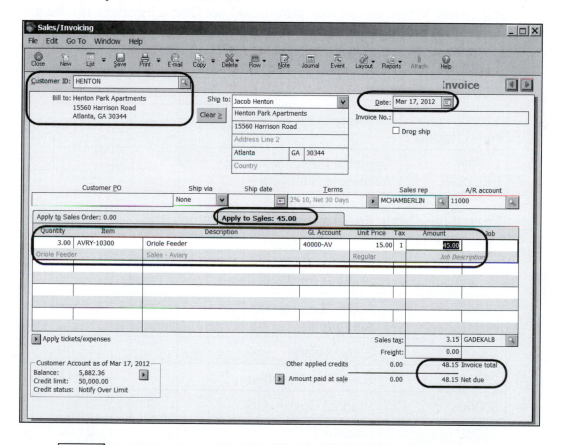

7. Click [Journal] to see how Peachtree journalizes this entry in the Sales Journal. Scroll down the Accounting Behind the Screens, Sales Journal window, to see the entire entry. Observe that in a perpetual inventory system (Peachtree's default) the cost of sales accounts (50000-AV, Product Cost-Aviary; and 12000, Inventory) are "To be calculated." Once the sales invoice is posted, the cost of sales

amounts will be calculated. Click [OK] to close the Accounting Behind the Screens window to return to the Sales/Invoicing window.

8. Click [Save] to post this sales invoice. Close the Sales/Invoicing window to return to the Customers & Sales Navigation Center.

Let's review the last two sections: Inventory and Purchases and Inventory and Sales. When Bellwether purchased six Oriole Feeders (an inventory stock item) on pages 184-186, the entry is recorded in the Purchase Journal with these accounts debited and credited.

Account #	Account Description	Debit	Credit
12000/ AVRY-10300	Inventory	42.00	
20000/ DEJULIA	Accounts Payable/DeJulia Wholesale Suppliers		42.00

When three Oriole Feeders were sold on pages 186-188, the entry in the Sales Journal was:

Account #	Account Description	Debit	Credit
11000/ HENTON	Accts. Rec./Henton Park Apartments	48.15	
40000-AV	Sales-Aviary		45.00
23100	Sales Tax Payable		3.15
50000-AV	Product Cost-Aviary	21.00	
12000	Inventory		21.00

When three Oriole feeders were sold, they were sold for $15 each, plus sales tax. The total sale to Henton Park Apartments is $45 plus sales tax of $3.15, for a total of $48.15. When Bellwether Garden Supply bought the Oriole Feeders from the vendor (DeJulia Wholesale Suppliers), they paid $7 each. The last two lines of the journal entry (Account nos. 50000-AV and 12000) reflect the product cost of the stock items, $7 X 3 = $21.

The journal entries shown on page 188 are examples of how purchases and sales are recorded in Peachtree's perpetual inventory system.

INVENTORY ADJUSTMENTS

It may become necessary to adjust the amount of Inventory Items due to faulty records, pilferage, spoilage, or inventory changes. You use the Inventory Adjustment Journal to make inventory adjustment entries.

In the example that follows, one of Bellwether's employees dropped two bird house kits which damaged them beyond repair. To adjust inventory for this loss, follow these steps.

1. From the Navigation Bar, click **Inventory & Services** ; **Inventory Adjustments** .
    The Inventory Adjustments window appears.

2. Type **AVRY-10100** (for Bird House Kit) in the Item ID field and the press **<Enter>** key six times. Your cursor is in the Adjust quantity by field.

3. Type **-2** in the Adjust quantity by field to decrease the current inventory by two. Press the **<Enter>** key. The New Quantity field shows that you have 28.00 bird house kits.

4. Type **Damaged** as the Reason to Adjust.

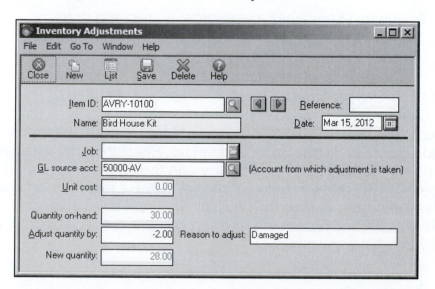

5. Click [Save] to post this adjustment, then close the Inventory Adjustments window.

Adjustments to inventory, like the one just made, only affect the average cost of the item. For example, let's say you purchased two bird house kits at $30 each and then damaged one. For accounting purposes you now have one bird house kit that costs $30.

SECURITY AND INTERNAL CONTROL

Internal control is an integrated system of people, processes, and procedures that minimize or eliminate business risks, protect assets, facilitate reliable accounting, and promote efficient operations. If changes are made to company records, Peachtree's *audit trail* provides documentation. An audit trail records all entries and changes related to the company's data, including actions by specific users.

Peachtree has several methods to track information. For example, a combination of the general ledger, journals, reports, and financial statements can be used to trace transactions and balances. If you want to track when an action is performed, Peachtree's audit trail provides this information. The audit trail provides accountability of users, deters users from fraudulent activity or mistakes, and tracks transaction history. Four internal control methods are built into the software:

- Setting up user names, passwords, and access rights.
- The ability to associate the user currently logged into the Peachtree company with the data that is being entered.
- Limit access to information in Peachtree's Navigation Centers.
- Audit Trail reports that show what each user entered.

In order to get the most use out of the audit trail feature, user records need to be set up. If User Security is set up, Peachtree can associate the user currently logged into the company with the data being entered. For example, USER1 adds a customer record. USER2 then logs on and modifies the customer record. The Audit Trail report will show that USER2 was the last person who worked with the customer record, and it will display what was changed.

By limiting access to accounting data, Peachtree's user security feature addresses an important purpose of internal control. For example, assigning users to one Navigation Center increases the accuracy of records and reports. Also, since one user assumes responsibility for repetitive tasks, the efficiency of operations increases. User security reduces the business's risk of users changing or deleting data inappropriately which also safeguards accounting data. User security establishes accountability and allows the company to track who has performed various maintenance and recording tasks.

User Security and Access to the Peachtree Navigation Centers

If you are an administrator responsible for setting up and maintaining user access to Peachtree, you can choose settings that will limit access to information in Peachtree's Navigation Centers. For example, if you want a user to have limited access to company revenue information, you could make sure the user has no access to the general ledger master list and transaction list reports or financial statements. However, you might want that same user to be able to view company budgets but not change them in any way.

When you set up Peachtree security, you can fine-tune settings to give users exactly the kind of access you want them to have. The Selected AccessRole Setup window has embedded Help for each security setting; just select a setting to see Help about it. This will aid you in deciding which areas users could have access to and which areas they don't.

Selected Access

The Selected Access window allows the administrator to grant rights to work in certain areas of the Peachtree program within the current company. Peachtree program areas include the following roles:

- Customers & Sales
- Vendors & Purchases
- Inventory & Services
- Employees & Payroll
- Banking & General Ledger
- System

In addition to full or no access, the administrator can set different levels of access within subareas such as maintenance, tasks, and reports. For example, in the Customers & Sales area, the administrator could choose to give a user limited access to Customer Information or Customer Beginning Balances. Drop-down lists let the administrator set different access levels for different subareas of the program; for example, Payments; Write Checks.

User Security

Peachtree allows custom access for different individuals. If you want to take advantage of this security feature, you set up user rights for each person who will be using Peachtree. When set up, each user is issued a user name and password that will be required before opening and working with company data.

Once user names and passwords are set up, Peachtree prompts each user for a user name and password whenever he or she opens a company. As long as users properly enter their passwords, they can access the areas of the program to which they have rights.

Setting Up Company Users, Passwords, and Access Rights

In order to have data security and password protection, you need to set up user records. When user names and passwords are set up, Peachtree prompts you for a user name and password when you open a company. This is a two-step process:

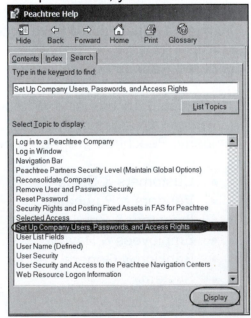

- Set up the company administrator.
- Set up individual users.

The steps below are for example purposes only. Check with your instructor to see if he or she would like you to set up user access. *Remember, if you set up a user name and password you have to use it each time you start Peachtree.* To learn

about setting up company users, passwords, and access rights, go to the
following Help windows.

1. From Peachtree's menu bar select, Help; Peachtree Accounting
   Help. Select the Search tab.
2. Type **Set Up Company Users, Passwords, and Access Rights** in
   the Type in the keyword to find.
3. Click List Topics .
4. Scroll down the topics list select Set Up Company Users,
   Passwords, and Access Rights to highlight it.
5. Click Display . The Set Up Company Users, Passwords, and
   Access Rights window appears. Enlarge the window. In the right
   pane, link to <u>Setting up the first user (administrator)</u>.
6. Link to <u>Setting up additional company users.</u> Read the information.
7. Link to <u>Setting up users with selected access.</u>
8. Read the information on this window. This Help window explains
   how to set up users, passwords and access rights.
9. Check with your instructor to see if he or she would like you do this.

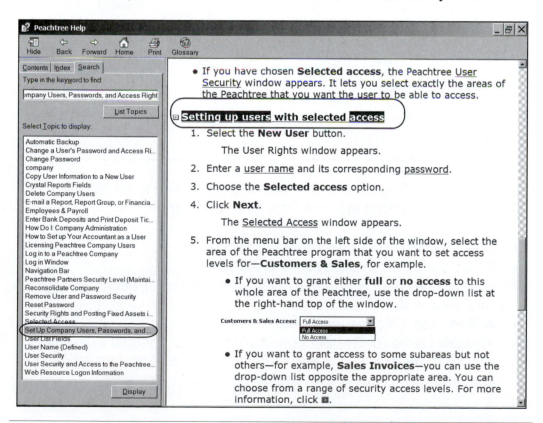

10. Click 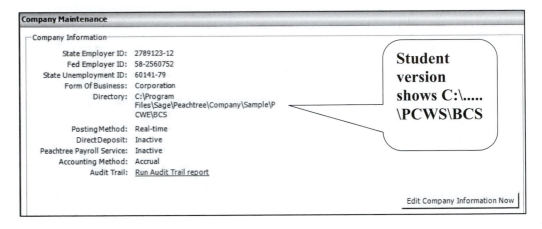 on the Peachtree Help title bar to close.

Audit Trail Report

The Audit trail is an historical record of financial data that is used to examine the data's correctness. Peachtree's audit trail feature records all entries and changes related to company data, including actions by specific users. The Audit Trail report can trace fraudulent activity and other accounting adjustments you may not know were completed.

The System Navigation Center shows a link to <u>Run Audit Trail report</u>. Once date options are selected, the Audit Trail report can be viewed from this link, or from the Reports & Forms, Company selection. On pages 196-197, the Audit Trial Report is displayed from the Reports & Forms menu.

Company Maintenance

Company Information

State Employer ID:	2789123-12
Fed Employer ID:	58-2560752
State Unemployment ID:	60141-79
Form Of Business:	Corporation
Directory:	C:\Program Files\Sage\Peachtree\Company\Sample\PCWE\BCS
Posting Method:	Real-time
Direct Deposit:	Inactive
Peachtree Payroll Service:	Inactive
Accounting Method:	Accrual
Audit Trail:	<u>Run Audit Trail report</u>

Student version shows C:\..... \PCWS\BCS

Edit Company Information Now

The audit trail feature records the following items with each activity performed while operating in the Peachtree company:

- Date: System (computer) date of action.
- Time: System (computer) time of action.
- User Name: User Name (if available); otherwise, Peachtree displays "Not Available."
- Action: Add, Change, or Delete.
- Window Name (or System Function): Name of window where action occurred (for example, Sales Orders) or name of system function implemented (for example, Unpost).

- Transaction ID: For maintenance records, the ID associated with the record; for tasks, the ID associated with the transaction after change.
- Transaction Reference: Reference number associated with the transaction after change.
- Amount: Amount of transaction after change.

Peachtree's audit trail tracks the following:

1. Records and Transactions

   Records include customers, vendors, employees, inventory items, etc. Transactions include quotes, sales orders, invoices, payments, general journal entries, inventory adjustments, etc.

   These include:

   - adding records or transactions (when Save is selected).
   - editing records or transactions (when Save is selected).
   - deleting records or transactions (when Delete is selected).
   - entering or maintaining record beginning balances (when OK or Save is selected).
   - voiding checks and paychecks.
   - making payments in Cash Manager and Payment Manager.

2. Miscellaneous Actions

   - reconciling accounts.
   - maintaining company information and options.
   - maintaining and loading user-maintained and Peachtree-maintained payroll tax tables.
   - importing data into the company.
   - adding transactions using Dynamic Data Exchange (DDE).

3. System Functions

   - posting and unposting journals (Batch mode only).
   - closing the fiscal year.
   - closing the payroll tax year.
   - backing up company data.

Displaying the Audit Trail Report & Find Transactions Report

Follow these steps to print an Audit Trail Report.

1. From the menu bar, select Reports & Forms; Company. The Select a Report or Form window appears. The Audit Trail Report is the default.

2. Click **Options**.

3. In the Date field, select Range.

4. Type **1/1/2006** in the From field. Press **<Tab>**.

5. Type **12/31/2012** in the To field. Press **<Tab>**.

   IMPORTANT: If the current date is *after* 12/31/2012, in the To field type today's date. The Audit Trail Report shows the dates that you recorded entries.

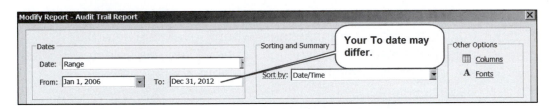

6. Click **OK**. The Audit Trail Report for the period from Jan 1, 2006 to Dec. 31, 2012 (*or, today's date*) appears. Observe that each transaction shows the Date; Time; User Name, Action, Window/ Description, Transaction ID, Transaction Reference, and Amount. If users had been set up, the User Name column would show that. Scroll down to see the whole report. A partial report is shown on the next page.

   Observe that the work completed in Chapters 1-5 is shown on the Audit Trail Report; for example, the employees added in Chapter 1 (CYACHT, or your name, and JWOOD); the vendors added (Maintain Vendors), purchases (Purchases/Receive Inventory), and payments to ARMSTRONG and POSTOFC in Chapter 2. Scroll down the Audit Trail Report to see your work. (Your date column will differ. It shows the date you recorded the entries.)

The Audit Trial Report provides a listing of the changes made to the maintenance items and transactions. Depending on when you made additions and changes, your time and date column will differ. The Audit Trail Report shows when the author made changes.

A partial Audit Trail Report is shown below. If you are working *after* December 31, 2012, your Audit Trail Report may show a different ending date.

Bellwether Garden Supply
Audit Trail Report
For the Period From Jan 1, 2006 to Dec 31, 2012

Filter Criteria includes: 1) All Actions.

Date	Time	User Name	Action	Window/Description	Transaction ID	Transaction Reference	Amount
3/14/10	11:00 A	Not Available	Change	Receipts	CHAPPLE	CC0001	40.25
3/14/10	11:01 A	Not Available	Change	Receipts	CUMMINGS	CASH-31503	423.89
3/19/10	5:35 PM	Not Available	Change	Maintain Customers/Prospects	CANNON		
3/19/10	5:37 PM	Not Available	Change	Backup Company Data Files			
2/28/11	10:50 P	Not Available	Change	Data Integrity Check	File Tests	Reindex EMPLOYEE.DA	
2/28/11	10:50 P	Not Available	Change	Data Integrity Check	File Tests	Reindex CHART.DAT	
2/28/11	10:50 P	Not Available	Change	Data Integrity Check	File Tests	Reindex CUSTOMER.DA	
2/28/11	10:50 P	Not Available	Change	Data Integrity Check	File Tests	Reindex VENDOR.DAT	
2/28/11	10:50 P	Not Available	Change	Data Integrity Check	File Tests	Reindex LINEITEM.DAT	
2/28/11	10:51 P	Not Available	Change	Data Integrity Check	File Tests	Reindex PROJECT.DAT	
2/28/11	10:51 P	Not Available	Change	Data Integrity Check	File Tests	Reindex PHASE.DAT	
2/28/11	10:51 P	Not Available	Change	Data Integrity Check	File Tests	Reindex COST.DAT	
2/28/11	10:51 P	Not Available	Change	Data Integrity Check	File Tests	Reindex JRNLROW.DAT	
8/15/11	1:07 PM	Not Available	Change	Maintain Company	BCS	Bellwether Garden Supply	
8/15/11	1:19 PM	Not Available	Change	Backup Company Data Files			
8/15/11	1:31 PM	Not Available	Change	Backup Company Data Files			
8/15/11	2:48 PM	Not Available	Change	Maintain Company	BCS	Bellwether Garden Supply	
8/16/11	11:01 A	Not Available	Change	Backup Company Data Files			
8/16/11	6:47 PM	Not Available	Change	Backup Company Data Files			
8/16/11	6:51 PM	Not Available	Change	Backup Company Data Files			
8/18/11	11:03 A	Not Available	Add	Maintain Employees & Sales Reps	CYACHT		
8/18/11	11:15 A	Not Available	Change	Backup Company Data Files			
8/18/11	11:16 A	Not Available	Change	Backup Company Data Files			
8/18/11	1:24 PM	Not Available	Add	Maintain Employees & Sales Reps	JWOOD		
8/18/11	1:31 PM	Not Available	Change	Backup Company Data Files			
8/18/11	1:32 PM	Not Available	Change	Backup Company Data Files			
8/22/11	2:21 PM	Not Available	Add	Purchase Orders	ABNEY	101	3,834.00
8/22/11	8:23 PM	Not Available	Add	Maintain Vendors	ARMSTRONG		
8/22/11	8:31 PM	Not Available	Add	Purchases/Receive Inventory	ARMSTRONG	ARM107	45.00
8/22/11	9:04 PM	Not Available	Change	Backup Company Data Files			
8/23/11	7:19 PM	Not Available	Add	Payments	ARMSTRONG		44.10
8/23/11	7:49 PM	Not Available	Change	Backup Company Data Files			
8/23/11	7:50 PM	Not Available	Change	Backup Company Data Files			
9/2/11	10:09 A	Not Available	Add	Maintain Vendors	POSTOFC		
9/2/11	10:12 A	Not Available	Add	Purchases/Receive Inventory	POSTOFC	H788	54.75
9/2/11	10:17 A	Not Available	Add	Payments	POSTOFC		53.65
9/2/11	10:39 A	Not Available	Change	Backup Company Data Files			
9/2/11	10:40 A	Not Available	Change	Backup Company Data Files			
9/3/11	11:17 A	Not Available	Add	Quotes	DASH		211.95
9/3/11	11:20 A	Not Available	Add	Quotes	DASH	10354	211.95

7. Close the Audit Trail Report. Then, display the Find Transactions Report from 3/15/12 to 3/15/12 (the default).

The Find Transactions Report provides a way to easily search for Peachtree Transactions. You can drill down to the original entry from each transaction.

A partial Find Transactions Report is shown on the next page.

*****EDUCATIONAL VERSION ONLY*****

Bellwether Garden Supply
Find Transactions Report
For the Period From Mar 15, 2012 to Mar 15, 2012

Filter Criteria includes: 1) All Transaction Types. Report order is by Date.

Date	Type	Reference	ID	Name	Amount
3/15/12	Credit Memo		ARCHER	Archer Scapes and Ponds	-49.99
3/15/12	Credit Memo		SAIA	Saia's Neighborhood Nursery	-49.99
3/15/12	General Journal Entry	ADJ0303103			0.11
3/15/12	General Journal Entry	Transfer			5,500.00
3/15/12	Inventory Adjustment		AVRY-10100	Bird House Kit	-2.00
3/15/12	Inventory Adjustment		AVRY-10050-LG-EFL	Prefabricated Birdhouse	4.00
3/15/12	Inventory Adjustment		AVRY-10050-SM-EFL	Prefabricated Birdhouse	8.00
3/15/12	Inventory Adjustment		AVRY-10050-SM-HTL	Prefabricated Birdhouse	8.00
3/15/12	Inventory Adjustment		AVRY-10050-SM-HTL	Prefabricated Birdhouse	6.00
3/15/12	Inventory Adjustment		AVRY-10050-SM-PYR	Prefabricated Birdhouse	4.00
3/15/12	Payment		ABNEY	Abney and Son Contractors	50.00
3/15/12	Payment	10210	SAFESTATE	Safe State Insurance Company	530.64
3/15/12	Payment	10212	PAYNE	Payne Enterprises	50.00
3/15/12	Payment	10213	CLINE	Cline Construction, Inc.	100.00
3/15/12	Payment	10214	HAWKINS	DPH Web Design	100.00
3/15/12	Payroll Entry	1250	ACHESTER	Amanda W. Chester	809.22
3/15/12	Payroll Entry	1251	ADUKE	Al L. Duke	379.50
3/15/12	Payroll Entry	1252	AHECTER	Anthony H. Hecter	787.54
3/15/12	Payroll Entry	1253	AKORNEL	Alex C. Kornel	845.06
3/15/12	Payroll Entry	1254	BHUGLEY	Brandon A. Hugley	612.75

8. Close the Find Transactions report. If necessary, close the Select a Report or Form window.

BACKING UP CHAPTER 5 DATA

Follow these steps to back up Chapter 5 data:

1. If necessary, insert your USB flash drive. From System Navigation Center, link to ⎡ Back Up Now ⎤. Make sure that the box next to Include company name in the backup file name is *unchecked*.

2. Click ⎡ Back Up ⎤.

3. In the Save in field, select the appropriate drive letter for your USB drive.[1] (*Or,* save to another location.) Type **Chapter 5** in the File name field.

4. Click [Save] .

5. When the window prompts This company backup will require approximately 1 diskette, click [OK] . When the window prompts Please insert the first disk, click [OK] . When the Back Up Company scale is 100% complete, you have successfully backed up to the current point in Chapter 5. (Step 5 will differ slightly if you are backing up to the default or other hard-drive location.)

SUMMARY AND REVIEW

Complete the following end-of-chapter activities:

1. Going to the net, pages 199-200.

2. Multiple-choice questions, pages 200-202.

3. Exercises 5-1 and 5-2, page 203.

4. Analysis question, page 204

5. Assessment rubric, page 204.

6. Chapter 5 Index, page 205.

GOING TO THE NET

Access this website http://www.nolo.com/legal-encyclopedia/bookkeeping-accounting-basics-29653.html.

---

[1]If you are having difficulty backing up to USB flash drive, backup to the desktop, then copy the file to a USB flash drive. Refer to Appendix A, Troubleshooting, pages 756-758—Problem Backing Up to USB Drive or Other External Media.

The McGraw-Hill Companies, Inc., *Computer Accounting with Peachtree by Sage Complete Accounting 2012, 16e*

Read the Bookkeeping and Accounting Basics article. (*Hint:* If this article is no longer available, link to another area from the Nolo.com website and write a brief essay—no more than 125 words—describing the link.) Going to the Net website links are on the textbook website at www.mhhe.com/yacht2012; link to Student Edition, select Chapter 5.

1. List the three steps for keeping your small business accounting records.

2. From this website, link to another area.

Multiple Choice Questions: The Online Learning Center includes these questions and the analysis question at www.mhhe.com/yacht2012, select Student Edition, Chapter 5, QA Templates.

_____1.   The inventory system used by PCA is called:

    a. Sum-of-the-years digits.
    b. Double-declining balance.
    c. Straight-line.
    d. Perpetual inventory.
    e. None of the above.

_____2.   A list of all the accounts used by a company showing an identifying number assigned to each account is called:

    a. A chart of accounts.
    b. Case-sensitive letters.
    c. An account number.
    d. A general ledger.
    e. None of the above.

_____3.   The account(s) added to Bellwether's Chart of Accounts in this chapter is:

    a. Account No. 10200, Regular Checking Account.
    b. Account No. 12000, Inventory.
    c. Account No. 10500, Money Market Fund.
    d. a. and c.
    e. All of the above.

_____4. After the March 15, 2012 transfer of funds, the General Ledger Trial Balance shows the following amount in the Money Market Fund account:

    a. $ 4,500.00.
    b. $ 7,500.00.
    c. $62,769.25.
    d. $ 5,004.90.
    e. None of the above.

_____5. On the Maintain Inventory Items window, the Oriole Feeder is which inventory type:

    a. Activity item.
    b. Description only.
    c. Assembly.
    d. Stock item.
    e. None of the above.

_____6. For Stock-Type Inventory Items, PCA tracks the following:

    a. Stock quantities.
    b. Unit prices.
    c. Descriptions.
    d. Cost of goods sold.
    e. All of the above.

_____7. The journal entry to purchase an inventory stock item is:

    a. Debit Accounts Payable/Vendor
       Credit Inventory
    b. Debit Inventory
       Credit Accounts Payable/Vendor
    c. Debit Account Receivable/Customer
       Credit Sales Tax Payable
    d. Debit Product Cost
       Credit Inventory
    e. None of the above.

_____8.   The journal entry or entries for the sale of an Inventory Item are:

a. Debit Accounts Receivable/Customer
    Credit Sales
b. Debit Accounts Receivable/Customer
    Credit Sales
    Credit Sales Tax Payable
    Debit Product Cost
    Credit Inventory
c. Debit Sales-Retail
    Debit Sales Tax Payable
    Credit Accounts Receivable/Customer
    Debit Product Cost
    Credit Inventory
d. Debit Inventory
    Credit Product Cost
e. None of the above.

_____9.   Shows all entries and changes related to the company's data, including actions by specific users.

a. Find transactions.
b. Report groups.
c. Audit trail.
d. Internal control.
e. All of the above.

_____10. The integrated system of people, processes, and procedures that minimize or eliminate business risks, protect assets, ensure reliable accounting, and promote efficient operation is called:

a. Peachtree's find transactions capability.
b. Peachtree's audit trail reports.
c. Internal control.
d. Setting up the administrator for access to all records.
e. None of the above.

Exercise 5-1: Follow the instructions below to complete Exercise 5-1.

1. Start PCA. Open Bellwether Garden Supply.

2. Restore data from the end of Chapter 5. This back up was made on pages 198-199.

3. Journalize and post the following transactions:

    Date   *Transaction Description*

    03/18/12   Transfer $1,200 from the Regular Checking Account to the Payroll Checking Account.

    03/19/12   Purchased two (2) Oriole Feeders from DeJulia Wholesale Suppliers, Invoice No. 94977, $14.

4. Continue with Exercise 5-2.

Exercise 5-2: Follow the instructions below to complete Exercise 5-2.

1. Print the General Ledger Trial Balance.

2. Back up Exercise 5-2. Use **Exercise 5-2** as the file name.

3. Export the General Ledger Trial Balance to Excel. Use **Exercise 5-2_General Ledger Trial Balance.xlsx** as the file name.

4. Save the General Ledger Trial Balance as a PDF file. Use **Exercise 5-2_General Ledger Trial Balance.pdf** as the file name.

    Check your figures:

    Account No. 10200, Regular Checking Account $9,046.52
    Account No. 10300, Payroll Checking Account   10,565.26
    Account No. 11000, Accounts Receivable   175,643.11
    Account No. 20000, Accounts Payable   80,682.01

5. Exit Peachtree.

ANALYSIS QUESTIONS

1. List four ways that Peachtree includes user security and internal control.

2. How is the audit trail associated with user security? Provide an example.

3. How does user security address the purpose of internal control?

ASSESSMENT RUBRIC

Complete the Assessment Rubric online at www.mhhe.com/yacht2012; Student Edition, select Chapter 5, Assessment Rubric link. To review Peachtree's journals, navigation centers, modules, and task windows, complete the blank fields online.

Date	Transaction	Navigation Center/Module	Task Window	Journal Dr./Cr.
3/18	Transfer $1,200 from the Regular Checking Account to the Payroll Checking Account.			
3/19	Purchased two (2) Oriole Feeders from DeJulia Wholesale Suppliers, Invoice No. 94977, $14.			

CHAPTER 5 INDEX

Chapter
6
Job Cost

LEARNING OBJECTIVES

1. Restore data from Exercise 5-2. (This backup was made on page 203.)
2. Learn about PCA's Job Cost system.
3. Set up a job.
4. Coordinate job costs with purchases, sales, and payroll.
5. Display the Job Profitability Report.
6. Make two backups, save one Excel file, and save one PDF file.

This chapter shows how to use PCA's Job Cost system. In Peachtree, you can assign Job ID codes to purchases, sales, and employee hours. In this way, Peachtree tracks how each of these factors impacts job costs. The diagram below illustrates how job costing works with purchases, sales, and payroll.

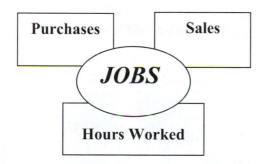

Peachtree's *job costing* feature allows you to track the costs incurred while performing a job. To use job costing, identify the project for which you want to track expenses and income and then determine how much detail is needed.

There are several advantages to using job costing:

* It allows you to track income and expenses for each project the company undertakes. You can create estimates for each job. As you

enter invoices for materials or services used in the job through accounts payable, they can be assigned to a job so actual costs can be compared with job estimates.

- You can exercise greater control over costs and revenues by tracking customer invoices and payments received for each job. You can print reports during a job's progress to find out the total amount spent and net revenues due for each job.

- You can also maintain statistics on various jobs including starting date, completion date, and the progress of each job and view these by printing various job-costing reports.

- If phases or cost codes are used, you can generate reports to display this information, showing whether a job is over or under budget for any phase or task involved. This helps control costs by adjusting one phase or task prior to the job's completion.

Job costing gives you greater insight into all the company's jobs or projects so that you know what you are spending, how long it is taking, and how much profit was made on each job.

The diagram below shows how Peachtree organizes job costing.

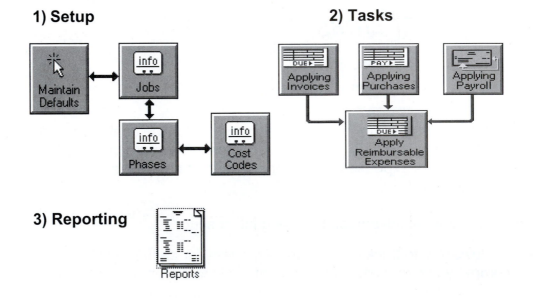

GETTING STARTED

Bellwether Garden Supply has a customer named Franklin Botanical Gardens. Once a Job ID is set up for Franklin Botanical Gardens, you can track supplies and employee hours charged to this customer.

1. Start PCA. Open Bellwether Garden Supply. (If Bellwether Garden Supply is not shown, restore A New Company. Refer to the Read me box on page 29.)

2. Restore your data from the Exercise 5-2 backup. (The Exercise 5-2.ptb backup was made on page 203.)

    a. Insert your USB flash drive. From the Navigation Bar, select | **System** |; click | Restore Now |.

    b. The Select Backup File window appears. Click | Browse |. Go to the Location of your Exercise 5-2.ptb file and select it. Click | Open |, then | Next > |.

    c. The Select Company window appears. The radio button next to An Existing Company is selected. The Company name field shows Bellwether Garden Supply. The Location field shows the default location on the hard drive for Bellwether Garden Supply. Click | Next > |.

    d. The Restore Options window appears. Make sure that the box next to Company Data is *checked*. Click | Next > |.

    e. The Confirmation window appears. Check the From and To fields to make sure they are correct. Click | Finish |. When the Restore Company scale is 100% complete, your data is restored. (*Hint:* The Student Version of Peachtree prompts that company data can be used for 14 months. After that time the data expires. Click | OK |. Bellwether Garden Supply opens.)

💾 To make sure you are starting in the appropriate place in the data (Exercise 5-2.ptb backup) check the General Ledger Trial Balance. A partial trial balance is shown below. The General Ledger Trial Balance was completed in Exercise 5-2, step 1, page 203.

Bellwether Garden Supply
General Ledger Trial Balance
As of Mar 31, 2012

Filter Criteria includes: Report order is by ID. Report is printed in Detail Format.

Account I	Account Description	Debit Amt	Credit Amt
10000	Petty Cash	327.55	
10100	Cash on Hand	1,850.45	
10200	Regular Checking Account	9,046.52	
10300	Payroll Checking Account	10,565.26	
10400	Savings Account	7,500.00	
10500	Money Market Fund	4,500.00	
11000	Accounts Receivable	175,643.11	
11400	Other Receivables	7,681.84	
11500	Allowance for Doubtful Account		5,000.00
12000	Inventory	12,537.81	
14000	Prepaid Expenses	14,221.30	
14100	Employee Advances	3,000.65	
14200	Notes Receivable-Current	11,000.00	
14700	Other Current Assets	120.00	

3. From the Navigation Bar, select  ;

, New Job. The Maintain Jobs window appears.

4. In the Job ID field, type **FRANKLIN** and press **<Enter>**. (*Hint: Peachtree is case sensitive: FRANKLIN is not the same as franklin.*)

5. In the Description field, type **Franklin Botanical Gardens** and press **<Enter>** two times.

6. Type **3/3/12** in the Start Date field. Press **<Enter>** go to the For Customer field. (*Hint:* Or, click on the For Customer field).

7. In the For Customer field, select FRANKLIN.

8. Click on the Job Type field. Select LAND. Compare your Maintain Jobs window to the one shown below.

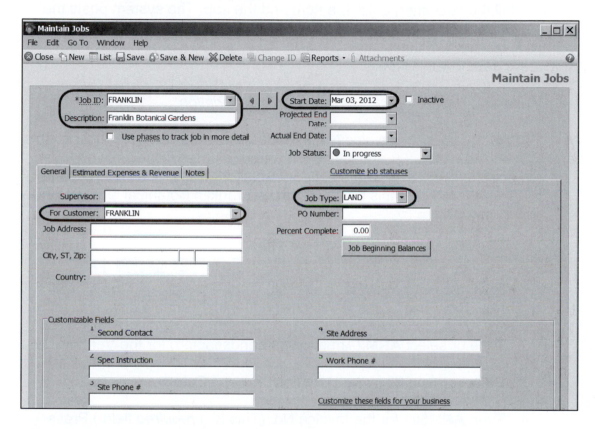

9. Save this job, then close the Maintain Jobs window to return to the Customers & Sales Navigation Center.

JOB COSTING AND PURCHASING: Purchasing Inventory Items for Jobs

This new job has some special circumstances; namely, Franklin Botanical Gardens has a new building overlooking a park. In the park, there are several picnic tables. According to the terms of the contract with Franklin Botanical Gardens, Bellwether Garden Supply purchases and provides a special wood treatment to the picnic benches.

When inventory items are purchased for jobs, you need to do the following:

➢ Record the purchase directly as a job expense. You could indicate a Non-stock or a Description only Inventory Item but not a Stock Item.

➢ Record the purchase into Inventory without entering a Job. When you bill the customer, enter the Item and the Job. The system posts the price as Job revenue and the Cost of Goods Sold as Job Expense.

Let's see how this works.

Date	Transaction Description
3/20/12	Invoice No. ARM501 was received from Armstrong's Landscaping for the purchase of special wood treatment, $85; terms 2% 10, Net 30 Days. Apply this purchase to the Franklin Botanical Gardens job.

1. From the Navigation Bar, select 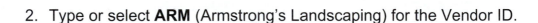; New Bill. The Purchases/Receive Inventory window displays.

2. Type or select **ARM** (Armstrong's Landscaping) for the Vendor ID.

3. Select or type **20** in the Date field. Press **<Enter>**.

4. Type **ARM501** for the Invoice No. (This is a *required* field.) Press **<Enter>**.

5. The Apply to Purchases tab is selected. Type **1** in the Quantity field and press **<Enter>** two times.

6. In the Description field, type **Special wood treatment** and press **<Enter>** two times.

7. Account No. 57200, Materials Cost, is the default account displayed in the GL Account field. Your cursor is in the Unit Price field. Type **85** and press **<Enter>** two times.

8. Type or select **FRANKLIN**, the new Job, in the Job field.

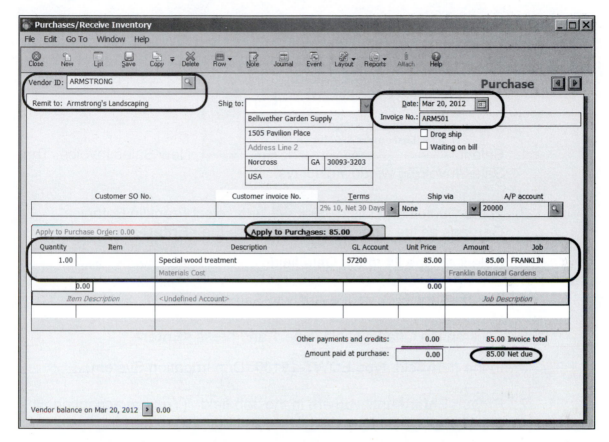

If your GL Account field and A/P Account field are *not* displayed on the Purchases/Receive Inventory window, see the instructions on page 18, step 1c, Hide General Ledger Accounts area.

9. Click  to post this purchase. Close the Purchases/Receive Inventory window to return to the Vendors & Purchases Navigation Center.

JOB COSTING AND SALES

Follow these steps to invoice Franklin Botanical Gardens for a drip irrigation system and apply this sale to Franklin Botanical Gardens, Job ID, FRANKLIN.

Date   *Transaction Description*

3/21/12   Bellwether Garden Supply sold one Bell-Gro Home
                           Irrigation System, Item No. EQWT-15100, to Franklin
                           Botanical Gardens on account, $129.99, plus $9.10
                           sales tax, total $139.09; terms 2% 10, Net 30 Days.

1. Select [Customers & Sales] ; [Sales Invoices] , New Sales Invoice. The
    Sales/Invoicing window displays.

2. In the Customer ID field, click [icon] and select Franklin Botanical
    Gardens as the Customer. Then, press the **<Enter>** key.

3. Select or type **21** in the Date field.

4. If necessary, click on the Apply to Sales tab.

5. Click on the Quantity field, type **1** and press **<Enter>**.

6. In the Item field, type **EQWT-15100** (Drip Irrigation System).

7. Press **<Enter>** until you are in the Job field. (You are accepting all
    of the displayed information when you do this.)

8. Type or select **FRANKLIN**, the Job ID for Franklin Botanical Gardens.

    Compare your Sales/Invoicing window with the one shown on the next
    page.

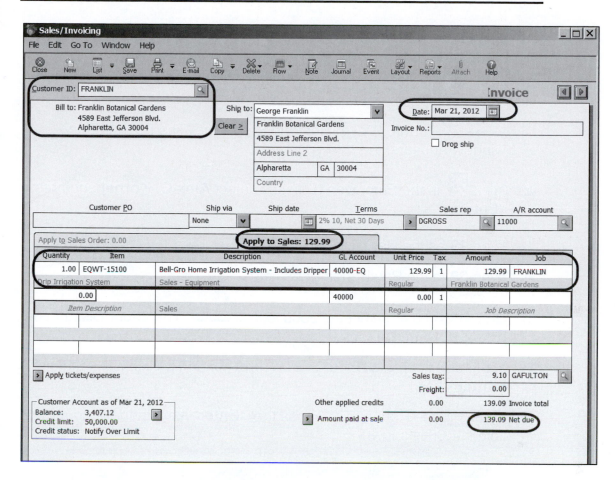

If your GL Account field and A/R Account field are *not* displayed on the Sales/Invoicing window, see the instructions on page 18, 1c, Hide General Ledger Accounts area.

9. Click [Save] to post this invoice. Close the Sales/Invoicing window to return to the Customers & Sales Navigation Center.

JOB COST AND PAYROLL

In the example that follows, one employee applied the special wood treatment to the picnic tables at Franklin Botanical Gardens. The employee spent one hour applying the wood treatment.

1. From the Navigation Bar, select  ;

   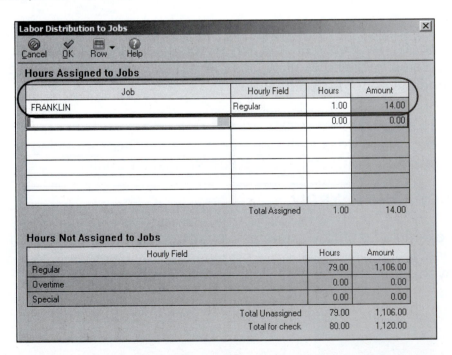
   , Enter Payroll for One Employee. The Payroll Entry window appears.

2. Click 🔍 in the Employee ID field. Select **Alex C. Kornel** and press **<Enter>**.

3. Type **29** as the Date. Press **<Enter>** two times.

4. Type **29** in the Pay Period Ends field.

5. On the icon bar, select the Jobs icon [Jobs] . The Labor Distribution to Jobs window appears.

6. In the Job field, click on the down arrow and FRANKLIN. Press the **<Enter>** key.

7. Type **1** in the Hours field. Press the **<Enter>** key. In the Amount field, 14.00 is shown.

Labor Distribution to Jobs

Cancel | OK | Row | Help

Hours Assigned to Jobs

Job	Hourly Field	Hours	Amount
FRANKLIN	Regular	1.00	14.00
		0.00	0.00
	Total Assigned	1.00	14.00

Hours Not Assigned to Jobs

Hourly Field	Hours	Amount
Regular	79.00	1,106.00
Overtime	0.00	0.00
Special	0.00	0.00
Total Unassigned	79.00	1,106.00
Total for check	80.00	1,120.00

8. Click [✓ OK] . You are returned to the Payroll Entry window.

9. Click [💾 Save] to post the paycheck. Close the Payroll Entry window to return to the Employees & Payroll window.

JOB COST REPORTS

Job cost reports tell you how jobs are progressing. Follow these steps to look at Job Cost Reports.

1. From the menu bar, select Reports & Forms; Jobs. The Select a Report or Form window displays.

2. In the Job Reports: Project Information list, double-click Job Profitability Report. The Job Profitability Report appears.

3. Scroll down to FRANKLIN.

FRANKLIN		40000-EQ	129.99			
		50000-EQ		59.95		
		57200		85.00		
		77500		14.00		
			129.99	158.95		
FRANKLIN	Total		129.99	158.95	-28.96	-22.28

The report breaks down each job according to what was spent or earned for each affected general ledger account. It also shows the profit or loss for each job.

4. Close the Job Profitability Report window. Close the Select a Report or Form window to return to the Employees & Payroll Navigation Center.

BACKING UP CHAPTER 6 DATA

Follow these steps to back up Chapter 6 data:

1. If necessary, insert your USB flash drive. From System Navigation Center, link to | Back Up Now |. Make sure that the box next to Include company name in the backup file name is *unchecked*.

2. Click | Back Up |.

3. In the Save in field, select the appropriate drive letter for your USB drive.[1] (*Or,* save to the hard-drive default location or other location.) Type **Chapter 6** in the File name field.

4. Click | Save |.

5. When the window prompts This company backup will require approximately 1 diskette, click | OK |. When the window prompts Please insert the first disk, click | OK |. When the Back Up Company scale is 100% complete, you have successfully backed up to the current point in Chapter 6. (Step 5 will differ slightly if you are backing up to the default or other hard-drive location.)

SUMMARY AND REVIEW

Complete the following end-of-chapter activities:

1. Going to the net, page 219.

2. Short-answer questions, pages 219-220.

3. Exercises 6-1 and 6-2, pages 220-221.

4. Analysis question, page 221.

---

[1]If you are having difficulty backing up to USB flash drive, backup to the desktop, then copy the file to a USB flash drive. Refer to Appendix A, Troubleshooting, pages 756-758—Problem Backing Up to USB Drive or Other External Media.

5. Assessment rubric, pages 221-222.

6. Chapter 6 Index, page 223.

GOING TO THE NET

Access the Sage website at www.sage.com. Link to Sage Worldwide. The URL is http://www.sage.com/ourbusiness/sageworldwide. Select North America (*or,* other location). Link to the USA. (Going to the Net links are on the textbook website at www.mhhe.com/yacht2012; link to Student Edition, select Chapter 6.)

1. In North America, how many small and medium sized businesses does Sage Software provide business management software to?
2. List Sage Software's brands.
3. Select the Our Business tab. Read the About Us information. Link to Our Products and Services. The URL is http://www.sage.com/ourbusiness/aboutus/ourproductsservices. How does Sage classify its products?

Short-Answer Questions: The Online Learning Center includes these questions and the analysis question at www.mhhe.com/yacht2012, select Student Edition, Chapter 6, QA Templates.

1. Draw the diagram that shows how the job cost system works with purchases, sales, and payroll.

2. What is the description of the Franklin Botanical Gardens job?

3. What is the customer ID for Franklin Botanical Gardens?

4. How much does Franklin Botanical Gardens owe for the one Bel-Gro Home Irrigation System (include the sales tax)?

5. What is the GL account (name and number) for the purchase of the wood treatment?

6. What is the name of the report that tells you about Bellwether's jobs?

7. When inventory items are purchased for jobs, what do you need to do?

8. How many hour(s) did Alex C. Kornel work on the Franklin Botanical Gardens job?

9. Summarize the advantage to using Peachtree's job costing feature.

10. What does the Job Profitability report show?

Exercise 6-1: Follow the instructions below to complete Exercise 6-1.

1. Start PCA. Open Bellwether Garden Supply.

2. Restore data from the end of Chapter 6. This backup was made on page 218.

3. Journalize and post the following transactions:

Date	Transaction Description
03/26/12	Sold two Bel-Gro Impulse Sprinklers (EQWT-15160) to Franklin Botanical Gardens, $64.18 (includes sales tax); terms 2% 10, Net 30 Days; Job ID Franklin Botanical Gardens.
03/26/12	Invoice No. ARM967 was received from Armstrong's Landscaping for the purchase of one container of special wood treatment for $85; terms 2% 10, Net 30 Days; Job ID Franklin Botanical Gardens. (Debit Materials Cost.)
03/29/12	Amanda W. Chester worked one hour on the Franklin Botanical Gardens job. Apply her paycheck to this job.

4. Continue with Exercise 6-2.

Exercise 6-2: Follow the instructions below to complete Exercise 6-2.

1. Print a Job Profitability Report.

2. Back up Exercise 6-2. Use **Exercise 6-2** as the file name.

> **Read Me**
> This backup is important. If you are using external media; for example, a USB drive, do *not* delete the Exercise 6-2.ptb file. You restore the Exercise 6-2.ptb backup file to complete work in Part 4, Chapters 16, 17, and 18.

3. Export the Job Profitability Report to Excel. Use **Exercise 6-2_Job Profitability Report.xlsx** as the file name.

4. Save the Job Profitability Repot as a PDF file. Use **Exercise 6-2_Job Profitability Report.pdf** as the file name.

Check Your Figures: Job Profitability Report, FRANKLIN

Actual Revenue, $189.97
Actual Expenses, $281.85
Profit dollars, -$91.88
Profit percentage, -48.37

ANALYSIS QUESTION

Explain the interrelations of jobs, purchases, sales and payroll.

ASSESSMENT RUBRIC

Complete the Assessment Rubric online at www.mhhe.com/yacht2012; Student Edition, select Chapter 6, Assessment Rubric link. To review Peachtree's journals, navigation centers, modules, and task windows, complete the blank fields online.

Date	Transaction	Navigation Center/Module	Task Window	Journal Dr./Cr.
3/26	Sold two Bel-Grow Impulse Sprinklers (EQWT-15160) to Franklin Botanical Gardens, $64.18 (includes sales tax); terms 2% 10, Net 30 days; Job ID Franklin Botanical Gardens.			

3/26	Invoice No. ARM967 was received from Armstrong's Landscaping for the purchase of special wood treatment, $85; terms 2% 10, Net 30 Days. Apply this purchase to the Franklin Botanical Gardens jobs.			
3/29	Amanda W. Chester worked one hour on the Franklin Botanical Gardens job. Apply her paycheck to this job.			

CHAPTER 6 INDEX

Chapter

7

Financial Statements

LEARNING OBJECTIVES

1. Restore data from Exercise 6-2. This backup was made on page 220.
2. Explore Peachtree's Help feature.
3. Print the financial statements.
4. Use drill down to go from the income statement to the general ledger, then to the original entry window.
5. Complete Bellwether Garden Supply project online at www.mhhe.com/yacht2012, Student Edition link.
6. Make an optional backup of Chapter 7, save one Excel file, and save six PDF files. (The Exercise 6-2.ptb backup, page 220, includes the data needed for Chapter 7.)

FINANCIAL STATEMENTS

In Chapters 1 through 6, you explored the sample company, Bellwether Garden Supply. You learned how PCA's user interface works and how to navigate the software. In Chapters 1 through 6, you also journalized and posted various types of transactions. Beginning with Chapter 9, you learn how to use these features to set up service businesses from scratch.

In Chapter 7, you learn about PCA's financial statements. Once journal entries have been recorded and posted, Peachtree automatically calculates financial statements. Since business managers and owners have the primary responsibility for the organization, they depend on accounting information in the form of financial statements to understand what is happening.

All the financial statements printed by PCA reflect the current month and year-to-date amounts.

In this chapter, six financial statements are printed.

1. Balance Sheet.

2. Gross Profit by Departments.

3. Income Statement.

4. Statement of Cash Flow.

5. Statement of Retained Earnings.

6. Statement of Changes in Financial Position (SCFP). Even though current accounting standards do not require a SCFP, Peachtree includes it. (Refer to Read Me on page 240.)

Balance Sheet

A balance sheet is a list of assets, liabilities, and capital of a business entity as of a specific date, such as the last day of an accounting period or the last day of the year.

Each financial statement may be modified to fit your needs. PCA includes a Design icon for that purpose. Later in this chapter, you learn about how to use PCA's Help feature to design financial statements. In Chapter 16, Customizing Forms, you learn more about modifying PCA's standard forms.

Gross Profit by Departments

A departmentalized accounting system provides information that management can use to evaluate the profitability or cost effectiveness of a department's activities. The Gross Profit by Departments financial statement is a custom report designed for Bellwether that details each department's year-to-date gross profit as of the current month.

Some of Bellwether's chart of account numbers have a dash, then an AV or a BK. For example, Account No. 40000-AV, Sales - Aviary; and Account No. 40000-BK, Sales - Books show the departmental designation.

PCA includes a feature called masking which allows organization of the business by department. Then, custom forms can be designed to

accommodate a departmentalized accounting system. The wrench [⬜] to the left of some of Bellwether's financial statements indicates custom-designed forms.

Income Statement

The income statement is a summary of the revenues and expenses a company accrues over a period of time, such as an accounting period or a year. Only revenue and expense accounts are displayed on the income statement. **Net income** is computed by subtracting total expenses from total revenues. Net income results when revenues exceed expenses. An excess of expenses over revenues results in a **net loss**. Bellwether's net loss for the current month, March 1 through March 31, 2012, is $2,625.61. A net loss is indicated on the income statement with parenthesis ($2,625.61). Bellwether's year-to-date net income is $25,476.82. On page 237, the Income Statement is shown.

In addition to dollar figures, the income statement also includes percentage-of-revenue columns for the current month and year to date. The percentages shown for each expense, total expenses, and net income (or net loss) indicate the relationship of each item to total revenues.

Statement of Cash Flow

The cash flow from operations is roughly the same as income from operations plus depreciation, depletion, and adjusted for any other operating transactions that had no effect on cash during the period. The statement of cash flow also reports cash transactions associated with the purchase or sale of fixed assets (Investing Activities) and cash paid to or received from creditors and owners (Financing Activities).

The statement of cash flow provides the answers to three questions:

1. Where did cash receipts come from?

2. What were cash payments used for?

3. What was the overall change in cash?

Statement of Retained Earnings

The Statement of Retained Earnings shows beginning and ending retained earnings amounts, adjustments made to retained earnings within the report period, and the detail for all Equity-gets closed accounts. The retained earnings balance is the cumulative, lifetime earnings of the company less its cumulative losses and dividends.

Statement of Changes in Financial Position

The statement of changes in financial position describes changes in a company's financial position that may not be obvious from other financial statements. The statement of changes shows the change in working capital, assets, and liabilities for a given period of time. (Peachtree includes this report. For more information, refer to Read me, page 240.)

Interrelationship of Financial Statements

The financial statements work together. The net income (or net loss) from the income statement is reported on the balance sheet's capital section. The net income or net loss is used to update the balance sheet's capital amount: Capital Beginning of the Year – Net Loss (or + Net Income) = Total Capital.

On the statement of retained earnings, the Ending Retained Earnings balance is $214,514.42. On the balance sheet, if you add the net income $25,476.82 to the balance sheet's retained earnings amount, $189,037.60, the result is $214,514.42. This amount, $214,514.42, is the same as the Ending Retained Earnings balance on the Statement of Retained Earnings.

The total of all the cash accounts on the Balance Sheet (Petty Cash, Cash on Hand, Regular Checking Account, Payroll Checking Account, Savings Account, and Money-Market Fund) is shown as the Cash Balance at End of Period on the statement of cash flow, $32,060.92. The statement of cash flow uses information from both the balance sheet and income statement.

The statement of changes in financial position uses information from the income statement and balance sheet. The net income is shown on the income statement. Current assets and current liabilities are derived from the balance sheet.

No single financial statement tells the entire story. The income statement indicates how much revenue a business has earned during a specific period of time, but it says nothing about how much of that amount has or has not been received in cash. For information about cash and accounts receivable, we have to look at the balance sheet, statement of cash flow, and statement of changes in financial position.

GETTING STARTED

1. If necessary, start PCA. Open the sample company, Bellwether Garden Supply. (If Bellwether Garden Supply is not shown, restore A New Company. Refer to Read me, page 29.)

2. If necessary, follow steps a. through e. to restore your data from the Exercise 6-2 back up. (The Exercise 6-2.ptb backup was made on page 220.)

   a. Insert your USB flash drive. From the Navigation Bar, select

      | System |; click | Restore Now |.

   b. The Select Backup File window appears. Click | Browse |. Go to the Location of your Exercise 6-2.ptb file and select it. Click | Open |, then | Next > |.

   c. The Select Company window appears. The radio button is next to An Existing Company. The Company name field shows Bellwether Garden Supply. The Location field shows the default location on the hard drive for Bellwether Garden Supply. Click | Next > |.

   d. The Restore Options window appears. Make sure that the box next to Company Data is *checked*. Click | Next > |.

   e. The Confirmation window appears. Check the From and To fields to make sure they are correct. Click | Finish |. When the Restore Company scale is 100% complete, your data is restored. (*Hint:* The Student Version of Peachtree prompts that company data can be used for 14 months. After that time the data expires. Click | OK |. Bellwether Garden Supply opens.)

To make sure you are starting in the appropriate place in the data (Exercise 6-2.ptb backup) check the Job Profitability Report. The results for Franklin Botanical Gardens are shown below.

FRANKLIN		40000-EQ	129.99			
			59.98			
		50000-EQ		59.95		
				23.90		
		57200		85.00		
				85.00		
		77500		14.00		
				14.00		
			189.97	281.85		
FRANKLIN	Total		189.97	281.85	-91.88	-48.37

USING PEACHTREE'S HELP FEATURE

In Chapter 5 on pages 166-167 you used PCA's Help feature to access the sample company's chart of accounts. Later in Chapter 5, on pages 192-194, you used Peachtree's Help feature to learn about security and internal controls. In this chapter, you learn how to access Peachtree's Help feature to learn more about financial statements.

Follow these steps to learn more about Help:

1. From the menu bar, click Help; Peachtree Accounting Help. The Peachtree Help window displays. If necessary, click on the Index tab.

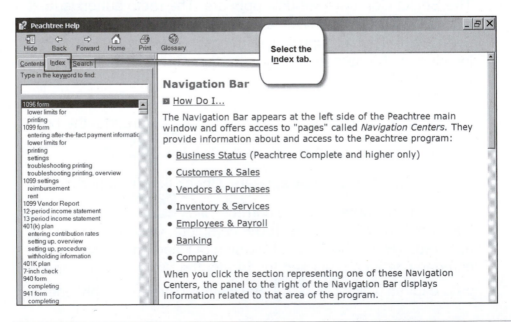

2. Type **balance sheet** in the Type in keyword to find field. Observe that Balance Sheet is highlighted.

3. Click [Display]. Read the information on the right pane.

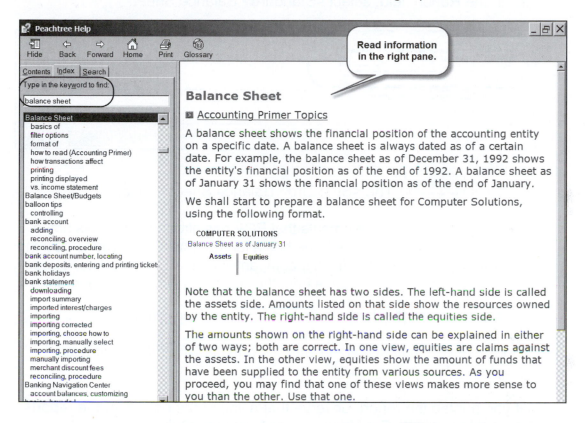

4. If necessary, on the Peachtree Help title bar click ▣ to enlarge the Peachtree Help window, *or* scroll down. Link to How Transactions Affect the Balance Sheet. Read the information. From this page you can link to Accounting Primer Topics, or you can scroll down and link to other areas.

5. Click ☒ on the Peachtree Help title bar to close the window.

DISPLAYING THE FINANCIAL STATEMENTS

You have already used the Reports & Forms menu to print PCA reports. In the steps that follow you use the Business Status Navigation Center to print financial statements.

---

1. From the Navigation Bar, click [Business Status]. In the Find a Report area's Category field, select Financial Statements.

2. In the Report field, select <Standard> Balance Sheet.

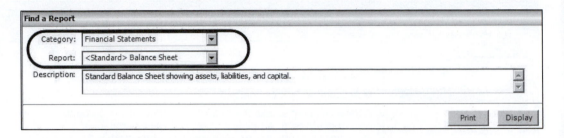

3. Click [Display]. The <Standard> Balance Sheet appears.

    Standard refers to statements that PCA has already set up. As noted in the Help window, Peachtree has a feature that allows you to design financial statements to fit your company's needs. For example, if you select Financial Statements from the Reports & Forms menu, reports

    with a wrench [ ] next to them are customized forms.

    Compare your balance sheet with the one shown on the next two pages.

    If you printed the report, observe that a line at the bottom of the reports says "Unaudited – For Management Purposes Only."

Bellwether Garden Supply
Balance Sheet
March 31, 2012

ASSETS

Current Assets		
Petty Cash	$ 327.55	
Cash on Hand	1,850.45	
Regular Checking Account	9,046.52	
Payroll Checking Account	8,836.40	
Savings Account	7,500.00	
Money Market Fund	4,500.00	
Accounts Receivable	175,846.38	
Other Receivables	7,681.84	
Allowance for Doubtful Account	(5,000.00)	
Inventory	12,453.96	
Prepaid Expenses	14,221.30	
Employee Advances	3,000.65	
Notes Receivable-Current	11,000.00	
Other Current Assets	120.00	
Total Current Assets		251,385.05
Property and Equipment		
Furniture and Fixtures	62,769.25	
Equipment	38,738.33	
Vehicles	86,273.40	
Other Depreciable Property	6,200.96	
Buildings	185,500.00	
Building Improvements	26,500.00	
Accum. Depreciation-Furniture	(54,680.57)	
Accum. Depreciation-Equipment	(33,138.11)	
Accum. Depreciation-Vehicles	(51,585.26)	
Accum. Depreciation-Other	(3,788.84)	
Accum. Depreciation-Buildings	(34,483.97)	
Accum. Depreciation-Bldg Imp	(4,926.28)	
Total Property and Equipment		223,378.91
Other Assets		
Deposits	15,000.00	
Organization Costs	4,995.10	
Accum Amortiz - Organiz Costs	(2,000.00)	
Notes Receivable- Noncurrent	5,004.90	
Other Noncurrent Assets	3,333.00	
Total Other Assets		26,333.00
Total Assets	$	501,096.96

LIABILITIES AND CAPITAL

Current Liabilities		
Accounts Payable	$ 80,852.01	
Accrued Expenses	3,022.55	
Sales Tax Payable	18,073.34	
Wages Payable	2,320.30	
401 K Deductions Payable	2,579.92	
Health Insurance Payable	(530.64)	
Federal Payroll Taxes Payable	42,381.73	

Unaudited - For Management Purposes Only

Bellwether Garden Supply
Balance Sheet
March 31, 2012

FUTA Tax Payable	258.20	
State Payroll Taxes Payable	6,946.31	
SUTA Tax Payable	658.67	
Local Payroll Taxes Payable	113.25	
Income Taxes Payable	11,045.75	
Other Taxes Payable	2,640.15	
Current Portion Long-Term Debt	5,167.00	
Contracts Payable- Current	2,000.00	
Other Current Liabilities	54.00	
Total Current Liabilities		177,582.54
Long-Term Liabilities		
Notes Payable-Noncurrent	4,000.00	
Total Long-Term Liabilities		4,000.00
Total Liabilities		181,582.54
Capital		
Common Stock	5,000.00	
Paid-in Capital	100,000.00	
Retained Earnings	189,037.60	
Net Income	25,476.82	
Total Capital		319,514.42
Total Liabilities & Capital	$	501,096.96

Unaudited - For Management Purposes Only

Follow these steps to display the Gross Profit by Departments financial statement for the current period.

1. Close the Balance Sheet. In the Find a Report area of the Business Status Navigation Center, the Category field shows Financial Statements. In the Report field, select Gross Profit by Departments.

2. Click [Display]. The Departmental Gross Profit Totals report appears. Compare yours with the one shown on the next page.

Bellwether Garden Supply
Departmental Gross Profit Totals
Year To Date Totals For the Month Ending March 31, 2012

	Aviary		Books		Equipment	
Revenues						
Sales	$ 51,697.86	100.00	$ 7,293.10	100.00	60,392.26	100.00
Total Revenues	51,697.86	100.00	7,293.10	100.00	60,392.26	100.00
Cost of Sales						
Product Cost - Aviary	20,954.25	40.53	0.00	0.00	0.00	0.00
Product Cost - Books	0.00	0.00	2,361.37	32.38	0.00	0.00
Product Cost - Equipment	0.00	0.00	0.00	0.00	24,238.80	40.14
Total Cost of Sales	20,954.25	40.53	2,361.37	32.38	24,238.80	40.14
Gross Profit	30,743.61	59.47	4,931.73	67.62	36,153.46	59.86

The Departmental Gross Profit Totals report lists the departmental gross profit totals for the following departments: Aviary, Books, and Equipment.

3. Close the Departmental Gross Profit Totals window.

Departmental Masking

The Departmental Gross Profit report shown above is separated into three departments: Aviary, Books, and Equipment. A feature included in Peachtree called **masking** allows you to departmentalize financial statements. Masking is the ability to limit information on the report to a single division, department, location, or type code.

For masking, account numbers could be set up like this.

When you print or display a report, you can filter the report using **wildcard** characters. In this example, you would type *****01 to include all departments ending in 01. You would type ****M** to show only main branch numbers on the report. You could type 10***** to find all asset-type accounts for all branches and departments (assuming your asset accounts all begin with 10).

Wildcards make it easy to select a range of account numbers. In Peachtree, the only valid wildcard character is an asterisk. An asterisk represents any number of characters.

You can filter or mask the information that appears on certain general ledger reports. This is done by the use of 15 characters that are allowed in the Account ID field of your general ledger accounts. To see the account masking option, do this.

1. Select Reports & Forms.
2. Select General Ledger.
3. Highlight the Chart of Accounts report.
4. On the toolbar, click [Options].
5. In the Select a filter area, highlight Department Mask.
6. In the Select an option area, select Use wildcards. Type **10*****.**

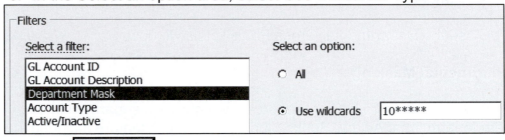

7. Click [OK]. The Chart of Accounts appears with account numbers starting with 10.
8. Close the Chart of Accounts and the Select a Report or Form window.

Bellwether Garden Supply masks departments by adding a suffix for the department name—AV for Aviary, BK for Books, etc.

Follow these steps to display the income statement:

1. In the Find a Report area of the Business Status Navigation Center, the Category field shows Financial Statements. In the Report field, select <Standard> Income Stmnt.

2. Click [Display]. When the Income Statement displays, click [Options], then uncheck Show Zero Amounts; [OK].

Bellwether Garden Supply
Income Statement
For the Three Months Ending March 31, 2012

		Current Month			Year to Date	
Revenues						
Sales	$	295.00	0.33	$	295.00	0.10
Sales - Aviary		7,172.71	8.09		51,697.86	18.38
Sales - Books		149.75	0.17		7,293.10	2.59
Sales - Equipment		18,038.77	20.33		60,392.26	21.47
Sales - Food/Fert		1,006.96	1.14		5,204.15	1.85
Sales - Hand Tools		729.67	0.82		7,058.12	2.51
Sales - Landscape Services		17,467.43	19.69		26,975.53	9.59
Sales - Miscellaneous		0.00	0.00		45.00	0.02
Sales - Nursery		33,795.03	38.10		67,637.11	24.04
Sales - Pots		7,919.31	8.93		11,483.74	4.08
Sales - Seeds		1,457.43	1.64		8,661.39	3.08
Sales - Soil		724.92	0.82		9,152.45	3.25
Other Income		100.00	0.11		25,600.00	9.10
Sales Discounts		(145.72)	(0.16)		(155.62)	(0.06)
Total Revenues		88,711.26	100.00		281,340.09	100.00
Cost of Sales						
Product Cost		(68.50)	(0.08)		(68.50)	(0.02)
Product Cost - Aviary		2,210.60	2.49		20,954.25	7.45
Product Cost - Books		14.27	0.02		2,361.37	0.84
Product Cost - Equipment		7,482.30	8.43		24,238.80	8.62
Product Cost - Food/Fert		398.80	0.45		2,060.04	0.73
Product Cost - Hand Tools		287.15	0.32		2,813.85	1.00
Product Cost - Pots		3,148.60	3.55		3,423.60	1.22
Product Cost - Seeds		584.45	0.66		3,450.65	1.23
Product Cost - Soil		310.72	0.35		4,075.97	1.45
Direct Labor - Nursery		1,750.00	1.97		3,062.50	1.09
Materials Cost		1,567.45	1.77		1,567.45	0.56
Materials Cost - Nursery		5,438.40	6.13		9,668.50	3.44
Subcontractors - Landscaping		335.50	0.38		335.50	0.12
Total Cost of Sales		23,459.74	26.45		77,943.98	27.70
Gross Profit		65,251.52	73.55		203,396.11	72.30
Expenses						
Freight		0.00	0.00		50.00	0.02
Advertising Expense		1,325.00	1.49		1,325.00	0.47
Auto Expenses		274.56	0.31		274.56	0.10
Bad Debt Expense		1,341.09	1.51		1,341.09	0.48
Bank Charges		18.00	0.02		18.00	0.01
Depreciation Expense		2,761.30	3.11		8,394.00	2.98
Legal and Professional Expense		150.00	0.17		510.00	0.18
Licenses Expense		150.00	0.17		150.00	0.05
Maintenance Expense		75.00	0.08		75.00	0.03
Office Expense		534.64	0.60		534.64	0.19
Payroll Tax Exp		5,854.46	6.60		16,115.88	5.73
Rent or Lease Expense		550.00	0.62		1,100.00	0.39
Repairs Expense		125.00	0.14		3,694.00	1.31
Supplies Expense		2,873.42	3.24		2,873.42	1.02
Utilities Expense		303.45	0.34		303.45	0.11
Wages Expense		51,086.42	57.59		140,705.46	50.01
Other Expense		464.90	0.52		464.90	0.17
Purchase Disc- Expense Items		(10.11)	(0.01)		(10.11)	0.00
Total Expenses		67,877.13	76.51		177,919.29	63.24
Net Income	$	(2,625.61)	(2.96)	$	25,476.82	9.06

For Management Purposes Only

Drill Down from the Income Statement to Original Entry

Follow these steps to follow an account balance from the income statement, to the general ledger, then to the original entry window. This is called drill down.

1. The income statement should be displayed. Place your cursor over 7,172.71, Sales – Aviary

   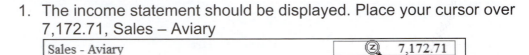

   Observe that the cursor becomes a magnifying glass icon with a Z in the middle. (Z is an abbreviation for zoom). Double-click with your left mouse button.

2. The General Ledger Account 40000-AV, Sales - Aviary, appears. From the general ledger you can drill down to the Receipts window. For example, double click on the 3/5/12 Cash Receipts Journal (CRJ) entry for $79.96.

3/5/12	CASH030503	CRJ	Retail (Cash) Sales - Item: AVRY-101	79.96

3. This takes you to the Receipts window. The original entry for 4 Thistle Bird Seed Mix-6 lb. (AVRY-10140) is shown (19.99 x 4 = 79.96). Close the Receipts window to go back to the General Ledger Account No. 40000-AV.

4. Drill down from one of the Sales Journal (SJ) entries. The Sales/Invoicing window appears.

5. When you are through using drill down, close the Sales/Invoicing window, General Ledger, and Income Statement windows to return to the Select a Report or Form window.

Follow these steps to display the Statement of Cash Flow.

1. In the Find a Report area of the Business Status Navigation Center, the Category field shows Financial Statements. In the Report field, select <Standard> Cash Flow.

2. Click **Display**. When the Statement of Cash Flow displays, click **Options**, uncheck Show Zero Amounts; **OK**. If printed, observe that the bottom of the report says "Unaudited - For Internal Use Only."

Bellwether Garden Supply
Statement of Cash Flow
For the three Months Ended March 31, 2012

	Current Month	Year to Date
Cash Flows from operating activities		
Net Income	$ (2,625.61) $	25,476.82
Adjustments to reconcile net income to net cash provided by operating activities		
Accum. Depreciation-Furniture	420.80	1,262.40
Accum. Depreciation-Equipment	385.05	1,265.25
Accum. Depreciation-Vehicles	1,437.89	4,313.67
Accum. Depreciation-Other	64.57	193.71
Accum. Depreciation-Buildings	396.37	1,189.11
Accum. Depreciation-Bldg Imp	56.63	169.87
Accounts Receivable	(10,905.71)	(172,747.94)
Other Receivables	0.00	(3,672.24)
Inventory	13,582.87	6,144.23
Accounts Payable	10,497.38	76,949.26
Sales Tax Payable	4,375.97	15,612.79
401 K Deductions Payable	825.32	2,135.22
Health Insurance Payable	(530.64)	(530.64)
Federal Payroll Taxes Payable	14,617.04	40,794.88
State Payroll Taxes Payable	2,138.64	5,960.98
Other Taxes Payable	50.00	50.00
Other Current Liabilities	150.00	150.00
Total Adjustments	37,562.18	(20,759.45)
Net Cash provided by Operations	34,936.57	4,717.37
Cash Flows from investing activities		
Used For		
Net cash used in investing	0.00	0.00
Cash Flows from financing activities		
Proceeds From		
Used For		
Net cash used in financing	0.00	0.00
Net increase <decrease> in cash	$ 34,936.57 $	4,717.37
Summary		
Cash Balance at End of Period	$ 32,060.92 $	32,060.92
Cash Balance at Beg of Period	2,875.54	(27,343.66)
Net Increase <Decrease> in Cash	$ 34,936.46 $	4,717.26

Unaudited - For Internal Use Only.

4. Close the Statement of Cash Flow.

Follow these steps to display the Statement of Retained Earnings:

1. In the Report field, select <Standard> Retained Earnings.

2. Click Display . When the Statement of Cash Flow displays, click Options, uncheck Show Zero Amounts; OK . The Statement of Retained Earnings appears.

Bellwether Garden Supply
Statement of Retained Earnings
For the Three Months Ending March 31, 2012

Beginning Retained Earnings	$	189,037.60
Adjustments To Date		0.00
Net Income		25,476.82
Subtotal		214,514.42
Ending Retained Earnings	$	214,514.42

For Management Purposes Only

---

3. Close the Statement of Retained Earnings.

Follow the steps on the next page to print the Statement of Changes in Financial Position.

 Read Me: Statement of Changes in Financial Position

Peachtree includes the Statement of Changes in Financial Position even though current accounting standards require that a statement of cash flow is needed as part of a full set of financial statements in place of a statement of changes in financial position.

---

1. In the Report field, select <Standard> Stmnt Changes, [Display].
   Select the option to uncheck Show Zero amounts.

Bellwether Garden Supply
Statement of Changes in Financial Position
For the three months ended March 31, 2012

	Current Month	Year To Date
Sources of Working Capital		
Net Income	$ (2,625.61)	$ 25,476.82
Add back items not requiring working capital		
Accum. Depreciation-Furniture	420.76	1,262.36
Accum. Depreciation-Equipment	384.99	1,265.19
Accum. Depreciation-Vehicles	1,437.89	4,313.67
Accum. Depreciation-Other	64.57	193.71
Accum. Depreciation-Buildings	396.36	1,189.10
Accum. Depreciation-Bldg Imp	56.63	169.87
Working capital from operations	135.59	33,870.72
Other sources		
Total sources	135.59	33,870.72
Uses of working capital		
Total uses	0.00	0.00
Net change	$ 135.59	$ 33,870.72
Analysis of componants of changes		
Increase <Decrease> in Current Assets		
Petty Cash	$ 227.55	$ 227.55
Regular Checking Account	(631.21)	(2,280.03)
Payroll Checking Account	30,840.12	2,269.74
Money Market Fund	4,500.00	4,500.00
Accounts Receivable	10,905.71	172,747.94
Other Receivables	0.00	3,672.24
Inventory	(13,582.87)	(6,144.23)
<Increase> Decrease in Current Liabilities		
Accounts Payable	(10,497.38)	(76,949.26)
Sales Tax Payable	(4,375.97)	(15,612.79)
401 K Deductions Payable	(825.32)	(2,135.22)
Health Insurance Payable	530.64	530.64
Federal Payroll Taxes Payable	(14,617.04)	(40,794.88)
State Payroll Taxes Payable	(2,138.64)	(5,960.98)
Other Taxes Payable	(50.00)	(50.00)
Other Current Liabilities	(150.00)	(150.00)
Net change	$ 135.59	$ 33,870.72

For Management Purposes Only

2. Close all windows.

BACKING UP CHAPTER 7 DATA (Optional Backup)

You have not added any new data in Chapter 7. If you would prefer to have another backup disk, follow these steps to back up Chapter 7:

1. If necessary, insert your USB flash drive. From System Navigation Center, link to [Back Up Now]. Make sure that the box next to Include company name in the backup file name is *unchecked*.

2. Click [Back Up].

3. In the Save in field, select the appropriate drive letter for your USB drive.[a] (*Or,* save to the hard-drive default location or other location.) Type **Chapter 7** in the File name field.

4. Click [Save].

5. When the window prompts This company backup will require approximately 1 diskette, click [OK]. When the window prompts Please insert the first disk, click [OK]. When the Back Up Company scale is 100% complete, you have successfully backed up to the current point in Chapter 7. (Step 5 will differ slightly if you are backing up to the default or other hard-drive location.)

EXPORT FINANCIAL STATEMENTS TO EXCEL

Follow these steps to have separate sheets for each financial statement on one Excel workbook.

1. Display the <Standard> Balance Sheet. From the Balance Sheet click [Excel].

2. The Copy Report to Excel window appears. The default File Option is Create a new Microsoft Excel workbook. The Default Report

---

[a]If you are having difficulty backing up to USB flash drive, backup to the desktop, then copy the file to a USB flash drive. Refer to Appendix A, Troubleshooting, pages 756-758—Problem Backing Up to USB Drive or Other External Media.

header option is Show header in Excel worksheet. If necessary, make these selections.

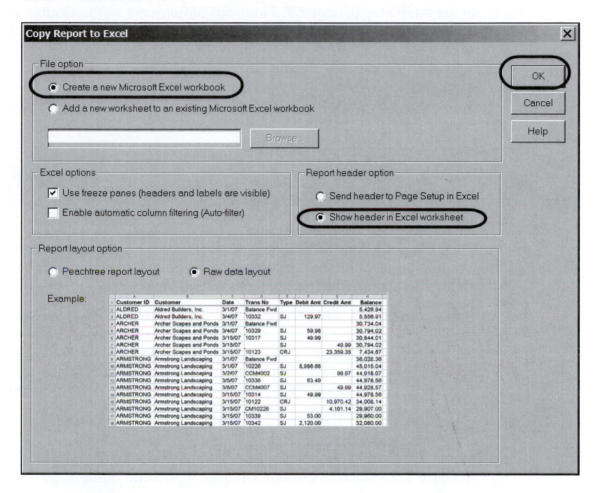

3. Click ⬛ OK ⬛ . The Balance Sheet appears as an Excel workbook.

4. Save. Use the file name **Chapter 7_Financial Statements.xlsx**. Minimize Excel.

5. Close Peachtree's Balance Sheet.

6. Display the <Standard> Income Statement. From the displayed

    Income Statement, click ⬛ Excel ⬛ .

7. On the Copy Report to Excel window, select Add a new worksheet to an Existing Microsoft Excel workbook. Then, Browse to the location of the saved file (Chapter 7_Financial Statements.xlsx). Double-click on the Chapter 7_Financial Statements file (or highlight it and click <Open>).

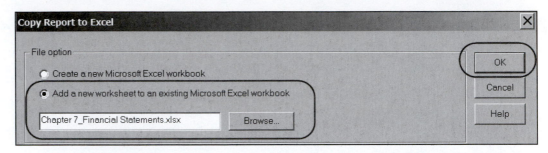

8. Click [OK]. Maximize Excel. (From the taskbar, click on the Microsoft Excel button.) Observe that the Excel file shows two sheets—Balance Sheet and Income Stmnt.

9. Save. Add the following financial statements to the Excel file: Gross Profit by Departments, Statement of Cash Flow, Retained Earnings Statement, and Statement of Changes in Financial Position. When you are finished, the Excel file should have 6 sheets: Balance Sheet, Income Stmnt, Gross Profit by Departments, Cash Flow, Retained Earnings, Stmnt Changes.

10. Save the financial statements as PDF files. Use the financial statement's name, then save. For example, use the file name Chapter 7_Balance Sheet.pdf, Chapter 7_Income Statement, etc.

Check your figures:

Total Liabilities & Capital	$501,096.96
Year to Date Gross Profit	203,396.11
Year-to-date Net Income	$ 25,476.82
Year-to-date Net Increase in Cash	$ 4,717.26
Ending Retained Earnings	$214,514.42

11. Save. Exit Excel.

SUMMARY AND REVIEW

Complete the following end-of-chapter activities:

1. Going to the net, page 245.

2. True/make true questions, page 246.

3. Exercises 7-1 and 7-2, page 247.

4. Bellwether Garden Supply Project, page 247.

5. Analysis questions, page 248.

6. Assessment rubric, page 248.

7. Chapter 7 Index, page 249.

GOING TO THE NET

Access the article How to Value Stocks: How to Read a Balance Sheet: at http://www.fool.com/investing/beginning/how-to-value-stocks-how-to-read-a-balance-sheet.aspx.
Read the article. (Going to the Net links are on the textbook website at www.mhhe.com/yacht2012, link to Student Edition, select Chapter 7.)

Answer the following questions.

1. What are liquid assets?

2. What are the liquid assets called on the balance sheet?

3. In the **More on reading a balance sheet** section, link to two other sites. Define each link; include the website address(es) in your answer.

True/Make True: The Online Learning Center includes these questions and the analysis question at www.mhhe.com/yacht2012, select Student Edition, Chapter 7, QA Templates.

1. Peachtree automatically calculates financial statements once journal entries have been journalized and posted.

2. In Chapter 7, you printed three financial statements.

3. The statement of cash flow is roughly the same thing as a balance sheet.

4. The balance sheet lists the revenues and expenses of the business.

5. The income statement is a summary of the revenue and expenses of a company for a period of time, such as an accounting period or a year.

6. The financial statements printed by Peachtree reflect month-to-date amounts only.

7. The financial statements are interrelated.

8. The term standard refers to financial statements that are designed by the company.

9. Bellwether Garden Supply showed a net loss for the current month, March 31, 2012.

10. The statement of changes in financial position derives its information from the income statement.

Exercise 7-1: Answer the following questions about the balance sheet and income statement:

1. The total assets are: _____

2. The total capital is: _____

3. Indicate the amount of the net income or
    (net loss) for the month of March: _____

4. The current month's gross profit is: _____

5. The current month's total expenses are: _____

Exercise 7-2: Answer the following questions about the statement of cash flow and the statement of retained earnings:

1. The current month's net cash provided
    by operations is: _____

2. The year-to-date's net cash provided by
    operations is: _____

3. The cash balance at end of period for the
    current month is: _____

4. The beginning Retained Earnings balance is: _____

5. The ending Retained Earnings balance is: _____

BELLWETHER GARDEN SUPPLY PROJECT

To answer questions about Bellwether Garden Supply, go online to www.mhhe.com/yacht2012; select Student Edition, link to Bellwether Garden Supply Project. In this project, you examine Bellwether's transactions, reports, and internal controls. The project includes comparing controlling account balances to the subsidiary ledgers and describing why some balances may differ.

ANALYSIS QUESTIONS

Explain the interrelationship of the financial statements. Specifically, answer these questions.

1. How are the income statement and balance sheet related to each other?

2. Using Bellwether Garden Supply as an example, what cash accounts does the statement of cash flow report?

3. Does the statement of cash flow use information from both the balance sheet and income statement?

ASSESSMENT RUBRIC

Complete the Assessment Rubric online at www.mhhe.com/yacht2012; Student Edition, select Chapter 7, Assessment Rubric link. To review Peachtree's navigation centers, menu selections, and windows, complete the blank fields online.

Report	Date	Menu	Window
Balance Sheet			
Income Statement			

CHAPTER 7 INDEX

Chapter 8

Stone Arbor Landscaping: Time & Billing

LEARNING OBJECTIVES

1. Start the sample company, Stone Arbor Landscaping.
2. Explore Peachtree's time and billing feature.
3. Use the time and billing feature to complete a time ticket, sales invoice, and payroll entry.
4. Make two backups, save two Excel files, and save four PDF files.

STONE ARBOR LANDSCAPING

When you installed Peachtree Complete Accounting 2012, two sample companies were included with the software: Bellwether Garden Supply and Stone Arbor Landscaping. In Chapters 1–7 you worked with Bellwether Garden Supply. Chapter 8 focuses on how the second sample company, Stone Arbor Landscaping, uses the time and billing feature.

TIME & BILLING

Time & Billing can track time spent on various activities and record internal use of company resources associated with customers or jobs. Recorded time and expenses can later be billed to customers on sales invoices. If you use payroll, timed activities can be applied to an employee's paycheck. Time & Billing can also be used to effectively manage administrative activities and overhead expenses for your business.

The purpose of PCA's time and billing feature is to provide the tools to record customer-related work or expenses. Time & Billing gives you a way to track expenses and time when working with customers. Time and expenses are recorded for customers, jobs, or administrative tasks.

Customers: Time and expenses can be associated with customers that you intend to bill later in Sales/Invoicing. Record time and expenses for customers only if you are not using job costing.

Jobs: If you are tracking jobs in Job Costs, you can record time and expense for jobs, phases, or cost codes. Then, you can apply billable time and expense items to the customer's invoice. The advantage of recording time and expense for jobs is that you can track details related to the completion of the project, including overhead and labor costs. Also, you can manage job profitability more effectively in reports.

Administrative: You can track internal activities to manage process control and overhead costs for the business. You may want to track the number of hours an employee spends preparing proposals or bookkeeping. Or, you may want to track an employee's mileage or travel expenses.

To track time and expenses, PCA uses two forms or tickets: the time ticket and the expense ticket. Each ticket type can be specific to a customer, job, or non-billable administrative tasks (miscellaneous items). Each ticket has its own special type of inventory item: the activity item for time tickets and the charge item for expense tickets.

Time Tickets

Time tickets are used to record time-based activities such as research or consultations. They record the activities of either an employee or a vendor. The two methods of entering time ticket information are weekly or daily.

The billing rate used for a recorded activity can be based on the employee who records the ticket or one of the five billing rates assigned to the activity item. Or, you can record the billing at the time you enter the time ticket.

Expense Tickets

Expense tickets are used to track and aid in the recovery of customer-related expenses. These expenses are *not* based on time. Expenses can be based on the various charges related to the service being offered. For example, if you were an accountant, you might charge your client for copying fees or faxing fees.

Both time and expense tickets can be used in the Sales/Invoicing window to bill your customers. The Sales/Invoicing window includes a feature called Apply Tickets/Reimbursable Expenses which takes you to the time and billing feature. The rate for expense tickets is determined by the unit price of the charge item multiplied by the quantity.

The chart below shows how time and billing works:

Time & Billing Ticket Types			
Ticket Type	**Inventory Item Class**	**Examples**	**Billing Amount Equals**
Time Ticket	Activity Item	Research Consultants Writing Reports	Billing Rate Times Activity Divisions
Expense Ticket	Charge Item	Copying Faxing Court Fees	Unit Price of the Charge Item Times Quantity

GETTING STARTED

1. Start PCA. From the startup window, select Explore a sample company. (*Hint: Stone Arbor Landscaping will be listed in the Company Name list after the first time it is opened.*)

2. The Explore a Sample Company window appears. Select Stone Arbor Landscaping.

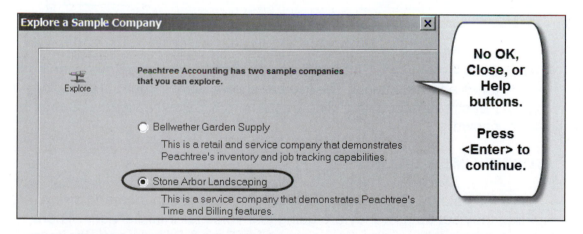

Troubleshooting: Why doesn't my Explore a Sample Company window show the <OK>, <Close>, and <Help> buttons?

Screen resolution affects how Peachtree's windows look. The recommended screen resolution is 1024X768 with small fonts (refer to page iv, Software Installation). You can use a higher resolution but some of the windows will look different. If you do not have an OK button, press <Enter> to start Stone Arbor Landscaping.

Software Expiration. If you are using the Student Version of PCA 2012 included with the textbook, a Peachtree Accounting window appears that says "You can use this company in the student version of Peachtree for the next 14 months and then it will expire. The company's expiration date can be found in the Company Information section of the System Navigation Center." For more information about the expiration date, refer to pages xv-xvi, Expiration Date, Student Version, PCA 2012.

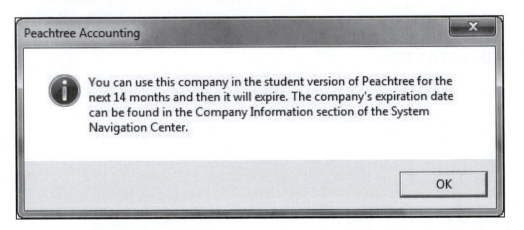

3. Click <u>OK</u>. The first time you start Stone Arbor Landscaping it takes a few moments. The title bar shows Stone Arbor Landscaping – Peachtree Accounting. The Customers & Sales Navigation Center is shown.

USING TIME & BILLING

Let's look at how Stone Arbor Landscaping has set up time and billing. First, they set up how they are going to invoice for their services. There are two special inventory item classes for Time & Billing: ***activity items*** and ***charge items***. Activity items are used on time tickets. Charge items are used on expense tickets. These inventory items must be set up prior to entering a time or expense ticket.

There are four steps to complete PCA's Time & Billing.

Step 1:   Set up the inventory item.
Step 2:   Enter the time ticket.
Step 3:   Record the sales invoice.
Step 4:   Payroll.

Inventory Item Maintenance

You use maintenance windows to set up defaults. Follow these steps to look at the inventory maintenance information for Stone Arbor Landscaping.

1. From the Navigation Bar, click [Inventory & Services] ; [Inventory Items], View and Edit Inventory Items. The Inventory List appears. Click once on INSTL HARD – COMM to highlight it.

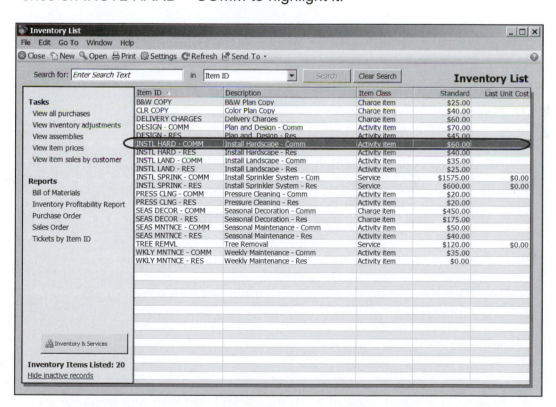

2. Double-click INSTL HARD – COMM. The Maintain Inventory Items window appears for INSTL HARD – COMM, Install Hardscape – Comm.

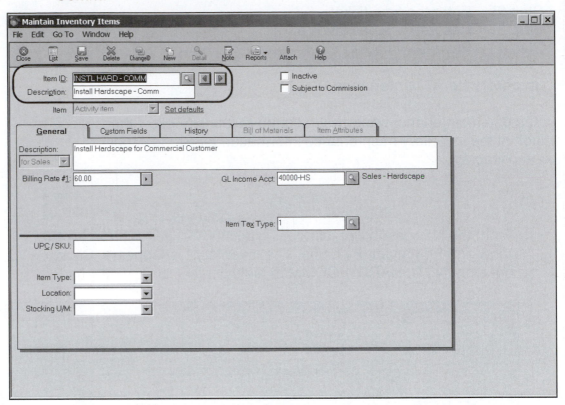

Review the information on the Maintain Inventory Items window. Observe that $60.00 is shown in the Billing Rate #1 field. Click on the right-arrow to see other billing rates, then close the Multiple Price Levels window. The GL Income Acct is Account No. 40000-HS, Sales – Hardscape. The Item Tax Type is 1 (for Taxable). This maintenance window is similar to ones that you have set up before. *Remember, defaults are set up in maintenance windows.*

3. Close all windows to return to the Inventory & Services Navigation Center.

Time Ticket

The Time Ticket shows how much was billed to the customer. To see how time is billed, look at a job that Alan Hardman has already completed.

Follow these steps to see time tickets.

1. From the Navigation Bar, click [Employees & Payroll] ; [Time and Expense Tickets],
    View and Edit Time Tickets. The Time Tickets List window appears.

2. Enlarge the window. Scroll down. Select Ticket No. 282, 3/12/2012,
    AHARDMAN, INSTL HARD –COMM, OHARA, 03-Installation. A
    partial Time Tickets List window is shown below.

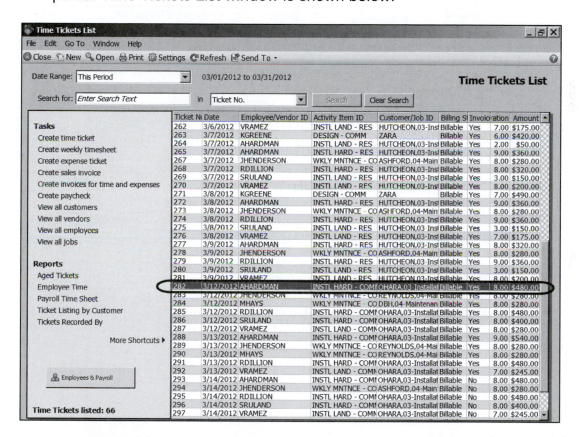

3. Click [Open]. The Time Tickets window appears. Notice that the
    Activity Item is for INSTL HARD – COMM, Install Hardscape -
    Comm, and that the Job name is O'Hara Homes Contract. The
    Invoice description is Installation of Decking/Patio. Mr. Hardman
    worked for eight hours on March 12, 2012; and the Bill amount is
    480.00. The Time Tickets window shows one instance, March 12,
    2012 (refer to the Ticket date field.)

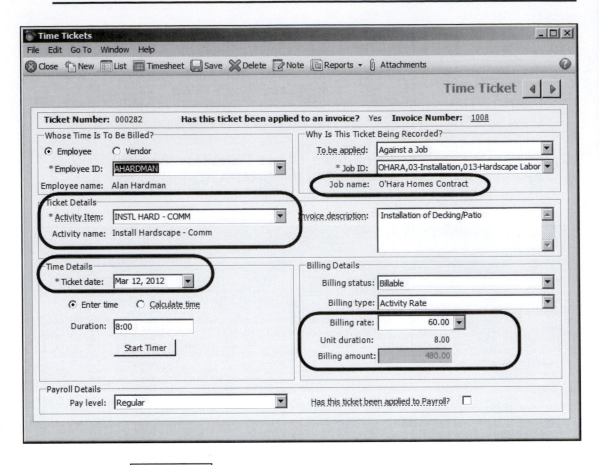

4. Click ⊞ Timesheet. The Time Ticket Weekly Timesheet Entry window appears. Your cursor should be over the OHARA,03 job row. The Time Ticket Weekly Timesheet Entry window is shown on the next page.

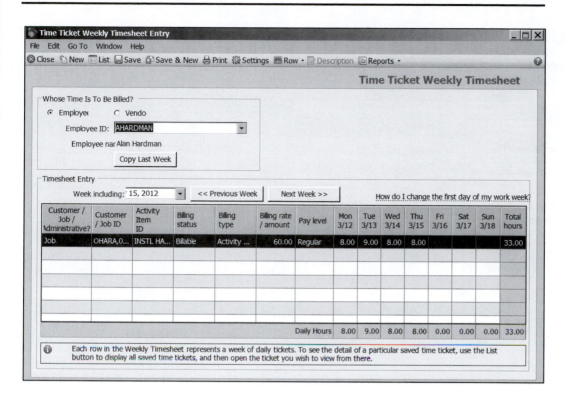

5. Close all windows.

Sales Invoice

In order to see how Mr. Hardman's charges were billed to the customer, O'Hara Homes, follow these steps.

1. From the Navigation Bar, click [Customers & Sales]; [Sales Invoices], View and Edit Sales Invoices. The Sales Invoice List appears. Click on OHARA, Invoice No. 1008, 3/13/2012 to highlight it.

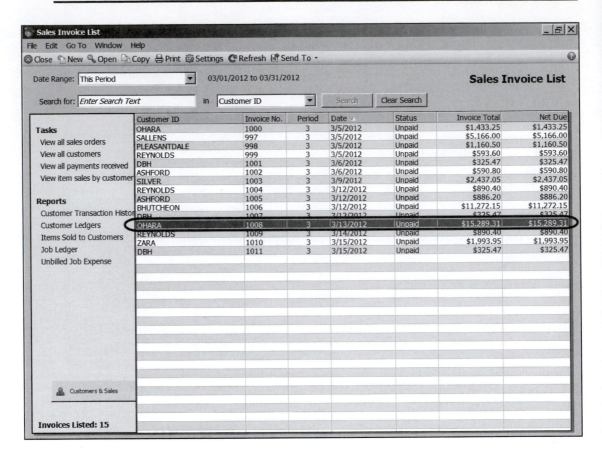

2. Double-click OHARA, Invoice 1008. The Sales/Invoicing window appears.

Compare your Sales/Invoicing window with the one shown on the next page.

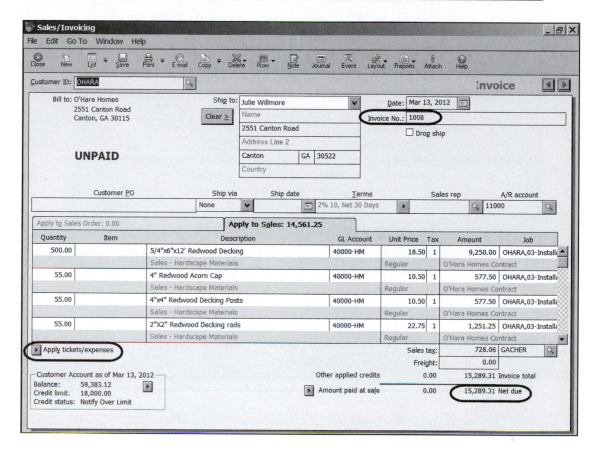

3. Click on the arrow next to Apply tickets/expenses
    ▶ Apply tickets/expenses . (*Hint: This is located in the lower left of the*
    window.)

4. The Apply Tickets/Reimbursable Expenses window appears.
    Observe that Alan Hardman's work on March 15 is billed, along with
    other employees that work on this customer's job.

    The Apply Tickets/Reimbursable Expenses window is shown on the
    next page.

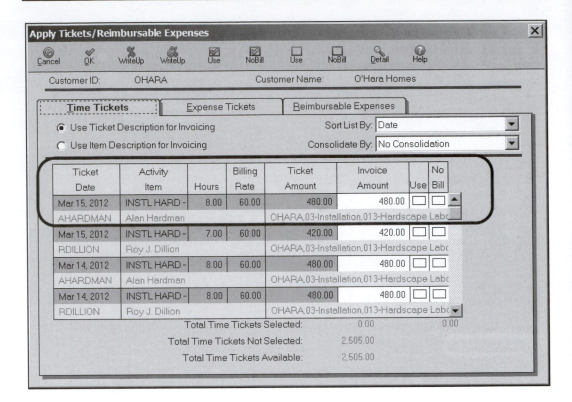

Observe that this time ticket shows that Alan Hardman's ticket amount is 480.00 for 8 hours at a billing rate of $60.00 ($60 x 8 = $480) on March 15, 2012.

5. Click [OK] to close the Apply Tickets/Reimbursable Expenses window. You are returned to the O'Hara Homes Sales/Invoicing window.

6. Close all windows to return to the Customers & Sales Navigation Center.

Payroll

Payroll also needs to be set up. You do this by selecting Hourly-Time Ticket Hours for employees. Let's see how Stone Arbor Landscaping sets this up.

1. From the Navigation Bar, click [Employees & Payroll]; [Employees],
   View and Edit Employees. The Employee List appears. Double-click
   AHARDMAN, Alan Hardman. Click on the Pay Info tab.

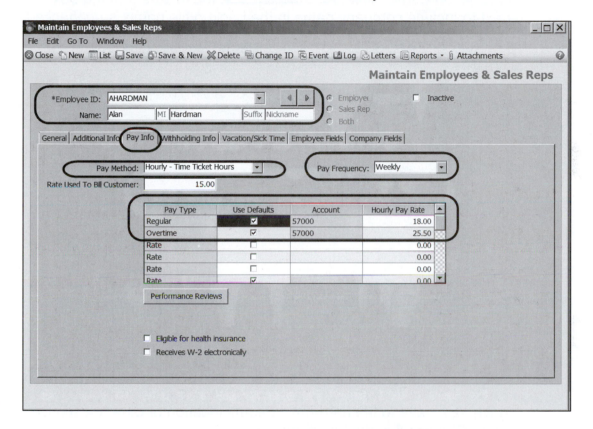

Observe that Mr. Hardman's Pay Method is Hourly – Time Ticket
Hours. He is paid weekly. Also notice that Mr. Hardman's regular pay
account number is 57000.

2. Close all windows. If prompted, do not save this record.

BACKING UP CHAPTER 8 DATA

Follow these steps to back up Chapter 8 data:

1. If necessary, insert your USB flash drive. From the System Navigation Center, link to [Back Up Now]. Make sure that the box next to Include company name in the backup file name is *unchecked*.

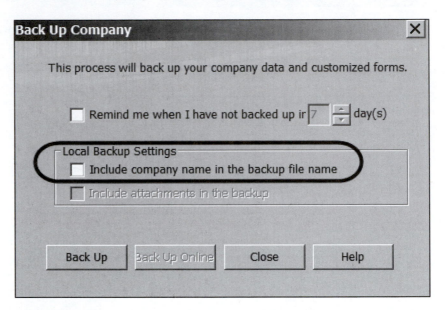

2. Click [Back Up].

3. In the Save in field, select the appropriate drive letter for your USB drive. (*Or,* save to the hard-drive default location or other location.) Type **Chapter 8** in the File name field.

4. Click [Save].

5. When the window prompts This company backup will require approximately 1 diskette, click [OK]. When the window prompts Please insert the first disk, click [OK]. When the Back Up Company scale is 100% complete, you have successfully backed up to the current point in Chapter 8. (Step 5 will differ slightly if you are backing up to the default or other hard-drive location.)

EXPORT TIME TICKET REGISTER TO EXCEL

Follow these steps to export the Time Ticket Register to Excel.

1. From the Reports & Forms menu, select Time/Expense.

2. From the Select a Report or Form window, click Time Ticket Register to highlight it.

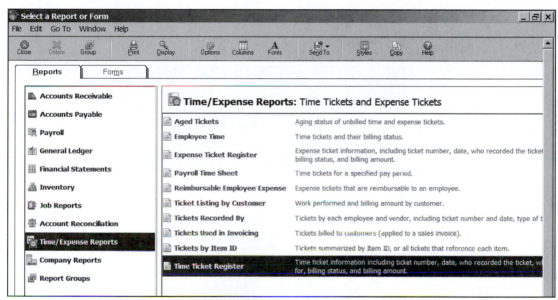

3. Click Send To, Excel.

4. The Modify Report – Time Ticket Register window appears, click OK .

5. The Copy Report to Excel window appears. In the File option area, make sure Create a new Microsoft Excel workbook is selected.

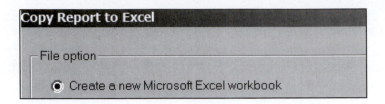

6. In the Report header option area, Show header in Excel worksheet should be selected.

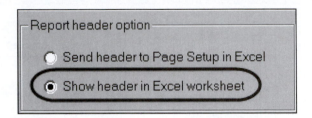

7. Click [OK]. Stone Arbor Landscaping's Time Ticket Register is exported to Excel. Scroll down the Register. Ticket No. 282 for AHardman is shown. The Time Tickets List window on page 257 also shows this job. A partial Time Ticket Register, which was exported to Excel, is shown on the next page.

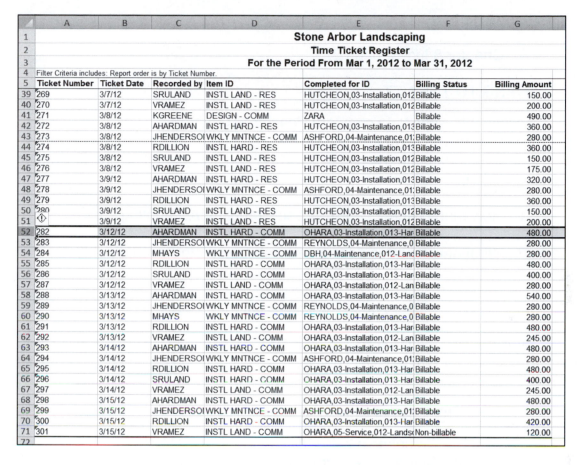

	Ticket Number	Ticket Date	Recorded by	Item ID	Completed for ID	Billing Status	Billing Amount
					Stone Arbor Landscaping		
					Time Ticket Register		
					For the Period From Mar 1, 2012 to Mar 31, 2012		
4	Filter Criteria includes: Report order is by Ticket Number.						
39	269	3/7/12	SRULAND	INSTL LAND - RES	HUTCHEON,03-Installation,012	Billable	150.00
40	270	3/7/12	VRAMEZ	INSTL LAND - RES	HUTCHEON,03-Installation,012	Billable	200.00
41	271	3/8/12	KGREENE	DESIGN - COMM	ZARA	Billable	490.00
42	272	3/8/12	AHARDMAN	INSTL HARD - RES	HUTCHEON,03-Installation,013	Billable	360.00
43	273	3/8/12	JHENDERSO	WKLY MNTNCE - COMM	ASHFORD,04-Maintenance,01:	Billable	280.00
44	274	3/8/12	RDILLION	INSTL HARD - RES	HUTCHEON,03-Installation,013	Billable	360.00
45	275	3/8/12	SRULAND	INSTL LAND - RES	HUTCHEON,03-Installation,012	Billable	150.00
46	276	3/8/12	VRAMEZ	INSTL LAND - RES	HUTCHEON,03-Installation,012	Billable	175.00
47	277	3/9/12	AHARDMAN	INSTL HARD - RES	HUTCHEON,03-Installation,013	Billable	320.00
48	278	3/9/12	JHENDERSO	WKLY MNTNCE - COMM	ASHFORD,04-Maintenance,01:	Billable	280.00
49	279	3/9/12	RDILLION	INSTL HARD - RES	HUTCHEON,03-Installation,013	Billable	360.00
50	280	3/9/12	SRULAND	INSTL LAND - RES	HUTCHEON,03-Installation,012	Billable	150.00
51	281	3/9/12	VRAMEZ	INSTL LAND - RES	HUTCHEON,03-Installation,012	Billable	200.00
52	282	3/12/12	AHARDMAN	INSTL HARD - COMM	OHARA,03-Installation,013-Har	Billable	480.00
53	283	3/12/12	JHENDERSO	WKLY MNTNCE - COMM	REYNOLDS,04-Maintenance,0	Billable	280.00
54	284	3/12/12	MHAYS	WKLY MNTNCE - COMM	DBH,04-Maintenance,012-Land	Billable	280.00
55	285	3/12/12	RDILLION	INSTL HARD - COMM	OHARA,03-Installation,013-Har	Billable	480.00
56	286	3/12/12	SRULAND	INSTL HARD - COMM	OHARA,03-Installation,013-Har	Billable	400.00
57	287	3/12/12	VRAMEZ	INSTL LAND - COMM	OHARA,03-Installation,012-Lan	Billable	280.00
58	288	3/13/12	AHARDMAN	INSTL HARD - COMM	OHARA,03-Installation,013-Har	Billable	540.00
59	289	3/13/12	JHENDERSO	WKLY MNTNCE - COMM	REYNOLDS,04-Maintenance,0	Billable	280.00
60	290	3/13/12	MHAYS	WKLY MNTNCE - COMM	REYNOLDS,04-Maintenance,0	Billable	280.00
61	291	3/13/12	RDILLION	INSTL HARD - COMM	OHARA,03-Installation,013-Har	Billable	480.00
62	292	3/13/12	VRAMEZ	INSTL LAND - COMM	OHARA,03-Installation,012-Lan	Billable	245.00
63	293	3/14/12	AHARDMAN	INSTL HARD - COMM	OHARA,03-Installation,013-Har	Billable	480.00
64	294	3/14/12	JHENDERSO	WKLY MNTNCE - COMM	ASHFORD,04-Maintenance,01:	Billable	280.00
65	295	3/14/12	RDILLION	INSTL HARD - COMM	OHARA,03-Installation,013-Har	Billable	480.00
66	296	3/14/12	SRULAND	INSTL HARD - COMM	OHARA,03-Installation,013-Har	Billable	400.00
67	297	3/14/12	VRAMEZ	INSTL LAND - COMM	OHARA,03-Installation,012-Lan	Billable	245.00
68	298	3/15/12	AHARDMAN	INSTL HARD - COMM	OHARA,03-Installation,013-Har	Billable	480.00
69	299	3/15/12	JHENDERSO	WKLY MNTNCE - COMM	ASHFORD,04-Maintenance,01:	Billable	280.00
70	300	3/15/12	RDILLION	INSTL HARD - COMM	OHARA,03-Installation,013-Har	Billable	420.00
71	301	3/15/12	VRAMEZ	INSTL LAND - COMM	OHARA,05-Service,012-Lands(	Non-billable	120.00

8. Save. Use the file name **Chapter 8_Time Ticket Register.xlsx**. Close all windows.

9. Save the Time Ticket Register as a PDF file. Use **Chapter 8_Time Ticket Register.pdf** as the file name.

SUMMARY AND REVIEW

Complete the following end-of-chapter activities:

1. Going to the net, page 268.

2. Multiple-choice questions, pages 268-270.

3. Exercises 8-1 and 8-2, pages 270-272.

4. Analysis question, page 272.

5. Assessment rubric, page 272.

6. Chapter 8 Index, page 273.

GOING TO THE NET

Access this website to compare Peachtree products www.peachtree.com/productsServices/compare/. (Going to the Net links are on the textbook website at www.mhhe.com/yacht2012; link to Student Edition, select Chapter 8.). Answer the following.

1. How many users can Peachtree Complete Accounting support?

2. What new features does Peachtree Complete Accounting 2012 include?

3. How many users does Peachtree Quantum support?

Multiple Choice Questions: The Online Learning Center includes these questions and the analysis question at www.mhhe.com/yacht2012, select Student Edition, Chapter 8, QA Templates.

_____1. The focus of Chapter 8 is to:

     a. Complete a sales invoice.
     b. Complete a payroll entry.
     c. Complete defaults.
     d. Look at PCA's time and billing features.
     e. None of the above.

_____2. In Chapter 8, you work with the sample company called:

     a. Bellwether Garden Supply.
     b. Stone Arbor Graphic Design.
     c. DBH Enterprises.
     d. Abbott's Landscaping.
     e. None of the above.

_____3.   The purpose of PCA's time and billing feature is to:

   a. Give you the tools to record customer-related work or expenses.
   b. Track how much an employee earns.
   c. Track how many sales invoices are completed in a month.
   d. Record employee payroll.
   e. None of the above.

_____4.   You use maintenance windows to set up:

   a. Payroll entries.
   b. Sales/Invoicing.
   c. Defaults.
   d. Time tickets.
   e. None of the above.

_____5.   Time tickets are used to:

   a. Record weekly or monthly information.
   b. Record payroll.
   c. Record time-based activities.
   d. Track sales invoices.
   e. None of the above.

_____6.   Expense tickets are used to:

   a. Track and aid in the recovery of customer-related expenses.
   b. Record time-based activities such as research or consultants.
   c. Track sales invoices.
   d. Record payroll.
   e. None of the above.

_____7.   Examples of expense ticket charge items are:

   a. Fixed asset accounts.
   b. Inventory accounts.
   c. Copying, faxing, court fees.
   d. Research, consultants, writing reports.
   e. None of the above.

_____8. How many hours did Mr. Hardman work on March 12, 2012 completing the installation of decking/patio for O'Hara Homes?

    a. Three hours.
    b. Four hours.
    c. Five hours.
    d. Six hours.
    e. None of the above.

_____9. Examples of time ticket activity items are:

    a. Copying, faxing, court fees.
    b. Research, consultants, writing reports.
    c. Inventory accounts.
    d. Fixed asset accounts.
    e. None of the above.

_____10. The time ticket shows:

    a. How much was billed to a vendor.
    b. How much was billed to a customer.
    c. How much was billed to an employee.
    d. Expenses minus revenue.
    e. None of the above.

Exercise 8-1: Complete the following time ticket, sales invoice, and payroll entry.

1. If necessary, restore the Chapter 8.ptb file. This backup was made on page 264.

2. Enter a new time ticket for the employee, Mike E. Hays. Complete the following Time Ticket fields.

Employee ID: Mike E. Hays
To be applied: Against a Job
Job ID: DBH, 04-
Maintenance, 012 Landscape
Labor.

Click on the plus sign next to DBH to expand the list. Expand 04-Maintenance, then select 012 Landscape Labor.

Activity item: Weekly Maintenance - Comm
Invoice description: Weekly Maintenance
Ticket Date: Mar 15, 2012
Duration: 8:00
Bill status: Billable
Billing type: Activity Rate

3. Record the following sales invoice.

   Date   *Description*

   03/22/12   Apply the completed time ticket to Invoice No. 1019. On
                 the Sales/Invoicing window, complete these fields:

                 Customer ID: DBH Enterprises
                 Date: March 22, 2012
                 Invoice No.:   1019

   Select [▸ Apply tickets/expenses]. The Time Ticket information is shown.
   Select the Use box to place a checkmark in it. Click <OK>. The Apply
   to Sales portion of the Sales/Invoicing window is completed. Observe
   that the Net due shows $295.40. Post the sales invoice.

4. Display the Time Ticket for Mike E. Hays. Observe that Invoice No.
   1019 is applied.

5. Record the following payroll entry.

   03/23/12   Pay employee, Mike E. Hays for 24 regular hours.
                 Select the Jobs icon to see the two jobs Mr. Hays
                 completed during this pay period. Post the payroll entry.
                 (The Timesheet also shows the jobs completed.)

6. Backup. The suggested file name is **Exercise 8-1.ptb**.

Exercise 8-2: To complete Exercise 8-2, do the following.

1. If necessary, restore the Exercise 8-1.ptb backup file.

2. Print the Job Ledger Report. (*Hint:* Reports & Forms, Jobs, Job
   Ledger.)

3. Print the Time Ticket Register. (*Hint:* Reports & Forms, Time/Expense Reports, Time Ticket Register.)

4. Print the Payroll Time Sheet. (*Hint:* Reports & Forms, Time/Expense Reports, Payroll Time Sheet.

5. Save the three Time & Billing Reports as an Excel file: Job Ledger, Time Ticket Register, and Payroll Time Sheet. The suggested file name is **Exercise 8-2_Time and Billing Reports.xlsx**.

6. Save three PDF files: **Exercise 8-2_Job Ledger.pdf**, **Exercise 8-2_Time Ticket Register.pdf**, and **Exercise 8-2_Payroll Time Sheet.pdf**.

ANALYSIS QUESTION

What is the purpose of Peachtree's time and billing feature? Briefly explain time and billing.

ASSESSMENT RUBRIC

Complete the Assessment Rubric online at www.mhhe.com/yacht2012; Student Edition, select Chapter 8, Assessment Rubric link.

Task	Navigation Center and Menu	Window
Timesheet		
Sales Invoice		
Payroll		

CHAPTER 8 INDEX

The McGraw-Hill Companies, Inc., *Computer Accounting with Peachtree by Sage Complete Accounting 2012, 16e*

In Part 2 of *Computer Accounting with Peachtree by Sage Complete Accounting 2012, 16th Edition,* you are the owner of an accounting practice. Your accounting business does monthly record keeping for local service businesses.

In Chapters 9, 10, 11, Projects 1 and 1A (Part 2), you use Peachtree to set up four service businesses, complete the accounting cycle, and close the fiscal year. In Part 2, entries are recorded in the Receipts window (Cash Receipts Journal) and the Write Checks window (Cash Disbursements Journal). Also, adjusting entries are recorded in the General Journal. At the end of each month, you reconcile the bank statement and print the general ledger trial balance and financial statements. At the end of the fourth quarter, you use Peachtree to complete end-of-quarter adjusting entries, print the adjusted trial balance, print financial statements, close the fiscal year, and print a postclosing trial balance.

After entering deposits and payments, the next step is to post them to the general ledger. One of the best features of a computerized accounting system is how quickly **posting** is done. Once entries are recorded and checked for accuracy, posting is a click of the mouse. All entries are posted to the correct accounts in the general ledger and account balances are calculated–fast, easy, and accurate. Think of it as a process where journalizing and posting is the first step, then ledgers and financial statements are next. The diagram below illustrates this process.

| Journalize and Post | General Ledger | Financial Statements |

Remember the accuracy of your general ledger and financial statement reports depends on the accuracy of the entries recorded on the Write Checks and Receipts windows. An added feature is that once entries are posted, account reconciliation is completed.

Chapters 9, 10 and 11 work together. The service businesses set up in Chapter 9 are continued in Chapters 10 and 11. Part 2 ends with two comprehensive projects. Part 2 includes:

Chapter 9:   New Company Setup and Beginning Balances
Chapter 10:   Maintaining Accounting Records for Service Businesses
Chapter 11:   Completing Quarterly Activities and Closing the Fiscal Year
Project 1:   Susan Babbage, Accounting
Project 1A: Student-Designed Service Business

Part 2 includes three chapters and two projects: Chapters 9, 10, and 11 and Projects 1 and 1A. In Chapters 9, 10, and 11, you set up two service businesses from scratch—Mark Foltz Designer and Design by Student Name (after Design by, students should use their first and last name). You complete accounting tasks for the fourth quarter–October, November and December 2012. You also complete end-of-quarter adjusting entries. At the end of Chapter 9, a new service business is set up in Exercise 9-1. The service business set up in Exercise 9-1 is continued in Exercises 9-2, 10-1, 10-2, 11-1 and 11-2.

In Project 1, you complete the accounting cycle for Susan Babbage, Accounting. This project gives you an opportunity to apply what you have learned in Chapters 9, 10, and 11. At the end of Project 1, there is a Check Your Progress assessment.

Project 1A is an opportunity to design a service business of your own. You select a chart of accounts, write and journalize transactions, reconcile the bank statement, and complete the accounting cycle for the business.

The chart on pages 277-278 shows the size of the backups, Excel files, and PDF files saved in Part 2–Chapters 9, 10, 11, and Project 1. The textbook shows how to back up to a USB drive. Backups can be made to the desktop, hard drive location, network location or external media.

Chapter	Peachtree Backup (.ptb) Excel (.xlsx) and Adobe (.pdf)	Kilobytes	Page Nos.
9	Chapter 9 Chart of Accounts.ptb	920 KB	296-298
	Chapter 9 Beginning Balances.ptb	958 KB	311-312
	Chapter 9_Chart of Accounts and Beginning Balances.xlsx	17 KB	312-314
	Chapter 9_Balance Sheet.pdf	8 KB	314-315
	Chapter 9_Chart of Accounts.pdf	39 KB	315
	Exercise 9-1.ptb	912 KB	320-322
	Exercise 9-2.ptb	916 KB	324
	Exercise 9-2_Chart of Accounts and Beginning Balances.xlsx	18 KB	324
	Exercise 9-2_Chart of Accounts.pdf	38 KB	324
	Exercise 9-2_Balance Sheet.pdf	8 KB	324
10	Chapter 10 Transaction Register October.ptb	977 KB	338-339
	Chapter 10 October.ptb	995 KB	351
	Chapter 10_October Trial Balance and Financial Statements.xlsx	21 KB	351-353
	Chapter 10_October Trial Balance.pdf	7 KB	353
	Chapter 10_October Balance Sheet.pdf	5 KB	353
	Chapter 10_October Income Statement.pdf	5 KB	353
	Exercise 10-1.ptb	949 KB	356
	Exercise 10-2.ptb	953 KB	358
	Exercise 10-2_October Trial Balance and Financial Statements.xlsx.	20 KB	358
	Exercise 10-2_October Trial Balance.pdf	37 KB	358
	Exercise 10-2_October Balance Sheet.pdf	8 KB	358
	Exercise 10-2_October Income Statement.pdf	9 KB	358
11	Chapter 11 November.ptb	1,010 KB	374-375
	Chapter 11 December UTB.ptb	1,011 KB	382-383
	Chapter 11 December.ptb	1,017 KB	383
	Chapter 11_Adjusted Trial Balance and Financial Statements.xlsx	30 KB	393-394
	Chapter 11_Adjusted Trial Balance.pdf	38 KB	394
	Chapter 11_December Balance Sheet.pdf	5 KB	394

The McGraw-Hill Companies, Inc., *Computer Accounting with Peachtree by Sage Complete Accounting 2012, 16e*

11	Chapter 11_December Income Statement.pdf	6 KB	394
	Chapter 11_December Statement of Cash Flow.pdf	5 KB	394
	Chapter 11_December Statement of Retained Earnings.pdf	4 KB	394
	Chapter 11 EOY.ptb	1,026 KB	400-401
	Chapter 11_Postclosing Trial Balance.xlsx	12 KB	401
	Chapter 11_Postclosing Trial Balance.pdf	51 KB	401
	Asset depreciation.xlsx (Going to the Net)	14 KB	402
	Exercise 11-1.ptb	973 KB	406
	Exercise 11-2 Unadjusted Trial Balance.ptb	1,008 KB	408
	Exercise 11-2 Financial Statements.ptb	1,011 KB	409
	Exercise 11-2_Adjusted Trial Balance and Financial Statements.xlsx	29 KB	409
	Exercise 11-2_Adjusted Trial Balance.pdf	53 KB	409
	Exercise 11-2_Balance Sheet.pdf	5 KB	409
	Exercise 11-2_Income Statement.pdf	6 KB	409
	Exercise 11-2_Statement of Cash Flow.pdf	5 KB	409
	Exercise 11-2_Statement of Retained Earnings.pdf	4 KB	409
	Exercise 11-2 End of Year.ptb	1,020 KB	409
	Exercise 11-2_Postclosing Trial Balance.xlsx	12 KB	409
	Exercise 11-2_Postclosing Trial Balance.pdf	50 KB	410
Project 1	Susan Babbage Chart of Accounts.ptb	914 KB	416
	Susan Babbage Beginning Balances.ptb	919 KB	417
	Susan Babbage UTB.ptb	943 KB	419
	Susan Babbage December.ptb	942 KB	420
	Susan Babbage_Adjusted Trial Balance and Financial Statements.xlsx	28 KB	420
	Project 1_Balance Sheet.pdf	5 KB	420
	Project 1_Income Statement.pdf	5 KB	420
	Project 1_Statement of Cash Flow.pdf	5 KB	420
	Project 1_Statement of Retained Earnings.pdf	4 KB	420
	Susan Babbage EOY.ptb	954 KB	420
	Susan Babbage_Postclosing Trial Balance.xlsx	12 KB	420
	Project 1_Postclosing Trial Balance.pdf	6 KB	420

The McGraw-Hill Companies, Inc., *Computer Accounting with Peachtree by Sage Complete Accounting 2012, 16e*

Chapter 9

New Company Setup and Beginning Balances

LEARNING OBJECTIVES

1. Set up company information for Mark Foltz Designer.
2. Select a Service Company from the simplified chart of accounts list.
3. Edit the chart of accounts.
4. Enter beginning balances.
5. Use Windows Explorer to see the company's file size.
6. Export the chart of accounts and beginning balances to Excel, and save PDF files.
7. Make four backups, save two Excel files, and save four PDF files.[1]

Chapter 9 begins Part 2 of the book–Peachtree Complete Accounting 2012 for Service Businesses. In this part of the book you are the owner of an accounting practice that does the monthly record keeping for several service businesses.

The chapters in Part 2 work together--the service businesses set up in Chapter 9 are continued in Chapters 10 and 11. The two businesses set up in Chapter 9 are Mark Foltz Designer, and another service business in Exercise 9-1, Design by Your Name. In Chapter 9, you set up a service business using one of PCA's sample companies. Then, edit a chart of accounts and enter beginning balances.

GETTING STARTED: NEW COMPANY SETUP

Mark Foltz is a designer and educator. His sources of income are: design work, book royalties, and part-time teaching at Green Bay Community College. He is single and has no dependents.

---

[1]Refer to the chart on pages 277-278 for the file names and size of backups, Excel files, and PDF files.

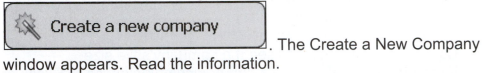 Follow these steps to set up the company, Mark Foltz Designer. (*Hint:* The arrow indicates a flash video at www.mhhe.com/yacht2012. Link to Student Edition; select Chapter 9, Flash Videos, Set up a new company.)

1. Start Peachtree. (If a company opens, click File; Close Company.)

2. At the Peachtree Accounting startup window, click

   Create a new company

   . The Create a New Company window appears. Read the information.

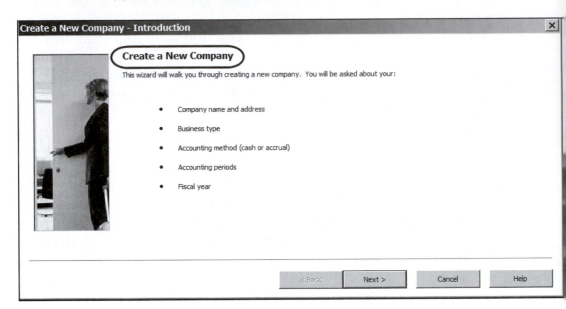

3. Click Next >. Type the company information shown on the next page. Press the **<Tab>** or **<Enter>** key between each field.

Company Information

Company Name: **Mark Foltz Designer (use your name)**[2]
Address Line 1:   **34511 Main Street**
City, State, Zip: **Green Bay, WI 54301**
Country: **USA**
Telephone: **920-555-8217**
Fax: **920-555-8219**
Business Type: Select Sole Proprietorship
Web Site: **www.markfoltz.com**
E-Mail: **info@markfoltz.com**

Compare the Enter your company information window to the one below. *The company name field should show your first and last name Designer. Do not complete the ID fields. (Hint: Observe that there is a red asterisk next to Company Name. The asterisk indicates a required field.)*

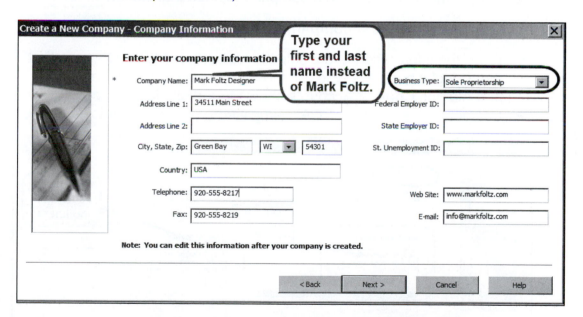

4. Check the information you just typed, then click [Next >]. The Select a method to create your company window appears.

---

[2]Boldface indicates information that you type. Substitute your name for Mark Foltz. If you use your first and last name Designer as the company name, Peachtree printouts show your name.

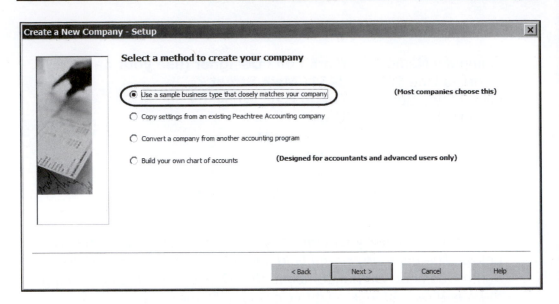

5. Accept the default to Use a sample business that closely matches your company **(Most companies choose this)**. Click Next > .

6. Read the information about selecting a business type. Observe that the Select a business type list shows Service Company selected, and that the Chart of Accounts shows four digits for the account numbers. This is one of PCA's simplified chart of accounts.

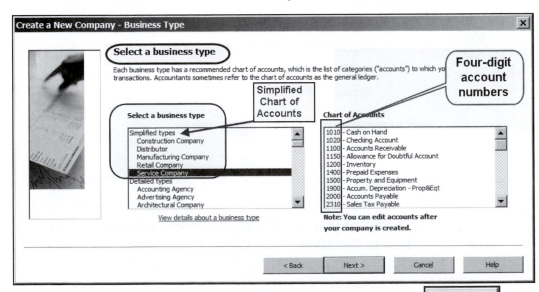

7. Make sure that Service Company is highlighted; click Next > . The Choose an accounting method window appears.

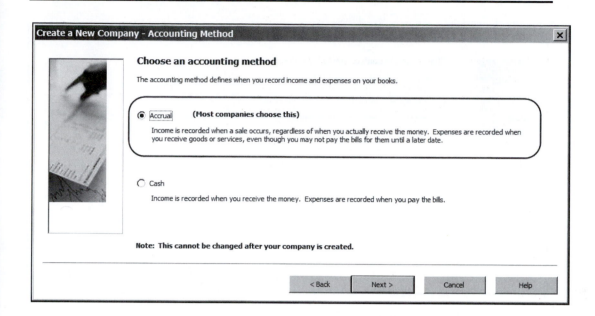

8. Accept the default for Accrual, by clicking . The Choose a posting method window appears.

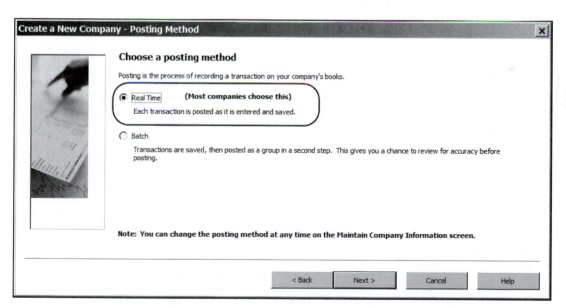

9. Accept the default for Real Time posting, by clicking Next >. The Choose an accounting period structure window appears.

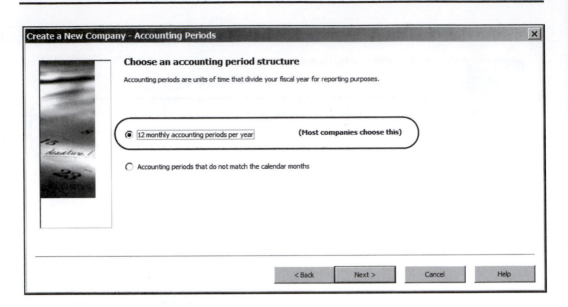

10. Accept the default for 12 monthly accounting periods per year by clicking [Next >]. The Choose the first period of your fiscal year window appears. Select 2012.

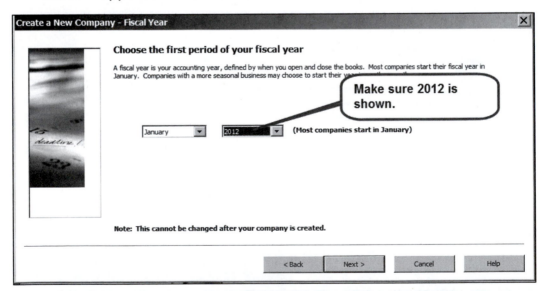

11. Make sure the Choose the first period of your fiscal year window shows January 2012. **This window is important. The year cannot be changed after your company is created**. Click [Next >]. You are ready to create your company window appears.

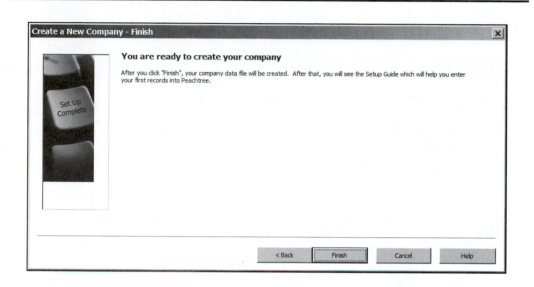

12. Read the information on the Finish window. Click [Finish]. If the screen prompts You can use this company in the student version of Peachtree for the next 14 months and then it will expire, click [OK]. After a few moments (be patient), the Mark Foltz Designer - Peachtree Accounting window appears. (Substitute your first and last name for Mark Foltz.)

13. When the Setup Guide window appears, click on the box next to [☑ Don't show this screen at startup.]. Click [Close]. Read the Peachtree Setup Guide window. Click [OK].

14. On the Navigation Bar, click [Business Status]. To set the Business Status Navigation Center as your default page, from the toolbar select [🏠 Make this the default page]. When you open Mark Foltz Designer, the Business Status Navigation Center will appear.

15. On the toolbar (below the menu bar and Business Status), click on the Period button [📅 Period]. The Change Accounting Period window appears. Click 10 – Oct 01, 2012 to Oct 31, 2012 to highlight it. Compare your Change Accounting Period window to the one shown on the next page.

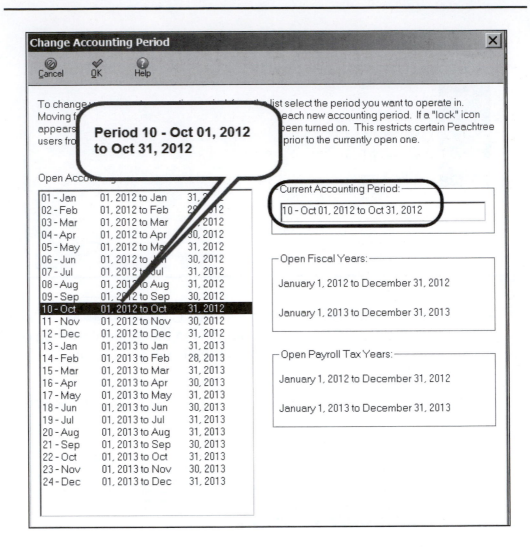

16. Make sure Period 10 is selected. October 2012 is the first month for recording transactions. Click ⟨OK⟩. If a window prompts that transactions may need to be reviewed, click on the box next to Do not display this message again. Then, click ⟨No⟩.

17. Check that Period 10 – 10/01/12-10/31/12 appears on the toolbar
    ![Period 10 - 10/01/12-10/31/12]. The Period appears next to the System
    Date, which is the current (today's) date. Compare your Business
    Status Navigation Center with the one shown below. A partial
    window is shown. Scroll down to see all the information. (*Hint:*
    Depending on your screen resolution, your Business Status
    Navigation Center may look different.)

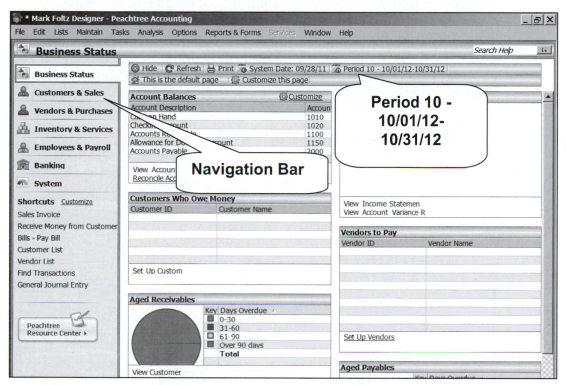

 Read Me: *What is Peachtree's shortened name?*

1. From the menu bar, select Help; Customer Support and Service, File Statistics.
    Peachtree displays the company's shortened name on the title bar. The Data File Statistics
    for XXXXXXDE window appears. (Substitute the Xs with your shortened name.) This
    represents the shortened name of the currently open company. Observe that there is also
    a Directory field at the bottom of the Data File Statistics window. The directory where Mark
    Foltz Designer resides on the computer is C:\Sage\Peachtree\Company\marfolde. (Since
    you used your first and last name, the first six characters of the shortened name will
    differ.) Your company directory may differ. The location of Mark Foltz Designer is shown in
    the next section, Company Maintenance Information.

2. Click [OK] to close the Data File Statistics window.

Company Maintenance Information

Follow these steps to see information.

1. From Peachtree's menu bar, select Maintain; Company Information.

2. Compare these fields to the company information on page 281. They should agree. Notice that the Directory field shows the default location where your company is stored: C:\Sage\Peachtree\ Company\marfolde. Since you used your first and last name, the Directory field ends with the shortened company name assigned by Peachtree. For example, if your company name is Janet Williams Designer, the Directory field ends in \janwilde. (*Hint:* Your Directory field may differ. Refer to Company Data Files Location, page xix.)

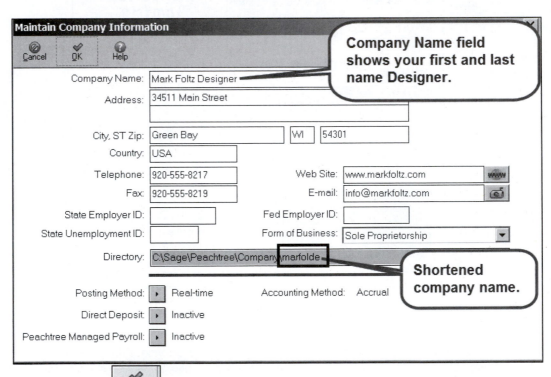

3. Click [OK] to return to the Business Status Navigation Center.

CHART OF ACCOUNTS

The chart of accounts is a list of all the accounts in the general ledger. When you selected Service Company from the list of business types, a chart of accounts was included. Follow these steps to edit PCA's sample chart of accounts.

Delete Accounts

1. From the Business Status Navigation Center, link to <u>View Account List</u>. The Account List appears. (*Or,* you can use the menu bar. Select Maintain; Chart of Accounts; in the Account ID field, click the down-arrow, continue with step 2.)

2. Double click Account ID, 1150, Allowance for Doubtful Account. The Maintain Chart of Accounts window appears.

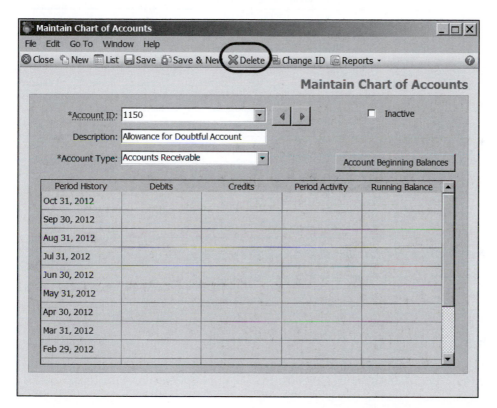

3. Click 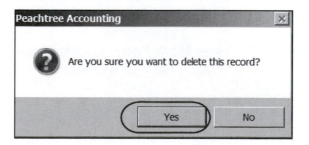 .

4. The Peachtree Accounting - Are you sure you want to delete this record? window appears.

5. Click [Yes] .

6. Delete the accounts shown on the chart below. (*Hint:* On the Maintain Chart of Accounts window, type the account number in the Account ID field to expedite editing the chart of accounts.)

Acct. ID	Account Description
2310	Sales Tax Payable
2320	Deductions Payable
2330	Federal Payroll Taxes Payable
2340	FUTA Payable
2350	State Payroll Taxes Payable
2360	SUTA Payable
2370	Local Taxes Payable
2500	Current Portion Long-Term Debt
2700	Long-Term Debt-Noncurrent
4300	Other Income
5900	Inventory Adjustments
6050	Employee Benefit Programs Exp
6250	Other Taxes Expense
6650	Commissions and Fees Expense
7100	Gain/Loss - Sale of Assets Exp

Change Accounts

To change the name of an account, follow these steps:

1. On the Maintain Chart of Accounts window, type **3920**; Press <Tab> or <Enter>. Owner's Contribution appears in the Description field.

2. Type **Mark Foltz, Capital** (use your first and last name, Capital). Press <Tab> or <Enter>.

3. In the Account Type field, click on the down arrow. Select Equity-doesn't close.

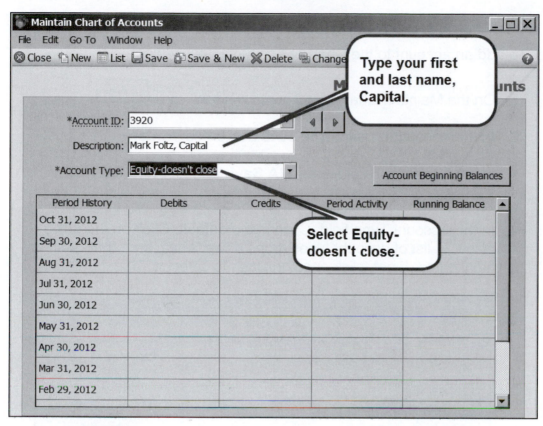

4. Click ⊟ Save .

5. Change the names of the accounts shown below. (*Hint:* When you change the Account Description, you do not need to change the Account Type.)

Acct. ID	Account Description	New Account Description
1010	Cash on Hand	**Money Market Account**
1400	Prepaid Expenses	**Prepaid Rent**
1500	Property and Equipment	**Computer Equipment**
1900	Accum. Depreciation – Prop&Eqt	**Accum. Depreciation – Comp Eqt**
2000	Accounts Payable	**VISA Payable**
2400	Customer Deposits	**Publisher Advances**
3930	Owner's Draw	**Mark Foltz, Draw** (your name, Draw)
4000	Professional Fees	**Teaching Income**
4050	Sales of Materials	**Royalty Income**
6100	Payroll Tax Expense	**Dues and Subscriptions**
6150	Bad Debt Expense	**Auto Registration**
6550	Other Office Expense	**Long Distance Co.**
6850	Service Charge Expense	**Bank Service Charge**
7050	Depreciation Expense	**Deprec. Exp. - Comp Eqt**

Add Accounts

To add an account to the Chart of Accounts, follow these steps:

1. On the Maintain Chart of Accounts window, click [New].

2. In the Account ID field, type **1040** and press **<Enter>**.

3. In the Description field, type **IRA Savings Account** and press **<Enter>**.

4. In the Account Type field, Cash is the default. Click on the down arrow. A list of account types drops down. Make sure that Cash is highlighted. If not, click once on Cash to select it.

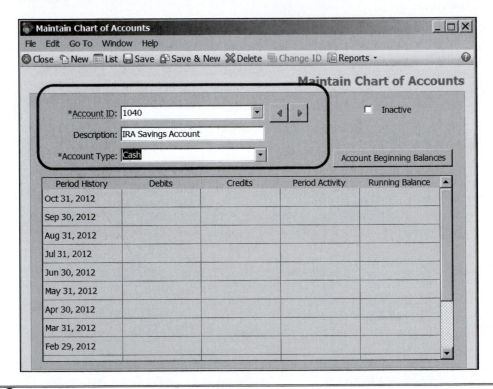

> **Read Me:** *Why is the Account Type field important?* Observe that the Account Type field shows Cash. This is an important field – the Account Type field classifies each account for the financial statements. For example, Account No. 1040, IRA Savings Account, is classified as Cash, which means this account will appear on the Balance Sheet, Statement of Cash Flow, and the Statement of Financial Position; but *not* on the Income Statement or Statement of Retained Earnings. *Always check that the Account Type field is correct so that accounts will be organized correctly on the financial statements.*

5. Click [Save & New] . (*Hint:* What is the difference between Save & New and Save? If you click Save, the Account Type does not change. If you have a couple of accounts with the same Account Type, click Save, then change the Account ID and Description. The Account Type stays the same.)

Add the following accounts:

Acct. ID	Account Description	Account Type
1045	**WI State Retirement**	Cash
1300	**Prepaid Insurance**	Other Current Assets
1450	**Supplies**	Other Current Assets
1510	**Furniture**	Fixed Assets
1520	**Automobile**	Fixed Assets
1910	**Accum. Depreciation – Furnitur**	Accumulated Depreciation
1920	**Accum. Depreciation – Automobi**	Accumulated Depreciation
6560	**Internet Service Provider**	Expenses
7060	**Deprec. Exp. - Furniture**	Expenses
7070	**Deprec. Exp. - Automobile**	Expenses

6. Click [Close] after completing the Chart of Accounts. If necessary, close all windows. You are returned to the Business Status Navigation Center.

Display the Chart of Accounts

1. From the menu bar, click Reports & Forms; General Ledger.

2. At the Select a Report or Form window, click on the Chart of Accounts to highlight it.

3. Select [Display] .

Comment

Move the mouse to the blue arrows ⊞ between columns. The cursor becomes a crossbar. Left click on the crossbar and drag the mouse to the right. After you have adjusted the Account Description column, click on the Print icon to print the chart of accounts. When you click on the Close icon, a window prompts that The report has been modified. Do you want to save it? Click No.

Mark Foltz Designer
Chart of Accounts
As of Oct 31, 2012

Filter Criteria includes: Report order is by ID. Report is printed with Accounts having Zero Amounts and in Detail Format.

Account I	Account Description	Active?	Account Type
1010	Money Market Account	Yes	Cash
1020	Checking Account	Yes	Cash
1040	IRA Savings Account	Yes	Cash
1045	WI State Retirement	Yes	Cash
1100	Accounts Receivable	Yes	Accounts Receivable
1200	Inventory	Yes	Inventory
1300	Prepaid Insurance	Yes	Other Current Assets
1400	Prepaid Rent	Yes	Other Current Assets
1450	Supplies	Yes	Other Current Assets
1500	Computer Equipment	Yes	Fixed Assets
1510	Furniture	Yes	Fixed Assets
1520	Automobile	Yes	Fixed Assets
1900	Accum. Depreciation - Comp Eqt	Yes	Accumulated Depreciation
1910	Accum. Depreciation - Furnitur	Yes	Accumulated Depreciation
1920	Accum. Depreciation - Automobi	Yes	Accumulated Depreciation
2000	VISA Payable	Yes	Accounts Payable
2380	Income Taxes Payable	Yes	Other Current Liabilities
2400	Publisher Advances	Yes	Other Current Liabilities
3910	Retained Earnings	Yes	Equity-Retained Earnings
3920	Mark Foltz, Capital	Yes	Equity-doesn't close
3930	Mark Foltz, Draw	Yes	Equity-gets closed
4000	Teaching Income	Yes	Income
4050	Royalty Income	Yes	Income
4100	Interest Income	Yes	Income
4200	Finance Charge Income	Yes	Income
4900	Sales/Fees Discounts	Yes	Income
5000	Cost of Sales	Yes	Cost of Sales
5400	Cost of Sales-Salary & Wage	Yes	Cost of Sales
6000	Wages Expense	Yes	Expenses
6100	Dues and Subscriptions	Yes	Expenses
6150	Auto Registration	Yes	Expenses
6200	Income Tax Expense	Yes	Expenses
6300	Rent or Lease Expense	Yes	Expenses
6350	Maintenance & Repairs Expense	Yes	Expenses
6400	Utilities Expense	Yes	Expenses
6450	Office Supplies Expense	Yes	Expenses
6500	Telephone Expense	Yes	Expenses
6550	Long Distance Co.	Yes	Expenses
6560	Internet Service Provider	Yes	Expenses
6600	Advertising Expense	Yes	Expenses
6800	Freight Expense	Yes	Expenses
6850	Bank Service Charge	Yes	Expenses
6900	Purchase Disc-Expense Items	Yes	Expenses
6950	Insurance Expense	Yes	Expenses
7050	Deprec. Exp. - Comp Eqt	Yes	Expenses
7060	Deprec. Exp. - Furniture	Yes	Expenses
7070	Deprec. Exp. - Automobile	Yes	Expenses

Carefully check the Account Type column. Peachtree's account types classify each account for the financial statements.

Observe that the chart of accounts is dated As of Oct 31, 2012. Since Peachtree posts on the last day of the month, your reports will show October 31, 2012 as the date.

Notice that Mark Foltz's chart of accounts includes Account No. 3910, Retained Earnings. At the end of every fiscal year, the temporary owner's equity accounts (revenues, expenses, and drawing) are closed to a permanent owner's equity account. In PCA, there are two permanent owner's equity accounts: the owner's capital account and the Retained Earnings account. PCA closes the temporary accounts to the Retained Earnings account. This will be discussed in more detail in Chapter 11 when you close the fiscal year. In order to post to the general ledger, Peachtree requires a Retained Earnings account.

4. To print the Chart of Accounts, click [Print]. When the Print window appears, make the selections to print.

5. Click [Close] two times to return to the Business Status Navigation Center. If you need to edit the Chart of Accounts, select Maintain, then Chart of Accounts, *or* from the Business Status Navigation Center, link to <u>View Account List</u>.

BACKING UP THE CHART OF ACCOUNTS

When using PCA, information is automatically saved to the hard drive of the computer. In a classroom setting, a number of students may be using the same computer. This means that when you return to the computer lab, your data will be gone. Backing up data simply means saving it to a hard drive location or external media. Saving data (backing up) means that it will be available when you want to work again.

In this textbook, detailed steps are shown for backing up to a USB drive. The chart on pages 277-278 shows the size of backup files. (*Hint:* Your default location may differ. Refer to File Management, pages xviii-xx).

When the backup is made, you are saving the new company set up information (pages 279-287) and the revised chart of accounts (pages 288-293).

Comment: Backup & Restore

When a back up is made, you are saving to the current point in Peachtree. Each backup made should have a different backup name (file name) to distinguish one backup from another. In this way, if you need to restore to an earlier backup, you have the data for that purpose.

Remember, you can Restore if you need to go back to an earlier point in the company's data. Without a backup file, you cannot go back to an earlier point in the data. Since Chapters 9, 10, and 11 work together, your backup files are important.

In the business world, backups are unique to each business: daily, weekly, monthly. *Remember, back up before you leave the computer lab!*

Follow these steps to back up Mark Foltz's company and the chart of accounts.

1. Insert your USB flash drive. From the Navigation Bar, click

   System ; Back Up Now . Make sure that the box next to Include company name in the backup file name is *unchecked*.

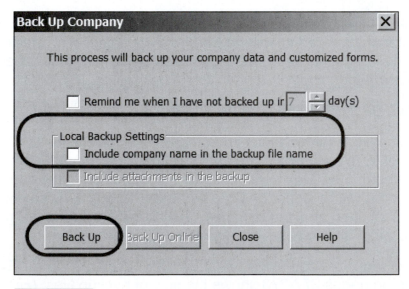

2. Click Back Up .

3. Go to the location of your USB drive. (*Or,* backup to the hard-drive or other location.) Type **Chapter 9 Chart of Accounts** in the File name field.

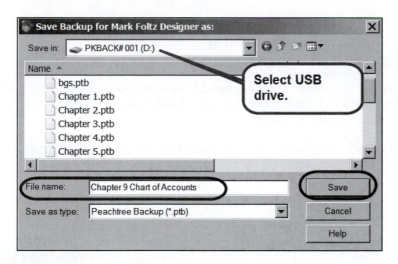

4. Click [Save] .

5. When the window prompts This company backup will require
   approximately 1 diskette, click [OK] . When the window
   prompts Please insert the first disk, click [OK] . When the Back
   Up Company scale is 100% complete, you have successfully backed
   up to the current point in Chapter 9. (This step will differ slightly if
   you are backing up to the default or other hard-drive location.)

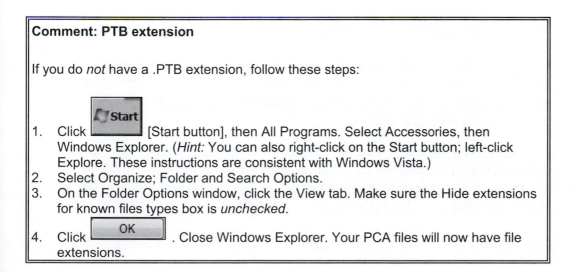

Comment: PTB extension

If you do *not* have a .PTB extension, follow these steps:

1. Click [Start] [Start button], then All Programs. Select Accessories, then
   Windows Explorer. (*Hint:* You can also right-click on the Start button; left-click
   Explore. These instructions are consistent with Windows Vista.)
2. Select Organize; Folder and Search Options.
3. On the Folder Options window, click the View tab. Make sure the Hide extensions
   for known files types box is *unchecked*.
4. Click [OK] . Close Windows Explorer. Your PCA files will now have file
   extensions.

> **Read Me: Problem Backing Up to USB Drive**
>
> If you encounter difficulties backing up to an external USB drive, backup to your desktop first. Then, copy the backup file from the desktop to the USB drive. Refer to Appendix A, Problem Backing Up to USB Drive or Other External Media, pages 756-758 for detailed steps.
>
> Some USB drives work better than others for backing up directly from Peachtree to the thumb drive.

Follow these steps to see the size of the backup file.

1. Right-click **Start** [start button]; left-click Open Windows Explorer.

2. Go to the location of your backup file; for example, the USB drive.

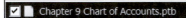

| ☑ 🗋 Chapter 9 Chart of Accounts.ptb | PTB File | 920 KB |

The Name of the file is Chapter 9 Chart of Accounts.ptb, the Type is PTB File, the Size of the file is 920 KB. (Your file size may differ.) As mentioned earlier, the textbook directions show how to back up to Peachtree's default hard drive location. Backups can also be made to other hard drive locations or external media. Close Windows Explorer.

RESTORING COMPANY DATA

After completing new company setup and editing the chart of accounts, you backed up (saved) Mark Foltz Designer company information. In order to start where you left off the last time you backed up, use Peachtree's Restore Wizard.

In the steps that follow you are shown how to restore the Peachtree backup file (.ptb extension). This backup was made on pages 296-297. Peachtree backups are compressed files which means that the file is made smaller.

1. If necessary, insert your USB flash drive. Start Peachtree.

2. These instructions assume that the Mark Foltz [your name] Designer - Peachtree Accounting window appears. If *not*, click File; Close

Company. If a screen prompts to keep two companies open, select
| No |. Open Mark Foltz [your name] Designer.

> ➤ **Troubleshooting: What if Mark Foltz Designer (or another name Designer) is not shown on Peachtree's title bar?**

a. Click File; Close Company.

b. From Peachtree's startup window, select
    | 🏢 Open an existing company |.

c. Click | Browse |. The Open Company window appears.

d. If Mark Foltz Designer (or, other name Designer) is shown select it, and then click | OK |. Go to page 300, step 3, and follow the steps to restore your data.

e. If *no Designer company is shown*, click | Cancel | then | Close |.

f. There are four menu bar options--| File Options Services Help |. Click File; Restore.

g. The Select Backup File window appears. Click | Browse |. In the Look in field, select the appropriate location of your backup file; for example, your USB drive.

h. Select the Chapter 9 Chart of Accounts.ptb backup file; click | Open |.

i. Make sure the Location field shows the Chapter 9 Chart of Accounts.ptb backup file. Click | Next > |.

j. The Select Company window appears. Click on the radio button next to A New Company.

Read Me

Observe that there are two options on the Select Company window: An Existing Company *and* A New Company. If you select A New Company, then the company will be named exactly the same as the backup file selected. You can restore an existing company—one that is previously set up—*or* you can restore a new company, bypassing the process of setting up a new company.

Let's say you wanted to restore a backup file for a company that was *not* set up in Peachtree. Some computer labs delete directories from the hard drive; for example, you have a back up file but the company, Mark Foltz [or your name] Designer, is *not* listed as a Peachtree company. If you start Peachtree and you *cannot* select the appropriate company, use the Restore Wizard to select A New Company. Using the backup file, and the selection for A New Company, you are able to start where you left off the last time you used Peachtree.

---

    k. The Company Name field shows Mark Foltz Designer. The Location field shows the location of your backup file. The last two letters of the location field shows "de." Click Next >. Continue with step 7 on page 301.

3. From the Navigation Bar, select System ; click Restore Now .

4. The Select Backup File window appears. Click Browse . The Open Backup File window appears. Go to the Location of your Chapter 9 Chart of Accounts.ptb file and select it.

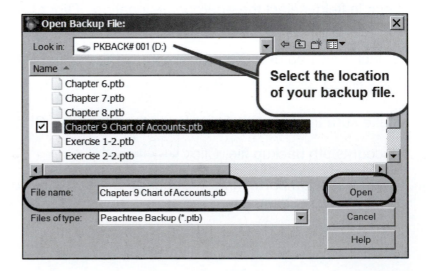

5. Click[Open]   The Select Backup File window shows the location of your backup file, X:\Chapter 9 Chart of Accounts.ptb. (Substitute X for your drive letter.) Click [Next >].

6. The Select Company window appears. The radio button next to An Existing Company is selected. The Company Name field shows Mark Foltz Designer (*or,* your first and last name, Designer). The Location field shows the default location on the hard drive for Mark Foltz Designer – C:\Sage\Peachtree\Company\marfolde.

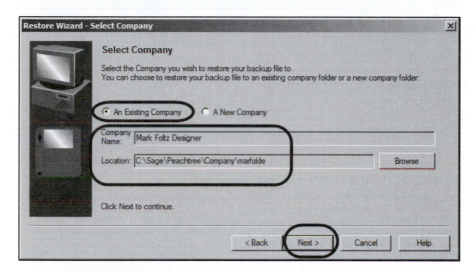

7. Click [Next >]. The Restore Options window appears. Make sure that the box next to Company Data is checked. Click [Next >].

8. The Confirmation window appears. Check the From and To fields to make sure they are correct. Click [Finish]. When the Restore Company scale is 100% complete, your data is restored. (*Hint:* The Student Version of Peachtree prompts that company data can be used for 14 months. After that time the data expires.

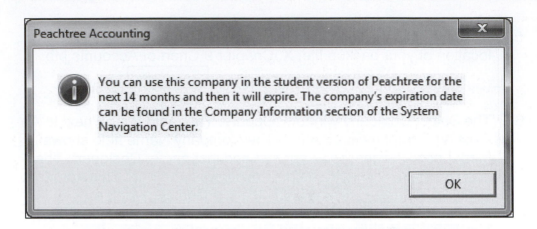

9. Click OK . Mark Foltz [your name] Designer opens.

Comment: Global Options

On pages xvi-xvii (step 1), you were instructed to select manual and 2 decimal places in the Decimal Entry and Number of Decimal Places fields. If you did *not* do this, follow these steps:

1. From the menu bar, click Options; Global.
2. In the Decimal Entry field, click Manual. When Manual is selected, a black circle is placed within a circle (radio button).
3. In the Quantity fields, Standard fields, and Unit Price fields make sure **2** is selected.
4. The boxes in the Hide General Accounts area should be *unchecked*.
5. Click OK .

In order for your windows to look like the ones shown in this textbook, you need to have the *same* global settings as the ones shown on pages xvi-xvii, steps 1-3. When global options are selected, this feature is in effect for all companies.

ENTERING CHART OF ACCOUNTS BEGINNING BALANCES

Mr. Foltz hired you to do his monthly record keeping. In order to begin accounting tasks for Mr. Foltz, you asked him for a ***Balance Sheet***. A Balance Sheet lists the types and amounts of assets, liabilities, and equity as of a specific date. A balance sheet is also called a ***statement of financial position***.

Mark Foltz Designer Balance Sheet **October 1, 2012**		
ASSETS		
Current Assets		
1010 - Money Market Account	$ 9,700.00	
1020 - Checking Account	9,750.75	
1040 - IRA Savings Account	27,730.35	
1045 - WI State Retirement	35,612.00	
1300 - Prepaid Insurance	2,100.00	
1400 - Prepaid Rent	600.00	
1450 - Supplies	1,771.83	
Total Current Assets		$ 87,264.93
Property and Equipment		
1500 - Computer Equipment	$ 6,800.00	
1510 - Furniture	5,000.00	
1520 - Automobile	19,000.00	
Total Property and Equipment		30,800.00
Total Assets		$ 118,064.93
LIABILITIES AND CAPITAL		
Current Liabilities		
2000 - VISA Payable	$ 5,250.65	
Total Current Liabilities		$ 5,250.65
Capital		
3920 - Mark Foltz, Capital		112,814.28
Total Liabilities and Capital		$ 118,064.93

The information in this Balance Sheet will be the basis for recording Mr. Foltz's beginning balances.

Follow these steps to record Mark Foltz's beginning balances.

1. From the menu bar, select Maintain, then Chart of Accounts.

2. Click [Account Beginning Balances].

> Observe that the balance sheet on page 303 is dated October 1, 2012. **Beginning balances must be set for the previous month– September 1 through 30, 2012**. You select 9/1/12 through 9/30/12 because Peachtree posts on the last day of the month. When 9/1/12 through 9/30/12 is selected as the chart of accounts beginning balance period, transaction windows start on October 1, 2012, and reports are dated October 31, 2012. **The September 30 ending balance is the October 1 beginning balance.**
>
> In Chapter 11, you print end-of-year financial statements. In order for your end-of-year financial statements to show the correct current month and year-to-date amounts, you *must* set your beginning balances for the previous month. *Remember, select September 1 through 30, 2012, as the period for setting beginning balances. The beginning balance period cannot be changed later.*

3. Scroll down the Select Period list. Click From 9/1/12 through 9/30/12 to highlight it.

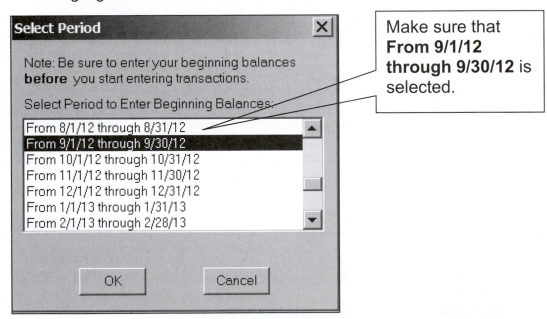

Make sure that **From 9/1/12 through 9/30/12** is selected.

IMPORTANT: Check the Select Period window. The period you select should be From 9/1/12 through 9/30/12. The period selected affects financial statement current month and year-to-date account balances. Make sure that **From 9/1/12 through 9/30/12** is selected.

4. Make sure that you have selected **From 9/1/12 through 9/30/12** on the Select Period window. You cannot change the period later. Click
   OK .

5. The Chart of Accounts Beginning Balances window appears. Below the icon bar, **Beginning Balances as of September 30, 2012** is shown. For Account ID 1010, Money Market Account, type **9700** in the Assets, Expenses field. Press **<Enter>**.

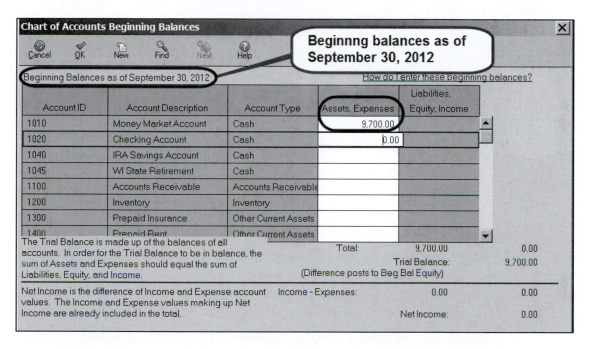

6. Account No. 1020, Checking Account is selected. Type **9750.75** and press **<Enter>**.

   Continue entering the beginning balances using the Balance Sheet on page 303. For credit balances, if necessary, click on the Liabilities, Equity, Income field. When you are finished, Assets, Expenses equals Liabilities, Equity, Income. This indicates that there are equal debits and credits.

   Compare your completed Chart of Accounts Beginning Balances window with the one shown on the next page.

Chart of Accounts Beginning Balances

Cancel	OK	New	Find	Next	Help

Entered beginning balances as of September 30, 2012.

Beginning Balances as of September 30, 2012

How do I enter these beginning balances?

Account ID	Account Description	Account Type	Assets, Expenses	Liabilities, Equity, Income
1910	Accum. Depreciation - Furnit	Accumulated Deprec		
1920	Accum. Depreciation - Auton	Accumulated Deprec		
2000	VISA Payable	Accounts Payable		5,250.65
2380	Income Taxes Payable	Other Current Liabiliti		
2400	Publisher Advances	Other Current Liabiliti		
3910	Retained Earnings	Equity-Retained Earn		
3920	Mark Foltz, Capital	Equity-doesn't close		112,814.28
3930	Mark Foltz, Draw	Equity-gets closed		0.00

The Trial Balance is made up of the balances of all accounts. In order for the Trial Balance to be in balance, the sum of Assets and Expenses should equal the sum of Liabilities, Equity, and Income.

Net Income is the difference of Income and Expense account values. The Income and Expense values making up Net Income are already included in the total.

Total:	118,064.93	118,064.93
Trial Balance:		0.00
(Difference posts to Beg Bal Equity)		
Income - Expenses:	0.00	0.00
Net Income:		0.00

Comment

What if your Trial Balance does *not* show 0.00? Make sure that debit balances for assets and credit balances for liabilities and capital accounts are entered correctly.

Make sure that your beginning balances are as of September 30, 2012. If you enter your balances for the wrong month (period), your financial statements will not show the current month and year-to-date amounts correctly. Remember, Chapters 9, 10 and 11 work together. If beginning balances are incorrect in Chapter 9, Chapters 10 and 11 financial statements will be incorrect.

7. Click [OK]. A window appears briefly that says Creating Journal Entries.

8. At the Maintain Chart of Accounts window, click [Close] to return to the Business Status Navigation Center.

To check your chart of accounts beginning balances, select Maintain, Chart of Accounts, [Account Beginning Balances]; then select the From 9/1/12 through 9/30/12, [OK]. Make any needed corrections. Refer to pages 303-307 for entering the chart of

accounts beginning balances. When through, click 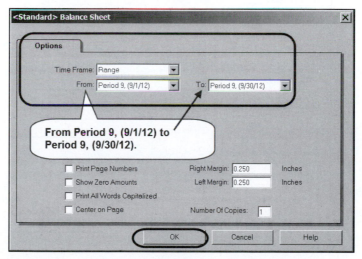 . Close the Maintain Chart of Accounts window.

Display the September 30, 2012 Balance Sheet

On page 303, the beginning balances for Mike Foltz Designer were shown on the October 1, 2012 Balance Sheet. It's important to record account beginning balances for the month *before* the business's start date. That means you should make sure that you entered the appropriate period for beginning balances–From 9/1/12 through 9/30/12 (refer to steps 2 and 3, page 304).

To check that you entered account beginning balances as of September 30, 2012, follow these steps. September 30 ending balances are October 1 beginning balances.

1. From the menu bar, select Reports & Forms, then Financial Statements. Double-click <Standard> Balance Sheet.

2. The <Standard> Balance Sheet Options window appears. In the Time Frame field, select Range.

3. In the From field, select Period 9, (9/1/12). In the To Field, select Period 9, (9/30/12). Click <OK>.

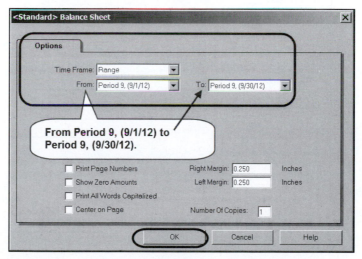

Compare the balance sheet with the one shown on the next page. The September 30, 2012 account balances match the ones shown on the October 1, 2012 balance sheet on page 303. If your account balances do not agree, or if they show zeroes, you should redo the account beginning balances. (*Hint:* Restore the Chapter 9 Chart of Accounts.ptb file completed on pages 296-297. Redo steps 1-8, pages 303-307.)

Mark Foltz Designer
Balance Sheet
September 30, 2012

ASSETS

Current Assets
Money Market Account	$ 9,700.00	
Checking Account	9,750.75	
IRA Savings Account	27,730.35	
WI State Retirement	35,612.00	
Prepaid Insurance	2,100.00	
Prepaid Rent	600.00	
Supplies	1,771.83	
Total Current Assets		87,264.93

Property and Equipment
Computer Equipment	6,800.00	
Furniture	5,000.00	
Automobile	19,000.00	
Total Property and Equipment		30,800.00

Other Assets

Total Other Assets		0.00
Total Assets		$ 118,064.93

LIABILITIES AND CAPITAL

Current Liabilities
VISA Payable	$ 5,250.65	
Total Current Liabilities		5,250.65

Long-Term Liabilities

Total Long-Term Liabilities		0.00
Total Liabilities		5,250.65

Capital
Mark Foltz, Capital	112,814.28	
Net Income	0.00	
Total Capital		112,814.28
Total Liabilities & Capital		$ 118,064.93

Unaudited - For Management Purposes Only

Observe that the report shows "Unaudited - For Management Purposes Only."

➤ **Troubleshooting: The companies set up in Chapter 9 continue in Chapters 10 and 11. If account beginning balances are <u>not</u> set up**

for September 30, 2012, your financial statements year-to-date column in Chapter 11 will not show the correct account balances.

4. Close the Balance Sheet and the Select a Report or Form windows.

5. On the Business Status Navigation Center's toolbar, click `↻ Refresh`. Notice that the account balances are updated. Balances shown in red are credit balances.

Account Balances		⚙ Customize
Account Description	**Account ID** △	**Balance** ▲
Money Market Account	1010	$9,700.00
Checking Account	1020	$9,750.75
IRA Savings Account	1040	$27,730.35
WI State Retirement	1045	$35,612.00
Accounts Receivable	1100	$0.00
VISA Payable	2000	($5.250.65) ▼

6. Link to View Account List to see all the accounts and their Running Balance. A partial Account List is shown below. (*Hint:* Accounts shown in red with a parenthesis are credit balances.) These account balances agree with the Balance Sheet shown on page 303.

Account ID △	Description	Type	Running Balance ▲
1010	Money Market Account	Cash	$9,700.00
1020	Checking Account	Cash	$9,750.75
1040	IRA Savings Account	Cash	$27,730.35
1045	WI State Retirement	Cash	$35,612.00
1100	Accounts Receivable	Accounts Receivable	$0.00
1200	Inventory	Inventory	$0.00
1300	Prepaid Insurance	Other Current Assets	$2,100.00
1400	Prepaid Rent	Other Current Assets	$600.00
1450	Supplies	Other Current Assets	$1,771.83
1500	Computer Equipment	Fixed Assets	$6,800.00
1510	Furniture	Fixed Assets	$5,000.00
1520	Automobile	Fixed Assets	$19,000.00
1900	Accum. Depreciation - Comp Eqt	Accumulated Depreciation	$0.00
1910	Accum. Depreciation - Furnitur	Accumulated Depreciation	$0.00
1920	Accum. Depreciation - Automobi	Accumulated Depreciation	$0.00
2000	VISA Payable	Accounts Payable	($5,250.65)
2380	Income Taxes Payable	Other Current Liabilities	$0.00
2400	Publisher Advances	Other Current Liabilities	$0.00
3910	Retained Earnings	Equity-Retained Earnings	$0.00
3920	Mark Foltz, Capital	Equity-does not close	($112,814.28)
3930	Mark Foltz, Draw	Equity-gets closed	$0.00

7. Close the Account List.

USING WINDOWS EXPLORER TO SEE THE FILE SIZE

To see the size of the Mark Foltz Designer file, following these steps.

1. Right-click 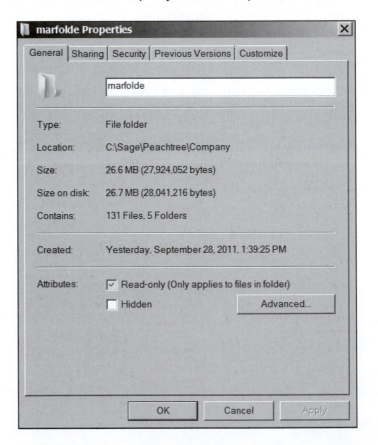 [start button]; left-click Open Windows Explorer.

2. Go to the location of the company data. The default location is C:\Sage\Peachtree\Company (or your company data location; refer to page xix). Click on the Company folder.

3. Right-click on the marfolde folder (or the one with your shortened name.). *Hint:* Peachtree shortens the company name using the first three letters of the first word, first three letters from the second word, and two letters from the third word. There are eight characters in Peachtree's shortened company name.

4. Left-click Properties. The default location is drive C. The title bar shows the shortened company name Properties.

Observe that the size of the file is 26.6 MB (27,924,052 bytes). To save all the data contained in the Mark Foltz [or your name] folder, use Windows Explorer to copy, then paste the marfolde folder from drive C to a USB drive, CD, or DVD. (Your file size may differ from the marfolde Properties window. This is okay.)

5. When you are finished comparing your properties window, click
    | OK |, then | x | on the Windows Explorer title bar.

BACKING UP BEGINNING BALANCES

Follow these steps to back up the work completed so far. This backup saves the Mark Foltz company set up on pages 279-287, the chart of accounts (pages 288-293), and the beginning balances (pages 303-307).

The idea is to make periodic backups so that, if needed, you can go back to an earlier point in the data. Use a different file name for each backup so that you can distinguish one file from another one.

1. If necessary, close all windows and insert your USB flash drive. From the System Navigation Center, select | Back Up Now |. (*Or,* from the menu bar, select File, then Back Up.)

2. If necessary, uncheck the box next to Include company name in the backup file name. Click | Back Up |.

3. In the Save in field, go to the location of your USB drive.

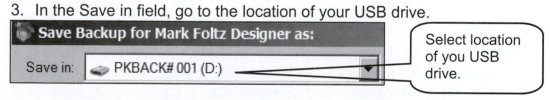

Select location of you USB drive.

4. Type **Chapter 9 Beginning Balances** in the File name field.

Type the file name.

5. Click | Save |.

6. When the window prompts that This company backup will require approximately 1 diskette, click [OK] . Click [OK] again when the window prompts Please insert the first disk. When the Back Up Company scale is 100% complete, you have successfully backed up to this point in Chapter 9. (This step will differ slightly if you are backing up to the default or other hard drive location.)

In Chapter 9, you learned how to set up a new Peachtree company, edit the chart of accounts, and how to use information from a balance sheet to enter beginning balances. Because two files were backed up in Chapter 9—the Chapter 9 Chart of Accounts.ptb file and the Chapter 9 Beginning Balances.ptb file—you could restore either file to start at that point in the data. For example, what if you notice a mistake and need to start at an earlier place in the data? By saving two files, you have two different backup files to restore. *Remember, in the business world backups are made frequently.*

EXPORT THE CHART OF ACCOUNTS AND BEGINNING BALANCES TO EXCEL

Follow these steps to export the October 1, 2012 Balance Sheet to Excel.

1. From the menu bar, select Reports & Forms, select General Ledger. Double-click Chart of Accounts. The Chart of Accounts appears. If needed, expand the Accounts Description and Account Type columns. (Click [↔] to widen the column.)

2. Click [Excel] . On the Copy Report to Excel window, in the file option area, Create a new Microsoft Excel workbook is selected. In the Report header option field, Show header in Excel worksheet is selected.

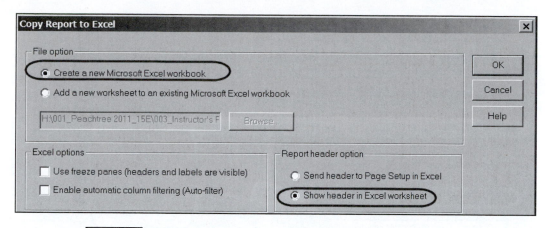

3. Click [OK]. The chart of accounts exports to Excel.

4. Save. Use the file name **Chapter 9_Chart of Accounts and Beginning Balances.xlsx**. (*Hint:* If you are using Excel 2003, your file extension is .xls.)

5. Go back to Peachtree's Select a Report or Form window. In the Reports list, select Financial Statements. Double-click <Standard> Balance Sheet. Click [OK].

6. Click [Excel]. On the Copy Report to Excel window, select Add a new worksheet to an existing Microsoft Excel workbook.

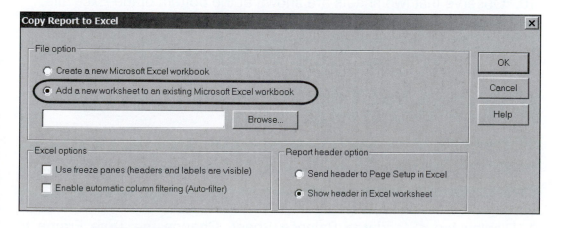

7. Click [Browse...] to go to the location of the Chapter 9_Chart of

Accounts and Beginning Balances.xlsx file. Click 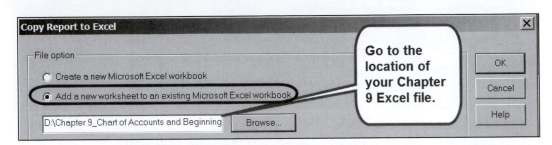. You are returned to the Copy Report to Excel window. Observe that the Browse field shows the location of the Chapter 9_Chart of Accounts and Beginning Balances file.

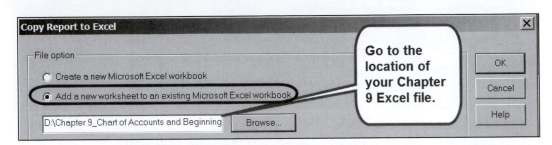

8. Click [OK].

9. The balance sheet appears in Excel. Change the date to **October 1, 2012**. (*Hint:* The balance sheet is shown on page 303.)

Mark Foltz Designer
Balance Sheet
October 1, 2012

10. Observe that two sheets are shown at the bottom of the Excel file: Chart of Accounts and Balance Sheet.

11. Save the file. Exit Excel. Close all Peachtree windows.

SAVE PDF FILES

Follow these steps to save the September 30, 2012 Balance Sheet and Chart of Accounts as Adobe PDF file.

1. Display the <Standard> Balance Sheet. Change the Time Frame to Range. Select From Period 9, (9/1/12) To Period 9, (9/30/12).

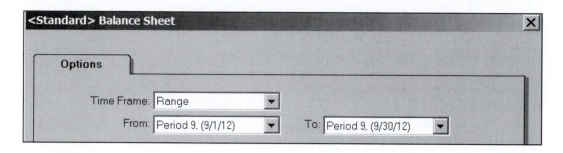

2. Click <OK>. The September 30, 2012 Balance Sheet appears. Click

   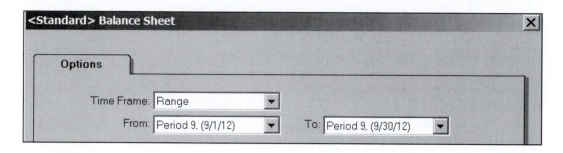. Select your USB drive. Save the file. The suggested file name is **Chapter 9_Balance Sheet.pdf**. (*Hint:* The September 30 ending balances are the October 1, 2012 beginning balances.) Compare the balance sheet to the one shown on page 303.

3. Display the Balance Sheet. Save as a PDF file. The suggested file name is **Chapter 9_Chart of Accounts.pdf.**

SUMMARY AND REVIEW

Complete the following end-of-chapter activities:

1. Going to the net, pages 315-316.

2. Multiple-choice questions, pages 316-318.

3. Exercises 9-1 and 9-2, pages 318-324.

4. Analysis questions, page 325.

5. Assessment rubric, page 325.

6. Chapter 9 Index, page 326.

GOING TO THE NET

Access information about the chart of accounts at http://en.wikipedia.org/wiki/Chart_of_accounts. Read the information on Wikipedia's chart of accounts website. (Going to the Net links are on the textbook website at www.mhhe.com/yacht2012; link to Student Edition, select Chapter 9, Going to the Net Exercises.)

1. What is the chart of accounts?
2. List four asset accounts, two liability accounts, two equity accounts, one revenue account, and three expense accounts.
3. What is the trial balance?

Multiple Choice Questions: The Online Learning Center includes these questions and the analysis question at www.mhhe.com/yacht2012, select Student Edition, Chapter 9, QA Templates.

_____ 1. In Part 2 of the book, you complete monthly accounting for which type of business?

   a. Corporate form of business.
   b. Merchandising business.
   c. Manufacturing business.
   d. Service business.
   e. None of the above.

_____ 2. Which type of accounting method does Mark Foltz Designer use?

   a. Cash basis accounting.
   b. Accrual accounting.
   c. PCA does not require you to make a choice.
   d. There is no difference between cash basis and accrual accounting.
   e. None of the above.

_____ 3. Mark Foltz's business type is a:

   a. Corporation.
   b. Partnership.
   c. Sole proprietorship.
   d. Non-profit.
   e. None of the above.

_____ 4. What chart of accounts did you select for Mr. Foltz's chart of accounts?

   a. Accounting firm.
   b. Merchandising company.
   c. Non-profit business.
   d. Service Company.
   e. None of the above.

_____ 5. Mr. Foltz uses which type of posting method?

    a. Batch posting.
    b. Real-time posting.
    c. There is no need to post his books.
    d. PCA does not require you to make a posting choice.
    e. None of the above.

_____ 6. You can restore data by making which menu bar selection?

    a. File; Restore.
    b. Tasks; Backup.
    c. Maintain; Restore.
    d. Maintain; Backup.
    e. None of the above.

_____ 7. The correct file name for backing up Mark Foltz Designer, the chart of accounts, and the October 1, 2012 beginning balances is:

    a. Chapter 9 Chart of Accounts October.
    b. Chapter 9 Beginning Balances.
    c. chap9.
    d. chap7.
    e. None of the above.

_____ 8. Peachtree assigns the following shortened company name to Mark Foltz Designer:

    a. \Company.
    b. \Peachtree.
    c. \marfolde.
    d. \Sage Software.
    e. None of the above.

_____ 9. The account type of Account No. 3920, Mark Foltz, Capital (or your name, Capital) is:

    a. \Cash.
    b. \Equity-gets closed.
    c. \Equity-doesn't close.
    d. \Current assets.
    e. None of the above.

_____10. When saving an Excel 2007 or 2010 file, the file extension is:

     a. docx
     b. xlsx
     c. pdf
     d. ptb
     e. None of the above.

Exercise 9-1: Follow the instructions below to complete Exercise 9-1:

1. Start Peachtree. If Mark Foltz [your name] Designer or other company opens, select File; New Company. When the window prompts, Do you want to keep Mark Foltz (your name) Designer open?, click | No | . The Create a New Company – Introduction window appears. Click | Next > | . (*Or,* from the startup window, select | 🪄 Create a new company |.)

2. Type the following company information:

Company Name:	Design by Your Name (*Use your first and last name*)
Address Line 1:	Your address
City, State, Zip	Your city, Your State, Your Zip code
Country:	USA
Telephone:	Your telephone number
Fax:	Your fax number (if any)
Business Type:	Sole Proprietorship
E-mail:	Type your email address

    Leave the Tax ID Numbers fields blank.

    The Company Name field should show Design *your first and last name*. The Business Type field shows Sole Proprietorship.

3. Click [Next >]. At the Select a method to create your company window, select Copy settings from an existing Peachtree Accounting company.

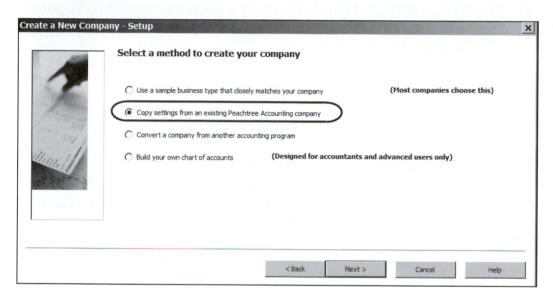

4. Click [Next >].

5. Highlight Mark Foltz [or your name] Designer, then click [Next >].

6. At the Copy Company Information window, accept the default selections by clicking [Next >].

7. Accept the default for accrual accounting by clicking [Next >].

8. Accept the default for Real Time posting by clicking [Next >].

9. At the You are ready to create your company window, click [Finish]. If the screen prompts You can use this company in the student version of Peachtree for the next 14 months and then it will expire, click [OK].

10. If the Setup Guide window appears, click on the box next to Don't show this screen at startup. Click [Close], then [OK].

11. The Design by Your Name - Peachtree Accounting window appears. Make sure the period is Period 10 - 10/01/12-10/31/12 –
[Period 10 - 10/01/12-10/31/12].

12. Make the following changes to the Chart of Accounts:

   a. Change the name of the following accounts:

   • Account No. 1020, Checking Account to Midwest Bank
   • Account No. 2000, VISA Payable to Accounts Payable
   • Account No. 3920, Mark Foltz, Capital to Your Name, Capital (Make sure the Account Type is Equity-doesn't close)
   • Account No. 3930, Mark Foltz, Draw to Your Name, Draw
   • Account No. 4050, Royalty Income to Design Income
   • Account No. 6800 Freight Expense to Conference Fees

   b. Delete the following accounts:

   • Account No. 1010, Money Market Account
   • Account No. 1040, IRA Savings Account
   • Account No. 1045, WI State Retirement
   • Account No. 2400, Publisher Advances

   c. Add the following accounts:

   • Account No. 6180, Automobile Expense
   • Account No. 6420, Water and Power Expense
   • Account No. 7400, Postage Expense

13. Print the chart of accounts.

14. Follow these steps to back up Exercise 9-1.

   a. Insert your USB flash drive. From the Navigation Bar, click [System]; [Back Up Now]. Make sure that the box next to Include company name in the backup file name is *unchecked*.

b. Click [Back Up]. Go to the location of your USB drive (or backup to another location). Type **Exercise 9-1** in the File name field.

c. Click [Save].

d. When the window prompts that This company backup will require approximately 1 diskette, click [OK]. Click [OK] when the window prompts Please insert the first disk. When the Back Up Company scale is 100% complete, you have successfully backed up to the current point in Chapter 9. (*Hint:* If you are backing up to a hard drive location, this step will differ slightly.)

15. Click File; Exit to exit Peachtree or continue.

Exercise 9-2: Follow the instructions below to complete Exercise 9-2. Exercise 9-1 *must* be completed before starting Exercise 9-2.

1. Start PCA. If necessary, open the company that you set up in Exercise 9-1, Design by Your Name. (*Hint:* If a different company opens, select File; Open Previous Company. When the screen prompts do you want to open two companies, select [No].)

2. Follow the steps on the next page to restore Exercise 9-1.[3] If you are continuing from Exercise 9-1, you do not need to restore.

    a. If necessary, insert your USB flash drive. From the Navigation Bar, select [System]; click [Restore Now].

    ---

    [3]You can restore from your back up file even if *no* Peachtree company exists. From the menu bar, click File; Close Company. Peachtree's startup window appears with four menu bar options-- [File Options Services Help]. Select File; Restore. Browse to the location of the Exercise 9-1.ptb backup file. On the Restore Wizard's Select Company window, select A New Company. The *A New Company* selection allows you to restore backup data *and* set up the company. For more information, refer to Troubleshooting on pages 299-300.

b. The Select Backup File window appears. Click Browse . In the Look in field, select the appropriate location of the Exercise 9-1.ptb back file. Click Open . Make sure the Location field shows the Exercise 9-1.ptb file. Click Next > .

c. The Select Company window appears. The radio button next to An Existing Company is selected. Check that the Company Name and Location fields are correct. Click Next > .

d. The Restore Options window appears. Make sure that the box next to Company Data is *checked*. Click Next > .

e. The Confirmation window appears. Check the From and To fields to make sure they are correct. Click Finish . When the Restore Company scale is 100% complete, your data is restored. (*Hint:* The Student Version of Peachtree prompts that company data can be used for 14 months. After that time the data expires. Click OK . Design by Student Name [your first and last name] opens.)

3. Use the Balance Sheet on the next page to record chart of accounts beginning balances. (Hint: Remember to select **9/1/12 through 9/30/12** as the period for entering chart of accounts beginning balances. Enter beginning balances as of September 30, 2012.)

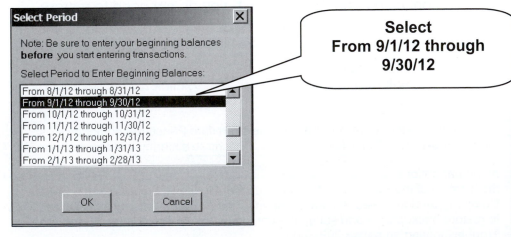

Enter the beginning balances as of September 30, 2012 from the Balance Sheet shown below.

Design by Your Name Balance Sheet October 1, 2012		
ASSETS		
Current Assets		
Midwest Bank	$14,500.00	
Prepaid Insurance	1,000.00	
Prepaid Rent	700.00	
Supplies	850.00	
Total Current Assets		$17,050.00
Property and Equipment		
Computer Equipment	6,500.00	
Furniture	3,500.00	
Automobile	19,000.00	
Total Property and Equipment		29,000.00
Total Assets		$ 46,050.00
LIABILITIES AND CAPITAL		
Current Liabilities		
Accounts Payable	$1,050.00	
Total Current Liabilities		$1,050.00
Capital		
Your Name, Capital		45,000.00
Total Liabilities and Capital		$ 46,050.00

4. Print the September 30, 2012 balance sheet. (*Hint:* Refer to pages 307-309 to change the date range for the balance sheet. September 30 ending balances are October 1, 2012 beginning balances.)

CHECK YOUR FIGURES: Chart of Accounts & Balance Sheet

Account No. 3930, Your Name, Draw
Account No. 4050, Design Income
Account No. 7400, Postage Expense
Account No. 1020, Midwest Bank, $14,500
Account No. 3920, Your Name, Capital, $45,000

5. Follow these steps to back up Exercise 9-2.

   a. Close all Peachtree windows. If necessary, insert your USB flash drive. From the System Navigation Center, click ⬚ Back Up Now ⬚.

   b. If necessary, uncheck the box next to Include company name in the backup file name. Click ⬚ Back Up ⬚.

   c. In the Save in field, select the location of your USB drive (or other location to back up).Type **Exercise 9-2** in the File name field.

   d. Click ⬚ Save ⬚.

   e. When the window prompts that This company backup will require approximately 1 diskette, click ⬚ OK ⬚. Click ⬚ OK ⬚ when the window prompts Please insert the first disk. When the Back Up Company scale is 100% complete, you have successfully backed up to the current point in Exercise 9-2.

6. Export the chart of accounts and beginning balances to Excel. Use the file name **Exercise 9-2_Chart of Accounts and Beginning Balances.xlsx**. Change the date on the balance sheet to October 1, 2012.

7. Save the Chart of Accounts and September 30, 2012 Balance Sheet as PDF files. Use the file names **Exercise 9-2_Chart of Accounts.pdf** and **Exercise 9-2_Balance Sheet.pdf** as the file names. Remember to change the Balance Sheet date to September 30, 2012. (*Hint:* Refer to pages 307-309 to change the date range for the balance sheet.)

ANALYSIS QUESTIONS

1. What chart of accounts beginning balance date is used for entering October 1, 2012 account balances in Peachtree?

2. How does the account beginning balance date affect the current month and year-to-date amounts on the financial statements?

ASSESSMENT RUBRIC

Complete the Assessment Rubric online at www.mhhe.com/yacht2012; Student Edition, select Chapter 9, Assessment Rubric link. To review Peachtree's navigation centers, menu selections, and windows, complete the blank fields online.

Task	Date	Selections	Window	Shortened Company Name
October 1, 2012 Beginning Balances				

CHAPTER 9 INDEX

Chapter 10 | Maintaining Accounting Records for Service Businesses

LEARNING OBJECTIVES

1. Restore data from Chapter 9. (This backup was made on pages 311-312.)[1]
2. Record and post deposits, checks and ATMs.
3. Complete account reconciliation.
4. Display the Account Register.
5. Display the Cash Receipts Journal, Cash Disbursements Journal, and General Journal.
6. Display the general ledger trial balance.
7. Print financial statements.
8. Export the October General Ledger Trial Balance, Balance Sheet and Income Statement to Excel and save as PDF files.
9. Make four backups, save two Excel files, and save four PDF files.[2]

In Chapter 10, you continue the work started in Chapter 9. You complete the computer accounting cycle for the month of October using your client's transaction register and bank statement as **source documents**. In accounting, you learn that source documents are used to show written evidence of a business transaction. For Mark Foltz Designer, the source documents used are his transaction register and bank statement. The **transaction register** shows Mr. Foltz's checking account activity.

Remember, Chapter 9 must be completed before starting Chapter 10.

GETTING STARTED

Follow the steps on the next page to continue using Mark Foltz [your first and last name] Designer company data.

---

[1]All activities in Chapter 9 must be completed before starting Chapter 10.

[2]Refer to the chart on pages 277-278 for the file names and size of backup files, Excel files, and Adobe PDF files.

The McGraw-Hill Companies, Inc., *Computer Accounting with Peachtree by Sage Complete Accounting 2012, 16e*

1. Start Peachtree. Open an existing company, Mark Foltz Designer (or your name Designer).[3] (*Hint:* If a different company opens, select File; Open a Previous Company; select Mark Foltz Designer. When the window prompts, Do you want to keep XXXXXX open?, click

   No . If you prefer to keep two companies open, click

   Yes .)

2. To restore Mark Foltz's data from Chapter 9, do the following. The Chapter 9 Beginning Balances.ptb backup was made on page 311-312.

   a. Insert your USB flash drive. From the System Navigation Center, click Restore Now . (*Or,* from the menu bar, click File, Restore.)

   b. The Select Backup File window appears. Click Browse . In the Look in field, select the appropriate location of your Chapter 9 Beginning Balances.ptb file. Click Open . Make sure the Location field shows the Chapter 9 Beginning Balances.ptb file. Click Next > .

   c. The Select Company window appears. The radio button next to An Existing Company is selected. Check that the Company Name and Location fields are correct. Click Next > .

   d. The Restore Options window appears. Make sure that the box next to Company Data is *checked*. Click Next > .

   e. The Confirmation window appears. Check the From and To fields to make sure they are correct. Click Finish . When the Restore Company scale is 100% complete, your data is restored. (*Hint:* The Student Version of Peachtree prompts that company

---

[3]You can restore from your back up file even if *no* designer company exists. From Peachtree's start up window, select File; Restore. Select the location of your backup file. On the Restore Wizard's Select Company window, select A New Company. The *A New Company* selection allows you to restore your backup data, bypassing the process of new company set up. For more information, refer to Troubleshooting on pages 299-300.

data can be used for 14 months. After that time the data expires. Click [OK]. Mark Foltz [your first and last name] Designer opens.)

To make sure you are starting in the appropriate place in the data (Chapter 9 Beginning Balances.ptb backup) check the balance sheet. A partial balance sheet is shown below. The complete balance sheet is shown on page 308.

Unless you changed the date range, the balance sheet shows October 31, 2011. Peachtree dates reports the last day of the period (month). On page 308, you changed the balance sheet's date range to check that you entered beginning balances as of September 30.

Mark Foltz Designer
Balance Sheet
October 31, 2012

ASSETS

Current Assets			
Money Market Account	$	9,700.00	
Checking Account		9,750.75	
IRA Savings Account		27,730.35	
WI State Retirement		35,612.00	
Prepaid Insurance		2,100.00	
Prepaid Rent		600.00	
Supplies		1,771.83	
Total Current Assets			87,264.93
Property and Equipment			
Computer Equipment		6,800.00	
Furniture		5,000.00	
Automobile		19,000.00	
Total Property and Equipment			30,800.00
Other Assets			
Total Other Assets			0.00
Total Assets	$		118,064.93

RECORDING DEPOSITS, CHECKS AND ATMs

In PCA, the Receipts window is used to record deposits. When you save a receipt, PCA automatically journalizes the entry in the Cash Receipts Journal. When Mr. Foltz writes a check, the disbursement is recorded in the Write Checks window. When you save the recorded check or ATM, the entry is automatically journalized in the Cash Disbursements Journal.

Peachtree's Write Checks window is a simplified version of the Payments window. In this chapter, use the Write Checks window to issue a check for expenses, assets, or owner's draw.

Mr. Foltz's transaction register has the information necessary to record entries for the month of October. Since Mr. Foltz is a new client, information from his Balance Sheet was used for an opening entry. His transaction register lists the information for the rest of the month.

Follow these steps to show the cash balance on the Receipts window and Payments window.

1. From the menu bar, click Options, Global.

2. Make sure the box next to Recalculate cash balance automatically in Receipts, Payments,

   Other Options

   ☑ Warn if a record was changed but not saved
   ☐ Hide inactive records
   ☑ Recalculate cash balance automatically in Receipts, Payments, and Payroll Entry
   ☐ Use Timeslips Accounting Link

   and Payroll Entry has a check mark next to it.

3. Click [OK]. When you use the Receipts window or Write Checks window, the transaction register balance agrees with the Cash Account balance shown on these windows.

Mr. Foltz's transaction register shows an October 1 deposit of $11,000. A section of Mr. Foltz's transaction register is shown.

Check Number	Date	Description of Transaction	Payment	Deposit	Balance
	9/30				9,750.75
	10/1	Deposit (publisher's advance)		11,000.00	20,750.75

▶ Follow these steps to record the October 1 deposit from Mr. Foltz's transaction register. (The arrow indicates a flash video at www.mhhe.com/yacht2012; Student Edition, select Chapter 9, Flash Videos, Deposits.)

1. From the menu bar, select Tasks, Receipts. The Select a Cash Account window displays. If necessary click on the down arrow to select Checking Account.

2. Click [OK]. The Receipts window displays.

3. Your cursor is in the Deposit ticket ID field. Type **10/01/12**. (*Hint: Use the date of the deposit for the Deposit ticket ID field.*)

4. Click on the Name field. Type **Deposit** in the Name field.

5. Click on the Reference field. Type **Advance** in the Reference field. Press **<Enter>** two times.

6. Accept the default for Oct 1, 2012 in the Date field by pressing **<Enter>**.

7. Verify that the Payment Method is Check and that Account 1020, Checking Account, is displayed in the Cash account field.

8. The Cash Account Balance field displays 9,750.75. This agrees with the partial transaction register balance shown on page 330 (and the Checking Account balance shown on the Balance Sheet, page 329).

9. Make sure that the Apply to Revenues tab is selected. Click once on the Quantity field. Type **1** in the Quantity field. Press the **<Enter>** key two times.

10. Type **Publisher's advance** in the Description field. Press **<Enter>**.

11. Click 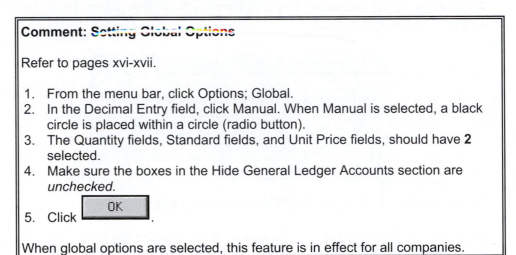 in the GL Account field. Select Account No. 2400, Publisher Advances.

12. Type **11000** in the Unit Price field.

Comment: Setting Global Options

Refer to pages xvi-xvii.

1. From the menu bar, click Options; Global.
2. In the Decimal Entry field, click Manual. When Manual is selected, a black circle is placed within a circle (radio button).
3. The Quantity fields, Standard fields, and Unit Price fields, should have **2** selected.
4. Make sure the boxes in the Hide General Ledger Accounts section are *unchecked.*
5. Click OK .

When global options are selected, this feature is in effect for all companies.

13. Press the **<Enter>** key two times. Compare your Receipts window to the one shown on the next page. If your window looks different, refer to Setting Global Options, pages xvi-xvii. (*Hint:* If the GL Account field is <u>not</u> shown, refer to the #4 in the Comment box. The boxes in the Hide General Ledger Accounts area must be *unchecked.*)

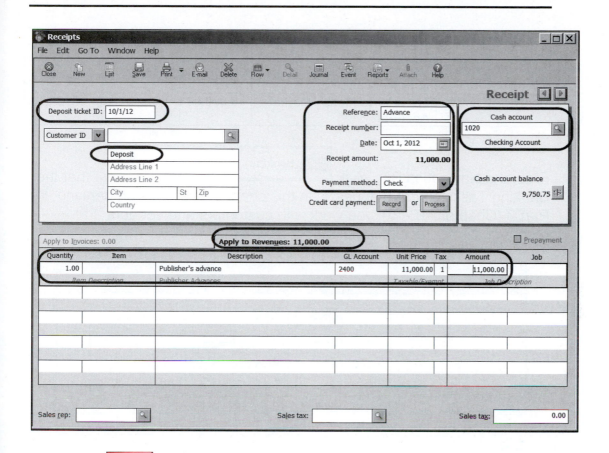

14. Click 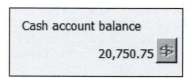 to post this entry. After you post, the Cash account balance field shows the same balance, $20,750.75, as the partial transaction register shown on the next page.

> Cash account balance
>
> 20,750.75

The Receipts window is ready for another entry. When the entry is saved, it is posted to the general ledger. The Cash Receipts Journal shows the debits and credits for this deposit.

15. Click **Close** to close the Receipts window.

▶ Use Write Checks for Check No. 4001. A section of the transaction register is shown on the next page. (The arrow indicates a flash video at www.mhhe.com/yacht2012. Link to Student Edition, select Chapter 9, Flash Videos, Checks.)

Ck. No.	Date	Description of Transaction	Payment	Deposit	Balance
					9,750.75
	10/1	Deposit (publisher's advance)		11,000.00	20,750.75
4001	**10/2**	**Transfer to Money Market Account**	**6,000.00**		**14,750.75**

From the Navigation Bar, click 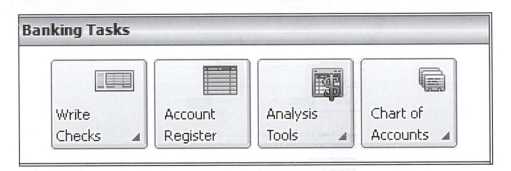 . Observe that the Banking Tasks diagram appears. In this chapter you focus on banking; in Part 3 (Chapters 12-15), you work with customers and vendors and record customer receipts and vendor payments.

Banking Tasks

Write Checks   Account Register   Analysis Tools   Chart of Accounts

---

Read Me: Navigation Bar or Menu Bar

In this textbook, you are going to use *both* menu bar selections and the Navigation Bar. In PCA 2012, there are two ways to access features. You can make selections from the menu bar *or* the Navigation Bar. Throughout the textbook, these two methods are shown.

Use these steps to enter Check No. 4001 and post to the Cash Disbursements Journal.

1. From the Banking Navigation Center, click ; New Check. The 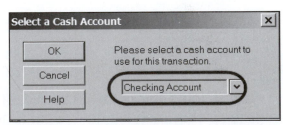 Select a Cash Account window appears. If necessary, click on the down- arrow to select the Checking Account.

2. Click  .

3. The Write Checks window displays. Click on the Pay to the order of, Name field. Type **Money Market Account**.

4. Click 🔍 in the Expense account field. The Chart of Accounts list is displayed. Even though you are *not* charging Check No. 4001 against an expense account, you use the Expense Account field to select the appropriate account. Select Account No.1010, Money Market Account. The Description field is automatically completed with Money Market Account.

5. Click on the Check number field. Type **4001** in the Check number field and press **<Enter>**.

6. Type **2** in the Date field and press **<Enter>**.

7. Verify that the Cash Account Balance field shows $20,750.75. This agrees with the partial transaction register on page 334 (beginning balance plus publisher's advance). If the Cash Account Balance field does not agree with your transaction register, see the instructions in on page 330, steps 1-3, for setting the global options for recalculating the cash balance for receipts, payments, and payroll.

8. Type **6000** in the $ field. Press **<Enter>**. Observe that the check is completed.

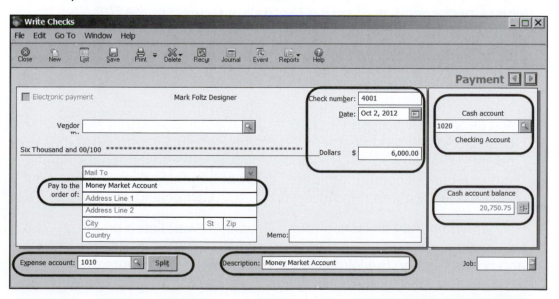

9. Click [Save] to post to the general ledger. The debits and credits for this entry are in the Cash Disbursements Journal. Verify that the Cash Account Balance field displays the October 2 balance (this is the same balance, $14,750.75, as the partial transaction register on page 334). You are ready for the next entry. (*Hint: you may need to change the date to 10/2/12 to see the correct cash balance.*)

10. Click [Close] to return to the Banking Navigation Center.

Comment

PCA automatically completes the Check number field once the first number is typed. After typing another reference in the Check number field (for example, ATM), you need to type the appropriate check number. ATM is an acronym for Automated Teller Machine. When an ATM card is used, cash is withdrawn from the checking account.

In accounting, you learn that source documents are used to show written evidence of a business transaction or event. Examples of source documents are sales invoices, purchase invoices, and in this case, Mr. Foltz's transaction registers which show checking account activity. Starting with the ATM withdrawal on October 3 for $200, record the entries shown on the transaction register on pages 337 and 338 in the Write Checks window (Banking Navigation Center) or the Receipts window (Tasks; Receipts). Assign each entry on the transaction register an appropriate account number from Mr. Foltz's Chart of Accounts. Record individual entries for each check number, deposit, or ATM transaction.

Each deposit (cash or check received) is a debit to Account No. 1020, Checking Account, and is recorded on the Receipts window (Cash Receipts Journal). On the Receipts window, you select the appropriate general ledger account for the credit part of the entry. The offsetting debit is automatically entered in Account No. 1020, Checking Account.

Each payment (check issued and ATM withdrawal) listed on the transaction register is a credit to Account No. 1020, Checking Account, and is recorded on the Write Checks window (Cash Disbursements Journal). On the Write Checks window, you select the appropriate general ledger account for the debit part of the entry. The offsetting credit is automatically entered in Account No. 1020, Checking Account.

After recording each check, deposit, or ATM, you should verify that the Balance field on the Write Checks window and Receipts window agrees with the transaction register balances below and on page 338. You have already recorded the first two entries for October 1 and October 2. Continue recording entries with the October 3 ATM transaction.

Remember, click *to post each entry (ATMs, Deposits, Checks). The transaction register entries are listed individually on the table below and on page 338.*

Read Me: *Why should I use Write Checks instead of the Payments window?*

The Write Checks window is a simplified version of the Payments window. Both Write Checks and Payments post to the Cash Disbursements Journal. In Chapter 10, you use the Write Checks window for checks and ATM withdrawals. You could use the Payments window for checks and ATMs but it is quicker to use Write Checks.

Transaction Register Mark Foltz Designer					
Ck. No.	**Date**	**Description of Transaction**	**Payment**	**Deposit**	**Balance**
	9/30				9,750.75
	10/1	Deposit (publisher's advance)		11,000.00	20,750.75
4001	10/2	Transfer to Money Market Fund	6,000.00		14,750.75
	10/3	**ATM[4]**	**200.00**		**14,550.75**
	10/4	Deposit (book royalty)		3,965.05	18,515.80
4002	10/4	Office Staples (computer equipment)	1,105.68		17,410.12
4003	10/9	U.S. Post Office[5]	44.00		17,366.12

---

[4]For each ATM use Account No. 3930, Mark Foltz, Draw [*or,* your name, Draw]. Type **ATM** in the Check number and Pay to the order of fields. For the next check, you need to type the check number in the Check number field.

[5]Add account No. 7400, Postage Expense. (*Hint:* In the Expense Account field, click ; New . In the Account Type field, select Expenses.)

4004	10/9	Courier News (newspaper subscription)[6]	45.00		17,321.12
4005	10/9	GPS Gas (utilities)	39.64		17,281.48
4006	10/10	Water and Power Co.[7]	98.59		17,182.89
4007	10/10	Century Telephone (telephone expense)	35.00		17,147.89
4008	10/10	Long Distance Co.	46.20		17,101.69
	10/13	Deposit (Green Bay Community College)		2,716.19	19,817.88
	10/14	ATM[8]	400.00		19,417.88
4009	10/15	Auto Parts (car headlight - automobile expense)[9]	201.00		19,216.88
4010	10/16	Matty Wills (install headlight)	110.00		19,106.88
4011	10/29	WI Dept. of Transportation (auto registration)	210.00		18,896.88
4012	10/29	Office Supplies & More (letterhead and envelopes)[10]	215.98		18,680.90
4013	10/30	Internet Service Provider	29.99		18,650.91

BACKING UP THE OCTOBER TRANSACTION REGISTER

Follow these steps to back up the October transaction register.

1. If necessary, close all windows and insert your USB flash drive. From the System Navigation Center, select | Back Up Now |. (*Or,* from the menu bar, select File, then Back Up.)

2. If necessary, uncheck the box next to Include company name in the backup file name. Click | Back Up |.

---

[6]Debit Account No. 6100, Dues and Subscriptions.

[7]Add Account No. 6420, Water and Power Expense.

[8]If you typed ATM in the Check number field for the October 3 withdrawal, a WARNING! That reference number has already been entered for this Cash Account displays. Click | OK |.

[9]Add Account No. 6180, Automobile Expense.

[10]Debit, Account No. 1450, Supplies.

3. In the Save in field, go to the location of your USB drive or back up to another location. Type **Chapter 10 Transaction Register October** in the File name field.

4. Click | Save |.

5. When the window prompts that This company backup will require approximately 1 diskette, click | OK |. Click | OK | again when the window prompts Please insert the first disk. When the Back Up Company scale is 100% complete, you have successfully backed up to this point in Chapter 10. (This step will differ slightly if you are backing up to the default or other hard drive location.)

ACCOUNT RECONCILIATION

Mark Foltz receives a bank statement every month for his checking account (Account No. 1020) from Prospect Bank. The bank statement shows which checks, ATMs, and deposits cleared the bank. PCA's Account Reconciliation feature allows you to reconcile his bank statement. Mr. Foltz's bank statement for his checking account is shown below and on then next page.

Statement of Account			Mark Foltz Designer	
Prospect Bank			34511 Main Street	
October 1 to October 31, 2012	Account No. 322955-70		Green Bay, WI 54301	
REGULAR CHECKING				
Previous Balance		$ 9,750.75		
3 Deposits (+)		17,681.24		
9 checks (-)		7,685.47		
2 Other Deductions (-)		600.00		
Service Charges (-)	10/31/12	10.00		
Ending Balance	10/31/12	**$19,136.52**		
DEPOSITS				
	10/4/12	11,000.00		
	10/7/12	3,965.05		
	10/17/12	2,716.19		
CHECKS (Asterisk * indicates break in check number sequence)				
	10/2/12	4001	6,000.00	
	10/6/12	4002	1,105.68	
	10/15/12	4003	44.00	
	10/16/12	4004	45.00	
	10/16/12	4006*	98.59	

	10/17/12	4007	35.00	
	10/20/12	4008	46.20	
	10/23/12	4009	201.00	
	10/30/12	4010	110.00	
OTHER DEDUCTIONS (ATM's)				
	10/3/12	ATM	200.00	
	10/14/12	ATM	400.00	

Follow these steps to reconcile Mr. Foltz's bank statement balance to Account No. 1020, Checking Account.

1. From the Navigation Bar, select [🏛 **Banking**] ; [⚖ Reconcile Accounts]. (*Hint:* You may also use the menu bar selections; Tasks, Account Reconciliation.) The Account Reconciliation window appears.

2. In the Account to Reconcile field, select Account No. 1020, Checking Account. If necessary, enlarge the window.

3. On the Account Reconciliation window, type **10** in the Service Charges field. The Date defaults to October 31, 2012. In the Account field, select Account No. 6850, Bank Service Charge.

4. In the Statement Ending Balance field (at the bottom of the window), type **19136.52**. (This is the ending balance on Mr. Foltz's bank statement.)

5. In the Deposit/Bank Credit; Check/Bank Debit table, place a check mark <✓> in the Status column for each deposit, check, and ATM that is listed on the bank statement. Observe that Clear appears with a checkmark in it for each deposit, check, and ATM. Do not check off the outstanding checks: 4005, 4011, 4012, 4013.

Comment

Observe that the Unreconciled Difference is zero (0.00). This zero balance is proof that Account No. 1020, Checking Account, is reconciled.

The GL (System) Balance is $18,640.91. The transaction register on page 338 shows an October 30 balance of $18,650.91. When you subtract the service charge of $10, the transaction register balance (18,650.91 – 10 = 18,640.91) agrees with the GL (System) Balance shown on the Account Reconciliation window.

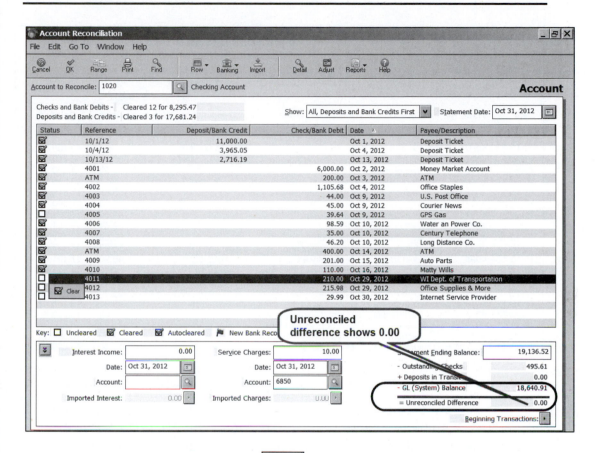

6. When you are finished, click .

The Account Reconciliation feature adjusts Mr. Foltz's bank statement. Another name for this is ***bank reconciliation*** – the process of bringing the balance of the bank statement and the balance of the cash account into agreement. The Account Reconciliation can be used with other accounts, too.

DISPLAYING THE ACCOUNT REGISTER

Entries for deposits and withdrawals are shown on PCA's Account Register.

1. From the Banking Navigation Center's Recently Used Banking Reports area, select <u>View</u> Account Register. Compare your Account Register to the one shown below.

Mark Foltz Designer
Account Register
For the Period From Oct 1, 2012 to Oct 31, 2012
1020 - Checking Account

Filter Criteria includes: Report order is by Date.

Date	Trans No	Type	Trans Desc	Deposit Am	Withdrawal Amt	Balance
			Beginning Balance			9,750.75
10/1/12	10/1/12	Deposit	Deposit	11,000.00		20,750.75
10/2/12	4001	Withdrawal	Money Market Account		6,000.00	14,750.75
10/3/12	ATM	Withdrawal	ATM		200.00	14,550.75
10/4/12	10/4/12	Deposit	Deposit	3,965.05		18,515.80
10/4/12	4002	Withdrawal	Office Staples		1,105.68	17,410.12
10/9/12	4003	Withdrawal	U.S. Post Office		44.00	17,366.12
10/9/12	4004	Withdrawal	Courier News		45.00	17,321.12
10/9/12	4005	Withdrawal	GPS Gas		39.64	17,281.48
10/10/12	4006	Withdrawal	Water and Power Co.		98.59	17,182.89
10/10/12	4007	Withdrawal	Century Telephone		35.00	17,147.89
10/10/12	4008	Withdrawal	Long Distance Co.		46.20	17,101.69
10/13/12	10/13/12	Deposit	Deposit	2,716.19		19,817.88
10/14/12	ATM	Withdrawal	ATM		400.00	19,417.88
10/15/12	4009	Withdrawal	Auto Parts		201.00	19,216.88
10/16/12	4010	Withdrawal	Matty Wills		110.00	19,106.88
10/29/12	4011	Withdrawal	WI Dept. of Transportation		210.00	18,896.88
10/29/12	4012	Withdrawal	Office Supplies & More		215.98	18,680.90
10/30/12	4013	Withdrawal	Internet Service Provider		29.99	18,650.91
10/31/12	10/31/12	Other	Service Charge		10.00	18,640.91
			Total	**17,681.24**	**8,791.08**	

2. The Account Register and Mr. Foltz's transaction register on pages 337-338 show the same results; *except* for the 10/31/12 service charge of 10.00. Similar to the transaction register, PCA's Account Register lists deposits (receipts) and withdrawals (payments). If you notice a discrepancy use drill down to follow the path of the entry's origin. Follow these steps to use drill down.

   a. Double-click on the first 10/4/12 entry (Deposit for $3,965.05). Notice that your cursor turns into a magnifying glass with a Z in the center.

10/4/12	10/4/12	ⓩ	Deposit	Deposit	3,965.05	18,515.80

   b. The Receipts window appears with the October 4, 2012 deposit shown.

   c. If there is no need to make a correction, close the Receipts window. You are returned to the Account Register window.

   Observe that the Account Register shows the Beginning Balance, Deposits, and Withdrawals (Checks, ATMs, bank service charge). It is okay if the Trans Desc (transaction descriptions) differs.

You can also drill down from the Account Register to the Write Checks, Receipts, or General Journal windows. Drill down shows the original entry. For example, if you double-click on the check number, you go to the Write Checks window; if you double-click on the 10/31/12 entry for the service charge (10.00) you go to the General Journal Entry window.

3. Close the Account Register and any other open windows.

4. Follow these steps to display the General Journal.

    a. From the menu bar, click Reports & Forms, and then select General Ledger.

    b. Click General Journal; then click , [Display] .

Mark Foltz Designer
General Journal
For the Period From Oct 1, 2012 to Oct 31, 2012
Filter Criteria includes: Report order is by Date. Report is printed with Accounts having Zero Amounts and with shortened descriptions and in Detail Format.

Date	Account ID	Reference	Trans Description	Debit Amt	Credit Amt
10/31/1	1020	10/31/12	Service Charge		10.00
	6850		Service Charge	10.00	
		Total		10.00	10.00

---

    c. Close the General Journal report.

PRINTING THE CASH RECEIPTS JOURNAL

Follow these steps to print the Cash Receipts Journal.

1. From the Select a Report or Form window, select Accounts Receivable in the Reports area. (*Hint:* If you are at the menu bar, select Reports & Forms; Accounts Receivable.)

2. Double-click Cash Receipts Journal. The Cash Receipts Journal appears.

				Mark Foltz Designer	
				Cash Receipts Journal	
				For the Period From Oct 1, 2012 to Oct 31, 2012	

Filter Criteria includes: Report order is by Check Date. Report is printed in Detail Format.

Date	Account ID	Transaction Ref	Line Description	Debit Amnt	Credit Amnt
10/1/12	2400	Advance	Publisher's advance		11,000.00
	1020		Deposit	11,000.00	
10/4/12	4050	Book royalty	Book royalty		3,965.05
	1020		Deposit	3,965.05	
10/13/12	4000	Green Bay CC	Teaching income		2,716.19
	1020		Deposit	2,716.19	
				17,681.24	17,681.24

Comment

The information in the Transaction Ref column may differ. The information in the Transaction Ref column is the same as what you typed in the Reference field of the Receipts window.

---

3. Close the Cash Receipts Journal.

PRINTING THE CASH DISBURSEMENTS JOURNAL

1. The Select a Report or Form window should be displayed. In the Reports area, highlight Accounts Payable.

2. Double-click the Cash Disbursements Journal.

			Mark Foltz Designer		
			Cash Disbursements Journal		
			For the Period From Oct 1, 2012 to Oct 31, 2012		
Filter Criteria includes: Report order is by Date. Report is printed in Detail Format.					
Date	**Check #**	**Account ID**	**Line Description**	**Debit Amount**	**Credit Amount**
10/2/12	4001	1010	Money Market Account	6,000.00	
		1020	Money Market Account		6,000.00
10/3/12	ATM	3930	Mark Foltz, Draw	200.00	
		1020	ATM		200.00
10/4/12	4002	1500	Computer Equipment	1,105.68	
		1020	Office Staples		1,105.68
10/9/12	4003	7400	Postage Expense	44.00	
		1020	U.S. Post Office		44.00
10/9/12	4004	6100	Dues and Subscriptions	45.00	
		1020	Courier News		45.00
10/9/12	4005	6400	Utilities Expense	39.64	
		1020	GPS Gas		39.64
10/10/12	4006	6420	Water and Power Expense	98.59	
		1020	Water and Power Co.		98.59
10/10/12	4007	6500	Telephone Expense	35.00	
		1020	Century Telephone		35.00
10/10/12	4008	6550	Long Distance Co.	46.20	
		1020	Long Distance Co.		46.20
10/14/12	ATM	3930	Mark Foltz, Draw	400.00	
		1020	ATM		400.00
10/15/12	4009	6180	Automobile Expense	201.00	
		1020	Auto Parts		201.00
10/16/12	4010	6180	Automobile Expense	110.00	
		1020	Matty Wills		110.00
10/29/12	4011	6150	Auto Registration	210.00	
		1020	WI Dept. of Transportation		210.00
10/29/12	4012	1450	Supplies	215.98	
		1020	Office Supplies & More		215.98
10/30/12	4013	6560	Internet Service Provider	29.99	
		1020	Internet Service Provider		29.99
	Total			**8,781.08**	**8,781.08**

3. Close the Cash Disbursements Journal; close the Select a Report or Form window.

EDITING JOURNAL ENTRIES

Compare your journal entries to the ones shown on pages 343–345. Some of the Line Descriptions may differ. This is okay. If your dates, check numbers, or account numbers are different, you should edit the journal entry. Follow these steps to edit the Cash Receipts Journal:

1. From the menu bar, click Tasks, Receipts. The Receipts window displays.

2. Click [List]. The Receipt List window appears showing the three deposits.

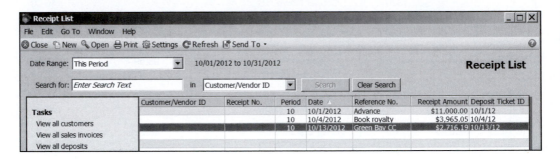

3. If you need to edit a deposit, double-click on it to drill down to the original entry on the Receipts window.

4. Make any necessary corrections, then click [Save] to post.

5. Close all windows. (*Hint:* From the menu bar, select Window, Close All.)

6. Editing the Cash Disbursements Journal is similar. Go to [Write Checks]; select View and Edit Checks. The Write Checks List appears. Drill down to the check or ATM that needs to be edited.

7. Close all windows.

DISPLAYING THE GENERAL LEDGER TRIAL BALANCE

Follow these steps to display the General Ledger Trial Balance.

1. From the menu bar, click Reports & Forms; General Ledger, General Ledger Trial Balance.

2. Click [Display]. Compare your General Ledger Trial Balance with the one shown below.

*****EDUCATIONAL VERSION ONLY*****

Mark Foltz Designer
General Ledger Trial Balance
As of Oct 31, 2012

Filter Criteria includes: Report order is by ID. Report is printed in Detail Format.

Account ID	Account Description	Debit Amt	Credit Amt
1010	Money Market Account	15,700.00	
1020	Checking Account	18,640.91	
1040	IRA Savings Account	27,730.35	
1045	WI State Retirement	35,612.00	
1300	Prepaid Insurance	2,100.00	
1400	Prepaid Rent	600.00	
1450	Supplies	1,987.81	
1500	Computer Equipment	7,905.68	
1510	Furniture	5,000.00	
1520	Automobile	19,000.00	
2000	VISA Payable		5,250.65
2400	Publisher Advances		11,000.00
3920	Mark Foltz, Capital		112,814.28
3930	Mark Foltz, Draw	600.00	
4000	Teaching Income		2,716.19
4050	Royalty Income		3,965.05
6100	Dues and Subscriptions	45.00	
6150	Auto Registration	210.00	
6180	Automobile Expense	311.00	
6400	Utilities Expense	39.64	
6420	Water and Power Expens	98.59	
6500	Telephone Expense	35.00	
6550	Long Distance Co.	46.20	
6560	Internet Service Provider	29.99	
6850	Bank Service Charge	10.00	
7400	Postage Expense	44.00	
	Total:	**135,746.17**	**135,746.17**

3. To print the general ledger trial balance, select [Print], then make the selections to print.

Observe that the Checking Account (Account No. 1020) balance on the General Ledger Trial Balance and the GL (System) Balance on the Account Reconciliation window on page 341 are the same: 18,640.91.

PRINTING FINANCIAL STATEMENTS

The Computer Accounting Cycle shows that adjusting entries are needed at this point. (See the Computer Accounting Cycle on pages 47-48.) There is no need to complete adjusting entries at the end of October since quarterly adjusting entries are done on December 31, 2012. Instead, print Mr. Foltz's financial statements.

Print the following financial statements:

1. <Standard> Balance Sheet. (*Hint:* Reports & Forms; Financial Statements. *Or,* from the Business Status Navigation Center's Find a Report area, in the *Select a Category* field, select Financial Statements. In the *Select a Report* field, select <Standard> Balance Sheet. Click [Display]. The October 31, 2012 balance sheet is shown on the next page.

Mark Foltz Designer
Balance Sheet
October 31, 2012

ASSETS

Current Assets
Money Market Account	$	15,700.00	
Checking Account		18,640.91	
IRA Savings Account		27,730.35	
WI State Retirement		35,612.00	
Prepaid Insurance		2,100.00	
Prepaid Rent		600.00	
Supplies		1,987.81	
Total Current Assets			102,371.07

Property and Equipment
Computer Equipment	7,905.68	
Furniture	5,000.00	
Automobile	19,000.00	
Total Property and Equipment		31,905.68

Other Assets

Total Other Assets		0.00
Total Assets	$	134,276.75

LIABILITIES AND CAPITAL

Current Liabilities
VISA Payable	$	5,250.65	
Publisher Advances		11,000.00	
Total Current Liabilities			16,250.65

Long-Term Liabilities

Total Long-Term Liabilities	0.00
Total Liabilities	16,250.65

Capital
Mark Foltz, Capital	112,814.28	
Mark Foltz, Draw	(600.00)	
Net Income	5,811.82	
Total Capital		118,026.10
Total Liabilities & Capital	$	134,276.75

Unaudited - For Management Purposes Only

2. Display or print the <Standard> Income Stmnt.

> **Comment**
>
> To print an Income Statement without zero balances, uncheck the Show Zero Amounts box on the <Standard> Income Statement Options window.

Mark Foltz Designer
Income Statement
For the Ten Months Ending October 31, 2012

	Current Month			Year to Date	
Revenues					
Teaching Income	$	2,716.19	40.65	$ 2,716.19	40.65
Royalty Income		3,965.05	59.35	3,965.05	59.35
Total Revenues		6,681.24	100.00	6,681.24	100.00
Cost of Sales					
Total Cost of Sales		0.00	0.00	0.00	0.00
Gross Profit		6,681.24	100.00	6,681.24	100.00
Expenses					
Dues and Subscriptions		45.00	0.67	45.00	0.67
Auto Registration		210.00	3.14	210.00	3.14
Automobile Expense		311.00	4.65	311.00	4.65
Utilities Expense		39.64	0.59	39.64	0.59
Water and Power Expense		98.59	1.48	98.59	1.48
Telephone Expense		35.00	0.52	35.00	0.52
Long Distance Co.		46.20	0.69	46.20	0.69
Internet Service Provider		29.99	0.45	29.99	0.45
Bank Service Charge		10.00	0.15	10.00	0.15
Postage Expense		44.00	0.66	44.00	0.66
Total Expenses		869.42	13.01	869.42	13.01
Net Income	$	5,811.82	86.99	$ 5,811.82	86.99

For Management Purposes Only

Observe that both the balance sheet and income statement include a line at the bottom of the report that says "For Management Purposes Only."

In addition to dollar amounts, observe that the income statement also includes percentage of revenue columns for both the current month and the year to date. The percentages shown for each expense, total expenses, and net income indicate the relationship of each item to total revenues.

More financial statements are printed at the end of the quarter.

BACKING UP CHAPTER 10 DATA

Follow these steps to back up Chapter 10 data to this point in your work. This backup saves the following data: new company set up (pages 279-287), chart of accounts (pages 288-293), beginning balances (pages 303-308), the entries recorded in the Receipts and Write Checks windows (transaction register, pages 337-338); Account Reconciliation (pages 339-341); the Account Register, General Journal, Cash Receipts Journal, Cash Disbursements Journal, the General Ledger Trial Balance, and Financial Statements (pages 341-345).

Each backup allows you to restore data to different points in the data. Observe that each time you backup, the instructions show a different file name. This allows you to distinguish one backup file from another one.

1. If necessary, close all windows and insert your USB flash drive. From the System Navigation Center, select [Back Up Now]. (*Or,* from the menu bar, select File, then Back Up.)

2. If necessary, uncheck the box next to Include company name in the backup file name. Click [Back Up].

3. In the Save in field, select the location of your USB drive (or other location.) Type **Chapter 10 October** in the File name field.

4. Click [Save].

5. When the window prompts that This company backup will require approximately 1 diskette, click [OK]. Click [OK] again when the screen prompts Please inset the first disk. When the Back Up Company scale is 100% complete, you have successfully backed up to this point in Chapter 10. (This step will differ slightly if you are backing up to a hard drive location.)

EXPORT THE GENERAL LEDGER TRIAL BALANCE, INCOME STATEMENT AND BALANCE SHEET TO EXCEL

Follow the steps on the next page to export the October general ledger trial balance and financial statements to Excel.

1. Display the General Ledger Trial Balance.

2. Click 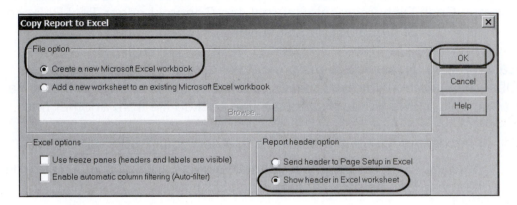. On the Copy Report to Excel window, in the file option area, Create a new Microsoft Excel workbook should be selected. In the Report header option field, Show header in Excel worksheet is selected.

3. Click [OK]. The general ledger trial balance appears in Excel. Save. Use the file name **Chapter 10_October Trial Balance and Financial Statements.xlsx**.

4. Maximize Peachtree. Go to Peachtree's Select a Report or Form window. Double-click <Standard> Income Statement. Uncheck Show Zero Amounts. Click [OK]. On the Income Statement window, click [Excel].

5. On the Copy Report to Excel window, select Add a new worksheet to an existing Microsoft Excel workbook. Click [Browse...] to go to the location of the saved file. Click [Open].

---

6. Go to Peachtree and add the <Standard> Balance Sheet to the Excel file.

7. Click OK . The Excel file opens. Observe that three sheets are shown at the bottom: General Ledger Trial Balance, Income Stmnt, Balance Sheet.

| ◄ ◄ ► ►| General Ledger Trial Balance | Income Stmnt | **Balance Sheet** |

8. Save the Excel file. Exit Excel. Close all Peachtree windows.

SAVE GENERAL LEDGER TRIAL BALANCE AND FINANCIAL STATEMENTS AS PDF FILES

1. Display the General Ledger Trial Balance. Click PDF . Save the **Chapter 10_October Trial Balance.pdf**.

2. Display the <Standard> Income Statement. Click PDF . Save the **Chapter 10_October Income Statement.pdf**.

3. Display the <Standard> Balance Sheet. Click PDF . Save the **Chapter 10_October Balance Sheet.pdf**.

SUMMARY AND REVIEW

Complete the following end-of-chapter activities:

1. Going to the net, pages 354.

2. Short-answer questions, pages 354.

3. Exercises 10-1 and 10-2, pages 355-358.

4. Analysis question, page 358.

5. Assessment rubric, 359.

6. Chapter 10 Index, page 360.

GOING TO THE NET

Access the Peachtree Quantum website
http://www.peachtree.com/quantum/ptQuantum/features.cfm. Answer
the following.

1. List nine Peachtree Quantum strengths.
2. Explain the Peachtree Quantum features that are industry specific.
   (Select the My Industry tab. The URL is
   http://www.peachtree.com/Quantum/industry.)

Short-Answer Questions: The Online Learning Center includes these
questions and the analysis question at www.mhhe.com/yacht2012, select
Student Edition, Chapter 10, QA Templates.

1. In Chapter 10, what source documents are used to complete Mr.
   Foltz's accounting? Include the month in your answer.

2. The file restored to begin Chapter 10 is _____?

3. To make sure you are starting in the appropriate place in the data,
   display this financial statement:

4. The Receipts window is also known as this journal _____.

5. The Write Checks window is also known as this journal _____.

6. When the Receipts window is used, what account is automatically
   debited? (Identify the account number and name.)

7. When the Write Checks window is used, what account is
   automatically credited? (Identify the account number and name.)

8. Explain Peachtree's account reconciliation feature. Define bank
   reconciliation.

9. What does the term transaction register refer to?

10. The transaction register shows payments and deposits. What are
    two examples of payments, and what Peachtree window is used?
    What Peachtree window is used to record deposits?

Exercise 10-1: Follow the instructions below to complete Exercise 10-1. Exercises 9-1 and 9-2 *must* be completed before starting Exercise 10-1.

1. Start PCA. Open the company that you set up in Exercise 9-1, Design by Your Name. The suggested company name in Exercise 9-1, page 318, is Design by your first and last name. (*Hint:* If a different company opens, select File; Open Previous Company. Select No to opening two companies.)

2. Follow these steps to restore Exercise 9-2.[11] This backup was made on page 324.

   a. Insert your USB flash drive. From the Navigation Bar, select

      | System | ; click | Restore Now | .

   b. The Select Backup File window appears. Click | Browse | . In the Look in field, select the appropriate location of the Exercise 9-2.ptb back file. Click | Open | . Make sure the Location field shows Exercise 9-2.ptb. Click | Next > | .

   c. The Select Company window appears. The radio button next to An Existing Company is selected. Check that the Company Name and Location fields are correct. Click | Next > | .

   d. The Restore Options window appears. Make sure that the box next to Company Data is *checked*. Click | Next > | .

   e. The Confirmation window appears. Check the From and To fields to make sure they are correct. Click | Finish | . When the Restore Company scale is 100% complete, your data is restored. (*Hint:* The Student Version of Peachtree prompts that company

---

[11]You can restore from your back up file even if *no* Peachtree company exists. From the menu bar, click File; Close Company. Peachtree's startup window appears with four menu bar options-- | File Options Services Help | . Select File; Restore. Browse to the location of the Exercise 9-2.ptb backup file. On the Restore Wizard's Select Company window, select A New Company. The *A New Company* selection allows you to restore backup data *and* set up the company (refer to Troubleshooting, pp. 299-300).

data can be used for 14 months. After that time data expires. Click [OK]. Design by Student Name [your first and last name] opens.)

3. To make sure you are starting in the correct place, display the Balance Sheet. Compare it to the one completed in Exercise 9-2, page 323, step 4.

4. Use the transaction register below to record and post checks, ATMs, and deposits. (*Hint:* From the Banking Navigation Center, use Write Checks for checks and ATMs. From the menu bar, use Tasks; Receipts for deposits.)

Transaction Register					
Ck. No.	Date	Description of Transaction	Payment	Deposit	Balance
	9/30/12	*Balance brought forward*			14,500.00
	10/1/12	Deposit (Design Income)		2,300.00	16,800.00
	10/2/12	ATM	100.00		16,700.00
1001	10/3/12	Accounts Payable	1,050.00		15,650.00
	10/8/12	Deposit (Teaching Income)		2,105.00	17,755.00
1002	10/9/12	Utilities Co.[12]	45.80		17,709.20
1003	10/10/12	Mullen Advertising, Inc.	115.00		17,594.20
1004	10/13/12	U.S. Post Office	44.00		17,550.20
1005	10/13/12	Design Workshop (conference)[13]	195.00		17,355.20
1006	10/15/12	Horizon Telephone	55.15		17,300.05
1007	10/16/12	DSL Service[14]	29.95		17,270.10
	10/20/12	ATM	100.00		17,170.10
1008	10/28/12	CTS Office Supplies[15]	137.80		17,032.30
	10/30/12	ATM	200.00		16,832.30

[12]Debit Account No. 6400, Utilities Expense.

[13]Debit Account No. 6800, Conference Fees.

[14] Debit Account No. 6560, Internet Service Provider.

[15]Debit Account No. 1450, Supplies.

5. Backup. The suggested file name is **Exercise 10-1.ptb**.
6. Exit Peachtree or continue with Exercise 10-2.

Exercise 10-2: Follow the instructions below to complete Exercise 10-2. Exercises 9-1, 9-2, and 10-1 must be completed before starting Exercise 10-2.

1. If necessary, start PCA. Open the company that you set up in Exercise 9-1, Design by Your Name.
2. If necessary, restore the Exercise 10-1.ptb backup file.
3. Use the Bank Statement below to complete Account Reconciliation. *Record the bank service charge on the Account Reconciliation window.*

Statement of Account Midwest Bank October 1 to October 31, 2012		Account No. 992834-20	Design by Your Name Your Address Your City, State, Zip	
REGULAR CHECKING				
Previous Balance	9/30/12	14,500.00		
2 Deposits(+)		4,405.00		
6 Checks (-)		1,479.75		
3 Other Deductions (-)		400.00		
Service Charges (-)	10/31/12	12.00		
Ending Balance	10/31/12	**17,013.25**		
DEPOSITS				
	10/6/12	2,300.00		
	10/8/12	2,105.00		
CHECKS (Asterisk * indicates break in check number sequence)				
	10/10/12	1001	1,050.00	
	10/10/12	1002	45.80	
	10/24/12	1003	115.00	
	10/24/12	1004	44.00	
	10/27/12	1005	195.00	
	10/30/12	1007*	29.95	
OTHER DEDUCTIONS (ATM's)				
	10/2/12	100.00	10/30/12	200.00
	10/20/12	100.00		

4. Print an Account Reconciliation report. (*Hint:* Reports & Forms; Account Reconciliation.)

5. Print the Account Register.

6. Print the General Journal.

7. Print the Cash Receipts Journal.

8. Print the Cash Disbursements Journal.

9. Print the General Ledger Trial Balance.

10. Print the Balance Sheet and Income Statement.

   Check Your Figures:

Account No 1020, Midwest Bank	$16,820.30
Total Liabilities & Capital	$48,508.10
Net Income	$3,908.10

11. Backup. The suggested file name is **Exercise 10-2.ptb**.

12. Export the General Ledger Trial Balance, Income Statement and Balance Sheet to Excel. Use the file name **Exercise 10-2_October Trial Balance and Financial Statements.xlsx**.

13. Save the General Ledger Trial Balance, Balance Sheet and Income Statement as PDF files. Use the files names **Exercise 10-2_October Trial Balance.pdf**, **Exercise 10-2_October Balance Sheet.pdf** and **Exercise 10-2_October Income Statement.pdf** as the file names.

14. Exit Peachtree.

ANALYSIS QUESTION

What is account reconciliation?

ASSESSMENT RUBRIC

Complete the Assessment Rubric online at www.mhhe.com/yacht2012; Student Edition, select Chapter 10, Assessment Rubric link. To review Peachtree's navigation centers, menu selections, and windows, complete the blank fields online.

Task	Date	Navigation Center	Task Window	Journal Dr. and Cr.
ATM (Exercise 10-1)	10/2/12			
Deposit (Exercise 10-1)	10/8/12			

CHAPTER 10 INDEX

Chapter 11 — Completing Quarterly Activities and Closing the Fiscal Year

LEARNING OBJECTIVES

1. Restore data from Chapter 10.[1] (This backup was made on page 351.)
2. Define Peachtree's General Ledger System.
3. Change accounting periods.
4. Record and post deposits, checks, and ATM transactions for November and December.
5. Complete account reconciliation.
6. Display Peachtree's data file statistics window.
7. Print a General Ledger Trial Balance (unadjusted).
8. Journalize and post end-of-quarter adjusting entries in the General Journal.
9. Print the Adjusted Trial Balance and financial statements.
10. Close the fiscal year.
11. Print a Postclosing Trial Balance.
12. Make eight backups, save four Excel files, and save eight PDF files.[2]

Chapters 9, 10 and 11 work together. In Chapter 11 you continue recording financial information for Mark Foltz Designer. You complete the computer accounting cycle for November and December. Mr. Foltz's transaction registers and bank statements are used as source documents. At the end of December, which is also the end of the fourth quarter, you complete adjusting entries, print financial statements, and close the fiscal year.

GENERAL LEDGER SYSTEM (GL)

Peachtree's *General Ledger System* is the complete collection of accounts (chart of accounts) of a company, transactions associated with these accounts, and account balances for a specified period of time. In Peachtree, the GL is the combination of all journal entries that have been

---

[1]All activities in Chapters 9 and 10 must be completed before starting Chapter 11.

[2]For the size of backup files, Excel files, and PDFs, refer to the chart on pages 277--278.

recorded and posted. The account balances are then collected and shown on the company's financial statements.

Similar to other modules, the General Ledger System is organized together within Peachtree's interface. On the Reports & Forms menu, the General Ledger selection shows the GL system in one place: Chart of Accounts, General Journal, General Ledger, etc. The Navigation Bar's Banking selection shows the Account Register, Chart of Accounts, General Journal Entry (three icons associated with the GL system). The journal associated with the General Ledger System is the general journal. Observe that the Tasks menu includes General Journal entry in one section-- General Journal Entry... .

The steps of the computer accounting cycle that are completed in Chapter 11 are shown below.

PCA's Computer Accounting Cycle
1. Change accounting periods.
2. Journalize entries.
3. Post entries to the General Ledger.
4. Account Reconciliation.
5. Print the General Ledger Trial Balance (unadjusted).
6. Journalize and post adjusting entries.
7. Print the General Ledger Trial Balance (adjusted).
8. Print the financial statements: Balance Sheet, Income Statement, Statement of Cash Flow, and Statement of Retained Earnings .
9. Close the fiscal year.
10. Interpret accounting information.

GETTING STARTED

Follow these steps to continue using Mark Foltz's company data.

1. Start Peachtree. Open an existing company, Mark Foltz Designer (or your name Designer).[3] (*Hint:* If a different company opens, select File; Open a Previous Company. Select Mark Foltz [your name] Designer. If the screen prompts Do you want to keep Design by Your Name open?, click [No].)

2. To restore Mark Foltz's data from Chapter 10, do the following. The Chapter 10 October.ptb backup was made on page 351.

    a. Insert your USB flash drive. From the System Navigation Center, click [Restore Now]. (*Or,* from the menu bar, click File, Restore.)

    b. The Select Backup File window appears. Click [Browse]. In the Look in field, select the appropriate location of your Chapter 10 October.ptb file. Click [Open]. Make sure the Location field shows the Chapter 10 October.ptb file. Click [Next >].

    c. The Select Company window appears. The radio button next to An Existing Company is selected. Check that the Company Name and Location fields are correct. Click [Next >].

    d. The Restore Options window appears. Make sure that the box next to Company Data is *checked*. Click [Next >].

    e. The Confirmation window appears. Check the From and To fields to make sure they are correct. Click [Finish]. When the Restore Company scale is 100% complete, your data is restored. (*Hint:* The Student Version of Peachtree prompts that company

---

[3]You can restore from your back up file even if *no* designer company exists. From Peachtree's start up window, select File; Restore. Select the location of your backup file. On the Restore Wizard's Select Company window, select A New Company. The *A New Company* selection allows you to restore your backup data, bypassing the process of new company set up. For more information, refer to Troubleshooting on pages 299-300.

data can be used for 14 months. After that time the data expires. Click [OK]. Mark Foltz [your first and last name] Designer opens.)

To make sure you are starting in the appropriate place in the data (Chapter 10 October.ptb backup) check the General Ledger Trial Balance. A partial General Ledger Trial Balance, showing asset account balances, is shown below. The complete General Ledger Trial Balance is shown in Chapter 10 on page 347.

*****EDUCATIONAL VERSION ONLY*****

Mark Foltz Designer
General Ledger Trial Balance
As of Oct 31, 2012

Filter Criteria includes: Report order is by ID. Report is printed in Detail Format.

Account I	Account Description	Debit Amt	Credit Amt
1010	Money Market Account	15,700.00	
1020	Checking Account	18,640.91	
1040	IRA Savings Account	27,730.35	
1045	WI State Retirement	35,612.00	
1300	Prepaid Insurance	2,100.00	
1400	Prepaid Rent	600.00	
1450	Supplies	1,987.81	
1500	Computer Equipment	7,905.68	
1510	Furniture	5,000.00	
1520	Automobile	19,000.00	

3. Follow these steps to change accounting periods:

   a. From the menu bar, select Tasks, then System.

   b. From the System menu, select Change Accounting Period.

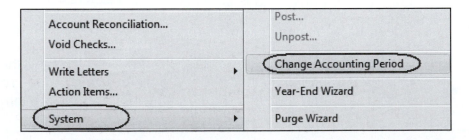

   c. From the Open Accounting Periods list, select 11-Nov 01, 2012 to Nov 30, 2012. Compare your Change Accounting Period window to the one on the next page.

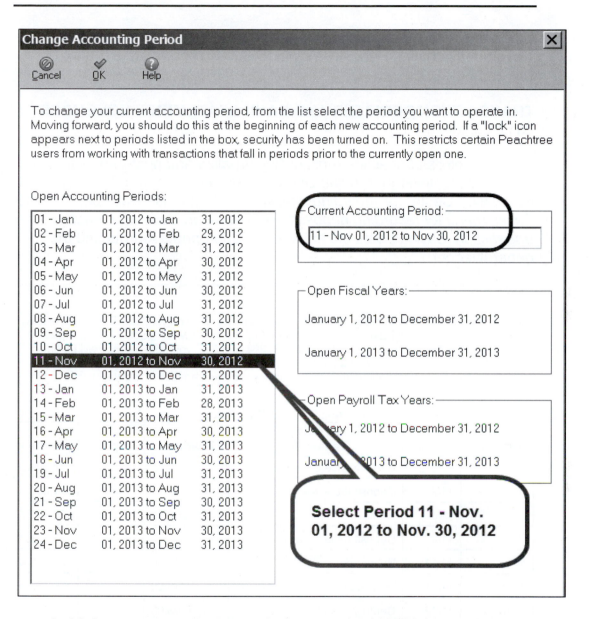

d. Make sure you selected period 11 - Nov 01, 2012 to Nov 30, 2012. Click [OK]. If necessary, click [No] when the Would you like to print your reports before continuing? window appears. If necessary, select [Business Status]. Observe that the toolbar shows [📅] Period 11 - 11/01/12-11/30/12.

When accounting periods are changed, you prepare Peachtree to record November's entries. Peachtree's windows and reports are updated to November 2012.

TRANSACTION REGISTER AND BANK STATEMENT: NOVEMBER 2012

Use Mr. Foltz's transaction register to journalize and post transactions for the month of November. (*Hint: Use Write Checks* from the Banking Navigation Center *for recording checks and ATMs; use Receipts from the Tasks menu for recording deposits. Remember to Save after each transaction.* Saving posts the entry to the appropriate journal and the general ledger.)

Comment
Before journalizing entries, make sure that you are starting with correct data. To do that, display the General Ledger Trial Balance and compare it to the one shown on page 347 in Chapter 10. Since you changed accounting periods on pages 364 and 365, your trial balance will be dated November 30, 2012. Verify that Account No. 1020, Checking Account, shows a balance of $18,640.91 which is the same as the starting balance on the transaction register below.

Transaction Register Mark Foltz Designer					
Check Number	**Date**	**Description of Transaction**	**Payment**	**Deposit**	**Balance**
	10/31	*Bank Service Charge*	*10.00*		*18,640.91*
	11/3	Deposit (book royalty)		2,455.85	21,096.76
	11/5	ATM	200.00		20,896.76
	11/6	Deposit (Green Bay CC)		2,716.19	23,612.95
4014	11/11	Water and Power Co.	90.50		23,522.45
4015	11/11	GPS Gas	53.90		23,468.55
4016	11/12	Century Telephone	45.08		23,423.47
4017	11/14	Long Distance Co.	81.50		23,341.97
	11/16	ATM	200.00		23,141.97
4018	11/27	VISA card payment	5,250.65		17,891.32
4019	11/28	Internet Service Provider	29.99		17,861.33
	11/28	ATM	200.00		17,661.33

Follow the steps on the next page to complete the computer accounting cycle.

1. Journalize and post the checks and deposits using the transaction register. (*Hint: Start entries with the November 3 deposit. Remember to record each transaction--checks, deposits, ATM withdrawals--as a separate entry. Save to post after each transaction*).

2. Use Mr. Foltz's bank statement to complete the account reconciliation for Account No. 1020, Checking Account.

   Remember to record the bank service charge (Account No. 6850) on the Account Reconciliation window.

Statement of Account Prospect Bank November 1 to November 30, 2012 Account No. 322955-70			Mark Foltz Designer 34511 Main Street Green Bay, WI 54301	
REGULAR CHECKING				
Previous Balance	10/31/12	19,136.52		
2 Deposits(+)		5,172.04		
8 checks (-)		766.59		
3 Other deduction (-)		600.00		
Service Charges (-)	11/30/12	10.00		
Ending Balance	11/30/12	**22,931.97**		
DEPOSITS				
	11/3/12	2,455.85		
	11/8/12	2,716.19		
CHECKS (Asterisk * indicates break in check number sequence)				
	11/3/12	4005*	39.64	
	11/3/12	4011	210.00	
	11/3/12	4012	215.98	
	11/5/12	4013	29.99	
	11/17/12	4014	90.50	
	11/27/12	4015	53.90	
	11/28/12	4016	45.08	
	11/28/12	4017	81.50	
Continued				

		OTHER DEDUCTIONS (ATM's)			
	11/5/12	200.00			
	11/16/12	200.00			
	11/28/12	200.00			

3. Follow these steps to display the Account Register.

   a. From Banking Navigation Center's Recently Used Banking Reports area, select <u>View</u> Account Register. (*Hint:* You can also go to the menu bar selection Reports & Forms, Account Reconciliation, Account Register.)

   b. Compare your Account Register to the transaction register on pages 366. If necessary, drill down to make corrections.

*****EDUCATIONAL VERSION ONLY*****

Mark Foltz Designer
Account Register
For the Period From Nov 1, 2012 to Nov 30, 2012
1020 - Checking Account

Filter Criteria includes: Report order is by Date.

Date	Trans No	Type	Trans Desc	Deposit Amt	Withdrawal Amt	Balance
			Beginning Balance			18,640.91
11/3/12	11/3/12	Deposit	Deposit	2,455.85		21,096.76
11/5/12	ATM	Withdrawal	ATM		200.00	20,896.76
11/6/12	11/6/12	Deposit	Deposit	2,716.19		23,612.95
11/11/12	4014	Withdrawal	Water and Power Co.		90.50	23,522.45
11/11/12	4015	Withdrawal	GPS Gas		53.90	23,468.55
11/12/12	4016	Withdrawal	Century Telephone		45.08	23,423.47
11/14/12	4017	Withdrawal	Long Distance Co.		81.50	23,341.97
11/16/12	ATM	Withdrawal	ATM		200.00	23,141.97
11/27/12	4018	Withdrawal	VISA card payment		5,250.65	17,891.32
11/28/12	4019	Withdrawal	Internet Service Provid		29.99	17,861.33
11/28/12	ATM	Withdrawal	ATM		200.00	17,661.33
11/30/12	11/30/12	Other	Service Charge		10.00	17,651.33
			Total	5,172.04	6,161.62	

4. Close the Account Register report.

5. Follow these steps to print an Account Reconciliation report:

   a. From the menu bar, click Reports & Forms; Account Reconciliation.

b. At the Select a Report window, highlight Account Reconciliation.

c. Click [Print]. The Modify Report – Account Reconciliation window appears. Observe that the As of field shows Current Period, and the GL Account ID field shows 1020. Click [OK].

d. At the Print window, click [OK].

Mark Foltz Designer
Account Reconciliation
As of Nov 30, 2012
1020 - Checking Account
Bank Statement Date: November 30, 2012

Filter Criteria includes: Report is printed in Detail Format.

Beginning GL Balanc		18,640.91
Add: Cash Receipts		5,172.04
Less: Cash Disburse		(6,151.62)
Add (Less) Other		(10.00)
Ending GL Balance		17,651.33
Ending Bank Balance		22,931.97
Add back deposits in		
Total deposits in tran		
(Less) outstanding ch		
Nov 27, 20 4018	(5,250.65)	
Nov 28, 20 4019	(29.99)	
Total outstanding che		(5,280.64)
Add (Less) Other		
Total other		
Unreconciled differen		0.00
Ending GL Balance		17,651.33

---

6. Close the account reconciliation report.

7. Print or display the Cash Receipts Journal.

*****EDUCATIONAL VERSION ONLY*****

Mark Foltz Designer
Cash Receipts Journal
For the Period From Nov 1, 2012 to Nov 30, 2012

Filter Criteria includes: Report order is by Check Date. Report is printed in Detail Format.

Date	Account ID	Transaction Ref	Line Description	Debit Amnt	Credit Amnt
11/3/12	4050	Book royalty	Royalty Income		2,455.85
	1020		Deposit	2,455.85	
11/6/12	4000	Green Bay CC	Teaching Income		2,716.19
	1020		Deposit	2,716.19	
				5,172.04	5,172.04

8. Print or display your Cash Disbursements Journal and compare it to the one shown.

*****EDUCATIONAL VERSION ONLY*****

Mark Foltz Designer
Cash Disbursements Journal
For the Period From Nov 1, 2012 to Nov 30, 2012

Filter Criteria includes: Report order is by Date. Report is printed in Detail Format.

Date	Check #	Account ID	Line Description	Debit Amount	Credit Amount
11/5/12	ATM	3930	Mark Foltz, Draw	200.00	
		1020	ATM		200.00
11/11/12	4014	6420	Water and Power Expense	90.50	
		1020	Water and Power Co.		90.50
11/11/12	4015	6400	Utilities Expense	53.90	
		1020	GPS Gas		53.90
11/12/12	4016	6500	Telephone Expense	45.08	
		1020	Century Telephone		45.08
11/14/12	4017	6550	Long Distance Co.	81.50	
		1020	Long Distance Co.		81.50
11/16/12	ATM	3930	Mark Foltz, Draw	200.00	
		1020	ATM		200.00
11/27/12	4018	2000	VISA Payable	5,250.65	
		1020	VISA card payment		5,250.65
11/28/12	4019	6560	Internet Service Provider	29.99	
		1020	Internet Service Provider		29.99
11/28/12	ATM	3930	Mark Foltz, Draw	200.00	
		1020	ATM		200.00
	Total			6,151.62	6,151.62

9. Print or display the general journal to see the bank service charge.

*****EDUCATIONAL VERSION ONLY*****

Mark Foltz Designer
General Journal
For the Period From Nov 1, 2012 to Nov 30, 2012

Filter Criteria includes: Report order is by Date. Report is printed with Accounts having Zero Amounts and with shortened descriptions and in Detail Format.

Date	Account I	Reference	Trans Description	Debit Amt	Credit Amt
11/30/12	1020	11/30/12	Service Charge		10.00
	6850		Service Charge	10.00	
		Total		10.00	10.00

If your journals do not agree with the ones shown, edit the journals and post again. (Refer to page 346 Editing Journal Entries.)

10. Print or display the General Ledger Trial Balance.

*****EDUCATIONAL VERSION ONLY*****

Mark Foltz Designer
General Ledger Trial Balance
As of Nov 30, 2012

Filter Criteria includes: Report order is by ID. Report is printed in Detail Format.

Account ID	Account Description	Debit Amt	Credit Amt
1010	Money Market Account	15,700.00	
1020	Checking Account	17,651.33	
1040	IRA Savings Account	27,730.35	
1045	WI State Retirement	35,612.00	
1300	Prepaid Insurance	2,100.00	
1400	Prepaid Rent	600.00	
1450	Supplies	1,987.81	
1500	Computer Equipment	7,905.68	
1510	Furniture	5,000.00	
1520	Automobile	19,000.00	
2400	Publisher Advances		11,000.00
3920	Mark Foltz, Capital		112,814.28
3930	Mark Foltz, Draw	1,200.00	
4000	Teaching Income		5,432.38
4050	Royalty Income		6,420.90
6100	Dues and Subscriptions	45.00	
6150	Auto Registration	210.00	
6180	Automobile Expense	311.00	
6400	Utilities Expense	93.54	
6420	Water and Power Expense	189.09	
6500	Telephone Expense	80.08	
6550	Long Distance Co.	127.70	
6560	Internet Service Provider	59.98	
6850	Bank Service Charge	20.00	
7400	Postage Expense	44.00	
	Total:	135,667.56	135,667.56

11. Print or display the Balance Sheet.

Mark Foltz Designer
Balance Sheet
November 30, 2012

ASSETS

Current Assets		
Money Market Account	$ 15,700.00	
Checking Account	17,651.33	
IRA Savings Account	27,730.35	
WI State Retirement	35,612.00	
Prepaid Insurance	2,100.00	
Prepaid Rent	600.00	
Supplies	1,987.81	
Total Current Assets		101,381.49
Property and Equipment		
Computer Equipment	7,905.68	
Furniture	5,000.00	
Automobile	19,000.00	
Total Property and Equipment		31,905.68
Other Assets		
Total Other Assets		0.00
Total Assets	$	133,287.17

LIABILITIES AND CAPITAL

Current Liabilities		
Publisher Advances	$ 11,000.00	
Total Current Liabilities		11,000.00
Long-Term Liabilities		
Total Long-Term Liabilities		0.00
Total Liabilities		11,000.00
Capital		
Mark Foltz, Capital	112,814.28	
Mark Foltz, Draw	(1,200.00)	
Net Income	10,672.89	
Total Capital		122,287.17
Total Liabilities & Capital	$	133,287.17

Unaudited - For Management Purposes Only

12. Print or display the Income Statement.

Mark Foltz Designer
Income Statement
For the Eleven Months Ending November 30, 2012

		Current Month			Year to Date	
Revenues						
Teaching Income	$	2,716.19	52.52	$	5,432.38	45.83
Royalty Income		2,455.85	47.48		6,420.90	54.17
Total Revenues		5,172.04	100.00		11,853.28	100.00
Cost of Sales						
Total Cost of Sales		0.00	0.00		0.00	0.00
Gross Profit		5,172.04	100.00		11,853.28	100.00
Expenses						
Dues and Subscriptions		0.00	0.00		45.00	0.38
Auto Registration		0.00	0.00		210.00	1.77
Automobile Expense		0.00	0.00		311.00	2.62
Utilities Expense		53.90	1.04		93.54	0.79
Water and Power Expense		90.50	1.75		189.09	1.60
Telephone Expense		45.08	0.87		80.08	0.68
Long Distance Co.		81.50	1.58		127.70	1.08
Internet Service Provider		29.99	0.58		59.98	0.51
Bank Service Charge		10.00	0.19		20.00	0.17
Postage Expense		0.00	0.00		44.00	0.37
Total Expenses		310.97	6.01		1,180.39	9.96
Net Income	$	4,861.07	93.99	$	10,672.89	90.04

For Management Purposes Only

➤ **Troubleshooting:** Why are my Current Month and Year to Date balances different than the Income Statement shown?

On the Income Statement shown above, the Year to Date column accumulates balances for October *and* November; the Current Month column reflects November only.

In Chapter 9, on page 304, step 2, the instructions said "beginning balances must be set for the previous month, September 1-30, 2012." If you did not set your chart of accounts beginning balances From 9/1/12 through 9/30/2012, the Current Month and Year to Date columns will differ from those shown above. To see when your beginning balances were set, display the General Ledger from Period 9 (9/1/2012) to Period 11 (11/30/2012).

To display the General Ledger from Sep 1, 2012 to Nov 30, 2012 do this:

a. From the Reports & Forms menu, select General Ledger, select General Ledger.

b. Click [Options].

c. In the From field, select Period 9, (9/1/12). The To field shows Period 11, (11/30/12).

d. Click [OK].

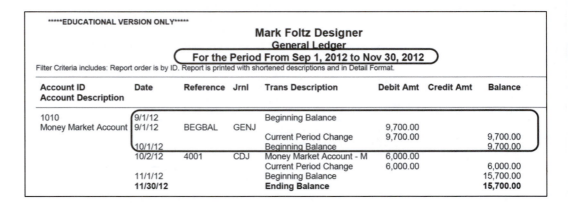

The beginning balance period cannot be changed. If you do not want to start again, ask your instructor for his or her advice.

BACKING UP NOVEMBER DATA

Follow these steps to back up Chapter 11 data:

1. If necessary, close all windows and insert your USB flash drive. From the System Navigation Center, select [Back Up Now]. (*Or*, from the menu bar, select File, then Back up.)

2. If necessary, uncheck the box next to Include company name in the backup file name. Click [Back Up].

3. In the Save in field, go to the location of your USB drive or back up to another location. Type **Chapter 11 November** in the File name field.

4. Click [Save] .

5. When the window prompts that This company backup will require approximately 1 diskette, click [OK] . Click [OK] again when the window prompts Please insert the first disk. When the Back Up Company scale is 100% complete, you have successfully backed up to the current point in Chapter 11. (This step will differ slightly if you are backing up to the default or other hard drive location.)

DATA FILE STATISTICS

To display information about your company data files, follow these steps.

1. From the menu bar, click Help; Customer Support and Service, File Statistics.

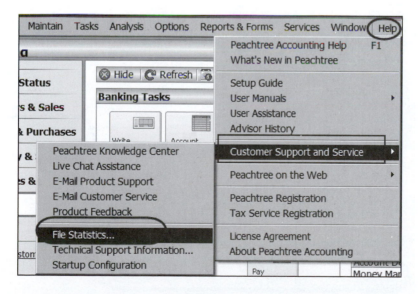

2. The Data File Statistics window lists the number of records and sizes in kilobytes for each data file for the company that is open. It also provides a grand total (scroll down).

Peachtree displays the company's shortened name (MARFOLDE) on the title bar.[4] This represents the name of the folder where the opened company resides. Observe that the Directory field shows where the company resides on your hard drive: C:\Sage\Peachtree\Company\marfolde [*or, your shortened name*].

In Chapter 9, pages 310-311, the marfolde Properties window also showed the shortened company name that Peachtree assigned. Compare your Data File Statistics window to the one shown below

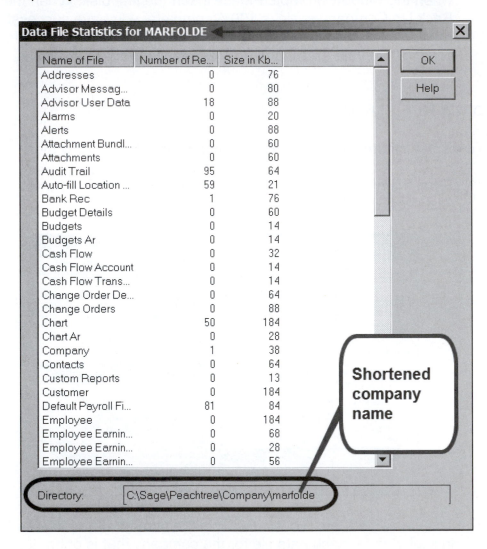

---

[4]If you used your name, the company's shortened name will differ.

The McGraw-Hill Companies, Inc., *Computer Accounting with Peachtree by Sage Complete Accounting 2012, 16e*

3. To close the Data File Statistics window, click OK .

CHANGING ACCOUNTING PERIODS

Follow these steps to change accounting periods:

1. From the menu bar, select Tasks, then System.

2. From the System menu, select Change Accounting Period.

   a. In the Open Accounting Periods list, select period 12 - Dec 01, 2012 to Dec 31, 2012.

   b. Click OK . When the window prompts Would you like to print your reports before continuing? window, click No . If necessary, select Business Status . Observe that your toolbar shows Period 12 - 12/01/12-12/31/12 .

TRANSACTION REGISTER AND BANK STATEMENT: DECEMBER 2012

1. Use Mr. Foltz's transaction register to journalize and post transactions for the month of December. His transaction register is shown on the next page.

Comment

Before you start journalizing entries, make sure that you are starting with correct data. To do that, display the General Ledger Trial Balance and compare it to the one shown on page 371.

		Transaction Register Mark Foltz Designer			
Check Number	Date	Description of Transaction	Payment	Deposit	Balance
	11/30	*Bank Service Charge*	*10.00*		*17,651.33*
	12/3^5	ATM	400.00		17,251.33
	12/8	Deposit (Green Bay CC)		2,716.19	19,967.52
4020	12/11	Water and Power Co.	75.45		19,892.07
4021	12/11	GPS Gas (utilities)	102.92		19,789.15
4022	12/12	Century Telephone	45.95		19,743.20
4023	12/15	R-Gallery (business cards - debit, Supplies)	115.25		19,627.95
4024	12/18	Long Distance Co.	75.49		19,552.46
4025	12/18	Internet Service Provider	29.99		19,522.47
	12/19	ATM	400.00		19,122.47
	12/29	ATM	400.00		18,722.47

2. Use Mr. Foltz's bank statement to complete account reconciliation. (*Remember to record the bank service charge on the Account Reconciliation window.*)

Statement of Account Prospect Bank December 1 to December 31, 2012 Account No. 433966-70			Mark Foltz Designer 34511 Main Street Green Bay, WI 54301	
REGULAR CHECKING				
Previous Balance	11/30/12	22,931.97		
1 Deposit(+)		2,716.19		
7 Checks (-)		5,695.70		
3 Other Deduction (-)		1,200.00		
Service Charges (-)	12/31/12	10.00		
Ending Balance	12/31/12	**18,742.46**		
Continued				

---

^{5}Start your journal transactions with the December 3 ATM transaction.

The McGraw-Hill Companies, Inc., *Computer Accounting with Peachtree by Sage Complete Accounting 2012, 16e*

DEPOSITS			
	12/8/12	2,716.19	

CHECKS (Asterisk * indicates break in check number sequence)			
	12/8/12	4018	5,250.65	
	12/8/12	4019	29.99	
	12/22/12	4020	75.45	
	12/29/12	4021	102.92	
	12/29/12	4022	45.95	
	12/31/12	4023	115.25	
	12/31/12	4024	75.49	

OTHER DEDUCTIONS (ATM's)			
	12/3/12	400.00	
	12/19/12	400.00	
	12/29/12	400.00	

3. Display the Account Register (Reports & Forms; Account Reconciliation, Account Register; Display). Compare the Account Register below to the transaction register on page 378.

*****EDUCATIONAL VERSION ONLY*****

Mark Foltz Designer
Account Register
For the Period From Dec 1, 2012 to Dec 31, 2012
1020 - Checking Account

Filter Criteria includes: Report order is by Date.

Date	Trans No	Type	Trans Desc	Deposit Amt	Withdrawal Amt	Balance
			Beginning Balance			17,651.33
12/3/12	ATM	Withdr	ATM		400.00	17,251.33
12/8/12	12/8/12	Deposit	Deposit	2,716.19		19,967.52
12/11/12	4020	Withdr	Water and Power Co.		75.45	19,892.07
12/11/12	4021	Withdr	GPS Gas		102.92	19,789.15
12/12/12	4022	Withdr	Century Telephone		45.95	19,743.20
12/15/12	4023	Withdr	R-Gallery		115.25	19,627.95
12/18/12	4024	Withdr	Long Distance Co.		75.49	19,552.46
12/18/12	4025	Withdr	Internet Service Provid		29.99	19,522.47
12/19/12	ATM	Withdr	ATM		400.00	19,122.47
12/29/12	ATM	Withdr	ATM		400.00	18,722.47
12/31/12	12/31/12	Other	Service Charge		10.00	18,712.47
			Total	2,716.19	1,655.05	

4. Print or display the Account Reconciliation report.

```
*****EDUCATIONAL VERSION ONLY*****
                                        Mark Foltz Designer
                                        Account Reconciliation
                                         As of Dec 31, 2012
                                       1020 - Checking Account
                                  Bank Statement Date: December 31, 2012
Filter Criteria includes: Report is printed in Detail Format.
```

Beginning GL Balanc				17,651.33
Add: Cash Receipts				2,716.19
Less: Cash Disburse				(1,645.05)
Add (Less) Other				(10.00)
Ending GL Balance				18,712.47
Ending Bank Balance				18,742.46
Add back deposits in				
Total deposits in tran				
(Less) outstanding ch				
	Dec 18, 20	4025	(29.99)	
Total outstanding che				(29.99)
Add (Less) Other				
Total other				
Unreconciled differen				0.00
Ending GL Balance				18,712.47

5. Print or display the General Journal.

```
*****EDUCATIONAL VERSION ONLY*****
                                        Mark Foltz Designer
                                        General Journal
                           For the Period From Dec 1, 2012 to Dec 31, 2012
Filter Criteria includes: Report order is by Date. Report is printed with Accounts having Zero Amounts and with shortened descriptions and in Detail Format.
```

Date	Account I	Reference	Trans Description	Debit Amt	Credit Amt
12/31/12	1020	12/31/12	Service Charge		10.00
	6850		Service Charge	10.00	
		Total		10.00	10.00

6. Print or display the Cash Receipts Journal.

*****EDUCATIONAL VERSION ONLY*****

Mark Foltz Designer
Cash Receipts Journal
For the Period From Dec 1, 2012 to Dec 31, 2012

Filter Criteria includes: Report order is by Check Date. Report is printed in Detail Format.

Date	Account ID	Transaction Ref	Line Description	Debit Amnt	Credit Amnt
12/8/12	4000	Green Bay CC	Teaching Income		2,716.19
	1020		Deposit	2,716.19	
				2,716.19	**2,716.19**

7. Print or display the Cash Disbursements Journal. Compare your cash disbursements journal to the one shown below.

*****EDUCATIONAL VERSION ONLY*****

Mark Foltz Designer
Cash Disbursements Journal
For the Period From Dec 1, 2012 to Dec 31, 2012

Filter Criteria includes: Report order is by Date. Report is printed in Detail Format.

Date	Check #	Account ID	Line Description	Debit Amount	Credit Amount
12/3/12	ATM	3930	Mark Foltz, Draw	400.00	
		1020	ATM		400.00
12/11/12	4020	6420	Water and Power Expense	75.45	
		1020	Water and Power Co.		75.45
12/11/12	4021	6400	Utilities Expense	102.92	
		1020	GPS Gas		102.92
12/12/12	4022	6500	Telephone Expense	45.95	
		1020	Century Telephone		45.95
12/15/12	4023	1450	Supplies	115.25	
		1020	R-Gallery		115.25
12/18/12	4024	6550	Long Distance Co.	75.49	
		1020	Long Distance Co.		75.49
12/18/12	4025	6560	Internet Service Provider	29.99	
		1020	Internet Service Provider		29.99
12/19/12	ATM	3930	Mark Foltz, Draw	400.00	
		1020	ATM		400.00
12/29/12	ATM	3930	Mark Foltz, Draw	400.00	
		1020	ATM		400.00
	Total			**1,645.05**	**1,645.05**

If your journals do not agree with the ones shown, edit and post again.

8. Display or print a General Ledger Trial Balance (unadjusted). Compare your trial balance to the one shown below.

*****EDUCATIONAL VERSION ONLY*****

Mark Foltz Designer
General Ledger Trial Balance
As of Dec 31, 2012

Filter Criteria includes: Report order is by ID. Report is printed in Detail Format.

Account ID	Account Description	Debit Amt	Credit Amt
1010	Money Market Account	15,700.00	
1020	Checking Account	18,712.47	
1040	IRA Savings Account	27,730.35	
1045	WI State Retirement	35,612.00	
1300	Prepaid Insurance	2,100.00	
1400	Prepaid Rent	600.00	
1450	Supplies	2,103.06	
1500	Computer Equipment	7,905.68	
1510	Furniture	5,000.00	
1520	Automobile	19,000.00	
2400	Publisher Advances		11,000.00
3920	Mark Foltz, Capital		112,814.28
3930	Mark Foltz, Draw	2,400.00	
4000	Teaching Income		8,148.57
4050	Royalty Income		6,420.90
6100	Dues and Subscriptions	45.00	
6150	Auto Registration	210.00	
6180	Automobile Expense	311.00	
6400	Utilities Expense	196.46	
6420	Water and Power Expense	264.54	
6500	Telephone Expense	126.03	
6550	Long Distance Co.	203.19	
6560	Internet Service Provider	89.97	
6850	Bank Service Charge	30.00	
7400	Postage Expense	44.00	
	Total:	138,383.75	138,383.75

BACKING UP THE UNADJUSTED TRIAL BALANCE

Follow the steps on the next page to back up Chapter 11 data.

1. Close all windows and insert your USB flash drive. From the System Navigation Center, select [Back Up Now]. (*Or,* from the menu bar, select File, then Back up.)

2. If necessary, uncheck the box next to Include company name in the backup file name. Click [Back Up].

3. In the Save in field, go to the location of your USB drive or back up to another location. Type **Chapter 11 December UTB** in the File name field. (UTB is an abbreviation of unadjusted trail balance.)

4. Click [Save].

5. When the window prompts that This company backup will require approximately 1 diskette, click [OK]. Click [OK] again when the window prompts Please insert the first disk. When the Back Up Company scale is 100% complete, you have successfully backed up to the current point in Chapter 11. (This step will differ slightly if you are backing up to the default or other hard drive location.)

6. Click File, Exit to exit Peachtree. Or, continue with the next section.

You print the financial statements after you journalize and post the end-of-quarter adjusting entries.

END-OF-QUARTER ADJUSTING ENTRIES

It is the policy of your accounting firm to record adjusting entries at the end of the quarter. Mr. Foltz's accounting records are complete through December 31, 2012. The adjusting entries are recorded in the General Journal. Use these steps for entering the seven adjusting entries shown on pages 384-386.

1. From the Banking Navigation Center, select [General Journal Entry]; New General Journal Entry. The General Journal Entry window appears. (*Or,* from the menu bar, click Tasks, then General Journal Entry.

2. Type **31** in the <u>D</u>ate field. Press **<Enter>** three times.

3. In the GL Account field, select the appropriate account to debit. Type the account name in the Description field (or type a description). Press the **<Enter>** key once to go to the Debit field. Type the debit amount, then press the **<Enter>** key three times.

4. In the GL Account field, select the appropriate account to credit. Type the account name in the Description field. (If you typed a description with the debit part of the entry, it appears automatically.) Press the **<Enter>** key two times to go to the Credit field. Type the credit amount. Press the **<Enter>** key.

5. Click [Save] to post each adjusting entry.

Journalize and post the following December 31, 2012 adjusting entries:

1. Office supplies on hand are $1,700.00. (It is the policy of Mr. Foltz's company to do an adjustment for supplies at the end of the quarter.)

Acct. #	Account Name	Debit	Credit
6450	Office Supplies Expense	403.06	
1450	Supplies		403.06

Computation: Supplies $2,103.06
               Office supplies on hand   - 1,700.00
               Adjustment $ 403.06

Hint: To post your transaction to the general ledger, click [Save] *after each general journal entry.*

2. Adjust three months of prepaid insurance ($2,100 X 3/12 = $525). Mr. Foltz paid a one year insurance premium on 10/1/12.

Acct. #	Account Name	Debit	Credit
6950	Insurance Expense	525.00	
1300	Prepaid Insurance		525.00

3. Adjust three months of prepaid rent ($200 X 3 = $600.)

Acct. #	Account Name	Debit	Credit
6300	Rent or Lease Expense	600.00	
1400	Prepaid Rent		600.00

4. Use straight-line depreciation for Mr. Foltz's computer equipment. His computer equipment has a three-year service life and a $1,000 salvage value. To depreciate computer equipment for the fourth quarter, use this calculation:

$7,905.68 – $1,000 ÷ 3 years × 3/12 = $575.47

Computer Equipment, 10/1/12	$6,800.00
Hardware Upgrade, 10/4/12	1,105.68
Total computer equipment, 12/31/12	$7,905.68

Acct. #	Account Name	Debit	Credit
7050	Deprec. Exp.- Comp Eqt	575.47	
1900	Accum. Depreciation - Comp Eqt		575.47

5. Use straight-line depreciation to depreciate Mr. Foltz's furniture. His furniture has a 5-year service life and a $500 salvage value. To depreciate furniture for the fourth quarter, use this calculation:

$5,000 – $500 ÷ 5 × 3/12 = $225.00

Acct. #	Account Name	Debit	Credit
7060	Deprec. Exp.- Furniture	225.00	
1910	Accum. Depreciation - Furniture		225.00

6. Mr. Foltz purchased his automobile on October 1, 2012. Use the following adjusting entry. The computation is:

$19,000 × 20% × 3/12 = $950.00

Acct. #	Account Name	Debit	Credit
7070	Deprec. Exp. - Automobile	950.00	
1920	Accum. Depreciation - Automobile		950.00

7. Mr. Foltz received a $11,000 advance from his publisher. This was recorded as **unearned revenue** on October 2, 2012. Unearned revenue is a liability account used to report advance collections from customers or clients. The amount of this adjusting entry is based on Mr. Foltz's royalty statement.

Acct. #	Account Name	Debit	Credit
2400	Publisher Advances	3,500.00	
4050	Royalty Income		3,500.00

8. After journalizing and posting the end-of-quarter adjusting entries, print the General Journal for December 31, 2012. Follow these steps to print your December 31, 2012 General Journal:

   a. From the menu bar, click Reports & Forms; General Ledger. Highlight General Journal.

   b. Click [Display]. The General Journal report appears.

   c. To see the account ID for each account debited and credited, click [Columns]. The General Journal Columns window appears. Select GL Account Description.

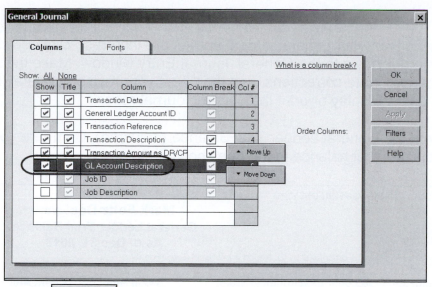

d. Click ⌐ OK ⌐. Adjust the report so it appears on one page. Observe that an Account Description column is added. If you used a description on the general journal entry window, you may want to show the account ID on the general journal report. The December 31 adjustments and bank charges, which post on 12/31/12, are shown below.

*****EDUCATIONAL VERSION ONLY*****

Mark Foltz Designer
General Journal
For the Period From Dec 1, 2012 to Dec 31, 2012
Filter Criteria includes: Report order is by Date. Report is printed with Accounts having Zero Amounts and with shortened descriptions and in Detail Format.

Date	Account I	Reference	Trans Description	Debit Amt	Credit Am	Account Description
12/31/12	6450		Office Supplies Expense	403.06		Office Supplies Expense
	1450		Supplies		403.06	Supplies
	6950		Insurance Expense	525.00		Insurance Expense
	1300		Prepaid Insurance		525.00	Prepaid Insurance
	6300		Rent or Lease Expense	600.00		Rent or Lease Expense
	1400		Prepaid Rent		600.00	Prepaid Rent
	7050		Deprec. Exp. - Comp Eqt	575.47		Deprec. Exp. - Comp Eqt
	1900		Accum. Depreciation - Co		575.47	Accum. Depreciation - Comp E
	7060		Deprec. Exp. - Furniture	225.00		Deprec. Exp. - Furniture
	1910		Accum. Depreciation - Fur		225.00	Accum. Depreciation - Furnitur
	7070		Deprec. Exp. - Automobile	950.00		Deprec. Exp. - Automobile
	1920		Accum. Depreciation - Aut		950.00	Accum. Depreciation - Automo
	2400		Publisher's Advances	3,500.00		Publisher Advances
	4050		Royalty Income		3,500.00	Royalty Income
12/31/12	1020	12/31/12	Service Charge		10.00	Checking Account
	6850		Service Charge	10.00		Bank Service Charge
		Total		**6,788.53**	**6,788.53**	

If any of your general journal entries are incorrect, click to drill down to the General Journal Entry window. Make the appropriate corrections, and then post your revised general journal entry. Display or print the general journal report.

9. Print the General Ledger Trial Balance (adjusted). Compare your adjusted trial balance to the one shown below.

*****EDUCATIONAL VERSION ONLY*****

Mark Foltz Designer
General Ledger Trial Balance
As of Dec 31, 2012

Filter Criteria includes: Report order is by ID. Report is printed in Detail Format.

Account ID	Account Description	Debit Amt	Credit Amt
1010	Money Market Account	15,700.00	
1020	Checking Account	18,712.47	
1040	IRA Savings Account	27,730.35	
1045	WI State Retirement	35,612.00	
1300	Prepaid Insurance	1,575.00	
1450	Supplies	1,700.00	
1500	Computer Equipment	7,905.68	
1510	Furniture	5,000.00	
1520	Automobile	19,000.00	
1900	Accum. Depreciation - Comp Eqt		575.47
1910	Accum. Depreciation - Furnitur		225.00
1920	Accum. Depreciation - Automobi		950.00
2400	Publisher Advances		7,500.00
3920	Mark Foltz, Capital		112,814.28
3930	Mark Foltz, Draw	2,400.00	
4000	Teaching Income		8,148.57
4050	Royalty Income		9,920.90
6100	Dues and Subscriptions	45.00	
6150	Auto Registration	210.00	
6180	Automobile Expense	311.00	
6300	Rent or Lease Expense	600.00	
6400	Utilities Expense	196.46	
6420	Water and Power Expense	264.54	
6450	Office Supplies Expense	403.06	
6500	Telephone Expense	126.03	
6550	Long Distance Co.	203.19	
6560	Internet Service Provider	89.97	
6850	Bank Service Charge	30.00	
6950	Insurance Expense	525.00	
7050	Deprec. Exp. - Comp Eqt	575.47	
7060	Deprec. Exp. - Furniture	225.00	
7070	Deprec. Exp. - Automobile	950.00	
7400	Postage Expense	44.00	
	Total:	**140,134.22**	**140,134.22**

10. Print the Balance Sheet.

Mark Foltz Designer
Balance Sheet
December 31, 2012

ASSETS

Current Assets		
Money Market Account	$ 15,700.00	
Checking Account	18,712.47	
IRA Savings Account	27,730.35	
WI State Retirement	35,612.00	
Prepaid Insurance	1,575.00	
Supplies	1,700.00	
Total Current Assets		101,029.82
Property and Equipment		
Computer Equipment	7,905.68	
Furniture	5,000.00	
Automobile	19,000.00	
Accum. Depreciation - Comp Eqt	(575.47)	
Accum. Depreciation - Furnitur	(225.00)	
Accum. Depreciation - Automobi	(950.00)	
Total Property and Equipment		30,155.21
Other Assets		
Total Other Assets		0.00
Total Assets	$	131,185.03

LIABILITIES AND CAPITAL

Current Liabilities		
Publisher Advances	$ 7,500.00	
Total Current Liabilities		7,500.00
Long-Term Liabilities		
Total Long-Term Liabilities		0.00
Total Liabilities		7,500.00
Capital		
Mark Foltz, Capital	112,814.28	
Mark Foltz, Draw	(2,400.00)	
Net Income	13,270.75	
Total Capital		123,685.03
Total Liabilities & Capital	$	131,185.03

Unaudited - For Management Purposes Only

11. Print the Income Statement.

Mark Foltz Designer
Income Statement
For the Twelve Months Ending December 31, 2012

	Current Month			Year to Date	
Revenues					
Teaching Income	$	2,716.19	43.70	$ 8,148.57	45.10
Royalty Income		3,500.00	56.30	9,920.90	54.90
Total Revenues		6,216.19	100.00	18,069.47	100.00
Cost of Sales					
Total Cost of Sales		0.00	0.00	0.00	0.00
Gross Profit		6,216.19	100.00	18,069.47	100.00
Expenses					
Dues and Subscriptions		0.00	0.00	45.00	0.25
Auto Registration		0.00	0.00	210.00	1.16
Automobile Expense		0.00	0.00	311.00	1.72
Rent or Lease Expense		600.00	9.65	600.00	3.32
Utilities Expense		102.92	1.66	196.46	1.09
Water and Power Expense		75.45	1.21	264.54	1.46
Office Supplies Expense		403.06	6.48	403.06	2.23
Telephone Expense		45.95	0.74	126.03	0.70
Long Distance Co.		75.49	1.21	203.19	1.12
Internet Service Provider		29.99	0.48	89.97	0.50
Bank Service Charge		10.00	0.16	30.00	0.17
Insurance Expense		525.00	8.45	525.00	2.91
Deprec. Exp. - Comp Eqt		575.47	9.26	575.47	3.18
Deprec. Exp. - Furniture		225.00	3.62	225.00	1.25
Deprec. Exp. - Automobile		950.00	15.28	950.00	5.26
Postage Expense		0.00	0.00	44.00	0.24
Total Expenses		3,618.33	58.21	4,798.72	26.56
Net Income	$	2,597.86	41.79	$ 13,270.75	73.44

For Management Purposes Only

Comment

If your income statement or other financial statements do *not agree* with the textbook illustrations, edit the journals, post, then reprint reports. If the Year to Date column *does not agree* with what is shown on the Income Statement (above), or Statement of Cash Flow (page 392), refer to Entering Chart of Accounts Beginning Balances in Chapter 9 on pages 302-309. Correct year-to-date balances depend on setting the beginning balances correctly for 9/1/12 through 9/30/12 (see the Select Period window on page 304, below step 3). To see if your beginning balances were set as of September 30, 2012, display the balance sheet for Period 9 (9/1/12 to 9/30/12). (Refer to pages 307-309.)

12. Follow these steps to print the Statement of Retained Earnings.

   a. In the Financial Statement list, click <Standard> Retained Earnings to highlight it.

   b. Click

   c. Uncheck Show Zero Amounts. Make the selections to print. Compare your Statement of Retained Earnings to the one shown below.

Mark Foltz Designer
Statement of Retained Earnings
For the Twelve Months Ending December 31, 2012

Beginning Retained Earnings	$	0.00
Adjustments To Date		0.00
Net Income		13,270.75
Subtotal		13,270.75
Mark Foltz, Draw		(2,400.00)
Ending Retained Earnings	$	10,870.75

The Statement of Retained Earnings shows the net income at the end of the Quarter, $13,270.75, minus Mr. Foltz's drawing, $2,400. When you close the fiscal year, the Ending Retained Earnings amount, $10,870.75, will be shown on the postclosing trial balance, page 400.

13. Print the Statement of Cash Flow. Compare it to the one shown on the next page.

Mark Foltz Designer
Statement of Cash Flow
For the twelve Months Ended December 31, 2012

	Current Month	Year to Date
Cash Flows from operating activities		
Net Income	$ 2,597.86	$ 13,270.75
Adjustments to reconcile net		
income to net cash provided		
by operating activities		
Accum. Depreciation - Comp Eqt	575.47	575.47
Accum. Depreciation - Furnitur	225.00	225.00
Accum. Depreciation - Automobi	950.00	950.00
Prepaid Insurance	525.00	(1,575.00)
Prepaid Rent	600.00	0.00
Supplies	287.81	(1,700.00)
Publisher Advances	(3,500.00)	7,500.00
Total Adjustments	(336.72)	5,975.47
Net Cash provided by Operations	2,261.14	19,246.22
Cash Flows from investing activities		
Used For		
Computer Equipment	0.00	(7,905.68)
Furniture	0.00	(5,000.00)
Automobile	0.00	(19,000.00)
Net cash used in investing	0.00	(31,905.68)
Cash Flows from financing activities		
Proceeds From		
Mark Foltz, Capital	0.00	112,814.28
Used For		
Mark Foltz, Draw	(1,200.00)	(2,400.00)
Net cash used in financing	(1,200.00)	110,414.28
Net increase <decrease> in cash	$ 1,061.14	$ 97,754.82
Summary		
Cash Balance at End of Period	$ 97,754.82	$ 97,754.82
Cash Balance at Beg of Period	(96,693.68)	0.00
Net Increase <Decrease> in Cash	$ 1,061.14	$ 97,754.82

Unaudited - For Internal Use Only.

BACKING UP DECEMBER DATA

Follow these steps to back up Mark Foltz's December data:

1. If necessary, close all windows and insert your USB flash drive. From the System Navigation Center, select [Back Up Now]. (*Or,* from the menu bar, select File, then Back up.)

2. If necessary, uncheck the box next to Include company name in the backup file name. Click [Back Up].

3. In the Save in field, go to the location of your USB drive or back up to another location. Type **Chapter 11 December** in the File name field.

4. Click [Save].

5. When the window prompts that This company backup will require approximately 1 diskette, click [OK]. Click [OK] again when the window prompts Please insert the first disk. When the Back Up Company scale is 100% complete, you have successfully backed up to the current point in Chapter 11. (This step will differ slightly if you are backing up to the default or other hard drive location.)

EXPORT FINANCIAL STATEMENTS TO EXCEL AND SAVE PDF FILES

Follow these steps to export the General Ledger Trial Balance (Adjusted), Balance Sheet, Income Statement, Statement of Cash Flow, and Statement of Retained Earnings to Excel and save as Adobe PDF files. For detailed steps exporting multiple reports to Excel, refer to pages 351-353.

1. Display the General Ledger Trial Balance.

2. Export the General Ledger Trial Balance to Excel. Create a new Microsoft Excel workbook.

3. Save. Use **Chapter 11_Adjusted Trial Balance and Financial Statements.xlsx** as the file name.

4. Display the Balance Sheet. Export to Excel. Add a new worksheet to an existing Microsoft Excel workbook. (*Hint:* Add the sheet to the file saved in step 3–Chapter 11_Adjusted Trial Balance and Financial Statements.xlsx.)

5. Display the Income Statement. (*Hint:* Select Options to uncheck Show Zero Amounts.) Export to Excel. Add a new worksheet to an existing Microsoft Excel workbook. *(Hint:* Add the sheet to the file saved in step 3—Chapter 11_Financial Statements.xlsx).

6. Display the Statement of Cash Flow. Export to Excel. Add this sheet to the saved file.

7. Display the Statement of Retained Earnings. Export to Excel. Add this sheet to the saved file.

8. Your Excel file should have five sheets: General Ledger Trial Balance, Balance Sheet, Income Stmnt, Cash Flow, and Retained Earnings.

9. Save the file. Exit Excel.

10. Save the General Ledger Trial Balance, Balance Sheet, Income Statement, Statement of Cash Flow, and Statement of Retained Earnings as PDF files. Use Chapter 11_Adjusted Trial Balance, Chapter 11_December Balance Sheet.pdf, Chapter 11_December Income Statement.pdf, etc. as the file names.

11. Close all Peachtree windows.

CLOSING THE FISCAL YEAR

The Retained Earnings account is updated at the close of the fiscal year with the ending balance of income and expenses (net income). The balance in the retained earnings account continues to accrue at the end of each fiscal year.

At the end of the year, PCA automatically completes the closing procedure. Follow these steps to close Mark Foltz's fiscal year:

1. If necessary, start Peachtree, then open Mark Foltz Designer. From the menu bar, select Tasks, System, Year-End Wizard.

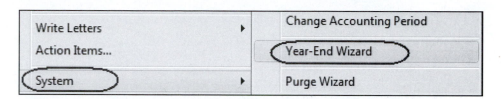

2. The Year-End Wizard - Welcome window appears. Read the information on the Welcome to the Peachtree Year-End Wizard window.

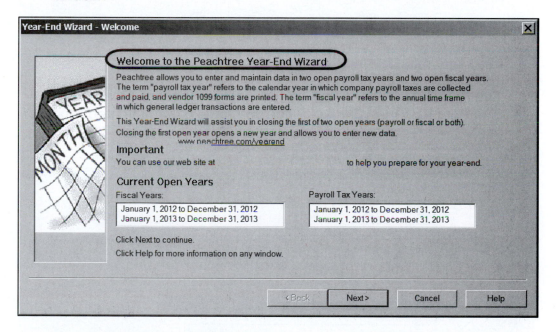

3. Click [Next >]. The Close Options window appears. In the Years to Close list, Fiscal and Payroll Tax Years is the default. Read the information on this window.

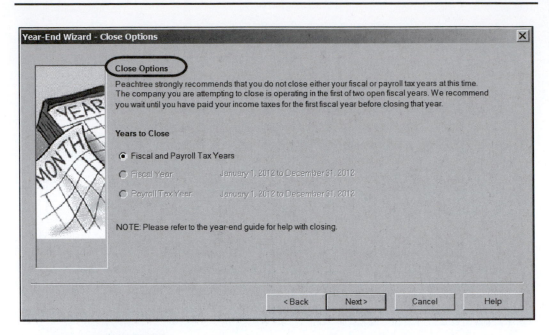

4. Click .

5. The Print Fiscal Year-End Reports window appears. Read the information on this window. Since you have already printed reports, click **Check None** to uncheck all.

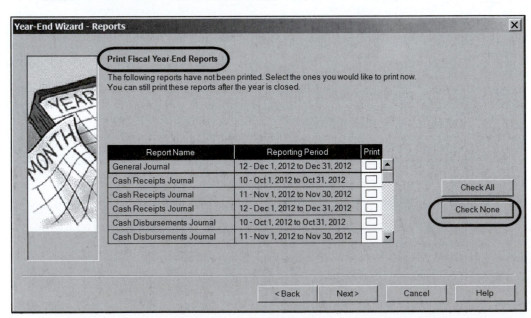

Hint: If you do not uncheck the boxes, the general ledger prints.

6. Click  .

7. The Internal Accounting Review window appears. Read the information on this window. Click [Next >] .

8. The Back Up Company Data window appears. You already made a back up on page 393 but you may want to make another one. Read the information on this window. Click [Back Up] . The Back Up Company window appears.

9. Observe that the box next to Include company name in the backup file name is checked. Click [Back Up] .

10. The Save Backup for Mark Foltz Designer as window appears. Observe that the File name field includes the name of the company and today's date.

11. Click [Save] . Make the selections to back up. Click [OK] .

12. After the backup is made, you are returned to the Back Up Company Data window. Click [Next >] .

13. The New Open Fiscal Years window appears. Read the information on this window.

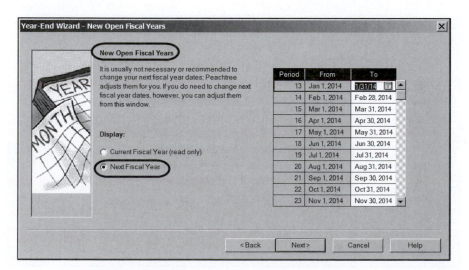

14. Accept the default for Next Fiscal Year by clicking on .

15. The Important - Confirm Year-End Close window appears. Read the information on this window.

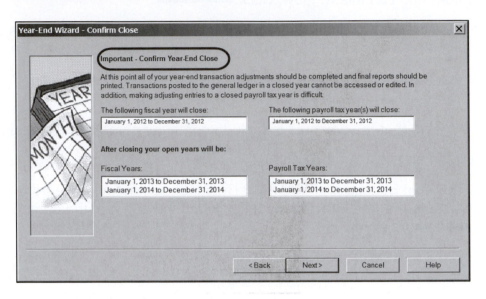

16. Click .

17. The Begin Close-Year Process window appears. Read the information on this window.

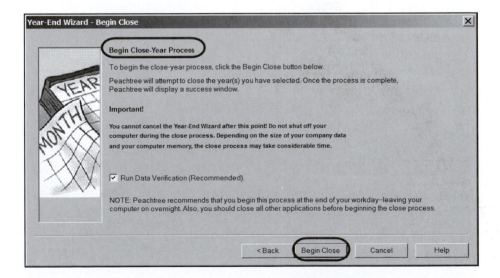

18. Click ▐ Begin Close ▌.

19. After a few moments the scale shows 100%. The Congratulations! window appears. Read the information on this window.

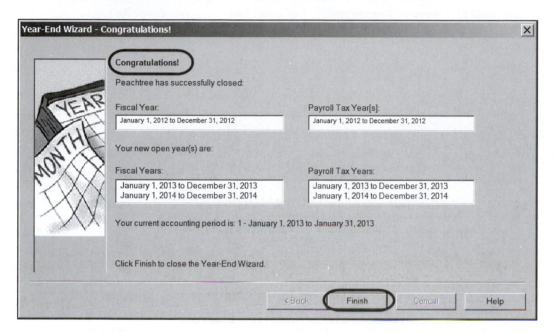

20. Click ▐ Finish ▌.

PRINTING THE POSTCLOSING TRIAL BALANCE

After the fiscal year is closed, a postclosing trial balance is printed. Only permanent accounts appear on the postclosing trial balance. All temporary accounts (revenues and expenses) have been closed. This completes the computer accounting cycle.

Follow these steps to print Mark Foltz's postclosing trial balance:

1. From the menu bar, select Reports & Forms, General Ledger, General Ledger Trial Balance.

2. Make the selections to print the postclosing trial balance. Compare your general ledger trial balance (postclosing) to the one shown on the next page.

*****EDUCATIONAL VERSION ONLY*****

Mark Foltz Designer
General Ledger Trial Balance
As of Jan 31, 2013

Filter Criteria includes: Report order is by ID. Report is printed in Detail Format.

Account ID	Account Description	Debit Amt	Credit Amt
1010	Money Market Account	15,700.00	
1020	Checking Account	18,712.47	
1040	IRA Savings Account	27,730.35	
1045	WI State Retirement	35,612.00	
1300	Prepaid Insurance	1,575.00	
1450	Supplies	1,700.00	
1500	Computer Equipment	7,905.68	
1510	Furniture	5,000.00	
1520	Automobile	19,000.00	
1900	Accum. Depreciation - Co		575.47
1910	Accum. Depreciation - Fu		225.00
1920	Accum. Depreciation - Au		950.00
2400	Publisher Advances		7,500.00
3910	Retained Earnings		10,870.75
3920	Mark Foltz, Capital		112,814.28
	Total:	**132,935.50**	**132,935.50**

Observe that the postclosing trial balance is dated January 31, 2013. The balance in retained earnings (Account No. 3910) is Mr. Foltz's year-to-date net income minus the total of his drawing accounts (13,270.75 – 2,400 = 10,870.75). The Retained Earnings balance was also shown on page 391, Statement of Retained Earnings.

BACKING UP YEAR-END DATA

Follow these steps to back up Mark Foltz's year-end data:

1. If necessary close all windows and insert your USB flash drive. From the System Navigation Center, select ⬚ Back Up Now . (*Or,* from the menu bar, select File, then Back up.)

2. Uncheck the box next to Include company name in the backup file name. Click ⬚ Back Up .

3. In the Save in field, go to the location of your USB drive or back up to another location. Type **Chapter 11 EOY** in the File name field.

4. Click  .

5. When the window prompts that This company backup will require approximately 1 diskette, click **OK** . Click **OK** again when the window prompts Please insert the first disk. When the Back Up Company scale is 100% complete, you have successfully backed up to the current point in Chapter 11. (This step will differ slightly if you are backing up the default or other hard drive location.)

EXPORT POSTCLOSING TRIAL BALANCE TO EXCEL AND SAVE PDF FILE

Follow these steps to export the postclosing trial balance to Excel.

1. Display the General Ledger Trial Balance.

2. Export to Excel. Create a new Microsoft Excel workbook. Change General Ledger Trial Balance to Postclosing Trial Balance. Change the date to December 31, 2012.

3. Save. Use **Chapter 11_Postclosing Trial Balance.xlsx** as the file name. On the Excel file, change title to Postclosing Trial Balance and date to December 31, 2012.

4. Save the General Ledger Trial Balance (postclosing) as a PDF file. The suggested file name is **Chapter 11_Postclosing Trial Balance.pdf**.

5. Close all windows.

SUMMARY AND REVIEW

Complete the following end-of-chapter activities:

1. Going to the net, page 402.

2. True/make true questions, page 403.

3. Exercises 11-1 and 11-2, pages 403-409

4. Analysis questions, page 410.

5. Assessment rubric, page 410.

6. Chapter 11 index, page 411.

GOING TO THE NET

Access the asset depreciation schedule at http://office.microsoft.com/en-us/templates/asset-depreciation-schedule-TC001046099.aspx. (*Hint:* Excel 2000 or later is required.) Click [Download]. Save the asset depreciation schedule. (*Hint:* If using Excel 2007, accept the default extension, .xlsx. *Or,* save the file as an .xls extension.) An Asset Depreciation worksheet appears. (Going to the Net links are on the textbook website at www.mhhe.com/yacht2012, link to Student Edition, select Chapter 11.)

Complete the following fields. Press <Enter> to move between fields.

Date:	1/1/2006
Initial cost:	7000
Salvage value:	0
Useful life (years)	7

1. Click on Asset Depreciation. Type **Furniture** to replace it.

2. From Excel's menu bar, make the selections to Print.

3. Save. The suggested file name is **Asset depreciation.xlsx**. If a window appears that says one or more of the following features are not supported, click [OK]. (Hint: This file is an Excel 2003 file with an .xls extension.)

4. What depreciation methods are shown?

True/Make True: The Online Learning Center includes these questions and the analysis question at www.mhhe.com/yacht2012, select Student Edition, Chapter 11, QA Templates.

1. You can complete the activities in Chapter 11 without completing Chapters 9 and 10.

2. Step 4 of PCA's Computer Accounting Cycle is reconciling the bank statement.

3. To change an accounting period, use the Maintain menu.

4. Mark Foltz's transaction register and bank statement are used as source documents for recording journal entries.

5. The account reconciliation feature can reconcile the cash account only.

6. The accounting periods used in Chapter 11 are November 1 - 30 and December 1 - 31, 2012.

7. PCA includes an editing feature so that records can be corrected.

8. To close the fiscal year, use the System menu selection, Year-End Wizard.

9. When the fiscal year is closed, an adjusted trial balance is displayed or printed.

10. The statement of retained earnings and the postclosing trial balance show the same balance for retained earnings.

Exercise 11-1: Follow the instructions below to complete Exercise 11-1. You must complete Exercises 9-1, 9-2, 10-1, and 10-2 *before* you can do Exercise 11-1.

1. Start Peachtree. Open the company that you started in Exercise 9-1. The company name is Design by your first and last name. (*Hint:* From the menu bar, select File, Open Previous Company, Design by your first and last name. When the screen prompts Do you want to keep Mark Foltz [or your name] Designer open, click <No>.)

2. Restore your data from Exercise 10-2.[6] This back up was made on page 358. (Hint: To make sure you are starting in the right place, display the general ledger trial balance and compare it to the one printed for Exercise 10 -2, step 9, page 358. Compare the Midwest Bank account balance on the general ledger trial balance with the 10/31/12 balance on the transaction register below.)

3. Change accounting period to November 1 through November 30, 2012.

4. Use the transaction register below to record and post checks, ATMs, and deposits. (*Hint: Use Write Checks for checks and ATMs; use Receipts for deposits.*)

Transaction Register					
Check Number	**Date**	**Description of Transaction**	**Payment**	**Deposit**	**Balance**
	10/31/12	Bank Service Charge	12.00		16,820.30
	11/2/12	ATM	100.00		16,720.30
	11/3/12	Deposit (Design income)		2,200.00	18,920.30
1009	11/3/12	Vincent's Maintenance and Repairs	75.00		18,845.30
	11/8/12	Deposit (Teaching income)		2,105.00	20,950.30
1010	11/9/12	Utilities Co.	55.75		20,894.55
1011	11/10/12	Mullen Advertising, Inc.	175.00		20,719.55
1012	11/13/12	U.S. Post Office	44.00		20,675.55
1013	11/15/12	Horizon Telephone	41.97		20,633.58
1014	11/16/12	DSL Service	29.95		20,603.63
	11/20/12	ATM	100.00		20,503.63
1015	11/28/12	CTS Office Supplies[7]	47.80		20,455.83
	11/29/12	ATM	200.00		20,255.83

---

[6]You can restore from your back up file even if *no* Peachtree company exists. From Peachtree's start up window, select File; Restore. Select the location of your backup file. On the Restore Wizard's Select Company window, select A New Company. The *A New Company* selection allows you to restore your backup data, bypassing the process of new company set up. For more information, refer to Troubleshooting on pages 299-300.

[7]Debit Account No. 1450, Supplies.

5. Use the Bank Statement below to complete Account Reconciliation.
    (*Hint: Remember to record the bank service charge on the Account
    Reconciliation window.*)

Statement of Account Midwest Bank November 1 to November 30, 2012		Account No. 992834-20	Design by Your Name Your Address Your city, state, Zip	
REGULAR CHECKING				
Previous Balance	10/31/12	17,013.25		
2 Deposits(+)		4,305.00		
6 Checks (-)		542.70		
3 Other Deductions (-)		400.00		
Service Charges (-)	11/30/12	12.00		
Ending Balance	11/30/12	**20,363.55**		
DEPOSITS				
	11/6/12	2,200.00		
	11/8/12	2,105.00		
CHECKS (Asterisk * indicates break in check number sequence)				
	11/10/12	1006*	55.15	
	11/10/12	1008	137.80	
	11/24/12	1009	75.00	
	11/24/12	1010	55.75	
	11/27/12	1011	175.00	
	11/30/12	1012	44.00	
OTHER DEDUCTIONS (ATM's)				
	11/2/12	100.00		
	11/20/12	100.00		
	11/29/12	200.00		

6. Print an Account Reconciliation report.

7. Print the Account Register.

8. Print the General Journal.

9. Print the Cash Receipts Journal.

The McGraw-Hill Companies, Inc., *Computer Accounting with Peachtree by Sage Complete Accounting 2012, 16e*

10. Print the Cash Disbursements Journal.

11. Print the General Ledger Trial Balance.

12. Print a Balance Sheet and Income Statement.

13. Backup your data. The suggested file name is **Exercise 11-1.ptb**.

Exercise 11-2: Follow the instructions below to complete Exercise 11-2. Exercises 9-1, 9-2, 10-1, 10-2 and 11-1 *must* be completed before starting Exercise 11-2.

1. Start PCA. Open the company that you set up in Exercise 9-1 (Design by your first and last name).

2. If necessary, restore Exercise 11-1.[8] To make sure you are starting in the correct place, display the General Ledger Trial Balance (refer to step 11, above).

3. Change accounting periods to December 1 through December 31, 2012.

4. Use the transaction register on the next page to record and post checks, ATMs, and deposits. (*Hint:* On the Business Status Navigation Center, the balance, $20,243.83, should match Account No. 1020 for Midwest Bank. In the Account Balances area, the balance shows $20,243.83; the same balance as the Transaction Register on the next page. You may need to click [Refresh].)

---

[8]You can restore from your backup file even if *no* Peachtree company exists. From Peachtree's start up window, select File; Restore. Select the location of your backup file. On the Restore Wizard's Select Company window, select A New Company. The *A New Company* selection allows you to restore your backup data, bypassing the process of new company set up. For more information, refer to Troubleshooting on pages 299-300.

Transaction Register					
Check Number	**Date**	**Description of Transaction**	**Payment**	**Deposit**	**Balance**
	11/30/12	Bank Service Charge	12.00		20,243,83
	12/2/12	ATM	100.00		20,143.83
	12/3/12	Deposit (Design Income)		2,850.00	22,993.83
1016	12/3/12	Mullen Advertising, Inc.	100.00		22,893.83
	12/7/12	Deposit (Teaching income)		2,105.00	24,998.83
1017	12/8/12	Vincent's Maintenance and Repairs	75.00		24,923.83
1018	12/9/12	Utilities Co.	95.75		24,828.08
1019	12/13/12	U.S. Post Office	44.00		24,784.08
1020	12/15/12	Horizon Telephone	45.05		24,739.03
1021	12/16/12	DSL Service	29.95		24,709.08
	12/20/12	ATM	100.00		24,609.08
1022	12/28/12	CTS Office Supplies[9]	137.80		24,471.28
	12/30/12	ATM	200.00		24,271.28

5. Use the Bank Statement below and on the next page to complete Account Reconciliation. *Record the bank service charge on the Account Reconciliation window.*

Statement of Account Midwest Bank December 1 to December 31, 2012 Account No. 992834-20			Design by Your Name Your Address Your City, State, Zip	
REGULAR CHECKING				
Previous Balance	11/30/12	20,363.55		
2 Deposits(+)		4,955.00		
6 Checks (-)		390.47		
3 Other Deductions (-)		400.00		
Service Charges (-)	12/31/12	12.00		
Ending Balance	12/31/12	**24,516.08**		*continued*

[9]Debit Account No. 1450, Supplies.

DEPOSITS				
	12/6/12	2,850.00		
	12/8/12	2,105.00		
CHECKS (Asterisk * indicates break in check number sequence)				
	12/10/12	1013	41.97	
	12/10/12	1014	29.95	
	12/24/12	1015	47.80	
	12/24/12	1016	100.00	
	12/27/12	1017	75.00	
	12/30/12	1018	95.75	
OTHER DEDUCTIONS (ATM's)				
	12/2/12	100.00		
	12/20/12	100.00		
	12/310/12	200.00		

6. Print an Account Reconciliation report.

7. Print the Account Register.

8. Print the General Journal.

9. Print the Cash Receipts Journal.

10. Print the Cash Disbursements Journal.

11. Print the General Ledger Trial Balance (unadjusted).

12. Back up your data. The suggested file name is **Exercise 11-2 Unadjusted Trial Balance.ptb**.

13. Complete the following end-of-quarter adjusting entries.

     a. Supplies on hand: $850.00.
     b. Depreciation for Computer Equipment: $458.33.
     c. Depreciation for Furniture: $150.00.
     d. Depreciation for the Automobile: $950.00.
     e. Adjust three months prepaid rent: $700.00.
     f. Adjust three months prepaid insurance: $250.00.

14. Print the December 31, 2012 general journal.

15. Print the General Ledger Trial Balance (adjusted).

16. Print the financial statements: Balance Sheet, Income Statement, Statement of Cash Flow, and Statement of Retained Earnings.

    Check Your Figures:

    Account No. 1020, Midwest Bank, $24,259.28
    Account No. 3920, Student Name, Capital, $45,000.00

17. Back up your data. The suggested filename is **Exercise 11-2 Financial Statements.ptb**.

18. Export the General Ledger Trial Balance (Adjusted), Balance Sheet, Income Statement, Statement of Cash Flow, and Statement of Retained Earnings to Excel. Use **Exercise 11-2_Adjusted Trial Balance and Financial Statements.xlsx** as the file name.

19. Save the General Ledger Trial Balance (Adjusted), Balance Sheet, Income Statement, Statement of Cash Flow and Statement of Retained Earnings as PDF files. Use Exercise 11-2 and the reports' title for each file name.

20. Close the fiscal year.

21. Print the General Ledger Trial Balance (Postclosing).

22. Back up your data. The suggested filename is **Exercise 11-2 End of Year.ptb**.

23. Export the Posting Closing Trial Balance to Excel. Create a new Microsoft Excel workbook. Change General Ledger Trial Balance to Postclosing Trial Balance. Change the date to December 31, 2012

24. Save. Use **Exercise 11-2_Postclosing Trial Balance.xlsx** as the file name. On the Excel file, change title and date (refer to step 23).

25. Save the Postclosing Trial Balance as a PDF file. Use **Exercise 11-2_Postclosing Trial Balance.pdf** as the file name.

26. Exit Peachtree.

ANALYSIS QUESTIONS

1. When using Peachtree why is it important to change accounting periods? (*Hint:* Do a search on Peachtree's Help window for Change Accounting Period.)

2. Does the balance in retained earnings differ on the adjusted trial balance and the postclosing trial balance?

3. How does the postclosing trial balance differ from the adjusted trial balance?

ASSESSMENT RUBRIC

Complete the Assessment Rubric online at www.mhhe.com/yacht2012; Student Edition, select Chapter 11 Assessment Rubric link. To review Peachtree's navigation centers, menu selections, and windows, complete the blank fields online.

Task	Date	Navigation Center	Task Window	Ending GL Balance
December bank reconciliation Mark Foltz Designer				

CHAPTER 11 INDEX

Project

1

Susan Babbage, Accounting

In Project 1, you complete the computer accounting cycle for Susan Babbage, Accounting. Ms. Babbage started her accounting practice on December 1, 2012 in Mesa, Arizona. Ms. Babbage employs two accounting technicians and one administrative assistant. Ms. Babbage's employees are independent contractors. Further study of payroll accounting will be done in Chapter 15.

In this project, you complete the accounting cycle for the month of December 2012. Susan Babbage's balance sheet, transaction register, and bank statement are provided as source documents.

At the end of Project 1, a checklist is shown listing the printed reports you should have. The step-by-step instructions remind you to print reports at certain intervals. Your instructor may require these printouts for grading purposes. Remember to make backups at periodic intervals.

Follow these steps to complete Project 1:

Step 1: Start Peachtree. If a company opens, select File; New Company. One company should be opened. The Create a New Company – Introduction window appears. Click **Next >**.

Step 2: Type the following company information:

Company Name:	**Susan Babbage, Accounting** (substitute your first and last name for Susan Babbage)
Address Line 1:	**1341 Saguaro Street**
City, State, Zip	**Mesa, AZ 85210**
Country:	**USA**
Telephone:	**480-555-4722**
Fax:	**480-555-4724**
Business Type:	Select Sole Proprietorship

Leave the Tax ID Numbers fields blank.

Web Site:	www.susanbabbage.com
E-mail:	info@susanbabbage.com

Step   3:   Accept the default to Use a sample business type that closely matches your company.

Step   4:   Select Service Company. (*Hint:* Simplified types.)

Step   5:   Accept the default for Accrual accounting.

Step   6:   Accept the default for Real Time posting.

Step   7:   Accept the default for Choose an accounting period structure, 12 monthly accounting periods per year.

Step   8:   The Choose the first period of your fiscal year window appears. Select January 2012.

Step   9:   At the You are ready to create your company window, click [Finish]. If the screen prompts You can use this company in the student version of Peachtree for the next 14 months and then it will expire, click [OK]. At the Peachtree Setup Guide window, click on the box next to Don't show this screen at startup. Click [Close].

Step 10:   Change the accounting period to Period 12 – 12/01/12 - 12/31/12. (*Hint:* On the toolbar, click [Period]; select 12 – Dec 01, 2012 to Dec 31, 2012. If a window appears suggesting that you select the Internal Accounting Review, click [No].

Step 11:   Make the following changes to the Chart of Accounts:

Delete these accounts:

1010	Cash on Hand
1150	Allowance for Doubtful Account
2310	Sales Tax Payable
2320	Deductions Payable
2330	Federal Payroll Taxes Payable

2340	FUTA Payable
2350	State Payroll Taxes Payable
2360	SUTA Payable
2370	Local Taxes Payable
2400	Customer Deposits
2700	Long-Term Debt–Noncurrent
4300	Other Income
5900	Inventory Adjustments
6250	Other Taxes Expense
6650	Commissions and Fees Expense
7100	Gain/Loss – Sale of Assets Exp

Change these accounts:[1]

1020	Checking Account	**Mesa Bank**
1400	Prepaid Expenses	**Prepaid Rent**
1500	Property and Equipment	**Computer Equipment**
1900	Accum. Depreciation-Prop&Eqt	**Accum. Depreciation-Comp Eqt**
2500	Current Portion Long-Term Debt	**Notes Payable**
3920	Owner's Contribution	**Susan Babbage, Capital** (Use your name; *Account Type: Equity-doesn't close*)
3930	Owner's Draw	**Susan Babbage, Draw** (Use your name)
4000	Professional Fees	**Accounting Fees**
6000	Wages Expense	**Wages Expense – Adm Asst**
6050	Employee Benefit Programs Exp.	**Wages Expense - Acctg Tech**
6150	Bad Debt Expense	**Subscriptions Expense**
6450	Office Supplies Expense	**Supplies Expense**
6550	Other Office Expense	**Internet Service**
7050	Depreciation Expense	**Deprec Exp – Comp Eqt**

---

[1]New account names are shown in boldface. Click between accounts.

Add these accounts:

1450	**Supplies**	Other Current Assets
1510	**Furniture and Fixtures**	Fixed Assets
1520	**Automobile**	Fixed Assets
1910	**Accum. Depreciation – Furn&Fix**	Accum. Depreciation
1920	**Accum. Depreciation – Automobi**	Accum. Depreciation
7060	**Deprec Exp - Furn&Fix**	Expenses
7070	**Deprec Exp - Automobile**	Expenses
7400	**Postage Expense**	Expenses

Step 12: Print the Chart of Accounts.

Step 13: Back up the chart of accounts. The suggested file name is **Susan Babbage Chart of Accounts.ptb**.

Step 14: Use Susan Babbage's Balance Sheet to enter the beginning balances. **Important:** When selecting the beginning balance period, use 11/1/12 through 11/30/12—Beginning Balances as of November 30, 2012.

Susan Babbage, Accounting Balance Sheet December 1, 2012		
ASSETS		
Current Assets		
Mesa Bank	$31,500.00	
Accounts Receivable	17,400.00	
Prepaid Rent	4,000.00	
Supplies	3,300.00	
Total Current Assets		$56,200.00
Property and Equipment		
Computer Equipment	12,600.00	
Furniture and Fixtures	15,000.00	
Automobile	21,500.00	
Total Property and Equipment		49,100.00
Total Assets		$105,300.00
Continued		

LIABILITIES AND CAPITAL		
Current Liabilities		
Accounts Payable	$11,200.00	
Notes Payable	8,400.00	
Total Current Liabilities		19,600.00
Capital		
Susan Babbage, Capital		85,700.00
Total Liabilities and Capital		$ 105,300.00

Step 15: Back up Ms. Babbage's beginning data. The suggested file name is **Susan Babbage Beginning Balances.ptb**.

Step 16: The transaction register below and on the next page provides the information necessary for December's journal entries. Remember to post (save) between each transaction.

		Transaction Register **Susan Babbage, Accounting**			
Ck. No.	**Date**	**Description of Transaction**	**Payment**	**Deposit**	**Balance**
	11/30				31,500.00
	12/1	Deposit (accounting fees)		3,500.00	35,000.00
9001	12/1	Mesa Bank (Notes Payable)	2,700.00		32,300.00
9002	12/1	Spencer's Office Equipment - laser printer (computer equipment)	625.87		31,674.13
9003	12/7	Administrative Asst.	1,250.00		30,424.13
9004	12/7	Acctg. Technician	690.00		29,734.13
9005	12/12	Grand Avenue Office Supplies (letterhead - supplies)	105.65		29,628.48
9006	12/14	Administrative Asst.	1,250.00		28,378.48
9007	12/14	Acctg. Technician	690.00		27,688.48
	12/16	Deposit (accounting fees)		3,500.00	31,188.48
9008	12/17	Western Telephone (telephone bill)	70.47		31,118.01
9009	12/17	U.S. Post Office	44.00		31,074.01
9010	12/17	Journal of Accounting (subscription)	545.00		30,529.01
Continued					

9011	12/21	Administrative Asst.	1,250.00		29,279.01
9012	12/21	Acctg. Technician	620.00		28,659.01
	12/23	Deposit (accounting fees)		4,000.00	32,659.01
9013	12/24	RSP Electric (utilities bill)	105.20		32,553.81
	12/24	Deposit (accounting fees)		4,000.00	36,553.81
9014	12/28	Administrative Asst.	1,250.00		35,303.81
9015	12/28	Acctg. Technician	750.00		34,553.81
	12/28	Deposit (payment received from client on account)		1,500.00	36,053.81
9016	12/28	Internet Service	29.99		36,023.82

Step 17: Susan Babbage's bank statement is shown below. (*Hint: Remember to record the bank service charge.*)

Statement of Account Mesa Bank December 1 to December 31, 2012		Account No. 4425-623301	Susan Babbage, Accounting 1341 Saguaro Street Mesa, AZ 85210		
		REGULAR CHECKING			
Previous Balance	11/30/12		31,500.00		
4 Deposits(+)			15,000.00		
12 Checks (-)			10,607.19		
Service Charges (-)	12/31/12		25.00		
Ending Balance	12/31/12		**35,867.81**		
		DEPOSITS			
	12/3/12		3,500.00	12/28/12	4,000.00
	12/17/12		3,500.00	12/30/12	4,000.00
	CHECKS (Asterisk * indicates break in check number sequence)				
	12/10/12	9001	2,700.00		
	12/11/12	9002	625.87		
	12/14/12	9003	1,250.00		
	12/14/12	9004	690.00		
	12/17/12	9005	105.65		
	12/17/12	9006	1,250.00		
	12/17/12	9007	690.00		
	12/24/12	9008	70.47		
	12/24/12	9011*	1,250.00		
Continued					

	12/24/12	9012	620.00	
	12/28/12	9013	105.20	
	12/31/12	9014	1,250.00	

Step 18: Print an Account Reconciliation report.

Step 19: Print the Account Register.

Step 20: Print a General Ledger Trial Balance (unadjusted).

Step 21: Back up the unadjusted trial balance. The suggested file name
is **Susan Babbage UTB.ptb**. (UTB is an abbreviation for
unadjusted trial balance.)

Step 22: Complete these adjusting entries:

a. Supplies on hand: $3,250.00.
b. Depreciation for Computer Equipment: $353.50.
c. Depreciation for Furniture and Fixtures: $166.67.
d. Depreciation for the Automobile: $358.33.
e. Rent was paid for two months on November 30, 2012.
Adjust one month's rent.[2]

Step 23: Print the General Journal (December 31, 2012), Cash Receipts
Journal, and Cash Disbursements Journal.

Step 24: Print the General Ledger Trial Balance (adjusted).

Step 25: Print the General Ledger. (*Hint: Select Reports & Forms;
General Ledger, highlight General Ledger, make the selections
to print.*)

Step 26: Print the financial statements: balance sheet, income
statement, statement of retained earnings, and statement of
cash flow.

---

[2]Refer to the December 1, 2012, Balance Sheet for the account balance in the
Prepaid Rent account.

Step 27: Back up December data. The suggested file name is **Susan Babbage December.ptb**.

Note: For grading purposes, your instructor may require that you turn in reports. Ask your instructor what type of files they prefer: Adobe (.pdf), Excel (.xlsx), or Peachtree backup (.ptb).

Step 28: Export the adjusted trial balance, balance sheet, income statement, statement of cash flow, and statement of retained earnings to Excel. Use **Susan Babbage_Adjusted Trial Balance and Statements.xlsx** as the file name. (Change the name of the General Ledger Trial Balance to Adjusted Trial Balance.)

Step 29: Save the financial statements as PDF files. Use Project 1, then the financial statement's title for the file name; for example, **Project 1_Balance Sheet.pdf**.

Step 30: Close the fiscal year. (If a window appears saying that The current Peachtree system date falls within the first of two open fiscal years. Do you still want to open the Year-End Wizard? Click [Yes]. Continue closing the fiscal year.)

Step 31: Print the Postclosing Trial Balance.

Step 32: Back up year-end data. The suggested file name is **Susan Babbage EOY.ptb**.

Step 33: Export the postclosing trial balance to Excel. Use **Susan Babbage_Postclosing Trial Balance.xlsx** as the file name; December 31, 2012 as the data. Change the name of the trial balance.

Step 34: Save the postclosing trial balance as a PDF file. **Use Project 1_Postclosing Trial Balance.pdf** as the file name.

Your instructor may want to collect this project. A Checklist of Printouts is shown below.

Checklist of Printouts, Project 1: Susan Babbage, Accounting
Chart of Accounts
Account Reconciliation
Account Register
General Ledger Trial Balance (unadjusted)
December 31, 2012 General Journal
Cash Receipts Journal
Cash Disbursements Journal
General Ledger Trial Balance (adjusted)
General Ledger
Balance Sheet
Income Statement
Statement of Retained Earnings
Statement of Cash Flow
Postclosing Trial Balance

Student Name_____ **Date**_____

CHECK YOUR PROGRESS: PROJECT 1, Susan Babbage, Accounting

1. What are the total debit and credit balances on your unadjusted trial balance? _____

2. What are the total debit and credit balances on your adjusted trial balance? _____

3. According to your account reconciliation report, what is the Ending GL Balance? _____

4. What is the depreciation expense for furniture and fixtures on December 31? _____

5. What is the depreciation expense for computer equipment on December 31? _____

6. What is the amount of total revenues as of December 31? _____

7. How much net income <or net loss> is reported on December 31? _____

8. What is the account balance in the Supplies account on December 31? _____

9. What is the account balance in the Accounts Payable account on December 31? _____

10. What is the total capital balance on December 31? _____

11. Is there an Increase or Decrease in cash for the the month of December? _____

12. Were any Accounts Payable incurred during the month of December? (Circle your answer). YES NO

Project 1A Student-Designed Service Business

In Chapters 9, 10, 11, and Project 1, you learned how to complete the Computer Accounting Cycle for a service business. Project 1A gives you a chance to design a service business of your own.

You create a service business, edit your business's Chart of Accounts, create source documents, and complete PCA's Computer Accounting Cycle. Project 1A also gives you an opportunity to review the software features learned so far.

You should think about the kind of business to create. Since you have been working on sole proprietorship service businesses in Part 2, you might want to design a business similar to these. Service businesses include: accountants, beauty salons, architects, hotels, airlines, cleaning stores, doctors, artists, etc. If you have a checking account and receive a monthly bank statement, you could use your own records for this project.

Before you begin you should design your business. You will need the following:

1. Company information that includes business name, address, and telephone number. (*Hint: Set your company up for Period 12, December 1 - 31, so that you can close the fiscal year.*)

2. One of PCA's sample companies.

3. A Chart of Accounts: 25 accounts minimum; 30 maximum.

4. One month's transactions for your business. You will need a Balance Sheet, check register, and bank statement. Your check register should include a minimum of 15 transactions and a maximum of 25. You should have at least four adjusting entries.

If you don't want to use a check register and bank statement, you could write 15 to 25 narrative transactions.

After you have designed your business, you should follow the steps of PCA's Computer Accounting Cycle to complete Project 1A.

For grading purposes, Project 1A should include the following printouts:

Checklist of Printouts **Project 1A** **Student-Designed Project**	
	Chart of Accounts
	Account Reconciliation
	Account Register
	General Ledger Trial Balance (unadjusted)
	Cash Receipts Journal
	Cash Disbursements Journal
	December 31, 20XX General Journal
	General Ledger Trial Balance (adjusted)
	General Ledger
	Balance Sheet
	Income Statement
	Statement of Retained Earnings
	Statement of Cash Flow
	Postclosing Trial Balance

Part 3 — Peachtree Complete Accounting 2012 for Merchandising Businesses

In Part 3 of *Computer Accounting with Peachtree by Sage Complete Accounting 2012*, 16th Edition, your accounting business is hired to do the monthly record keeping for three merchandising businesses: Cynthia's Service Merchandise, the end-of-chapter exercise, Your Name Sales and Service, and Sports Emporium.

Part 3 includes four chapters and two projects.

Chapter 12: Vendors & Purchases

Chapter 13: Customers & Sales

Chapter 14: Inventory & Services

Chapter 15: Employees, Payroll and Account Reconciliation

Project 2: Sports Emporium

Project 2A: Student-Designed Merchandising Business

Merchandising businesses purchase products ready-made from a vendor and then resell these products to their customers. (Merchandising businesses are also called retail businesses.) Items purchased by a retail business for resale are referred to as merchandise. A merchandising business earns revenue from buying and selling goods. Items purchased for use by the business are *not* merchandise; for example, supplies or computer equipment are *not* sold to customers.

In Part 1 you were shown how the sample company, Bellwether Garden Supply, used Peachtree's customer, vendor, payroll, and inventory features. The chapters that follow illustrate these features in detail.

Chapters 12 through 15 are cumulative. This means that the businesses you set up in Chapter 12, Cynthia's Service Merchandise; and Exercise 12-1, Student Name Sales and Service, are continued in Chapters 13, 14, and 15.

The McGraw-Hill Companies, Inc., *Computer Accounting with Peachtree by Sage Complete Accounting 2012, 16e*

At the end of Part 3, you complete Project 2, Sports Emporium, which reviews PCA's merchandising business features. At the end of Project 2, there is a Check Your Progress assessment that your instructor may want you to turn in. Project 2A, Student-Designed Merchandising Business, gives you an opportunity to create a merchandising business from scratch.

The chart below shows the size of the backups, Excel files, and Adobe PDF files in Part 3–Chapters 12, 13, 14, 15, and Project 2. The textbook shows how to back up to a USB drive. Backups can be made to the desktop, hard drive location, network location, or external media.

Chapter	Backup (.ptb extension) Excel (.xlsx)	Kilobytes	Page Nos.
12	Chapter 12 Starting Balance Sheet.ptb	971 KB	442-443
	Chapter 12 Begin.ptb	981 KB	456
	Chapter 12.ptb	1,017 KB	481-482
	Chapter 12_CofA_PJ_CDJ_ VL_GLTB.xlsx	29 KB	482-484
	Exercise 12-1_Starting Balance Sheet.ptb	914 KB	488
	Exercise 12-1.ptb	939 KB	491
	Exercise 12-2.ptb	953 KB	493
	Exercise 12-2_ CofA_PJ_CDJ_ VL_GLTB. xlsx	28 KB	493
	Exercise 12-2_Chart of Accounts.pdf	60 KB	493
	Exercise 12-2_Purchase Journal.pdf	50 KB	493
	Exercise 12-2_Cash Disbursements Journal.pdf	51 KB	493
	Exercise 12-2_Vendor Ledgers.pdf	50 KB	493
	Exercise 12-2_General Ledger Trial Balance.pdf	51 KB	493
13	Chapter 13 Begin.ptb	1,052 KB	510
	Chapter 13.ptb	1,082 KB	538
	Chapter 13_SJ_CRJ_CL_GLTB.xlsx	24 KB	539
	Exercise 13-1.ptb	967 KB	544
	Exercise 13-2.ptb	984 KB	546
	Exercise 13-2_SJ_CRJ_CL_GLTB.xlsx	23 KB	546
	Exercise 13-2_Sales Journal.pdf	6 KB	546
Continued			

Chapter	Backup (.ptb extension) Excel (.xlsx) and Adobe (.pdf)	Kilobytes	Page Nos.
13	Exercise 13-2_Cash Receipts Journal.pdf	6 KB	546
	Exercise 13-2_Customer Ledgers.pdf	6 KB	546
	Exercise 13-2_General Ledger Trial Balance.pdf	6 KB	546
14	Chapter 14 Begin.ptb	1,091 KB	559
	Chapter 14.ptb	1,119 KB	572
	Chapter 14_ CL_ VL_CGSJ_IAJ_IPR_GLTB.xlsx	32 KB	572-573
	Exercise 14-1.ptb	993 KB	575
	Exercise 14-2_ CRJ_PJ_CGSJ_IAJ_IPR_GLTB.xlsx	30 KB	576
	Exercise 14-2_Cash Receipts Journal.pdf	7 KB	576
	Exercise 14-2_Purchase Journal.pdf	6 KB	576
	Exercise 14-2_Cost of Goods Sold Journal.pdf	6 KB	576
	Exercise 14-2_Inventory Adjustment Journal.pdf	5 KB	576
	Exercise 14-2_Inventory Profitability Report.pdf	6 KB	576
	Exercise 14-2_General Ledger Trial Balance.pdf	6 KB	576
15	Chapter 15 Begin.ptb	1,128 KB	598-599
	Chapter 15.ptb	1,169 KB	621
	Chapter 15_PayJ_GLTB_BS_IS_SCF.xlsx	33 KB	621
	Exercise 15-1.ptb	1,011 KB	628
	Exercise 15-2.ptb	1,039 KB	631
	Exercise 15-2_EL_CL_VL_IVR_ PayJ_ GLTB_ BS_IS_SCF.xlsx	47 KB	631
	Exercise 15-1_Employee List.pdf	54 KB	631
	Exercise 15-2_Vendor Ledgers.pdf	6 KB	631
	Exercise 15-2_Customer Ledgers.pdf	6 KB	631
	Exercise 15-2_Inventory Valuation Report.pdf	6 KB	631
	Exercise 15-2_Payroll Journal.pdf	61 KB	631
	Exercise 15-2_General Ledger Trial Balance.pdf	7 KB	631
	Exercise 15-2_Balance Sheet.pdf	6 KB	631
	Exercise 15-2_Income Statement.pdf	5 KB	631
	Exercise 15-2_Statement of Cash Flow.pdf	5 KB	631

Chapter	Backup (.ptb extension) Excel (.xlsx) and Adobe (.pdf)	Kilobytes	Page Nos.
Project 2	Sports Emporium Chart of Accounts.ptb	934 KB	638
	Sports Emporium Starting Balance Sheet.ptb	936 KB	638
	Sports Emporium Begin.ptb	972 KB	646
	Sports Emporium January.ptb	1,037 KB	650
	Sports Emporium_CofA_CL_VL_ GLTB_AcctRec_ BS_ IS_ SCF.xlsx	43 KB	650
	Project 2_Chart of Accounts.pdf	119 KB	650
	Project 2_Customer Ledgers.pdf	6 KB	650
	Project 2_Vendor Ledgers.pdf	6 KB	650
	Project 2_General Ledger Trial Balance.pdf	7 KB	650
	Project 2_Account Reconcilation.pdf	88 KB	650
	Project 2_Balance Sheet.pdf	5 KB	650
	Project 2_Income Statement.pdf	5 KB	650
	Project 2_Statement of Cash Flow.pdf	6 KB	650

The size of your files may differ from those shown.

The extension for Excel 2007 and 2010 files is .xlsx. If you are using Excel 2003, the extension is .xls.

Chapter 12 | Vendors & Purchases

LEARNING OBJECTIVES

1. Set up company information for Cynthia's Service Merchandise, a merchandising business.
2. Enter the following general ledger information: chart of accounts and beginning balances.
3. Enter the following accounts payable information: vendor defaults and vendor records.
4. Enter the following inventory information: inventory defaults, inventory items, and inventory beginning balances.
5. Record and post Vendors & Purchases transactions.
6. Make six backups, save two Excel files, and save five PDF files.[1]

Chapter 12 begins Part 3 of the book: Peachtree Complete Accounting 2012 for Merchandising Businesses. Merchandising businesses are retail stores that resell goods and services. In this chapter, you set up a merchandising business called Cynthia's Service Merchandise. Cynthia's Service Merchandise is a partnership owned by Eric Lerette and Cynthia Barber. Mr. Lerette and Ms. Barber divide their income equally.

Merchandising businesses purchase the merchandise they sell from suppliers known as **vendors**. Vendors are the businesses that offer Cynthia's Service Merchandise credit to buy merchandise and/or assets, or credit for expenses incurred. When Cynthia's Service Merchandise makes purchases on account from vendors, the transactions are known as **accounts payable transactions**.

PCA organizes and monitors Cynthia's Service Merchandise's **accounts payable**. Accounts Payable is the amount of money the business owes to suppliers or vendors.

When entering a purchase, you enter a vendor code first. The vendor's name and address information, the standard payment terms, and the

---

[1]Refer to the chart on page 426 for the size of files backed up and saved.

general ledger purchase account are automatically entered in the appropriate places. This information can be edited if any changes are needed. This works similarly for accounts receivable.

Once you have entered purchase information, printing a check to pay for a purchase is simple. When you enter the vendor's code, a list of purchases displays. You simply select the ones you want to pay and click on the Pay box. You can print the check or wait to print a batch of checks later. You can also pay a whole batch of vendors at one time, using the Select for Payment option. The diagram below illustrates how vendors are paid.

In Chapter 12, the merchandising businesses that you set up are continued in Chapters 13, 14, and 15.

GETTING STARTED

Cynthia's Service Merchandise started operations on January 1, 2012. It is a partnership owned by Eric Lerette and Cynthia Barber and is located in Tempe, AZ. Follow these steps to set up the company.

1. Start Peachtree. If a company opens, select File; New Company, click 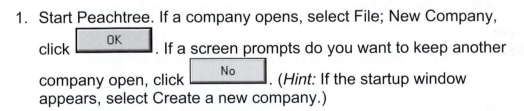. If a screen prompts do you want to keep another company open, click [No]. (*Hint:* If the startup window appears, select Create a new company.)

2. The Create a New Company – Introduction window appears. Click

   [Next >]

3. The Enter your company information window appears. (Observe that
   a red asterisk (*) indicates a required field.) Complete the following
   fields. Press the **<Tab>** key between each field.

Company Information

Company Name:	**Cynthia's Service Merchandise** *(use your first name then Service Merchandise)*
Address Line 1:	**2117 Oak Street**
City, State, Zip:	**Tempe, AZ 85281**
Country:	**USA**
Telephone:	**480-555-9900**
Fax:	**480-555-9902**
Business Type:	Select Partnership

Tax ID Information

Federal Employer ID:	**53-4433889**
State Employer ID:	**23-8991243**
State Unemployment ID:	**2334119-2**
Web Site:	**www.cynthiaservmdse.biz**
E-mail:	**info@cynthiaservmdse.biz**

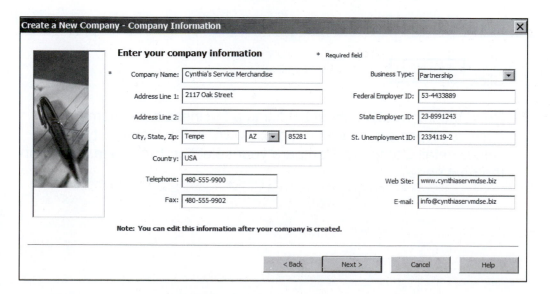

> **Comment**
>
> If you use your name in the Company Name field, the name of your company will appear on all printouts.

4. Check the information you just typed, then click [Next >]. The Select a method to create your Company window appears.

   Accept the default for Use a sample business type that closely matches your company.

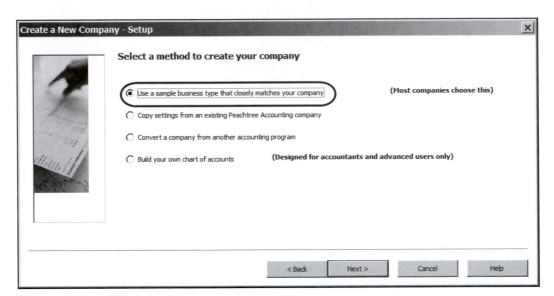

5. Click [Next >].

6. Read the information about selecting a business type. Numerous business types are available. Scroll down. In the Detailed types list, select Retail Company. Compare your selection to the one shown on the next page.

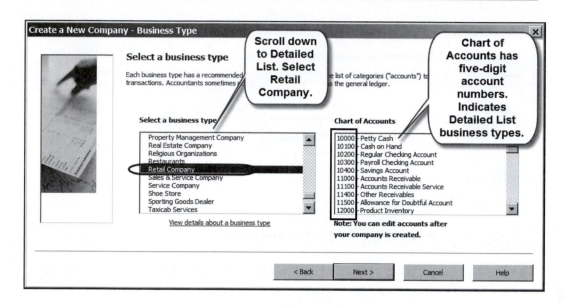

IMPORTANT: Make sure that Retail Company is selected from the **Detailed types list** <u>not</u> the Simplified types list. Check the Chart of Accounts on the right pane. The Detailed types list has a more extensive chart of accounts than the Simplified types list. Observe that the chart of accounts has account numbers with five digits; for example, 10000 – Petty Cash. (The Simplified types list has four-digit account numbers.)

7. Make sure that Retail Company is selected from the Detailed types list. Click [Next >] .

8. Read the information about the Accounting Method. Accept the default for Accrual by clicking [Next >] .

9. Read the information about Posting Method. Peachtree Software recommends real-time posting for networked computers. Accept the default for real-time posting by clicking [Next >] .

10. At the Choose an accounting period structure window, accept the default for 12 monthly accounting periods per year by clicking [Next >] .

11. The Choose the first period of your fiscal year window appears. Select **2012** as the year.

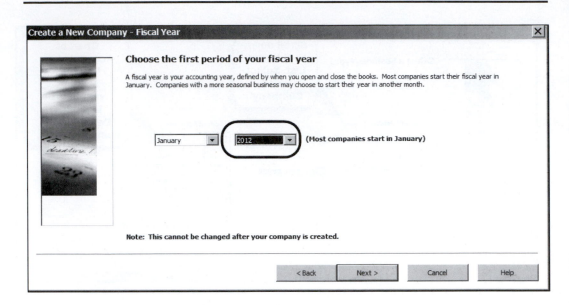

Check this window carefully. You cannot change it later.

12.   Click Next > .

13.   The You are ready to create your company window appears. Click
   Finish . If the screen prompts You can use this company in the
   student version of Peachtree for the next 14 months and then it will
   expire, click OK .

14.   The Peachtree Setup Guide window appears. Click on the box next
   to Don't show this screen at startup to place a checkmark in it--
   ☑ Don't show this screen at startup. . Click Close . Cynthia's (your
   name) Service Merchandise - Peachtree Accounting appears on the
   title bar (above the menu bar).

15.   The Period shown on the toolbar defaults to the current period
   (month). If necessary, change the accounting period to 01 – Jan
   01,2012 to Jan 31,2012; Period 1 - 01/01/12-01/31/12 . (*Hint:* Click on
   the Period shown on the toolbar to change accounting periods.)

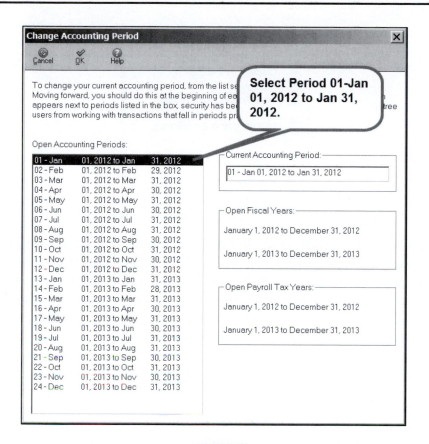

16. After selecting Period 1, click [OK].

17. Click [Business Status]. The Business Status Navigation
    Center shows the following sections:

    - Account Balances
    - Customers Who Owe Money
    - Aged Receivables
    - Find a Report
    - Revenue: Year to Date
    - Vendors to Pay
    - Aged Payables

In Chapters 12 through 15, you use links from the Business Status
Navigation Center and the Navigation Bar to record transactions.
Observe that the Navigation Bar's selections include:

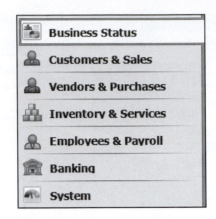

These selections provide ways to navigate the software for Cynthia's Service Merchandise, a retail business. The Navigation Bar's selections also indicate Peachtree's modules: Business Status represents an overview of the company; Customers & Sales is the accounts receivable system; Vendors & Purchases is the accounts payable system, etc. A Navigation Bar is used with other Windows software, for example, Microsoft Outlook and Microsoft Dynamics GP use a Navigation Bar. QuickBooks has a Home page that includes Vendors, Customers, Company and Banking modules. Similar to Peachtree's Business Status center, Account Balance are includes on QuickBooks' home page.

To make the Business Status Navigation Center the default, on the toolbar, click **Make this the default page**. This icon changes to This is the default page **This is the default page**.

GENERAL LEDGER

Peachtree's general ledger system includes the collection of accounts of a company (chart of accounts), then summarizes the transactions associated with these accounts and their related account balances for a specified period of time. After setting up a new company, the next step is editing the chart of accounts, and then entering the beginning balances. Peachtree's general ledger system is used for that purpose. Think of the general ledger as the core of an accounting system.

Observe how the general ledger system is organized within Peachtree's user interface; for example, the Navigation Bar's Banking selection shows general ledger system choices such as the chart of accounts general journal entries, and banking reports. Also, the Reports & Forms menu shows the general ledger system's contents.

Most accounting software organizes the user interface into system modules: Accounts Payable (Vendors & Purchases); Accounts Receivable (Customers & Sales), Banking, etc. For this reason, Peachtree, QuickBooks, and Microsoft Dynamics GP work similarly.

The major differences between accounting software applications include the depth of processing, enhanced features and functions, and the size of the **database** (an organized body of related information). As the database gets larger, the depth of processing increases and more features and functions are available. As companies grow in size, their accounting software needs change.

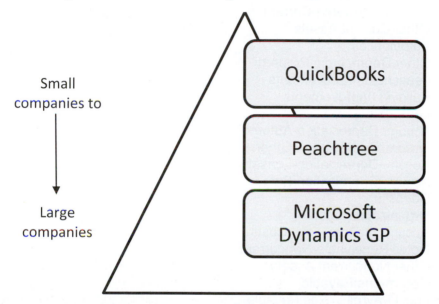

Peachtree and QuickBooks are used by small companies. As the company grows to mid-size, Peachtree and Microsoft Dynamics GP can be used. Large companies use Microsoft Dynamics GP.

Company size	No. of Employees
Small business	1-20 employees
Medium-sized business	20-500 employees
Large business	500+ employees

Chart of Accounts

From the Navigation Bar, click 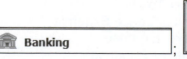; , View and Edit Accounts.

1. Delete the following accounts.

> **Comment**
>
> Double-click on the account you want to delete. Then, click ⊠ Delete . From the Maintain Chart of Accounts window, you can also type the account number into the Account ID field, then delete.

    10000 Petty Cash
    10100 Cash on Hand
    11400 Other Receivables
    14100 Employee Advances
    14200 Notes Receivable-Current
    14700 Other Current Assets
    15200 Automobiles
    15300 Other Depreciable Property
    15400 Leasehold Improvements
    15600 Building Improvements
    16900 Land
    17200 Accum. Depreciation-Automobi
    17300 Accum. Depreciation-Other
    17400 Accum. Depreciation-Leasehol
    17600 Accum. Depreciation-Bldg Imp
    19000 Deposits
    19100 Organization Costs
    19150 Accum. Amortiz -Org. Costs
    19200 Notes Receivable-Noncurrent
    19900 Other Noncurrent Assets
    23300 Deductions Payable
    23800 Local Payroll Taxes Payable
    24800 Other Current Liabilities
    24900 Suspense-Clearing Account
    58000 Cost of Sales-Other
    60500 Amortization Expense
    61000 Auto Expenses
    62500 Cash Over and Short
    63000 Charitable Contributions Exp
    63500 Commissions and Fees Exp
    65000 Employee Benefit Programs Exp
    68000 Laundry and Cleaning Exp
    73000 Other Taxes
    74000 Rent or Lease Expense
    76500 Travel Expense
    77000 Salaries Expense

2. Change the following accounts.

10200	Regular Checking Account	**Southwest Bank**
10400	Savings Account	**Arizona Savings & Loan**
12000	Product Inventory	**Merchandise Inventory**
14000	Prepaid Expenses	**Prepaid Insurance**
15100	Equipment	**Computers & Equipment**
17000	Accum. Depreciation-Furniture	**Accum. Depreciation - Furn&Fix**
17100	Accum. Depreciation-Equipment	**Accum. Depreciation - Comp&Eqt**
24000	Other Taxes Payable	**FICA Employee Taxes Payable**
24100	Employee Benefits Payable	**FICA Employer Taxes Payable**
24200	Current Portion Long-Term Debt	**Medicare Employee Taxes Payabl**
24400	Customer Deposits	**Medicare Employer Taxes Payabl**
27000	Notes Payable-Noncurrent	**Long-Term Notes Payable**
27400	Other Long Term-Liabilities	**Mortgage Payable**
39006	Partner's Contribution	**Eric Lerette, Capital** *(Note: Account Type, Equity-doesn't close)*
39007	Partner's Draw	**Eric Lerette, Drawing**
40000	Sales-Merchandise	**Sales-Hardware**
40200	Sales-Services	**Sales-Wall**
40400	Sales-Clearance	**Sales-Floor**
40600	Interest Income	**Service Fees**
50000	Cost of Goods Sold	**Cost of Sales-Hardware**
50500	Cost of Sales-Service	**Cost of Sales-Wall**
57000	Cost of Sales-Salaries and Wag	**Cost of Sales-Floor**
64000	Depreciation Expense	**Deprec Exp-Furn & Fixtures**
64500	Dues and Subscription Exp	**Deprec Exp-Computers & Equip**

3. Add the following accounts.

Account Type:

13000	**Supplies**	Other Current Assets
39008	**Cynthia Barber, Capital**	Equity-doesn't close
39009	**Cynthia Barber, Drawing**	Equity- gets closed
64600	**Deprec Exp-Building**	Expenses
72510	**FICA Expense**	Expenses
72520	**Medicare Expense**	Expenses

72530	FUTA Expense	Expenses
72540	SUTA Expense	Expenses
77600	Overtime Expense	Expenses

Beginning Balances

1. From the Maintain Chart of Accounts window, click
   [Account Beginning Balances].

2. The Select Period window appears. Highlight From 12/1/11 through 12/31/11. Beginning balances *must* be set for the previous month. The starting balance sheet on pages 441-442 is dated January 1, 2012. This means that the period for entering beginning balances must be from December 1 through December 31, 2011 the month *before* the starting balances.

Comment

Select December 1 - 31, 2011 as your Chart of Accounts Beginning Balance period so that your journals will start on January 1, 2012. Your reports will be dated January 31, 2012. Remember, Peachtree posts on the last day of the month. The December 31, 2011 balances are the January 1, 2012 starting balances.

---

3. Compare your Select Period window to the one shown below. Make sure From 12/1/11 through 12/31/11 is selected.

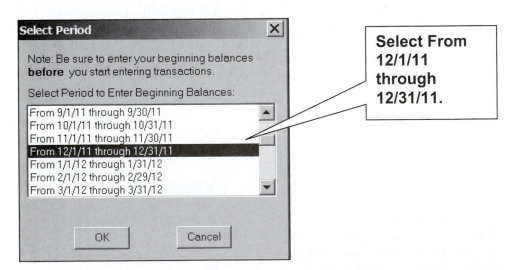

Select From 12/1/11 through 12/31/11.

Check the Select Period window carefully. Once the beginning balance period is selected, you cannot change it later.

4. Click [OK]. The Chart of Accounts Beginning Balances window appears. Observe that this window shows that you are going to enter Beginning Balances as of December 31, 2011.

Beginning Balances as of December 31, 2011.

5. Eric Lerette and Cynthia Barber purchased Cynthia's Service Merchandise in December 2011. Use the Balance Sheet below and on the next page to record the Chart of Accounts Beginning Balances. If you need to review how to record beginning balances, see Chapter 9 pages 303-307, steps 1-8.

Cynthia's Service Merchandise		
Balance Sheet		
January 1, 2012		
ASSETS		
Current Assets:		
10200 - Southwest Bank	$73,500.00	
10400 - Arizona Savings & Loan	22,000.00	
12000 - Merchandise Inventory	27,740.00	
13000 - Supplies	1,750.00	
14000 - Prepaid Insurance	2,400.00	
Total Current Assets		$127,390.00
Property and Equipment:		
15000 - Furniture and Fixtures	5,000.00	
15100 - Computers & Equipment	7,500.00	
15500 - Building	100,000.00	
Total Property and Equipment		112,500.00
Total Assets		$239,890.00

LIABILITIES AND CAPITAL		
Long-Term Liabilities:		
27000 - Long-Term Notes Payable	20,500.00	
27400 - Mortgage Payable	75,000.00	
Total Long-Term Liabilities		$95,500.00
Continued		
Capital:		
39006 - Eric Lerette, Capital	72,195.00	
39008 - Cynthia Barber, Capital	72,195.00	
Total Capital		144,390.00
Total Liabilities and Capital		$239,890.00

6. When you are finished entering the beginning balances, click
     .

7. Close the Maintain Chart of Accounts window.

BACKING UP BEGINNING BALANCES

Follow these steps to back up the work completed so far. This backup saves the new company set on pages 430-435, the general ledger chart of accounts, pages 437-440, and the beginning balances, pages 440-442.

1. Insert your USB flash drive. From the Navigation Bar, select

    System ; click Back Up Now . Make sure the box next to Include company name in the backup file name is *unchecked*.

2. Click Back Up .

3. Go to the location of your USB drive. (Or, backup to another location.) Type **Chapter 12 Starting Balance Sheet** in the File name field.

4. Click [Save].

5. When the window prompts This company backup will require approximately 1 diskette, click [OK]. When the window prompts Please insert the first disk, click [OK]. When the Back Up Company scale is 100% complete, you have successfully backed up to the current point in Chapter 12. (If you are backing up to the default or another location, this step will differ slightly.)

ACCOUNTS PAYABLE: VENDORS

The next section shows how to set up Accounts Payable defaults. This is where you set up information about the vendors who offer credit to Cynthia's Service Merchandise. Vendors offer Cynthia's Service Merchandise a 2 percent discount for invoices paid within 10 days (2% 10, Net 30 Days).

In Chapter 2, Vendors, you used Bellwether Garden Supply to explore Peachtree's accounts payable system. The accounts payable system provides the information needed for the entry that credits the Accounts Payable account and debits asset or expense accounts that vendor invoices represent. Since the company set up in Chapter 12, Cynthia's Service Merchandise, buys on credit from various vendors, the business wants to keep track of the amount owed and the due dates of bills. The accounts payable system does that.

Follow these steps to enter vendor default information.

1. From the Navigation Bar, select [Vendors & Purchases] ; [Vendors] , Set Up Vendor Defaults. The Vendor Defaults window appears.

2. Due in number of days is selected in the Standard Terms list. In the Discount in field, type **10** for the number of days. Press <Tab>.

3. In the Discount % field, type **2** then press **<Tab>**.

4. In the Credit Limit field, type **10000** then press **<Tab>**.

5. In the Expense Account field, click 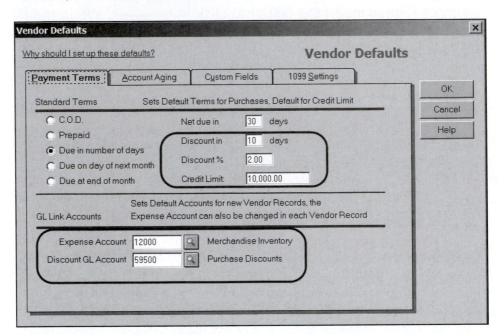. Select Account No. 12000, Merchandise Inventory.

6. In the Discount GL Account field, click . Select Account No. 59500, Purchase Discounts.

Make sure that the Expense Account field shows Account No. 12000, Merchandise Inventory; and that the Discount GL Account field shows Account No. 59500, Purchase Discounts. This sets up the default accounts for merchandise purchases and vendor discounts.

In PCA, the Merchandise Inventory account contains summary information about the total cost of the merchandise on hand and available for sale. In addition, PCA tracks vendor discounts in Account No. 59500, Purchase Discounts. PCA also keeps a detailed inventory record for each item of merchandise in stock. PCA automatically updates subsidiary records every time there is a change in the Merchandise Inventory account caused by a purchase, sale, or return of merchandise.

7. Click OK. You are returned to the Vendors & Payables Navigation Center.

8. Click ; New Vendor. The Maintain Vendors window displays. Follow these steps to enter vendor information:

a. In the Vendor ID field, type **JJH06** (use a zero) then press the **<Enter>** key.

b. In the Name field, type **Jimmy Jackson Hardware** then press the **<Enter>** key four times.

c. In the Mailing Address field, type **7709 Santa Monica Blvd.** then press the **<Enter>** key two times.

d. In the City, ST Zip field, type **Los Angeles** then press the **<Enter>** key. Click on the down arrow ▼ then select CA from the list of states. Press the **<Enter>** key. Type **90036** as the Zip code, press **<Enter>**.

e. In the Country field, type **USA** then press **<Enter>**.

f. In the Vendor Type field, type **hardware** then press **<Enter>**.

g. In the 1099 Type field, click on the down arrow ▼ and select Independent Contractor. Press the **<Enter>** key. Observe that the Expense Account automatically displays 12000. This is the default Expense Account entered on page 444, step 5.

h. In the Telephone 1 field, type **213-555-1234** then press **<Enter>** two times.

i. In the Fax field, type **213-555-1244** then press **<Enter>**.

j. In the E-mail field, type **jimmy@jacksonhardware.com** and then press <Enter>.

k. Type **www.jacksonhardware.com** in the Web Site field. Compare your Maintain Vendor window to the one shown on the next page.

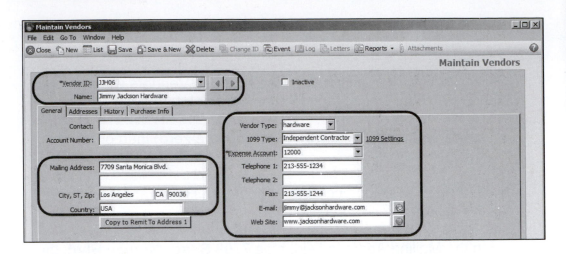

9. Click on the Purchase Info tab. Follow these steps to complete the fields:

   a. Type **28-3124986** in the Tax ID Number field. Observe that the credit terms entered on page 444 are shown. Compare your Maintain Vendors/Purchase Info window to the one shown below.

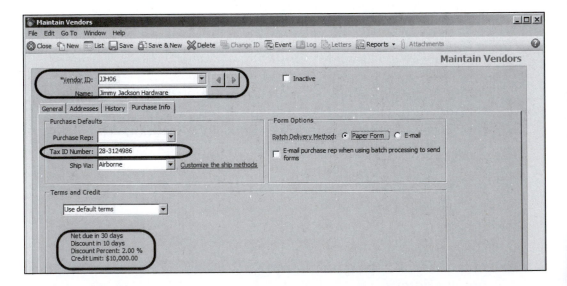

Comment
The Ship Via field on this window shows Airborne. You complete shipping information when you set the defaults for inventory.

b. Click [🗐 Save & New] .

c. Click on the General tab. Add the next vendor.

1) Vendor ID: **LLP07**
    Name: **Lee Lanning Products**
    Mailing Address: **3700 University Drive**
    City, ST Zip   **San Diego, CA 97022**
    Country: **USA**
    Vendor Type: **floor**
    1099 Type: **Independent Contractor**
    Expense Account: Defaults to 12000
    Telephone 1:   **619-555-9043**
    Fax: **619-555-9045**
    E-mail: **lee@lanningproducts.com**
    Web Site: **www.lanningproducts.com**

Purchase Info:

    Tax ID Number: **12-9988776**
    Terms and Credit: Defaults to 2% 10 Net 30

2) Vendor ID: **RBF08**
    Name: **Ronald Becker Fabrics**
    Mailing Address: **203 North Cactus Road**
    City, ST Zip   **Mesa, AZ 85233**
    Country: **USA**
    Vendor Type: **wall**
    1099 Type: **Independent Contractor**
    Expense Account: Defaults to 12000
    Telephone 1:   **602-555-0030**
    Fax: **602-555-7711**
    E-mail: **ronald@beckerfabrics.biz**
    Web Site: **www.beckerfabrics.biz**

Purchase Info:

    Tax ID Number: **55-1230989**
    Terms and Credit: Defaults to 2% 10 Net 30

10. Check your vendor information carefully. When you are finished entering vendor information, close the Maintain Vendors window.

How does vendor information work? The diagram below shows how vendor maintenance information, vendor default information and purchases and payments work together.

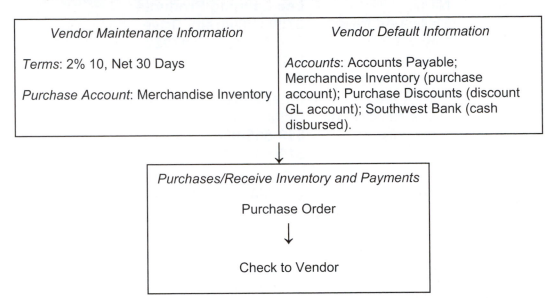

Vendor Maintenance Information	Vendor Default Information
Terms: 2% 10, Net 30 Days *Purchase Account*: Merchandise Inventory	*Accounts*: Accounts Payable; Merchandise Inventory (purchase account); Purchase Discounts (discount GL account); Southwest Bank (cash disbursed).

Purchases/Receive Inventory and Payments

Purchase Order
↓
Check to Vendor

On the Vendors & Purchases Navigation Center, Peachtree illustrates its accounts payable system. In Chapter 12, you work with vendors, entering bills, credits and returns, paying vendor bill, and issuing checks for expenses and owners' withdrawals, (*Hint:* To see Vendors, click Refresh .)

Compare your Vendors to the one shown below

Vendors			View Detailed List
Vendor ID	Vendor Name	Telephone 1	Balance
JJH06	Jimmy Jackson Hardware	213-555-1234	$0.00
LLP07	Lee Lanning Products	619-555-9043	$0.00
RBF08	Ronald Becker Fabrics	602-555-0030	$0.00

INVENTORY & SERVICES

The Inventory & Services Navigation Center displays information and access points related to the company's inventory items. It includes a summary of item information, access to recently used inventory reports, and a graphic analysis of how the cost of sales is trending. In addition, the Inventory & Services Navigation Center shows the flow of inventory-related tasks and takes you where you need to go to perform those tasks. Peachtree's inventory system is an example of another module within its user interface.

In the next section, default information for inventory items is completed. Because the Merchandise Inventory account is increased or decreased for every purchase, sale or return, its balance in the general ledger is current.

Inventory Defaults

Follow these steps to set up inventory items.

1. From the Navigation Bar, select **Inventory & Services**. Observe how the Inventory & Services Tasks are organized. The workflow diagram illustrates a sequence of connected steps within Peachtree's inventory system.

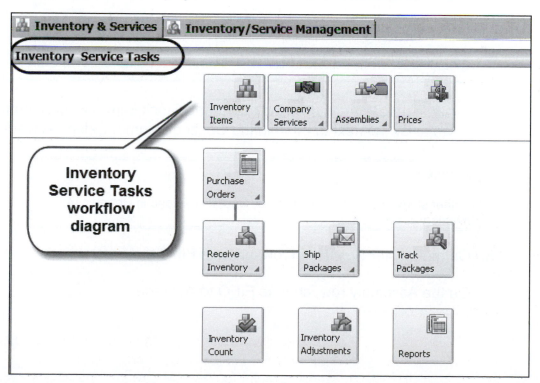

2. Click 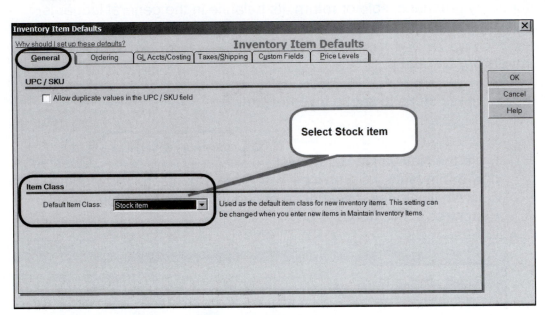; Set Up Inventory Defaults. The Inventory Item Defaults window appears.

3. Click on the General tab. In the Default Item Class field, select Stock item.

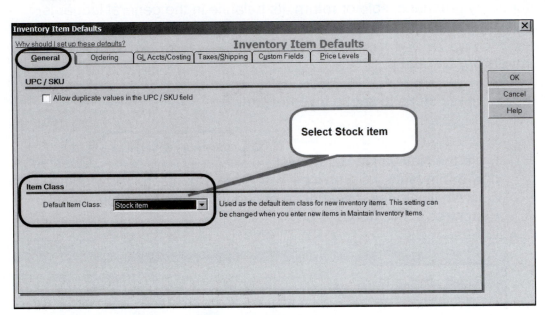

4. Click on the GL Accts/Costing tab. In the Stock item row, click on the down arrow ▾ next to FIFO in the Costing column. Select Average.

Comment

Further study of inventory costing methods will be done in Chapter 14, Inventory & Services.

---

5. On the Master Stock item row, change FIFO to Average.

6. On the Assembly row, change FIFO to Average.

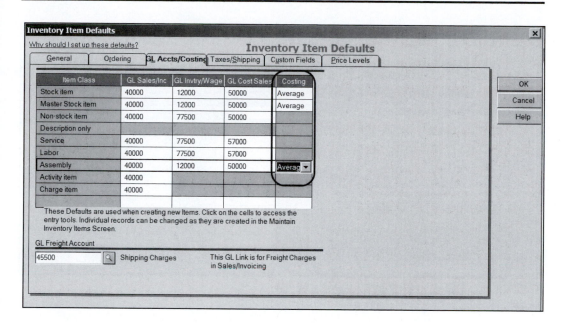

7. Make sure Average is selected in the Costing column. Click
    OK .

Inventory Items

1. Click [Inventory Items] ; New Inventory item. Follow these steps to add inventory items.

    a. In the Item I<u>D</u> field, type **001hardware**, then press the **<Enter>** key.

    b. In the Description field, type **hardware** then press **<Enter>**. In the Item field, Stock item appears automatically. (Refer to step 3, page 450.) Press **<Enter>** two times.

    c. In the Description: for Sales field, type **restoration hardware** then press **<Enter>**.

    d. Click on the right arrow [▸] in the Price Level 1 field. The Multiple Price Levels window appears. Type **150** in the Price field of Price Level 1, then press **<Enter>**.

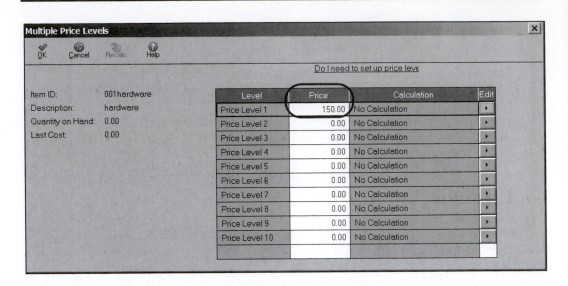

e. Click  .

Comment: What if your Price Level 1 field does not display 150.00 but 1.50? Follow these steps to set the decimal point:

1. From the menu bar, click Options, then Global. If necessary, select the Accounting tab.
2. In the Decimal Entry field, click Manual. Make sure that the number 2 is shown in the Number of decimal places field.
3. Click [OK]. This sets your decimal place globally. That means from now on all numbers with decimal places will be set automatically; for example, 150 will display as 150.00.

---

f. Type **50** in the Last Unit Cost field. Press **<Enter>**.

g. Accept the default for Account No. 40000, Sales-Hardware as the GL Sales Acct.

h. Accept the default for Account No. 12000, Merchandise Inventory, as the GL Inventory Acct by pressing **<Enter>**

i. Accept the default for Account No. 50000, Cost of Sales-Hardware as the GL Cost of Sales Acct by pressing **<Enter>** three times.

j. In the Item Type field, type **hardware** then press **<Enter>** two times.

k. In the Stocking U/M field (U/M is an abbreviation for Unit of Measure), type **each** then press **<Enter>** two times.

l. In the Minimum Stock field, type **10** then press **<Enter>**.

m. In the Reorder Quantity field, type **4** then press **<Enter>**.

n. In the Preferred Vendor ID field, click 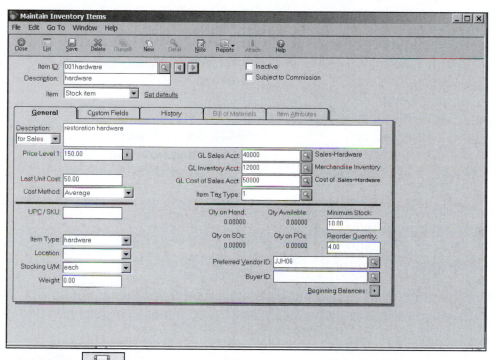. Select Jimmy Jackson Hardware, JJH06, as the vendor. Compare your Maintain Inventory Items window with the one below.

o. Click [Save].

p. Click [New].

Enter the following stock items:

1) Item ID: **002wall**
    Description: **wall**
    Item Class: Stock item
    Description for Sales: **wall coverings**

Price Level 1:	**100**
Last Unit Cost:	**30**
GL Sales Acct:	**40200 Sales-Wall**
GL Inventory Acct:	**12000 Merchandise Inventory**
GL Cost of Sales Acct:	**50500 Cost of Sales-Wall**
Item Type:	**wall**
Stocking U/M:	**each**
Minimum Stock:	**10**
Reorder Quantity:	**4**
Preferred Vendor ID:	**RBF08**

2)

Item ID:	**003floor**
Description:	**floor**
Item Class:	Stock item
Description for Sales:	**flooring**
Price Level 1:	**160**
Last Unit Cost:	**54**
GL Sales Acct:	**40400 Sales-Floor**
GL Inventory Acct:	**12000 Merchandise Inventory**
GL Cost of Sales Acct:	**57000 Cost of Sales-Floor**
Item Type:	**floor**
Stocking U/M:	**each**
Minimum Stock:	**25**
Reorder Quantity:	**10**
Preferred Vendor ID:	**LLP07**

2. Save then click Beginning Balances. The Inventory Beginning Balances window displays. Follow these steps to record beginning balances.

   a. In the Item ID table, click on 001hardware. Press the **<Tab>** key.

   b. In the Quantity field, type **90** then press **<Enter>**.

   c. In the Unit Cost field, type **50** then press **<Enter>**.

   d. The Total Cost field displays 4,500.00. Press the **<Enter>** key.

   e. Enter the beginning balances for walls and floors:

Item ID	Description	Quantity	Unit Cost	Total Cost
002wall	wall	148	30	4,440.00
003floor	floor	200	54	10,800.00

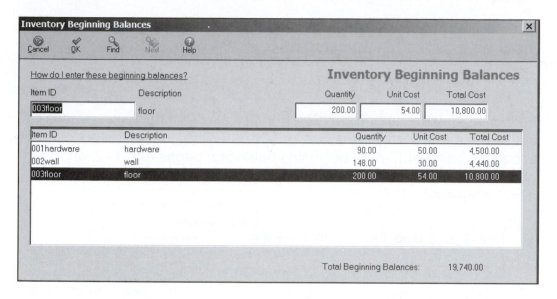

f. Observe that the Total Beginning Balance is 19,740. You add additional inventory in Chapter 14, Inventory & Services.[2] Click OK.

g. Close the Maintain Inventory Items window.

When you have completed entering Inventory items, the Inventory & Services Navigation Center shows these Inventory items. (*Hint:* If necessary, click Refresh.)

Inventory			View Detailed List
Item ID △	Description	No. Units Sold	Qty on Hand
001hardware	hardware	0.00	90.00
002wall	wall	0.00	148.00
003floor	floor	0.00	200.00

Inventory/Service Management

On the Inventory & Services Navigation Center, there is a tab for Inventory/Service Management. When you select Inventory/Service Management, you can access windows where you enter/maintain

---

[2]If you compare the total beginning balance in inventory, $19,740, to the balance sheet on pages 441-442, observe that the Merchandise Inventory account has a $27,740 balance. Additional inventory valued at $8,000 is added in Chapter 14 on pages 557-558.

inventory items and services. This page shows inventory item detail, totals, sales orders, backorders, and purchase orders.

BACKING UP YOUR DATA

Follow these steps to back up Chapter 12 data. This back up saves data to this point: new company setup, pages 430-435; general ledger chart of accounts, pages 437-440; beginning balances, pages 440-442; and accounts payable defaults, vendors, inventory defaults, and inventory items, pages 443-455.

1. Insert your USB flash drive. Select [System];
   [Back Up Now].

2. Make sure that the Include company name field is *unchecked*. Click
   [Back Up].

3. Go to the location of your USB drive. (Or, backup to another location.) Type **Chapter 12 Begin** in the File name field.

4. Click [Save].

5. When the window prompts that This company backup will require approximately 1 diskette, click [OK]. When the window prompts Please insert the first disk, click [OK]. When the Back Up Company scale is 100% complete, you have successfully backed up to the current point in Chapter 12. (This step will differ slightly if you are backing up the default or other hard-drive location.)

6. Continue or click File; Exit to exit Peachtree.

VENDORS & PURCHASES: PURCHASES/RECEIVE INVENTORY

The Vendors & Purchases Tasks workflow diagram includes a selection for Enter Bills; New Bill. This selection takes you to the Purchases/ Receive Inventory window. In PCA, all information about a purchase is recorded in the Purchases/Receive Inventory window. Then, PCA takes the necessary information from the window and journalizes the transaction in the Purchase Journal.

In Peachtree, the Purchases/Receive Inventory window is the **Purchase Journal**. On the Purchases/Receive Inventory window, you can enter vendor purchase invoices or receive inventory for purchase orders. The Purchases/Receive Inventory window includes two tabs.

- **Apply to Purchase Order**: When you select a vendor who has open purchase orders, Peachtree displays this tab, allowing you to select which purchase order to receive items against.
- **Apply to Purchases**: If you select a vendor with no open purchase orders, by default Peachtree displays this tab, where you can enter a purchase that did not originate on a purchase order. In addition, if items were included on the purchase invoice that are not included on the purchase order, you can add them here.

After recording vendor purchases in the Purchases/Receive Inventory window, you can display or print the Purchase Journal by selecting Reports, then Accounts Payable and highlighting the Purchase Journal. These steps are included in this chapter. Just remember, each time you use the Purchases/Receive Inventory window you are also journalizing in the Purchase Journal.

Purchases are posted both to the General Ledger and to the **Vendor Ledger** or **Accounts Payable Ledger**. You can also apply purchases to Inventory Items or Jobs.

Purchases work hand in hand with paying bills. On the Vendors & Purchases Tasks flowchart, Pay Bills is one of the selections. Once you have entered and posted a purchase (vendor invoice), that invoice is available when you enter the Vendor's ID code in Payments. You can select the invoice, then save (post) the payment; PCA distributes the appropriate amounts.

▶ Recording Purchases: Purchases/Receive Inventory Window

(*Hint:* This icon, ▶, means there is a flash video at www.mhhe.com/yacht2012.)

1. If you exited Peachtree, start Peachtree. Then, open Cynthia's Service Merchandise and, if necessary, restore the Chapter 12 Begin.ptb backup file.

2. From the Navigation Bar, select [**Vendors & Purchases**] ; [Enter Bills] , New Bill. The Purchases/Receive Inventory window displays. Observe that the window looks like a typical purchase order or invoice form.

    Check that *both* the A/P Account lookup field and GL Account field are shown on your Purchases/Receive Inventory window. If *not*, read the paragraph below the Purchases/Receive Inventory window. (*Hint:* To see multiple lines in the Apply to Purchases table, use your cursor to enlarge the Purchases/Receive Inventory window.)

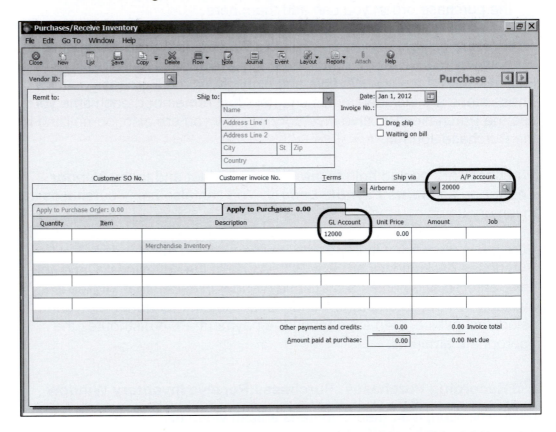

If the A/P Account lookup field and GL Account field are *not* shown, check your global settings. To do that, click Options, Global. If necessary, select the Accounting tab. The boxes in the Hide General Ledger Accounts section *must* be unchecked. (See steps 1-3 pages xvi-xvii.)

On the Purchases/Receive Inventory window, your cursor is in the Vendor ID field. There are three ways to select a vendor or add a new vendor.

➢ In the Vendor ID field, type a question mark **<?>** and the vendor list displays.

➢ With the mouse pointer in the Vendor ID field, click on the right mouse button. The vendor list displays.

➢ In the Vendor ID field, click 🔍 and the vendor list displays.

The transaction that you are going to work is shown below.

Date	*Transaction Description*
01/03/12	Invoice No. 56JJ was received from Jimmy Jackson Hardware for the purchase of six curtain rods for a unit cost of $50.00 each, and a total of $300.00. (Cynthia's Service Merchandise classifies curtain rods as hardware.)

3. In the Vendor ID field, select JJH06, Jimmy Jackson Hardware.

The name and address information is automatically completed when you select an existing vendor. Observe that when you select Jimmy Jackson Hardware, the Ship To, Ship Via, Terms, and A/P Account[3] fields are automatically completed.

4. In the Date field type **3** (or select 3).

5. In the Invoice # field, type **56JJ** and press the **<Enter>** key.

6. Click on the Quantity field and type **6** then press the **<Enter>** key.

---

[3]If the A/P Account lookup field does not display, click Options, Global. The boxes in the Hide General Ledger Accounts section *must* be unchecked. (See pages xvi-xvii, Setting Global Options.)

7. In the Item field, click 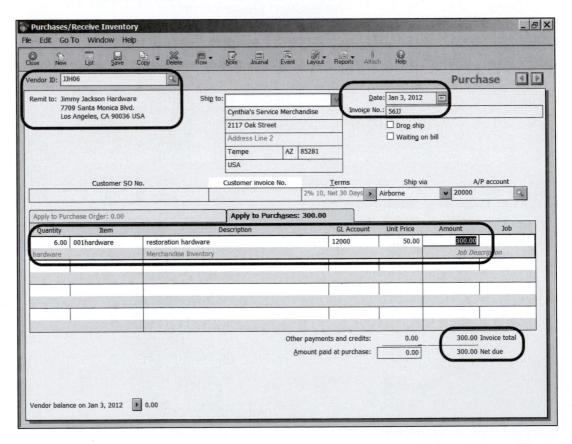 and select 001hardware. Accept the description. Press the **<Tab>** key. Observe that the following purchase information is automatically completed:

   a. Description field, restoration hardware.
   b. GL Account 12000, Merchandise Inventory. (If the account name, Merchandise Inventory does *not* show, go to Options; Global, General tab. In the Line Item Entry Display area, make sure 2 Line is selected; click OK. Click on the Purchases/Receive Inventory button on the taskbar to enlarge the window.)
   c. Unit Price 50.00.
   d. Amount 300.00.
   e. Invoice Total and Net Due, 300.00
   f. Vendor Balance on Jan 3, 2012: 0.00.

> **Read Me**
>
> On the Purchases/Receive Inventory window, if the Quantity, Item, Description, GL Account, Unit Price, and Amount table does *not* show multiple lines you can use the arrows next to the Job field to scroll through the multiple lines. *Or,* try using the cursor to enlarge the window.
>
> The number of lines on the Quantity, Item/Description table is determined by how the screen resolution is set. If your Purchases/Receive Inventory window shows one line on the Quantity, Item table, then your computer is probably set up for 800 X 600 pixels. If your screen resolution is set at 1024 X 768 pixels, your Purchases/Receive Inventory window shows multiple lines in the Quantity/Item area. To check your screen resolution, go to the desktop and right click; left click Properties, select the Settings tab. The screen resolution area shows the number of the monitor's pixels.

Invoice Total: The Invoice Total keeps a running total of the entry lines you have added to the Purchase Journal. Before you post a Purchase Journal entry, you should check to see that the amount field is the same as the total invoice amount (Net Due) on the vendor invoice.

The total that shows in the Amount field is automatically credited to the accounts payable account (Account No. 20000, Accounts Payable and the vendor account, Jimmy Jackson Hardware). The information entered on the Purchases/Receive Inventory window will be recorded in the Purchase Journal.

8. Click **Journal** to see this entry in the Purchases Journal.

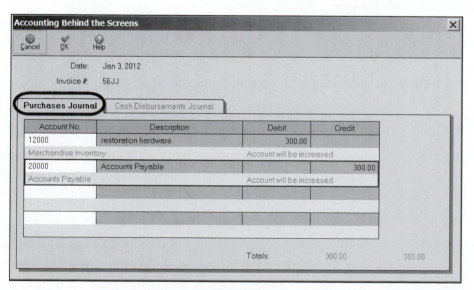

Inventory Items and Purchases: Since you entered an Inventory Item (hardware), the debit amount is shown in the merchandise inventory account (Account No. 12000). (On page 444, step 5, you set up the Expense Account default for Account No. 12000, Merchandise Inventory.)

9. Click [OK] to return to the Purchases/Receive Inventory window.

10. Click [Save] to post this entry. The Purchases/Receive Inventory window is ready for the next transaction. When you enter and post purchases of inventory items, three things happen:

   a. The amount or stock level of the item is updated.

   b. The **Average Cost** is updated based on the Unit Price entered. Average cost is computed using the **weighted-average method** for inventory. The Average Cost is used by PCA to compute Cost of Goods Sold when these Inventory Items are entered as Sales.

   c. For Stock-Type items, the Inventory account is debited and Accounts Payable is credited (debit, Account No. 12000, Merchandise Inventory; credit, Account No. 20000, Accounts Payable/Vendor.)

Additional Purchases

The following transactions need to be entered in the Purchases Journal. Remember to click [Save] after each transaction to post.

Date	Transaction Description
01/20/12	Invoice 90 was received from Lee Lanning Products for the purchase of eight rolls of vinyl flooring at $54 each, for a total of $432. (*Hint: Select 003floor as the inventory item.*)
01/20/12	Invoice 210 was received from Ronald Becker Fabrics for four pairs of curtains at $30 each, for a total vendor

invoice of $120. (*Hint: Select 002wall as the inventory item.*)

01/20/12   Invoice 78JJ was received from Jimmy Jackson Hardware for the purchase of 10 curtain rods at $50 each, for a total of $500. (*Hint: Select 001hardware as the inventory item.*)

CASH PURCHASES: Write Checks Window

Cynthia's Service Merchandise pays cash for some purchases. Usually these cash disbursements are for expenses. All payments of cash are recorded in the ***cash disbursements journal***. Follow these steps to see how cash purchases are entered.

 Read Me:

The Write Checks window is a simplified version of the Payments window. Both the Write Checks window and the Payments window post to the Cash Disbursements Journal.

---

1. From the Vendors & Purchases Navigation Center, click [Write Checks], New Check. When the Select a Cash Account window appears, make sure Southwest Bank is selected. Then, click [OK]. The Write Checks window displays.

   Date   *Transaction Description*

   01/24/12   Cynthia's Service Merchandise issued check 3030 in the amount of $160 to David Allison for cleaning (debit Account No. 70000, Maintenance Expense). Print Check No. 3030.

> **Comment**
>
> Your Write Checks window will show a cash account balance in the Balance field. Your Cash Account Balance field shows the same amount as the January 1, 2012 balance sheet, page 441, Southwest Bank.

2. Click on the Pay to the order of Name field and type **David Allison**.

3. Type **24** in the Date field and press **<Enter>**.

4. Type **160** in the $ field.

5. In the Expense Account field, select Account No. 70000, Maintenance Expense.

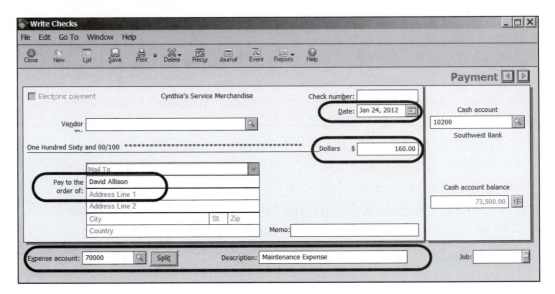

Printing the Check

Follow these steps to print the check:

1. The Write Checks window with David Allison's check should be displayed.

2. Click [Print].

3. Type **3030** in the First check number field.

Comment

Step 4 instructs you to select OCR AP Laser Preprinted as the form to print. If this form does *not* print, select another one. The form you select is tied to the kind of printer you are using. Depending on your printer, you may need to make a different selection.

---

4. The Print Forms: Disbursement Checks window appears. Click .
    Select Form Then select OCR AP Laser Preprinted to highlight it.

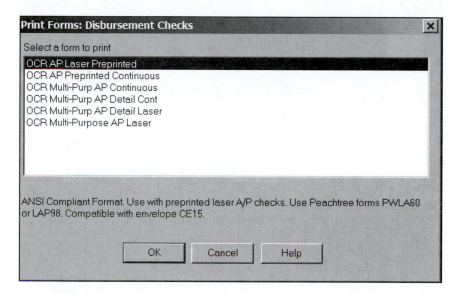

5. Click OK .

6. The Print Forms: Disbursements Checks window appears. The Use this form field shows OCR AP Laser Preprinted; the First Check Number shows 3030. (*Hint:* The check number, 3030, was entered in step 3 above.)

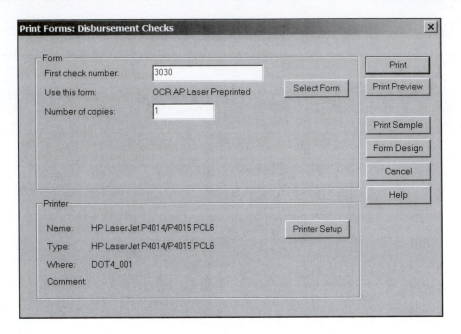

7. Peachtree automatically sequences check numbers after the first one is entered. Click 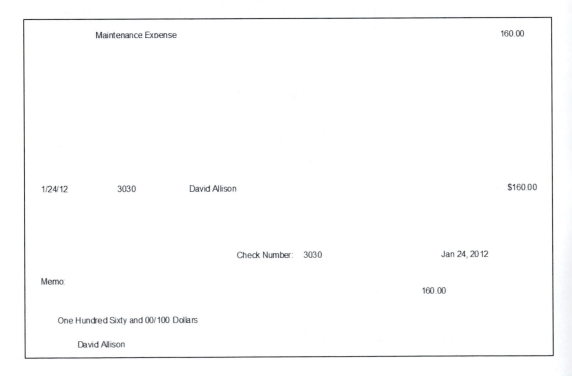 The check starts to print.

Comment

If your check does not show the same amount, go back to the Write Checks window and click . Double-click Check No. 3030, 1/24/2012; the Write Checks window appears. Make the necessary corrections. When you reprint Check No. 3030, Duplicate will be shown on the printout.

After you print a check, the Write Checks window is ready for another payment. Remember, the check form that you select is tied to the kind of printer you are using. If necessary, select a different form to print.

8. Record the additional payments shown below. Since you are *not* going to print Check Nos. 3031-3035, type the appropriate check number in the Check Num**b**er field on the Write Checks window.

   Date   *Transaction Description*

   01/24/12   Cynthia's Service Merchandise issued Check No. 3031 in the amount of $45.00 to the U.S. Post Office (*Hint: Since you are not going to print checks, type Check No.* **3031** *in the Check Num**b**er field. Click*

   ⊞ Save *after each entry.*)

   01/24/12   Issued Check No. 3032 in the amount of $107.65 to Broadway Office Supplies for letterhead paper, envelopes, and note pads. (Debit Account No. 75500, Supplies Expense.)

   01/24/12   Issued Check No. 3033 in the amount of $72.14 to RCI Phone Co.

   01/25/12   Issued Check No. 3034 to Eric Lerette for $500.

   01/25/12   Issued Check No. 3035 to Cynthia Barber for $500.

9. Click ⊞ List to see if you have issued Check Nos. 3030 through 3035.

---

10. If you have any transactions to edit, highlight the line. Double-click. When the Write Checks window appears, make the necessary corrections. Remember to click [Save] for any revised transactions. If no corrections are needed, close the Write Checks List window.

11. Close the Write Checks window and the Write Checks List window.

PURCHASE RETURNS: CREDITS & RETURNS

Sometimes it is necessary to return merchandise that has been purchased from a vendor. When entering a purchase return, you need to record it as a vendor credit memo.

The following transaction is for merchandise returned to a vendor:

Date   *Transaction Description*

01/25/12   Returned one roll of vinyl flooring to Lee Lanning Products, Invoice 90 and paid the invoice on the same day.

Follow these steps to enter a purchase return:

1. From the Vendors & Purchases Navigation Center, click [Credits and Returns]. New Vendor Credit Memo. The Vendor Credit Memos window appears.

2. In the Vendor ID field, select Lee Lanning Products.

3. Type **25** in the <u>D</u>ate field.

4. Type **VCM90** in the Credit No field. For the credit number you are using the abbreviation VCM for Vendor Credit Memo, then the invoice number.

5. The Apply to In<u>v</u>oice No. tab is selected. Click on the down-arrow to select 90.

Observe that the Item, Quantity, Description, GL Account, and Unit Price fields are completed.

6. Type **1** in the Returned field; Press <Enter>. After you type 1 in the Returned field, the Amount field shows 54.00. Also, notice that the Credit Applied to Invoice shows 54.00. This agrees with the Credit Total.

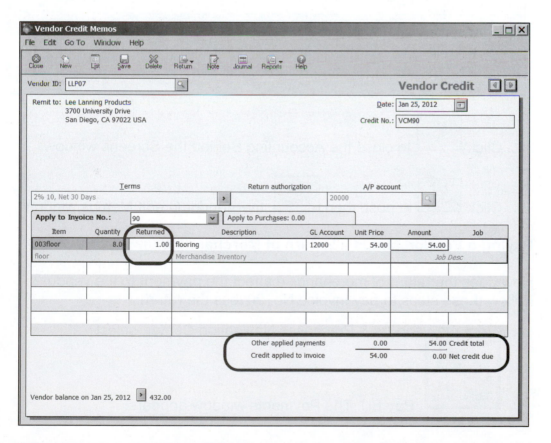

7. To see how the vendor credit memo is journalized, click 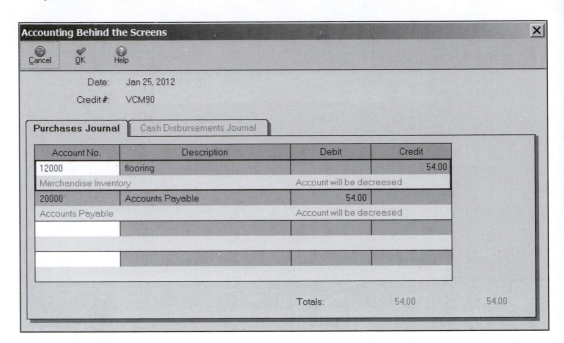. Notice that Account No. 12000, Merchandise Inventory, is credited for $54.00 and Account No. 20000, Account Payable, is debited for $54.00.

Accounting Behind the Screens

Cancel   OK   Help

Date: Jan 25, 2012
Credit #:   VCM90

Purchases Journal   Cash Disbursements Journal

Account No.	Description	Debit	Credit
12000	flooring		54.00
Merchandise Inventory		Account will be decreased	
20000	Accounts Payable	54.00	
Accounts Payable		Account will be decreased	
	Totals:	54.00	54.00

8. Click [OK] to close the Accounting Behind the Screens window.

9. Click [Save] to post, then [Close] the Vendor Credit Memos window.

Paying a Vendor, Minus a Return of Merchandise

How does the return of merchandise affect the payment to the vendor? Follow these steps to pay Invoice No. 90 less the return.

1. From the Vendors & Purchases Navigation Center, select , Pay Bill. The Payments window appears.

Date	Transaction Description
01/25/12	Cynthia's Service Merchandise issued Check No. 3036 to Lee Lanning Products in payment of Invoice No. 90 (less the return of merchandise). Print Check No. 3036.

2. In the Vendor ID field, select Lee Lanning Products.

3. Type **25** in the Date field. Observe that the Apply to Invoices tab is selected and that the Invoice, 90; Date Due (Feb 19, 2012) and Amount Due 378.00 fields are completed. Cynthia's Service Merchandise owes Lee Lanning Products $378 ($432, original invoice amount, less the $54 return). Lee Lanning Products extends a 2% vendor discount to Cynthia's Service Merchandise. Type **7.56** in the Discount field (.02 x 378 = 7.56). Press <Enter>. Observe that the Pay box is checked. The payment was calculated as follows:

Jan. 20	Invoice 90	$432.00
Jan. 25	Less, VCM90	54.00
Jan. 25	Less, Purchase discount	7.56
Total Paid		$370.44

Compare your Payments window to the one shown on the next page. Make sure that Discount field is shows 7.56 and that the Discount Account field shows Account No. 59500, Purchase Discounts.

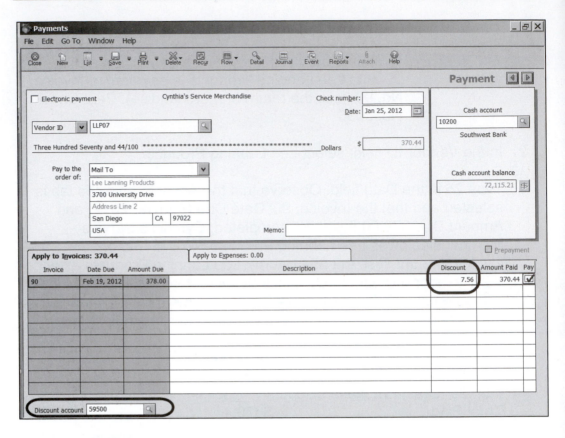

> ➤ **Troubleshooting Tip:** What if your Cash Account Balance field does not show an amount? Close the Payments window without saving. Then, from the menu bar, go to Options; Global. A checkmark should be placed next to Recalculate cash balance automatically in Receipts, Payments, and Payroll Entry. If necessary, click on the appropriate field, then OK . Go back to step 1, on page 470.

4. Click  .

5. The Print Forms: Disbursement Checks window displays. Type **3036** in the First Check Number field.

6. The Use this form field shows OCR AP Laser Preprinted. If this selection is *not* made, click Select Form , then select OCR AP Laser Preprinted.

7. Click [Print] . Check No. 3036 starts to print. Make sure the check amount is $370.44.

90		1/20/12	432.00	7.56	370.44

1/25/12   3036   Lee Lanning Products   7.56 $370.44

Check Number: 3036   Jan 25, 2012

Memo:
                                                             370.44

   Three Hundred Seventy and 44/100 Dollars

      Lee Lanning Products
      3700 University Drive
      San Diego, CA 97022
      USA

8. Close the Payments window.

9. Record the following purchase return and payment:

Date	Transaction Description

01/28/12   Returned two curtain rods (001hardware) to Jimmy Jackson Hardware, Invoice No. 78JJ; VCM78JJ. Cynthia's Service Merchandise paid $50 each for the two curtain rods; credit total, $100.00.

01/28/12   Issued Check No. 3037 to pay Jimmy Jackson Hardware for Invoice No. 78JJ (minus returned merchandise). (*Hint: Type the check number in the Check Number field instead of printing it. The discount is 8.00*)

▶ PAYING SPECIFIC VENDOR INVOICES

Once you have entered a vendor invoice in the Purchases/Receive Inventory window, you can apply payments to specific invoices. You enter the vendor invoice using the Purchases/Receive Inventory window; then when you post, the purchase journal is updated. To pay for the merchandise purchased, you select the specific invoice from the vendor's transaction list. When you print a check, you are also posting to the cash disbursements journal. The journal entry below shows a specific vendor payment.

Account Name	Debit	Credit
Accounts Payable/Ronald Becker Fabrics	$120.00	
Purchase Discounts		$2.40
Southwest Bank		$117.60

You should take advantage of both the Purchases/Receive Inventory and Payments features. Because amounts are disbursed and discounts are tracked automatically, your job is made easier. This also provides a detailed and complete audit trail. An audit trail is the path from the source document to the accounts. (Refer to pages 190-198 for more information about Peachtree's internal controls and audit trail.)

The diagram below shows how Purchases/Receive Inventory works together with Payments.

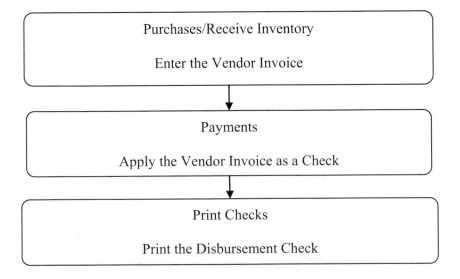

Date   *Transaction Description*

01/28/12   Issued Check No. 3038 to Ronald Becker Fabrics in
              payment of Invoice No. 210.

Follow these steps to pay vendor invoice 210:

1. From the Payments window, select Ronald Becker Fabrics as the
    vendor.

2. If necessary, type **3038** in the Check Number field.

3. Type **28** in the Date field.

4. The Apply to Invoices tab should already be selected. For Invoice
    No. 210, click on the Pay box.

5. Click ![Save] to post.

Editing Payments

If you have already paid a vendor, you can edit payments. Follow these
steps to see what vendors have been paid:

1. Display the Payments window.

2. Click ![List]. The Payment List window appears. Compare your
    Payment List window to the one shown below.

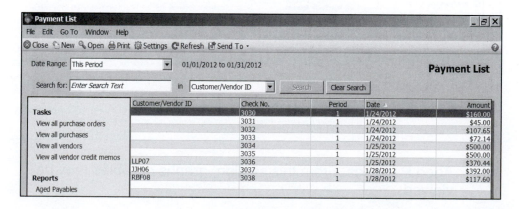

---

3. If you need to edit a payment, double-click on the appropriate one. Or, if no corrections are needed, close the Payment List window.

4. Make any necessary changes, then post.

5. When you are finished close the Payments window.

PRINTING THE PURCHASE JOURNAL AND CASH DISBURSEMENTS JOURNAL

Observe that the Vendors & Purchases Navigation Center shows the following sections.

- Vendors & Purchases Tasks: The flowchart that shows the Peachtree's accounts payable system.
- Vendors: Each vendor is shown. You can link to individual vendors or <u>View Detailed List</u>.
- Recently Used Vendor Reports: You can link to view or print vendor reports from this section or <u>View All Vendor & Purchases Reports</u>.

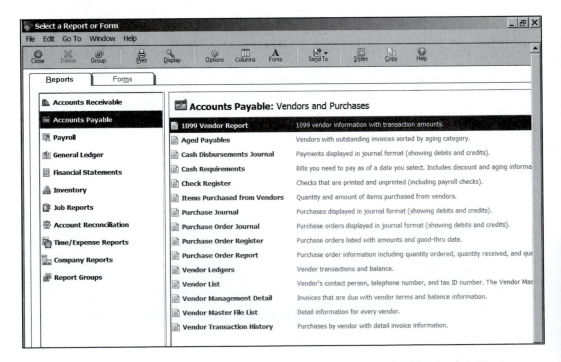

- Aged Payables: From this section, graphs or tables may be viewed.

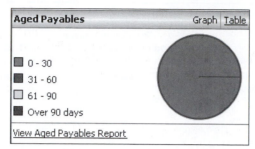

- Peachtree Solutions: Checks and Forms and Online Bill Pay are available through third party vendors who supply checks and online services to Peachtree.

Peachtree Solutions

Checks & Forms   Online Bill Pay

1. From the Recently Used Vendor Reports area, go to the Purchase Journal <u>Print</u> or <u>View</u> link.

2. If you selected <u>Print</u>, the Modify Report - Purchase Journal window appears. Click [OK]. (*Hint:* If you selected <u>View</u>, the Purchase Journal appears.)

3. The Print window appears. Click [OK].

*****EDUCATIONAL VERSION ONLY*****

Cynthia's Service Merchandise
Purchase Journal
For the Period From Jan 1, 2012 to Jan 31, 2012

Filter Criteria includes: 1) Includes Drop Shipments. Report order is by Date. Report is printed in Detail Format.

Date	Account ID Account Description	Invoice/CM #	Line Description	Debit Amount	Credit Amount
1/3/12	12000 Merchandise Inventory 20000 Accounts Payable	56JJ	restoration hardware Jimmy Jackson Hardware	300.00	300.00
1/20/12	12000 Merchandise Inventory 20000 Accounts Payable	210	wall coverings Ronald Becker Fabrics	120.00	120.00
1/20/12	12000 Merchandise Inventory 20000 Accounts Payable	78JJ	restoration hardware Jimmy Jackson Hardware	500.00	500.00
1/20/12	12000 Merchandise Inventory 20000 Accounts Payable	90	flooring Lee Lanning Products	432.00	432.00
1/25/12	12000 Merchandise Inventory 20000 Accounts Payable	VCM90	flooring Lee Lanning Products	54.00	54.00
1/28/12	12000 Merchandise Inventory 20000 Accounts Payable	VCM78JJ	restoration hardware Jimmy Jackson Hardware	100.00	100.00
				1,506.00	1,506.00

4. To print the Cash Disbursements Journal, close the Purchase Journal. Link to <u>Print</u> (or <u>View</u>) for the Cash Disbursements Journal.

*****EDUCATIONAL VERSION ONLY*****

Cynthia's Service Merchandise
Cash Disbursements Journal
For the Period From Jan 1, 2012 to Jan 31, 2012

Filter Criteria includes: Report order is by Date. Report is printed in Detail Format.

Date	Check #	Account ID	Line Description	Debit Amount	Credit Amount
1/24/12	3030	70000	Maintenance Expense	160.00	
		10200	David Allison		160.00
1/24/12	3031	73500	Postage Expense	45.00	
		10200	U.S. Post Office		45.00
1/24/12	3032	75500	Supplies Expense	107.65	
		10200	Broadway Office Supplies		107.65
1/24/12	3033	76000	Telephone Expense	72.14	
		10200	RCI Phone Co.		72.14
1/25/12	3034	39007	Eric Lerette, Drawing	500.00	
		10200	Eric Lerette		500.00
1/25/12	3035	39009	Cynthia Barber, Drawing	500.00	
		10200	Cynthia Barber		500.00
1/25/12	3036	59500	Discounts Taken		7.56
		20000	Invoice: 90	378.00	
		10200	Lee Lanning Products		370.44
1/28/12	3037	59500	Discounts Taken		8.00
		20000	Invoice: 78JJ	400.00	
		10200	Jimmy Jackson Hardware		392.00
1/28/12	3038	59500	Discounts Taken		2.40
		20000	Invoice: 210	120.00	
		10200	Ronald Becker Fabrics		117.60
Total				2,282.79	2,282.79

Comment

Observe that the Line Description on the Cash Disbursements Journal shows the account name (e.g. Account No. 70000, Maintenance Expense) for the debit amount. The person to whom the check was written (e.g. David Allison) is shown for the amount credited. Your Line Description fields may differ.

VENDOR LEDGERS

Follow these steps to print a Vendor Ledger for Cynthia's Service Merchandise.

1. From the Recently Used Vendor Reports area, link to <u>View All Vendor & Purchases Reports</u>. The Select a Report or Form window appears.

2. Double-click Vendor Ledgers then make the selections to print.

*****EDUCATIONAL VERSION ONLY*****							
Cynthia's Service Merchandise							
Vendor Ledgers							
For the Period From Jan 1, 2012 to Jan 31, 2012							
Filter Criteria includes: Report order is by ID.							
Vendor ID **Vendor**	**Date**	**Trans No**	**Type**	**Paid**	**Debit Amt**	**Credit Amt**	**Balance**
JJH06	1/3/12	56JJ	PJ			300.00	300.00
Jimmy Jackson Hardware	1/20/12	78JJ	PJ	*		500.00	800.00
	1/28/12	VCM78JJ	PJ	*	100.00		700.00
	1/28/12	3037	CDJ		8.00	8.00	700.00
	1/28/12	3037	CDJ		400.00		300.00
LLP07	1/20/12	90	PJ	*		432.00	432.00
Lee Lanning Products	1/25/12	VCM90	PJ	*	54.00		378.00
	1/25/12	3036	CDJ		7.56	7.56	378.00
	1/25/12	3036	CDJ		378.00		0.00
RBF08	1/20/12	210	PJ	*		120.00	120.00
Ronald Becker Fabrics	1/28/12	3038	CDJ		2.40	2.40	120.00
	1/28/12	3038	CDJ		120.00		0.00
Report Total					**1,069.96**	**1,369.96**	**300.00**

3. Close the Vendor Ledgers.

PRINTING THE GENERAL LEDGER TRIAL BALANCE

1. In the Reports list, highlight General Ledger. Then, select General Ledger Trial Balance.

2. Make the selections to print. Compare your printout with the one shown on the next page.

*****EDUCATIONAL VERSION ONLY*****

Cynthia's Service Merchandise
General Ledger Trial Balance
As of Jan 31, 2012

Filter Criteria includes: Report order is by ID. Report is printed in Detail Format.

Account ID	Account Description	Debit Amt	Credit Amt
10200	Southwest Bank	71,235.17	
10400	Arizona Savings & Loan	22,000.00	
12000	Merchandise Inventory	28,938.00	
13000	Supplies	1,750.00	
14000	Prepaid Insurance	2,400.00	
15000	Furniture and Fixtures	5,000.00	
15100	Computers & Equipment	7,500.00	
15500	Building	100,000.00	
20000	Accounts Payable		300.00
27000	Long-Term Notes Payable		20,500.00
27400	Mortgage Payable		75,000.00
39006	Eric Lerette, Capital		72,195.00
39007	Eric Lerette, Drawing	500.00	
39008	Cynthia Barber, Capital		72,195.00
39009	Cynthia Barber, Drawing	500.00	
59500	Purchase Discounts		17.96
70000	Maintenance Expense	160.00	
73500	Postage Expense	45.00	
75500	Supplies Expense	107.65	
76000	Telephone Expense	72.14	
	Total:	**240,207.96**	**240,207.96**

3. Close all windows.

BACKING UP CHAPTER 12 DATA

Follow these steps to back up Chapter 12 data.

1. If necessary, close all window and insert your USB flash drive. From the System Navigation Center, select | Back Up Now |.

2. Click | Back Up |.

3. In the Save in field, go to the location of your USB drive (or another location). Type **Chapter 12** in the File name field.

4. Click | Save |.

5. When the window prompts that This company backup will require approximately 1 diskette, click [OK]. Click [OK] when the window prompts Please insert the first disk. When the Back Up Company scale is 100% complete, you have successfully backed up to the current point in Chapter 12. (If you are backing up to the default or other hard drive location, this step will differ slightly.)

6. Continue or click File; Exit to exit Peachtree.

EXPORT REPORTS TO EXCEL

Follow these steps to export the following Peachtree reports to Excel: Chart of Accounts, Purchase Journal, Cash Disbursements Journal, Vendors Ledgers, General Ledger Trial Balance.

1. From the menu bar, select Reports & Forms, select General Ledger. Double-click Chart of Accounts. The Chart of Accounts appears.

   Expand the Account Description column. (Click [↔] to widen the column.)

2. Click [Excel]. On the Copy Report to Excel window, accept the default for Create a new Microsoft Excel workbook. In the Report header option field, Show header in Excel worksheet is selected.

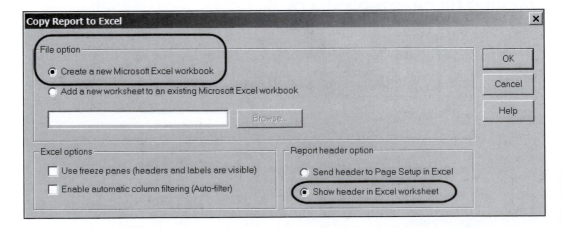

3. Click [OK]. The chart of accounts exports to Excel.

4. Save. Use the file name **Chapter 12_CofA_PJ_CDJ_VL_GLTB. xlsx**. (Abbreviations are Chart of Accounts, Purchase Journal, Cash Disbursements Journal, Vendor Ledgers, and General Ledger Trial Balance.)

5. Go back to Peachtree's Select a Report or Form window. In the Reports list, select Accounts Payable. Double-click Purchase Journal.

6. Click [Excel]. On the Copy Report to Excel window, select Add a new worksheet to an existing Microsoft Excel workbook.

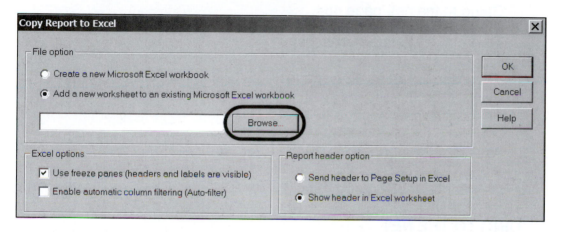

7. Click [Browse...] to go to the appropriate file. (*Hint:* File name is Chapter 12_CofA_PJ_CDJ_VL_GLTB.xlsx.) Click [Open]. You are returned to the Copy Report to Excel window. Observe that the Browse field shows the location of the file selected. Click [OK].

8. Observe that two sheets are shown at the bottom of the Excel file: Chart of Accounts and Purchase Journal. Save the file.

9. Repeat steps 5, 6, 7, and 8 to export the Cash Disbursements Journal, Vendor Ledgers, and General Ledger Trial Balance to the Excel File. There should be five sheets: Chart of Accounts, Purchase Journal, Cash Disbursements Journal, Vendor Ledgers, and General Ledger Trial Balance. When you are through, the Excel file has five sheets.

10. Save. Exit Excel.

   NOTE: If your instructor would like you to save the Chart of Accounts, Purchase Journal, Cash Disbursements Journal, Vendor Ledgers, and General Ledger Trial Balance as PDF files, refer to page 353, Save General Ledger Trial Balance and Financial Statements as PDF files. The suggested file name is **Chapter 12_Chart of Accounts.pdf**, etc.

SUMMARY AND REVIEW

Complete the following end-of-chapter activities:

1. Going to the net, page 484.

2. True/Make true questions, pages 485.

3. Exercises 12-1 and 12-2, pages 485-493.

4. Analysis question, page 493.

5. Assessment rubric, page 494.

6. Chapter 12 Index, page 495.

GOING TO THE NET

Watch the Vendor Management Center video at http://www.peachtree.com/productsServices/whatsNew/. To watch the video, link to . (Going to the Net links are on the textbook website at www.mhhe.com/yacht2012 link to Student Edition, select Chapter 12.) Answer these questions.

1. What Peachtree feature allows the user to simplify vendor searches?

2. What was the result of being able to negotiate with the vendor?

The website http://www.peachtree.com/productsServices/whatsNew/ also includes additional videos. Watch those videos too.

True/Make True: The Online Learning Center includes these questions at www.mhhe.com/yacht2012, select Student Edition, Chapter 12, QA Templates.

1. Accounts Payable is money you pay to customers.

2. Vendor default information needs to be set up to establish the criteria used when computing vendor discounts.

3. Each time you use the Write Checks window, you are journalizing in the Cash Disbursements Journal.

4. The purchase discount offered to Cynthia's Service Merchandise from their vendors is 2% 10, Net 30 Days

5. Each time you use the Payments window, you are journalizing in the Purchases Journal.

6. The merchandise that Cynthia's Service Merchandise buys from Ronald Becker Fabrics is classified as wall coverings.

7. The detailed types list includes chart of accounts numbers with five digits.

8. The Maintain Vendors window is used to enter information about vendors from whom you purchase merchandise.

9. All accounting software applications, regardless of the size of the company, are the same.

10. Each accounting software application (for example, Peachtree, QuickBooks, and Microsoft Dynamics GP) has a unique system design.

Exercise 12-1: Follow the instructions below to complete Exercise 12-1.

1. Start Peachtree. From the menu bar, select File; New Company. (One company should be open.) Set up a retail business using *your first and last name*; for example, *Your Name Sales and Service.* For the address, use 1010 Sycamore Avenue; Norcross, GA 30092; telephone, 404-555-8900; Fax, 404-555-8833. Your company is a

Sole Proprietorship. For the Tax ID information, use the following:

Federal Employer ID:	43-1823359
State Employer ID:	82-9157844
State Unemployment ID:	824511-7

Leave the Web Site and E-mail address fields blank.

2. At the New Company – Setup; Chart of Accounts window, select Copy settings from an existing Peachtree Accounting company.

3. Highlight Cynthia's Service Merchandise (*or,* your name Service Merchandise), then click ⌈Next >⌉ .

4. Observe that the information on the Copy Company Information window includes a selection for Accounting Periods. Since this company is using the same accounting period (January 1 - 31, 2012) as Cynthia's Service Merchandise, leave that box checked. For purposes of Exercise 12-1 accept all the defaults on the Copy Company Information window by clicking on ⌈Next >⌉ .

5. Read the information about the Accounting Method. Accept the default for accrual accounting by clicking on ⌈Next >⌉ .

6. Accept the default for Real Time posting by clicking on ⌈Next >⌉ .

7. At the Create a New Company – Finish window, click ⌈Finish⌉ . If the screen prompts You can use this company in the student version of Peachtree for the next 14 months and then it will expire, click ⌈OK⌉ .

8. Close the Setup Guide. (*Hint:* Click on the box next to Don't show this screen at startup to place a checkmark in it.)

9. Make sure the Period shows Period 1 - 01/01/12-01/31/12 ⌈Period 1 - 01/01/12-01/31/12⌉ .

General Ledger

1. Delete the following accounts:

   3900A Owner's Draw
   40400   Sales-Floor

   Change the following accounts:

10200	Southwest Bank	**Caliber Bank**
10400	Arizona Savings & Loan	**City Savings & Loan**
39009	Owner's Contribution	**Student Name, Capital** (Equity–doesn't close)
40200	Sales-Wall	**Sales-Tools**
50500	Cost of Sales-Wall	**Cost of Sales-Tools**
57000	Cost of Sales-Floor	**Cost of Sales**

   Add the following account:

23755	**SUTA2 Payable**	Other Current Liabilities
39010	**Student Name, Drawing**	Equity-gets closed
72545	**SUTA2 Expense**	Expenses

2. Use the Balance Sheet to record chart of accounts beginning balances. You purchased the retail business in December 2011. Remember to select the period From 12/1/11 through 12/31/11. Record beginning balances as of December 31, 2011. The January 1, 2012 balance sheet is shown below and on the next page.

Student Name Sales and Service Balance Sheet January 1, 2012		
ASSETS		
Current Assets		
10200 - Caliber Bank	$62,500.00	
10400 - City Savings & Loan	13,300.00	
12000 - Merchandise Inventory	14,750.00	
13000 - Supplies	1,000.00	
14000 - Prepaid Insurance	2,400.00	
Total Current Assets		$93,950.00

Property and Equipment		
15000 - Furniture and Fixtures	$3,500.00	
15100 - Computers & Equipment	5,500.00	
15500 - Building	85,000.00	
Total Property and Equipment		$94,000.00
Total Assets		$187,950.00
LIABILITIES AND CAPITAL		
Long Term Liabilities		
27000 - Long-Term Notes Payable	10,000.00	
27400 - Mortgage Payable	60,000.00	
Total Long-Term Liabilities		$70,000.00
Capital		
39009 - Student Name, Capital		117,950.00
Total Liabilities and Capital		$187,950.00

3. Print the chart of accounts.

4. Print the December 31, 2011 balance sheet.

5. Back up. The suggested file name is **Exercise 12-1 Starting Balance Sheet.ptb**.

Accounts Payable

Follow the instructions below to set up vendor information.

1. From the Vendors & Purchases Navigation Center, click Vendors;
   Set up Vendor Defaults. Make sure the follow defaults are set. If not, set them up.

   Standard Terms: Due in number of days
   Net due in: 30 days

Discount in:	10 days
Discount %:	2.00
Credit Limit:	10,000.00
GL Link Accounts:	
Expense Account:	12000 Merchandise Inventory
Discount GL Account:	59500 Purchase Discounts

2. Click ; New Vendor. Set up the following vendors:

a.
Vendor ID:	**CPT12**
Name:	**Carson Phillips Tools**
Contact:	**Carson Phillips**
Mailing Address:	**2301 Thunderbird Avenue**
City, ST Zip	**Phoenix, AZ 85120**
Country:	**USA**
Vendor Type:	**tools**
1099 Type:	select Independent Contractor
Expense Account:	12000 Merchandise Inventory
Telephone 1:	**602-555-3832**
Fax:	**602-555-3834**
E-mail:	**info@carsonphillips.com**
Web Site:	**www.carsonphillips.com**

Purchase Info:

Tax ID Number:	**32-8844192**

b.
Vendor ID:	**SJH14**
Name:	**Sara Jensen Hardware**
Contact:	**Sara Jensen**
Mailing Address:	**3700 Highland Avenue**
City, ST Zip	**Los Angeles, CA 90036**
Country:	**USA**
Vendor Type:	**hardware**
1099 Type:	select Independent Contractor
Expense Account:	12000 Merchandise Inventory
Telephone 1:	**310-555-8311**

Fax:	**310-555-8313**
E-mail:	**info@jensenhardware.net**
Web Site:	**www.jensenhardware.net**
Purchase Info:	
Tax ID Number:	**68-7738812**

Inventory

Follow these steps to set up inventory defaults:

1. From the Inventory & Services Navigation Center, click , Set Up Inventory Defaults.

2. On the General tab, the Default Item Class field shows Stock item. If not, select Stock item.

3. Select the GL Accts/Costing tab. If necessary, set up Average as the inventory costing method (Stock item, Master Stock item, Assembly).

4. If necessary, select Account No. 45500, Shipping Charges. This GL Link is for Freight Charges in Sales/Invoicing.

5. Click ; New Inventory Item. Set up the following inventory stock items:

   a. | | | |
   |---|---|---|
   | | Item ID: | **002tools** |
   | | Description: | **tools** |
   | | Item Class: | Stock item |
   | | Description for Sales: | **tools** |
   | | Price Level 1: | **85** |
   | | Last Unit Cost: | **30** |
   | | Cost Method: | Average |
   | | GL Sales Acct: | **40200 Sales-Tools** |
   | | GL Inventory Acct: | **12000 Merchandise Inventory** |
   | | GL Cost of Sales Acct: | **50500 Cost of Sales-Tools** |

Item Tax Type:	1 Regular Taxable
Item Type:	**tools**
Stocking U/M:	**each**
Minimum Stock:	**10**
Reorder Quantity:	**4**
Preferred Vendor ID:	**CPT12, Carson Phillips Tools**

b.

Item ID:	**003hardware**
Description:	**hardware**
Item Class:	Stock item
Description for Sales:	**copper hardware**
Price Level 1:	**150**
Last Unit Cost:	**50**
Cost Method:	Average
GL Sales Acct:	**40000 Sales-Hardware**
GL Inventory Acct:	**12000 Merchandise Inventory**
Cost of Sales Acct:	**50000 Cost of Sales-Hardware**
Item Tax Type:	1 Regular Taxable
Item Type:	**hardware**
Stocking U/M:	**each**
Minimum Stock:	**10**
Reorder Quantity:	**4**
Preferred Vendor ID:	**SJH14, Sara Jensen Hardware**

6. Click on <u>B</u>eginning Balances. Record the beginning balances shown below.

Item ID	Description	Quantity	Unit Cost	Total Cost
002tools	tools	175	30	5,250.00
003hardware	hardware	190	50	9,500.00

7. Click [OK] .

8. Back up. The suggested file name is **Exercise 12-1.ptb**.

Exercise 12-2: Follow the instructions below to complete Exercise 12-2. Exercise 12-1 *must* be completed before starting Exercise 12-2.

1. If necessary, restore the Exercise 12-1.ptb file.[4]

2. Journalize and post the following transactions and print each check.

01/3/12   Invoice No. 480CP was received from Carson Phillips Tools for the purchase of 10 tool kits for a unit cost of $30.

01/5/12   Invoice No. SJH52 was received from Sara Jensen Hardware for the purchase of 8 hardware sets at a unit cost of $50.

01/6/12   Returned two tool kits to Carson Phillips Tools, Invoice No. 480CP. Paid $30 for each tool kit; VCM480CP.

01/10/12   Issued Caliber Bank Check No. 2020 to pay Sara Jensen Hardware for Invoice No. SJH52. (*Hint: Type the check number, 2020, in the Check Number field.*)

01/10/12   Issued Check No. 2021 to pay Carson Phillips Tools for merchandise purchased on January 3, less the January 6 return, Invoice No. 480CP. (*Hint: Remember to calculate, then type the correct discount amount in the Discount field.*)

01/13/12   Issued Check No. 2022 to Sally Caron for $125 for cleaning and maintenance.

01/16/12   Issued Check No. 2023 to the U.S. Post Office for $45.

01/16/12   Issued Check No. 2024 to Avenue Office Supplies for $145.72 for cell phone. (Debit Account No. 71000, Office Expense.)

---

[4]You can restore from your back up file even if *no* Peachtree company exists. From Peachtree's start up window, select File; Restore. Select the location of your backup file. On the Restore Wizard's Select Company window, select A New Company. The *A New Company* selection allows you to restore your backup data, bypassing the process of new company set up. For more information, refer to Troubleshooting on pages 299-300.

01/16/12   Issued Check No. 2025 to RDA Telephone for $46.65 to pay the telephone bill.

01/26/12   Issued Check No. 2026 to the owner of the business for $400.

3. Print the Purchase Journal.

4. Print the Cash Disbursements Journal.

5. Print the Vendor Ledgers.

6. Print the General Ledger Trial Balance.

    Check Your Figures:

10200, Caliber Bank:	$61,110.13
12000, Merchandise Inventory	15,390.00
20000, Accounts Payable	0.00
59500, Purchase Discounts	12.80

    mine is 61,110.43

7. Back up. The suggested file name is **Exercise 12-2.ptb**.

8. Export the following reports to Excel – Chart of Accounts, Purchase Journal, Cash Disbursements Journal, Vendor Ledgers, and General Ledger Trial balance. The suggested file name is **Exercise 12-2_ CofA _PJ_CDJ_VL_GLTB.xlsx**.

9. Save these files as PDFs: Chart of Accounts, Purchase Journal, Cash Disbursements Journal, Vendor Ledgers, and General Ledger Trial Balance. The suggested file name is **Exercise 12-2_Chart of Accounts.pdf**, etc.

ANALYSIS QUESTION

What is the balance in the Accounts Payable account, Cynthia's Service Merchandise? Why? (*Hint:* Remember, analysis questions refer to the company set up within the chapter, <u>not</u> the company set up in Exercise 12-1.)

ASSESSMENT RUBRIC

Complete the Assessment Rubric online at www.mhhe.com/yacht2012; Student Edition, select Chapter 12, Assessment Rubric link. To review Peachtree's navigation centers, menu selections, and windows, complete the blank fields online.

Date	Transaction	Navigation Center/Module	Task Window	Journal Dr./Cr.
1/3	Invoice No. 480CP was received from Carson Phillips Tools for the purchase of 10 tool kits for a unit cost of $30.			
1/6	Returned two tool kits to Carson Phillips Tools, Invoice No. 480CP. Paid $30 for each tool kit: VCM480CP.			
1/10	Issued Check No. 2021 to Carson Phillips Tools for merchandise purchased on January 3, less the January 6 return, Invoice No. 480CP.			

CHAPTER 12 INDEX

Chapter 13 Customers & Sales

LEARNING OBJECTIVES

1. Restore data from Chapter 12. (This backup was made on pages 481-482.)
2. Set up customer default information.
3. Set up sales tax information.
4. Set up customer maintenance information.
5. Record credit sales, cash sales, and sales returns.
6. Record customer receipts, partial payments, and edit invoices.
7. Make four backups, save two Excel files, and save three PDF files.[1]

In Chapter 12, you learned how to use PCA's Purchases/Receive Inventory and Payments features. Now that you have purchased merchandise from vendors, you are ready to sell that merchandise. To do that, you use PCA's Customers & Sales Navigation Center.

In Chapter 3, Customers, when you entered a sales invoice for Bellwether Garden Supply, the unit price, description, account number, and sales taxes were automatically calculated for you. (See pages 115-126.)

Before using the Sales/Invoicing window, you need to set up customer defaults, sales tax information, and customer maintenance information. After you set up these defaults, PCA will use this information when you record a sale.

Chapter 13 explains how PCA's accounts receivable system works. *Accounts receivable* are what customers owe your business. Credit transactions from customers are called *accounts receivable transactions*.

---

[1]For the size of files backed up and saved, refer to the chart on pages 426-427.

The McGraw-Hill Companies, Inc., *Computer Accounting with Peachtree by Sage Complete Accounting 2012, 16e*

Customer receipts work similarly to paying vendor invoices. When a customer pays an existing *invoice* there are two steps:

1. Enter the customer's ID code so that a list of existing invoices for the customer displays.

2. Select the invoice that applies to the customer's check, then select the Pay box.

This diagram illustrates PCA's accounts receivable system.

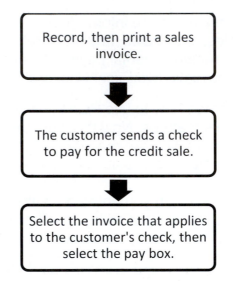

On the Customers & Sales Navigation Center, Peachtree illustrates the accounts receivable system. In Chapter 13, you work with customers, sales invoices, credits and returns, and receipts from customers.

The Customers & Sales Navigation Center shows the flow of customer-related tasks and takes you where you need to go to perform those tasks. In Peachtree, this represents the accounts receivable module or accounts receivable system.

The Customers & Sales workflow diagram is shown on the next page.

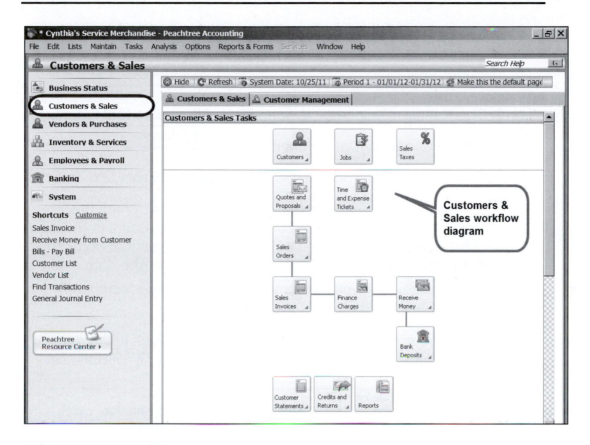

GETTING STARTED

1. Start Peachtree. Open Cynthia's Service Merchandise, or if you used a unique name, select it. This company was set up in Chapter 12 on pages 430–435. (*Hint:* If another company opens, click File; Open Previous Company, select Cynthia's [your name] Service Merchandise. Open one company.)

2. Follow these steps to restore data from Chapter 12. This file was backed up on pages 481-482.

    a. Insert your USB flash drive. From the System Navigation Center, click | Restore Now |.

    b. The Select Backup File window appears. Click | Browse |. In the Look in field, select the location of the Chapter 12.ptb file. Click | Open |, then | Next > |.

c. The Select Company window appears. The radio button next to An Existing Company is selected. Check that the Company Name and Location fields are correct. Click [Next >].

d. The Restore Options window appears. Make sure that the box next to Company Data is *checked*. Click [Next >].

e. The Confirmation window appears. Check the From and To fields to make sure they are correct. Click [Finish]. When the Restore Company scale is 100% complete, your data is restored. (*Hint:* The Student Version of Peachtree prompts that company data can be used for 14 months. After that time, the data expires. Click [OK]. Cynthia's (or your name) Service Merchandise opens.)

To make sure you are starting in the appropriate place in the data (Chapter 12.ptb backup) display the General Ledger Trial Balance.

*****EDUCATIONAL VERSION ONLY*****

Cynthia's Service Merchandise
General Ledger Trial Balance
As of Jan 31, 2012

Filter Criteria includes: Report order is by ID. Report is printed in Detail Format.

Account ID	Account Description	Debit Amt	Credit Amt
10200	Southwest Bank	71,235.17	
10400	Arizona Savings & Loan	22,000.00	
12000	Merchandise Inventory	28,938.00	
13000	Supplies	1,750.00	
14000	Prepaid Insurance	2,400.00	
15000	Furniture and Fixtures	5,000.00	
15100	Computers & Equipment	7,500.00	
15500	Building	100,000.00	
20000	Accounts Payable		300.00
27000	Long-Term Notes Payable		20,500.00
27400	Mortgage Payable		75,000.00
39006	Eric Lerette, Capital		72,195.00
39007	Eric Lerette, Drawing	500.00	
39008	Cynthia Barber, Capital		72,195.00
39009	Cynthia Barber, Drawing	500.00	
59500	Purchase Discounts		17.96
70000	Maintenance Expense	160.00	
73500	Postage Expense	45.00	
75500	Supplies Expense	107.65	
76000	Telephone Expense	72.14	
	Total:	**240,207.96**	**240,207.96**

This is the same trial balance shown in Chapter 12 on page 481.

Setting Up Customer Defaults

In Chapter 12, you entered General Ledger, Accounts Payable, and Inventory Item defaults. The directions that follow show how to enter customer defaults.

1. From the Navigation Bar, select  ;
    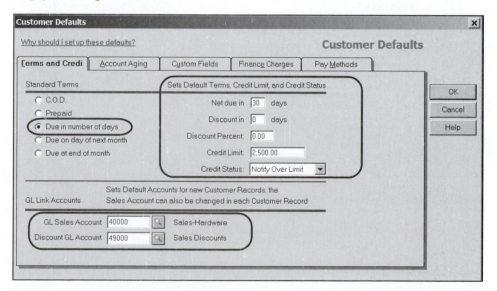 , Set Up Customer Defaults. The Customer Defaults window appears.

2. If necessary, click on the Discount % field. Type **0** (zero) in the Discount % field, then press **<Enter>**. Cynthia's Service Merchandise does *not* offer a discount to its credit customers.

3. If necessary, type **2500** in the Credit Limit field, press **<Enter>**.

4. Accept the default for GL Sales Account 40000, Sales-Hardware by pressing **<Enter>**. (When you set up individual customers, you will select a GL Sales Account for that customer.)

5. Accept the default for Discount GL Account 49000, Sales Discounts by pressing **<Enter>**.

Observe that the default for Standard Terms is Due in number of days.

6. Click OK .

Setting Up Sales Tax Defaults

You can enter sales tax default information for these areas:

➢ Sales Tax Authorities: codes for governments or other tax authorities and their tax rates. These are used to assemble the sales tax codes.

➢ Sales Tax Codes: the overall rate applied to taxable items on invoices to customers. This is composed of rates entered as Sales Tax Authorities.

Follow these steps to set up sales tax defaults.

1. From the Customers & Sales Navigation Center, click Sales Taxes . The Sales Taxes window appears. Set up a new sales tax is the default.

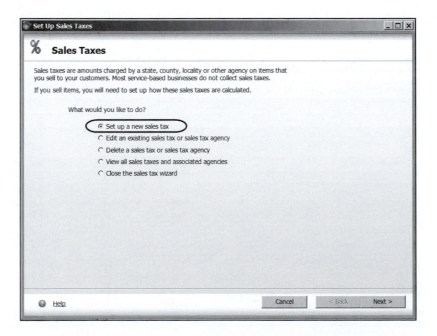

2. Click [Next >]. The Set Up New Sales Tax window appears.

3. Type **8.00**% in the What is the total rate that you will charge? Press <Enter>. Accept the default for 1 in the How many individual rates make up this total rate? field.

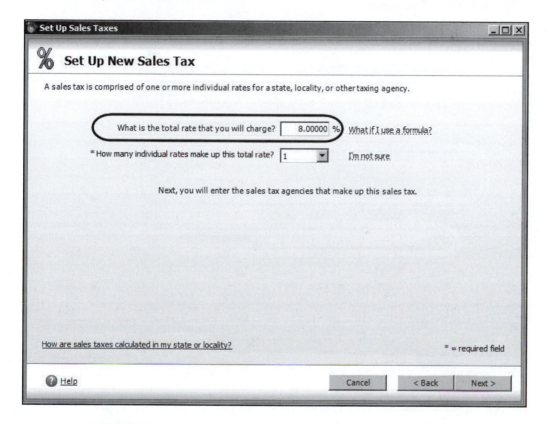

4. Click [Next >]. The Add Sales Tax Agency window appears.

5. Type **AZ** in the Sales tax agency ID field. Press **<Enter>**.

6. Type **Arizona Dept. of Revenue** in the Sales tax agency name field.

7. Accept the default by single rate in the How are sales taxes calculated for this agency? field.

8. Type **8.00**% in the Rate field. Press **<Enter>**.

9. Select Account No. 23100, Sales Tax Payable in the Select an account to track sales taxes field. Press **<Enter>**.

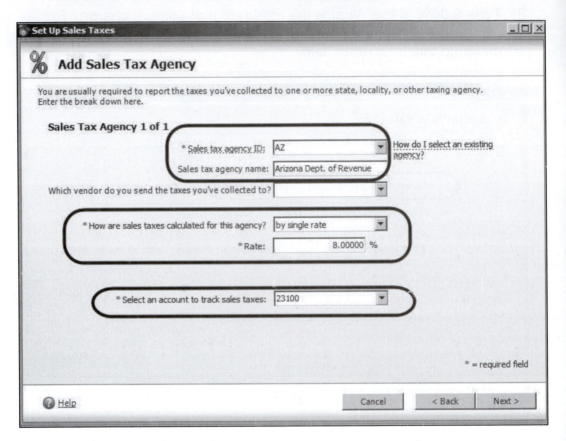

10. Click [Next >]. The Sales Tax Entered window appears.

11. Type **AZ** in the Sales Tax ID field. Press **<Enter>**.

12. Type **Arizona sales tax** in the Sales tax name field. Compare your Sales Tax Entered window to the one shown on the next page.

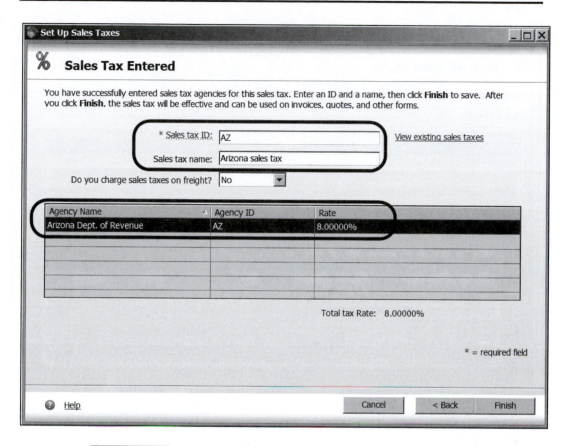

13. Click [Finish]. The Sales Taxes window appears. To make sure
    you have set up sales taxes for Cynthia's Service Merchandise
    select View all sales taxes and associated agencies. Click
    [Next >].

14. The View All Sales Taxes window appears and shows the sales tax
    that was set up on pages 502-505. The 8.00% sales tax rate for
    Arizona is shown. Compare your View All Sales Taxes window with
    the one shown on the next page.

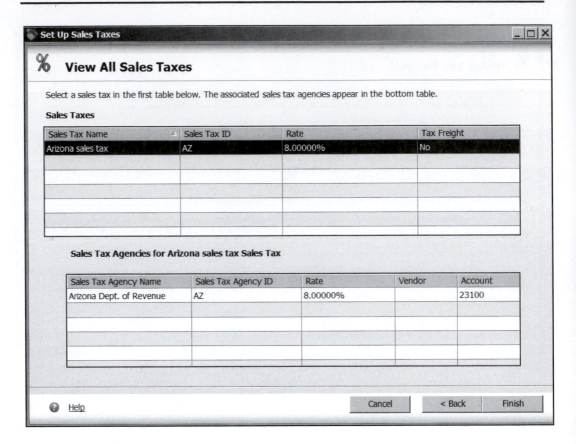

15. Click Finish . Click ☒ on the title bar to close the Set Up Sales Taxes window.

Setting Up Customer Maintenance Information

To enter default information about your customers, follow these steps:

1. Select Customers ; New Customer. The Maintain Customers/Prospects window appears.

2. Complete the following fields.

   Customer ID: **ap001** (Use lowercase letters and zeroes)
   Name: **Aileen Parker**
   Billing Address: **490 Northern Avenue**
   City, ST Zip: **Phoenix, AZ 85603**

Country: **USA**
Sales Tax: Select AZ (for Arizona sales tax)
Customer Type: **MAR**[2]
Telephone 1:   **602-555-1889**
Fax: **602-555-1901**
E-mail: **ap@phoenix.com**
Web Site: **www.phoenix.com/aileen**

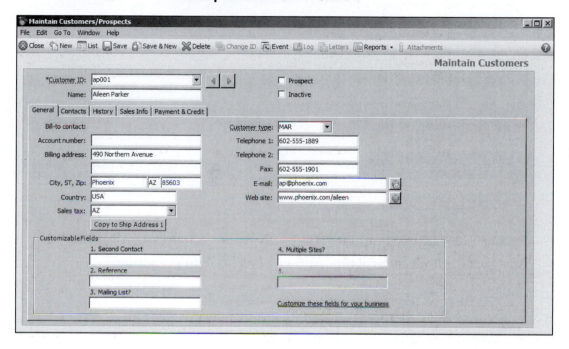

3. Click on the Sales Info tab.

4. In the GL Sales Acct field, if necessary, select Account No. 40000, Sales-Hardware.

---

[2]It is important to indicate Customer Type. This groups similar customers together. In this case, customers from Phoenix (MAR) are grouped together. MAR is an abbreviation of Maricopa County.

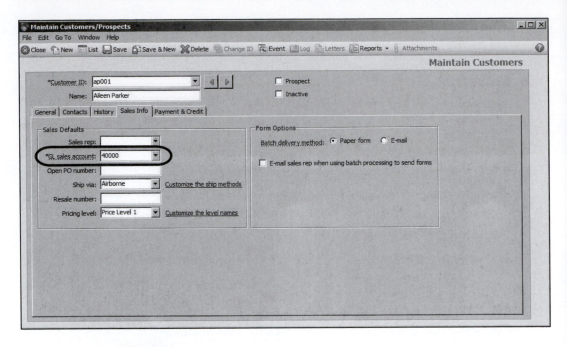

5. Click .

6. Click on the General tab. Add in the following customers.

> **Customer ID:** **bb002**
> Name: **Betty Barlow**
> Billing Address: **4113 Broadway**
> City, ST Zip: **Phoenix, AZ 85302**
> Country: **USA**
> Sales Tax: **AZ**
> Customer Type: **MAR**
> Telephone 1: **602-555-0632**
> Fax: **602-555-3203**
> E-mail: **betty@mail.com**
> Web Site: **www.mail.com/barlow**

> In the Sales Info tab, select the GL Sales Acct 40200,
> Sales-Wall for Betty Barlow.

> **Customer ID:** **dc003**
> Name: **Diane Conlin**
> Billing Address: **78898 W. Farrington Rd.**

City, ST Zip: **Ft. Lauderdale, FL 33074**
Country: **USA**
Sales Tax: Skip this field--see footnote.[3]
Customer Type: **FL**
Telephone 1:   **954-555-5955**
Fax: **954-555-5965**
E-mail: **diane@mail.net**
Web Site: **www.mail.net/dianeC**

In the Sales Info tab, select the GL Sales Acct 40400, Sales-Floor for Diane Conlin.

Customer ID: **jp004**
Name: **Joann Poe**
Billing Address: **8009 School Street**
City, ST Zip: **Phoenix, AZ 85221**
Country: **USA**
Sales Tax: **AZ**
Customer Type: **MAR**
Telephone 1:   **602-555-2389**
Fax: **602-555-3290**
E-mail: **poe@phxmail.com**
Web Site: **www.phxmail.com/joann**

In the Sales Info tab, select the GL Sales Acct 40000, Sales-Hardware for Joann Poe.

Customer ID: **pm005**
Name: **Paul Moore**
Billing Address: **799 East 14th Street**
City, ST Zip: **Phoenix, AZ 85002**
Country: **USA**
Sales Tax: **AZ**
Customer Type: **MAR**
Telephone 1:   **602-555-9412**
Fax: **602-555-9414**
E-mail: **paul@mymail.com**
Web Site: **www.mymail.com/paul**

---

[3]Since this customer is out of state, there is no Sales Tax.

In the Sales Info tab, select the GL Sales Acct 40200, Sales-Wall for Paul Moore. Close the Maintain Customers/Prospects window.

BACKING UP YOUR DATA

Follow these steps to back up Chapter 13 data:

1. If necessary, insert your USB flash drive. From the System Navigation Center, click [Back Up Now]. Make sure the box next to include company name in the backup file name is *unchecked.*

2. Click [Back Up].

3. Go to the location of your USB drive. (Or, backup to another location.) Type **Chapter 13 Begin** in the File name field.

4. Click [Save].

5. When the window prompts that This company backup will require approximately 1 diskette, click on [OK]. When the window prompts Please insert the first disk, click [OK]. When the Back Up Company scale is 100% complete, you have successfully backed up to the current point in Chapter 13. (If you are backing up to the default or another location, this step will differ slightly.)

RECORDING SALES

Two types of sales are entered in PCA:

> ➢ Credit sales or invoiced sales—sales where you enter an invoice.
> ➢ Cash sales—sales where you do not enter an invoice.

In PCA, all the information about a sale is recorded on the Sales/ Invoicing window. Then, PCA takes the necessary information from the window and automatically journalizes the transaction in the *sales journal*. Only sales on account are recorded in the sales journal. You can also print sales invoices.

Cash sales are entered on the Receipts window. Then, PCA takes the necessary information from the window and automatically journalizes the transaction in the *cash receipts journal*.

On the Sales/Invoicing window, enter invoices for the customers stored in PCA's customer file. You entered five credit customers for Cynthia's Service Merchandise. (Click [Refresh] on the Customers & Sales Navigation Center to see the customer list.)

Customers			View Detailed List
Customer ID △	Customer Name	Telephone 1	Balance
ap001	Aileen Parker	602-555-1889	$0.00
bb002	Betty Barlow	602-555-0632	$0.00
dc003	Diane Conlin	954-555-5955	$0.00
jp004	Joann Poe	602-555-2389	$0.00
pm005	Paul Moore	602-555-9412	$0.00

All journal entries made to the Sales Journal (Sales/Invoicing window) are posted both to the General Ledger and to the Customer Ledger or **Accounts Receivable Ledger**. You can apply transactions to inventory items and jobs.

Entering sales works hand in hand with entering receipts. Once an invoice is posted it is simple to show that a customer has paid. Just display the appropriate invoice and click on the Pay box. PCA takes care of all the correct accounting distributions for you.

▶ **Entering Invoices for Credit Sales** (Remember, the icon means there is a flash video at www.mhhe.com/yacht2012.)

In the steps that follow, you record the following transaction:

Date   *Transaction Description*

01/06/12   Sold two doorknobs on account to Aileen Parker; $324 ($300 plus $24, sales tax). (*Hint: Doorknobs are classified as hardware.*)

1. From the Customers & Sales Navigation Center, select [Sales Invoices ▴]; New Sales Invoice. The Sales/Invoicing window appears.

2. Your cursor is in the <u>C</u>ustomer ID field. Click [🔍] and select **Aileen Parker**. PCA supplies the customer default information: billing

address, payment terms, GL account default, A/R Account default, and the sales tax code. (*Hint: If the GL Account field and A/R Account field do* not *display Account Nos. 40000 and 11000, refer step 1, pages xvi-xvii. The Hide General Ledger Accounts boxes should be unchecked.*)

3. Type **6** in the Date field and press **<Enter>**. Since the invoice is printed later, skip the Invoice # field. When the invoice is printed, PCA automatically numbers the invoices.

4. Click on the Quantity field, type **2** and press **<Enter>**.

5. In the Item field, click 🔍. Select **001hardware** for hardware.

6. In the Description field, type **Two doorknobs** and press **<Enter>**. Notice that the GL Account,[4] Unit Price, Amount field, A/R Account, and Sales Tax Code are automatically completed.

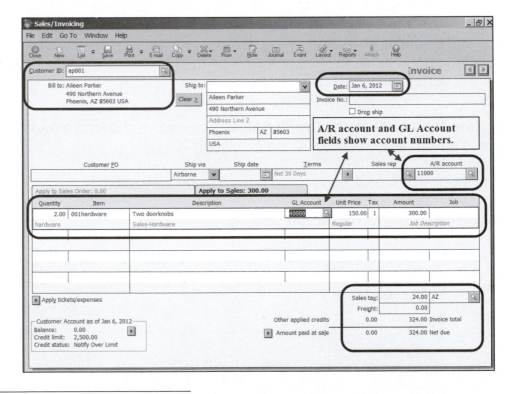

---

[4]If the G/L Account field and A/R Account fields are *not* displayed on your Sales/Invoicing window, click on Options, Global. Make sure the boxes in the Hide General Ledger Accounts section are unchecked.

Printing Sales Invoices

When you print the sales invoice, it also posts the transaction to the
Sales Journal. To print this sales invoice, follow these steps:

1. Click .

2. The Print Forms: Invoices window appears. Click Select Form .

3. The Print Forms: Invoices/Pkg. Slips window appears. If necessary,
   select Invoice.

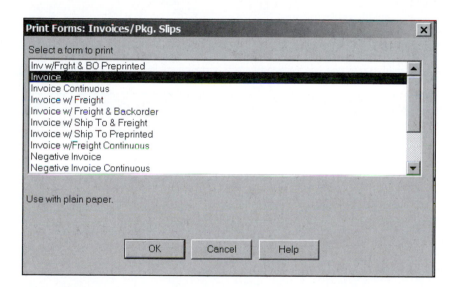

4. Click OK .

5. The Print Forms: Invoices window appears. The First invoice number
   field shows 101. PCA numbers subsequent invoices consecutively.
   The Use this form field shows Invoice.

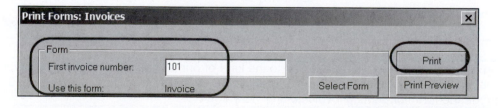

6. Click [Print]. The invoice starts to print. (*Hint:* When you print the invoice, it also posts to the sales journal.)

Cynthia's Service Merchandise
2117 Oak Street
Tempe, AZ 85281
USA

INVOICE

Invoice Number: 101
Invoice Date: Jan 6, 2012
Page: 1

Voice: 480-555-9900
Fax: 480-555-9902

Bill To:	Ship to:
Aileen Parker 490 Northern Avenue Phoenix, AZ 85603 USA	Aileen Parker 490 Northern Avenue Phoenix, AZ 85603 USA

Customer ID	Customer PO	Payment Terms	
ap001		Net 30 Days	
Sales Rep ID	**Shipping Method**	**Ship Date**	**Due Date**
	Airborne		2/5/12

Quantity	Item	Description	Unit Price	Amount
2.00	001hardware	Two doorknobs	150.00	300.00
			Subtotal	300.00
			Sales Tax	24.00
			Total Invoice Amount	324.00
Check/Credit Memo No:			Payment/Credit Applied	
			TOTAL	**324.00**

Comment: The form you select is tied to the kind of printer you are using. If your invoice does not print, you should select a different form to print. Refer to step 2 on page 513 to change the form for printing invoices.

7. The Sales/Invoicing window is ready for the next sales invoice. (*Hint:* When you printed the invoice, the transaction was posted to the sales journal, accounts receivable account in the general ledger, and customer account in the customer ledger. Once the transaction is posted, cost of sales is also calculated.)

8. Record the following credit sales in the Sales/Invoicing window:

Date   *Transaction Description*

01/06/12   Sold four rolls of vinyl flooring on account to Diane Conlin. Print Invoice No. 102. (*Hint: Vinyl flooring is classified as floor. Ms. Conlin's sales invoice shows no tax because this sale is made to an out-of-state customer.*)

Cynthia's Service Merchandise
2117 Oak Street
Tempe, AZ 85281
USA

Voice: 480-555-9900
Fax: 480-555-9902

INVOICE

Invoice Number: 102
Invoice Date: Jan 6, 2012
Page: 1

Bill To:	Ship to:
Diane Conlin 78898 W. Farrington Rd. Ft. Lauderdale, FL 33074 USA	Diane Conlin 78898 W. Farrington Rd. Ft. Lauderdale, FL 33074 USA

Customer ID	Customer PO	Payment Terms	
dc003		Net 30 Days	
Sales Rep ID	**Shipping Method**	**Ship Date**	**Due Date**
	Airborne		2/5/12

Quantity	Item	Description	Unit Price	Amount
4.00	003floor	Four rolls of vinyl flooring	160.00	640.00

Subtotal		640.00
Sales Tax		
Total Invoice Amount		640.00
Payment/Credit Applied		
TOTAL		**640.00**

Check/Credit Memo No.

Date   *Transaction Description*

01/06/12   Sold four pairs of curtains on account to Paul Moore. Print
                  Invoice No.103. (*Hint: Curtains are classified as wall.*)

Cynthia's Service Merchandise
2117 Oak Street
Tempe, AZ 85281
USA

INVOICE

Invoice Number: 103
Invoice Date: Jan 6, 2012
Page: 1

Voice: 480-555-9900
Fax: 480-555-9902

Bill To:	Ship to:
Paul Moore 799 East 14th Street Phoenix, AZ 85002 USA	Paul Moore 799 East 14th Street Phoenix, AZ 85002 USA

Customer ID	Customer PO	Payment Terms	
pm005		Net 30 Days	
Sales Rep ID	**Shipping Method**	**Ship Date**	**Due Date**
	Airborne		2/5/12

Quantity	Item	Description	Unit Price	Amount
4.00	002wall	Four pairs of curtains	100.00	400.00

Subtotal		400.00
Sales Tax		32.00
Total Invoice Amount		432.00
Payment/Credit Applied		
TOTAL		**432.00**

Check/Credit Memo No:

Date | Transaction Description

01/06/12   Sold three curtain rods on account to Joann Poe. Print
            Invoice No. 104. (*Hint: Curtain rods are classified as
            hardware.*)

Cynthia's Service Merchandise
2117 Oak Street
Tempe, AZ 85281
USA

Voice: 480-555-9900
Fax: 480-555-9902

INVOICE

Invoice Number: 104
Invoice Date: Jan 6, 2012
Page: 1

Bill To:	Ship to:
Joann Poe 8009 School Street Phoenix, AZ 85221 USA	Joann Poe 8009 School Street Phoenix, AZ 85221 USA

Customer ID	Customer PO	Payment Terms
jp004		Net 30 Days

Sales Rep ID	Shipping Method	Ship Date	Due Date
	Airborne		2/5/12

Quantity	Item	Description	Unit Price	Amount
3.00	001hardware	Three curtain rods	150.00	450.00

Subtotal	450.00
Sales Tax	36.00
Total Invoice Amount	486.00
Payment/Credit Applied	
TOTAL	**486.00**

Check/Credit Memo No:

Entering a Service Invoice

Cynthia's Service Merchandise sells and repairs household items. When repairs are done, a *service invoice* is used. A service invoice is an alternative to the standard invoice. It is used when you want to create an invoice without inventory items.

Follow these steps to enter a service invoice:

Date	Transaction Description
01/10/12	Repaired curtains for Betty Barlow, $49.89, plus sales tax of $3.99, for a total of $53.88.

1. From the Sales/Invoicing window, click [Layout]. Then select <Predefined> Service.

   The Sales/Invoicing window changes to include only the information necessary for a service invoice. This means that you no longer can select inventory items. When you complete the service transaction, click [Layout] again. Then, you are ready to enter an inventory sale on the Sales/Invoicing window.

2. In the Customer ID field, select Betty Barlow.

3. Type **10** in the Date field, then press **<Enter>**.

4. Click on the Description field. Type **Repair** and press **<Enter>**.

5. In the GL Account field, select Account No. 40600, Service Fees.

6. Type **49.89** in the Amount field. Compare your Sales/Invoicing window to the one shown on the next page.

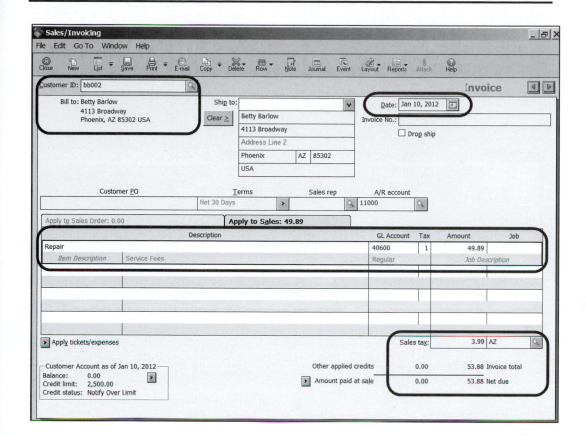

7. Print Invoice No. 105 and compare it to the one shown on the next
    page.

Cynthia's Service Merchandise
2117 Oak Street
Tempe, AZ 85281
USA

Voice: 480-555-9900
Fax: 480-555-9902

INVOICE

Invoice Number: 105
Invoice Date: Jan 10, 2012
Page: 1

Bill To:	Ship to:
Betty Barlow 4113 Broadway Phoenix, AZ 85302 USA	Betty Barlow 4113 Broadway Phoenix, AZ 85302 USA

Customer ID	Customer PO	Payment Terms	
bb002		Net 30 Days	
Sales Rep ID	**Shipping Method**	**Ship Date**	**Due Date**
	Airborne		2/9/12

Quantity	Item	Description	Unit Price	Amount
		Repair		49.89
			Subtotal	49.89
			Sales Tax	3.99
			Total Invoice Amount	53.88
Check/Credit Memo No:			Payment/Credit Applied	
			TOTAL	**53.88**

8. Click , then <Predefined> Product. Click [Close] .

Sales Returns: Credits & Returns

A sales return, or credit memo, is used when merchandise is returned by a customer. Credit memos for sales returns are entered similarly to vendor credit memos.

Before you can apply a credit, you must post the invoice. Invoice Nos. 101–105 were posted to the sales journal when you printed the sales invoices (see pages 514-520). This work must be completed *before* you can apply a sales return. When a credit memo is entered, select the customer's ID code and the appropriate invoice number. Then, the return will be applied to that invoice and the customer's account balance will be adjusted.

In the steps that follow, you record the following transaction:

Date	Transaction Description
01/13/12	Paul Moore returned one pair of curtains that he purchased on January 6, Invoice No. 103. He also paid the balance of that invoice.

1. From the Customers & Sales Navigation Center, select ; New Credit Memo.

2. In the Customer ID field, select Paul Moore.

3. In the Date field, type **13** and press **<Enter>**.

4. Type **CM103** in the Credit No. field. (CM is an abbreviation for Credit Memo; use the sales invoice number to identify the credit memo.) Press **<Enter>**.

5. The Apply to Invoice No. tab is selected. Click on the down-arrow and select 103.

6. Type **1** in the Returned field. Press **<Enter>**

7. Type **Returned one pair of curtains** in the Description field.

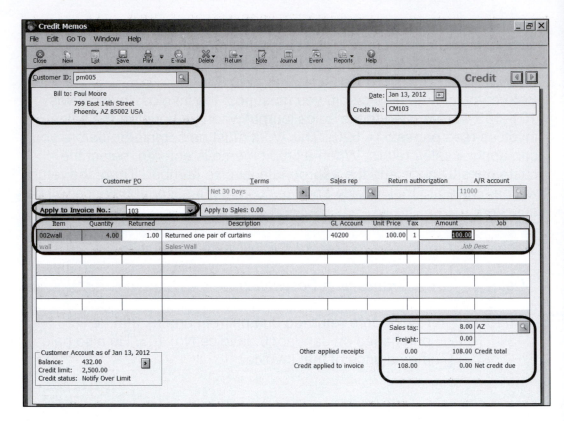

8. Click ![Save] to post, then click ![Close].

Apply a sales return: Follow these steps:

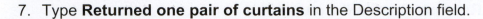

1. From the Customers & Sales Navigation Center, select ![Receive Money];
   Receive Money From Customer. At the Select a Cash Account
   window, accept the default for Southwest Bank by clicking ![OK].

2. Type **01/13/12** in the Deposit ticket ID field. Press **<Enter>**.

3. In the Customer ID field, select Paul Moore.

4. In the Reference field, type **Invoice 103** then press the **<Enter>** key two times.

5. In the Date field, type **13**, then press the **<Enter>** key two times.

6. Observe that the Payment Method field displays Check; and that the Cash Account field displays Account No. 10200, Southwest Bank. In the Apply to Invoices list, click on the Pay box. Observe that the Receipt Amount shown is 324.00 ($432 original invoice - $108, return).

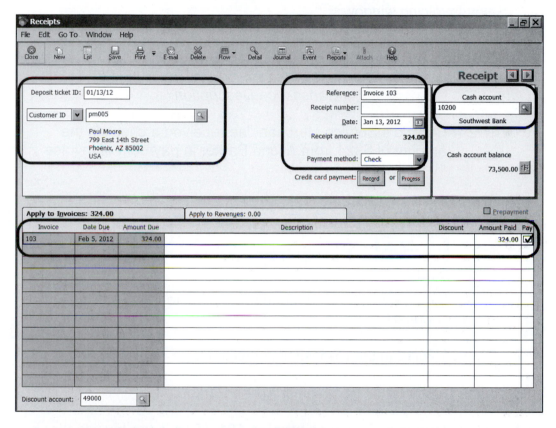

7. Click ![Save] to post, then click ![Close].

RECORDING RECEIPTS AND CASH SALES

The Receipts window is used for recording checks, cash, and credit card sales that are received and deposited in the checking account. Then, PCA takes the necessary information from the Receipts window and automatically journalizes the transactions in the Cash Receipts Journal. If the receipt is from a credit customer, then the receipt is posted to the customer's subsidiary ledger as well.

There are two categories for receipts that result from sales:

➤ Receipts for which an invoice was entered in the Sales/Invoicing window.

➤ Direct sales receipts for which no invoice was entered in the Sales/Invoicing window.

▶ Entering A Receipt

Date   *Transaction Description*

01/20/12   Cynthia's Service Merchandise received a check in the amount of $324 from Aileen Parker in payment of Invoice 101.

Follow these steps to enter this receipt:

1. Select ; Receive Money From Customer. The Receipts window appears.

2. Type **01/20/12** in the Deposit ticket ID field.

3. In the Customer ID field, select Aileen Parker.

4. In the Reference field, type **Invoice 101**. (This is the Invoice that is being paid.) Press the **<Enter>** key two times.

5. Type **20** in the Date field.

6. Verify that Account No. 10200, Southwest Bank, is displayed in the Cash Account field. The Apply to Invoices tab is selected. Click on the Pay box for Invoice 101. Compare your Receipts window to the one shown on the next page.

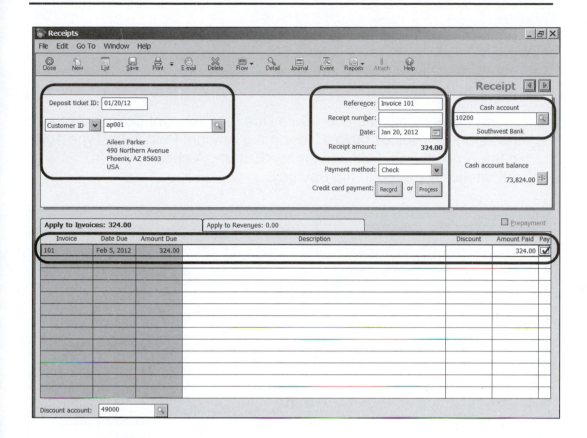

7. Click ![Save] to post this receipt. The Receipts window is ready for another transaction.

In the preceding steps, each customer paid the invoice in full. What if a customer made a partial payment on an invoice?

Date   *Transaction Description*

01/23/12   Joann Poe paid $105 on account, Invoice No. 104.

Follow these steps for partial payment:

1. The Receipts window should be displayed. Type **01/23/12** in the Deposit ticket ID field.

2. Select Joann Poe as the customer.

3. Type **Invoice 104** in the Reference field. Press the **<Enter>** key two times.

4. Type **23** in the Date field.

5. Joann Poe's Invoice number, Date Due, and Amount Due display in the Apply to Invoices table. Click on the Amount Paid field. Type **105** in the Amount Paid field and press **<Enter>**. A check mark is automatically placed in the Pay box.

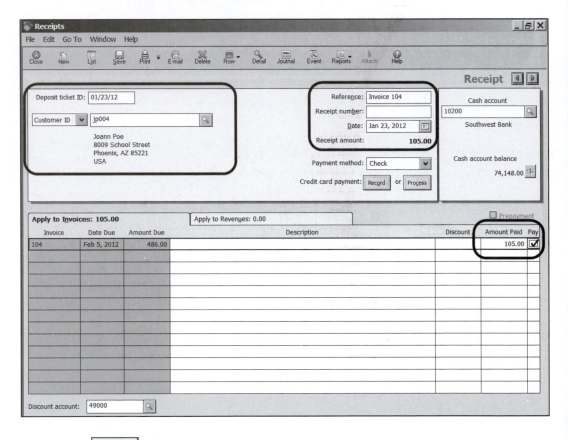

6. Click [Save] to post.

Enter the following receipts:

Date	Transaction Description
Date	*Transaction Description*

01/27/12   Received a check in the amount of $53.88 from Betty Barlow in full payment of Invoice No. 105.

01/27/12   Received a check in the amount of $640 from Diane Conlin in full payment of Invoice No. 102.

Cash Sales

Follow these steps to record a cash sale.

Date	Transaction Description
Date	*Transaction Description*

01/29/12   Sold two pairs of curtains for cash to Barbara Williams, $200.

1. On the Receipts window, type **01/30/12** in the Deposit ticket ID field.

2. Click on the Name field, then type **Barbara Williams**. You do not enter address information for a cash sale.

3. Since this is a cash sale, type **Cash** in the Reference field. Press **<Enter>** two times.

4. Type **30** as the date.

5. Verify that account 10200, Southwest Bank, is displayed in the Cash Account field.

6. Make sure that the Apply to Revenues tab is selected.

   PCA assumes you are going to apply the receipt to revenue unless you select a customer with open invoices.

   You can also apply a portion of the receipt to both invoices and revenue. You do this by selecting each heading, then entering the distribution information for that portion of the receipt. A running subtotal is kept to show how much of the receipt has been applied.

7. Type **2** in the Quantity field.

8. Select 002wall as the inventory item.

9. Type **Two pairs of curtains** as the Description and press the **<Enter>** key.

10. Observe that the GL Account field, shows Account No. 40200, Sales-Wall (this is the default account). (*Hint:* Make sure the correct sales account is selected.)

11. In the Sales Tax field, select AZ. Observe that 16.00 is automatically calculated in the Sales Tax field.

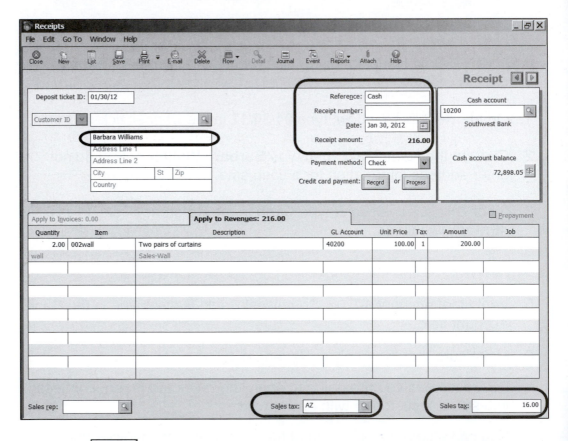

12. Click [Save], then close the Receipts window.

Finance Charges

PCA includes a feature in the Tasks menu for computing finance or interest charges. This option computes and applies finance charges for customers and/or prints a report listing all finance charges.

You use this feature by selecting the Finance Charge option. You may want to try this out on your own. Use the Tasks menu and select Finance Charge to see how this feature works.

PRINTING CUSTOMER FORMS

PCA provides forms for the following types of customer correspondence:

➢ Invoices.

➢ Statements.

➢ Mailing labels.

➢ Collection letters.

These reports can be accessed by selecting Reports & Forms from the menu bar, then Forms. Select a predefined form to print customer information or design your own form. In Part 4 of this book you will learn more about Custom Forms.

Printing Invoices

You can print a single invoice from the Sales/Invoicing window by selecting ⊟Print▾. This saves and prints the invoice.

A batch of invoices can be printed from the Reports & Forms menu by selecting Forms, then Invoices and Packing Slips. There are several types of predefined invoices available for printing customer information or you can design your own form.

Printing Statements

The information that is printed on customer statements is defined in the Statement/Invoices Defaults which are set up from the Maintain menu. You can set up collection letters and also select from these print options.

➢ Whether to print your company name, address, phone, and fax on the statement.

➢ Whether to print zero and credit balance statements.

➢ The minimum balance necessary to print a statement.

➢ The number of grace days before printing a statement.

➢ Whether to print statements for accounts with no activity.

You can print or display statements. Or, if you want to display customer information before printing, display or print the customer ledger.

Statements can be printed from the Reports & Forms menu by selecting Forms, then Invoices and Packing Slips. There are several types of predefined statements available for printing customer account balances. Select the form that best suits your needs. As mentioned before, you can also design your own statement.

When the statements stop printing, a message box displays, asking if the statements printed okay and if you want to update the customer file. Look at your printed statements carefully before you answer Yes to this question. When you answer Yes, PCA records the statement date in the customer record. This is used as the balance brought forward date the next time you print a statement. This way the ending balance on one statement is the same as the beginning balance on the next statement.

You should enter, print, and post all invoices prior to printing statements. In this way the Balance Forward amounts are correct from month to month.

Printing Mailing Labels

Labels can be printed by selecting the Reports & Forms menu, Accounts Receivable, Forms, then Customer Labels and Letters. Select one of Customer Labels, then print. There are several predefined labels available for printing. You can elect to use these forms or design your own. When printing labels you can do the following.

➢ Select a range of customers.

➢ Enter all or part of a Zip code to limit the mailing labels to customers in a certain area.

> Print labels for customers, prospects, or both.

> Enter a Status for customers so that you print labels for all, active, or inactive customers.

> Enter a Type Code for customers so that only customers of a specific Type Code will print.

Preparing Collection Letters

What if credit customers are slow to pay their bills? Collection letters can play an important role in generating revenue from customers who are slow to pay off their balances. Sometimes just a friendly reminder is all that is needed.

The table below shows how important it is to get paid on time because the longer a bill remains unpaid, the less chance there is of collecting.

Number of Days Overdue	Percent Uncollectible
1 to 30 days	2%
31 to 60 days	10%
61 to 90 days	20%
91 to 180 days	30%
181 to 365 days	50%
over 365 days	90%

Collection letters are an effective way to remind customers to pay their unpaid balances. Most customers will pay after they receive a friendly reminder of a past-due account. It is worthwhile to send these letters because past-due amounts can be a burden on a company's cash flow.

Depending on how late the payment is, collection letters vary in tone and urgency. For example, a friendly reminder may be all that's needed for someone who is 30 days past due, but a different letter may be needed for someone who is more than 90 days past due. Remember that while it is important to collect past-due amounts, you would also like to keep the customer.

PCA's letters are grouped by lateness of payment and severity of tone. The less than 30 days overdue letter is soft while the 61-90 days overdue letter is much firmer. You may edit all of these letters to suit your needs.

To print a collection letter you use the analysis menu. Follow these steps to do that:

1. From the menu bar, click on Analysis, then Collection Manager.

2. Type **01/31/12** in the As of Date field. Press **<Enter>**. The Collection Aging bar graph appears.

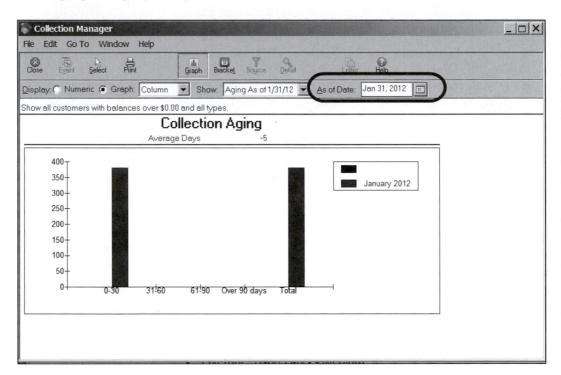

3. Click [Bracket]. The Total Bracket table lists an invoice for Joann Poe.

4. Click on the Letter box on the Total Bracket table to place a check

	Total Bracket					
Age	Name	Ref	Document Date	Due Date	Total Amount	Letter
-5	Joann Poe	104	1/6/12	2/5/12	381.00	☑

mark in it [table]. Then, click [Letter].

5. The Print Forms: Collection Letters window appears. Click
    Select Form . You may want to try one of these selections and see
    what Peachtree's collection letters look like. The sample letters are
    sorted as follows.

    ➤ Overdue < 30 Days - Soft
    ➤ Overdue >90 Days
    ➤ Overdue >90 Days - Coll Agency
    ➤ Overdue 31-60 Days - Medium
    ➤ Overdue 61-90 Days - Firm

6. Select a form to print, then click OK .

7. Click Print . A collection letter prints. Read the letter that you
    printed. The collection letter that prints is an example. When the
    window prompts, Did the collection letters print properly?, click
    Yes . Since Ms. Poe does *not* have an overdue bill, no
    amount shows in the letter's Amount Overdue field.

8. Close the Collection Manager.

PRINTING THE SALES JOURNAL

The Sales/Invoicing window is the Sales Journal. Credit sales are
recorded in the Sales/Invoicing window. Follow these steps to print the
Sales Journal:

1. From the Recently Used Customer Reports area on the Customers &
    Sales Navigation Center, link to Print the Sales Journal.

2. The Modify Report – Sales Journal window appears. Click
    OK . Make the selections to print. Compare your sales
    journal report to the one shown on the next page.

*****EDUCATIONAL VERSION ONLY*****

Cynthia's Service Merchandise
Sales Journal
For the Period From Jan 1, 2012 to Jan 31, 2012

Filter Criteria includes: Report order is by Invoice/CM Date. Report is printed in Detail Format.

Date	Account ID	Invoice/CM #	Line Description	Debit Amnt	Credit Amnt
1/6/12	23100	101	AZ: Arizona Dept. of Revenue		24.00
	40000		Two doorknobs		300.00
	50000		Cost of sales	100.00	
	12000		Cost of sales		100.00
	11000		Aileen Parker	324.00	
1/6/12	40400	102	Four rolls of vinyl flooring		640.00
	57000		Cost of sales	216.00	
	12000		Cost of sales		216.00
	11000		Diane Conlin	640.00	
1/6/12	23100	103	AZ: Arizona Dept. of Revenue		32.00
	40200		Four pairs of curtains		400.00
	50500		Cost of sales	120.00	
	12000		Cost of sales		120.00
	11000		Paul Moore	432.00	
1/6/12	23100	104	AZ: Arizona Dept. of Revenue		36.00
	40000		Three curtain rods		450.00
	50000		Cost of sales	150.00	
	12000		Cost of sales		150.00
	11000		Joann Poe	486.00	
1/10/12	23100	105	AZ: Arizona Dept. of Revenue		3.99
	40600		Repair		49.89
	11000		Betty Barlow	53.88	
1/13/12	23100	CM103	AZ: Arizona Dept. of Revenue	8.00	
	40200		Returned one pair of curtains	100.00	
	50500		Cost of sales		30.00
	12000		Cost of sales	30.00	
	11000		Paul Moore		108.00
		Total		**2,659.88**	**2,659.88**

PRINTING THE CASH RECEIPTS JOURNAL

In PCA, the Receipts window is the Cash Receipts Journal. Payments from customers and cash sales are recorded in the Receipts window. Follow these steps to print the Cash Receipts Journal.

1. From the Recently Used Customer Reports area on the Customers & Sales Navigation Center, link to <u>Print</u> the Cash Receipts Journal. If the Cash Receipts Journal is not listed, link to <u>View All Customer & Sales Reports</u>. (Or, from the menu bar select Reports, then Accounts Receivable, then highlight Cash Receipts Journal.)

2. The Modify Report - Cash Receipts Journal window displays. Click

    | OK |

    . Make the selections to print.

```
*****EDUCATIONAL VERSION ONLY*****
                                        Cynthia's Service Merchandise
                                             Cash Receipts Journal
                                  For the Period From Jan 1, 2012 to Jan 31, 2012
Filter Criteria includes: Report order is by Check Date. Report is printed in Detail Format.
```

Date	Account ID	Transaction Ref	Line Description	Debit Amnt	Credit Amnt
1/13/12	11000	Invoice 103	Invoice: 103		324.00
	10200		Paul Moore	324.00	
1/20/12	11000	Invoice 101	Invoice: 101		324.00
	10200		Aileen Parker	324.00	
1/23/12	11000	Invoice 104	Invoice: 104		105.00
	10200		Joann Poe	105.00	
1/27/12	11000	Invoice 105	Invoice: 105		53.88
	10200		Betty Barlow	53.88	
1/27/12	11000	Invoice 102	Invoice: 102		640.00
	10200		Diane Conlin	640.00	
1/30/12	23100	Cash	AZ: Arizona Dept. of Revenue		16.00
	40200		Two pairs of curtains		200.00
	50500		Cost of sales	60.00	
	12000		Cost of sales		60.00
	10200		Barbara Williams	216.00	
				1,722.88	1,722.88

PRINTING THE CUSTOMER LEDGERS

Follow these steps to print the Customer Ledgers for Cynthia's Service Merchandise:

1. From the Recently Used Customer Reports area on the Customers & Sales Navigation Center, link to <u>View All Customer & Sales Reports</u>. The Select a Report or Form window appears.

2. In the Accounts Receivable: Customers and Sales list, select Customer Ledgers. Then, make the selections to print.

Cynthia's Service Merchandise
Customer Ledgers
For the Period From Jan 1, 2012 to Jan 31, 2012

Filter Criteria includes: Report order is by ID. Report is printed in Detail Format.

Customer ID Customer	Date	Trans No	Type	Debit Amt	Credit Amt	Balance
ap001	1/6/12	101	SJ	324.00		324.00
Aileen Parker	1/20/12	Invoice 101	CRJ		324.00	0.00
bb002	1/10/12	105	SJ	53.88		53.88
Betty Barlow	1/27/12	Invoice 105	CRJ		53.88	0.00
dc003	1/6/12	102	SJ	640.00		640.00
Diane Conlin	1/27/12	Invoice 102	CRJ		640.00	0.00
jp004	1/6/12	104	SJ	486.00		486.00
Joann Poe	1/23/12	Invoice 104	CRJ		105.00	381.00
pm005	1/6/12	103	SJ	432.00		432.00
Paul Moore	1/13/12	CM103	SJ		108.00	324.00
	1/13/12	Invoice 103	CRJ		324.00	0.00
Report Total				**1,935.88**	**1,554.88**	**381.00**

PRINTING THE GENERAL LEDGER TRIAL BALANCE

1. In the Reports list, highlight General Ledger. Then, in the General Ledger: Account Information list highlight General Ledger Trial Balance.

2. Make the selections to print. Compare your general ledger trial balance to the one shown on the next page.

*****EDUCATIONAL VERSION ONLY*****

Cynthia's Service Merchandise
General Ledger Trial Balance
As of Jan 31, 2012

Filter Criteria includes: Report order is by ID. Report is printed in Detail Format.

Account ID	Account Description	Debit Amt	Credit Amt
10200	Southwest Bank	72,898.05	
10400	Arizona Savings & Loan	22,000.00	
11000	Accounts Receivable	381.00	
12000	Merchandise Inventory	28,322.00	
13000	Supplies	1,750.00	
14000	Prepaid Insurance	2,400.00	
15000	Furniture and Fixtures	5,000.00	
15100	Computers & Equipment	7,500.00	
15500	Building	100,000.00	
20000	Accounts Payable		300.00
23100	Sales Tax Payable		103.99
27000	Long-Term Notes Payable		20,500.00
27400	Mortgage Payable		75,000.00
39006	Eric Lerette, Capital		72,195.00
39007	Eric Lerette, Drawing	500.00	
39008	Cynthia Barber, Capital		72,195.00
39009	Cynthia Barber, Drawing	500.00	
40000	Sales-Hardware		750.00
40200	Sales-Wall		500.00
40400	Sales-Floor		640.00
40600	Service Fees		49.89
50000	Cost of Sales-Hardware	250.00	
50500	Cost of Sales-Wall	150.00	
57000	Cost of Sales-Floor	216.00	
59500	Purchase Discounts		17.96
70000	Maintenance Expense	160.00	
73500	Postage Expense	45.00	
75500	Supplies Expense	107.65	
76000	Telephone Expense	72.14	
	Total:	242,251.84	242,251.84

EDITING RECEIPTS

Is your Customer Ledger correct? Joann Poe's account is used to show how to edit the Customer Ledger. Follow these steps to see how the editing feature works:

1. From the Customers & Sales Navigation Center, select ; View and Edit Payments Received.

2. The Receipt List appears. Click on Invoice 104, $105.00 to highlight it.

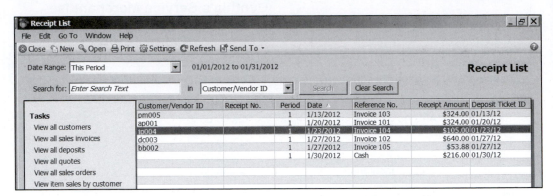

3. Click [🔍 Open]. The original Receipts window with Joann Poe's partial payment appears. Make any necessary corrections, then <u>S</u>ave.

4. Close the Receipts window and Receipt List window.

BACKING UP CHAPTER 13 DATA

Follow these steps to back up Chapter 13 data:

1. If necessary, insert your USB flash drive. From the System Navigation Center, click [Back Up Now]. Make sure the box next to include company name in the backup file name is *unchecked.*

2. Click [Back Up].

3. Go to the location of your USB drive. (Or, backup to another location.) Type **Chapter 13** in the File name field.

4. Click [Save].

5. When the window prompts that This company backup will require approximately 1 diskette, click [OK]. When the window prompts Please insert the first disk, click [OK]. When the Back Up Company scale is 100% complete, you have successfully backed up to the current point in Chapter 13. (If you are backing up to the default or another location, this step will differ slightly.)

EXPORT REPORTS TO EXCEL

1. Export the following Peachtree reports to Excel:

   - Sales Journal
   - Cash Receipts Journal
   - Customer Ledgers
   - General Ledger Trial Balance.

2. If needed, refer to pages 482-484 for detailed steps to add multiple sheets to one Excel file. Use the file name **Chapter 13_ SJ_ CRJ_ CL_GLTB.xlsx.**

   NOTE: If your instructor would like you to save the Sales Journal, Cash Receipts Journal, Customer Ledgers, and General Ledger Trial Balance as PDF files, refer to page 353. The suggested file name is **Chapter 13_Sales Journal.pdf**, etc.

SUMMARY AND REVIEW

Complete the following end-of-chapter activities:

1. Going to the net, pages 539-540.

2. Multiple-choice questions pages 540-543.

3. Exercises 13-1 and 13-2, pages 543-546.

4. Analysis question, page 546.

5. Assessment rubric, page 547.

6. Chapter 13 Index, page 548.

GOING TO THE NET

Access the Business Owner's Toolkit website at http://www.toolkit.com/small_business_guide/sbg.aspx?nid=P06_1430. Read the accounts receivable information. Answer the following questions.

1. What is the common abbreviation for accounts receivable?
2. What is the control account for customer sales on account?

---

3. How is the ending accounts receivable total computed?

Multiple Choice Questions: The Online Learning Center includes these questions at www.mhhe.com/yacht2012, select Student Edition, Chapter 13, QA Templates.

_____ 1. Cynthia's Service Merchandise charges sales tax to all sales made in:

    a. Georgia
    b. Oregon.
    c. Washington.
    d. Arizona.
    e. None of the above.

_____ 2. The money that your customers owe to the business is known as:

    a. Accounts payable.
    b. Revenue.
    c. Accounts receivable.
    d. Cash in bank.
    e. None of the above.

_____ 3. The sales tax rate is:

    a. 6%.
    b. 7%.
    c. 8%.
    d. 9%.
    e. None of the above.

_____ 4. Use the following Navigation Bar options to record entries in the Cash Receipts Journal:

    a. Customers & Sales; Receive Money, Receive Money from Customer.
    b. Customers & Sales; Customers, Receive Money, View and Edit Payment Received.
    c. Vendor & Payments; Customers, Receive Money, Receive Money from Customer.
    d. Tasks; Sales/Invoicing.
    e. None of the above.

_____ 5. Use the following Navigation Bar options to record entries in the Sales Journal:

  a. Maintain/Customers Prospects.
  b. Customers & Sales; Customers, Set Up Customer Defaults.
  c. Customers & Sales; Sales Invoices, New Sales Invoice.
  d. Maintain; Default Information, Customers.
  e. None of the above.

_____ 6. The owner(s) of Cynthia's Service Merchandise are:

  a. Eric Lerette.
  b. Cynthia Barber.
  c. both a. and b.
  d. Joann Poe.
  e. None of the above.

_____ 7. PCA's accounts receivable system allows you to set up all of the following, EXCEPT:

  a. Customers.
  b. Inventory items.
  c. Finance charges.
  d. Vendors.
  e. None of the above.

_____ 8. All journal entries made to the Sales Journal are posted to the General ledger and to the:

  a. Accounts payable ledger.
  b. Customer ledger.
  c. Job cost ledger.
  d. Payroll register.
  e. None of the above.

_____ 9. The sales tax payable account is:

  a. Account No. 52000.
  b. Account No. 53000.
  c. Account No. 23100.
  d. Account No. 12000.
  e. None of the above.

_____10.   The Customer ID for Aileen Parker is:

a. AAP001.
b. ap001.
c. ap002.
d. AP002.
e. None of the above.

_____11.   The Cash Account number is shown on which of the following windows:

a. Sales/Invoicing.
b. Purchases/Receive Inventory.
c. Receipts.
d. General Journal Entry.
e. None of the above.

_____12.   The account used for hardware sales is:

a. Account No. 40000.
b. Account No. 40800.
c. Account No. 40200.
d. Account No. 40400.
e. None of the above.

_____13.   A sales return is also called a/an:

a. Credit memo.
b. Debit memo.
c. Invoice.
d. Receipt.
e. None of the above.

_____14.   To back up all of Chapter 13's data, the following file name is used:

a. Chapter 13 Begin.
b. Chapter 13b.
c. Backup.
d. Chapter 13.
e. None of the above.

_____15. The GL Sales Account for wall is:

       a. Account No. 44200.
       b. Account No. 44300.
       c. Account No. 44400.
       d. Account No. 40200.
       e. None of the above.

Exercise 13-1: You must complete Exercises 12-1 and 12-2 before starting Exercise 13-1.

1. Start PCA. Open the company that you set up in Exercise 12-1 on pages 485-486, Your Name Sales and Service.

2. Restore your data from Exercise 12-2. (*Hint: This backup was made on page 493.*) To make sure you are starting in the right place, display Exercise 12-2's general ledger trial balance (step 6, page 493).

3. If necessary, enter the following customer defaults:

    a.   Standard Terms: Due in number of days

    b.   Net due in: 30 days
        Discount in: 0 days
        Discount %:   0.00
        Credit Limit: 2,500.00
        GL Sales Account: 40000 Sales Hardware
        Discount GL Account: 49000 Sales Discounts

4. Set up GA sales taxes. The sales tax rate is 8.00%. (*Hint:* Refer to pages 502-506. Use Georgia Dept. of Revenue and Georgia sales tax.)

5. Enter the following customers:

    a.   Customer ID: **ac001**
        Name: **Alan Clark**
        Billing Address: **223 W. Peachtree Blvd.**
        City, ST Zip: **Norcross, GA 30092**
        Country: **USA**
        Sales Tax: **GA**
        Customer Type: **GWI** (for Gwinnett Country)

Telephone 1:	**770-555-3422**
Fax:	**770-555-5525**
E-mail:	**info@alanclark.com**
Web Site:	**www.alanclark.com**

In the Sales Info tab, select the GL Sales Acct 40200, Sales-Tools for Alan Clark.

b.
Customer ID:	**bb002**
Name:	**Bill Brenner**
Billing Address:	**248 E. Mesa Verde Avenue**
City, ST Zip:	**Atlanta, GA 30342**
Country:	**USA**
Sales Tax:	**GA**
Customer Type:	**FUL** (for Fulton Country)
Telephone 1:	**404-555-8900**
Fax:	**404-555-8902**
E-mail:	**info@billbrenner.net**
Web Site:	**www.billbrenner.net**

In the Sales Info tab, select the GL Sales Acct 40000, Sales-Hardware for Bill Brenner.

c.
Customer ID:	**rn003**
Name:	**Rebekah Nash**
Billing Address:	**15590 Horseshoe Bend Drive**
City, ST Zip:	**Atlanta, GA 30341**
Country:	**USA**
Sales Tax:	**GA**
Customer Type:	**FUL**
Telephone 1:	**404-555-7310**
Fax:	**404-555-3138**
E-mail:	**info@rebekahnash.com**
Web Site:	**www.rebekahnash.com**

In the Sales Info tab, select the GL Sales Acct 40000, Sales-Hardware for Rebekah Nash.

6. Make a backup of your work. (Use **Exercise 13-1** as the file name.)

Exercise 13-2: Exercise 13-1 must be completed before Exercise 13-2.

1. Start PCA. Open your Sales and Service company.

2. If necessary, restore data from Exercise 13-1.

3. Record the following transactions:

01/06/12	Sold five tool kits on account to Alan Clark, Customer ac001. Type **101** in the Invoice No. field. Subsequent invoices will be numbered automatically.
01/06/12	Sold three hardware sets on account to Bill Brenner, Customer bb002.
01/06/12	Sold six hardware sets on account to Rebekah Nash, Customer rn003.
01/10/12	Alan Clark returned one of the tool kits that he purchased on January 6, Invoice No. 101, CM101. Mr. Clark also paid the balance of Invoice 101. (*Hint: This transaction requires two entries.* If necessary, select Account No. 10200, Caliber Bank as the cash account.)
01/13/12	Received a check in full payment of Invoice No. 102 from Bill Brenner.
01/17/12	Sold two hardware sets *and* two tool kits for cash to Sybil Gallagher. (*Hint:* Remember to enter two quantities and two items. Make sure GA sales tax is being charged.)
01/18/12	Sold three tool kits for cash to Randall Richards.

4. Print the Sales Journal.

5. Print the Cash Receipts Journal.

6. Print the Customer Ledgers.

7. Print the General Ledger Trial Balance.

Check Your Figures:

10200, Caliber Bank:	$62,746.63
11000, Accounts Receivable	972.00
12000, Merchandise Inventory	14,570.00
23100, Sales Tax Payable	193.20
40000, Sales-Hardware	1,650.00
40200, Sales-Tools	765.00

8. Make a backup. Use **Exercise 13-2** as the file name.

9. Export the following reports to Excel: Sales Journal, Cash Receipts Journal, Customer Ledgers, General Ledger Trial Balance. Use the file name **Exercise 13-2_SJ_CRJ_CL_GLTB.xlsx**.

10. Save these files as PDFs: Sales Journal.pdf, Cash Receipts Journal.pdf, and General Ledger Trial Balance.pdf. The suggestion file name is Exercise 13-2_Sales Journal.pdf, etc.

ANALYSIS QUESTION

What is the balance in the Accounts Receivable account, Cynthia's Service Merchandise? Why? (*Hint:* Analysis questions refer to Cynthia's [or your name] Service Merchandise, <u>not</u> the company set up in the exercise.)

ASSESSMENT RUBRIC

Complete the Assessment Rubric online at www.mhhe.com/yacht2012; Student Edition, select Chapter 13, Assessment Rubric link.

Date	Transaction	Navigation Center/Module	Task Window	Journal Dr./Cr.
1/6	Sold five tool kits on account to Alan Clark, Invoice 101.			
1/10	Alan Clark returned one of the tool kits purchased on 1/6, Invoice No. 101, CM101. Mr. Clark also paid the balance of Invoice 101.			

CHAPTER 13 INDEX

LEARNING OBJECTIVES

1. Restore data from Chapter 13. (This backup was made on page 538.)
2. Enter inventory maintenance and default information.
3. Enter inventory item information, including S ales account, Merchandise Inventory account, and Cost of Sales account.
4. Enter item codes when recording purchases and sales.
5. Enter inventory adjustments.
6. Make three backups, save two Excel files, and save five PDF files.

Merchandise inventory includes all goods owned by the business and held for sale. The account used for merchandise inventory is Account No. 12000, Merchandise Inventory.

Peachtree's inventory system tracks inventory items at both the purchasing and sales level. When you set up an inventory item, you establish the General Ledger accounts that are updated by purchases and sales. Peachtree keeps track of cost of goods sold, stock levels, sales prices, and vendors.

PCA uses a perpetual inventory system. In a perpetual inventory system a *merchandising business* continuously updates inventory each time an item is purchased or sold.

Inventory calculations include FIFO, LIFO, and average cost methods. The *FIFO* (first in, first out) method assumes that the items in the beginning inventory are sold first. The *LIFO* (last in, first out) method assumes that the goods received last are sold first. The average cost method (also known as weighted average method) is the default that PCA uses for inventory items sold. The formula used is: Average Cost x Quantity Sold = Cost of Sales.

PCA tracks the inventory items that you buy and sell. After you post, PCA automatically updates the cost and quantity of each inventory item.

Generally, all of your inventory should use the same costing method.

Tracking inventory is a three-step process:

➢ Enter item information, including Sales account, Merchandise Inventory account, and Cost of Sales account.

➢ Use item codes when entering purchases and sales. PCA automatically calculates and tracks average cost, which is the default, using this to calculate and enter the Cost of Sales. You can change the cost method to LIFO (last in, first out) or FIFO (first in, first out). This chapter explains these inventory cost methods in detail.

➢ If necessary, enter inventory adjustments.

PCA does the rest automatically: adjusts inventory levels each time you post a purchase or sale of an inventory item, tracks the cost of each item, and makes a Cost of Goods Sold journal entry at the end of the accounting period.

COST METHODS

PCA includes three types of cost methods for inventory: average cost, LIFO, and FIFO. Once you select the costing method for an inventory item, you cannot change it if transactions have been posted. Therefore, if you want to change the cost method for an item with posted transactions, you must enter the item again.

Average Cost

When you set up inventory items for Cynthia's Service Merchandise, you selected the Average cost method. In Chapter 12, Cynthia's Service Merchandise purchased four pairs of curtains from Ronald Becker Fabrics for $30 each (Invoice 210, pages 462-463). What happens when these curtains are sold?

The journal entries would look like this:

Purchased four pairs of curtains from Ronald Becker Fabrics at $30 each (Invoice 210, pages 462-463).

Account ID	Account Description, Purchase Invoice 210	Debit	Credit
12000	Merchandise Inventory	120.00	
20000/RBF08	Accounts Payable/Ronald Becker Fabrics		120.00

Sold four pairs of curtains to Paul Moore for $100 each (Invoice 103, page 516).

Account ID	Account Description, Sales Invoice 103	Debit	Credit
50500	Cost of Sales-Wall	120.00	
11000/pm005	Accounts Receivable/Paul Moore	432.00	
12000	Merchandise Inventory		120.00
40200	Sales-Wall		400.00
23100	Sales Tax Payable		32.00

You can see from these journal entries that the Merchandise Inventory account is updated with each purchase and sale. After these transactions, the balance in Merchandise Inventory looks like this:

Merchandise Inventory, Account No. 12000

Purchased inventory	120.00	Sold Inventory	120.00
Balance	0.00		

LIFO (Last In, First Out)

The LIFO (last in, first out) method of inventory pricing assumes that the last goods received are sold first. LIFO assumes that cost is based on replacement and that the last price paid for merchandise is more accurate.

Accountants recommend that you select LIFO when you desire to charge the most recent inventory costs against revenue. LIFO yields the lowest amount of net income in periods of rising costs because the cost of the most recently acquired inventory more closely approximates the replacement cost.

FIFO (First In, First Out)

The FIFO (first in, first out) method of inventory pricing assumes that the items in the beginning inventory are sold first. FIFO costs your sales and values your inventory as if the items you sell are the ones that you have had in stock for the longest time.

Accountants recommend that you select FIFO when you desire to charge costs against revenue in the order in which costs occur. FIFO yields a higher amount of profit during periods of rising costs. This happens because merchandise was acquired prior to the increase in cost.

TYPES OF INVENTORY ITEMS

There are nine types of inventory items in PCA:

➤ Stock item: This is the default in the Item Class list. It is the traditional inventory item where the program tracks descriptions, unit prices, stock quantities, and cost of sales. For stock items, you should complete the entire window. Once an item has been designated as a stock item, the type cannot be changed.

➤ Master Stock Item: PCA uses this item class as a special item that does not represent inventory stocked but contains information (item attributes) shared with a number of substock items.

➤ Non-stock item: PCA tracks the description and a unit price for sales. You can also track default accounts. You might use this type for service items such as hours where the unit price is set.

➤ Description only: PCA keeps track of the description of an Inventory Item. This saves time when entering purchases and sales because you don't have to retype the description. You might use this type for service items where the price fluctuates.

➤ Service: This is for services you can apply to your salary and wages account.

➤ Labor: This is for labor you can apply to your salary and wages account. You cannot purchase labor items but you can sell them.

➤ Assembly: You can specify items as assembly items and create a bill of materials for a unit made up of component stock or subassembly items.

➤ Activity item: To indicate how time is spent when performing services for a customer, for a job, or for internal administrative work. Activity items are used with the Time & Billing feature.

➤ Charge item: Expenses recorded by an employee or vendor when company resources are used for a customer or job.

GETTING STARTED

In the preceding chapters, you set up inventory items. The instructions that follow show how to add inventory items to Cynthia's Service Merchandise.

1. Start Peachtree. Open Cynthia's Service Merchandise. If you used your name Service Merchandise, select it.

2. Follow these steps to restore data from Chapter 13. This backup was made on page 538.

    a. Start Peachtree. Open Cynthia's Service Merchandise. This company was set up in Chapter 12 on pages 430-435. (*Hint:* If another company opens, click File; Open Previous Company, select Cynthia's [your name] Service Merchandise. Open one company.)

    b. If necessary, insert your USB flash drive. From the System Navigation Center, click [Restore Now].[1]

    c. The Select Backup File window appears. Click [Browse]. In the Look in field, select the location of the Chapter 13.ptb file. Click [Open], then [Next >].

    d. The Select Company window appears. The radio button next to An Existing Company is selected. Check that the Company Name and Location fields are correct. Click [Next >].

---

[1]You can restore from your back up file even if *no* Peachtree company exists. From Peachtree's start up window, select File; Restore. Select the location of your backup file. On the Restore Wizard's Select Company window, select A New Company. The *A New Company* selection allows you to restore backup data, bypassing the process of new company set up. For more information, refer to Troubleshooting on pages 299-300.

e. The Restore Options window appears. Make sure that the box next to Company Data is *checked*. Click Next >.

f. The Confirmation window appears. Check the From and To fields to make sure they are correct. Click Finish. When the Restore Company scale is 100% complete, your data is restored. (*Hint:* The Student Version of Peachtree prompts that company data can be used for 14 months. After that time, the data expires. Click OK. Cynthia's [or your name] Service Merchandise opens.)

💾 To make sure you are starting in the appropriate place in the data (Chapter 13.ptb backup) display the General Ledger Trial Balance. This trial balance is also shown on page 537, Chapter 13.

*****EDUCATIONAL VERSION ONLY*****

Cynthia's Service Merchandise
General Ledger Trial Balance
As of Jan 31, 2012

Filter Criteria includes: Report order is by ID. Report is printed in Detail Format.

Account ID	Account Description	Debit Amt	Credit Amt
10200	Southwest Bank	72,898.05	
10400	Arizona Savings & Loan	22,000.00	
11000	Accounts Receivable	381.00	
12000	Merchandise Inventory	28,322.00	
13000	Supplies	1,750.00	
14000	Prepaid Insurance	2,400.00	
15000	Furniture and Fixtures	5,000.00	
15100	Computers & Equipment	7,500.00	
15500	Building	100,000.00	
20000	Accounts Payable		300.00
23100	Sales Tax Payable		103.99
27000	Long-Term Notes Payable		20,500.00
27400	Mortgage Payable		75,000.00
39006	Eric Lerette, Capital		72,195.00
39007	Eric Lerette, Drawing	500.00	
39008	Cynthia Barber, Capital		72,195.00
39009	Cynthia Barber, Drawing	500.00	
40000	Sales-Hardware		750.00
40200	Sales-Wall		500.00
40400	Sales-Floor		640.00
40600	Service Fees		49.89
50000	Cost of Sales-Hardware	250.00	
50500	Cost of Sales-Wall	150.00	
57000	Cost of Sales-Floor	216.00	
59500	Purchase Discounts		17.96
70000	Maintenance Expense	160.00	
73500	Postage Expense	45.00	
75500	Supplies Expense	107.65	
76000	Telephone Expense	72.14	
	Total:	**242,251.84**	**242,251.84**

INVENTORY DEFAULTS

1. From the Navigation Bar, select ; 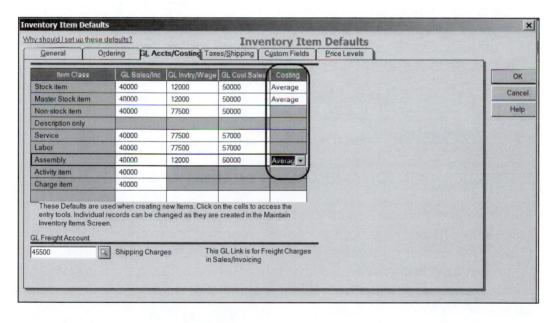 Set Up Inventory Defaults. The Inventory Item Defaults window displays. Observe that the General tab shows the Default Item Class as Stock item . If Stock item is not selected, select it.

2. Click on the GL Accts/Costing tab. The default for inventory costing is the Average method. Since this is what Cynthia's Service Merchandise uses, there is no need to make any changes to this window. These inventory defaults were set up in Chapter 12, pages 449-451.

3. Click on the Taxes/Shipping tab.

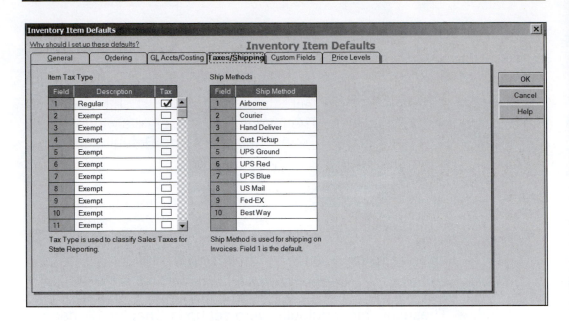

The Regular tax type is selected with a check mark. This is correct because there is an 8% sales tax in Arizona. The Ship Methods that appear on this tab are also shown on the Sales/Invoicing and Purchases/Receive Inventory windows. You can also use these ship methods to set up defaults for customers and vendors.

3. Click [OK] to close this window. (Remember: If you click [Cancel], you close the window without saving any changes.)

ENTERING INVENTORY ITEM MAINTENANCE INFORMATION

Inventory items are set up on the Maintain Inventory Items window. You can establish general ledger accounts, vendors, tax exemptions, sales prices and reorder quantities. The information on the Maintain Inventory Items window displays three active tabs: General, Custom Fields, and History; two tabs are inactive–Bill of Materials, and Item Attributes. Select an active tab to view its fields.

Follow the steps on the next page to enter inventory maintenance information.

1. From the Inventory & Services Navigation Center, select ,
    New Inventory Item. The Maintain Inventory Items window appears.

2. Complete the following information:

Item ID:	**004lights**
Description:	**lighting**
Item Class:	Stock Item
Description(for Sales):	**light fixtures**
Price Level 1:	**175**
Last Unit Cost:	**64**
Cost Method:	Average
GL Sales Acct:	Add Account No. **40500 Sales-Lights** (Account Type, Income)
GL Inventory Acct:	**12000 Merchandise Inventory**
GL Cost of Sales Acct:	Add Account No. **57050 Cost of Sales-Lights** (Account Type, Cost of Sales)
Item Tax Type:	1
Item Type:	**lights**
Stocking U/M:	**each**
Minimum Stock:	**8**
Reorder Quantity:	**4**

    Preferred Vendor ID:

    You need to add a new vendor. To add a vendor, click in the

    Preferred Vendor ID field, then click . The Maintain Vendors window displays.

Vendor ID:	**TSS09**
Name:	**Thomas Sales and Service**
Mailing Address:	**3489 Union Street**
City, ST Zip:	**Mesa, AZ 85022**
Country:	**USA**
Vendor Type:	**lights**
1099 Type:	**Independent Contractor**
Expense Account:	12000 Merchandise Inventory

Telephone 1:	**480-555-2200**
Fax:	**480-555-2302**
E-Mail:	**info@thomas.com**
Web Address:	**www.thomas.com**

Purchase Info:

Tax ID Number:	**41-8819302**

a. Click 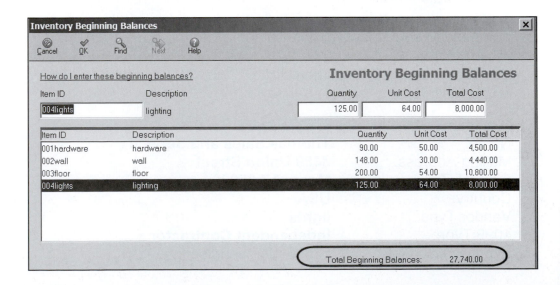 Save , then close the Maintain Vendors window. You are returned to the Maintain Inventory Items window. In the Preferre<u>d</u> Vendor ID field, select Thomas Sales and Service as the vendor. Click Save .

b. Click on the Beginning Balances arrow (lower right corner of the Maintain Inventory Items window.) The Inventory Beginning Balances window displays. Select lighting. Complete the following:

Quantity:	125
Unit Cost:	64.00
Total Cost:	8,000.00 (completed automatically)

3. Observe that the Total Beginning Balances field shows 27,740.00. This amount agrees with the Merchandise Inventory balance on page 441 (Chapter 12's January 1, 2012 balance sheet).

Inventory Beginning Balances

Cancel | OK | Find | Next | Help

How do I enter these beginning balances?

Inventory Beginning Balances

Item ID	Description	Quantity	Unit Cost	Total Cost
004lights	lighting	125.00	64.00	8,000.00

Item ID	Description	Quantity	Unit Cost	Total Cost
001hardware	hardware	90.00	50.00	4,500.00
002wall	wall	148.00	30.00	4,440.00
003floor	floor	200.00	54.00	10,800.00
004lights	lighting	125.00	64.00	8,000.00

Total Beginning Balances: 27,740.00

4. Click  to close the Inventory Beginning Balances window.

5. Make sure, TSS09, Thomas Sales and Service, is shown in the Preferred Vendor ID field. Save, then close the Maintain Inventory Items window.

6. Save, then close the Maintain Inventory Items window.

BACKING UP YOUR DATA

Follow these steps to back up Chapter 14 data:

1. If necessary, insert your USB flash drive. From the System Navigation Center, click [Back Up Now].

2. Click [Back Up].

3. Go to the location of your USB drive or another location. Type **Chapter 14 Begin** in the File name field.

4. Click [Save].

5. When the window prompts that This company backup will require approximately 1 diskette, click [OK]. When the window prompts Please insert the first, disk click [OK]. When the Back Up Company scale is 100% complete, you have successfully backed up to the current point in Chapter 14. (If you are backing up to the default or another location, this step will differ slightly.)

6. Continue or click File; Exit to exit Peachtree.

INVENTORY ADJUSTMENTS

Follow these steps to record a purchase and inventory adjustment.

Date	*Transaction Description*
01/13/12	Thomas Sales and Service sent Invoice No. 112 for the purchase of eight light fixtures for a unit cost of $64 each, and a total of $512.

1. From the Vendors & Purchases Navigation Center, select 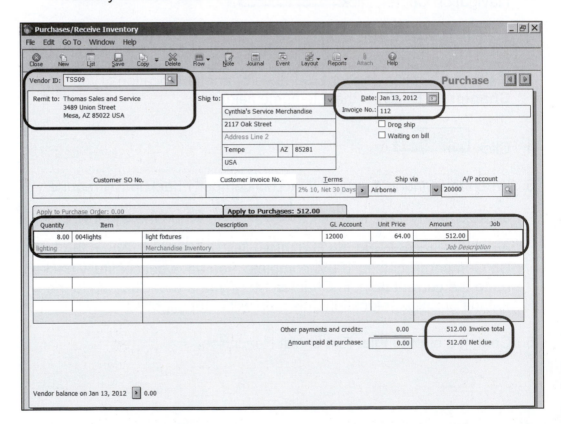 ; New Bill. The Purchases/Receive Inventory window appears. Record the January 13, 2012 transaction. Compare your Purchases/Receive Inventory window with the one shown below.

2. Save to post, then close.

Record the following transaction.

Date	Transaction Description

01/16/12   Two light fixtures were damaged when they were dropped on the floor by the owner, Eric Lerette.

Follow the steps below to make an inventory adjustment.

1. From the Inventory & Services Navigation Center, select <span></span>. The Inventory Adjustments window appears.

2. In the Item ID field, select lighting.

3. In the Reference field, type **EL** (Eric Lerette's initials).

4. Type **16** in the Date field.

5. Type **-2** in the Adjust Quantity By field. (PCA calculates the New Quantity after you enter the adjustment.)

6. In the Reason to Adjust field, type **Two damaged light fixtures**.

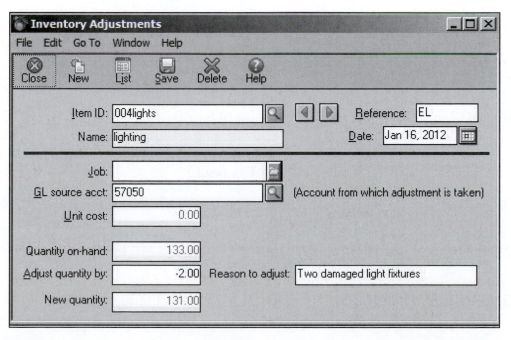

7. Click ![Save] to post, then close the Inventory Adjustments window.

ADDITIONAL TRANSACTIONS

Record the following transactions for Cynthia's Service Merchandise.

Date	Transaction Description
01/19/12	Sold two doorknobs on account to Aileen Parker. Type **106** in the Invoice No. field. Subsequent invoices will be numbered automatically. (*Hint: Select hardware as the inventory item for doorknobs. Make sure the Sales Ta*x *field shows 24.00, or 8% of the sales amount for AZ sales taxes.*)
01/19/12	Sold two rolls of vinyl flooring on account to Diane Conlin, Invoice No. 107. There is no sales tax because merchandise is being shipped out of state.
01/19/12	Sold two pairs of curtains on account to Paul Moore, Invoice No. 108. (*Hint: Select wall as the inventory item for curtains. Remember to check Sales Ta*x *field for 16.00 AZ sales taxes.*)
01/20/12	Cynthia's Service Merchandise completed repair work for Betty Barlow at a cost of $75, plus 6.00 sales taxes, Invoice No. 109. (*Hint: Remember to credit Account No. 40600, Service Fees.*)
01/23/12	Cash sales in the amount of $1,404 ($1,300 plus $104, AZ sales taxes) were deposited at Southwest Bank: 10 pairs of curtains, $1,000; 2 doorknobs, $300. (*Hint: Remember to select AZ in the Sa*l*es Tax field.*)
01/24/12	Received a check in the amount of $324 from Aileen Parker in full payment of Invoice 106.
01/26/12	Received a check in the amount of $216 from Paul Moore in full payment of Invoice No. 108.
01/30/12	Issued Check No. 3039 to EMD Mortgage Co. in the amount of $685.80. Type **685.80** in the Dollars field. To

distribute this amount between the principal amount of $587.95 and Interest Expense of $97.85, click Split .

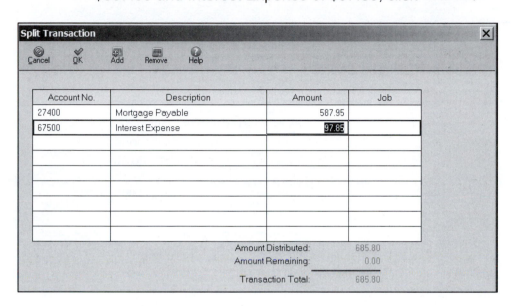

Click OK to accept the split transaction. These steps assume you are using the Write Checks window. (*Hint: On the Write Checks window, type **3039** in the Check number field.*)

01/30/12   Issued Check No. 3040 in the amount of $500 to Eric Lerette.

01/30/12   Issued Check No. 3041 in the amount of $500 to Cynthia Barber.

01/30/12   Cash sales in the amount of $2,376 ($2,200 plus $176, AZ sales taxes) were deposited at Southwest Bank: 8 doorknobs, $1,200; 10 pairs of curtains, $1,000. (*Remember to select AZ sales taxes.*)

PRINTING REPORTS

1. Print the Sales Journal.

Cynthia's Service Merchandise
Sales Journal
For the Period From Jan 1, 2012 to Jan 31, 2012

Filter Criteria includes: Report order is by Invoice/CM Date. Report is printed in Detail Format.

Date	Account ID	Invoice/CM #	Line Description	Debit Amnt	Credit Amnt
1/6/12	23100	101	AZ: Arizona Dept. of Revenue		24.00
	40000		Two doorknobs		300.00
	50000		Cost of sales	100.00	
	12000		Cost of sales		100.00
	11000		Aileen Parker	324.00	
1/6/12	40400	102	Four rolls of vinyl flooring		640.00
	57000		Cost of sales	216.00	
	12000		Cost of sales		216.00
	11000		Diane Conlin	640.00	
1/6/12	23100	103	AZ: Arizona Dept. of Revenue		32.00
	40200		Four pairs of curtains		400.00
	50500		Cost of sales	120.00	
	12000		Cost of sales		120.00
	11000		Paul Moore	432.00	
1/6/12	23100	104	AZ: Arizona Dept. of Revenue		36.00
	40000		Three curtain rods		450.00
	50000		Cost of sales	150.00	
	12000		Cost of sales		150.00
	11000		Joann Poe	486.00	
1/10/12	23100	105	AZ: Arizona Dept. of Revenue		3.99
	40600		Repair		49.89
	11000		Betty Barlow	53.88	
1/13/12	23100	CM103	AZ: Arizona Dept. of Revenue	8.00	
	40200		Returned one pair of curtains	100.00	
	50500		Cost of sales		30.00
	12000		Cost of sales	30.00	
	11000		Paul Moore		108.00
1/19/12	23100	106	AZ: Arizona Dept. of Revenue		24.00
	40000		Two doorknobs		300.00
	50000		Cost of sales	100.00	
	12000		Cost of sales		100.00
	11000		Aileen Parker	324.00	
1/19/12	40400	107	two rolls of vinyl flooring		320.00
	57000		Cost of sales	108.00	
	12000		Cost of sales		108.00
	11000		Diane Conlin	320.00	
1/19/12	23100	108	AZ: Arizona Dept. of Revenue		16.00
	40200		Two pairs of curtains		200.00
	50500		Cost of sales	60.00	
	12000		Cost of sales		60.00
	11000		Paul Moore	216.00	
1/20/12	23100	109	AZ: Arizona Dept. of Revenue		6.00
	40600		Repair		75.00
	11000		Betty Barlow	81.00	
		Total		**3,868.88**	**3,868.88**

If any of your transactions do *not* agree with the Sales Journal, you can drill-down ( ) to the original entry, make any needed corrections, then save and reprint.

2. Print the Cash Receipts Journal.

*****EDUCATIONAL VERSION ONLY*****

Cynthia's Service Merchandise
Cash Receipts Journal
For the Period From Jan 1, 2012 to Jan 31, 2012

Filter Criteria includes: Report order is by Check Date. Report is printed in Detail Format.

Date	Account ID	Transaction Ref	Line Description	Debit Amnt	Credit Amnt
1/13/12	11000	Invoice 103	Invoice: 103		324.00
	10200		Paul Moore	324.00	
1/20/12	11000	Invoice 101	Invoice: 101		324.00
	10200		Aileen Parker	324.00	
1/23/12	11000	Invoice 104	Invoice: 104		105.00
	10200		Joann Poe	105.00	
1/23/12	23100	Cash	AZ: Arizona Dept. of Revenue		104.00
	40200		Ten pairs of curtains		1,000.00
	50500		Cost of sales	300.00	
	12000		Cost of sales		300.00
	40000		Two doorknobs		300.00
	50000		Cost of sales	100.00	
	12000		Cost of sales		100.00
	10200		Cash	1,404.00	
1/24/12	11000	Invoice 106	Invoice: 106		324.00
	10200		Aileen Parker	324.00	
1/26/12	11000	Invoice 108	Invoice: 108		216.00
	10200		Paul Moore	216.00	
1/27/12	11000	Invoice 105	Invoice: 105		53.88
	10200		Betty Barlow	53.88	
1/27/12	11000	Invoice 102	Invoice: 102		640.00
	10200		Diane Conlin	640.00	
1/30/12	23100	Cash	AZ: Arizona Dept. of Revenue		16.00
	40200		Two pairs of curtains		200.00
	50500		Cost of sales	60.00	
	12000		Cost of sales		60.00
	10200		Barbara Williams	216.00	
1/30/12	23100	Cash	AZ: Arizona Dept. of Revenue		176.00
	40000		Eight doorknobs		1,200.00
	50000		Cost of sales	400.00	
	12000		Cost of sales		400.00
	40200		Ten pairs of curtains		1,000.00
	50500		Cost of sales	300.00	
	12000		Cost of sales		300.00
	10200		Cash sales	2,376.00	
				7,142.88	7,142.88

3. Print the Customer Ledgers.

Cynthia's Service Merchandise
Customer Ledgers
For the Period From Jan 1, 2012 to Jan 31, 2012

Filter Criteria includes: Report order is by ID. Report is printed in Detail Format.

Customer ID Customer	Date	Trans No	Type	Debit Amt	Credit Amt	Balance
ap001	1/6/12	101	SJ	324.00		324.00
Aileen Parker	1/19/12	106	SJ	324.00		648.00
	1/20/12	Invoice 101	CRJ		324.00	324.00
	1/24/12	Invoice 106	CRJ		324.00	0.00
bb002	1/10/12	105	SJ	53.88		53.88
Betty Barlow	1/20/12	109	SJ	81.00		134.88
	1/27/12	Invoice 105	CRJ		53.88	81.00
dc003	1/6/12	102	SJ	640.00		640.00
Diane Conlin	1/19/12	107	SJ	320.00		960.00
	1/27/12	Invoice 102	CRJ		640.00	320.00
jp004	1/6/12	104	SJ	486.00		486.00
Joann Poe	1/23/12	Invoice 104	CRJ		105.00	381.00
pm005	1/6/12	103	SJ	432.00		432.00
Paul Moore	1/13/12	CM103	SJ		108.00	324.00
	1/13/12	Invoice 103	CRJ		324.00	0.00
	1/19/12	108	SJ	216.00		216.00
	1/26/12	Invoice 108	CRJ		216.00	0.00
Report Total				**2,876.88**	**2,094.88**	**782.00**

4. Print the Purchase Journal and compare it to the one shown on the next page.

*****EDUCATIONAL VERSION ONLY*****

Cynthia's Service Merchandise
Purchase Journal
For the Period From Jan 1, 2012 to Jan 31, 2012

Filter Criteria includes: 1) Includes Drop Shipments. Report order is by Date. Report is printed in Detail Format.

Date	Account ID / Account Description	Invoice/CM #	Line Description	Debit Amount	Credit Amount
1/3/12	12000 Merchandise Inventor	56JJ	restoration hardware	300.00	
	20000 Accounts Payable		Jimmy Jackson Hardware		300.00
1/13/12	12000 Merchandise Inventor	112	light fixtures	512.00	
	20000 Accounts Payable		Thomas Sales and Service		512.00
1/20/12	12000 Merchandise Inventor	210	wall coverings	120.00	
	20000 Accounts Payable		Ronald Becker Fabrics		120.00
1/20/12	12000 Merchandise Inventor	78JJ	restoration hardware	500.00	
	20000 Accounts Payable		Jimmy Jackson Hardware		500.00
1/20/12	12000 Merchandise Inventor	90	flooring	432.00	
	20000 Accounts Payable		Lee Lanning Products		432.00
1/25/12	12000 Merchandise Inventor	VCM90	flooring		54.00
	20000 Accounts Payable		Lee Lanning Products	54.00	
1/28/12	12000 Merchandise Inventor	VCM78JJ	restoration hardware		100.00
	20000 Accounts Payable		Jimmy Jackson Hardware	100.00	
				2,018.00	2,018.00

5. Print the Cash Disbursements Journal and compare it to the one shown on the next page.

*****EDUCATIONAL VERSION ONLY*****

Cynthia's Service Merchandise
Cash Disbursements Journal
For the Period From Jan 1, 2012 to Jan 31, 2012

Filter Criteria includes: Report order is by Date. Report is printed in Detail Format.

Date	Check #	Account ID	Line Description	Debit Amount	Credit Amount
1/24/12	3030	70000	Maintenance Expense	160.00	
		10200	David Allison		160.00
1/24/12	3031	73500	Postage Expense	45.00	
		10200	U.S. Post Office		45.00
1/24/12	3032	75500	Supplies Expense	107.65	
		10200	Broadway Office Supplies		107.65
1/24/12	3033	76000	Telephone Expense	72.14	
		10200	RCI Phone Co.		72.14
1/25/12	3034	39007	Eric Lerette, Drawing	500.00	
		10200	Eric Lerette		500.00
1/25/12	3035	39009	Cynthia Barber, Drawing	500.00	
		10200	Cynthia Barber		500.00
1/25/12	3036	59500	Discounts Taken		7.56
		20000	Invoice: 90	378.00	
		10200	Lee Lanning Products		370.44
1/28/12	3037	59500	Discounts Taken		8.00
		20000	Invoice: 78JJ	400.00	
		10200	Jimmy Jackson Hardware		392.00
1/28/12	3038	59500	Discounts Taken		2.40
		20000	Invoice: 210	120.00	
		10200	Ronald Becker Fabrics		117.60
1/30/12	3039	27400	Mortgage Payable	587.95	
		67500	Interest Expense	97.85	
		10200	EMD Mortgage Co.		685.80
1/30/12	3040	39007	Eric Lerette, Drawing	500.00	
		10200	Eric Lerette		500.00
1/30/12	3041	39009	Cynthia Barber, Drawing	500.00	
		10200	Cynthia Barber		500.00
	Total			3,968.59	3,968.59

6. Print the Vendor Ledgers.

Vendor ID Vendor	Date	Trans No	Type	Paid	Debit Am	Credit Amt	Balance
***** EDUCATIONAL VERSION ONLY *****							
Cynthia's Service Merchandise							
Vendor Ledgers							
For the Period From Jan 1, 2012 to Jan 31, 2012							
Filter Criteria includes: Report order is by ID.							
JJH06	1/3/12	56JJ	PJ			300.00	300.00
Jimmy Jackson Hardware	1/20/12	78JJ	PJ	*		500.00	800.00
	1/28/12	VCM78JJ	PJ	*	100.00		700.00
	1/28/12	3037	CDJ		8.00	8.00	700.00
	1/28/12	3037	CDJ		400.00		300.00
LLP07	1/20/12	90	PJ	*		432.00	432.00
Lee Lanning Products	1/25/12	VCM90	PJ	*	54.00		378.00
	1/25/12	3036	CDJ		7.56	7.56	378.00
	1/25/12	3036	CDJ		378.00		0.00
RBF08	1/20/12	210	PJ	*		120.00	120.00
Ronald Becker Fabrics	1/28/12	3038	CDJ		2.40	2.40	120.00
	1/28/12	3038	CDJ		120.00		0.00
TSS09	1/13/12	112	PJ			512.00	512.00
Thomas Sales and Service							
Report Total					**1,069.96**	**1,881.96**	**812.00**

7. Follow these steps to print the Cost of Goods Sold Journal and the Inventory Adjustment Journal:

    a. From the Reports area of the Select a Report or Form window, select Inventory.

    b. Highlight Cost of Goods Sold Journal, then make the selections to print. Compare your printout to the one shown on the next page.

Cynthia's Service Merchandise
Cost of Goods Sold Journal
For the Period From Jan 1, 2012 to Jan 31, 2012

Filter Criteria includes: Report order is by Date. Report is printed in Detail Format and with shortened descriptions.

Date	GL Acct I	Reference	Qty	Line Description	Debit Amo	Credit Amount
1/6/12	12000	101	2.00	Two doorknobs		100.00
	50000		2.00	Two doorknobs	100.00	
1/6/12	12000	102	4.00	Four rolls of vinyl flooring		216.00
	57000		4.00	Four rolls of vinyl flooring	216.00	
1/6/12	12000	103	4.00	Four pairs of curtains		120.00
	50500		4.00	Four pairs of curtains	120.00	
1/6/12	12000	104	3.00	Three curtain rods		150.00
	50000		3.00	Three curtain rods	150.00	
1/13/12	12000	CM103	-1.00	Returned one pair of curtain	30.00	
	50500		-1.00	Returned one pair of curtain		30.00
1/19/12	12000	106	2.00	Two doorknobs		100.00
	50000		2.00	Two doorknobs	100.00	
1/19/12	12000	107	2.00	two rolls of vinyl flooring		108.00
	57000		2.00	two rolls of vinyl flooring	108.00	
1/19/12	12000	108	2.00	Two pairs of curtains		60.00
	50500		2.00	Two pairs of curtains	60.00	
1/23/12	12000	Cash	10.00	Ten pairs of curtains		300.00
	50500		10.00	Ten pairs of curtains	300.00	
	12000		2.00	Two doorknobs		100.00
	50000		2.00	Two doorknobs	100.00	
1/30/12	12000	Cash	2.00	Two pairs of curtains		60.00
	50500		2.00	Two pairs of curtains	60.00	
	12000		8.00	Eight doorknobs		400.00
	50000		8.00	Eight doorknobs	400.00	
	12000		10.00	Ten pairs of curtains		300.00
	50500		10.00	Ten pairs of curtains	300.00	
		Total			**2,044.00**	**2,044.00**

c. Highlight the Inventory Adjustment Journal, then make the selections to print.

Cynthia's Service Merchandise
Inventory Adjustment Journal
For the Period From Jan 1, 2012 to Jan 31, 2012

Filter Criteria includes: Report order is by Date. Report is printed in Detail Format and with shortened descriptions.

Date	GL Acct ID	Reference	Qty	Line Description	Debit Amount	Credit Amount
1/16/12	12000	EL	-2.00	lighting		128.00
	57050		-2.00	Two damaged light fixtures	128.00	
		Total			**128.00**	**128.00**

8. Print the Inventory Profitability Report.

*****EDUCATIONAL VERSION ONLY*****

Cynthia's Service Merchandise
Inventory Profitability Report
For the Period From Jan 1, 2012 to Jan 31, 2012
Filter Criteria includes: 1) Stock/Assembly. Report order is by ID. Report is printed with shortened descriptions.

Item ID Item Description	Units Sold	Sales($)	Cost($)	Gross Profit($)	Gross Profit(%)	% of Total
001hardware hardware	17.00	2,550.00	850.00	1,700.00	66.67	40.23
002wall wall	27.00	2,700.00	810.00	1,890.00	70.00	44.72
003floor floor	6.00	960.00	324.00	636.00	66.25	15.05
004lights lighting						
	50.00	6,210.00	1,984.00	4,226.00		100.00

9. Print the General Ledger Trial Balance.

*****EDUCATIONAL VERSION ONLY*****

Cynthia's Service Merchandise
General Ledger Trial Balance
As of Jan 31, 2012
Filter Criteria includes: Report order is by ID. Report is printed in Detail Format.

Account ID	Account Description	Debit Amt	Credit Amt
10200	Southwest Bank	75,532.25	
10400	Arizona Savings & Loan	22,000.00	
11000	Accounts Receivable	782.00	
12000	Merchandise Inventory	27,338.00	
13000	Supplies	1,750.00	
14000	Prepaid Insurance	2,400.00	
15000	Furniture and Fixtures	5,000.00	
15100	Computers & Equipment	7,500.00	
15500	Building	100,000.00	
20000	Accounts Payable		812.00
23100	Sales Tax Payable		429.99
27000	Long-Term Notes Payable		20,500.00
27400	Mortgage Payable		74,412.05
39006	Eric Lerette, Capital		72,195.00
39007	Eric Lerette, Drawing	1,000.00	
39008	Cynthia Barber, Capital		72,195.00
39009	Cynthia Barber, Drawing	1,000.00	
40000	Sales-Hardware		2,550.00
40200	Sales-Wall		2,700.00
40400	Sales-Floor		960.00
40600	Service Fees		124.89
50000	Cost of Sales-Hardware	850.00	
50500	Cost of Sales-Wall	810.00	
57000	Cost of Sales-Floor	324.00	
57050	Cost of Sales-Lights	128.00	
59500	Purchase Discounts		17.96
67500	Interest Expense	97.85	
70000	Maintenance Expense	160.00	
73500	Postage Expense	45.00	
75500	Supplies Expense	107.65	
76000	Telephone Expense	72.14	
	Total:	246,896.89	246,896.89

BACKING UP CHAPTER 14 DATA

If your reports agree with the ones shown, make a backup of Chapter 14 data. If your printouts do not agree with the ones shown, make the necessary corrections.

Follow the steps below to back up Chapter 14 data.

1. If necessary, insert your USB flash drive. From the System Navigation Center, click | Back Up Now |.

2. Click | Back Up |.

3. Go to the location of your USB drive or another location. Type **Chapter 14** in the File name field.

4. Click | Save |.

5. When the window prompts that This company backup will require approximately 1 diskette, click | OK |. When the window prompts Please insert the first disk, click | OK |. When the Back Up Company scale is 100% complete, you have successfully backed up to the current point in Chapter 14. (If you are backing up to the default or another location, this step will differ slightly.)

6. Continue or click File; Exit to exit Peachtree.

7. Exit PCA or continue.

EXPORT REPORTS TO EXCEL

1. Export the following Peachtree reports to Excel:

   - Customer Ledgers
   - Vendor Ledgers
   - Cost of Goods Sold Journal
   - Inventory Adjustment Journal
   - Inventory Profitability Report

- General Ledger Trial Balance

Check with your instructor to see if he or she also wants you to include the following journals to this Excel file: Purchase Journal, Cash Disbursements Journal, Sales Journal, and Cash Receipts Journal.

2. If needed, refer to pages 482-484 for detailed steps to add multiple sheets to one Excel file. Use the file name **Chapter 14_ CL_ VL_CGSJ_IAJ_IPR_GLTB.xlsx**.

NOTE: If your instructor would like you to save reports as PDF files, refer to page 353. The suggested file name is **Chapter 14_Customer Ledgers.pdf**, etc.

SUMMARY AND REVIEW

Complete the following end-of-chapter activities:

1. Going to the Net, page 573

2. Short-Answer Questions, page 574

3. Exercises 14-1 and 14-2, pages 574-576

4. Analysis question, page 576

5. Assessment rubric, page 577

6. Chapter 14 Index, page 578

GOING TO THE NET

Access the Small Business Knowledge Base website at http://www.bizmove.com/finance/m3d3.htm. Scroll down the window to Merchandise Inventories: Perpetual Inventory. (*Hint:* To find areas on the website, use <Ctrl+F>.) Answer these questions about perpetual inventory.

1. What is a perpetual inventory at retail?
2. When is a physical count of inventory necessary?

Short-Answer Questions: The Online Learning Center includes these questions at www.mhhe.com/yacht2012, select Student Edition, Chapter 14, QA Templates.

1. Identify and explain the three-step process for tracking inventory.

2. Explain how PCA uses a perpetual inventory system.

3. Define the term merchandise inventory.

4. Explain the terms Average Cost, LIFO and FIFO.

5. What do Invoice Nos. 106, 107, and 108 show? Identify to whom the merchandise was sold, what was purchased, and the amount of the invoice.

6. What are the journal entries for the following transactions when a perpetual inventory system is used: Purchased four pairs of curtains from Ronald Becker Fabrics at $30 each? Sold four pairs of curtains to Paul Moore for $400?

7. What kind of invoice is No. 109? Identify this transaction and the amount.

Exercise 14-1: You must complete Exercises 12-1, 12-2, 13-1, and 13-2 before starting Exercise 14-1.

1. Start PCA. Open the company that you set up in Exercise 12-1, Your Name Sales and Service.

2. Restore the data that you backed up in Exercise 13-2. (This backup was made on page 546.) To make sure you are starting in the right place, display Exercise 13-2's general ledger trial balance (step 7, page 545).

3. Make the following inventory purchase.

   01/27/12   Carson Phillips Tools sent Invoice No. 732CP for the purchase of 8 tool kits for a unit cost of $30.

4. Make the following inventory adjustment:

> 01/30/12   Two tool kits purchased from Carson Phillips Tools on 1/27/12 were accidentally damaged by the owner. (*Hint:* Use your initials.)

Complete the following additional transactions:

> 01/30/12   Received check in the amount of $972 from Rebekah Nash in payment of Invoice No. 103.
>
> 01/31/12   Cash Sales in the amount of $4,752, ($4,400 plus $352, GA sales taxes) were deposited at Caliber Bank: 20 tool kits, $1,700; 18 hardware sets, $2,700.

5. Make a backup of Exercise 14-1. (Use **Exercise 14-1** as the file name.)

Exercise 14-2: Follow the instructions below to complete Exercise 14-2.

1. Print the Cash Receipts Journal.

2. Print the Purchase Journal.

3. Print the Cost of Goods Sold Journal.

4. Print the Inventory Adjustment Journal.

5. Print the Inventory Profitability Report.

6. Print the General Ledger Trial Balance.

Check Your Figures:

10200, Caliber Bank:	$68,470.63
11000, Accounts Receivable	0.00
12000, Merchandise Inventory	13,250.00
23100, Sales Tax Payable	545.20
50000, Cost of Sales-Hardware	1,450.00
50500, Cost of Sales-Tools	930.00
59500, Purchase Discounts	12.80

7. Export the following reports to Excel.

   a. Cash Receipts Journal
   b. Purchase Journal
   c. Cost of Goods Sold Journal
   d. Inventory Adjustment Journal
   e. Inventory Profitability Report
   f. General Ledger Trial Balance

8. Save the Excel file as **Exercise 14-2_CRJ_PJ_ CGSJ_ IAJ_ IPR_ GLTB.xlsx**.

9. Save these reports as PDFs: Cash Receipts Journal, Cost of Goods Sold Journal, Inventory Adjustment Journal, Purchase Journal, Inventory Profitability Report, and General Ledger Trial Balance. The suggested file name is **Exercise 14-2_Cash Receipts Journal.pdf**, etc.

10. There is no need to backup Exercise 14-2. The Exercise 14-1.ptb file has the data needed to print Exercise 14-2's reports.

ANALYSIS QUESTION

Which one of Cynthia's Service Merchandise inventory items shows the highest gross profit percentage? Why?

ASSESSMENT RUBRIC

Complete the Assessment Rubric online at www.mhhe.com/yacht2012;
Student Edition, select Chapter 14, Assessment Rubric link.

Date	Transaction	Navigation Center/Module	Task Window	Journal Dr./Cr.
1/30	Two tool kits purchased from Carson Phillips Tools on 1/27 were damaged by the owner.			
1/31	Cash sales in the amount of $4,752, ($4,400 plus $352 sales taxes) were deposited at Caliber Bank: 20 tool kits, $1,700; 18 hardware sets $2,700.			

CHAPTER 14 INDEX

Chapter 15

Employees, Payroll, and Account Reconciliation

LEARNING OBJECTIVES

1. Restore data from Chapter 14. (This backup was made on page 572.)
2. Complete the Payroll Setup Wizard.
3. Enter employee and employer default information.
4. Journalize and post Payroll Journal entries.
5. Print paychecks.
6. Reconcile the Southwest Bank account and the Payroll Checking Account.
7. Compare the vendor ledgers, customer ledgers, and inventory valuation report to the associated general ledger accounts.
8. Print the financial statements.
9. Make four backups, save two Excel files, and save nine PDF files.

In accounting you learn that employees and employers are required to pay local, state, and federal payroll taxes. Employers must withhold taxes from each employee's paycheck. The amount withheld for federal taxes is determined from tax tables published by the Internal Revenue Service (IRS). Circular E, Employer's Tax Guide, is available from the IRS. It shows the applicable tax tables and forms that are necessary for filing employee payroll information. PCA has payroll tax tables built into the software. In this chapter you learn how to access and use the payroll tax tables.

The amount withheld also depends on the employee's earnings and the number of *exemptions* or *withholding allowances* claimed by the employee. The number of withholding allowances usually includes one for the employee, one for the employee's spouse, and one for each dependent.

Also deducted from employees' paychecks are *FICA taxes* or social security taxes. This deduction from wages provides qualified workers who retire at age 62 or older with monthly payments from the federal government. The retiree also receives medical benefits called **Medicare** after reaching age 65. In addition to these retirement benefits, social security also provides payments to the surviving family of a qualified deceased worker.

By January 31 of each year employers are required to issue **W-2 Forms** to employees and to the Internal Revenue Service. The W-2 Form is an annual report of the employee's wages subject to FICA and federal income tax and shows the amounts that were withheld.

In PCA, the employee's W-2 Form shows the Federal Income Tax, State Income Tax, Social Security, and Medicare withheld. In 2012, yearly income up to $110,100 is subject to the social security portion of the FICA tax. FICA is actually two taxes—the Social Security portion and the Medicare portion.

In 2012, the maximum taxable earnings subject to social security taxes is $110,100. For additional information, refer to this website www.imercer.com/content/social_security_figures.aspx.

The following table compares 2011 and 2012 FICA tax rates and maximum social security earnings for tax contributions.

Social Security	2011*	2012 (Pending Legislation)
FICA tax rate:		
• Social Security for employees	4.2%	6.2%
• Social Security for employers	6.2%	6.2%
• Medicare	1.45%	1.45%
Maximum Social Security earnings for tax contributions	$106,800	$110,100
Medicare taxable earnings	No limit	No limit

*Peachtree's automatic payroll withholding calculations are based on 2011 legislation. *Remember, Peachtree's payroll tax calculations are for example purposes only.* Payroll products can be purchased from Sage after annual federal legislation (www.peachtree.com/productsservices/payrollsolutions).

Employees may also voluntarily deduct other amounts from wages. These voluntary deductions include: charitable contributions, medical insurance premiums, U.S. savings bonds, or union dues.

It is the purpose of this chapter to show you how to use PCA to enter payroll default information, add employees, make journal entries for payroll, and to print the various payroll reports. Once you set up the default information and employee information, PCA automates the payroll process.

You establish the following default information for processing payroll:

1. The cash account that is credited when disbursing paychecks. Cynthia's Service Merchandise credits Account No. 10300, Payroll Checking Account.

2. The accounts that comprise the employee's fields.

3. The accounts that comprise the employer's fields.

4. The payroll fields that go on the W-2 form.

5. The employee-paid taxes.

6. The employer-paid taxes.

At the Maintain Employees level, you enter the following types of information:

1. The employee name, address, telephone number, and information from the Employee's Withholding Allowance Certificate, Form W-4.

2. Information about employee pay: hourly, salaried, and amount.

3. The tax filing status of the employee for federal, state, and local purposes, including withholding allowances.

If you use the payroll tables included with the student version or educational version software, the payroll tax withholdings are calculated automatically. Once payroll defaults are set up, all you need to do is select the employee you want to pay, date the paycheck and pay period, and post the paycheck. For a yearly fee, Peachtree's payroll tax service offers the appropriate state's payroll tax amounts. For more information, go online to Peachtree's website at www.peachtree.com/productsServices/payrollSolutions/.

The diagram below shows the steps for setting up and using PCA's payroll system.

Default and Setup Information	
Deductions:	*Cash Account:*
FICA, Federal Payroll Tax, State Payroll Tax	10300, Payroll Checking Account

↓

Maintain Employees	
Rate of Pay:	*Frequency:*
$12.50 per hour, regular rate $18.75 per hour, overtime rate	Weekly

↓

Payroll Journal

Paycheck, net pay: $439.73

Wages Expense	537.50	
FICA: Soc. Sec.		22.58
FICA: Medicare		7.79
Federal Payroll Tax		55.72
State Payroll Tax		11.68
Payroll Checking Account		439.73

GETTING STARTED

Follow these steps to start PCA:

1. Start Peachtree. Open Cynthia's Service Merchandise. If you used a unique name, select it. (*Hint:* If a different company opens, select File; Open Previous Company. Open one company.)

2. Restore the Chapter 14.ptb file. This backup was made on page 572.

a. If necessary, insert your USB flash drive. From the System Navigation Center, click 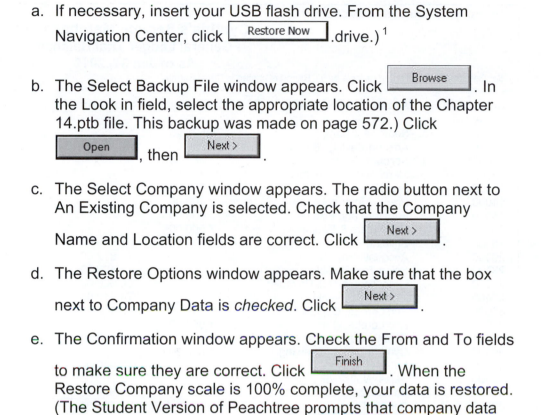 Restore Now .drive.)[1]

b. The Select Backup File window appears. Click Browse . In the Look in field, select the appropriate location of the Chapter 14.ptb file. This backup was made on page 572.) Click Open , then Next > .

c. The Select Company window appears. The radio button next to An Existing Company is selected. Check that the Company Name and Location fields are correct. Click Next > .

d. The Restore Options window appears. Make sure that the box next to Company Data is *checked*. Click Next > .

e. The Confirmation window appears. Check the From and To fields to make sure they are correct. Click Finish . When the Restore Company scale is 100% complete, your data is restored. (The Student Version of Peachtree prompts that company data can be used for 14 months. After that time, the data expires. Click OK . Cynthia's [or your name] Service Merchandise opens.)

To make sure you are starting in the appropriate place in the data (Chapter 14.ptb backup) display the General Ledger Trial Balance. The trial balance shown on the next page is also shown in Chapter 14 on page 571.

---

[1]You can restore from your back up file even if *no* Peachtree company exists. From Peachtree's start up window, select File; Restore. Select the location of your backup file. On the Restore Wizard's Select Company window, select A New Company. The *A New Company* selection allows you to restore your backup data, bypassing the process of new company set up. For more information, refer to Chapter 9, Troubleshooting on pages 299-300.

The McGraw-Hill Companies, Inc., *Computer Accounting with Peachtree by Sage Complete Accounting 2012, 16e*

```
*****EDUCATIONAL VERSION ONLY*****
                                        Cynthia's Service Merchandise
                                          General Ledger Trial Balance
                                               As of Jan 31, 2012
Filter Criteria includes: Report order is by ID. Report is printed in Detail Format.
```

Account ID	Account Description	Debit Amt	Credit Amt
10200	Southwest Bank	75,532.25	
10400	Arizona Savings & Loan	22,000.00	
11000	Accounts Receivable	782.00	
12000	Merchandise Inventory	27,338.00	
13000	Supplies	1,750.00	
14000	Prepaid Insurance	2,400.00	
15000	Furniture and Fixtures	5,000.00	
15100	Computers & Equipment	7,500.00	
15500	Building	100,000.00	
20000	Accounts Payable		812.00
23100	Sales Tax Payable		429.99
27000	Long-Term Notes Payable		20,500.00
27400	Mortgage Payable		74,412.05
39006	Eric Lerette, Capital		72,195.00
39007	Eric Lerette, Drawing	1,000.00	
39008	Cynthia Barber, Capital		72,195.00
39009	Cynthia Barber, Drawing	1,000.00	
40000	Sales-Hardware		2,550.00
40200	Sales-Wall		2,700.00
40400	Sales-Floor		960.00
40600	Service Fees		124.89
50000	Cost of Sales-Hardware	850.00	
50500	Cost of Sales-Wall	810.00	
57000	Cost of Sales-Floor	324.00	
57050	Cost of Sales-Lights	128.00	
59500	Purchase Discounts		17.96
67500	Interest Expense	97.85	
70000	Maintenance Expense	160.00	
73500	Postage Expense	45.00	
75500	Supplies Expense	107.65	
76000	Telephone Expense	72.14	
	Total:	**246,896.89**	**246,896.89**

Establishing the Payroll Account

In order to establish the payroll checking account, transfer funds from Southwest Bank (Account No. 10200) to the Payroll Checking Account (Account No. 10300). Journalize and post the following General Journal transaction:

Date   *Transaction Description*

01/05/12   Cynthia's Service Merchandise transferred $6,500 from
              Account No. 10200, Southwest Bank, to Account No.
              10300, Payroll Checking Account.

After posting this general journal entry, display the general journal. (*Hint:
Click on Reports & Forms; General Leger, General Journal, Display.*)

Cynthia's Service Merchandise
General Journal
For the Period From Jan 1, 2012 to Jan 31, 2012
Filter Criteria includes: Report order is by Date. Report is printed with Accounts having Zero Amounts and with shortened descriptions and in Detail Format.

Date	Account ID	Reference	Trans Description	Debit Amt	Credit Amt
1/5/12	10300		Payroll Checking Account	6,500.00	
	10200		Southwest Bank		6,500.00
		Total		6,500.00	6,500.00

Close the General Journal window and the Select a Report or Form
window.

PAYROLL SETUP WIZARD

The Payroll Setup wizard walks you through setting up most payroll
defaults and standard payroll fields. As you answer the prompts in the
wizard, Peachtree creates most of the common payroll fields used in
calculating deductions and taxes.

The Peachtree Payroll Setup Wizard establishes the following:

- State and locality defaults.
- State unemployment percentage.
- Common federal and state payroll fields for employee-paid and
  company-paid taxes.
- General ledger account defaults for payroll fields.
- Optional payroll fields for tips, meals, 401K contributions, etc.

1. From the Navigation Bar, select 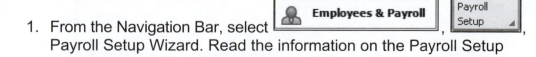 ,
   Payroll Setup Wizard. Read the information on the Payroll Setup

Wizard window. Observe that the left pane shows Home, Payroll Options, Company Information, Benefits, Taxes, Setup Complete.

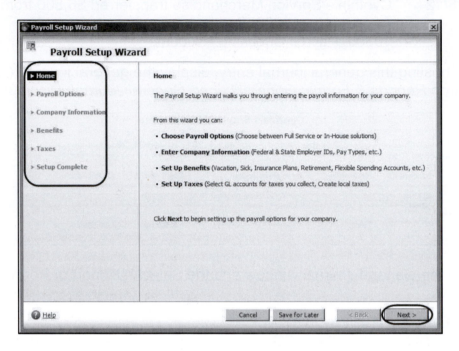

2. Click Next >. Payroll Options is selected. Read the information. Accept the default for Do It Yourself In-House.

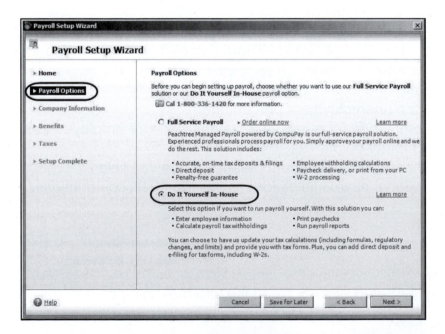

3. Click [Next >]. The Payroll Options – Do It Yourself In-House window appears. Select Do It Yourself.

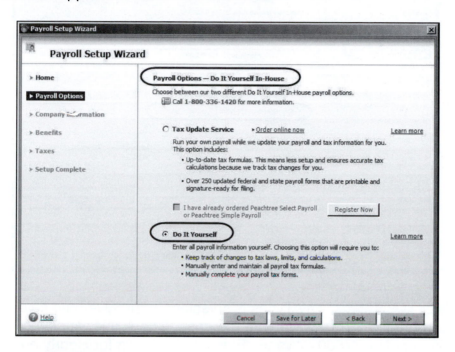

4. Click [Next >]. Read the Other Payroll Options, Direct Deposit, and E-Filing areas.

5. Then click [Next >]. Company Information is selected. The Federal Employer ID, State Employer ID, State (AZ), and State Unemployment ID are automatically completed. These fields agree with the company information entered on page 431 in Chapter 12.

6. Type **3.4** in the State Unemployment Rate field. The Arizona Administration Assessment Tax rate is shown and No is selected for Do you want to record employee means and tips. Compare your Company Information window to the one shown on the next page.

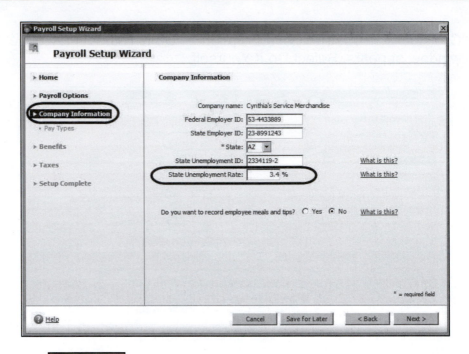

7. Click 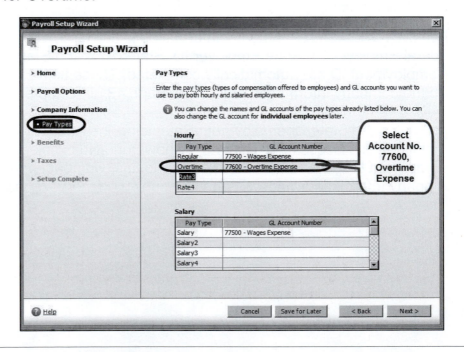. Pay Types is selected. In the Overtime field, select Account No. 77600, Overtime Expense. Check this window carefully. Account No. 77500 – Wages Expense is shown for Hourly and Salary regular pay types. Account No. 77600 – Overtime Expense for Overtime.

8. Click | Next > | . The Benefits window appears. Do not make any selections. Click | Next > | to continue.

9. The Payroll Taxes window appears. Observe that the Tax liability acct no. (23400) and Tax Expense acct no. (72000) is selected. To accept these defaults, click | Next > | .

10. The Setup Complete window appears, click | Finish | . After completing employee defaults in the next section, you return to the Payroll Setup Wizard to assign employee and company-paid tax fields.

ENTERING EMPLOYEE AND EMPLOYER DEFAULT INFORMATION

Follow these steps to enter employee and employer default information:

1. From the Employees & Payroll Navigation Center, click | Employees ⬧ | ; Set Up Employee Defaults. The Employee Defaults window displays. In the Employee Defaults window, you enter account numbers that serve as the basis for payroll withholdings.

    There are five tabs:
    ➢ General
    ➢ Employee Fields
    ➢ Company Fields
    ➢ Review Ratings
    ➢ Employment Status

2. Select the Employee Fields tab.

3. The Fed_Income line shows the default G/L Account as 23400 (Federal Payroll Taxes Payable) for FIT. Account No. 23400, Federal Payroll Taxes Payable, is the correct account for the Fed Income line.

4. Click on the G/L Account field for Soc_Sec and select Account No. 24000, FICA Employee Taxes Payable.

5. Click on the G/L Account field for MEDICARE and select Account No. 24200, Medicare Employee Taxes Payable.

6. Click on the G/L Account field for St_Income and select Account No. 23600, State Payroll Taxes Payable.

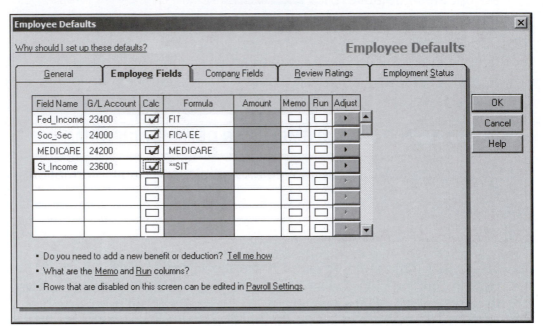

7. Click on the Company Fields tab. Change the following account numbers:

	Liability Column	*Expense Column*
Soc_Sec_C	24100, FICA Employer Taxes Payable	72510, FICA Expense
Medicare_C	24400, Medicare Employer Taxes Payable	72520, Medicare Expense
Fed_Unemp_C	23500, FUTA Tax Payable	72530, FUTA Expense
State_Unemp_C	23700, SUTA Payable	72540, SUTA Expense

Compare your Employee Defaults/Company Fields window, to the one shown on the next page. Make sure the Liability and Expense accounts are correctly selected.

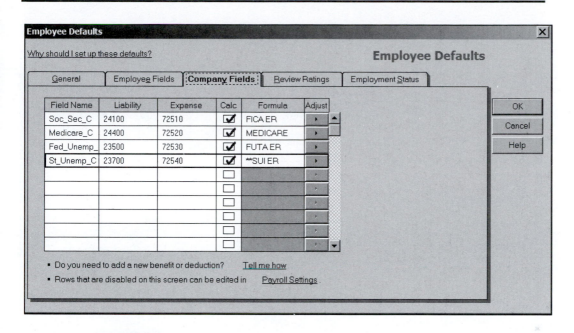

8. Click OK to save your changes and return to the menu bar.

COMPLETING PAYROLL SETUP

After completing the initial payroll setup and entering employee defaults, the next step is to use the Payroll Setup Wizard to assign tax fields. Follow these steps to do that.

1. From the Employees & Payroll Navigation Center, click ![Payroll Setup], Payroll Setup Wizard. On the left pane select Taxes. Then, select Assign Tax Fields.

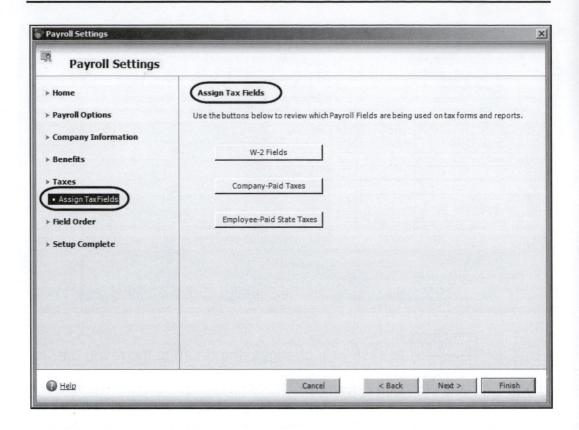

2. The Assign Tax Fields Taxes window appears. There are three buttons: W-2 Fields, Company-Paid Taxes, and Employee-Paid State Taxes. Click W-2 Fields. The Assign Tax Fields for W-2s window appears. These selections appear. (If not, select them.)

Federal income tax withheld: Fed_Income
Social Security tax withheld: Soc_Sec
Medicare tax withheld: MEDICARE
State income tax: St_Income

Compare your Assign Tax Fields for W-2s window to the one shown on the next page.

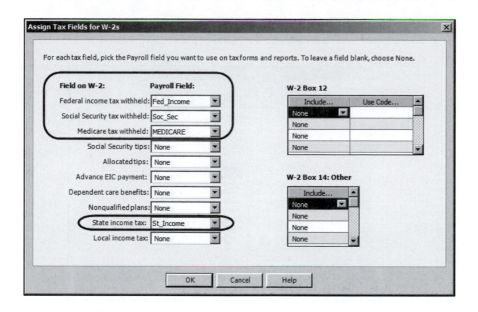

3. Click [OK]. You are returned to the Assign Tax Fields window.

4. Click [Company-Paid Taxes]. The Assign Company-Paid Tax Fields window appears. These selections appear. (If not, select them.)

Federal Unemployment (FUTA):   Fed_Unemp_C
State Unemployment (SUTA):   St_Unemp_C

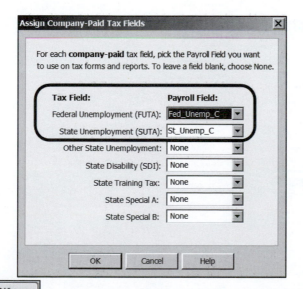

5. Click [OK]. You are returned to the Assign Tax Fields window.

6. Click [Employee-Paid State Taxes]. Do not make any changes.

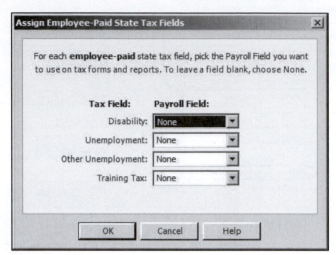

7. Click [OK]. You are returned to the Assign Tax Fields window. Click [Next >].

8. The Field Order window appears. Do not make any changes. Click [Next >].

9. The Setup Complete window appears. Read the information.

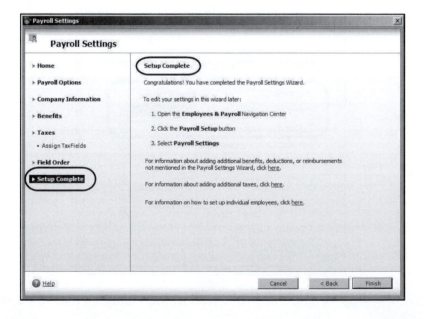

10. Click [Finish] .

ENTERING EMPLOYEE MAINTENANCE INFORMATION

The Maintain Employees/Sales Reps window includes information about
your employees or sales representatives. The information is displayed as
seven tabs: General, Additional Info, Pay Info, Withholding Info,
Vacation/Sick Time, Employee Fields, and Company Fields.
Follow these steps to set up employee maintenance information.

1. Select [Employees ▲] , New Employee. The Maintain Employees & Sales
    Reps window appears.

2. Complete the following fields.

    Employee ID: **A001** (use zeroes)
    Name: **Tom Ashton**
    Accept the default for Employee
    Address: **3875 E. Lakeshore Dr.**
    City, ST Zip: **Tempe, AZ 85021**
    E-mail   **tom@mail.com**
    Home phone: **480-555-4390**
    Social Security No   **020-00-1234**
    Type: **FULL**

3. Click on the Withholding Info tab. Complete the following fields.

    Filing Status: Single for Federal, State, and Local
    Allowances: **1** for Federal, State, and Local
    State Addl Withholding: **11.68** (Type **11.68** in the State,
                                  Additional Withholding field.)

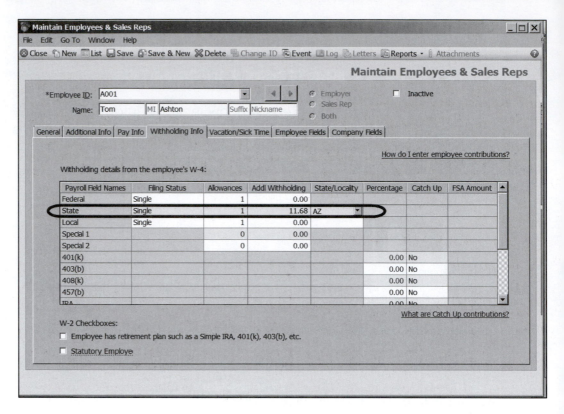

4. Click on the Pay Info tab.

5. Type **12.50** in the Hourly Pay Rate column. Press the **<Enter>** key two times.

6. Type **18.75** in the Hourly Pay Rate column for Overtime. Press the **<Enter>** key. Make sure that the Pay Method field displays Hourly - Hours per Pay Period, and that the Pay Frequency field displays Weekly. Compare your Maintain Employees & Sales Reps/Pay Info window to the one shown on the next page.

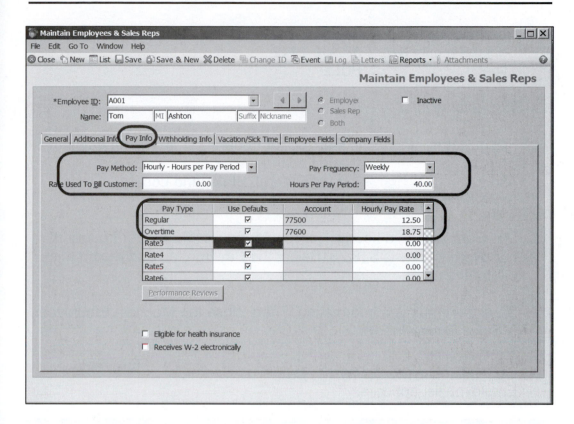

7. Select the Employee Fields tab. Notice that the accounts selected for Fed_Income, Soc_Sec, MEDICARE, and St_Income match the accounts shown on page 590, Employee Defaults/Employee Fields window.

8. Click on the Company Fields tab. These are the employer payroll tax liabilities. Notice that the accounts match the Employee Defaults/Company Fields window shown on page 591.

9. Click [Save & New].

10. Click on the General tab. Enter another employee.

Employee ID:	**G001**
Name:	**Lauren Gomez**
Accept the default for Employee.	
Address:	**6054 E. Pinecrest Dr.**
City, ST Zip:	**Phoenix, AZ 85033**
E-mail:	**lauren@mail.com**

Home phone:	**602-555-0722**
Social Security No:	**002-00-2212**
Type:	**FULL**

Withholding Info:

Filing Status:	**Married** for Federal, State (Married/Jointly), and Local
Allow:	**2** for Federal, State, and Local
State Addl Withholding:	**5.04**

11. Ms. Gomez is paid hourly. Her regular pay is $12.50 per hour and her overtime pay is $18.75. Select the Pay Info tab and record this information.

12. Save the employee information. Then, close the Maintain Employees & Sales Reps window.

13. On the Employees & Payroll Navigation Center, click ⟳ Refresh . The Employee list appears.

Employees				🖩 View Detailed List
Employee ID △	Last Name	First Name	Home Phone	Pay Method
A001	Ashton	Tom	480-555-4390	Hourly - Hours per Pa
G001	Gomez	Lauren	602-555-0722	Hourly - Hours per Pa

BACKING UP YOUR DATA

Follow these steps to back up Chapter 15 data:

1. If necessary, insert your USB flash drive. From the System Navigation Center, click Back Up Now .

2. Click Back Up .

3. Go to the location of your USB drive or another location. Type **Chapter 15 Begin** in the File name field.

4. Click Save .

5. When the window prompts that This company backup will require approximately 1 diskette, click `OK`. When the window prompts Please insert the first disk, click `OK`. When the Back Up Company scale is 100% complete, you have successfully backed up to the current point in Chapter 15. (If you are backing up to the default or another location, this step will differ slightly.)

6. Continue or click on File, Exit to exit Peachtree.

PAYROLL ENTRY

Once the defaults for payroll are set up, you have very little work to do. In Chapter 4, Employees, Bellwether Garden Supply already had the default information set up. Since the payroll tax tables were included for the sample company, all you needed to do for payroll was:

➢ Enter or select the Employee ID.

➢ Specify the pay period (period-ending date).

➢ Verify the information the window displays (name and address of employee, amount of hours, and employee/employer fields.)

➢ Print or post the paycheck.

In Chapter 15, you use the payroll tax tables included with the software. These tables are for example purposes only and are not meant for exact computation of payroll withholding amounts.

In Peachtree, the Payroll Entry window is also the ***payroll journal***. All entries made in the Payroll Entry window show up in the payroll journal, and then are posted to both the General Ledger and to the Employee file.

Payroll entry is a simple process after completing the Payroll Setup Wizard and employee and company (employer) default and maintenance information. When employee and company defaults are selected, you are setting up the payroll liability and expense accounts for payroll entry. The employee maintenance information includes the employee's name; address; social security number; Federal, State, and Local withholding allowances; and pay levels.

All journal entries made to the Payroll Journal are posted both to the General Ledger and to the Employee file. Once an Employee ID is selected, the rest of the employee information is completed automatically. Enough information is entered in the Maintain Employees record, Default Information, and the payroll tax tables included with the software to determine what the paycheck amount should be. If the information is correct, you print or post the paycheck and proceed to the next employee.

The check amount (or net pay) is automatically credited to Account No. 10300, Payroll Checking Account. The withholding amounts are calculated based on the Payroll Fields which were defined in the Default Information that you previously entered. The rate and frequency of pay were set up in the Employee/Sales Rep record. For Cynthia's Service Merchandise, employees are paid weekly.

1. From the Employees & Payroll Navigation Center, click , Enter Payroll For One Employee.

2. The Select a Cash Account window displays. Select the Payroll Checking Account.

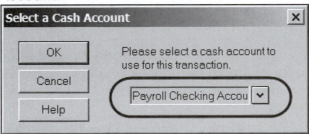

3. Click [OK].

4. In the Employee ID field, select Tom Ashton.

5. Leave the Check Number field blank. Type or select **6** as the Date.

6. Make sure that Account No. 10300, Payroll Checking Account, is displayed in the Cash Account field.

7. In the Pay Period End field, type **6** and press **<Enter>**.

8. Accept the default for Weeks in Pay Period which is 1 week.

9. In the Hours Worked table go to the Overtime Hours field. Type **2** and press **<Enter>**.

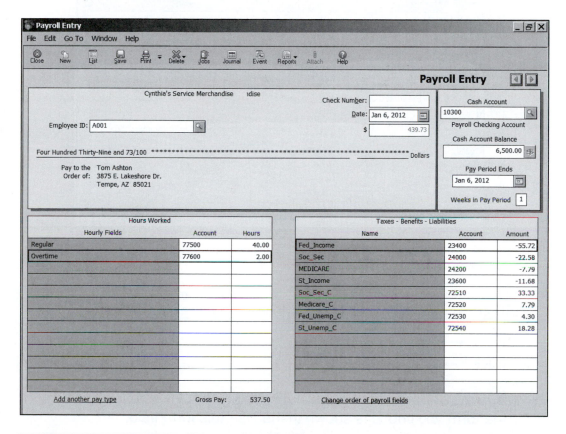

Comment

Observe that the Taxes- Benefits - Liabilities table on the Payroll Entry window includes withholding amounts. These amounts are for example purposes only and do not reflect accurate payroll taxes. For an explanation of Peachtree's payroll calculations, refer to the chart on page 580.

A separate service provided by Peachtree at an additional cost includes payroll tax tables. More information about Peachtree's Payroll Tax Service is included on their website at www.peachtree.com/productsServices/payrollSolutions/.

---

10. Click .

---

11. The Print Forms: Payroll Checks window appears. Click Select Form .
    Select OCR Multi-Purpose PR Laser.

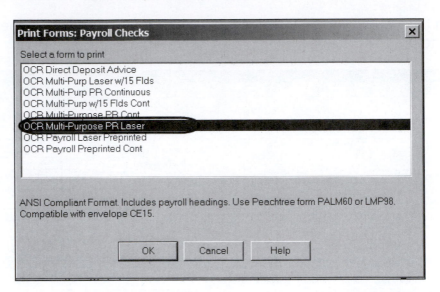

Comment
The form you select is tied to the kind of printer you are using. You may need to make a different selection depending on your printer.

12. Click OK .

13. The Print Forms: Payroll Checks window appears. Make sure that the form you chose is shown in the Use this form field.

14. Type **101** as the First check number.

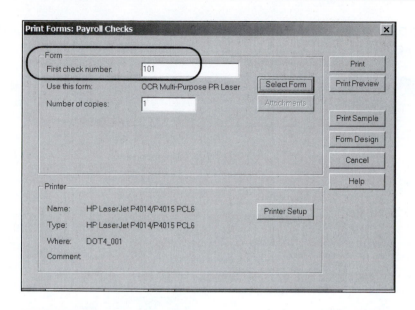

15. Click [Print]. Your check starts to print.

Tom Ashton			Employee ID: A001		
	This Check	Year to Date	Social Sec # xxx-xx-1234		
Gross	537.50	537.50	Hours	Rate	Total
Fed Income	-55.72	-55.72 Regular	40.00	12.50	500.00
Soc Sec	-22.58	-22.58 Overtime	2.00	18.75	37.50
MEDICARE	-7.79	-7.79			
St Income	-11.68	-11.68			

Net Check: $439.73   Total   42.00   537.50

Pay Period Beginning: Dec 31, 2011   Check Date: 1/6/12
Pay Period Ending: Jan 6, 2012   Weeks in Pay Period: 1

Check Number: 101   Jan 6, 2012

439.73

Four Hundred Thirty-Nine and 73/100 Dollars

Tom Ashton
3875 E. Lakeshore Dr.
Tempe, AZ 85021

16. Make the selections to pay Ms. Gomez on January 6, 2012. She worked 40 regular hours for Cynthia's Service Merchandise.

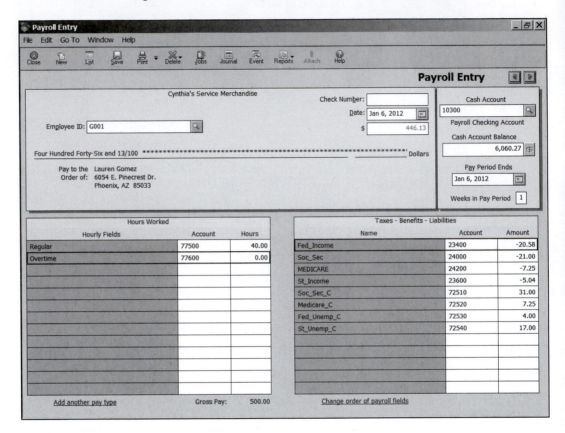

17. Print Check No. 102. Compare your check with the one shown on the next page.

```
      Lauren Gomez                                    Employee ID: G001
                                                      Social Sec # xxx-xx-2212
                        This Check    Year to Date
  Gross                  500.00          500.00       Hours        Rate        Total
  Fed Income             -20.58          -20.58  Regular  40.00    12.50       500.00
  Soc Sec                -21.00          -21.00
  MEDICARE                -7.25           -7.25
  St Income               -5.04           -5.04



  Net Check:            $446.13          Total        40.00                    500.00
            Pay Period Beginning: Dec 31, 2011              Check Date: 1/6/12
            Pay Period Ending: Jan 6, 2012               Weeks in Pay Period: 1


                      Check Number:   102                      Jan 6, 2012


                                                              446.13


  Four Hundred Forty-Six and 13/100 Dollars

      Lauren Gomez
      6054 E. Pinecrest Dr.
      Phoenix, AZ  85033
```

18. Make the following payroll entries for Tom Ashton and Lauren Gomez.

Date	Name	Hours Worked	Overtime	Check No.
1/13/12	T. Ashton	40	2	103
	L. Gomez	40		104
1/20/12	T. Ashton	40	2	105
	L. Gomez	40		106
1/27/12	T. Ashton	40	2	107
	L. Gomez	40		108

After recording the paycheck information, type the check number, then click **Save** to post. You do *not* need to print the paychecks.

19. Close the Payroll Entry window.

PRINTING THE PAYROLL JOURNAL

From the Recently Used Employee Reports area of the Employees &
Payroll Navigation Center, link to <u>Print</u> the Payroll Journal.

*****EDUCATIONAL VERSION ONLY*****

Page: 1

Cynthia's Service Merchandise
Payroll Journal
For the Period From Jan 1, 2012 to Jan 31, 2012

Filter Criteria includes: Report order is by Check Date. Report is printed in Detail Format.

Date Employee	GL Acct ID	Reference	Debit Amt	Credit Amt
1/6/12 Tom Ashton	77500	101	500.00	
	77600		37.50	
	23400			55.72
	24000			22.58
	24200			7.79
	23600			11.68
	24100			33.33
	24400			7.79
	23500			4.30
	23700			18.28
	72510		33.33	
	72520		7.79	
	72530		4.30	
	72540		18.28	
	10300			439.73
1/6/12 Lauren Gomez	77500	102	500.00	
	23400			20.58
	24000			21.00
	24200			7.25
	23600			5.04
	24100			31.00
	24400			7.25
	23500			4.00
	23700			17.00
	72510		31.00	
	72520		7.25	
	72530		4.00	
	72540		17.00	
	10300			446.13
1/13/12 Tom Ashton	77500	103	500.00	
	77600		37.50	
	23400			55.72
	24000			22.58
	24200			7.79
	23600			11.68
	24100			33.33
	24400			7.79
	23500			4.30
	23700			18.28
	72510		33.33	
	72520		7.79	
	72530		4.30	
	72540		18.28	
	10300			439.73
1/13/12 Lauren Gomez	77500	104	500.00	
	23400			20.58
	24000			21.00
	24200			7.25
	23600			5.04
	24100			31.00
	24400			7.25
	23500			4.00
	23700			17.00
	72510		31.00	
	72520		7.25	
	72530		4.00	
	72540		17.00	
	10300			446.13
1/20/12	77500	105	500.00	

Page: 2

Cynthia's Service Merchandise
Payroll Journal
For the Period From Jan 1, 2012 to Jan 31, 2012

Filter Criteria includes: Report order is by Check Date. Report is printed in Detail Format.

Date Employee	GL Acct ID	Reference	Debit Amt	Credit Amt
Tom Ashton	77600		37.50	
	23400			55.72
	24000			22.58
	24200			7.79
	23600			11.68
	24100			33.33
	24400			7.79
	23500			4.30
	23700			18.28
	72510		33.33	
	72520		7.79	
	72530		4.30	
	72540		18.28	
	10300			439.73
1/20/12 Lauren Gomez	77500	106	500.00	
	23400			20.58
	24000			21.00
	24200			7.25
	23600			5.04
	24100			31.00
	24400			7.25
	23500			4.00
	23700			17.00
	72510		31.00	
	72520		7.25	
	72530		4.00	
	72540		17.00	
	10300			446.13
1/27/12 Tom Ashton	77500	107	500.00	
	77600		37.50	
	23400			55.72
	24000			22.58
	24200			7.79
	23600			11.68
	24100			33.33
	24400			7.79
	23500			4.30
	23700			18.28
	72510		33.33	
	72520		7.79	
	72530		4.30	
	72540		18.28	
	10300			439.73
1/27/12 Lauren Gomez	77500	108	500.00	
	23400			20.58
	24000			21.00
	24200			7.25
	23600			5.04
	24100			31.00
	24400			7.25
	23500			4.00
	23700			17.00
	72510		31.00	
	72520		7.25	
	72530		4.00	
	72540		17.00	
	10300			446.13
			4,641.80	**4,641.80**

ACCOUNT RECONCILIATION

In Chapters 12-15, you worked with Peachtree's accounts payable, accounts receivable, inventory, and payroll systems. PCA's general ledger is integrated with the other parts of the program. For example, when a vendor is paid, that entry is recorded in *both* the general ledger, Southwest Bank *and* Accounts Payable accounts, and the individual vendor's account. In other words, the subsidiary ledger (vendor ledger) works together with the general ledger.

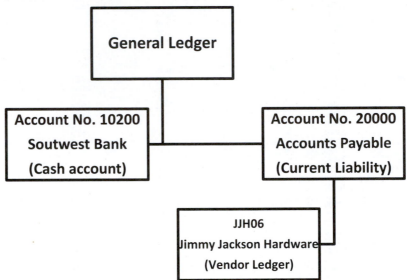

To see how this works, you are going to reconcile two bank statements.

- The January 31, 2012 bank statement from Southwest Bank, page 609.

- The January 31, 2012 bank statement from the Payroll Checking Account, page 610.

Then, you are going to check the accounts receivable, accounts payable, and merchandise inventory account balances against the general ledger. This shows you that Peachtree's subsidiary ledgers (customer ledgers, vendor ledgers, and inventory valuation) are in agreement with the associated general ledger accounts.

Southwest Bank Statement

You may want to review the steps for Account Reconciliation in Chapter 10, pages 339-341.

Statement of Account Southwest Bank January 1 to January 31, 2012		Account No. 30092-23-10		Cynthia's Service Merchandise 2117 Oak Street Tempe, AZ 85345	
REGULAR CHECKING					
Previous Balance	12/31/11	73,500.00			
9 Deposits(+)		3,390.88			
11 Checks (-)		9,450.63			
Service Charges (-)	1/31/12	18.00			
Ending Balance	1/31/12	**67,422.25**			
DEPOSITS					
1/16/12	324.00	1/25/12	1,404.00	1/28/12	53.88
1/23/12	324.00	1/26/12	324.00	1/31/12	640.00
1/25/12	105.00	1/27/12	216.00		
CHECKS (Asterisk * indicates break in check number sequence)					
		1/5/12	Transfer	6,500.00	
		1/26/12	3030	160.00	
		1/26/12	3031	45.00	
		1/26/12	3032	107.65	
		1/27/12	3033	72.14	
		1/27/12	3034	500.00	
		1/27/12	3035	500.00	
		1/28/12	3036	370.44	
		1/30/12	3037	392.00	
		1/30/12	3038	117.60	
		1/30/12	3039	685.80	

NOTE: Deposits that are recorded on the same day may be added together on the Account Reconciliation window. For example, $1,509 may be shown for $1,404 plus $105 and $693.88 for $53.88 plus $640.

Payroll Checking Account Bank Statement

Statement of Account Payroll Checking Account January 1 to January 31, 2012		Account No. 891-7823142	Cynthia's Service Merchandise 2117 Oak Street Tempe, AZ 85345	
REGULAR CHECKING				
Previous Balance	12/31/11	0.00		
1 Deposits(+)		6,500.00		
6 Checks (-)		2,657.58		
Service Charges (-)	1/31/12	15.00		
Ending Balance	1/31/12	**3,827.42**		
DEPOSITS				
	1/5/12	6,500.00		
CHECKS (Asterisk * indicates break in check number sequence)				
	1/9/12	101	439.73	
	1/9/12	102	446.13	
	1/16/12	103	439.73	
	1/16/12	104	446.13	
	1/23/12	105	439.73	
	1/23/12	106	446.13	

Printing Reports: Account Reconciliation, Accounts Receivable, Accounts Payable, and Inventory

1. Print the Southwest Bank account reconciliation report.

*****EDUCATIONAL VERSION ONLY*****

Cynthia's Service Merchandise
Account Reconciliation
As of Jan 31, 2012
10200 - Southwest Bank
Bank Statement Date: January 31, 2012

Filter Criteria includes: Report is printed in Detail Format.

Beginning GL Balance				73,500.00
Add: Cash Receipts				5,982.88
Less: Cash Disbursements				(3,950.63)
Add (Less) Other				(6,518.00)
Ending GL Balance				69,014.25
Ending Bank Balance				67,422.25
Add back deposits in transit				
	Jan 30, 20	01/30/12	2,592.00	
Total deposits in transit				2,592.00
(Less) outstanding ch				
	Jan 30, 20	3040	(500.00)	
	Jan 30, 20	3041	(500.00)	
Total outstanding checks				(1,000.00)
Add (Less) Other				
Total other				
Unreconciled difference				0.00
Ending GL Balance				69,014.25

2. Print the Payroll Checking Account reconciliation report. (*Hint:* On the Account Reconciliation Select a Report or Form window, click

⚙ Options . In the Select a filter field, select Account No. 10300, Payroll Checking Account.)

```
*****EDUCATIONAL VERSION ONLY*****          Cynthia's Service Merchandise
                                              Account Reconciliation
                                                As of Jan 31, 2012
                                          10300 - Payroll Checking Account
                                          Bank Statement Date: January 31, 2012
Filter Criteria includes: Report is printed in Detail Format.
```

Beginning GL Balance		
Add: Cash Receipts		
Less: Cash Disbursements	(3,543.44)	
Add (Less) Other	6,485.00	
Ending GL Balance	2,941.56	
Ending Bank Balance	3,827.42	
Add back deposits in transit		
Total deposits in transit		
(Less) outstanding checks		
Jan 27, 20 107	(439.73)	
Jan 27, 20 108	(446.13)	
Total outstanding checks	(885.86)	
Add (Less) Other		
Total other		
Unreconciled difference	0.00	
Ending GL Balance	2,941.56	

3. Print the General Ledger accounts 10200 and 10300. (*Hint:* On the General Ledger Select a Report or Form window, select General Ledger, then click ⚙ Options . On the Modify Report - General Ledger window, select the filter GL Account ID. Select One or more, then place a checkmark in the boxes next to 10200 and 10300. Click <OK>. Observe that Account No. 10200, Southwest Bank; and Account No. 10300, Payroll Checking Account agree with the Ending GL Balances shown on the account reconciliation reports on pages 611 and 612: $69,014.25 and $2,941.56, respectively.

Cynthia's Service Merchandise
General Ledger
For the Period From Jan 1, 2012 to Jan 31, 2012

Filter Criteria includes: 1) IDs from 10200 to 10300. Report order is by ID. Report is printed with shortened descriptions and in Detail Format.

Account ID Account Description	Date	Reference	Jrnl	Trans Description	Debit Amt	Credit A	Balance
10200	1/1/12			Beginning Balance			73,500.00
Southwest Bank	1/5/12		GENJ	Southwest Bank		6,500.00	
	1/13/12	Invoice 103	CRJ	Paul Moore	324.00		
	1/20/12	Invoice 101	CRJ	Aileen Parker	324.00		
	1/23/12	Invoice 104	CRJ	Joann Poe	105.00		
	1/23/12	Cash	CRJ	Cash	1,404.00		
	1/24/12	3030	CDJ	David Allison		160.00	
	1/24/12	3031	CDJ	U.S. Post Office		45.00	
	1/24/12	3032	CDJ	Broadway Office Su		107.65	
	1/24/12	3033	CDJ	RCI Phone Co.		72.14	
	1/24/12	Invoice 106	CRJ	Aileen Parker	324.00		
	1/25/12	3034	CDJ	Eric Lerette		500.00	
	1/25/12	3035	CDJ	Cynthia Barber		500.00	
	1/25/12	3036	CDJ	Lee Lanning Product		370.44	
	1/26/12	Invoice 108	CRJ	Paul Moore	216.00		
	1/27/12	Invoice 105	CRJ	Betty Barlow	53.88		
	1/27/12	Invoice 102	CRJ	Diane Conlin	640.00		
	1/28/12	3037	CDJ	Jimmy Jackson Har		392.00	
	1/28/12	3038	CDJ	Ronald Becker Fabri		117.60	
	1/30/12	Cash	CRJ	Barbara Williams	216.00		
	1/30/12	3039	CDJ	EMD Mortgage Co.		685.80	
	1/30/12	3040	CDJ	Eric Lerette		500.00	
	1/30/12	3041	CDJ	Cynthia Barber		500.00	
	1/30/12	Cash	CRJ	Cash sales	2,376.00		
	1/31/12	01/31/12	GENJ	Service Charge		18.00	
				Current Period Chan	5,982.88	10,468.63	-4,485.75
	1/31/12			**Ending Balance**			69,014.25
10300	1/1/12			Beginning Balance			
Payroll Checking Accoun	1/5/12		GENJ	Payroll Checking Ac	6,500.00		
	1/6/12	101	PRJ	Tom Ashton		439.73	
	1/6/12	102	PRJ	Lauren Gomez		446.13	
	1/13/12	103	PRJ	Tom Ashton		439.73	
	1/13/12	104	PRJ	Lauren Gomez		446.13	
	1/20/12	105	PRJ	Tom Ashton		439.73	
	1/20/12	106	PRJ	Lauren Gomez		446.13	
	1/27/12	107	PRJ	Tom Ashton		439.73	
	1/27/12	108	PRJ	Lauren Gomez		446.13	
	1/31/12	01/31/12	GENJ	Service Charge		15.00	
				Current Period Chan	6,500.00	3,558.44	2,941.56
	1/31/12			**Ending Balance**			2,941.56

4. Print the general ledger account balance for Account No. 11000, Accounts Receivable.

*****EDUCATIONAL VERSION ONLY*****

Cynthia's Service Merchandise
General Ledger
For the Period From Jan 1, 2012 to Jan 31, 2012
Filter Criteria includes: 1) IDs from 11000 to 11000. Report order is by ID. Report is printed with shortened descriptions and in Detail Format.

Account ID Account Descriptio	Date	Reference	Jrnl	Trans Description	Debit Amt	Credit Amt	Balance
11000	1/1/12			Beginning Balance			
Accounts Receivable	1/6/12	101	SJ	Aileen Parker	324.00		
	1/6/12	102	SJ	Diane Conlin	640.00		
	1/6/12	103	SJ	Paul Moore	432.00		
	1/6/12	104	SJ	Joann Poe	486.00		
	1/10/12	105	SJ	Betty Barlow	53.88		
	1/13/12	CM103	SJ	Paul Moore		108.00	
	1/13/12	Invoice 103	CRJ	Paul Moore - Invoice: 10		324.00	
	1/19/12	106	SJ	Aileen Parker	324.00		
	1/19/12	107	SJ	Diane Conlin	320.00		
	1/19/12	108	SJ	Paul Moore	216.00		
	1/20/12	Invoice 101	CRJ	Aileen Parker - Invoice: 1		324.00	
	1/20/12	109	SJ	Betty Barlow	81.00		
	1/23/12	Invoice 104	CRJ	Joann Poe - Invoice: 104		105.00	
	1/24/12	Invoice 106	CRJ	Aileen Parker - Invoice: 1		324.00	
	1/26/12	Invoice 108	CRJ	Paul Moore - Invoice: 10		216.00	
	1/27/12	Invoice 105	CRJ	Betty Barlow - Invoice: 1		53.88	
	1/27/12	Invoice 102	CRJ	Diane Conlin - Invoice: 1		640.00	
				Current Period Change	2,876.88	2,094.88	782.00
	1/31/12			Ending Balance			782.00

5. Compare the general ledger's accounts receivable balance to the customer ledgers balance.

*****EDUCATIONAL VERSION ONLY*****

Cynthia's Service Merchandise
Customer Ledgers
For the Period From Jan 1, 2012 to Jan 31, 2012
Filter Criteria includes: Report order is by ID. Report is printed in Detail Format.

Customer ID Customer	Date	Trans No	Type	Debit Amt	Credit Amt	Balance
ap001	1/6/12	101	SJ	324.00		324.00
Aileen Parker	1/19/12	106	SJ	324.00		648.00
	1/20/12	Invoice 101	CRJ		324.00	324.00
	1/24/12	Invoice 106	CRJ		324.00	0.00
bb002	1/10/12	105	SJ	53.88		53.88
Betty Barlow	1/20/12	109	SJ	81.00		134.88
	1/27/12	Invoice 105	CRJ		53.88	81.00
dc003	1/6/12	102	SJ	640.00		640.00
Diane Conlin	1/19/12	107	SJ	320.00		960.00
	1/27/12	Invoice 102	CRJ		640.00	320.00
jp004	1/6/12	104	SJ	486.00		486.00
Joann Poe	1/23/12	Invoice 104	CRJ		105.00	381.00
pm005	1/6/12	103	SJ	432.00		432.00
Paul Moore	1/13/12	CM103	SJ		108.00	324.00
	1/13/12	Invoice 103	CRJ		324.00	0.00
	1/19/12	108	SJ	216.00		216.00
	1/26/12	Invoice 108	CRJ		216.00	0.00
Report Total				**2,876.88**	**2,094.88**	**782.00**

6. Print the general ledger account balance for Account No. 20000, Account Payable. (A minus sign in front of a general ledger balance means it is a credit balance.)

*****EDUCATIONAL VERSION ONLY*****

Cynthia's Service Merchandise
General Ledger
For the Period From Jan 1, 2012 to Jan 31, 2012
Filter Criteria includes: 1) IDs from 20000 to 20000. Report order is by ID. Report is printed with shortened descriptions and in Detail Format.

Account ID Account Descri	Date	Reference	Jrnl	Trans Description	Debit Amt	Credit Amt	Balance
20000	1/1/12			Beginning Balance			
Accounts Payable	1/3/12	56JJ	PJ	Jimmy Jackson Hardware		300.00	
	1/13/12	112	PJ	Thomas Sales and Service		512.00	
	1/20/12	90	PJ	Lee Lanning Products		432.00	
	1/20/12	210	PJ	Ronald Becker Fabrics		120.00	
	1/20/12	78JJ	PJ	Jimmy Jackson Hardware		500.00	
	1/25/12	VCM90	PJ	Lee Lanning Products	54.00		
	1/25/12	3036	CDJ	Lee Lanning Products - Invo	378.00		
	1/28/12	VCM78JJ	PJ	Jimmy Jackson Hardware	100.00		
	1/28/12	3037	CDJ	Jimmy Jackson Hardware -	400.00		
	1/28/12	3038	CDJ	Ronald Becker Fabrics - Inv	120.00		
				Current Period Change	1,052.00	1,864.00	-812.00
	1/31/12			**Ending Balance**			-812.00

7. Compare the general ledger's accounts payable balance to the vendor ledgers balance.

*****EDUCATIONAL VERSION ONLY*****

Cynthia's Service Merchandise
Vendor Ledgers
For the Period From Jan 1, 2012 to Jan 31, 2012
Filter Criteria includes: Report order is by ID.

Vendor ID Vendor	Date	Trans No	Type	Paid	Debit Amt	Credit Amt	Balance
JJH06	1/3/12	56JJ	PJ			300.00	300.00
Jimmy Jackson Hardware	1/20/1	78JJ	PJ	*		500.00	800.00
	1/28/1	VCM78JJ	PJ	*	100.00		700.00
	1/28/1	3037	CDJ		8.00	8.00	700.00
	1/28/1	3037	CDJ		400.00		300.00
LLP07	1/20/1	90	PJ	*		432.00	432.00
Lee Lanning Products	1/25/1	VCM90	PJ	*	54.00		378.00
	1/25/1	3036	CDJ		7.56	7.56	378.00
	1/25/1	3036	CDJ		378.00		0.00
RBF08	1/20/1	210	PJ	*		120.00	120.00
Ronald Becker Fabrics	1/28/1	3038	CDJ		2.40	2.40	120.00
	1/28/1	3038	CDJ		120.00		0.00
TSS09	1/13/1	112	PJ			512.00	512.00
Thomas Sales and Service							
Report Total					1,069.96	1,881.96	812.00

8. Print the general ledger account balance for Account No. 12000, Merchandise Inventory.

```
*****EDUCATIONAL VERSION ONLY*****
```
Cynthia's Service Merchandise
General Ledger
For the Period From Jan 1, 2012 to Jan 31, 2012
Filter Criteria includes: 1) IDs from 12000 to 12000. Report order is by ID. Report is printed with shortened descriptions and in Detail Format.

Account ID Account Description	Date	Reference	Jrnl	Trans Description	Debit Amt	Credit Amt	Balance
12000	1/1/12			Beginning Balance			27,740.00
Merchandise Inventory	1/3/12	56JJ	PJ	Jimmy Jackson Har	300.00		
	1/6/12	101	COGS	Aileen Parker - Item:		100.00	
	1/6/12	102	COGS	Diane Conlin - Item:		216.00	
	1/6/12	103	COGS	Paul Moore - Item: 0		120.00	
	1/6/12	104	COGS	Joann Poe - Item: 00		150.00	
	1/13/12	CM103	COGS	Paul Moore - Item: 0	30.00		
	1/13/12	112	PJ	Thomas Sales and S	512.00		
	1/16/12	EL	INAJ	lighting		128.00	
	1/19/12	106	COGS	Aileen Parker - Item:		100.00	
	1/19/12	107	COGS	Diane Conlin - Item:		108.00	
	1/19/12	108	COGS	Paul Moore - Item: 0		60.00	
	1/20/12	90	PJ	Lee Lanning Product	432.00		
	1/20/12	210	PJ	Ronald Becker Fabri	120.00		
	1/20/12	78JJ	PJ	Jimmy Jackson Har	500.00		
	1/23/12	Cash	COGS	Cash - Item: 002wall		300.00	
	1/23/12	Cash	COGS	Cash - Item: 001har		100.00	
	1/25/12	VCM90	PJ	Lee Lanning Product		54.00	
	1/28/12	VCM78JJ	PJ	Jimmy Jackson Har		100.00	
	1/30/12	Cash	COGS	Barbara Williams - It		60.00	
	1/30/12	Cash	COGS	Cash sales - Item: 0		400.00	
	1/30/12	Cash	COGS	Cash sales - Item: 0		300.00	
				Current Period Chan	1,894.00	2,296.00	-402.00
	1/31/12			**Ending Balance**			**27,338.00**

9. Compare the general ledger's merchandise inventory account balance to the Inventory Valuation Report's item value. (*Hint:* From the Reports list, select Inventory; Inventory Valuation Report.)

```
*****EDUCATIONAL VERSION ONLY*****
```
Cynthia's Service Merchandise
Inventory Valuation Report
As of Jan 31, 2012
Filter Criteria includes: 1) Stock/Assembly. Report order is by ID. Report is printed with shortened descriptions.

Item ID Item Class	Item Descriptio	Stocking U/	Cost Metho	Qty on Han	Item Value	Avg Cost	% of Inv Value
001hardware Stock item	hardware	each	Average	87.00	4,350.00	50.00	15.91
002wall Stock item	wall	each	Average	125.00	3,750.00	30.00	13.72
003floor Stock item	floor	each	Average	201.00	10,854.00	54.00	39.70
004lights Stock item	lighting	each	Average	131.00	8,384.00	64.00	30.67
					27,338.00		**100.00**

PRINTING THE GENERAL LEDGER TRIAL BALANCE

*****EDUCATIONAL VERSION ONLY*****

Cynthia's Service Merchandise
General Ledger Trial Balance
As of Jan 31, 2012

Filter Criteria includes: Report order is by ID. Report is printed in Detail Format.

Account ID	Account Description	Debit Amt	Credit Amt
10200	Southwest Bank	69,014.25	
10300	Payroll Checking Account	2,941.56	
10400	Arizona Savings & Loan	22,000.00	
11000	Accounts Receivable	782.00	
12000	Merchandise Inventory	27,338.00	
13000	Supplies	1,750.00	
14000	Prepaid Insurance	2,400.00	
15000	Furniture and Fixtures	5,000.00	
15100	Computers & Equipment	7,500.00	
15500	Building	100,000.00	
20000	Accounts Payable		812.00
23100	Sales Tax Payable		429.99
23400	Federal Payroll Taxes Payabl		305.20
23500	FUTA Tax Payable		33.20
23600	State Payroll Taxes Payable		66.88
23700	SUTA Payable		141.12
24000	FICA Employee Taxes Payabl		174.32
24100	FICA Employer Taxes Payabl		257.32
24200	Medicare Employee Taxes Pa		60.16
24400	Medicare Employer Taxes Pa		60.16
27000	Long-Term Notes Payable		20,500.00
27400	Mortgage Payable		74,412.05
39006	Eric Lerette, Capital		72,195.00
39007	Eric Lerette, Drawing	1,000.00	
39008	Cynthia Barber, Capital		72,195.00
39009	Cynthia Barber, Drawing	1,000.00	
40000	Sales-Hardware		2,550.00
40200	Sales-Wall		2,700.00
40400	Sales-Floor		960.00
40600	Service Fees		124.89
50000	Cost of Sales-Hardware	850.00	
50500	Cost of Sales-Wall	810.00	
57000	Cost of Sales-Floor	324.00	
57050	Cost of Sales-Lights	128.00	
59500	Purchase Discounts		17.96
62000	Bank Charges	33.00	
67500	Interest Expense	97.85	
70000	Maintenance Expense	160.00	
72510	FICA Expense	257.32	
72520	Medicare Expense	60.16	
72530	FUTA Expense	33.20	
72540	SUTA Expense	141.12	
73500	Postage Expense	45.00	
75500	Supplies Expense	107.65	
76000	Telephone Expense	72.14	
77500	Wages Expense	4,000.00	
77600	Overtime Expense	150.00	
	Total:	**247,995.25**	**247,995.25**

PRINTING THE FINANCIAL STATEMENTS: BALANCE SHEET

Cynthia's Service Merchandise
Balance Sheet
January 31, 2012

ASSETS

Current Assets		
Southwest Bank	$ 69,014.25	
Payroll Checking Account	2,941.56	
Arizona Savings & Loan	22,000.00	
Accounts Receivable	782.00	
Merchandise Inventory	27,338.00	
Supplies	1,750.00	
Prepaid Insurance	2,400.00	
Total Current Assets		126,225.81
Property and Equipment		
Furniture and Fixtures	5,000.00	
Computers & Equipment	7,500.00	
Building	100,000.00	
Total Property and Equipment		112,500.00
Other Assets		
Total Other Assets		0.00
Total Assets	$	238,725.81

LIABILITIES AND CAPITAL

Current Liabilities		
Accounts Payable	$ 812.00	
Sales Tax Payable	429.99	
Federal Payroll Taxes Payable	305.20	
FUTA Tax Payable	33.20	
State Payroll Taxes Payable	66.88	
SUTA Payable	141.12	
FICA Employee Taxes Payable	174.32	
FICA Employer Taxes Payable	257.32	
Medicare Employee Taxes Payabl	60.16	
Medicare Employer Taxes Payabl	60.16	
Total Current Liabilities		2,340.35
Long-Term Liabilities		
Long-Term Notes Payable	20,500.00	
Mortgage Payable	74,412.05	
Total Long-Term Liabilities		94,912.05
Total Liabilities		97,252.40
Capital		
Eric Lerette, Capital	72,195.00	
Eric Lerette, Drawing	(1,000.00)	
Cynthia Barber, Capital	72,195.00	
Cynthia Barber, Drawing	(1,000.00)	
Net Income	(916.59)	
Total Capital		141,473.41
Total Liabilities & Capital	$	238,725.81

Print the <Standard> Income Stmnt (Income Statement).

Cynthia's Service Merchandise
Income Statement
For the One Month Ending January 31, 2012

	Current Month			Year to Date	
Revenues					
Sales-Hardware	$	2,550.00	40.25	$	2,550.00	40.25
Sales-Wall		2,700.00	42.62		2,700.00	42.62
Sales-Floor		960.00	15.15		960.00	15.15
Service Fees		124.89	1.97		124.89	1.97
Total Revenues		6,334.89	100.00		6,334.89	100.00
Cost of Sales						
Cost of Sales-Hardware		850.00	13.42		850.00	13.42
Cost of Sales-Wall		810.00	12.79		810.00	12.79
Cost of Sales-Floor		324.00	5.11		324.00	5.11
Cost of Sales-Lights		128.00	2.02		128.00	2.02
Purchase Discounts		(17.96)	(0.28)		(17.96)	(0.28)
Total Cost of Sales		2,094.04	33.06		2,094.04	33.06
Gross Profit		4,240.85	66.94		4,240.85	66.94
Expenses						
Bank Charges		33.00	0.52		33.00	0.52
Interest Expense		97.85	1.54		97.85	1.54
Maintenance Expense		160.00	2.53		160.00	2.53
FICA Expense		257.32	4.06		257.32	4.06
Medicare Expense		60.16	0.95		60.16	0.95
FUTA Expense		33.20	0.52		33.20	0.52
SUTA Expense		141.12	2.23		141.12	2.23
Postage Expense		45.00	0.71		45.00	0.71
Supplies Expense		107.65	1.70		107.65	1.70
Telephone Expense		72.14	1.14		72.14	1.14
Wages Expense		4,000.00	63.14		4,000.00	63.14
Overtime Expense		150.00	2.37		150.00	2.37
Total Expenses		5,157.44	81.41		5,157.44	81.41
Net Income	$	(916.59)	(14.47)	$	(916.59)	(14.47)

For Management Purposes Only

Print the <Standard> Cash Flow.

Cynthia's Service Merchandise
Statement of Cash Flow
For the one Month Ended January 31, 2012

		Current Month		Year to Date
Cash Flows from operating activities				
Net Income	$	(916.59)	$	(916.59)
Adjustments to reconcile net income to net cash provided by operating activities				
Accounts Receivable		(782.00)		(782.00)
Merchandise Inventory		402.00		402.00
Accounts Payable		812.00		812.00
Sales Tax Payable		429.99		429.99
Federal Payroll Taxes Payable		305.20		305.20
FUTA Tax Payable		33.20		33.20
State Payroll Taxes Payable		66.88		66.88
SUTA Payable		141.12		141.12
FICA Employee Taxes Payable		174.32		174.32
FICA Employer Taxes Payable		257.32		257.32
Medicare Employee Taxes Payabl		60.16		60.16
Medicare Employer Taxes Payabl		60.16		60.16
Total Adjustments		1,960.35		1,960.35
Net Cash provided by Operations		1,043.76		1,043.76
Cash Flows from investing activities				
Used For				
Net cash used in investing		0.00		0.00
Cash Flows from financing activities				
Proceeds From				
Used For				
Mortgage Payable		(587.95)		(587.95)
Eric Lerette, Drawing		(1,000.00)		(1,000.00)
Cynthia Barber, Drawing		(1,000.00)		(1,000.00)
Net cash used in financing		(2,587.95)		(2,587.95)
Net increase <decrease> in cash	$	(1,544.19)	$	(1,544.19)
Summary				
Cash Balance at End of Period	$	93,955.81	$	93,955.81
Cash Balance at Beg of Period		(95,500.00)		(95,500.00)
Net Increase <Decrease> in Cash	$	(1,544.19)	$	(1,544.19)

Unaudited - For Internal Use Only.

BACKING UP CHAPTER 15 DATA

Follow these steps to back up Chapter 15 data:

1. If necessary, insert your USB flash drive. From the System Navigation Center, click | Back Up Now | .

2. Click | Back Up | .

3. Go to the location of your USB drive or another location. Type **Chapter 15** in the File name field.

4. Click | Save | .

5. When the window prompts that This company backup will require approximately 1 diskette, click | OK | . When the window prompts Please insert the first, disk click | OK | . When the Back Up Company scale is 100% complete, you have successfully backed up to the current point in Chapter 15 (If you are backing up to the default or another location, this step will differ slightly.)

6. Continue or click on File, Exit to exit Peachtree.

EXPORT REPORTS TO EXCEL

1. Export the following reports to Excel:

   - Payroll Journal
   - General Ledger Trial Balance
   - Balance Sheet
   - Income Statement
   - Statement of Cash Flow

2. Save. Use the file name **Chapter 15_PayJ_GLTB_BS_IS_SCF.xlsx**.

   NOTE: If your instructor would like you to save reports as PDF files, refer to page 353. The suggested file name is **Chapter 15_Payroll Journal.pdf**, etc. Your instructor may require additional reports.

SUMMARY AND REVIEW

Complete the following end-of-chapter activities:

1. Going to the net, pages 622.

2. Multiple-choice questions, pages 622-625.

3. Exercises 15-1 and 15-2, pages 625-631.

4. Analysis question, page 631.

5. Assessment rubric, page 632.

6. Chapter 15 Index, page 633.

GOING TO THE NET

Access the Employer Reporting and Instructions website at http://www.ssa.gov/employer/. Link to General W-2 Filing Information, then answer these questions.

1. What are dates that employers must send W-2 information to the Social Security Administration? (Include the dates for *both* electronic and paper filing.)
2. When must employers give employees their W-2?
3. What two forms do employers send to the Social Security Administration?

Multiple-Choice Questions: The Online Learning Center includes these questions and the analysis question at www.mhhe.com/yacht2012, select Student Edition, Chapter 15, QA Templates.

_____ 1. The cash account to credit when disbursing checks for Cynthia's Service Merchandise employees is:

    a. Account No. 10200, Southwest Bank.
    b. Account No. 10300, Payroll Checking Account.
    c. Account No. 23200, Wages Payable.
    d. Account No. 77500, Wages Expense.
    e. None of the above.

_____ 2. The amount withheld from employees' paychecks depend on:

    a. How many employees a company has.
    b. The amount withheld changes on every paycheck.
    c. There are no withholdings.
    d. The number of withholding allowances.
    e. None of the above.

_____ 3. Guidelines for employee and employer withholdings are found in the following IRS publication:

    a. Circular E, Employer's Tax Guide.
    b. Form 941, Employer's Quarterly Federal Tax Return.
    c. Circular F, Employee/Employer Tax Guide.
    d. Both a. and b.
    e. None of the above.

_____ 4. On the Maintain Employees/Sales Reps window, you enter the following types of information:

    a. Employee name, address, and telephone number.
    b. The way an employee is paid.
    c. Tax filing status and withholding allowances.
    d. All of the above.
    e. None of the above.

_____ 5. Tom Ashton received a January 6 paycheck in the amount of:

    a. $495.00.
    b. $439.73
    c. $400.00.
    d. $550.00.
    e. None of the above.

_____ 6. The entry in the General Journal for the transfer of funds on January 5, 2012 is:

a. Debit, Account No. 10200, Southwest Bank, $6,500; Credit, Account No. 10300, Payroll Checking Account, $6,500.
b. Debit, Account No. 10300, Payroll Checking Account, $6,500; Credit, Account No. 10200, Southwest Bank, $6,500.
c. Debit, Account No. 10400, First Street Savings, $6,000; Credit, Account No. 10200, Southwest Bank, $6,000.
d. Debit, Account No. 10200, Southwest Bank, $6,500; Credit, Account No. 10400, First Street Savings, $6,500.
e. None of the above.

_____ 7. All of these payroll tax deductions are subtracted from an employee's gross pay EXCEPT:

a. Federal income tax (FIT).
b. Social security tax (FICA).
c. Medicare tax.
d. Federal unemployment tax (FUTA).
e. None of the above.

_____ 8. The Gross Pay Account is:

a. Account No. 72000, Payroll Tax Expense.
b. Account No. 23400, Federal Payroll Taxes Payable.
c. Account No. 77500, Wages Expense.
d. Account No. 24000, FICA Employee Tax Payable.
e. None of the above.

_____ 9. Lauren Gomez received a January 13 paycheck in the amount of:

a. $449.02.
b. $338.59.
c. $446.13.
d. $360.00.
e. None of the above.

_____10. The maximum taxable earnings subject to social security taxes can change due to:

    a. Federal legislation.
    b. The amount of monthly wages.
    c. The number of exemptions.
    d. The Medicare tax.
    e. None of the above.

Exercise 15-1: Follow the instructions below to complete Exercise 15-1. Exercises 12-1, 12-2, 13-1, 13-2, 14-1, and 14-2 must be completed before starting Exercise 15-1.

1. Start PCA. Open the company that you set up in Exercise 12-1, Your Name Sales and Service.

2. Restore your data from Exercise 14-1 which was backed up on page 575. To make sure you are starting with the correct data, display Exercise 14-2's General Ledger Trial balance (step 6, page 575).

3. Journalize and post the following General Journal entry:

    01/05/12   Transferred $5,450 from Account No. 10200, Caliber Bank, to Account No. 10300, Payroll Checking Account.

4. Print the January 5, 2012 General Journal.

5. For setting up payroll, refer to the Payroll Setup Wizard, pages 585-589. Use the following information:

State: GA
State Unemployment Rate: **3.4%**
Georgia Administrative Assessment Tax Rate: **.08**

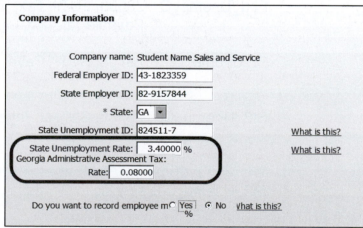

Overtime Expense: Account No. 77600, Overtime Expense

6. For entering employee and employer defaults, refer to pages 589-591. Use the Employee Fields shown below.

Field Name	GL Account
Fed_Income	23400, Federal Payroll Taxes Payable
Soc_Sec	24000, FICA Employee Taxes Payable
MEDICARE	Account No. 24200, Medicare Employee Taxes Payable
St_Income	Account No. 23600, State Payroll Taxes Payable

Verify your Employee Fields window with the one shown on page 590.

7. Use the following Company Fields.

Field Name	Liability column	Expense column
Soc_Sec_C	24100, FICA Employer Taxes Payable	72510, FICA Expense
Medicare_C	24400 Medicare Employer Taxes Payable	72520, Medicare Expense
Fed_Unemp_C	23500, FUTA Tax Payable	72530, FUTA Expense
St_Unemp_C	23700, SUTA Payable	72540, SUTA Expense
St2_Unemp_C	23755, SUTA2 Payable	72545, SUTA2 Expense

Verify you Company Fields window with the one shown on page 591. St2_Unemp_C is specific to Georgia payroll tax.

8. Refer to pages 591-595 to complete the payroll setup wizard. The Assign Company-Paid Taxes window shows ST2_Unemp_C for Other State Unemployment which is specific to GA payroll taxes. (*Hint:* Other State Unemployment is not shown on page 593 for an Arizona company.)

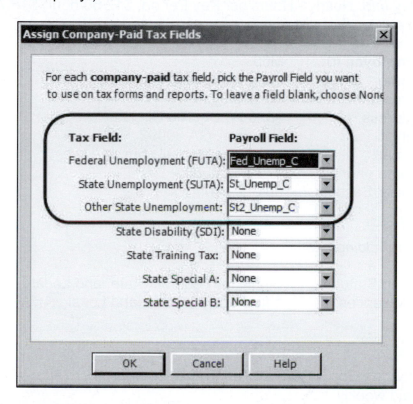

9. Add the following employees.

    Employee ID: C50
    Name: Richard Clinton
    Accept the default for Employee
    Address: 571 North Palisade Dr.
    City, ST Zip: Norcross, GA 30092
    E-mail: clinton@email.com
    Home phone: 404-555-0220
    Social Security #:   003-00-0011
    Type: FULL

Withholding Info:

Filing Status: Single for Federal, State, and Local
Allowances: 1 for Federal, State, and Local

Pay Info: Hourly - Hours per Pay Period, $12.50/hour; $18.75/hour, overtime; paid weekly

Employee ID: M60
Name: Mary Mouritsen
Accept the default for Employee
Address: 4820 W. Del Rio Circle
City, ST Zip: Norcross, GA 30092
E-mail: mouritsen@email.com
Home phone: 770-555-0090
Social Security #:   001-00-9877
Type: FULL

Withholding Info:

Filing Status: Single for Federal, State, and Local
Allowances: 1 for Federal, State, and Local

Pay Info:

Hourly - Hours Per Pay Period, $12.50/hour; $18.75/hour, overtime; paid weekly

10. Print an employee list. (*Hint:* Reports & Forms; Payroll, Employee List.)

11. Back up. (Use **Exercise 15-1** as the file name.)

12. Exit PCA or continue.

Exercise 15-2: Follow the instructions below to complete Exercise 15-2.

1. Start PCA. Open your company.

2. If necessary, restore data from Exercise 15-1.

3. On January 6, 2012, issue payroll check 6050 to Richard Clinton. Mr. Clinton worked 40 regular hours. Issue paychecks from the Payroll Checking Account. Type **6050** in the Check Number field. To post, save after each payroll transaction.

4. On January 6, 2012, issue payroll check 6051 to Mary Mouritsen. Ms. Mouritsen worked 40 regular hours.

5. Make the following payroll entries for Richard Clinton and Mary Mouritsen.

Date	Name	Hours Worked	Overtime	Check No.
1/13/12	R. Clinton	40		6052
	M. Mouritsen	40		6053
1/20/12	R. Clinton	40		6054
	M. Mouritsen	40		6055
1/27/12	R. Clinton	40		6056
	M. Mouritsen	40		6057

After recording the paycheck information, type the check number, then post. You do *not* need to print paychecks 6050–6057.

6. Print the Payroll Journal.

7. Complete account reconciliation for Caliber Bank.

Statement of Account Caliber Bank January 1 to January 31, 2012		Account No. 382-0312-19	Student Name Sales and Service Student Address Student City, State, Zip	
		REGULAR CHECKING		
Previous Balance	12/31/11	$62,500.00		
6 Deposits(+)		7,360.20		
8 Checks (-)		6,839.57		
Service Charges (-)	1/31/12	12.00		
Ending Balance	1/31/12	**63,008.63**		
		DEPOSITS		
1/15/12	367.20	1/24/12	275.40	
1/22/12	486.00	1/30/12	972.00	
1/23/12	507.60	1/31/12	4,752.00	

CHECKS (Asterisk * indicates break in check number sequence)			
	1/15/12	Transfer	5,450.00
	1/15/12	2020	392.00
	1/24/12	2021	235.20
	1/24/12	2022	125.00
	1/27/12	2023	45.00
	1/27/12	2024	145.72
	1/27/12	2025	46.65
	1/30/12	2026	400.00

8. Complete account reconciliation for the Payroll Checking Account.

Statement of Account Payroll Checking Account January 1 to January 31, 2012		Account No. 613-4588770	Student Name Sales and Service Student Address Student City, State, Zip	
REGULAR CHECKING				
Previous Balance	12/31/11	0.00		
1 Deposits(+)		5,450.00		
8 Checks (-)		3,208.56		
Service Charges (-)	1/31/12	15.00		
Ending Balance	1/31/12	**2,226.44**		
DEPOSITS				
	1/5/12	5,450.00		
CHECKS (Asterisk * indicates break in check number sequence)				
	1/7/12	6050	401.07	
	1/7/12	6051	401.07	
	1/14/12	6052	401.07	
	1/14/12	6053	401.07	
	1/21/12	6054	401.07	
	1/21/12	6055	401.07	
	1/28/12	6056	401.07	
	1/28/12	6057	401.07	

9. Print the account reconciliation reports for Caliber Bank and the Payroll Checking Account.

10. Print the Customer Ledgers; Vendor Ledgers; and Inventory Valuation Report.

11. Print the General Ledger Trial Balance.

12. Print the following financial statements: Balance Sheet, Income Statement, and Statement of Cash Flow.

    Check Your Figures:

Total Assets:	$189,185.07
Gross Profit	4,447.80
Net Increase in Cash	2,735.07

13. Make a backup. (Use **Exercise 15-2** as the file name.)

14. Export the following files to Excel:

    - Employee List
    - Customer Ledgers
    - Vendor Ledgers
    - Inventory Valuation Report
    - Payroll Journal

    - General Ledger Trial Balance
    - Balance Sheet
    - Income Statement
    - Statement of Cash Flow.

15. Use the file name **Exercise 15-2_EL_CL_VL_IVR_PayJ_GLTB_ BS_IS_SCF.xlsx.**

16. Save these reports as PDF files: Employee List, Customer Ledgers, Vendor Ledgers, Inventory Valuation Report, Payroll Journal, General Ledger Trial Balance, Balance Sheet, Income Statement, and Statement of Cash Flow.

ANALYSIS QUESTION

Peachtree's automatic payroll withholding calculations are based on what year? Explain.

ASSESSMENT RUBRIC

Complete the Assessment Rubric online at www.mhhe.com/yacht2012;
Student Edition, select Chapter 15, Assessment Rubric link.

Date	Transaction	Navigation Center/Module	Task Window	Journal Dr./Cr.
1/7	Issue payroll Check No. 6050 to Richard Clinton for 40 regular hours.			

CHAPTER 15 INDEX

Project

2 | Sports Emporium

In Project 2, you complete the Computer Accounting Cycle for Sports Emporium, a merchandising business. Sports Emporium sells mountain bicycles, road bicycles, and children's bicycles. It is organized as a corporation. You purchased Sports Emporium in December 2011.

It is the purpose of Project 2 to review what you have learned in Part 3 of the book, Peachtree Complete Accounting for Merchandising Businesses. Accounts payable, accounts receivable, payroll, and inventory transactions are included in this project. Account reconciliation is also completed.

Vendors offer Sports Emporium a purchase discount of 2% 15, Net 30 days. Sports Emporium is located in OR where there is no sales tax.

At the end of Project 2, a checklist is shown listing the printed reports that you should have. The step-by-step instructions also remind you to print reports and back up.

Follow these steps to complete Project 2, Sports Emporium:

Step 1: Start Peachtree.

Step 2: If a company opens, from the menu bar, select File; New Company; No keeping another company open, Next. (*Or,* from the startup window, select Create a new Company.)

Step 3: Complete the following company information:

Company Name:	Sports Emporium (use your last name, then the company name; for example Smith Sports Emporium)
Address Line 1:	8700 Orange Grove Avenue
City, State, Zip:	Eugene, OR 97401
Country:	USA

Telephone:	541-555-4239
Fax:	541-555-4344
Business Type:	Corporation
Federal Employer ID:	80-8314425
State Employer ID:	54-3179845
State Unemployment ID:	543122-7
Web Site:	www.sportsemporium.com
E-mail:	mail@sportsemporium.com

Step 4: Accept the default for Use a sample business type that closely matches your company.

Step 5: Scroll down the list. In the **Detailed types** list, select Retail Company. (*Hint:* Account numbers are five digits.)

Step 6: Accept the default for Accrual accounting.

Step 7: Accept the default for Real Time posting.

Step 8: Accept the default for 12 monthly accounting periods.

Step 9: The Choose the first period of your fiscal year window appears. If necessary, select 2012 as the year.

Step 10: At the You are ready to create your company window, click Finish. When the Peachtree Setup Guide window appears, click on the box next to Don't show this screen at startup to place a checkmark in it. Close the Setup Guide window.

Step 11: Change the accounting period to 01-Jan 01,2012 to Jan 31, 2012—Period 1 - 01/01/12-01/31/12.

General Ledger

1. Delete the accounts shown below and on the next page.

10000	Petty Cash
10100	Cash on Hand
10300	Payroll Checking Account

11500	Allowance for Doubtful Account
14200	Notes Receivable-Current
15400	Leasehold Improvements
15500	Building
15600	Building Improvements
16900	Land
17400	Accum. Depreciation - Leasehold
17500	Accum. Depreciation - Building
17600	Accum. Depreciation - Bldg Imp
19000	Deposits
19200	Note Receivable-Noncurrent
19900	Other Noncurrent Assets
23000	Accrued Expenses
24200	Current Portion Long-Term Debt
60500	Amortization Expense
63000	Charitable Contributions Exp
63500	Commissions and Fees Exp
65000	Employee Benefit Programs Exp
66000	Gifts Expense
68000	Laundry and Cleaning Exp
89000	Other Expense

Change these account names:

10200	Regular Checking Account to Wells Bank
10400	Savings Account to Downtown Savings & Loan
12000	Product Inventory to Inventory-Mountain Bikes
14000	Prepaid Expenses to Prepaid Insurance
23300	Deductions Payable to Medicare Employee Taxes Payabl
24000	Other Taxes Payable to FICA Employee Taxes Payable
24100	Employee Benefits Payable to FICA Employer Taxes Payable
24800	Other Current Liabilities to Short-Term Notes Payable
27000	Notes Payable-Noncurrent to Long-Term Notes Payable
40000	Sales-Merchandise to Sales-Mountain Bikes
50000	Cost of Goods Sold to Cost of Sales-Mountain Bikes
72500	Penalties and Fines Exp to FUTA Expense
73000	Other Taxes to SUTA Expense
74000	Rent or Lease Expense to Rent-Mall Space

Add these accounts:

12020	Inventory-Road Bikes	Inventory
12030	Inventory-Children's Bikes	Inventory
23350	Medicare Employer Taxes Payable	Other Current Liabilities
40020	Sales-Road Bikes	Income

40030	Sales-Children's Bikes	Income
50020	Cost of Sales-Road Bikes	Cost of Sales
50030	Cost of Sales-Children's Bikes	Cost of Sales
73200	FICA Expense	Expenses
73300	Medicare Expense	Expenses
73350	Local Payroll Taxes Expense	Expenses

2. Back up. Use the file name is **Sports Emporium Chart of Accounts.ptb**.

3. Record chart of accounts beginning balances as of December 31, 2011. Use the Balance Sheet below to record the chart of account beginning balances.

Sports Emporium, Balance Sheet January 1, 2012		
ASSETS		
Current Assets		
Wells Bank	$ 83,400.00	
Downtown Savings & Loan	14,000.00	
Inventory-Mountain Bikes	6,000.00	
Inventory-Road Bikes	8,250.00	
Inventory-Children's Bikes	4,050.00	
Prepaid Insurance	2,400.00	
Total Current Assets		$118,100.00
Property and Equipment: Furniture and Fixtures	6,000.00	
Total Property and Equipment and Other Assets		6,000.00
Total Assets		$124,100.00
LIABILITIES AND STOCKHOLDERS' EQUITY		
Short-Term Notes Payable	4,000.00	
Long-Term Notes Payable	5,500.00	
Total Liabilities		$9,500.00
Stockholder's Equity: Common Stock		114,600.00
Total Liabilities and Stockholders' Equity		$124,100.00

4. Back up. Use the file name is **Sports Emporium Starting Balance Sheet.ptb**.

Accounts Payable

Follow the instructions below to set up vendor information for Sports Emporium.

1. Set up the following vendor defaults.

Standard Terms:	Due in number of days
Net due in:	30 days
Discount in:	15 days
Discount %	2.00
Credit Limit:	15,000.00

   GL Link Accounts:

Expense Account:	12000 Inventory-Mountain Bikes
Discount GL Account:	59500 Purchase Discounts

2. Set up the following vendors.

Vendor ID:	ABC111
Name:	ABC Mountain Bikes
Contact:	Alene Dutton
Mailing Address:	801 Alameda Street
City, ST Zip:	Los Angeles, CA 90046
Vendor Type:	mountain
1099 Type:	Independent Contractor
Expense Account:	12000, Inventory-Mountain Bikes
Telephone 1:	213-555-7808
Fax:	213-555-7810
E-Mail:	info@abcmountainbikes.biz
Web Site:	www.abcmountainbikes.biz

   Purchase Info:

Tax ID Number:	38-9154822

Vendor ID:	ERB112
Name:	Empire Road Bikes
Contact:	Daniel Empire
Mailing Address:	3005 West 3rd Street
City, ST Zip:	El Paso, TX 76315

Vendor Type: road
1099 Type: Independent Contractor
Expense Account: 12020, Inventory-Road Bikes
Telephone 1: 915-555-3988
Fax: 915-555-9833
E-mail: empire@roadbikes.com
Web Site: www.roadbikes.com

Purchase Info:

Tax ID Number: 44-8843419

Vendor ID: TTW113
Name: Tiny Tots Wheels
Contact: Michael West
Mailing Address: 1800 Milton Street
City, ST Zip: Flagstaff, AZ 86001
Vendor Type: children
1099 Type: Independent Contractor
Expense Account: 12030, Inventory-Children's Bikes
Telephone 1: 928-555-3144
Fax: 928-555-3146
E-mail: info@tinytotswheels.biz
Web Site: www.tinytotswheels.biz

Purchase Defaults:

Tax ID Number: 78-8994144

Accounts Receivable

Follow these steps to set up customer information for Sports Emporium.

1. Set up the following customer defaults.

Standard Terms: Due in number of days
Net due in: 30 days
Discount in: 0 days
Discount %: 0.00
Credit Limit: 5,000.00
GL Sales Account: 40000 Sales-Mountain Bikes
Discount GL Account: 49000 Sales Discounts

2. Set up the following customers.

Customer ID:	DB001
Name:	David Bartels
Billing Address:	70 Rimrock Road
City, ST Zip:	Eugene, OR 97402
Customer Type:	LANE (for Lane County)
Telephone 1:	541-555-3912
Fax:	541-555-3388
E-mail	bartels@eugene.com
Web Site:	www.eugene.com/bartels

Sales Info:

GL Sales Acct:	40000, Sales-Mountain Bikes

Customer ID:	RL002
Name:	Rich Larson
Billing Address:	93 North Montana Drive
City, ST Zip:	Eugene, OR 97404
Customer Type:	LANE
Telephone 1:	541-555-8933
Fax:	541-555-4302
E-mail:	rich@eugene.com
Web Site:	www.eugene.com/larson

Sales Info:

GL Sales Acct:	40020, Sales-Road Bikes

Customer ID:	SW003
Name:	Sally Watson
Billing Address:	9013 Mustang Drive
City, ST Zip:	Eugene, OR 97401
Customer Type:	LANE
Telephone 1:	541-555-5488
Fax:	541-555-5490
E-mail:	watson@eugene.com
Web Site:	www.eugene.com/sally

Sales Info:

GL Sales Acct:	40030, Sales-Children's Bikes

Payroll

1. Use the following information for the Payroll Setup Wizard:

   State: OR
   State Unemployment Rate: 3.4%
   Do you have any localities for which you collect taxes in the state of OR?   **Yes**

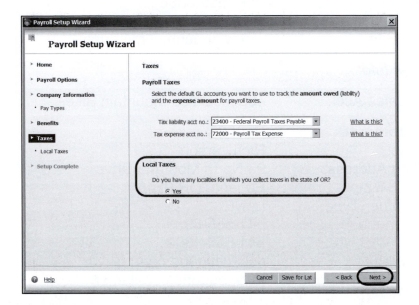

Locality: **Tri-Met**

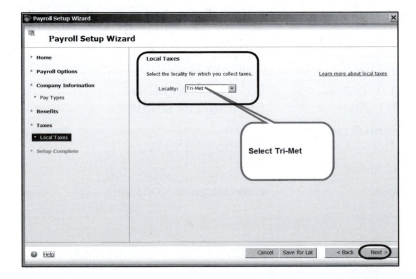

2. For entering employee and employer default information, refer to pages 589-591. Use the Employee Fields shown below.

Field Name	GL Account
Fed_Income	23400, Federal Payroll Taxes Payable
Soc_Sec	24000, FICA Employee Taxes Payable
MEDICARE	23300, Medicare Employee Taxes Payable
St_Income	23600, State Payroll Taxes Payable

3. Use the Company Fields shown below.

Field	Liability column	Expense column
Soc_Sec_C	24100, FICA Employer Taxes Payable	73200, FICA Expense
Medicare_C	23350 Medicare Employer Taxes Payable	73300, Medicare Expense
Fed_Unemp_C	23500, FUTA Tax Payable	72500, FUTA Expense
LIT_ER	23800, Local Payroll Taxes Payable	73350, Local Payroll Taxes Expense
St_Unemp_C	23700, SUTA Payable	73000, SUTA Expense

4. Refer to pages 591-595 to complete the Payroll Setup Wizard's Taxes and Assign Tax Fields.

    a. Compare your Assign Tax Fields for W-2s to page 593.

    b. Compare your Assign Company-Paid Tax Fields to page 593. The State Special A field shows Loc_IncomeC.

    c. Compare Employee-Paid State Taxes to page 594.

5. Add the following employees.

Employee ID:	1ML
Name:	Mike Lowen

Accept the default for Employee

Address:	5551 Valley Avenue
City, ST Zip:	Eugene, OR 97402
E-mail:	mike@mail.net
Home phone:	541-555-8814
Social Security #:	003-00-0012
Type:	FULL

Withholding Info:

Filing Status:	Married for Federal, State Local (Married/Jointly)
Allow:	2 for Federal, State and Local

Pay Info: Salary, $500 per week. (*Hint:* Remember to select Salary as the Pay Method. Weekly is the default.)

Employee ID:	2JW
Name:	Jessica Wills

Accept the default for Employee

Address:	690 Birch Ave., Apt. 1B
City, ST Zip:	Eugene, OR 97404
E-mail:	jessica@mail.net
Home phone:	541-555-9099
Social Security #:	090-00-0200
Type:	FULL

Withholding Info:

Filing Status:	Married for Federal, State Local (Married/Jointly)
Allow:	2 for Federal, State and Local

Pay Info: Salary, $500 per week.

8. Close.

Inventory

1. Set up the following inventory defaults. On the General Tab select Stock item as the Default Item Class.

2. Click on the GL Accts/Costing tab.Set up LIFO as the inventory costing method.

3. Set up the following Inventory items.

Item ID:	mbikes
Description:	mountain bikes
Item Class:	Stock item
Description for Sales:	mountain bikes
Price Level 1:	300.00
Last Unit Cost:	150.00
Cost Method:	LIFO
GL Sales Acct:	40000 Sales-Mountain Bikes
GL Inventory Acct:	12000, Merchandise Inventory-Mountain Bikes
GL Cost of Sales Acct:	50000, Cost of Sales-Mountain Bikes
Item Tax Type:	1
Item Type:	mountain
Stocking U/M:	each
Minimum Stock:	10
Reorder Quantity:	5
Preferred Vendor ID:	ABC Mountain Bikes

Beginning Balances:	mountain bikes
Quantity:	40.00
Unit Cost:	150.00
Total Cost:	6,000.00

Item ID:	rbikes
Description:	road bikes
Item Class:	Stock item
Description for Sales:	road bikes
Price Level 1:	150.00
Last Unit Cost:	75.00
Cost Method:	LIFO

GL Sales Acct:	40020, Sales-Road Bikes
GL Inventory Acct:	12020, Inventory-Road Bikes
GL Cost of Sales Acct:	50020, Cost of Sales-Road Bikes
Item Tax Type:	1
Item Type:	road
Stocking U/M:	each
Minimum Stock:	10
Reorder Quantity:	5
Preferred Vendor ID:	Empire Road Bikes

Beginning Balances: Road Bikes

Quantity:	110.00
Unit Cost:	75.00
Total Cost:	8,250.00

Item ID:	cbikes
Description:	children's bikes
Item Class:	Stock item
Description for Sales:	children's bikes
Price Level 1:	90.00
Last Unit Cost:	45.00
Cost Method:	LIFO
GL Sales Acct:	40030, Sales-Children's Bikes
GL Inventory Acct:	12030, Inventory-Children's Bikes
Cost of Sales Acct:	50030, Cost of Sales-Children's Bikes
Item Tax Type:	1
Item Type:	children
Stocking U/M:	each
Minimum Stock:	10
Reorder Quantity:	5
Preferred Vendor ID:	Tiny Tots Wheels

Beginning Balances: children's bikes

Quantity:	90.00
Unit Cost:	45.00
Total Cost:	4,050.00

4. Back up. Use **Sports Emporium Begin.ptb** as the filename.

Journalize and post the following transactions:

Date   *Description of Transaction*

01/06/12   Issued pay checks 5001 and 5002 from Wells Bank to Mike Lowen and Jessica Wills. Type the check number on the Payroll Entry window.

01/06/12   Invoice No. 74A was received from ABC Mountain Bikes for 10 mountain bikes at $150 each.

01/06/12   Invoice No. 801 was received from Tiny Tots Wheels for 15 children's bikes at $45 each.

01/06/12   Invoice No. ER555 was received from Empire Road Bikes for 12 road bikes at $75 each.

01/11/12   Deposited cash sales of $2,670: 4 mountain bikes, $1,200; 5 road bikes, $750; 8 children's bikes, $720. Cash sales are deposited in the Wells Bank account. (*Hint: Make sure the correct Sales account is credited.*)

01/13/12   Deposited cash sales of $1,950: 5 children's bikes, $450; 4 road bikes, $600; and 3 mountain bikes, $900.

01/13/12   Issued pay checks 5003 and 5004 for Mike Lowen and Jessica Wills. (*Hint: If necessary, complete the Check Number field.*)

01/14/12   Sold one mountain bike to David Bartels on account, Sales Invoice 101. (*Hint: Type the invoice number in the Invoice No. field. If necessary, select Layout, <Predefined> Product as the Invoice type.*)

01/18/12   Deposited cash sales of $1,920: 3 children's bikes, $270; 2 mountain bikes, $600; 7 road bikes, $1,050.

01/20/12   Issued No. 5005 to ABC Mountain Bikes in payment of purchase Invoice No. 74A. Complete the Check Number field. Issue checks from the Wells Bank account. (Make sure that the Discount Account field shows 59500 for Purchase Discounts.)

01/20/12 Issued Check No. 5006 to Empire Road Bikes in payment of purchase Invoice No. ER555.

01/20/12 Issued Check No. 5007 to Tiny Tots Wheels in payment of purchase Invoice No. 801.

01/20/12 Issued pay checks 5008 and 5009 for Mike Lowen and Jessica Wills.

01/23/12 Issued Check No. 5010 to Greene Rentals for $1,350 in payment of mall space rent for Sports Emporium. (*Hint: Remember to complete the Check Number field.*)

01/24/12 Deposited cash sales of $3,810: 6 mountain bikes, $1,800; 8 road bikes, $1,200; 9 children's bikes, $810.

01/25/12 Sold one children's bike to Sally Watson on account, Sales Invoice 102. (*Hint: Type the invoice number in the Invoice No. field.*)

01/25/12 Invoice No. 88A was received from ABC Mountain Bikes for three mountain bikes at $150 each.

01/25/12 Invoice No. 962 was received from Tiny Tots Wheels for five children's bikes at $45 each.

01/25/12 Invoice No. ER702 was received from Empire Road Bikes for five road bikes at $75 each.

01/27/12 Deposited cash sales of $3,240: 6 mountain bikes, $1,800; 6 road bikes, $900; 6 children's bikes, $540.

01/27/12 Issued pay checks 5011 and 5012 for Mike Lowen and Jessica Wills.

01/30/12 Issued Check No. 5013 to Bob Allen for $245 in payment of Short-Term Notes Payable.

01/30/12 Issued Check No. 5014 to Wells Bank for $175.80 in payment of Long-Term Notes Payable.

01/30/12   Issued Check No. 5015 to Local Utilities for $226.65 in
                payment of utilities.

Complete account reconciliation for the Wells Bank account. The January
31, 2012 bank statement is shown below.

Statement of Account Wells Bank January 1 to January 31, 2012		Account No. 345911-2901		Sports Emporium 87001 Orange Grove Avenue Eugene, OR 30353	
REGULAR CHECKING					
Previous Balance	12/31/11	$83,400.00			
5 Deposits(+)		13,590.00			
12 Checks (-)		7,341.32			
Service Charges (-)	1/31/12	15.00			
Ending Balance	1/31/12	**89,633.68**			
DEPOSITS					
1/12/12	2,670.00	1/23/12	3,810.00		
1/15/12	1,950.00	1/30/12	3,240.00		
1/18/12	1,920.00				
CHECKS (Asterisk * indicates break in check number sequence)					
		1/12/12	5001	426.17	
		1/12/12	5002	426.17	
		1/19/12	5003	426.17	
		1/19/12	5004	426.17	
		1/26/12	5005	1,470.00	
		1/26/12	5006	882.00	
		1/26/12	5007	661.50	
		1/27/12	5008	426.17	
		1/27/12	5009	426.17	
		1/27/12	5010*	1,350.00	
		1/31/12	5013	245.00	
		1/31/12	5014	175.80	

Print the following reports:

1. Print the General Ledger Trial Balance.

2. Print the Account Reconciliation report for the Wells Bank.

3. Print the Inventory Valuation Report.

4. Print the financial statements: Balance Sheet, Income Statement, and Statement of Cash Flow.

5. Print the Customer Ledgers and Vendor Ledgers.

6. Back up. Use the file name **Sports Emporium January.ptb**.

7. Export the following reports to Excel: Chart of Accounts, Customer Ledgers, Vendor Ledgers, General Ledger Trial Balance, Account Reconciliation, Balance Sheet, Income Statement, Statement of Cash Flow. Use the file name **Sports Emporium_CofA_CL_VL_GLTB_AcctRec_BS_IS_SCF.xlsx**.

8. Save the following reports as PDF files: Chart of Accounts, Customer Ledgers, Vendors Ledger, General Ledger Trial Balance, Account Reconciliation, Balance Sheet, Income Statement, and Statement of Cash Flow. (Your instructor may require more reports saved as PDF files.)

		CHECKLIST OF PRINTOUTS, Sports Emporium	
	1	General Ledger Trial Balance	
	2	Account Reconciliation – Wells Bank	
	3	Inventory Valuation Report	
	4	Balance Sheet	
	5	Income Statement	
	6	Statement of Cash Flow	
	7	Customer Ledgers	
	8	Vendor Ledgers	
		OPTIONAL PRINTOUTS	
	9	Chart of Accounts	
	10	General Ledger	
	11	Customer List	
	12	Vendor List	
	13	Purchase Journal	
	14	Cash Disbursements Journal	
	15	Sales Journal	
	16	Cash Receipts Journal	
	17	Payroll Journal	
	18	Cost of Goods Sold Journal	

Student Name_____**Date**_____

CHECK YOUR PROGRESS: PROJECT 2, Sports Emporium

1. What are the total debit and credit balances on your
    General Ledger Trial Balance?   _____

2. What are the total assets on January 31?   _____

3. What is the balance in the Wells Bank account
    on January 31?   _____

4. How much are total revenues as of January 31?   _____

5. How much net income (net loss) is reported on
    January 31?   _____

6. What is the balance in the Inventory-Mountain Bikes
    account on January 31?   _____

7. What is the balance in the Inventory-Road Bikes
    account on January 31?   _____

8. What is the balance in the Inventory-Children's Bikes
    account on January 31?   _____

9. What is the balance in the Short-Term Notes Payable
    account on January 31?   _____

10. What is the balance in the Common Stock account
    on January 31?   _____

11. What are the total expenses reported on January 31?   _____

12. Were any Accounts Payable incurred during the
    month of January? (Circle your answer.)   YES   NO

Project 2A

Student-Designed Merchandising Business

In Chapters 12, 13, 14, 15 and Project 2, you learned how to complete the Computer Accounting Cycle for merchandising businesses. Project 2A gives you a chance to design a merchandising business of your own.

You select the type of merchandising business you want, edit your business's Chart of Accounts, create an opening Balance Sheet and transactions, and complete PCA's computer accounting cycle. Project 2A also gives you an opportunity to review the software features learned so far.

You should think about the kind of business you want to create. In Chapters 12, 13, 14 and 15 you worked with Cynthia's Service Merchandise, a partnership form of business; and Your Name Sales and Service, a sole proprietorship. In Project 2, you worked with Sports Emporium, a corporate form of business. You might want to design businesses similar to these. Other merchandising businesses include: jewelry store, automobile dealer, convenience store, florist, furniture dealer, etc.

Before you begin, you should design your business. You need the following:

1. Company information that includes business name, address, telephone number, and form of business.
2. One of PCA's sample companies.
3. A Chart of Accounts: 80 accounts minimum, 110 accounts maximum.
4. A Balance Sheet for your business.
5. One month's transactions for your business. These transactions must include accounts receivable, accounts payable, inventory, and payroll. You should have a minimum of 25 transactions; a maximum of 35 transactions. Your transactions should result in a net income.
6. A bank statement.
7. Complete another month of transactions that result in a net loss.

After you have created your business, you should follow the steps of PCA's computer accounting cycle to complete Project 2A.

After completing the Student-Designed Merchandising Business, you should have the following printouts.

CHECKLIST OF PRINTOUTS		
Student-Designed Merchandising Business		
	1	General Ledger Trial Balance
	2	Account Reconciliation Report
	3	Inventory Valuation Report
	4	Balance Sheet
	5	Income Statement
	6	Statement of Cash Flow
	7	Customer Ledgers
	8	Vendor Ledgers
OPTIONAL PRINTOUTS		
	9	Chart of Accounts
	10	General Ledger
	11	Customer List
	12	Vendor List
	13	Purchase Journal
	14	Cash Disbursements Journal
	15	Sales Journal
	16	Cash Receipts Journal
	17	Payroll Journal
	18	Cost of Goods Sold Journal

<table>
<tr><td>**Part**
4</td><td># Advanced Peachtree
Complete Accounting 2012
Applications</td></tr>
</table>

Part 4 includes three chapters and three projects.

Chapter 16:   Customizing Forms

Chapter 17:   Import/Export

Chapter 18:   Microsoft Word and Templates

Project 3:   Chicago Computer Club (a nonprofit company)

Project 4:   BR Manufacturing, Inc.

Project 4A: Student-Designed Project

Chapter 16, Customizing Forms, shows how to change the preprinted forms included with the software.

Chapter 17, Import/Export, shows how to use PCA 2012 with a word processing program.

Chapter 18, Microsoft Word and Templates, shows you how to copy Peachtree reports to Microsoft Word, use Peachtree's write letters feature, and create templates.

Projects 3 and 4 complete your study of *Computer Accounting with Peachtree by Sage Complete Accounting 2012, 16th Edition*. All features of the software are included for review in these projects.

Project 4A gives you an opportunity to add another month's worth of transactions to any of the projects that you have completed.

The chart on the next page shows the size of the files saved and Peachtree backups made in Part 4--Chapters 16, 17, 18, Project 3 and Project 4. You may back up or save to a USB flash drive, the hard drive, or network. *To complete work in Chapters 16-18, the Exercise 6-2.ptb file is restored.*

The McGraw-Hill Companies, Inc., *Computer Accounting with Peachtree by Sage Complete Accounting 2012, 16e*

Chapter	Peachtree Backup (.ptb) Excel (.xlsx) and Adobe (.pdf)	Kilobytes	Page No.
16	Exercise 16-2.ptb	3,685 KB	680
	Exercise 16-2_Copy of Income Stmnt.pdf	9 KB	680
17	customer.csv	34 KB	690
	customer.txt	34 KB	691
	Exercise 17-2.ptb	956 KB	700
	Exercise 17-2_Vendor List_Chart of Accounts.xlsx	21 KB	700
	Exercise 17-2_Vendor List.pdf	52 KB	701
	Exercise 17-2_Chart of Accounts.pdf	87 KB	701
18	Bellwether Garden Supply.docx	11 KB	705
	Customer Letters.docx	3,131 KB	707
	Bellwether Sales Special.doc	578 KB	711
	Exercise 18-1.docx	3,131 KB	715
	Exercise 18-2.docx	3,131 KB	715
Project 3	Chicago Computer Club Chart of Accounts.ptb	925 KB	723
	Chicago Computer Club Starting Balance Sheet.ptb	927 KB	724
	Chicago Computer Club January.ptb	946 KB	726
	Chicago Computer Club_CofA_ CDJ_CRJ_ GLTB_ BS_ IS_ SCF_SRE_xlsx	40 KB	726
	Project 3_Chart of Accounts.pdf	55 KB	726
	Project 3_General Ledger Trial Balance.pdf	98 KB	726
	Project 3_Balance Sheet.pdf	5 KB	726
	Project 3_Income Statement.pdf	5 KB	726
	Project 3_Statement of Cash Flow.pdf	5 KB	726
	Project 3_Statement of Retained Earnings.pdf	4 KB	726
Project 4	BR Mftg Chart of Accounts.ptb	927 KB	731
	BR Mftg Starting Balance Sheet.ptb	929 KB	732
	BR Mftg Begin.ptb	953 KB	742
	BR Mftg January.ptb	1,092 KB	747
	BR Mftg_CofA_GLTB_BS_IS_SCF_ SRE.xlsx	37 KB	747
	Project 4_Chart of Accounts.pdf	13 KB	747
	Project 4_General Ledger Trial Balance.pdf	7 KB	747
	Project 4_Balance Sheet.pdf	6 KB	747
	Project 4_Income Statement.pdf	6 KB	747
	Project 4_Statement of Cash Flow.pdf	6 KB	747
	Project 4_Statement of Retained Earnings.pdf	4 KB	747

The size of your backup files may differ from the amounts shown on the table.

Chapter

16 Customizing Forms

LEARNING OBJECTIVES

1. Define Peachtree forms.
2. Customize a form (invoice).
3. Print a practice form.
4. Use design tools.
5. Use the Financial Statement Wizard.
6. Make one backup and save one PDF file.

You have used many different kinds of forms: invoices, statements, checks, etc. There may be times when you want to create your own form or customize one of the formats that come with PCA. You can customize forms with PCA's Forms Designer.[1]

PRINTING FORMS

There are three types of documents that can be accessed from the Reports & Forms menu:

➢ Reports

➢ Financial Statements

➢ Forms

The rules for each type of document are different for printing and designing. This chapter will explain the rules for designing forms.

WHAT IS A FORM?

A form in Peachtree is a document that you exchange with customers, vendors, or employees. The forms that come with PCA include checks, tax forms, invoices, statements, mailing labels, quotes, and collection letters.

---

[1]You need a mouse to use the forms designer.

The McGraw-Hill Companies, Inc., *Computer Accounting with Peachtree by Sage Complete Accounting 2012, 16e*

Usually, these documents are printed on preprinted forms, but you can also design a form and print on blank paper. When you are ready to print or design a form, you select Reports & Forms, then select Forms. Select the appropriate form from the Forms Types list. The illustration below shows the Checks selection. From the Forms list, additional selections can be made.

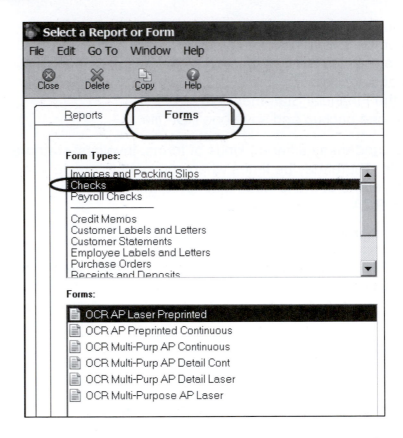

The Select a Report or Form window lists all the reports and forms currently set up in Peachtree. Reports include financial statements, aging reports, etc. Forms are usually tied to a transaction, such as an invoice or check. Letters are also listed on the Forms tab.

The following table lists the forms that can be printed or edited:

Accounts Receivable	Accounts Payable	Payroll
Collection letters	1099 Forms	Payroll checks
Credit memos	Disbursement checks	Employee mailing labels
Customer labels	Purchase orders	
Customer quotes	Vendor mailing labels	
Customer statements		
Invoices/packing slips		
Receipts		
Sales orders		

Preprinted paper forms require special attention because the forms must be aligned in the printer correctly and the printer must be configured to accommodate the form. That is why forms cannot be displayed on your screen prior to printing. You can print practice forms to test alignment and printer configuration, or you can view the layout of the form.

GETTING STARTED

In this chapter, you are going to use Bellwether Garden Supply (the sample company that you used in Chapters 1 through 7).

1. Start Peachtree.

2. Open the sample company, Bellwether Garden Supply. (The instructions in this chapter assume that you are using data from the Exercise 6-2.ptb backup made on page 220. No new data was added in Chapter 7.) If necessary, restore the Exercise 6-2.ptb file.

Comment

You can use beginning Bellwether Garden Supply data or any subsequent Bellwether backup. To install Bellwether's starting data, restore the bgs.ptb backup file. Steps for restoring the bgs.ptb backup file are on pages 29-32.

To verify Exercise 6-2 data, display the balance sheet. A partial balance sheet is shown below. Chapter 7's balance sheet is shown on pages 233-234. (If you restored the bgs.ptb backup file, your balance sheet will differ.)

	Bellwether Garden Supply Balance Sheet March 31, 2012	
	ASSETS	
Current Assets		
Petty Cash	$ 327.55	
Cash on Hand	1,850.45	
Regular Checking Account	9,046.52	
Payroll Checking Account	8,836.40	
Savings Account	7,500.00	
Money Market Fund	4,500.00	
Accounts Receivable	175,846.38	
Other Receivables	7,681.84	
Allowance for Doubtful Account	(5,000.00)	
Inventory	12,453.96	
Prepaid Expenses	14,221.30	
Employee Advances	3,000.65	
Notes Receivable-Current	11,000.00	
Other Current Assets	120.00	
Total Current Assets		251,385.05
Property and Equipment		
Furniture and Fixtures	62,769.25	
Equipment	38,738.33	
Vehicles	86,273.40	
Other Depreciable Property	6,200.96	
Buildings	185,500.00	
Building Improvements	26,500.00	
Accum. Depreciation-Furniture	(54,680.57)	
Accum. Depreciation-Equipment	(33,138.11)	
Accum. Depreciation-Vehicles	(51,585.26)	
Accum. Depreciation-Other	(3,788.84)	
Accum. Depreciation-Buildings	(34,483.97)	
Accum. Depreciation-Bldg Imp	(4,926.28)	
Total Property and Equipment		223,378.91
Other Assets		
Deposits	15,000.00	
Organization Costs	4,995.10	
Accum Amortiz - Organiz Costs	(2,000.00)	
Notes Receivable- Noncurrent	5,004.90	
Other Noncurrent Assets	3,333.00	
Total Other Assets		26,333.00
Total Assets		$ 501,096.96

CUSTOMIZING A FORM

1. From the Navigation Bar, select 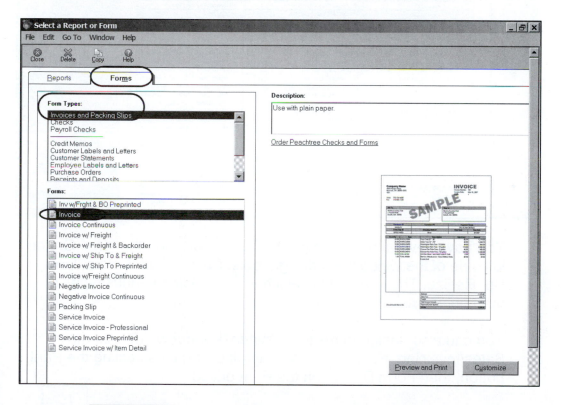 [**Customers & Sales**]. In the Recently Used Customer Reports area, link to <u>View All Customer & Sales Reports</u>. The Select a Report or Form window displays.

2. Select the For<u>m</u>s tab. In the Form Types list, Invoices and Packing Slips is highlighted.

3. In the Forms list, select Invoice. Observe that the Description field shows Use with plain paper.

4. Click [Cu<u>s</u>tomize]. The window for designing an invoice form appears. A partial Invoice window is shown on the next page. This window allows you to create new customized forms or edit existing forms to match your business's needs.

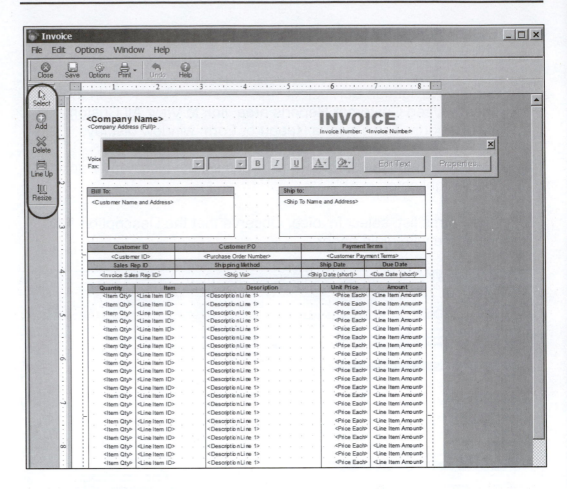

You have several options available for customizing the form. On the left side of the window are design tools: Select, Add, Delete, Line Up, Resize. These assist in selecting and adding various types of form objects.

You can also design forms in certain task windows (for example, Sales/Invoicing, Payments, and Payroll Entry) by selecting the Print button, then Form Design on the Print dialog.

5. To select an object for customizing, use the Selection tool [Select]. With your mouse pointer, you can drag and drop objects to move them around. Click Select . Then move your mouse cursor to the inside of the form (inside the red outline). Click on the <Company Name> field to select it (field selection is indicated by a box).

6. With the <Company Name> field selected (blue box is around it), right-click.

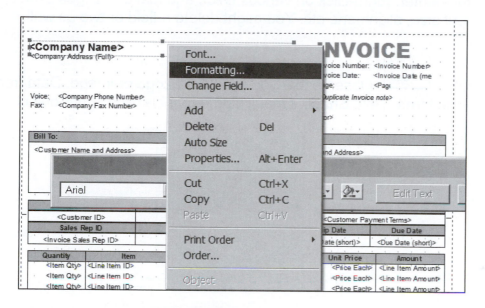

You can also click 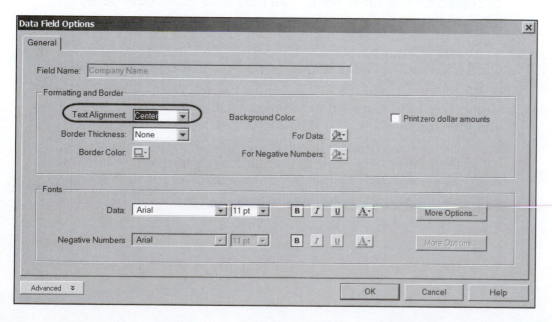 on the window within the Invoice.

7. Left-click Formatting. The Data field Options window appears. In the Text alignment field, select Center.

8. Click 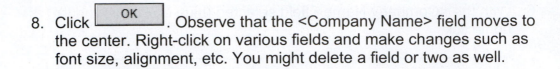 . Observe that the <Company Name> field moves to the center. Right-click on various fields and make changes such as font size, alignment, etc. You might delete a field or two as well.

9. Click [+ Add] . Observe that you can add a Logo or image, Data from Peachtree, Text, Shape, Line, Column to table, and Other object.

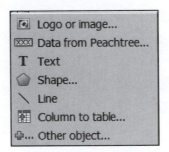

10. On the icon bar of the Forms Designer, click [Options] . The Forms Design Options window appears.

    Select the Display tab to select various display options. Select the Grid/Copies tab to adjust grid options and specify a default number of copies for this form. (*Hint:* You may also accept the default selections.)

11. Click [OK] to close the Forms Design Options window.

12. When finished designing the form, select [Save] . The Save As window appears.

13. Type **Practice** in the Form Name field. Observe that the Filename field shows the path for this form. Compare your Save As window with the one shown on the next page.

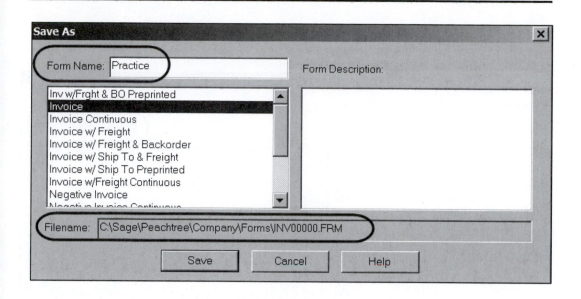

14. Click [Save]. Click [Close]. Observe that Practice is shown on the Forms list with a wrench next to it. A wrench indicates a Custom Peachtree form. Select Practice.

15. Click [Preview and Print].

PRINTING CUSTOMIZED FORMS

The Preview and Print Invoices and Packing Slips window should be displayed. Follow these steps to see the redesigned Invoice.

1. Make the following selections on the Preview and Print Invoices and Packing Slips window

   a. The Invoices to print/e-mail field shows Unprinted invoices through Mar 15, 2012.

   b. The Number the first invoice field shows 103.

   c. The Use this form field shows Practice.

   d. The Delivery method field shows Print and e-mail.

e. Click  .

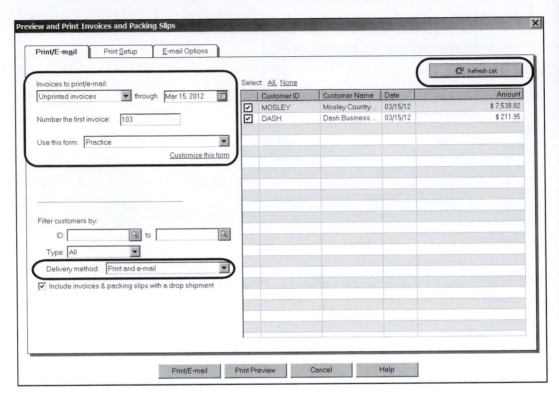

2. Click [Print Preview]. Invoice Number 103 appears. Notice in the illustration on the next page that Bellwether Garden Supply and its address information is centered. Your Invoice may differ depending on which fields you changed. A partial Invoice is shown on the next page.

Bellwether Garden Supply
1505 Pavilion Place
Norcross, GA 30093-3203
USA

INVOICE

Invoice Number: 103
Invoice Date: Mar 15, 2012
Page: 1

Voice: 770-724-4000
Fax: 770-555-1234

Bill To:	Ship to:
Mosley Country Club 1 Howell Walk Duluth, GA 30096	Mosley Country Club 1 Howell Walk Duluth, GA 30096

Customer ID	Customer PO	Payment Terms	
MOSLEY		2% 10, Net 30 Days	
Sales Rep ID	**Shipping Method**	**Ship Date**	**Due Date**
SPRICHARD	None		4/14/12

Quantity	Item	Description	Unit Price	Amount
20.00	NURS-21900	Ficus Tree 22" - 26"	55.95	1,119.00
25.00	NURS-22000	Ginko Tree 14" - 16"	49.95	1,248.75
10.00	NURS-23000	Washington Palm Tree - 5 Gallon	49.00	490.00
20.00	NURS-23010	Washington Palm Tree - 10 gallon	119.00	2,380.00
10.00	NURS-24000	Chinese Fan Palm Tree - 5 gallon	49.95	499.50
10.00	NURS-24010	Chinese Fan Palm Tree - 10 gallon	122.00	1,220.00
15.00	SOIL-34160	GA Pine Straw - wire tied 4 cubic ft. bale	6.99	104.85
1.00	TOOL-35300	Bell-Gro Wheelbarrow - Green Metal; Holds 6 cubic feet	49.99	49.99

3. Click [Next] to see Invoice Number 104. Click [Print]. When the Did the Invoices print and e-mail properly window appears, click [Yes].

4. Close the Select a Report or Form window.

EDITING A FORM DESIGN

1. From the menu bar, select Reports & Forms; Forms, Invoices and Packing Slips.

2. In the Forms list, select Practice.

3. Click [Customize]. Select the fields you want to change.

4. On the Practice window's icon bar, click [Options]. Select the Display

tab to select various display options. Select the Grid/Copies tab to adjust grid options and specify a default number of copies for this form.

5. When through, click [OK].

6. Save the form. Use the same filename, Practice.

DESIGN TOOLS

The forms designer includes design tools: Select, Add, Delete, Line Up, Resize. These terms are defined as follows:

Object Toolbar

[Select]   Select: Select this to use the Selection tools to highlight or select one or more form objects.

[Add]   Add: Select Add to add an object to the form. You can add an image or logo, data field, text field, column field, shape, line or other object using this tool.

[Delete]   Delete: Select Delete to delete the object or objects that you have selected on the form.

[Line Up]   Line Up: Select Line Up to align the objects that you have selected on the form. You can Line Up-Left, Right, Top, Bottom.

[Resize]   Resize: Select Resize to resize the objects that you have selected on the form. You can resize the width and height.

Click  to return to the Select a Report or Form window. Close to return to the menu bar.

Formatting Toolbar

Use the formatting toolbar to change the format of the selected object on your form. Use this toolbar to change the font, color, and background color of the selected object. If you have selected a text object, you can click the Edit Text button to change the text. Clicking the Properties button will open the corresponding property window, where you can modify the object's properties. The Fonts section of the Data Field Options window is shown below.

Fonts						
Data:	Arial	11 pt	**B**	*I*	U	**A**▾
Negative Numbers	Arial	11 pt	**B**	*I*	U	**A**▾

You may want to experiment with the Practice form to see some of these design features.

FINANCIAL STATEMENT DESIGN TOOLS

When you design a financial statement, use the financial statement Design Tools window. It has three major areas: the toolbar at the top of the window, the design toolbar at the side of the window where you select the type of fields you want to place on the designer, and the design area where you actually create the financial statement.

When you create a financial statement, you work with five areas: 1) the header; 2) lines of text; 3) columns; 4) totals; 5) footer. Follow these steps to see the designing tools that are available on the Statement of Cash Flow.

1. From the Reports & Forms menu, select Financial Statements, <Standard> Cash Flow.

2. Click 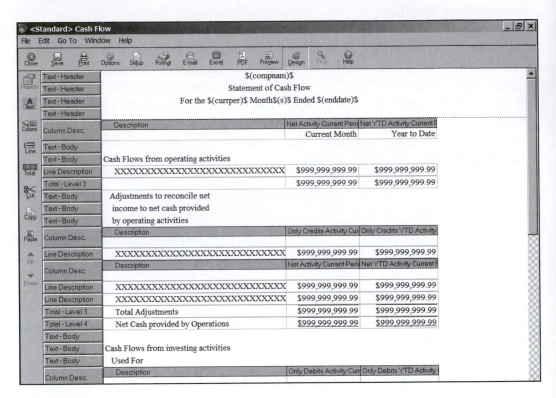. The \<Standard> Cash Flow window includes the design tools necessary for customization. Compare yours with the one shown below.

On the left side of the design window, observe that each row has a button next to it that defines the row; for example, Text – header, Column Desc., Text – Body, etc. The icon bar at the top of the window contains the following buttons: Close, Save, Print, Options, Setup, Format, E-mail, Excel, PDF, Preview, Design, and Help.

The information that follows is for explanation purposes only. You may want to experiment with some of the design tools to make changes to Peachtree's \<Standard> Cash Flow.

When designing a new form or modifying an existing one, you need to save the form to record your changes. If you change one of the standard forms (those that came with Peachtree), you must rename the form before saving your changes. You cannot save changes to the standard forms using the original form name. This allows you to keep the standard form in case you make a design error and need to start over.

A custom form appears on the report list with a different icon than a <Standard> form. Predefined or standard forms and reports are included with the software.

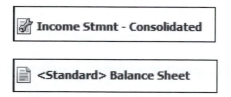

The financial statement design tools are shown below.

Use the Property tool to work with the properties window for the selected row type. For example, if you select a text row, the text window opens.

Use the Text tool to insert text that you will not change from statement to statement (for example, section headings).

Use the Column tool to define columns, enter a title for each column, select the alignment of each column title (left, right, or center) and select the style, size and color of the text.

Once the columns are defined, use the Line tool to define what data to put in each row of a column. Line objects are placed below column objects.

Use the Total tool to tell the program how to calculate totals and subtotals.

Use the Cut tool to remove the selected row and copy it to the Windows Clipboard.

Use the Copy tool to copy the selected row to the Windows Clipboard.

Use the Paste tool to insert the current row from the Windows Clipboard.

Use the Up tool to move the selected row up one position in the list of rows.

Use the Down tool to move a selected row down one position in the list of rows.

You can select multiple rows in the window and then apply the cut, copy, and paste functions to all of them. To select multiple rows, hold down the Ctrl key, and then with the cursor select the buttons that define the rows you want.

FINANCIAL STATEMENT WIZARD

The Financial Statement Wizard walks you through the process of designing financial statements. Follow these steps to use the Financial Statement Wizard.

1. If necessary start Peachtree. Open Bellwether Garden Supply.

2. From the Reports & Forms menu, select Financial Statements.

3. Link to <u>Financial Statement Wizard</u> (upper right side of window).

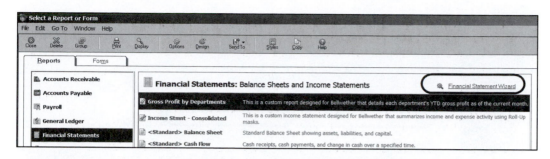

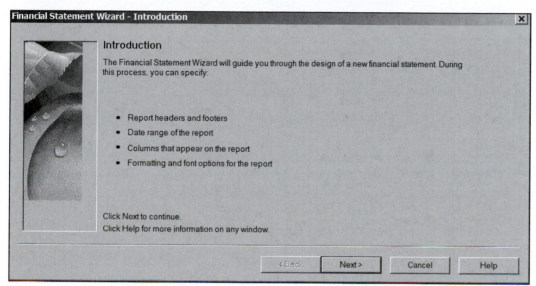

4. After reading the information on the Introduction window, click Next >.

5. Make sure <Standard> Balance Sheet appears in the Financial Statement Template field. If necessary, select it.

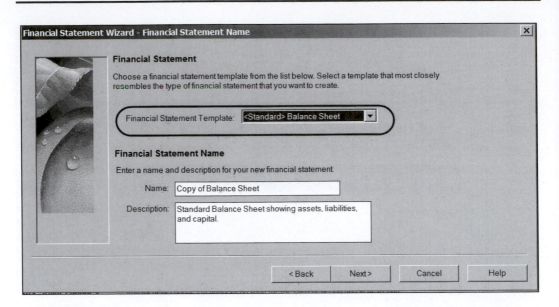

6. After reading the information on the Financial Statement window, click
    | Next > | . The Headers and Footers window appears.

7. The Headers and Footers window allows you to change information at
    the top and bottom of the balance sheet. For purposes of this
    exercise, click on the Header 1 line, then type **your name** followed by
    a comma and a space.

8. In the Header 3 line, click on the beginning of the line, then click
    | Insert ▼ | (down arrow next to Insert). Select Today's Date from the
    drop-down list. Type a comma and a space between $(Date)$, and
    $(enddate)$. The Header 3 line looks like this:

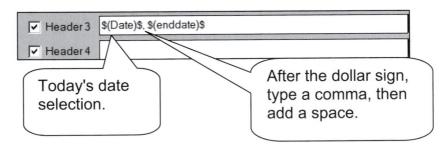

    Compare your Headers and Footers window with the one shown on
    the next page.

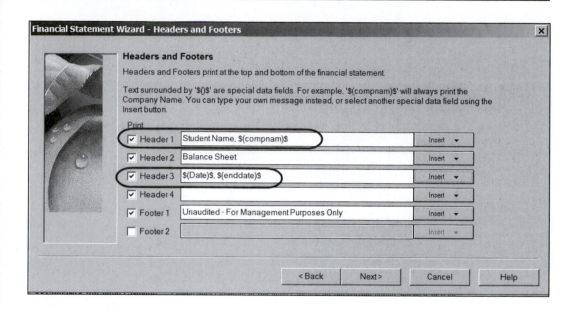

9. Click [Next >]. The Date Range and Account Masking window appears. Read the information in the Dates and General Ledger Account Masking sections. Accept the defaults on this window, by clicking on [Next >].

10. Accept the defaults on the Column Properties window by clicking on [Next >].

11. Accept the defaults on the Column Options window by clicking on [Next >].

12. Unless you want to change fonts, accept the defaults on the Fonts window by clicking on [Next >].

13. Accept the defaults on the Formatting and Default Printer window by clicking on [Next >].

14. The Congratulations window appears. To display your new financial statement, click [Finish]. The Copy of Balance Sheet window appears, click [OK].

Compare your balance sheet to the partial one shown below. Observe that the header shows your name on line one; today's date is shown on line 3 before March 31, 2012 (your current date will differ). This balance sheet is from the Exercise 6-2.ptb backup file. In Chapter 7 on pages 233-234, you printed Bellwether Garden Supply's balance sheet.

		Student Name, Bellwether Garden Supply
	Line 1 and Line 3 of header	Balance Sheet
		November 9, 2011, March 31, 2012
		ASSETS

Current Assets		
Petty Cash	$ 327.55	
Cash on Hand	1,850.45	
Regular Checking Account	9,046.52	
Payroll Checking Account	8,836.40	
Savings Account	7,500.00	
Money Market Fund	4,500.00	
Accounts Receivable	175,846.38	
Other Receivables	7,681.84	
Allowance for Doubtful Account	(5,000.00)	
Inventory	12,453.96	
Prepaid Expenses	14,221.30	
Employee Advances	3,000.65	
Notes Receivable-Current	11,000.00	
Other Current Assets	120.00	
Total Current Assets		251,385.05
Property and Equipment		
Furniture and Fixtures	62,769.25	
Equipment	38,738.33	
Vehicles	86,273.40	
Other Depreciable Property	6,200.96	
Buildings	185,500.00	
Building Improvements	26,500.00	
Accum. Depreciation-Furniture	(54,680.57)	
Accum. Depreciation-Equipment	(33,138.11)	
Accum. Depreciation-Vehicles	(51,585.26)	
Accum. Depreciation-Other	(3,788.84)	
Accum. Depreciation-Buildings	(34,483.97)	
Accum. Depreciation-Bldg Imp	(4,926.28)	
Total Property and Equipment		223,378.91
Other Assets		
Deposits	15,000.00	
Organization Costs	4,995.10	
Accum Amortiz - Organiz Costs	(2,000.00)	

15. Close the balance sheet window. Observe a wrench is shown next to Copy of Balance Sheet, which indicates a custom form.

Copy of Balance Sheet	Standard Balance Sheet showing assets, liabilities, and capital.

16. Close the Select a Report or Form window. Exit Peachtree or continue.

SUMMARY AND REVIEW

Complete the following end-of-chapter activities:

1. Going to the net, page 677

2. Multiple-choice questions, pages 677-679

3. Exercises 16-1 and 16-2, page 680

4. Analysis questions, page 680

5. Assessment rubric, page 681

6. Chapter 16 Index, page 682

GOING TO THE NET

Access the Sage Newsroom at www.sagenorthamerica.com/Newsroom. (Going to the Net links are on the textbook website at www.mhhe.com/yacht2012; link to Student Edition, select Chapter 16.)

1. Select two articles.

2. Write a brief summary (no more than 100 words for each article). Identify the name and date of the articles and the website address in your answer.

Multiple-choice questions: The Online Learning Center includes these questions and the analysis question at www.mhhe.com/yacht2012, select Student Edition, Chapter 16, QA Templates.

_____ 1. The definition of a form in Peachtree is:

    a. Preprinted paper forms that can be displayed on your screen.
    b. A document that you exchange with customers, vendors, or employees.
    c. Reports that are selected from the menu bar.
    d. Options selected from the menu bar.
    e. None of the above.

_____ 2. The three types of documents accessed from the Reports & Forms menu are:

    a. Reports, Financial Statements, Forms.
    b. Payroll Checks, Disbursements Checks, Invoices.
    c. Sales Invoices, Purchase Invoices, Cash Receipts.
    d. Filter, Forms Designer, Report List.
    e. None of the above.

_____ 3. The Accounts Payable forms that can be printed or edited are:

    a. Payroll Checks, W2s, 940's and 941's, State Quarterly Tax Forms, Employee Mailing Labels.
    b. Disbursement Checks, 1099 Forms, Purchase Orders, Vendor Mailing Labels.
    c. Invoices, Statements, Customer Mailing Labels, Quotes, Collection Letters.
    d. All of the above.
    e. None of the above.

_____ 4. The Accounts Receivable forms that can be printed or edited are:

    a. Payroll checks, 940's and 941's.
    b. Purchase Orders, 1099 Forms, Disbursement Checks, Vendor Mailing Labels.
    c. Invoices/Packing Slips, Customer Statements, Customer Labels, Collection Letters.
    d. All of the above.
    e. None of the above.

_____ 5. To use Peachtree's forms designer, make this selection:

    a. Customize.
    b. Select.
    c. Customers & Sales.
    d. View All customer & Sales Reports.
    e. None of the above.

_____   6.   These buttons are called design tools:

     a.   Select.
     b.   Add.
     c.   Delete.
     d.   Line Up and Resize.
     e.   All of the above.

_____   7.   In Chapter 16, the Windows 7 default location for saving the Practice form is:

     a.   C:\Peachtree\Program Files\INV00000.FRM
     b.   C:\Program Files\Practice
     c.   C:\Program Files\Sage Software\Invoice\Practice
     d.   C:\Sage\Peachtree\ Company\Forms\INV00000.FRM
     e.   None of the above.

_____   8.   To add an object to the form, make this selection:

     a.   Select.
     b.   Add.
     c.   Delete.
     d.   Resize.
     e.   All of the above.

_____   9.   This selection walks you through the process of designing financial statements.

     a.   Customizing forms.
     b.   Financial statement wizard.
     c.   Financial statement template.
     d.   The Navigation Bar selection, Company.
     e.   None of the above.

_____10.   The top and the bottom of financial statements include the following:

     a.   Object toolbar.
     b.   Design tools.
     c.   Fonts selections.
     d.   Headers and footers.
     e.   None of the above.

Exercise 16-1: Use the forms designer to customize a Service Invoice.

1. From the Customers & Sales Navigation Center, link to View All Customer and Sales Reports.

2. From the Forms list, select Service Invoice. Select Customize.

3. Center the Company Name and Company Address.

4. Change Company Name's font size to 14.

5. Change the font size of the Company Address to Arial 11.

6. Change the font size of the Customer Name and Address to Arial 11.

7. Save the Service Invoice as Exercise 16-1.

8. Preview and print the service invoices. (*Hint:* Remember to Refresh List.)

Exercise 16-2: Use the Financial Statement Wizard.

1. Use the Financial Statement Wizard to add your name and today's date to <Standard> Income Statement.

2. Print the income statement. (*Hint:* Uncheck Show Zero Amounts.)

3. Backup. The suggested file name is **Exercise 16-2.ptb**.

4. Save the Copy of the Income Statement as a PDF file. The suggested file name is **Exercise 16-2.Copy of Income Stmnt.pdf**. Check with your instructor to see if he or she would also like an Excel file.

ANALYSIS QUESTIONS

1. What is a Peachtree form?

2. What is a predefined or standard report?

ASSESSMENT RUBRIC

Complete the Assessment Rubric online at www.mhhe.com/yacht2012; Student Edition, select Chapter 16, Assessment Rubric link. To review Peachtree's navigation centers, menu selections, and windows, complete the blank fields online.

Report	Date	Menu	Icon ID
Customized Balance Sheet			

CHAPTER 16 INDEX

Chapter

17 Import/Export

LEARNING OBJECTIVES

1. Export information from Peachtree to a word processing program. (In this chapter Microsoft Word 2010 and Windows 7 are used. Microsoft Word 2007 can also be used.)
2. Select the customer list from Bellwether Garden Supply to export.
3. Import Bellwether Garden Supply's chart of accounts into a new company.
4. Save two files: a comma separated value file (.csv) and a text file (.txt).
5. Make one backup, save one Excel file, and save two PDF files.

Importing translates data from other programs into a format that Peachtree can use. The diagram below shows how importing works. Data can be imported into Peachtree.

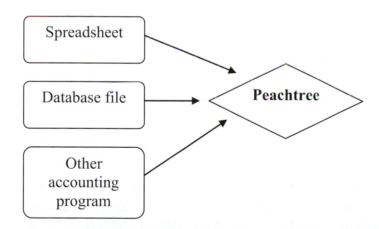

Exporting copies Peachtree data into a format that other programs can read and use. The diagram on the next page illustrates exporting. Data is exported from Peachtree.

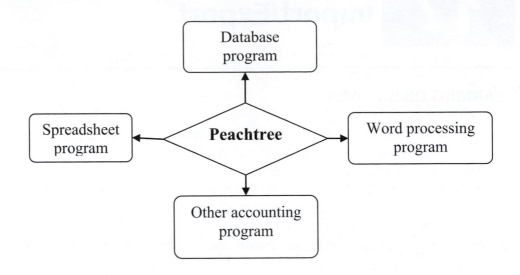

The chart below shows how Peachtree organizes data.

| Customer | **Files** | Journal |

Records

| General Journal | Purchase Journal | Cash Disbursements Journal | Sales Journal | Cash Receipts Journal |

Fields

| Invoice Number | Account Number | Debit Amount | Credit Amount |

➢ **Files** are a group of related records; for example, customer files and journal files.

➢ **Records** are a group of fields that contain information on one subject; for example, the general journal, purchase journal, cash disbursements journal, sales journal, or cash receipts journal.

➢ **Fields** are an individual piece of data; for example, invoice numbers, account numbers, debit amount, credit amount.

Files

When you import or export files, you use templates to format the data. The templates included in Peachtree are:

> Accounts Receivable: Customer List, Sales Journal, and Cash Receipts Journal

> Accounts Payable: Vendor List, Purchase Journal, and Cash Disbursements Journal

> Payroll: Employee List

> General Ledger: Chart of Accounts and General Journal

> Inventory: Inventory Item List

> Job Reports: Jobs List

Records

When you select a file to export, you can define which information you want. For instance, when you select the Customer List, you can select which customers you want to export.

Fields

When export is used, you export individual fields of information. You can see what fields are exported by selecting the Format tab. You may uncheck fields to exclude them from being exported or move fields around to change their order.

When you export, the information is exported in a **comma separated values** (CSV) format. This means that the fields for each record are written in one line, with commas between them. You see how this looks when you export one of Peachtree's customer lists into Microsoft Word 2007 or 2010. Common separated value files (CSV extensions) are commonly used for transferring data between applications in a text-based format.

The file created during the export process is an **ASCII** file, which contains only text characters. Each record is on a separate line. ASCII is an acronym for American Standard Code for Information Interchange. It is one of the standard formats used for representing characters on a computer. Most word processing, spreadsheet, and database programs can read ASCII files.

GETTING STARTED: EXPORTING

1. Start Peachtree.

2. Open Bellwether Garden Supply. (In this chapter data is used from the Exercise 6-2.ptb backup file made on page 220.)

3. Restore the Exercise 6-2.ptb file. (*Hint:* Any Bellwether Garden Supply file can be used to complete work in Chapter 17.)

4. From the menu bar, select File; then Select Import/Export. The Select Import/Export window appears.

5. In the Accounts Receivable list, highlight Customer List.

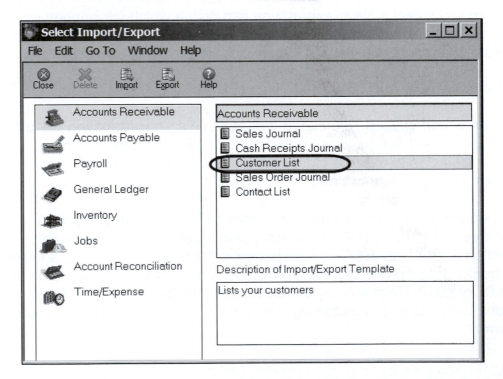

6. Click 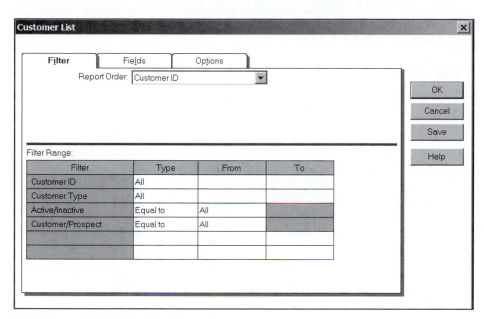. The Customer List window appears.

7. Click on the Fields tab, then click 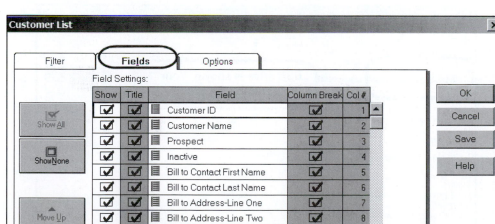.

> **Comment**
>
> Show <u>A</u>ll places a check mark in all the fields.

8. Click on the Op<u>t</u>ions tab.

> **Comment**
>
> The radio button next to Ask, Then Overwrite is the default.

9. Insert a USB flash drive. Click on the arrow [▸] below Import/Export File. The Open window appears. The File name field shows CUSTOMER.CSV File name: CUSTOMER.CSV . The field to the right shows Import/Export Files (*.CSV)  .

10. Select the appropriate drive letter for your USB drive.

   In this example, drive D is shown.
   Then click Open .

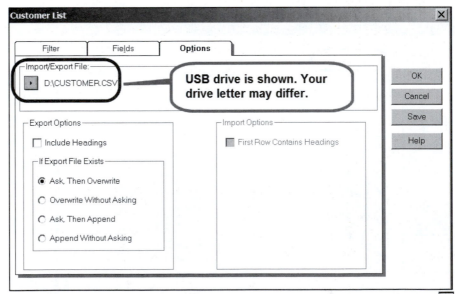

Observe that D:\CUSTOMER.CSV is shown next to the arrow [▸] under Import/Export File. (Substitute your drive letter for D.)

11. Click [Save]. The Save As window appears. Type **Customers** in the Template Name field.

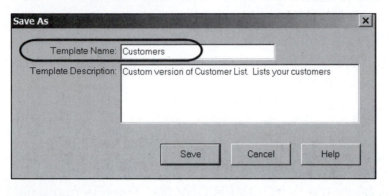

12. Click [Save].

13. You are returned to the Customer List Options window. Make sure X:\CUSTOMER.CSV is shown as the Import/Export File name.

(Substitute your drive letter for X.) Click [OK]. The Select Import/Export window shows Customers with a red arrow. Select it. The Description field describes the custom version.

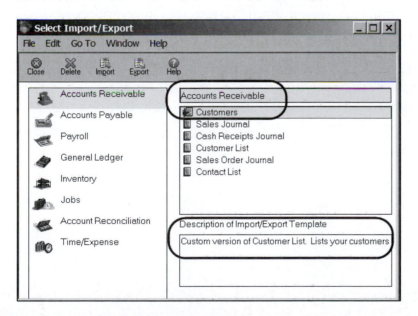

14. Close the Select Import/Export window.

15. If necessary, go to the desktop. Start your word processing program. You can also use Microsoft Word 2010 (2007 or 2003), or any word processing program that supports ASCII.

16. Follow these steps to open the Peachtree file from Microsoft Word.

    a. Start Word or other word processing program. Click 🗁 (the open file icon).

    b. Select the appropriate location of the CUSTOMER.CSV file. Make sure All Files (*.*) is shown | All Files (*.*) ▼ |.

    c. Highlight the CUSTOMER.CSV file. The File name field is completed | File name: CUSTOMER.CSV ▼ | All Files (*.*) ▼ |.

    d. Click | Open |. (*Hint:* If a convert file window appears, select Plain Text, then <OK>.)

    The data on your window was exported in a comma separated format. The fields for each record are written in one line, with commas between them. To use this information, you would need to edit its contents, then save it.

    Compare your window to the one shown on the next page. If you used a different word processing program, your window will look different but the text portion of the data is the same.

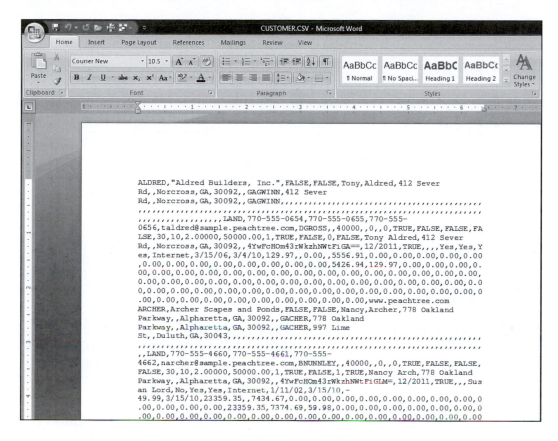

e. To keep the original ASCII file, use Word's Save <u>A</u>s command and rename the file **CUSTOMER.txt**. When you save, the file converts to a text document file from its original ASCII format. If a File Conversion – CUSTOMER.txt window appears, click

    [OK].

f. Exit the word processing program.

TEXT AND COMMA SEPARATED VALUES FILES

To look at the files you just created, do this:

1. Right-click the Start button; left-click Open Windows Explorer.

2. Go to the location of the CSV file.

3. Observe that the CUSTOMER.CSV file is an Excel file saved as Comma Separated Values. The CUSTOMER.txt file is a Text document.

CUSTOMER.CSV	Microsoft Office Excel Comma Separated Values File	34 KB
CUSTOMER.txt	Text Document	34 KB

4. Double-click CUSTOMER.CSV to see the Excel file created from Bellwether Garden Supply's customer list. Close the window.

5. Double-click CUSTOMER.txt to see the text file.

6. Close the Notepad window and Windows Explorer.

IMPORTING

Importing data from another accounting, database, or spreadsheet program into Peachtree works similarly to exporting. Any information that is entered in Peachtree during setup and maintenance can be imported.

In Peachtree, the Maintain windows allow you to perform tasks associated with lists, such as the Customer List, Employee List, Chart of Accounts, etc. The Tasks windows allow you to perform tasks that consist of journalizing transactions. When you import data, it is important to know that Peachtree allows you to import new transactions, for example, tasks performed within the Tasks windows. Once transactions are imported they cannot be edited.

In the example that follows, you are going to copy Bellwether Garden Supply's chart of accounts to another company. To start this process, you export the chart of accounts list first, then import the chart into a newly set up company.

Import a Chart of Accounts

To import the chart of accounts from Bellwether Garden Supply to another company, do the following.

1. If necessary start Peachtree and open Bellwether Garden Supply. From the File menu, click Select Import/Export.

2. Select General Ledger, then Chart of Accounts List.

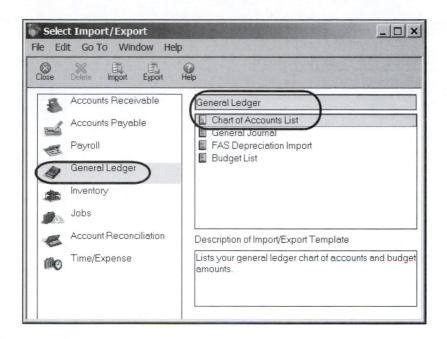

3. Click 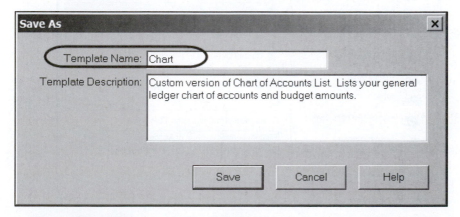. The Chart of Accounts List window appears. Select the Options tab. Observe the default location for the CHART.CSV file. The file will be imported from that location. The default location on Windows 7 computers is C:\Users\[computer name]\ Documents\ CHART.CSV.

4. Click **Save**. In the Template Name field, type **Chart**.

5. Click **Save**. The Chart window appears. Observe the location where the CHART.CSV file is stored.

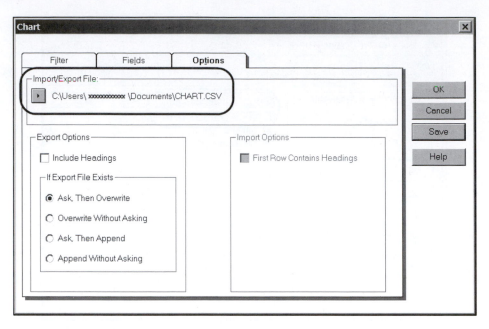

Substitute the X's for your computer name.

6. Click OK. The Select/Import Export window shows the custom version of the Chart listed.

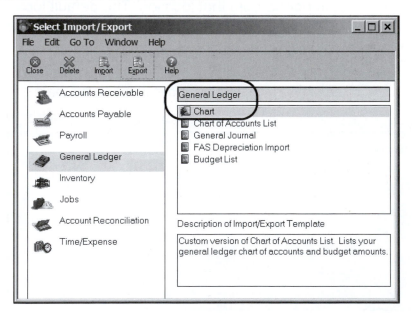

7. Close the Select Import/Export window.

8. Set up a new company. From the menu bar, select File; New Company. When the window prompts, do you want to keep Bellwether Garden Supply open, select No . The Create a New Company window appears. Click Next >

    a. Use your first name Company; for example, Carol Company.

    b. Accept the default for Corporation. Click Next > .

    c. On the Select a method to create your company, select Build your own chart of accounts.

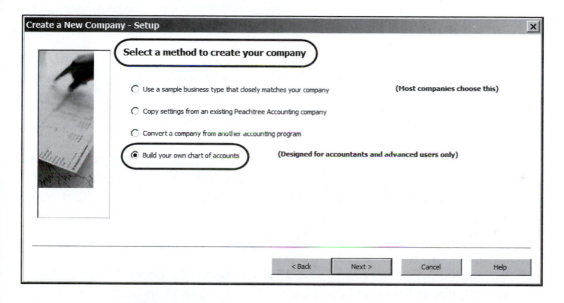

    d. Click Next > until the Choose the first period of your fiscal year window appears. Select January 2012.

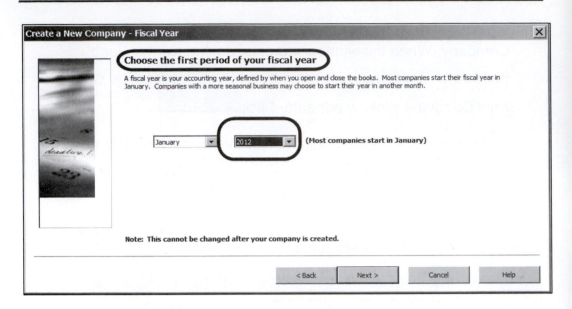

e. Click [Next >], then [Finish]. If the screen prompts You can use this company in the student version of Peachtree for the next 14 months and then it will expire, click [OK].

9. If necessary, close the Setup Guide. The title bar shows Your Name Company - Peachtree Accounting. From the File menu, click Select Import/Export. Select General Ledger; Chart of Accounts List. Then, [Import].

10. On the Chart of Accounts List window, select Options. Observe that the file name location is the same as the illustration at the top of page 694. (Substitute the x's for your computer name.)

11. Click [OK]. When the screen prompts You should make a backup before attempting to import. Would you like to continue?, click [Yes]. Close the Select Import/Export window.

The McGraw-Hill Companies, Inc., *Computer Accounting with Peachtree by Sage Complete Accounting 2012, 16e*

12. Display your Chart of Accounts (Reports & Forms; General Ledger, Chart of Accounts). Your company shows the same chart of accounts as Bellwether Garden Supply. A partial chart of accounts is shown below. The month on your chart of accounts may differ from the one shown. The month defaults to the period when the company was set up.

Carol Company
Chart of Accounts
As of Nov 30, 2012

Filter Criteria includes: Report order is by ID. Report is printed with Accounts having Zero Amounts and in Detail Format.

Account ID	Account Description	Active?	Account Type
10000	Petty Cash	Yes	Cash
10100	Cash on Hand	Yes	Cash
10200	Regular Checking Account	Yes	Cash
10300	Payroll Checking Account	Yes	Cash
10400	Savings Account	Yes	Cash
10500	Money Market Fund	Yes	Cash
11000	Accounts Receivable	Yes	Accounts Receivable
11100	Contracts Receivable	Yes	Accounts Receivable
11400	Other Receivables	Yes	Accounts Receivable
11500	Allowance for Doubtful Account	Yes	Accounts Receivable
12000	Inventory	Yes	Inventory
14000	Prepaid Expenses	Yes	Other Current Assets
14100	Employee Advances	Yes	Other Current Assets
14200	Notes Receivable-Current	Yes	Other Current Assets
14700	Other Current Assets	Yes	Other Current Assets
15000	Furniture and Fixtures	Yes	Fixed Assets
15100	Equipment	Yes	Fixed Assets
15200	Vehicles	Yes	Fixed Assets
15300	Other Depreciable Property	Yes	Fixed Assets
15400	Leasehold Improvements	Yes	Fixed Assets
15500	Buildings	Yes	Fixed Assets
15600	Building Improvements	Yes	Fixed Assets
16900	Land	Yes	Fixed Assets
17000	Accum. Depreciation-Furniture	Yes	Accumulated Depreciation
17100	Accum. Depreciation-Equipment	Yes	Accumulated Depreciation
17200	Accum. Depreciation-Vehicles	Yes	Accumulated Depreciation
17300	Accum. Depreciation-Other	Yes	Accumulated Depreciation
17400	Accum. Depreciation-Leasehold	Yes	Accumulated Depreciation
17500	Accum. Depreciation-Buildings	Yes	Accumulated Depreciation
17600	Accum. Depreciation-Bldg Imp	Yes	Accumulated Depreciation
19000	Deposits	Yes	Other Assets
19100	Organization Costs	Yes	Other Assets
19150	Accum Amortiz - Organiz Costs	Yes	Other Assets
19200	Notes Receivable- Noncurrent	Yes	Other Assets
19900	Other Noncurrent Assets	Yes	Other Assets
20000	Accounts Payable	Yes	Accounts Payable
23000	Accrued Expenses	Yes	Other Current Liabilities
23100	Sales Tax Payable	Yes	Other Current Liabilities
23200	Wages Payable	Yes	Other Current Liabilities
23300	401 K Deductions Payable	Yes	Other Current Liabilities
23350	Health Insurance Payable	Yes	Other Current Liabilities

In this chapter, you exported and imported data. To learn more about these features, use Peachtree's Help feature. Exit Peachtree, or continue.

SUMMARY AND REVIEW

1. Going to the net, page, 698.
2. Multiple-choice questions, page 698-700.
3. Exercises 17-1 and 17-2, pages 700-701.
4. Analysis question, page 701.
5. Assessment rubric, page 701.
6. Chapter 17 Index, page 702.

GOING TO THE NET

Access the Peachtree Add-Ons website at
www.peachtree.com/productsServices/peachtreeAddOns/.
Complete the following.

1. List nine Peachtree add-ons.
2. Link to Third-Party Add-Ons, then Point of Sale. The URL is
   http://sagepss.com/Solutions.aspx?p=2&v=111%2c112%2c130%2c
   141&b=207%2c208%2c209%2c210%2c211%2c212%2c213. Briefly
   explain the Point of Sale application.

Multiple-Choice Questions: The Online Learning Center includes these
questions and the analysis question at www.mhhe.com/yacht2012, select
Student Edition, Chapter 17, QA Templates.

_____ 1. A group of related records is called a/an:

      a. File.
      b. Record.
      c. Field.
      d. Balance Sheet.
      e. All of the above.

_____ 2. A group of fields that contains information on one subject is
called a/an:

      a. File.
      b. Record.
      c. Field.
      d. Income statement.
      e. All of the above.

_____ 3. An individual piece of data such as an account number or customer's name is called a/an:

    a. File.
    b. Record.
    c. Field.
    d. Income statement.
    e. All of the above.

_____ 4. Exporting copies Peachtree data into a format that the following programs can read and use:

    a. Spreadsheet programs.
    b. Database programs.
    c. Accounting programs.
    d. Word processing programs.
    e. All of the above

_____ 5. Importing allows you to translate data from the following types of programs:

    a. Spreadsheet programs.
    b. Database programs.
    c. Accounting programs.
    d. All of the above.
    e. None of the above.

_____ 6. Information that appears on Peachtree's reports can be:

    a. Imported.
    b. Exported.
    c. Formatted into an ANSI file.
    d. A macro.
    e. None of the above.

_____ 7. The name of the company from which you exported data is:

    a. Mark Foltz Designer.
    b. Susan Babbage, Accounting.
    c. Sports Emporium.
    d. Cynthia's Service Merchandise.
    e. None of the above.

_____ 8. When you import or export files, you use one of the following to format the data:

    a. Template.
    b. File.
    c. Field.
    d. Record.
    e. None of the above.

_____ 9. The type of file that is exported into a word processing program is called a/an:

    a. DOS text file.
    b. ANSI file.
    c. ASCII file.
    d. WordStar file.
    e. None of the above.

_____10. The data on your window was exported in the following format:

    a. Comma separated.
    b. Line separated.
    c. Field separated.
    d. File separated.
    e. None of the above.

Exercise 17-1: Follow the instructions below to complete Exercise 17-1.

1. Import Bellwether Garden Supply's vendor list into the company set up in Chapter 17, Your Name Company. Save the vendor list as List of Vendors.

2. Print the Vendor List.

Exercise 17-2: Follow the instructions below to complete Exercise 17-2.

1. Print the Chart of Accounts.

2. Backup. The suggested file name is **Exercise 17-2.ptb**.

3 Save the Vendor List and Chart of Accounts as an Excel file. The suggested file name is **Exercise 17-2_Vendor List_Chart of Accounts.xlsx**.

4   Save your company's Vendor list and Chart of Accounts as a PDF
    file. The suggested file name is **Exercise 17-2_Vendor List.pdf** and
    Exercise 17-2_Chart of Accounts.pdf.

ANALYSIS QUESTION

What is the purpose of importing and exporting?

ASSESSMENT RUBRIC

Complete the Assessment Rubric online at www.mhhe.com/yacht2012;
Student Edition, select Chapter 17, Assessment Rubric link. To review
Peachtree's navigation centers, menu selections, and windows, complete
the blank fields online.

Report	Menu Selections and Links	File Name, Extension, and Report ID
Customer List		

The McGraw-Hill Companies, Inc., *Computer Accounting with Peachtree by Sage Complete Accounting 2012, 16e*

CHAPTER 17 INDEX

Chapter 18

Microsoft Word and Templates

LEARNING OBJECTIVES

1. Copy Peachtree report data to Microsoft Word.
2. Use the write letters feature.
3. Edit and save letter templates.
4. Save Word files.
5. Extract the PAWMail.zip folder.
6. Search Peachtree's knowledgebase.
7. Save five Word files.

Peachtree's write letters feature allows you to send information to a large number of people quickly. For example, you can send personally addressed letters to all the company's customers. The Tasks menu and the Select a Report or Forms window include a selection for write letters. Use Peachtree's write letters feature to create mailings or e-mail messages from existing or custom letter templates using customer, vendor, and employee information. A *template* is a document pattern or part of a document that is stored so that it can be used again.

You can create mailings such as newsletters, announcements, collection letters, individual letters, e-mail messages, and other types of mailings. Peachtree integrates with Microsoft Word's mail merge feature, using Word to edit and create custom templates, then generates mailings using selected Peachtree information.

GETTING STARTED

1. Start Peachtree. Open Bellwether Garden Supply.

2. If necessary, restore the Exercise 6-2 file. This backup was made on page 220.

The McGraw-Hill Companies, Inc., *Computer Accounting with Peachtree by Sage Complete Accounting 2012, 16e*

> **Comment**
>
> If you no longer have your Exercise 6-2 back up file, use starting data for Bellwether Garden Supply. Refer to pages 29-32, Using Peachtree's Restore Wizard, to restore Bellwether's starting data.

COPYING PEACHTREE REPORT DATA TO MICROSOFT WORD

A displayed PCA report or financial statement can be copied to the Windows clipboard. Then you can paste that data into other applications, such as Microsoft Word or another word processing program. The steps that follow show you how to copy and paste a report using Microsoft Word 2003 or higher.

1. If necessary start PCA. Open the sample company, Bellwether Garden Supply.

2. From Bellwether's menu bar, select Reports & Forms; Financial Statements; <Standard> Retained Earnings. Click Display. The Statement of Retained Earnings displays.

3. Click Options. Uncheck Print Page Numbers and Show Zero Amounts. Click OK.

4. From the menu bar, click Edit, Copy.

5. Start Microsoft Word or other word processing program. Click Paste. Or, right-click on the document, left-click Paste. Bellwether's statement of retained earnings appears. You need to format the statement in order for it to look like the one shown on the next page. (These account balances reflect data from the Exercise 6-2.ptb backup file. If you are using a different backup file, your account balances will differ.)

```
                    Bellwether Garden Supply
                   Statement of Retained Earnings
              For the Three Months Ending March 31, 2012


    Beginning Retained Earning        $     189,037.60
    Adjustments To Date                            0.00
    Net Income                                25,476.82

    Subtotal                                 214,514.42

    Ending Retained Earnings          $     214,514.42

                   For Management Purposes Only
```

The file copied was formatted with Microsoft Word.

6. Click ![icon], Save As. In the Save in field, select the appropriate drive. Accept the file name Bellwether Garden Supply.docx. Observe that the File as type field shows Word Document (*.docx). (*Hint:* If you are using Word 2003, the default file extension is .doc.)

7. Click Save .

8. Exit Word.

9. Close all Peachtree windows.

CREATE A MAILING TO CUSTOMERS

Follow these steps to use one of Peachtree's Write Letters templates.

1. From the Tasks menu, select Write Letters; Customer Letters.

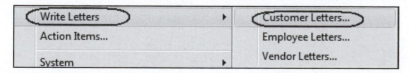

2. The Select a Report or Form window appears. Observe that the Form Types list shows Customer Labels and Letters highlighted. Select Bellwether Sales Special. The Description field shows 2nd Qtr Sales Promotion letter.

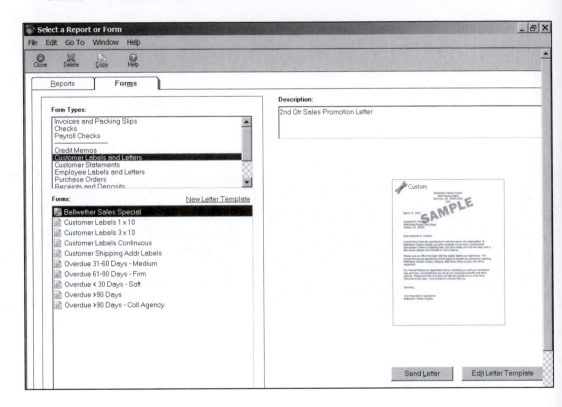

3. Click $\boxed{\text{Send Letter}}$. The Write Letters - Bellwether Sales Special window appears. Observe there are two tabs: Select Recipients and E-mail Options. Select Recipients is the default.

4. Click $\boxed{\text{Word}}$. Wait a few moments for the first customer letter to appear. Observe that the taskbar shows Page 1 of 34— $\boxed{\text{Page: 1 of 34}}$. This means there are 34 customer letters. The Aldred Builders, Inc. letter is shown on your screen and on the next page. Read the letter.

GARDEN SUPPLY
1505 Pavilion Place
Norcross, GA 30093-3203
770-724-4000

BUY ONE ITEM GET THE 2nd ITEM 50% OFF PROMOTION!!!

Aldred Builders, Inc.
412 Sever Rd
Norcross, GA 30092

Dear Tony Aldred:

As one of our loyal customers, we would like to **thank you** by extending you a **special offer**. Buy any item in our catalog at the regular price and receive any **2nd** item (at an equal or lesser value) for **50%** off.

This offer is also good for purchases made online!! Check us out on the web at **www.peachtree.com**.

Again, thank you for your continued business.

Regards,

Derrick P. Gross
Sales Representative

Go to pages 2, 3, etc. Observe that each customer receives an individually addressed letter.

5. To save the letter, click ; Save As. The suggested filename is **Customer Letters**. If you are using Word 2003, save the file by accepting the default extension, .doc. In Word 2007 or 2010, when the screen prompts, You are about to save your document to one of the new file formats, click OK.

6. Close the document.

7. If necessary, on the taskbar, click [⚙ Select a Report or Form ☒] to return to the Select a Report or Form window.

EDIT LETTER TEMPLATES

Follow these steps to create a letter template from the promotion letter shown on page 707.

1. From the Select a Report window, make sure Bellwether Sales Special is selected. (If necessary, select Tasks; Write Letters, Customers Letters.)

2. Click [Edit Letter Template]. The Edit Letter Template – Bellwether Sales Special window appears. Observe that the Letter Template Description shows 2nd Qtr Sales Promotion Letter. Compare your Edit Letter Template window with the one shown below.

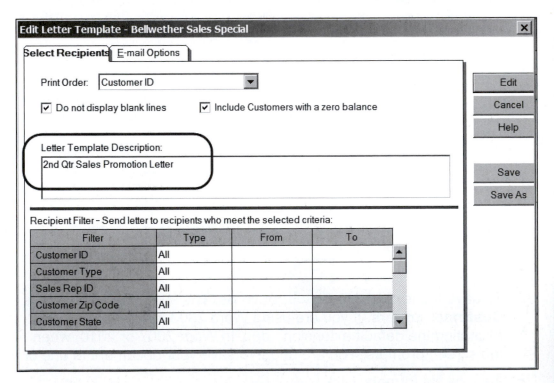

3. Review the information on the Edit Template window. Click [Edit]. The letter appears with fields identified.

«Company_Address_Line_1»
«Company_Address_Line_2»
«Company_City», «Company_State» «Company_Zip_Code»
«Company_Telephone_Number»

BUY ONE ITEM GET THE 2nd ITEM 50% OFF PROMOTION!!!

«Customer_Name»
«Customer_Full_Address»

Dear «Customer_Contact»:

As one of our loyal customers, we would like to *thank you* by extending you a *special offer*. Buy any item in our catalog at the regular price and receive any 2nd item (at an equal or lesser value) for **50%** off.

This offer is also good for purchases made online!! Check us out on the web at **«Company_Website_Address»**.

You can use this letter as a template or model to create a similar letter. Observe that the information in the letter is the same as the customer letter shown on page 707, *except* for the customizable information—<<Company_Address_Line_1>>, etc.

4. To add a date to the letter, click on a line or two above

   <<Customer_Name>>. Select Date & Time [🖹 Date & Time] from Word's Insert selections. Select the appropriate format and the date is inserted.

5. Select 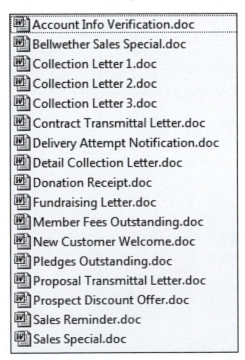, click Save As. A list of letter templates appears. (*Hint:* If you do not see the list of customer letter templates, you may need to extract the PAWMail.zip folder. Unzipping or extracting the PAWMail.zip folder is shown on pages 711-712.)

| Account Info Verification.doc |
| Bellwether Sales Special.doc |
| Collection Letter 1.doc |
| Collection Letter 2.doc |
| Collection Letter 3.doc |
| Contract Transmittal Letter.doc |
| Delivery Attempt Notification.doc |
| Detail Collection Letter.doc |
| Donation Receipt.doc |
| Fundraising Letter.doc |
| Member Fees Outstanding.doc |
| New Customer Welcome.doc |
| Pledges Outstanding.doc |
| Proposal Transmittal Letter.doc |
| Prospect Discount Offer.doc |
| Sales Reminder.doc |
| Sales Special.doc |

6. Accept the default file name Bellwether Sales Special.doc. (*Hint:* Peachtree's letter templates default to .doc files.) Insert your USB flash drive. Select the appropriate drive letter. Click [Save] .

PAWMail.Zip FOLDER

The letter templates are included in Peachtree's program path. Follow these instructions to see all the letters.

1. Right-click [Start] (Start); left-click Open Windows Explorer.

2. Go to Peachtree's program path: C:\Sage\Peachtree\Company\ Letters.

3. Copy the PAWMail.zip folder to the desktop.

4. Extract the files. (Right-click on the PAWMail.Zip folder. Left-click Extract All. Click [Extract] .) Open the templates from these folders: Customer; Employee; Vendor.

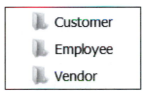

a. The Customer folder includes these documents. These templates were also shown on page 710.

Name	Type
Account Info Verification.doc	Microsoft Office Word 97 - 2003 Document
Collection Letter 1.doc	Microsoft Office Word 97 - 2003 Document
Collection Letter 2.doc	Microsoft Office Word 97 - 2003 Document
Collection Letter 3.doc	Microsoft Office Word 97 - 2003 Document
Contract Transmittal Letter.doc	Microsoft Office Word 97 - 2003 Document
Delivery Attempt Notification.doc	Microsoft Office Word 97 - 2003 Document
Detail Collection Letter.doc	Microsoft Office Word 97 - 2003 Document
Donation Receipt.doc	Microsoft Office Word 97 - 2003 Document
Fundraising Letter.doc	Microsoft Office Word 97 - 2003 Document
Member Fees Outstanding.doc	Microsoft Office Word 97 - 2003 Document
New Customer Welcome.doc	Microsoft Office Word 97 - 2003 Document
Pledges Outstanding.doc	Microsoft Office Word 97 - 2003 Document
Proposal Transmittal Letter.doc	Microsoft Office Word 97 - 2003 Document
Prospect Discount Offer.doc	Microsoft Office Word 97 - 2003 Document
Sales Reminder.doc	Microsoft Office Word 97 - 2003 Document
Sales Special.doc	Microsoft Office Word 97 - 2003 Document

    b. The Employee folder includes the Employee Welcome.doc file.

    c. The Vendor folder includes two documents: Disputed Charge.doc and Request Credit Increase.doc.

5. Observe that the letters end in a .doc extension which means that the Peachtree templates were saved as Word 97-2003 files. Double-click the Request Credit Increase.doc.

«Company_Name»
«Company_Full_Address»

«Todays_Date_Long»

«Vendor_Name»
«Vendor_Full_Address»

Re: Request for increase in credit limit

Dear «Vendor_Contact»:

«Company_Name» has enjoyed doing business with your company for the past twelve months. We are very happy with your product, and are looking forward to a continued business relationship. After reviewing the past year's records, I would like you to consider increasing our credit limit. An increase of available credit in the amount of $500.00 should suffice.

Thank you for your consideration in this matter. If you have any questions, please feel free to contact me at my direct extension.

Sincerely,

Office Manager
«Company_Name»

---

6. Close the Request for increase in credit limit letter.

7. To see the Customer Templates, go to your desktop and open the Customers folder. These are the same letters shown on pages 710 and 711.

8. Double-click Contract Transmittal Letter.

«Company_Name»
«Company_Full_Address»

«Todays_Date_Long»

«Customer_Contact»
«Customer_Name»
«Customer_Full_Address»

Dear «Customer_Contact»:

Enclosed are two copies of the contract. If it meets with your approval, please sign both copies and return one in the enclosed, preaddressed envelope.

Please do not hesitate to contact me should you have any questions or concerns.

We at «Company_Name» are pleased to come to this agreement and look forward to working with you.

Sincerely,

«Customer_Sales_Rep_Name»
«Company_Name»
«Company_Telephone_Number»
«Company_Full_Address»

9. Look at some of the other templates.

10. Exit Word without saving documents.

11. If necessary, maximize Peachtree. Close all windows.

12. Exit Peachtree.

PEACHTREE'S KNOWLEDGE CENTER

The Knowledge Center offers help for the most frequently asked Peachtree questions. You can search by product, category, keywords, Answer ID or phrases. Feedback can also be emailed to Peachtree.

1. From the desktop, click .

2. After selecting the Peachtree Knowledge Center, the Sage Peachtree Find Answers page appears. (The web site address is

www.peachtree.com/supporttraining/findanswers?WT.mc_id=RD_pe
achtree.com/inproduct_KnowledgeCenter.) Link to Search the
Knowledgebase.

2. Select Sage Peachtree - .

3. For purposes of this example, type **Import/Export** in the Search field

.

4. Click [Search]. A list of documents appears. Link to one or more
   documents for feedback about Import/Export.

5. Experiment. Change the search field to look at Peachtree's
   knowledgebase.

SUMMARY AND REVIEW

Complete the following end-of-chapter activities.

1. Going to the net, page 714-715

2. Short-answer questions, page 715

3. Exercises 18-1 and 18-2, page 715

4. Analysis question, pages 716

5. Assessment rubric, page 716

6. Chapter 18 Index, page 717

GOING TO THE NET

Access the MSDN Online Library website at
http://msdn.microsoft.com/library/. Answer the following questions.

1. What is the MSDN library?

2. Type **What are templates?** in the Search for field. Click 🔍 to search.

3. Link to an article of interest about templates. Write a brief essay about what you find (minimum length is 75 words; maximum length 150 words). Include website addresses in your answer.

Short-answer questions: The Online Learning Center includes these questions and the analysis question at www.mhhe.com/yacht2012, select Student Edition, Chapter 18, QA Templates.

1. What does the Write Letters feature do?

2. How many customers does Bellwether Garden Supply have?

3. What type of promotion is Bellwether offering its customers?

4. How do customers receive this special offer?

5. What toolbar is used to change or add template fields?

6. What is a template?

7. What is the program and data path for Bellwether's letter templates?

8. List four customer letter templates.

Exercise 18-1: Follow the instructions below to complete Exercise 18-1.

1. Print the sales promotion letter to Chapple Law Offices. Use March 15, 2012 as the date. (*Hint:* Use the Bellwether Special letter template. Send a letter to Chapple Law Office.)

2. Save the file as Exercise 18-1.

Exercise 18-2: Follow the instructions below to complete Exercise 18-2.

1. Print a sales promotion letter to Cummings Construction. (Use the current date.)

2. Save the file as Exercise 18-2.

ANALYSIS QUESTION

1. What is included in the PAWMail.zip folder?
2. How do you see its contents?

ASSESSMENT RUBRIC

Complete the Assessment Rubric online at www.mhhe.com/yacht2012; Student Edition, select Chapter 18, Assessment Rubric link.

File	Location	Extracted Folders
PAWMail.zip		

CHAPTER 18 INDEX

Project
3
Chicago Computer Club

In Project 3, you complete the computer accounting cycle for the Chicago Computer Club which is located in Chicago, IL. The Chicago Computer Club is a nonprofit business organized as a corporation.

Because the Chicago Computer Club is a nonprofit business, observe that there are some differences in its Chart of Accounts and some of its transactions. For example, revenues are derived from membership fees and seminars. Club members also contribute computers to local schools. When you work with this project, you see how these transactions are handled.

The club sponsors a trip to the International Consumer Electronics Show (CES), a trade show in Las Vegas, Nevada. The trip involves expenses for bus rental, motel rooms, meals, and entrance fees to the trade show. Since so many club members attend CES, a special rate is offered to them.

In this project, you complete the accounting cycle for the month of January 2012. Chicago Computer Club's Balance Sheet, transaction register, and bank statement are provided as source documents.

At the end of this project there is a Checklist that shows the printed reports you should have. The step-by-step instructions also remind you when to print. Your instructor may ask you to turn in these printouts for grading purposes. Remember to make backups at periodic intervals.

Follow these steps to complete Project 3, Chicago Computer Club:

Step 1:   Start Peachtree.

Step 2:   Make the selections to create a new company.

The McGraw-Hill Companies, Inc., *Computer Accounting with Peachtree by Sage Complete Accounting 2012, 16e*

Step   3:   The company information for Chicago Computer Club is:

Company Name:	Chicago Computer Club
Address Line 1:	544 South Fourth Street
City, State, Zip:	Chicago, IL 60605
Country:	USA
Phone:	312-555-8720
Fax:	312-555-5113
Business Type:	Corporation
Federal Employer ID:	23-8755313
State Employer ID:	41-3148955
State Unemployment ID:	410810-2
Web Site:	www.chicagocomputerclub.com
E-mail:	info@chicagocomputerclub.com

Step   4:   Accept the default to Use a sample business that closely matches your company.

Step   5:   Select Non-Profit Organizations. (*Hint:* Scroll down the Detailed types list.)

Step   6:   Accept the default for Accrual accounting.

Step   7:   Accept the default for Real Time posting.

Step   8:   Accept the default for Choose an accounting period structure, 12 monthly accounting periods per year.

Step   9:   The Choose the first period of your fiscal year window appears. If necessary, select January 2012.

Step 10:   At the You are ready to create your company window, click
[Finish]. If the screen prompts You can use this company in the student version of Peachtree for the next 14 months and then it will expire, click [OK]. If necessary, close the Setup Guide.

Step 11:   Change the accounting period to Period 1 – 01/01/12 to 01/31/12 - [Period 1 - 01/01/12-01/31/12].

Step 12:   Delete, add, and change the following General Ledger accounts in the Chart of Accounts:

Delete these accounts:

Acct. # Account Name

10000	Petty Cash
10100	Cash on Hand
10300	Payroll Checking Account
10500	Special Account
10600	Cash-Restricted Fund
10700	Investments
11400	Other Receivables
11500	Allowance for Doubtful Account
12100	Inventory-Kitchen
12150	Inventory-Golf & Tennis
12200	Inventory-Snack Stand
14100	Employee Advances
14700	Other Current Assets
15200	Automobiles
15300	Other Depreciable Property
15400	Leasehold Improvements
15500	Building
15600	Building Improvements
16900	Land
17200	Accum. Depreciation-Automobi
17300	Accum. Depreciation-Other
17400	Accum. Depreciation-Leasehol
17500	Accum. Depreciation-Building
17600	Accum. Depreciation-Bldg Imp
19000	Deposits
19150	Accum. Amortiz. - Org. Costs
19200	Note Receivable-Noncurrent
19900	Other Noncurrent Assets
23000	Accrued Expenses
23100	Sales Tax Payable
23300	Deductions Payable
23400	Federal Payroll Taxes Payable
23500	FUTA Tax Payable
23600	State Payroll Taxes Payable

23700	SUTA Payable
23800	Local Payroll Taxes Payable
24000	Other Taxes Payable
24100	Employee Benefits Payable
24200	Current Portion Long-Term Debt
24800	Other Current Liabilities
24900	Suspense-Clearing Account
27000	Notes Payable-Noncurrent
27100	Deferred Revenue
27400	Other Long-Term Liabilities
40200	Sales-Kitchen/Dining Room
40400	Sales-Golf/Tennis
40600	Sales-Snack Stand
40800	Sales-Other
41000	Contributions-Unrestricted
41200	Grants
41400	Program Service Revenue
41800	Investment Income
42000	Realized gain in Investment
42200	Miscellaneous Income
42400	Contributions-Restricted
42600	Investment Income-Restricted
43000	Other Income
48000	Fee Refunds
58000	Cost of Sales-Other
59000	Purchase Returns and Allowance
60000	Default Purchase Expense
60100	Grant and Allocation Exp.
61500	Bad Debt Expense
65000	Employee Benefit Programs Exp
65500	Other Employee Benefits
72000	Payroll Tax Expense
76500	Compensation of Officers
77000	Salaries Expense
89000	Other Expense

Change these accounts:

Acct. #	Account Name	New Account Name
10200	Regular Checking Account	Federal Bank

12000	Inventory-Bar	Inventory-Computers/Schools
14000	Prepaid Expenses	Prepaid Rent
15100	Equipment	Computer Equipment
17000	Accum. Depreciation-Furnitur	Accum. Depreciation-Furn&Fix
17100	Accum. Depreciation-Eq.	Accum. Depreciation-Comp Equip
20000	Accounts Payable	Credit Card Payable
40000	Sales-Bar	Fees-Seminars/Classes
66000	Supplies Expense	Office Supplies Expense
67500	Occupancy Expense	Rent Expense
70000	Travel Expense	Bus Rental-CES
72500	Depreciation Expense	Depr. Exp.-Furniture & Fixture

Add these accounts:

Acct. #	Account Name	Account Type
39002	Membership Contributions	Equity-doesn't close
60000	Advertising Expense	Expenses
60400	Bank Service Charge	Expenses
70010	Meals-CES	Expenses
70020	Motel-CES	Expenses
70030	Fees-CES	Expenses
72520	Depr. Exp.-Comp Equip	Expenses

Read Me: How do I show my name on printouts?

Follow these steps to add your name to the company name.

1. From the menu bar, select Maintain; Company Information. The Maintain Company Information window appears.
2. Type your first and last name after Chicago Computer Club. The Company Name field shows: Chicago Computer Club—Your first and last name.
3. Click .

Step 13: Back up. The suggested file name is **Chicago Computer Club Chart of Accounts.ptb**.

Step 14: Use the Chicago Computer Club Balance Sheet to record the chart of accounts beginning balances.

Chicago Computer Club Balance Sheet January 1, 2012		
ASSETS		
Current Assets		
Federal Bank	$18,250.00	
Inventory-Computers/Schools	500.00	
Inventory-Office	1,500.00	
Total Current Assets		$20,250.00
Property and Equipment		
Furniture and Fixtures	1,500.00	
Computer Equipment	3,000.00	
Total Property and Equipment		4,500.00
Total Assets		$24,750.00
LIABILITIES		
Credit Card Payable	250.00	
Total Liabilities		250.00
CAPITAL		
Retained Earnings		24,500.00
Total Liabilities and Capital		$24,750.00

Step 15: Back up your data. The suggested file name is **Chicago Computer Club Starting Balance Sheet.ptb**.

Step 16: The transaction register on the next page provides you with the information necessary for Chicago Computer Club's Cash Receipts Journal and Cash Disbursements Journal entries for January. The Chicago Computer Club issues checks and makes deposits to the Federal Bank.

		Chicago Computer Club Transaction Register			
Ck. No.	Date	Description of Transaction	Payment	Deposit	Balance
	12/31/11				18,250.00
	1/3/12	Deposit (membership dues)[1]		2,850.00	21,100.00
8001	1/10/12	Payment - Credit Card	250.00		20,850.00
8002	1/10/12	Schultz Advertising	205.00		20,645.00
8003	1/10/12	Office Supplies on Main	155.65		20,489.35
8004	1/17/12	Meals-CES	800.00		19,689.35
8005	1/17/12	Bus Rental-CES	600.00		19,089.35
8006	1/17/12	Entrance Fees-CES	725.00		18,364.35
8007	1/17/12	Motel Rooms-CES	835.27		17,529.08
8008	1/26/12	Chicago Telephone	41.76		17,487.32
8009	1/26/12	Shipping Charges	45.00		17,442.32
	1/29/12	Deposit (seminar fees)		800.00	18,242.32

Step 17: *Additional journal entry*: On January 31, a club member donated a computer system and printer to the club. The value of the computer and printer is $250. (Debit, Inventory - Computers/Schools; Credit, Membership Contributions. Use the General Journal for this entry)

Step 18: Chicago Computer Club's bank statement is shown on the next page. Complete the Account Reconciliation for the Federal Bank.

[1]For each deposit shown on the transaction register, type the date of the transaction in the Deposit ticket ID field. For each check, use Banking; Write Checks.

Statement of Account Federal Bank Jan. 1 to Jan. 31, 2012 Account No. 871-993310			Chicago Computer Club 544 South Fourth Street Chicago, IL 60605	
REGULAR CHECKING				
Previous Balance	12/31/11	$ 18,250.00		
2 Deposits(+)		3,650.00		
7 Checks (-)		2,887.68		
Service Charges (-)		12.00		
Ending Balance	1/31/12	**$ 19,000.32**		
DEPOSITS				
	1/3/12	2,850.00	1/31/12	800.00
CHECKS (Asterisk * indicates break in check number sequence)				
	1/14/12	8001	250.00	
	1/14/12	8002	205.00	
	1/17/12	8003	155.65	
	1/26/12	8004	800.00	
	1/28/12	8005*	600.00	
	1/29/12	8007	835.27	
	1/31/12	8008	41.76	

Step 19:   Make a backup. The suggested file name is **Chicago Computer Club January.ptb**.

Step 20:   Export these reports to Excel: Chart of Accounts, Cash Receipts Journal, Cash Disbursements Journal, General Ledger Trial Balance, Balance Sheet, Income Statement, Statement of Cash Flow, Statement of Retained Earnings. Use the file name **Chicago Computer Club_CofA_CRJ_CDJ_ GLTB_ BS_ IS_ SCF_SRE.xlsx**.

Step 21:   Save the following reports as PDF files: Chart of Accounts, General Ledger Trial Balance, Balance Sheet, Income Statement, Statement of Cash Flow, Statement of Retained Earnings. The suggested file name is **Project 3_Chart of Accounts.pdf**, etc. Your instructor may require additional PDF files.

Your instructor may want to collect this project. A Checklist of Printouts is shown below.

Checklist of Printouts, Project 3: Chicago Computer Club		
1		Chart of Accounts
2		Account Reconciliation
3		Account Register – Federal Bank
4		Cash Disbursements Journal
5		Cash Receipts Journal
6		General Journal
7		General Ledger Trial Balance
8		General Ledger
9		Balance Sheet
10		Income Statement
11		Statement of Cash Flow
12		Statement of Retained Earnings

The McGraw-Hill Companies, Inc., *Computer Accounting with Peachtree by Sage Complete Accounting 2012,* 16e

Student Name_____**Date**_____

CHECK YOUR PROGRESS: PROJECT 3
CHICAGO COMPUTER CLUB

1. What are the total debit and credit balances on your
   general ledger trial balance?   _____

2. What is the total amount of checks outstanding?   _____

3. How much are the total expenses on January 31?   _____

4. How much are the total revenues on January 31?   _____

5. How much is the net income (net loss) on January 31?   _____

6. What is the account balance in the Membership
   Contributions account on January 31?   _____

7. What are the total assets on January 31?   _____

8. What is the ending retained earnings on
   January 31, 2012?   _____

9. What is the balance in the Credit Card Payable
   account on January 31?   _____

10. What is the balance in the Office Supplies Expense
    account on January 31?   _____

11. Is there an Increase or Decrease in cash for the
    month of January?   _____

12. Was any Credit Card Payable incurred during the
    month of January? (Circle your answer)   YES   NO

Project
4

BR Manufacturing, Inc.

In Project 4, you complete the computer accounting cycle for BR Manufacturing, Inc. This company manufactures backpacks, sleeping bags, and tents.

BR Manufacturing, Inc. offers its customers a sales discount of 2% 15, Net 30 days. Vendors offer BR Manufacturing, Inc. a purchase discount of 1% 15, Net 30 days.

Follow these steps to complete Project 4, BR Manufacturing, Inc.

Step 1:   Start Peachtree.

Step 2:   Make the selections to create a new company.

Step 3:   Type the following company information for BR Manufacturing, Inc.:

Company Name:	BR Manufacturing, Inc. (*use your initials, then Manufacturing, Inc.*)
Address Line 1:	30091 National Avenue
City, State, Zip:	Philadelphia, PA 19120
Country:	USA
Phone:	215-555-4331
Fax:	215-555-4333
Business Type:	Corporation
Federal Employer ID:	98-8505301
State Employer ID:	43-4844312
State Unemployment ID:	430207-7
Web Site:	www.phila.net/brmftg
E-mail:	brmftg@phila.net

Step 4:   Accept the default for Use a sample business type that closely matches your company.

Step   5:   Scroll down the list. In the **Detailed types** list, select Manufacturing Company. (*Hint:* The Chart of Accounts has five-digit account numbers.)

Step   6:   Accept the default for Accrual accounting.

Step   7:   Accept the default for Real Time posting.

Step   8:   Accept the default for 12 monthly accounting periods.

Step   9:   The Choose the first period of your fiscal year window appears. If necessary, select January 2012 as the month and year.

Step 10:   At the You are ready to create your company window, click Finish . If the screen prompts You can use this company in the student version of Peachtree for the next 14 months and then it will expire, click OK .

Step 11:   When the Peachtree Setup Guide window appears, click on the box next to Don't show this screen at startup to place a checkmark in it. Close the Setup Guide Window.

Step 12:   Change the accounting period to 01-Jan 01,2012 to Jan 31, 2012—. Period 1 - 01/01/12-01/31/12 .

General Ledger

1. Delete the following accounts:

    10100   Cash on Hand
    10400   Savings Account
    10500   Special Account
    10600   Investments-Money Market
    15400   Leasehold Improvements
    16900   Land
    17300   Accum. Depreciation-Other
    17400   Accum. Depreciation-Leasehold
    24800   Other Current Liabilities

2. Change these account names:

    10200   Regular Checking Account to Franklin Bank
    10300   Payroll Checking Account to Philadelphia Savings and Loan
    14000   Prepaid Expenses to Prepaid Insurance
    15100   Equipment to Computers & Equipment
    15200   Automobiles to Trucks/Autos
    17100   Accum. Depreciation - Equipment to Accum. Depreciation - Comp&Eq
    17200   Accum. Depreciation - Automobil to Accum. Depreciation - Trks/Aut
    23300   Deductions Payable to Medicare Employee Taxes Payabl
    24000   Other Taxes Payable to FICA Employee Taxes Payable
    24100   Employee Benefits Payable to FICA Employer Taxes Payable
    27000   Notes Payable-Noncurrent to Mortgage Payable
    40000   Sales #1 to Sales-Backpacks
    40200   Sales #2 to Sales-Sleeping Bags
    40400   Sales #3 to Sales-Tents
    72500   Penalties and Fines Exp to Employer FUTA Expense
    73000   Other Taxes to Employer SUTA Expense

3. Add these accounts:

Acct. ID	Acct. Description	Account Type
12010	Inventory-Backpacks	Inventory
12020	Inventory-Sleeping Bags	Inventory
12030	Inventory-Tents	Inventory
22000	Credit Card Payable	Other Current Liabilities
23350	Medicare Employer Taxes Payabl	Other Current Liabilities
23650	Employee SUI Taxes Payable	Other Current Liabilities
73200	Employer FICA Taxes Expense	Expenses
73300	Employer Medicare Expense	Expenses

4. Back up. The suggested file name is **BR Mftg Chart of Accounts.ptb**.

5. You purchased BR Manufacturing, Inc. in December 2011. Use the Balance Sheet below to record the chart of account beginning balances.

BR Manufacturing, Inc. Balance Sheet January 1, 2012		
ASSETS		
Current Assets		
Franklin Bank	$77,650.00	
Philadelphia Savings and Loan	31,300.00	
Investments-Cert. of Deposit	14,500.00	
Inventory-Backpacks	1,612.50	
Inventory-Sleeping Bags	1,760.00	
Inventory-Tents	2,679.60	
Prepaid Insurance	3,600.00	
Total Current Assets		$133,102.10
Property and Equipment		
Furniture and Fixtures	2,500.00	
Computers & Equipment	6,000.00	
Trucks/Autos	25,000.00	
Building	105,000.00	
Total Property and Equipment		138,500.00
Total Assets		$271,602.10
LIABILITIES AND STOCKHOLDER'S EQUITY		
Credit Card Payable	15,900.00	
Mortgage Payable	97,500.00	
Total Liabilities		$113,400.00
Stockholder's Equity: Common Stock		158,202.10
Total Liabilities and Stockholder's Equity		$271,602.10

6. **Backup.** The suggested filename is **BR Mftg Starting Balance Sheet.ptb**.

Accounts Payable

1. Set up the following vendor defaults.

Standard Terms:	Due in number of days
Net due in:	30 days
Discount in:	15 days
Discount %:	1.00
Credit Limit:	20,000.00

GL Link Accounts:

Expense Account:	12010 Inventory-Backpacks
Discount GL Account:	59500 Purchase Discounts

2. Set up the following vendors:

Vendor ID:	dd22
Name:	David Dash Fabrics
Contact:	David Dash
Mailing Address:	131 East Oak Lane
City, ST Zip:	Hartford, CT 06108
Vendor Type:	slpg bgs
1099 Type:	Independent Contractor
Expense Account:	12020 Inventory-Sleeping Bags
Telephone 1:	860-555-1200
Fax:	860-555-2112
E-mail:	david@ddfabrics.com
Web Site:	www.ddfabrics.com

Purchase Info:

Tax ID Number:	19-3384204

Vendor ID:	ep33
Name:	Ellis Products
Contact:	Doris Ellis
Mailing Address:	143 Heights Boulevard
City, ST Zip:	Cleveland, OH 44192
Vendor Type:	tents
1099 Type:	Independent Contractor

Expense Account:	12030 Inventory-Tents
Telephone 1:	216-555-9209
Fax:	216-555-4210
E-mail:	doris@ellisproducts.com
Web Site:	www.ellisproducts.com

Purchase Info:

Tax ID Number:	38-2880081

Vendor ID:	rk44
Name:	RK Supplies
Contact:	Roslyn Kalman
Mailing Address:	401 Princeton Road
City, ST Zip:	Trenton, NJ 07092
Vendor Type:	backpack
1099 Type:	Independent Contractor
Expense Accounting:	12010 Inventory-Backpacks
Telephone 1:	609-555-8900
Fax:	609-555-8999
E-mail:	info@rkproducts.net
Web Site:	www.rkproducts.net

Purchase Info:

Tax ID Number:	32-1484187

Accounts Receivable

1. Set up the following customer default settings:

Standard Terms:	Due in number of days
Net due in:	30 days
Discount in:	15 days
Discount %:	2.00
Credit Limit:	$15,000.00
GL Sales Account:	40000 Sales-Backpacks
Discount GL Account:	49000 Sales Discounts

2. Enter the following customer records:

Customer ID:	001BOS
Name:	Benson's Outdoor Suppliers
Billing Address:	3102 Palmetto Avenue
City, ST Zip:	Gainesville, FL 32652
Customer Type:	FL (for Florida)
Telephone 1:	352-555-1192
Fax:	352-555-1194
E-mail:	info@bensonoutdoor.biz
Web Site:	www.bensonoutdoor.biz

Contacts:

Contact name:	Vincent Benson

Sales Info:

G/L Sales Acct:	40000, Sales-Backpacks
Resale Number:	7312440-4

Customer ID:	002SCS
Name:	Sharon's Camping Store
Billing Address:	1341 Woodlands Ave.
City, ST Zip:	Philadelphia, PA 19133
Customer Type:	PA (for Pennsylvania)
Telephone 1:	215-555-3900
Fax:	215-555-8633
E-mail:	sharon@campingstore.biz
Web Site	www.campingstore.biz

Contacts:

Contact name:	Sharon Carson

Sales Info:

G/L Sales Acct:	40200, Sales-Sleeping Bags
Resale Number:	9392193-6

Customer ID:	003WST
Name:	West's Store
Billing Address:	1400 Clarkson Ave.
City, ST Zip:	Cincinnati, OH 45227
Customer Type:	OH (for Ohio)
Telephone 1:	513-555-1209
Fax:	513-555-1211
E-mail:	jane@weststore.com
Web Site:	www.weststore.com

Contacts:

Contact name: Jane West

Sales Info:

G/L Sales Acct: 40400, Sales-Tents
Resale Number: 8876804-2

Payroll

1. Use the following information for the Payroll Setup Wizard.

   State: PA
   State Unemployment Rate: **3.4**
   Hourly Pay Type: Select 51000 - Direct Labor Costs
   Salary Pay Type: Select 77000 - Salaries Expense

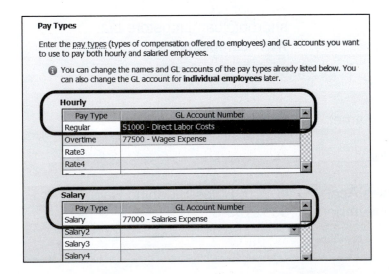

Do you have any localities for which you collect taxes in the state of PA? **Yes**

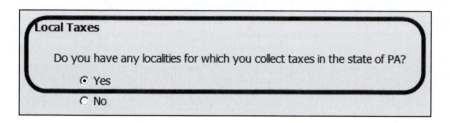

Locality: **Phila**
Tax rate: **1.0**

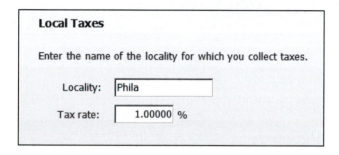

2. Set up these employee defaults. Use the Employee Fields information shown below.

Field Name	G/L Account
Fed_Income	Account No. 23400, Federal Payroll Taxes Payable
Soc_Sec	Account No. 24000, FICA Employee Taxes Payable
MEDICARE	Account No. 23300, Medicare Employee Taxes Payable
St_Income	Account No. 23600, State Payroll Taxes Payable
Loc_Income	Account No. 23800, Local Payroll Taxes Payable
St_Unemp	Account No. 23650, Employee SUI Taxes Payable

3. Use the Company Fields shown below.

Field Name	Liability column	Expense column
Soc_Sec_C	24100, FICA Employer Taxes Payable	73200, Employer FICA Taxes Expense
Medicare_C	23350 Medicare Employer Taxes Payable	73300, Employer Medicare Expense
Fed_Unemp_C	23500, FUTA Tax Payable	72500, Employer FUTA Expense
St_Unemp_C	23700, SUTA Payable	73000, Employer SUTA Expense

4. Complete the Payroll Setup Wizard's Taxes and Assign Tax Fields.

5. Add the following employee.

Employee ID: EK40
Name: Elaine King
Accept the default for Employee
Address: 1215 Haverford Avenue
City, ST Zip: Upper Darby, PA 19112
E-mail: elaine@mail.net
Home phone: 215-555-5133
Social Security #:   000-02-0023
Type: FULL

Pay Info:

Salary, $1,500. Ms. King is paid monthly.

Withholding Info:

Filing Status: Single for Federal, State, and Local
Allow: 1 for Federal, State and Local

Employee ID: JS50
Name: Janice Sullivan
Accept the default for Employee

Address:	1341 Brockton Court
City, ST Zip:	Philadelphia, PA 19191
E-mail:	janice@mail.net
Home phone:	215-555-8230
Social Security #:	002-00-0011
Type:	FULL

Pay Info: Hourly, $13.00 per hour; Overtime, $19.50. Ms. Sullivan is paid weekly.

Withholding Info:

Filing Status:	Married for Federal, State, and Local
Allow:	2 for Federal, State and Local

Employee ID: LS60
Name: Lee Smith
Accept the default for Employee

Address:	8192 City Line Avenue, Apt. 3C
City, ST Zip:	Philadelphia, PA 19122
E-mail:	lee@mail.net
Home phone:	215-555-3490
Social Security #:	007-00-0020
Type:	FULL

Pay Info: Hourly, $13.00 per hour; Overtime, $19.50. Mr. Smith is paid weekly.

Withholding Info:

Filing Status:	Married for Federal, State, and Local
Allow:	2 for Federal, State and Local

Employee ID: OW70
Name: Oscar Watson
Accept the default for Employee

Address:	1490 Broad Street, Apt. 1003
City, ST Zip:	Philadelphia, PA 19135
E-mail:	oscar@mail.net
Home phone	215-555-5522
Social Security #:	000-01-1301

Type: FULL

Pay Info: Hourly, $13.00 per hour; Overtime, $19.50. Mr. Watson is paid weekly.

Withholding Info:

Filing Status: Married for Federal, State, and Local
Allow: 2 for Federal, State and Local

Inventory

1. Set up inventory defaults. On the General Tab, select Stock item as the Default Item Class.

2. Make sure that FIFO is the default inventory costing method.

3. Set up the following inventory items:

Item ID:	backpacks
Description:	backpacks
Item Class:	Stock item
Description for Sales:	backpacks
Price Level 1:	150.00
Last Unit Cost:	37.50
Cost Method:	FIFO
GL Sales Acct:	40000 Sales-Backpacks
GL Inventory Acct:	12010, Inventory-Backpacks
GL Cost of Sales Acct:	50500, Raw Material Purchases
Item Tax Type:	2 Exempt
Item Type:	backpack
Stocking U/M:	each
Minimum Stock:	10
Reorder Quantity:	5
Preferred Vendor ID:	rk44, RK Supplies

Beginning Balances: backpacks

Quantity:	43.00
Unit Cost:	37.50
Total Cost:	1,612.50

Item ID:	sleeping bags
Description:	sleeping bags
Item Class:	Stock item
Description for Sales:	sleeping bags
Price Level 1:	105.00
Last Unit Cost:	27.50
Cost Method:	FIFO
GL Sales Acct:	40200, Sales-Sleeping Bags
GL Inventory Acct:	12020, Inventory-Sleeping Bags
GL Cost of Sales Acct:	50500, Raw Material Purchases
Item Tax Type:	2 Exempt
Item Type:	slpg bgs
Stocking U/M:	each
Minimum Stock:	10
Reorder Quantity:	5
Preferred Vendor ID:	dd22, David Dash Fabrics

Beginning Balances: sleeping bags

Quantity:	64.00
Last Unit Cost	27.50
Total Cost:	1,760.00

Item ID:	tents
Description:	tents
Item Class:	Stock item
Description for Sales:	tents
Price Level 1:	175.00
Last Unit Cost:	47.85
Cost Method:	FIFO
GL Sales Acct:	40400, Sales-Tents
GL Inventory Acct:	12030, Inventory-Tents
GL Cost of Sales Acct:	50500, Raw Material Purchases
Item Tax Type:	2 Exempt
Item Type:	tents
Stocking U/M:	each
Minimum Stock:	10
Reorder Quantity:	5
Preferred Vendor ID:	ep33, Ellis Products

Beginning Balances: tents

Quantity: 56.00
Unit Cost: 47.85
Total Cost: 2,679.60

Jobs

1. Set up the following job records:

    Job ID: 13-221
    Description: backpacks
    For Customer: 001BOS
    Start Date: 1/2/12
    Projected End Date: 12/31/12
    Job Type: backpack

    Job ID: 14-331
    Description: sleeping bags
    For Customer: 002SCS
    Start Date: 1/2/12
    Projected End Date: 12/31/12
    Job Type: slpg bgs

    Job ID: 15-441
    Description: tents
    For Customer: 003WST
    Start Date: 1/2/12
    Projected End Date: 12/31/12
    Job Type: tents

2. Back up. Use **BR Mftg Begin.ptb** as the filename.

3. Exit or continue.

Journalize and post the following transactions:

Date   *Description of Transaction*

01/06/12 Invoice No. 315 was received from David Dash Fabrics for 15 sleeping bags @ $27.50 each for a total of $412.50. Post invoice 315.

01/06/12   Invoice No. 45 was received from RK Supplies for 20 backpacks @ $37.50 each for a total of $750.00. Post invoice 45.

01/06/12   Invoice No. 800 was received from Ellis Products for 16 tents @ $47.85 each for a total of $765.60. Post invoice 800.

01/06/12   Pay the factory employees for 40 hours of direct labor. Select Account No. 10300, Philadelphia Savings and Loan, as the Cash Account. In the Check Number field, type **101** for Ms. Sullivan's paycheck. The check numbers for Mr. Smith and Mr. Watson will be automatically completed. (Do *not* print the payroll checks.) Remember, click [Jobs] to complete the following:

Check No.	Employee	Job	Hours
101	Janice Sullivan	15-441	40
102	Lee Smith	14-331	40
103	Oscar Watson	13-221	40

Remember to click [Save] *after each payroll entry.*

01/11/12   Sold 20 backpacks on account to Benson's Outdoor Suppliers for a total of $3,000.00, Job 13-221. In the Invoice # field, type **101**.[1] Post sales invoice 101.

01/11/12   Sold 12 sleeping bags on account to Sharon's Camping Store for a total of $1,260.00, Job 14-331. Post sales invoice 102.

01/11/12   Sold 20 tents on account to West's Store for a total of $3,500.00, Job 15-441. Post sales invoice 103.

01/13/12   Pay the factory employees for 40 hours of direct labor. (Refer to the information on the next page.) *Remember to post each payroll entry.*

---

[1]Since you are not printing sales invoices, it is necessary to complete this field.

Check No.	Employee	Job	Hours
104	Janice Sullivan	15-441	40
105	Lee Smith	14-331	40
106	Oscar Watson	13-221	40

01/13/12 Issued Check No. 1001 to RK Supplies in payment of purchase Invoice No. 45. Select Account No. 10200, Franklin Bank as the cash account. In the Check Number field, type **1001**. Do *not* print vendor checks. In the Discount Account field, make sure that Account No. 59500, Purchase Discounts is shown. Post Check No. 1001 in the amount of $742.50.

01/13/12 Issued Check No. 1002 to David Dash Fabrics in payment of purchase Invoice No. 315. Post Check No. 1002 in the amount of $408.37.

01/13/12 Issued Check No. 1003 to Ellis Products in payment of purchase Invoice No. 800. Post Check No. 1003 in the amount of $757.94.

01/18/12 Invoice No. 328 was received from David Dash Fabrics for 15 sleeping bags @ $27.50 each for a total of $412.50. Post invoice 328.

01/18/12 Invoice No. 900 was received from Ellis Products for 20 tents @ $47.85 each for a total of $957.00. Post invoice 900.

01/20/12 Pay the factory employees for 40 hours of direct labor. *Remember to click on* S*ave after each payroll check is recorded.*

Check No.	Employee	Job	Hours
107	Janice Sullivan	15-441	40
108	Lee Smith	14-331	40
109	Oscar Watson	13-221	40

01/25/12 Received payment from Benson's Outdoor Suppliers for sales invoice 101. Select Account No. 10200, Franklin Bank, as the cash account. Use the date of the transaction in the Deposit ticket ID field. In the Reference field, type **Inv. 101**. Post this receipt in the amount of $2,940.

01/25/12 Received payment from Sharon's Camping Store for sales invoice 102. In the Reference field, type **Inv. 102**. Post this receipt in the amount of $1,234.80.

01/25/12 Received payment from West's Store for sales invoice 103. In the Reference field, type **Inv. 103**. Post this receipt in the amount of $3,430.

01/25/12 Sold 25 sleeping bags on account to Sharon's Camping Store for a total of $2,625.00, Job 14-331. In the Invoice # field, type **104**. Post sales invoice 104.

01/25/12 Sold 21 tents on account to West's Store for a total of $3,675.00, Job 15-441. Post sales invoice 105.

01/27/12 Pay the factory employees for 40 hours of direct labor. *Remember to click on* S*ave after each payroll check is recorded.*

Check No.	Employee	Job	Hours
110	Janice Sullivan	15-441	40
111	Lee Smith	14-331	40
112	Oscar Watson	13-221	40

01/27/12 Pay the salaried employee, Elaine King. In the Salary Amounts table, make sure that account 77000, Salaries Expense, is shown in the Account column. If not, select that account. *Post Check No. 113.*

01/27/12 Issued Check No. 1004 to Franklin Bank for $709.23 in payment of Mortgage Payable; split the mortgage payment between principal in the amount of $584.06, and interest in the amount of $125.17. In the Check Number field, type **1004**. (Use the Write Checks task and the split feature. Make sure that account 10200, Franklin Bank, is selected as the Cash Account.) Post Check No. 1004.

01/27/12   Issued Check No. 1005 to Philadelphia Savings and Loan for $800 in payment of Credit Card Payable. Post Check No. 1005.

01/27/12   Issued Check No. 1006 to the PHL Power Company for $204.75 in payment of utilities. (Debit Utilities Expense, Account No. 78000.) Post Check No. 1006.

01/27/12   Issued Check No. 1007 to Phila. Telephone for $189.10 in payment of telephone bill. Post Check No. 1007.

01/30/12   Received payment from West's Store for sales invoice 105. In the Reference field, type **Inv. 105**. Post this receipt in the amount of $3,601.50.

Account Reconciliation

1. Complete the bank reconciliation for Franklin Bank and Philadelphia Savings and Loan. The January 31, 2012, bank statements are shown below and on the next page.

Bank Statement: Franklin Bank

Statement of Account Franklin Bank January 1 to January 31, 2012 Account #40012			BR Manufacturing, Inc. 30091 National Avenue Philadelphia, PA 19120	
REGULAR CHECKING				
Previous Balance	12/31/11	$77,650.00		
2 Deposits(+)		11,206.30		
3 Checks (-)		1,908.81		
Service Charges (-)	1/31/12	22.00		
Ending Balance	1/31/12	**$86,925.49**		
DEPOSITS				
	1/26/12	7,604.80		
	1/31/12	3,601.50		
CHECKS (Asterisk * indicates break in check number sequence)				
	1/28/12	1001	742.50	
	1/30/12	1002	408.37	
	1/30/12	1003	757.94	

Bank Statement: Philadelphia Savings and Loan

Statement of Account Philadelphia Savings and Loan January 1 to January 31, 2012 Account #982-789120			BR Manufacturing, Inc. 30091 National Avenue Philadelphia, PA 19120	
PAYROLL CHECKING				
Previous Balance	12/31/11	31,300.00		
Deposits(+)				
9 Checks (-)		4,018.14		
Service Charges (-)	1/31/12	20.00		
Ending Balance	1/31/12	**27,261.86**		
DEPOSITS				
CHECKS (Asterisk * indicates break in check number sequence)				
	1/13/12	101	446.46	
	1/13/12	102	446.46	
	1/13/12	103	446.46	
	1/20/12	104	446.46	
	1/20/12	105	446.46	
	1/20/12	106	446.46	
	1/27/12	107	446.46	
	1/27/12	108	446.46	
	1/27/12	109	446.46	

2. Back up. Use **BR Mftg January.ptb** as the file name.

   Export the following reports to Excel: Chart of Accounts, General Ledger Trial Balance, Balance Sheet, Income Statement, Statement of Cash Flow, and Statement of Retained Earnings. Use the file name **BR Mftg_GLTB_ BS_IS_SCF_SRE.xlsx**.

3. Save the following reports as PDF files: General Ledger Trial Balance, Balance, Sheet, Income Statement, Statement of Cash Flow, Statement of Retained Earnings. The suggested file name is **Project 4_Chart of Accounts.pdf**, etc. Your instructor may require additional reports.

Your instructor may want to collect this project. A Checklist of Printouts is shown below.

		CHECKLIST OF PRINTOUTS, BR MANUFACTURING, INC.
	1	Account Reconciliation Report: Franklin Bank
	2	Account Reconciliation Report: Philadelphia Savings and Loan
	3	Account Register: Franklin Bank
	4	Account Register: Philadelphia Savings and Loan
	5	General Ledger Trial Balance
	6	General Ledger
	7	Balance Sheet
	8	Income Statement
	9	Statement of Cash Flow
	10	Statement of Retained Earnings
	11	Customer Ledgers
	12	Vendor Ledgers
	13	Job Ledger
	14	Job Profitability Report
	15	Inventory Profitability Report
	16	Payroll Register
		Optional printouts, BR Manufacturing, Inc.
	17	Chart of Accounts
	18	Customer List
	19	Vendor List
	20	Payroll Journal
	21	Purchase Journal
	22	Cash Disbursements Journal
	23	Sales Journal
	24	Cash Receipts Journal
	25	Cost of Goods Sold Journal
	26	General Journal

Student Name_____**Date**_____

CHECK YOUR PROGRESS: PROJECT 4
BR MANUFACTURING, INC.

1. What are the total debit and credit balances on your
    General Ledger Trial Balance?   _____

2. What are the total assets on January 31?   _____

3. What is the balance in the Franklin Bank
    account on January 31?   _____

4. What is the balance in the Philadelphia Savings and
    Loan account on January 31?   _____

5. What is Sharon's Camping Store account balance
    on January 31?   _____

6. What are the direct labor costs on January 31?   _____

7. How many backpacks were sold during the month
    of January?   _____

8. How many sleeping bags were sold during the
    month of January?   _____

9. How many tents were sold during the month of
    January?   _____

10. What is the ending retained earnings amount on
    on January 31?   _____

11. What are the total expenses reported on January 31?   _____

12. Was any Accounts Payable incurred during the
    month of January? (Circle your answer)   YES   NO

Project

4A Student-Designed Project

You have completed four projects: Susan Babbage, Accounting; Sports Emporium; Chicago Computer Club; and BR Manufacturing, Inc. In each project you completed the Computer Accounting Cycle for one month.

It is the purpose of Project 4A, to have you write the next month's transactions for one of the four projects. You pick the project and complete the accounting cycle: Project 1, Susan Babbage, Accounting, a service business; Project 2, Sports Emporium, a merchandising business; Project 3, Chicago Computer Club, a nonprofit business; or Project 4, BR Manufacturing, Inc., a manufacturing business. At the end of your month's transactions, you are required to complete adjusting entries.

Good luck! It is your turn to create the transactions for another month and complete the Computer Accounting Cycle. Remember to back up periodically.

Appendix A
Troubleshooting

Appendix A, Troubleshooting, includes the following.

1. Troubleshooting Installation, page 753

   a. System Requirements Warning, page 753
   b. Peachtree Installer: IPV4 vs. IPV6, page 754
   c. 1628: Failed to Complete Installation, page 754
   d. Remove PCWxxx.ini Files, pages 754-755

2. PDF Files, pages 755
3. Opening the Sample Companies, page 755-756
4. Problem Backing Up to USB Drive or Other External Media, pages 756-758
5. Restoring Starting Data for the Sample Companies, page 758
6. Serial Number in Use, page 758
7. Deleting Peachtree, pages 759

TROUBLESHOOTING INSTALLATION

System Requirements Warning

If a System Requirements window warns RAM is not large enough or processing speed is too slow, you may continue installation but Peachtree 2012 may run slower.

The minimum requirements for Peachtree 2012 installation is 512 MB of RAM for single user, 1GB of RAM for multiple users, and 1 GHz of processor speed. Refer to pages iv-vi for System Requirements. Peachtree's system configuration is also online at http://www.peachtree.com/productsservices/complete/system

Peachtree Installer: IPV4 vs. IPV6

During installation, if a window prompts "Your computer is currently using a default network protocol, IPV6, that may cause Peachtree to run slowly. Would you like to change to a default protocol, IPV4, that will make Peachtree run faster? Click <Yes>.

The database engine that Peachtree uses internally is not compatible with IPV6. It requires the use of IPV4. In some configurations, it can cause Peachtree to run very slowly. Very few network installations actually use IPV6, so it is generally safe to make the switch to IPV4.

More information is included on Peachtree's knowledgebase article at https://customers.sagenorthamerica.com/irj/go/km/docs/sageKM/Peachtree%20by%20Sage/Ungated%20Customers/peachtree21345.html.

1628: Failed to Complete Installation

Go to Task Manager (Ctrl+Alt+Del). Under the Processes tab if you see the file IDRIVER.exe in the list highlight it and click End Task or End Process. Close the Task Manager when done.

Next, download and update the Windows Installer to the 4.5 version.

1. Go online to http://support.microsoft.com/kb/942288. Run Windows Installer version 4.5.

2. Restart your computer.

3. Reinstall Peachtree 2012.

This article refers to the Windows Vista or Windows XP operating system. If you are using Windows 7, follow the link on the Microsoft Support website to "Visit the Windows 7 Solution Center."

Remove PCWxxx.ini Files

If you are having difficulty installing Peachtree 2012, do a search to check if a PCWXXX.ini file resides on your hard drive.

Search and then delete these files:

1. PCW160.ini (Peachtree 2009)
2. PCW170.ini (Peachtree 2010)
3. PCW180.ini (Peachtree 2011)

Once the PCWXXX.ini file is deleted, try reinstalling Peachtree.

PDF FILES

To convert Peachtree reports to PDF files, you need Adobe Reader software, an Adobe Corporation product. This software lets you view, navigate, and print the contents of a file. Free Adobe Reader software is available at www.adobe.com.

If you are having difficulty using Peachtree's PDF feature, do the following:

1. Update to the latest version of Adobe Reader (www.adobe.com).
2. Exit Peachtree. Insert the Peachtree Complete Accounting DVD and select Repair.

OPENING THE SAMPLE COMPANIES

When selecting one of the sample companies – Bellwether Garden Supply or Stone Arbor Landscaping – the Explore a Sample Company Window does <u>not</u> show the OK, Close, or Help buttons.

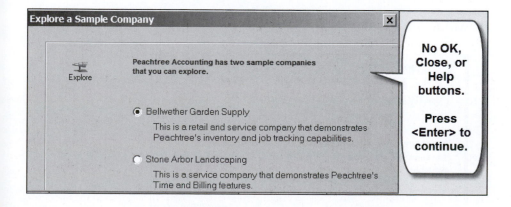

Screen resolution affects how Peachtree's windows look. The recommended screen resolution is 1024X768 with small fonts. Page iv includes this recommended system requirement:

- At least high color (16-bit) SVGA video; supports 1024x768 resolution with small fonts required.

Higher screen resolution may be used. Higher resolution will not affect how the software functions, but the user interface might look different. For example, if you do not have an OK button, press <Enter> to start Bellwether Garden Supply or Stone Arbor Landscaping.

PROBLEM BACKING UP TO USB DRIVE OR OTHER EXTERNAL MEDIA

When I back up to USB media (thumb or flash drive), this message appears.

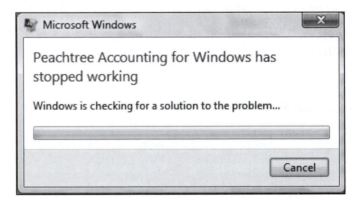

Then, this window appears:

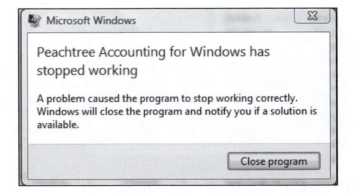

Click [Close program] . You are returned to the Windows desktop.

Make a backup, using the Desktop as the destination. Then, copy the backup from your desktop to a USB drive. Follow the steps shown below to do that.

1. From the Navigation Bar, select [System] ;
   [Back Up Now] .

2. Click [Back Up] .

3. In the Save in field, select Desktop.

4. In the File name field, type the appropriate file name. (In the example Chapter 3 is shown.)

5. Click [Save] .

6. When This Company backup will require approximately X.XXMB window appears (substitute correct number for Xs.), click

   [OK] . When the Back Up Company scale is 100% complete, you have successfully backed up. Minimize Peachtree to go to your desktop. The Chapter 3.ptb file is shown on the Windows desktop.

7. Right click on the Chapter 3.ptb file; left-click Copy.

8. Right click on the Start button; left-click Explore.

9. Go to your USB drive location. Right-click on the USB drive; left-click Paste.

RESTORING STARTING DATA FOR THE SAMPLE COMPANIES: BELLWETHER GARDEN SUPPLY AND STONE ARBOR LANDSCAPING

To start the sample companies from the beginning (before any data was added), restore these files:

1. In Chapter 1, on pages 23-25, you backed up Bellwether Garden Supply. This back up was made *before* any data was added. Restore the bgs.ptb file. Refer to Using Peachtree's Restore Wizard on pages 29-32 for detailed steps. Once the bgs.ptb file is restored you have starting (beginning) data for Bellwether Garden Supply.

2. In Chapter 8, on page 264, you backed up Stone Arbor Landscaping. Restore the Chapter 8.ptb file.

SERIAL NUMBER IN USE; YOU CANNOT USE PEACHTREE BECAUSE IT HAS REACHED ITS MAXIMUM NUMBER OF USERS

If you are receiving Serial Number in use, Another Peachtree user is using the same serial number, or Peachtree has reached its maximum number of users, do the following.

1. If necessary, exit Peachtree.

2. Go to Task Manager by pressing the CTRL+ALT+DEL keys and on the Processes tab look for W3DBSMGR.EXE, click to highlight and choose End Task. The W3DBSMGR.EXE file is the Pervasive database which sometimes takes time to end. You may have exited Peachtree and then tried to start it *before* Pervasive stopped running.

3. Restart Peachtree.

DELETING PEACHTREE

Follow these steps to delete Peachtree Complete Accounting 2012. (Use similar steps to delete Peachtree 2011.)

1.   Insert the Peachtree DVD. Select Run autorun.exe.

2.   When the Welcome to Peachtree Accounting window appears, select <u>R</u>emove or Modify Peachtree Accounting. When the User Account Control window appears, select <Yes>.

3.   Select Peachtree Complete Accounting 2012. A Preparing to Install window appears. Be patient, this will take a few minutes. When a screen prompts that setup has detected an installation of Peachtree Release 2012 on this computer, click <OK>.

4.   Select Remove, then click <Next>. A window prompts, This will remove Peachtree Accounting 2012 (all versions), click <OK>. Removing Peachtree will take a few minutes.

5.   When the Select Country window appears, select the country for this installation; for example, United States. Click <Next>.

6.   When the Maintenance Complete window appears, click <Finish>. Close the Welcome to Peachtree Accounting window.

7.   Remove the DVD.

After removal, you may want to delete these two folders:

1.   C:\Sage
2.   C:\Program Files (x86)\Sage

<u>Before</u> removing the folders, backup data that you want to keep. Once the Sage folder is deleted, all company data files are removed. (*Hint:* In Windows Vista and XP, the Sage folder is within C:\Program Files.) After removing the folders, empty the recycle bin.

These steps are also shown on pages xxi-xxii.

Appendix B

Accounting Information Systems

In *Computer Accounting with Peachtree by Sage Complete Accounting 2012, 16e,* you learn about the relationship between Peachtree and fundamental accounting principles and procedures. Throughout the textbook, you are shown how the initial decisions for setting up a company, setting defaults, processing transactions, and generating reports relates to what is learned in other accounting courses.

Another feature of the textbook explains how Peachtree's user interface organizes and processes data. Peachtree is an example of an accounting information system. The following section defines *accounting information systems (AIS)* and their key components.

ACCOUNTING INFORMATION SYSTEMS

An accounting information system is the method of recordkeeping a business uses to maintain its financial information. This includes purchases, sales, and other financial processes of the business. The purpose of AIS is to accumulate data and provide decision makers (investors, creditors, and managers) with information.

Key characteristics of an accounting information system include providing timely accurate financial information to management and external users (creditors, investors, regulatory authorities, and taxation authorities). AIS software uses various modules to record data and produce reports. Users can easily produce financial statements or obtain information to manage the day-to-day activities of a business. This was previously a paper-based process but most businesses now use accounting software. In an electronic financial accounting system, the steps in the accounting cycle are built on the system itself.

Accounting information systems not only record the financial transactions of a business but also combine the study and practice of accounting within the design, implementation, and monitoring of records. Such systems use information technology resources together with traditional accounting controls and methods to provide users the financial information necessary to manage their organizations.

The key components of an accounting information system are:

Input. The input devices commonly associated with AIS include: standard personal computers or workstations, scanning devices for standardized data entry, electronic communication devices for electronic data interchange (EDI) and e-commerce. In addition, many financial systems come Web-enabled to allow devices to connect to the Internet

Process. Basic processing is achieved through computer systems ranging from individual personal computers to large-scale enterprise servers. The underlying model is the double-entry accounting system initially introduced in Italy in the fifteenth century.

Output. Output devices used include computer displays, printers, and electronic communication devices for electronic data exchange and e-commerce. The output content may encompass almost any type of financial reports from budgets and tax reports to multinational financial statements.

ACCOUNTS PAYABLE SYSTEM: PEACHTREE AND QUICKBOOKS

Peachtree and QuickBooks are two popular small business accounting software applications. To exemplify an accounting information system, let's look at how these two software applications process accounts payable.

Both software applications contain modules that reflect business processes. Typical business processes include sales, cash receipts, purchases, cash payments, and human resource functions such as payroll.

Peachtree

Peachtree includes a Navigation Bar and Navigation Centers which take you to various business process areas or system modules. Another way to go to Peachtree's modules is to make selections from the menu bar. In order to show Peachtree's accounts payable system, the Vendors & Purchases Navigation Center is shown on the next page.

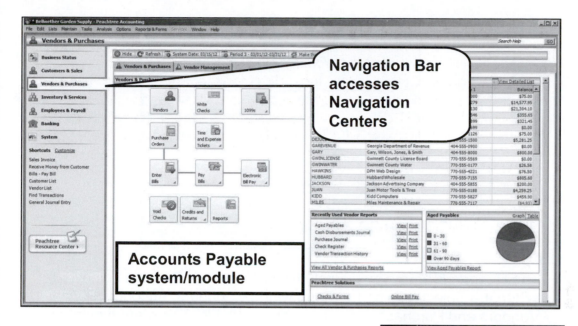

When Vendors & Purchases is selected, the Vendors & Purchases Navigation Center appears. A task diagram shows the flow of data through the accounts payable system. Other areas on the Vendors & Purchases Navigation Center include the Vendors list, Recently Used Vendor Reports, Aged Payables, and Peachtree solutions. This is all in Peachtree's accounts payable system or accounts payable module.

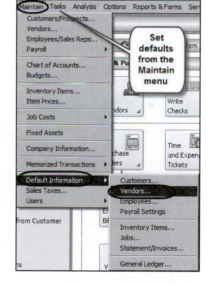

Another way to use the accounts payable system is to make selections from the menu bar. The Maintain menu is where defaults are set up. The Maintain menu includes a Vendors selection and a selection for Default Information, Vendors. The menu bar's Tasks menu is also organized by module. For example, the accounts payable selections are in one area. The Tasks menu A/P area is shown on the next page.

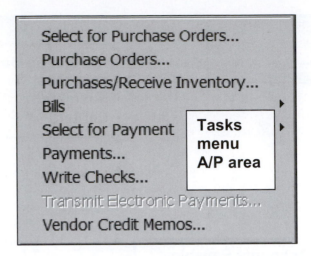

The Reports & Forms menu includes an Accounts Payable selection. When the Select a Report or Form window appears, Accounts Payable: Vendors and Purchases selections are available. There are two tabs: Reports and Forms. The Forms tab allows you to select the appropriate accounts payable form. Notice that the Reports list includes each Peachtree module: Accounts Receivable, Accounts Payable, Payroll, General Ledger, Inventory, etc.

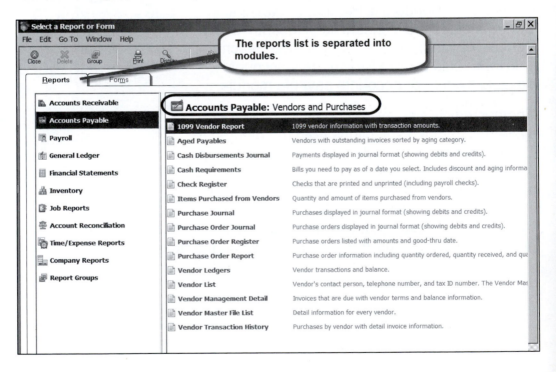

In addition, various system controls exist to ensure the accuracy and reliability of the data recorded. For example, preformatted screens facilitate the accuracy and completeness of data entry. Fields are restricted to either text or numeric data or a specific number of characters. Values are automatically calculated. The system prompts or requests the user to enter specific data and processing will not continue until the appropriate data is entered. Drop down lists or look-up tables allow the user to access master tables.

Master tables are used to set and maintain constant data, i.e. defaults. When a user enters a specific identification code such as a vendor number, the system accesses the master table and automatically completes information about the vendor within the transaction window. From these examples, you can see how Peachtree's accounts payable system is organized. Now let's look at QuickBooks and you will see many similarities as well as differences between the two accounting information systems.

QuickBooks

QuickBooks's home page shows Centers or areas; for example, Vendors, Customers, Employees, Company, Banking. If you compare this to Peachtree's Navigation Bar you see a similar organization—QuickBooks's Centers vs. Peachtree's Navigation Bar and Navigation Centers.

QuickBooks's home page is shown on the next page.

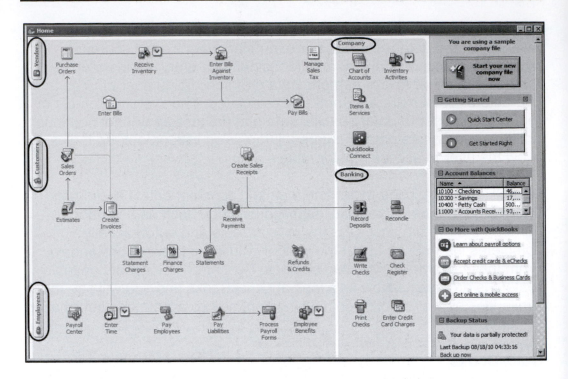

The QuickBooks Home page provides a big picture of how essential business tasks fit together. Tasks are organized into groups (Customers, Vendors, Employees, Company, and Banking) with

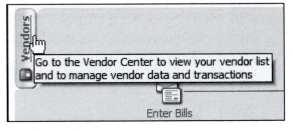

workflow arrows to help you learn how tasks relate to each other, and help decide what to do next. When the Vendors button is selected, the Vendor Center appears. If the Customers button or Employees button is selected, their Centers appear.

Another way to access the accounts payable module is to make selections from QuickBooks's icon bar or menu bar. For example, from

the icon bar, you can go to the Vendor Center by selecting [Vendor Center] .

The menu bar Reports selection also includes Vendors & Payables and Purchases reports. The Reports; Vendors & Payables selection is shown below.

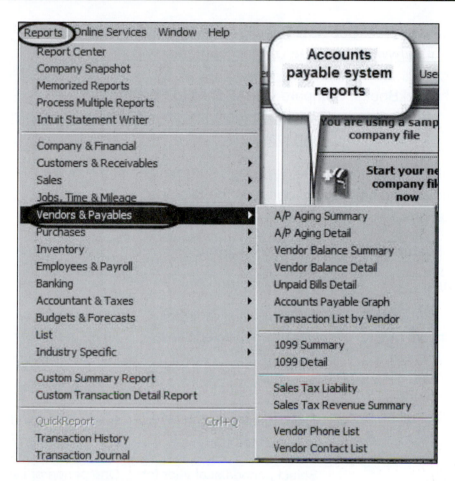

The Reports menu Purchases selection includes more accounts payable reports.

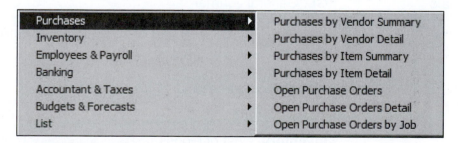

Similarities and Differences

To read about the similarities and differences between Peachtree and QuickBooks, visit these websites.

1. Peachtree: See how Peachtree compares to QuickBooks – http://www.peachtree.com/accountants/switch/.

2. QuickBooks: Compare QuickBooks to Peachtree – http://quickbooks.intuit.com/qb/components/landing_pages/switcher_center/compchart.jsp

The table below and on the next page summarizes some of the similarities and differences between the two accounting software applications.

Features	Peachtree	QuickBooks
Modules Customers (A/R) Vendors (A/P) Employees Banking Inventory	**Navigation Bar** Transaction windows include debit/credit fields LIFO/FIFO, and average inventory User-maintained payroll *or* third-party	**Centers** Transaction window dr./cr. defaults cannot be changed Average inventory Intuit payroll add-on or third-party
Periods	Select period/fiscal year for accounting	One period or list for all entries
Journals	**GL:** General Journal **A/P:** Purchase Journal and Cash Payments Journal **A/R:** Sales Journal and Cash Receipts Journal **Inventory:** Cost of Goods Sold Journal; Inventory Adjustments Journal **Payroll:** Payroll Journal	Transaction Journal

Features	Peachtree	QuickBooks
General Ledger **Subsidiary Ledgers** **Financial Statements**	YES	YES
Audit Trail	Audit Trail Report (shows time and date of entry) Find Transactions Report	Audit Trail Report (does not show time of entry) NO
Backup/Restore/ Open Company	One file extension - .PTB - for backups/restore/open company	Backup extensions include .QBB, .QBM, .QBA. Open company, .QBW extension

Peachtree and QuickBooks are examples of accounting information systems that are used for small business accounting. Even though the user interface looks different, the processing of accounting data and the reports generated are similar.

Accounting Software

Accounting information systems use software applications like Peachtree and QuickBooks, as well as numerous other software programs, to process and manage business transactions.
There are a lot of software packages for accounting. To look at some product comparisons, go online to http://accounting-software-review.toptenreviews.com/ which compares ten accounting software products.

The major differences between accounting software products include the depth of processing, enhanced features and functions, and the size of the database. As the database gets larger, the depth of processing increases and more features and functions are available. As companies grow in size, their accounting software needs change.

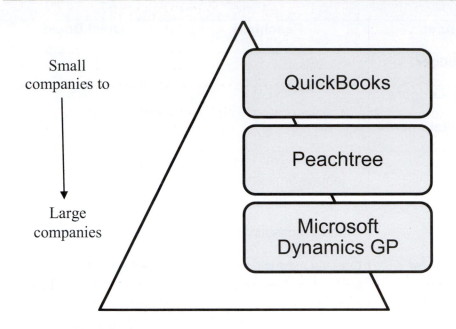

Peachtree and QuickBooks are used by small companies. As the company grows to mid-size, Peachtree and Microsoft Dynamics GP can be used. Large companies use Microsoft Dynamics GP.

Company size	No. of Employees
Small business	1-50 employees
Medium-sized business	50-500 employees
Large business	500+ employees

You can see that accounting software addresses small, medium and large businesses. The high-end accounting software applications are generally referred to as *enterprise resource planning (ERP)* systems. ERP systems are designed to integrate all of the major functions of a business to promote efficient operations. ERP systems are usually company-wide software applications which manage and coordinate all the resources, information, and functions of a business from shared data sources.

Appendix C

Review of Accounting Principles

Computer Accounting with Peachtree by Sage Complete Accounting 2012, 16th Edition, is for students who are studying accounting or have used accounting in business. Some of you may have completed one or two semesters of accounting using *Fundamental Accounting Principles*, 20e, Wild et al., McGraw-Hill/Irwin, ©2011, or another accounting textbook. Appendix C is a review of basic accounting principles and procedures.

Accounting is concerned with how transactions and other economic events should be described and reported. The Computer Accounting Cycle is shown below. This series of steps (2 through 11) is repeated each month for a business's transactions. (Step 1, New Company Setup and the chart of accounts is completed when the business is created.)

	Peachtree Complete Accounting Computer Accounting Cycle
1.	New Company Set up and the chart of accounts.
2.	Analyze transactions.
3.	Journalize entries.
4.	Post to the ledger.
5.	Print general ledger trial balance (unadjusted).
6.	Account reconciliation.
7.	Journalize and post adjusting entries.
8.	Print the general ledger trial balance (adjusted).
9.	Print the financial statements.
10.	Change accounting periods.
11.	Interpret accounting information.

In the service businesses featured in this book, you used the Cash Payments Journal and Cash Receipts Journal for business transactions. Then you post these transactions to the General Ledger. In a merchandising business you use Peachtree's Accounts Payable system and Accounts Receivable system. Special journals are used in conjunction with the Accounts Payable and Accounts Receivable ledgers. The special journals include: Cash Receipts Journal, Sales Journal, Cash Disbursements Journal, and Purchase Journal. The General Ledger, Accounts Payable and Accounts Receivable systems are taught in Parts 1, 2 and 3 of *Computer Accounting with Peachtree by Sage Complete Accounting 2012, 16e.*

Standard accounting procedures are based on the double-entry system. This means that for each business transaction, one or more debits and one or more credits must be made in a journal and posted to the ledger. The debits must equal the credits.

The double-entry accounting system is based on the following premise: each account has two sides–a debit (left) side and credit (right) side. This is stated in the ***accounting equation*** as:

Assets = Liabilities + Owner's Equity

Assets are the economic resources and other properties that a business owns. Asset accounts include: Cash, Accounts Receivable, Office Supplies, Equipment, Land, Buildings, etc.

Liabilities are the business's debts. Liability accounts include: Accounts Payable, Loans Payable, Unearned Rent, etc.

Equity is the difference between the organization's assets and liabilities. Equity accounts for organizations that are sole proprietorships or partnerships include: Capital and Withdrawals. Equity accounts for organizations that are corporations include contributed capital accounts like common stock which represent external ownership and retained earnings and dividends accounts which represent internal ownership interests. Temporary equity-related accounts known as revenue and expense accounts recognize an organization's income activities during the period.

Since assets are on the left side of the accounting equation, the left side of the account increases. This is the usual balance, too; assets increase on the left side and have a debit balance. Liabilities and Equity accounts are on the right side of the equation. Therefore, they increase on the right side and normally carry credit balances.

Another way to show the accounting equation and double-entry is illustrated below.

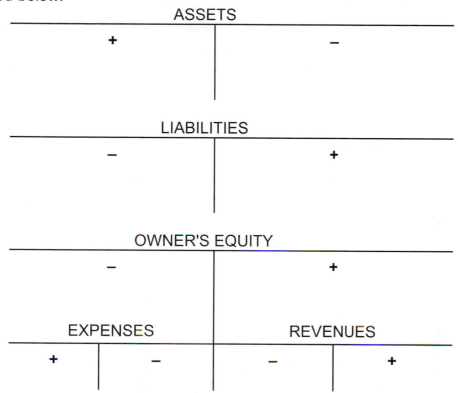

Each element of the accounting equation, Assets, Liabilities, and Equity, behaves similarly to their placement in the equation. Assets have debit balances; Liabilities have credit balances; Equities have credit balances; Expenses have debit balances because they decrease equity; and Revenues have credit balances because they increase equity.

In computerized accounting it is important to number each account according to a system. This is called the Chart of Accounts. The Chart of Accounts is a listing of all the general ledger accounts. The Chart of Accounts identifies accounts with a number (five digits in Peachtree's detailed chart; four digits in Peachtree's simplified chart). The account number is shown in the Account ID column; the name of the account in the Account Description column; the next column shows whether account is Active; and the Account Type column classifies accounts for the financial statements. On Peachtree's chart of accounts, the Account Type column classifies accounts as cash, accounts receivable, inventory, fixed assets, accumulated depreciation accounts, liability accounts, etc. A partial chart of accounts is shown below.

Page: 1

BR Manufacturing, Inc.
Chart of Accounts
As of Jan 31, 2012

Filter Criteria includes: Report order is by ID. Report is printed with Accounts having Zero Amounts and in Detail Format.

Account ID	Account Description	Active?	Account Type
10000	Petty Cash	Yes	Cash
10200	Franklin Bank	Yes	Cash
10300	Philadelphia Savings and Loan	Yes	Cash
10700	Investments-Cert. of Deposit	Yes	Cash
11000	Accounts Receivable	Yes	Accounts Receivable
11400	Other Receivables	Yes	Accounts Receivable
11500	Allowance for Doubtful Account	Yes	Accounts Receivable
12000	Raw Materials Inventory	Yes	Inventory
12010	Inventory-Backpacks	Yes	Inventory
12020	Inventory-Sleeping Bags	Yes	Inventory
12030	Inventory-Tents	Yes	Inventory
12050	Supplies Inventory	Yes	Inventory
12100	Work in Progress Inventory	Yes	Inventory
12150	Finished Goods Inventory	Yes	Inventory
14000	Prepaid Insurance	Yes	Other Current Assets
14100	Employee Advances	Yes	Other Current Assets
14200	Notes Receivable-Current	Yes	Other Current Assets
14300	Prepaid Interest	Yes	Other Current Assets
14700	Other Current Assets	Yes	Other Current Assets
15000	Furniture and Fixtures	Yes	Fixed Assets
15100	Computers & Equipment	Yes	Fixed Assets
15200	Trucks/Autos	Yes	Fixed Assets
15300	Other Depreciable Property	Yes	Fixed Assets
15500	Building	Yes	Fixed Assets
15600	Building Improvements	Yes	Fixed Assets
17000	Accum. Depreciation - Furnitur	Yes	Accumulated Depreciation
17100	Accum. Depreciation - Comp&Eq	Yes	Accumulated Depreciation
17200	Accum. Depreciation - Trks/Aut	Yes	Accumulated Depreciation
17500	Accum. Depreciation - Building	Yes	Accumulated Depreciation
17600	Accum. Depreciation - Bldg Imp	Yes	Accumulated Depreciation
19000	Deposits	Yes	Other Assets
19100	Organization Costs	Yes	Other Assets
19150	Accum. Amortiz. - Org. Costs	Yes	Other Assets
19200	Note Receivable-Noncurrent	Yes	Other Assets
19900	Other Noncurrent Assets	Yes	Other Assets
20000	Accounts Payable	Yes	Accounts Payable
22000	Credit Card Payable	Yes	Other Current Liabilities
23000	Accrued Expenses	Yes	Other Current Liabilities
23100	Sales Tax Payable	Yes	Other Current Liabilities
23200	Wages Payable	Yes	Other Current Liabilities
23300	Medicare Employee Taxes Payabl	Yes	Other Current Liabilities
23350	Medicare Employer Taxes Payabl	Yes	Other Current Liabilities
23400	Federal Payroll Taxes Payable	Yes	Other Current Liabilities
23500	FUTA Tax Payable	Yes	Other Current Liabilities
23600	State Payroll Taxes Payable	Yes	Other Current Liabilities
23650	Employee SUI Taxes Payable	Yes	Other Current Liabilities
23700	SUTA Payable	Yes	Other Current Liabilities
23800	Local Payroll Taxes Payable	Yes	Other Current Liabilities
23900	Income Taxes Payable	Yes	Other Current Liabilities
24000	FICA Employee Taxes Payable	Yes	Other Current Liabilities
24100	FICA Employer Taxes Payable	Yes	Other Current Liabilities
24200	Current Portion Long-Term Debt	Yes	Other Current Liabilities
24400	Deposits from Customers	Yes	Other Current Liabilities
24900	Suspense-Clearing Account	Yes	Other Current Liabilities
27000	Mortgage Payable	Yes	Long Term Liabilities
27100	Deferred Revenue	Yes	Long Term Liabilities
27400	Other Long-Term Liabilities	Yes	Long Term Liabilities
39003	Common Stock	Yes	Equity-doesn't close
39004	Paid-in Capital	Yes	Equity-doesn't close
39005	Retained Earnings	Yes	Equity-Retained Earnings
39007	Dividends Paid	Yes	Equity-gets closed
40000	Sales-Backpacks	Yes	Income
40200	Sales-Sleeping Bags	Yes	Income

Peachtree includes over 75 sample companies from which you can copy default information, including detailed and simplified Chart of Accounts examples. If you want to see which sample companies are included in Peachtree, select Help from the menu bar, then select Contents and Index. If necessary, select the Contents tab; then double-click Help about Your Specific Type of Business. Double -click on the A-Z List of Business Types. An alphabetic list of company types displays. Move your mouse to a company that you want to see and single click. To see the chart of accounts, click on <u>Display a sample chart of accounts for this</u>

<u>type of business</u>. If you want a printout, click [Print]. Click

[Back] to select another business type; or click [X] on the title bar to close the Peachtree Help screen.

Report information in the form of financial statements is important to accounting. The Balance Sheet reports the financial position of the business. It shows that assets are equal to liabilities plus equity—the accounting equation. The Income Statement shows the difference between revenue and expenses for a specified period of time (month, quarter, year). The Statement of Cash Flow reports the operating, financial, and investing activities for the period.

Peachtree tracks income and expense data for an entire year. At the end of the year, all revenue and expense accounts are closed to equity. All you need to do is select Tasks, System, then Year-End Wizard. This step closes all revenue and expense accounts to equity. The income and expense accounts have zero balances and you are ready to start the next year. Peachtree includes 24 periods so it is possible to accumulate data for two years.

In accounting you learn that asset, liability, and equity accounts are included on the balance sheet. Revenue (income) and expense accounts are placed on the Income Statement. The Cash Flow Statement shows the sources of cash coming into the business and the destination of the cash going out.

The most important task you have is recording transactions into the appropriate accounts. Peachtree helps you by organizing the software into Business Status, Customers & Sales, Vendors & Purchases,

Inventory & Services, Employees & Payroll, Banking, and Company navigation centers. You record transactions into the right place using easy-to-complete forms. Once transactions are entered, the data is organized into journal entries, ledgers, reports, and analysis capabilities. Another important task is deciding how to enter transactions. Recording and categorizing business transactions will determine how Peachtree uses that information. For instance, observe that the chart of accounts for BR Manufacturing, Inc. shows Account 10200 – Franklin Bank, classified as the Account Type, Cash; Account No. 11000, Accounts Receivable, classified as Accounts Receivable. The Chart of Accounts Account Type column classifies the account for the financial statements—Assets, Liability, and Equity accounts go on the balance sheet; Income, Cost of Sales, and Expense accounts go on the Income Statement.

As you work with Peachtree, you see how the accounts, recording of transactions, and reports work to provide your business with the information necessary for making informed decisions.

Another important aspect of accounting is determining whether the basis for recording transactions is cash or accrual. In the cash basis method, revenues and expenses are recognized when cash changes hands. In other words, when the customer pays for their purchase, the transaction is recorded. When the expense is paid the transaction is recorded. In the accrual method of accounting, revenues and expenses are recognized when they occur. In other words, if the company purchases inventory from a vendor on April 1, the transaction is recorded on April 1. If inventory is sold on account on April 15, the transaction is done on April 15 *not* when cash is received. Accrual basis accounting is seen as more accurate because assets, liabilities, income, and expenses are recorded when they actually happen.

The charts on the next two pages summarize Appendix C, Review of Accounting Principles.

ACCOUNTING EQUATION:	Assets =	Liabilities +	Owners Equities +	Revenues –	Expenses
Definition:	Something that has future or potential value "resources"	Responsibilities to others "Payables" "Unearned"	Internal and External ownership	Recognition of value creation	Expired, used, or consumed costs or resources
Debit Rules:DR	Increase	Decrease	Decrease	Decrease	Increase
Credit Rules:CR	Decrease	Increase	Increase	Increase	Decrease
Account Types and Examples	**Current Assets:** Cash, Marketable Securities, Accounts Receivable, Inventory, Prepaids **Plant Assets:** Land, Buildings, Equipment, Accumulated Depreciation **Noncurrent Assets:** Investments, Intangibles	**Current Liabilities:** Accounts Payable, Unearned Revenue, Advances from Customer **Noncurrent or Long-term Liabilities:** Bonds Payable, Notes Payables, Mortgage Payable	**Sole Proprietor:** (both internal and external) Name, Capital; Name, Withdrawals **Partnership:** (both internal and external) Partner A, Capital; Partner A, Withdrawals, etc. **Corporation:** External: Common Stock, Preferred Stock, Paid-in Capital Internal: Retained Earnings, Dividends	**Operating Revenue:** Sales: Fees Earned, Rent Income, Contract Revenue **Other Revenue:** Interest Income	**Product/Services Expenses:** Cost of Goods Sold, Cost of Sales **Prepaid Expenses:** Selling Expenses, Administrative Expense, General Expense, Salary Expense, Rent Expense, Depreciation Expense, Insurance Expense **Other Expenses:** Interest Expense

T-Account Rules

Assets		Liabilities		Owners Equities		Revenues		Expenses	
Acquire resources	Consume resources	Pay bills Recognize earnings	Buy on credit Receive cash or other assets before earning it	Internal: Net Loss External: Owners reduce ownership thru withdrawals or dividends	Internal: Net Income External: Investment made by owners in company	Sales returns Sales discount given	Sales Earned Income	Resources used consumed expired	
increase	*decrease*	*decrease*	*increase*	*decrease*	*increase*	*decrease*	*increase*	*increase*	*decrease*

Basic Financial Statement Rules:

Income Statement
Revenue = Net Income (NI) or Net Loss (NL)
(Prepare first)

Statement of Equity
Beginning* + NI or – NL – (Withdrawals) = Ending*
*for Sole Proprietors and Partnerships use Capital; for Corporations use Retained Earnings
(Prepare second)

Balance Sheet
Assets = Liabilities + Owners Equities
(Prepare third)

Statement of Cash Flows
Operating +/– Investing +/–
Financing+Beginning Cash = Ending Cash
(Prepare last)

Appendix D Glossary

Appendix D lists a glossary of terms used in *Computer Accounting with Peachtree by Sage Complete Accounting 2012, 16th Edition*. Appendix D is also included on the textbook website at www.mhhe.com/yacht2012, link to Student Edition, then select Glossary.

accounting equation
The accounting equation is stated as assets = liabilities + owner's equity. (p. 772)

accounting information systems (AIS)
The method of recordkeeping a business uses to maintain its financial information. This includes purchases, sales, and other financial processes. Accounting information systems use information technology resources together with traditional accounting controls and methods to provide users the financial information necessary to manage their organizations. (p. 761)

accounts payable
The money a company owes to a supplier or vendor. (p. 429)

accounts payable ledger
Shows the account activity for each vendor. (p. 457)

accounts payable module
The Vendors & Purchases Navigation Center includes Vendors & Purchases Tasks and its accompanying workflow diagram, Vendors, Recently Used Vendor Reports, Aged Payables, and Peachtree Solutions. (p. 60).

accounts payable system	Keeps track of the amount owed and the due dates of bills. In order to have the cash needed to pay bills, knowing why bills are due. The accounts payable system provides the summary information needed for the entry that credits Accounts Payable and debits the various asset and expense accounts that vendor invoices represent. (p. 60)
accounts payable transactions	Purchases of merchandise for resale, assets, or expenses incurred on credit from vendors. (p. 429)
accounts receivable	Accounts receivable represents amounts owed by customers for items or services sold to them when cash is not received at the time of sale. (p. 497)
accounts receivable ledger	Shows the account activity for each customer. (p. 511)
accounts receivable module	The Customers & Sales Navigation center shows the accounts receivable system. There are also individual tabs for Customers and Sales and Customer Management. (p. 103)
accounts receivable system	A summary of customer information, includes access to recently used customer reports, an overview of the company's aged receivables, lists of information regarding transactions, customer history, invoices, receipts, and finance charges. See accounts receivable module. (p. 103)

accounts receivable transactions   Credit transactions from customers. (p. 497)

activity items   An item class for time and billing. (p. 254)

ASCII   An acronym for American Standard Code for Information Interchange. A standard format for representing characters on a computer. Most word processing, spreadsheet, and database programs can read ASCII files. (p. 686)

assets   The economic resources and other properties that a business owns. (p. 772)

audit trail   The path from the source document to the accounts. (p. 190)

average cost   A method of computing inventory. (See weighted-average method.) (p. 462)

backing up   A copy of a data file typically stored on the hard drive or external media. (p. 22)

balance sheet   Lists the types and amounts of assets, liabilities, and equity as of a specific date. (p. 302)

bank reconciliation   The process of bringing the balance of the bank statement and the balance of the cash account into agreement. (p. 341)

batch posting	Journal entries are held in temporary storage on your disk and not made part of the permanent records of the company until you decide you are satisfied with them and select Post from the icon bar. After you post, the General Ledger and all other accounting reports are updated. (p. 123)
business status navigation center	The Business Status Navigation Center displays a variety of general business information, including account balances, revenue figures, receivables and payables data, and action items. Like a car's dashboard it tells you what you need to know in one place. (See dashboard.) (p. 8)
case sensitive	Refers to the use of lowercase and uppercase letters. When coding a customer or vendor, you must use either a capital or lowercase letter. For example, a vendor code that is A002 will not be recognized if a002 is typed. (p. 74)
cash disbursements journal	All payments of cash are recorded in the cash disbursements journal. In Peachtree, the Payments task is the cash disbursements journal. (p. 463)
cash receipts journal	In Peachtree the receipts task posts to the cash receipts journal. (p. 510)
charge items	An item class for time and billing. (p. 254)
chart of accounts	A list of all the accounts used by a company, showing the identifying number assigned to each account. PCA has over 70 sample charts of accounts. (p. 20)

coding system	A combination of letters and numbers that are used to identify customers and vendors. The coding system is case sensitive, for example, A002 is not the same as a002. (See case sensitive.) (p. 73)
comma separated values values (CSV)	Files that are commonly used for trans- ferring data between applications. (p. 685)
credit memos	Refunds for merchandise that is returned by a customer. Also known as a credit invoice. (p. 133)
customer ledgers	Customer Ledgers lists customers with detail transaction information including outstanding balances for each customer. The bottom of the report provides debit, credit, and balance totals. (p. 132)
dashboard	The Business Status Navigation Center shows you in one place what you need to know about the business—data relating to account balances, who owes you what and what bills need to be paid, who your most profitable customers are, etc. (See business status) (p. 8).
database	An organized body of related information. A database is a structured collection of records or data that is stored in a computer system. The structure is achieved by organizing the data. (p. 437)
default	The built-in or suggested variable. For example, when you install Peachtree, the Windows 7 default for backing up or saving company data is C:\Sage\Peachtree \Company. The system will automatically revert to certain defaults if no other choices are made. (p. 34)

desktop	Depending on how your computer is set up, various icons appear on your desktop when you start Windows. (p. 9)
dialog boxes	A window that appears when the system requires further information. You type information into dialog boxes to communicate with the program. Some dialog boxes display warnings and messages. (p. 33)
drill down	The function that allows you to follow a path to its origin for further analysis. Some of the data that appears in the Peachtree Navigation Centers can be drilled down on. These spots are marked by blue text; just click to go to a related window displaying detailed information. You can also use drill down from reports. (p. 85)
drop-down list	The down arrow means that the field contains a list of information from which you can make a selection. When you click on the arrow next to a field, the list appears. You can press <Enter> or click your mouse on an item to select it from the list. (p. 13)
ellipsis (...)	A punctuation mark consisting of three successive periods (...). Choosing a menu item with an ellipsis opens a dialog box. See glossary item, dialog box. (p. 33)
employees and payroll system	The payroll system includes employees information and earnings. (p. 141)

enterprise resource planning (ERP)	ERP systems are company-wide software products that manage and coordinate all the resources, information, and functions of a business from shared data sources. ERP systems are used by large companies. (p. 770)
equity	The difference between the assets and liabilities or what the business has left after the debts are paid. (p. 772)
exemptions	These are withholding allowances claimed by the employee. The number of exemptions or withholding allowances usually includes one for the employee, one for the employee's spouse, and one for each dependent. (p. 579)
expense tickets	Used to track and aid in the recovery of customer-related expenses. (p. 252)
exporting	Copies Peachtree data into a format that other programs can read and use. (p. 683)
external media	Examples of external media include floppy disks; CD-R; DVD-R; USB flash drive; Zip disks. External media of this type can be used for backing up Peachtree data. (p. 23)
FICA taxes	This deduction from wages is also called the social security tax and provides qualified workers who retire at age 62 or older with monthly payments from the federal government. A portion of this tax is for Medicare. (See Medicare.) (p. 579)

fields	An individual piece of data, for example, the account number for sales or a customer's name. (p. 684)
FIFO	First in, first out method of inventory assumes that the items in the beginning inventory are sold first. (p. 549)
files	A group of related records; for example, customer files and journal files. (p. 684)
filter	Filtering allows you to select specific types of activities and events. (p. 12)
general ledger system or module (GL)	The complete collection of accounts (chart of accounts) of a company, transactions associated with these accounts, and account balances for a specified period of time. The GL is the combination of all journal entries that have been recorded and posted. The account balances are then collected and shown on the company's financial statements. (p. 21; 361)
global options	Settings that affect the entire program. When you set global options for one company, you set them for all companies. You can access these settings from the Options menu. (p. 18)
graphical user interface (GUI)	Consists of procedures which enable you to interact with PCA. The key is the Windows environment: the menus, dialog boxes, and list boxes. A mouse simplifies use of the GUI, but it is not required. (p. 1)
home page	The Business Status page is also known as the home page. (p. 15)
HTML	HTML is an abbreviation for Hypertext Markup Language. Peachtree's Help topics are displayed in HTML. (p. 166)

icons	Small graphic symbols that represent an application or command. Icons appear on the screen when Windows programs are used: file folder, eraser, clock, hour-glass, etc. (p. 1)
icon bar	The icon bar shows pictures of commands or additional information that pertain to the window. (p. 11)
input	The input devices commonly associated with AIS include: standard personal computers or workstations, scanning devices for, electronic communication devices for electronic data interchange (EDI) and e-commerce. In addition, many financial systems come Web-enabled to allow devices to connect to the World Wide Web. (p. 762)
internal control	An integrated system of people, processes, and procedures that minimize or eliminate business risks, protect assets, ensure reliable accounting, and promote efficient operations. (190)
inventory system	Peachtree's Inventory & Services Navigation Center shows Peachtree's inventory system, another module within the software. The Inventory & Services page displays information and access points related to the company's inventory items, includes a summary of item information, access to recently used inventory reports, a graphic analysis of how the cost of sales is trending, shows the flow of inventory-related tasks, and takes you where you need to go to perform those tasks. (p. 178)
importing	Translates data from other programs into a format that Peachtree can use. (p. 683)
invoice	A bill that shows an itemized list of goods shipped or services rendered, stating quantities, prices, fees, and shipping charges. (p. 498)

job costing	The job costing feature allows you to track the cost incurred while performing a job. (p. 207)
liabilities	The business' debts. (p. 772)
LIFO	Last in, first out method of inventory assumes that the last goods received are sold first. (p. 549)
line items	These rows appear on many of Peachtree's windows. On color monitors, a magenta line is placed around the row you select. (p. 12)
masking	The ability to limit information on the report to a single division, department, location, or type code. Financial statements can be departmentalized. See wildcards (p. 235)
Medicare	A portion of FICA taxes (also called social security taxes) deducted from wages of qualified workers. Retirees receive medical benefits called Medicare after reaching age 65. (p. 580)
merchandise inventory	Includes all goods owned by the business and held for resale. (p. 549)
merchandising business	Retail stores that resell goods and/or perform services. (p. 549)
module	Modules organize Peachtree's transaction windows and reports. The menu bar selections, Tasks and Reports & Forms, are also organized by module; for example, Accounts Receivable, Accounts Payable, General Ledger, etc. (p. 20)
mouse	A pointing device that is used to interact with images on the screen. The left mouse button is used in PCA. (p. 1)

navigation bar	The navigation bar appears on the left side of the Peachtree main window and offers access to seven navigation centers: Business Status; Customers & Sales; Vendors & Purchases; Inventory & Services; Employees & Payroll; Banking; and Company. Also called a dashboard. (p. 20)
navigation centers	Each navigation bar selection takes you to the navigation center pages, which provide information and access to the Peachtree program. (p. 20)
net income	A net income results when revenues exceed expenses. (p. 227)
net loss	A net loss results when expenses exceed revenues. (p. 227)
option button	Circles in dialog boxes which toggle options on and off. Options signal an either or choice. For example, there are two option buttons on the Maintain Employees dialog box: Salary or Hourly pay. You select one or the other; you cannot select both. (p. 39)
output	Output devices used include computer displays, impact and nonimpact printers, and electronic communication devices for electronic data exchange and e-commerce. (p. 762)
payroll journal	The Payroll Entry window is also the payroll journal. The Payroll Entry window posts to the General Ledger and to the Employee file. (p. 599)

payroll system	Peachtree's Employees & Payroll Navigation Center displays information and access points related to the company's employees. It includes a summary of employee information including 1099 vendors, and access to recently used employee reports. There is also a section called Peachtree Solutions, with links to information about their-party features such as checks and forms. (p. 141)
PCA	Abbreviation for Peachtree Complete Accounting. (p. 1)
perpetual inventory	In a perpetual inventory system, an up-to-date record of inventory is maintained and the inventory account is revised each time a purchase or sale is made. (p. 165)
posting	The process of transferring information from the journal to the ledger. (p. 275)
process	Basic processing is achieved through computer systems ranging from individual personal computers to large-scale enterprise servers. The underlying processing model is the double-entry accounting system initially introduced in the fifteenth century. (p. 762)
purchase discount	Cash discounts from vendors in return for early payment of an invoice, for example, 2% 10 days, net 30. (p. 57)
purchase journal	In the Purchase Journal, or Purchases/Receive Inventory window, you can enter invoices received from vendors or enter and print purchase orders. In manual accounting, a Purchase Journal is a multi-columnar journal in which all purchases on account are recorded. (p. 457)

purchase order

A purchase order is used to request items from a vendor. Purchase Orders, abbreviated PO, authorize the vendor to ship the ordered merchandise at the stated price and terms. When the Apply to Purchase Order tab is selected on the Purchases/Receive Inventory window and the transaction is posted, accounting information (inventory, accounts payable subsidiary ledger, general ledger) is updated. (p. 62)

queue

A list of files waiting to be printed (p. 36)

radio button

Commands that can be turned on from a list of choices in a dialog box or window. (p. 39)

real-time posting

Journal transactions are posted to the General Ledger at the time they are entered and saved. Peachtree Software recommends real-time posting for networked computers. (p. 122).

records

A group of fields that contain information on one subject, for example, the general journal, purchase journal, cash disbursements journal, sales journal, or cash receipts journal. (p. 684)

restore

Previously backed up data can be restored or retrieved from the Company page; or, from the menu bar by selecting File, Restore selection. (p. 23)

sales discount

A cash discount that is offered to customers for early payment of their sales invoices. For example, Bellwether Garden Supply offers Teesdale Real Estate a 5% discount for payments received within 15 days of the invoice date. In PCA the discount period (number of days) and discount percentage can be changed. (p. 114)

sales journal	The Sales/Invoicing task in Peachtree is the sales journal. (p. 510)
sales order	A document containing a list of items or services that a customer wants to buy. A sales order is a request for a sale. (p. 101)
service invoice	An alternative to the standard invoice. Use it when you want to create an invoice without inventory items. (p. 518)
shortcut keys	Enable you to perform some operations by pressing two or more keys at the same time. For example **<Alt> + <F4>** closes an application window. (p. 6)
source documents	Written evidence of a business transaction. Examples of source documents are sales invoices, purchase invoices, transaction register, and a bank statement. (p. 327)
statement of financial position	Another name for a balance sheet. (See balance sheet.) (p. 302).
tabs	There are various tabs shown on Peachtree's windows. For example, in the Maintain Customers/Prospects window there are tabs for General, Sales Defaults, Payment Defaults, Custom Fields, and History. You can select one of these tabs to open a window so that more information will display about a customer. (p. 13)
taskbar	In Windows 7/Vista/XP, the Start button and taskbar are located at the bottom of your screen. (p. 9)
template	A document pattern or part of a document that you keep stored so that it can be used again. (p. 703)

time tickets	Used to record time-based activities such as research or consultations. A record of activities of either a vendor or an employee. (p. 252)
title bar	The top line of every window is a bar which contains the name of the application or menu in that window. (p. 9)
touchpad	A touchpad pointing device usually consists of two mouse-like buttons and one scroll button. It is used to control the movement of the cursor. (p. 1)
transaction register	A term used to identify checking account activity. (p. 327)
unearned revenue	A liability account used to report advance collections from customers. (p. 386)
USB drive	USB is an abbreviation of Universal Serial Bus. USB drives are known as flash drives, pen drives, etc. USBs are used as storage media. (p. 22)
user interface	The user interface is also called the graphical user interface. Refer to glossary term, graphical user interface. (p. 1)
vendor credit memos	Returns to vendors. (p. 85)
vendor ledger	Shows the account activity for each vendor. (p. 457)
vendors	In PCA, this term refers to businesses that offer credit for merchandise or assets purchased or expenses incurred. (p. 429)

W-2 forms Annual report of an employee's wages subject to FICA and federal income tax that shows withholding amounts. (p. 580)

weighted-average method This method of inventory pricing divides the cost of the inventory purchased by the quantity of merchandise purchased. This unit cost is multiplied by the ending inventory. (p. 462)

wildcard Reports can be filtered using wildcard characters. In Peachtree, a valid wildcard character is an asterisk (*). (See making.) (p. 235)

WIMP The acronym, WIMP, stands for Windows, Icons, Menus, and Pull-downs. This acronym is used to describe the way personal computer software looks and works. (p. 1)

windows A visual (instead of typographic) format for computer operations. (p. 1)

withholding allowances Exemptions claimed by the employee. The number of exemptions or withholding allowances often includes one for the employee, one for the employee's spouse, and one for each dependent. (p. 579)

workflow diagram A workflow diagram shows a sequence of connected steps. For example, the Vendors & Purchases diagram shows the flow of data through the accounts payable system. (See module.) (p. 20)

Index

The McGraw-Hill Companies, Inc., *Computer Accounting with Peachtree by Sage Complete Accounting 2012, 16e*